Ford Transit Diesel Owners Workshop Manual

John S Mead

Models covered

All Ford Transit models with normally-aspirated and turbocharged 2.5 litre Diesel engines

Does not cover petrol engine models, Transit 4 x 4, or specialist bodywork/conversions

ABCDE
FGHIJ
KLMNO
PQRST

Haynes Publishing
Sparkford Nr Yeovil
Somerset BA22 7JJ England

Haynes North America, Inc
861 Lawrence Drive
Newbury Park
California 91320 USA

Acknowledgements

Thanks are due to Champion Spark Plug, who supplied replacement component information, to Holt Lloyd Limited who supplied the illustrations showing bodywork repair, and to Duckhams Oils, who provided lubrication data. Certain other illustrations are the copyright of the Ford Motor Company Limited, and are used with their permission. Thanks are also due to Sykes-Pickavant Limited, who provided some of the workshop tools, and to all those people at Sparkford and Newbury Park who helped in the production of this manual.

© Haynes Publishing 1995

A book in the **Haynes Owners Workshop Manual Series**

Printed by J. H. Haynes & Co. Ltd., Sparkford, Nr Yeovil, Somerset BA22 7JJ, England

All rights reserved. No part of this book may be reproduced or transmitted in any form or by any means, electronic or mechanical, including photocopying, recording or by any information storage or retrieval system, without permission in writing from the copyright holder.

ISBN 1 85960 019 0

British Library Cataloguing in Publication Data
A catalogue record for this book is available from the British Library.

We take great pride in the accuracy of information given in this manual, but vehicle manufacturers make alterations and design changes during the production run of a particular vehicle of which they do not inform us. No liability can be accepted by the authors or publishers for loss, damage or injury caused by any errors in, or omissions from, the information given.

Contents

	Page
Preliminary sections	
Acknowledgements	0-2
About this manual	0-5
Introduction to the Ford Transit Diesel	0-5
General dimensions and weights	0-6
Jacking, towing and wheel changing	0-7
Buying spare parts and vehicle identification numbers	0-9
Safety first!	0-11
General repair procedures	0-13
Tools and working facilities	0-15
Booster battery (jump starting)	0-19
Radio/cassette unit anti-theft system	0-19
Conversion factors	0-20
Fault diagnosis	0-21
MOT test checks	0-28

Chapter 1
Routine maintenance and servicing 1-1
Lubricants, fluids and capacities 1-3

Chapter 2
Part A: in-vehicle engine repair procedures 2A-1
Part B: Engine removal and general engine overhaul procedures 2B-1

Chapter 3
Cooling, heating and ventilation systems 3-1

Chapter 4
Fuel, exhaust and emissions control systems 4-1

Chapter 5
Engine electrical systems 5-1

Chapter 6
Clutch 6-1

Chapter 7
Part A: Manual transmission 7A-1
Part B: Automatic transmission 7B-1

Chapter 8
Propeller shaft and rear axle 8-1

Chapter 9
Braking system 9-1

Chapter 10
Suspension and steering 10-1

Chapter 11
Bodywork and fittings 11-1

Chapter 12
Body electrical systems 12-1
Wiring diagrams 12-24

Index IND-1

1986 model Transit 100L long-wheelbase

1995 model Transit 80 short-wheelbase

About this manual

Its aim

The aim of this manual is to help you get the best value from your vehicle. It can do so in several ways. It can help you decide what work must be done (even should you choose to get it done by a garage), provide information on routine maintenance and servicing, and give a logical course of action and diagnosis when random faults occur. However, it is hoped that you will use the manual by tackling the work yourself. On simpler jobs, it may even be quicker than booking the vehicle into a garage and going there twice, to leave and collect it. Perhaps most important, a lot of money can be saved by avoiding the costs a garage must charge to cover its labour and overheads.

The manual has drawings and descriptions to show the function of the various components so that their layout can be understood. Then the tasks are described and photographed in a clear step-by-step sequence.

Its arrangement

The manual is divided into Chapters, each covering a logical sub-division of the vehicle. The Chapters are each divided into Sections, numbered with single figures, eg 5; and the Sections are divided into numbered paragraphs.

It is freely illustrated, especially in those parts where there is a detailed sequence of operations to be carried out. The reference numbers used in illustration captions pinpoint the pertinent Section and the paragraph within that Section. That is, illustration 3.2 means that the illustration refers to Section 3, and paragraph 2 within that Section.

There is an alphabetical index at the back of the manual as well as a contents list at the front. Each Chapter is also preceded by its own individual contents list.

References to the "left" or "right" of the vehicle are in the sense of a person in the driver's seat facing forward.

Unless otherwise stated, nuts and bolts are removed by turning anti-clockwise, and tightened by turning clockwise.

Vehicle manufacturers continually make changes to specifications and recommendations, and these, when notified, are incorporated into our manuals at the earliest opportunity.

We take great pride in the accuracy of information given in this manual, but vehicle manufacturers make alterations and design changes during the production run of a particular vehicle of which they do not inform us. No liability can be accepted by the authors or publishers for loss, damage or injury caused by any errors in, or omissions from, the information given.

Project vehicles

The main project vehicle used in the preparation of this manual, and appearing in many of the photographic sequences, was a 1992 short-wheelbase 2.5 litre Diesel panel Van. Additional vehicles were used to highlight procedural differences where necessary.

Introduction to the Ford Transit Diesel

The latest Ford Transit range of models was introduced in February 1986, and is the third generation of this popular range of vehicles. This manual covers the 2.5 litre Diesel engine models.

The most obvious and distinctive features of the new range is the wedge-front styling, adopted to improve the aerodynamics.

The 2.5 litre direct-injection Diesel engine is an overhead valve, water-cooled design with cast-iron cylinder head and cylinder block. Normally-aspirated and turbocharged versions are available. The engine is mounted in-line and, depending on model, is coupled to a four-speed, four-speed plus overdrive, or five-speed manual transmission, or a four-speed automatic transmission.

The steering and suspension on the short-wheelbase (LCX) models is new, being rack-and-pinion type with MacPherson strut independent front suspension. The long-wheelbase (LCY) models up to the 1992 model year continue with the worm-and-nut steering gear, and beam axle with leaf springs as used on earlier models. From 1992 onwards, all models are with rack-and-pinion steering and independent front suspension.

Telescopic double-acting shock absorbers are fitted to the front and rear suspension on all models.

Drive to the rear wheels is by a two- or three-piece propeller shaft to the rear axle, which is suspended by single or multiple leaf springs on each side.

All models are fitted with dual-circuit servo-assisted brakes, with discs at the front and self-adjusting drum brakes at the rear.

Seemingly innumerable variations of body types and styles of Transit are available, from the Pick-up to the Caravanette. All body styles and variants are mounted on a long- or short-wheelbase chassis as necessary.

General dimensions and weights

Dimensions
	Short-wheelbase	Long-wheelbase
Overall length:		
Pre-1992 model year	4606 mm	5358 mm
1992 model year onwards	4616 mm	5368 mm
Overall width:		
Pre-1992 model year	1938 mm	1972 mm
1992 model year onwards	1972 mm	1972 mm
Wheelbase:		
Pre-1992 model year	2815 mm	3020 mm
1992 model year onwards	2835 mm	3570 mm

Weights
Due to the wide range of models available, the kerb weights given are a representative selection for reference only, and are for a vehicle with a full fuel tank and basic equipment. The vehicle types are standard panel vans with side-loading door. For other models and non-standard types, consult a Ford dealer for details.

Short-wheelbase:
- 80 model .... 1533 kg
- 100 model .... 1547 kg
- 120 model .... 1599 kg
- 150 model .... 1644 kg

Long-wheelbase:
- 100 model .... 1673 kg
- 150 model .... 1750 kg
- 190 model .... 1759 kg

Jacking, towing and wheel changing

Jacking

The jack supplied with the vehicle tool kit should only be used for changing the roadwheels - see *"Wheel changing"* later in this Section. When carrying out any other kind of work, raise the vehicle using a hydraulic jack, and always supplement the jack with axle stands positioned under the vehicle jacking points, chassis members or axles. Ensure that the jack is of sufficient capacity to lift the vehicle safely.

When using a hydraulic jack, always position the jack head under one of the relevant jacking points, or centrally under the front or rear axle, or front crossmember **(see illustration)**. Whenever the rear of the vehicle is being raised (for whatever purpose), do not jack up under the centre of the axle when the vehicle is fully loaded. Do not raise the vehicle higher than is necessary. **Never** *work under, around, or near a raised vehicle, unless it is adequately supported in at least two places.*

Towing

Towing eyes are provided at the front and rear of the vehicle **(see illustrations)**.

When being towed, the ignition switch should be in position "II",

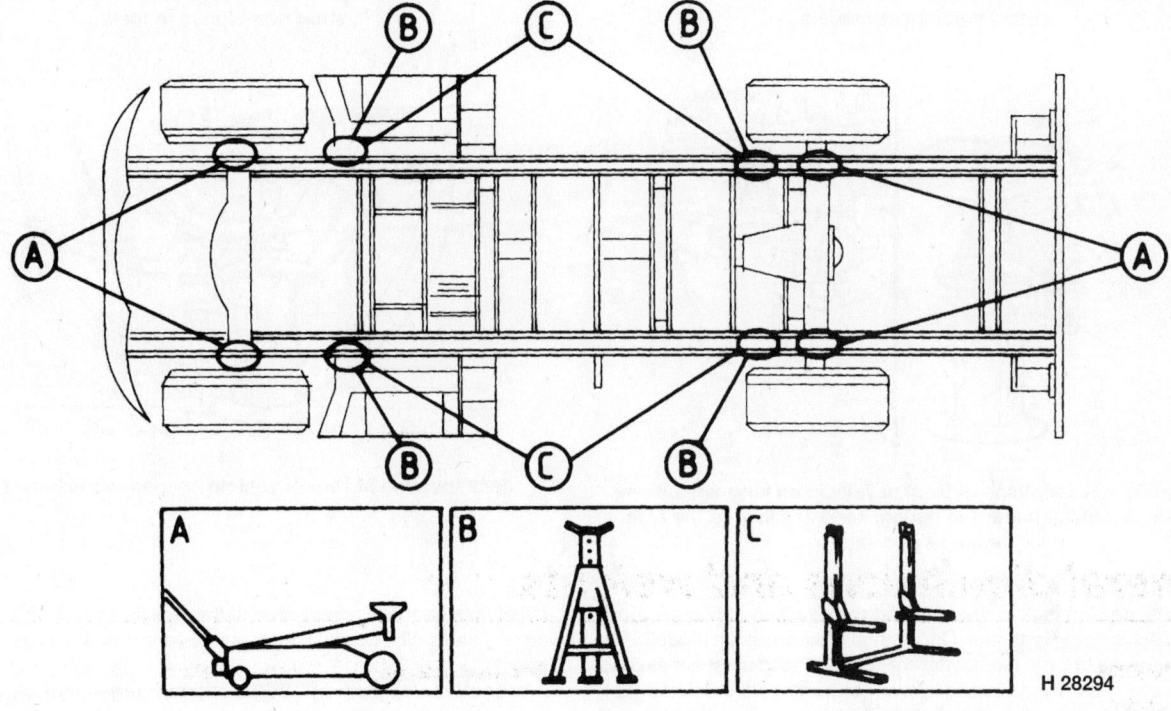

Typical workshop jacking point locations - long-wheelbase Chassis Cab model illustrated

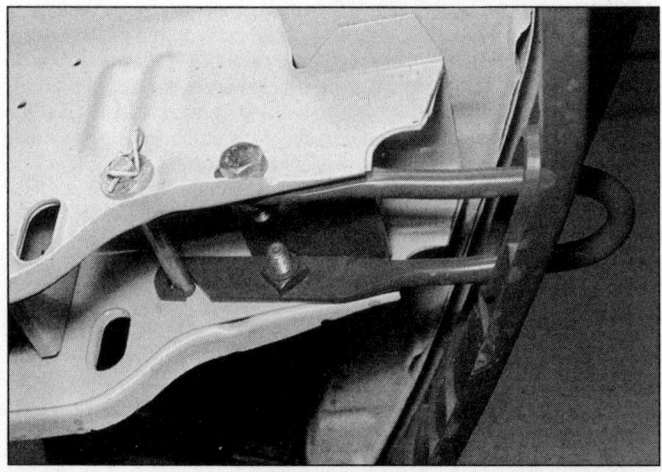

Front towing eye

Rear towing eye

0-8 Jacking, towing and wheel changing

Scissor jack location at front of vehicle on short-wheelbase models

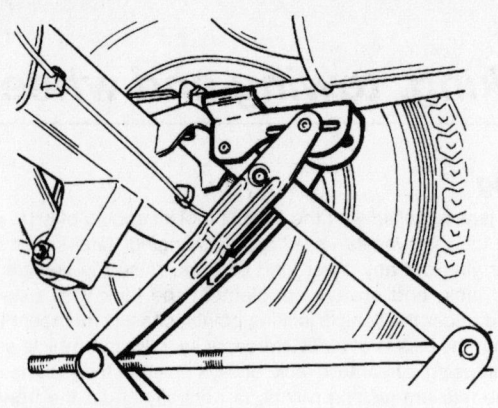

Scissor jack location at rear of vehicle on short-wheelbase models

Alternative jack locations at front of vehicle on long-wheelbase models. If jacking under the spring, keep as close to the axle beam as possible

Jack location at rear of vehicle on long-wheelbase models

so that the steering lock is released and the direction indicators, horn and stop lights are operational. On automatic transmission models, the selector lever must be in neutral (N), the towing speed must not exceed 30 mph, and the towing distance must not exceed 30 miles (50 km). For longer distances, the propeller shaft should be removed, or the rear of the vehicle lifted clear of the ground.

Push- or tow-starting is not possible on vehicles fitted with automatic transmission, and is not recommended on manual transmission models, owing to the extremely high compression pressures in a Diesel engine.

Remember that if the vehicle is to be towed and the engine is not running, there will be no servo assistance to the brakes, and therefore additional pressure will be required to operate them.

If towing another vehicle, attach the tow-rope to the towing eyes.

Wheel changing

To change a wheel in an emergency, use the jack supplied with the vehicle. Ensure that the roadwheel nuts are loosened (but not removed) before jacking up the vehicle. When changing a wheel on pre-1992 model year vehicles fitted with six-stud wheels, note that the wheel nuts on the left-hand side of the vehicle have a *left-hand thread*, ie they undo *clockwise*. These nuts and studs are marked with the letter "L".

The type of jack and its location is dependent on model. On short-wheelbase models, a scissor jack is supplied, and this should be located at the points shown **(see illustrations)**. On long-wheelbase models, a pillar jack or heavy-duty scissor jack is supplied, and this should also be located as indicated **(see illustrations)**. On later models, the jack head engages with specific indented areas on the sill panel. When jacking up under a roadspring, position the jack as close to the axle as possible. Ensure that the jack is fully engaged at the lift point before raising the vehicle. Wherever possible, jack up on a firm, level surface. Fully apply the handbrake, and engage reverse gear (or set the selector lever at "P" on automatic transmission models). Chock the roadwheels on the side opposite that being raised.

Having changed the wheel, tighten the nuts moderately before lowering the vehicle, then tighten them fully with the vehicle on the ground. Check the tightness of the wheel nuts using a torque wrench at the earliest opportunity. Have the puncture repaired as soon as possible (where applicable).

Buying spare parts and vehicle identification numbers

Buying spare parts

Spare parts are available from many sources, including maker's appointed garages, accessory shops, and motor factors. To be sure of obtaining the correct parts, it will sometimes be necessary to quote the vehicle identification number. If possible, it can also be useful to take the old parts along for positive identification. Items such as starter motors and alternators may be available under a service exchange scheme - any parts returned should always be clean.

Our advice regarding spare part sources is as follows.

Officially-appointed garages

This is the best source of parts which are peculiar to your vehicle, and are not otherwise generally available (eg badges, interior trim, certain body panels, etc). It is also the only place at which you should buy parts if the vehicle is still under warranty.

Accessory shops

These are very good places to buy materials and components needed for the maintenance of your vehicle (oil, air and fuel filters, plugs, light bulbs, drivebelts, oils and greases, brake pads, touch-up paint, etc). Components of this nature sold by a reputable shop are of the same standard as those used by the car manufacturer.

Besides components, these shops also sell tools and general accessories, usually have convenient opening hours, charge lower prices, and can often be found not far from home. Some accessory shops have parts counters where the components needed for almost any repair job can be purchased or ordered.

Motor factors

Good factors will stock all the more important components which wear out comparatively quickly, and can sometimes supply individual components needed for the overhaul of a larger assembly (eg brake seals and hydraulic parts, bearing shells, pistons, valves, alternator brushes). They may also handle work such as cylinder block reboring, crankshaft regrinding and balancing, etc.

Tyre and exhaust specialists

These outlets may be independent, or members of a local or national chain. They frequently offer competitive prices when compared with a main dealer or local garage, but it will pay to obtain several quotes before making a decision. When researching prices, also ask what "extras" may be added - for instance, fitting a new valve and balancing the wheel are both commonly charged on top of the price of a new tyre.

Other sources

Beware of parts or materials obtained from market stalls, car boot sales or similar outlets. Such items are not invariably sub-standard, but there is little chance of compensation if they do prove unsatisfactory. In the case of safety-critical components such as brake pads, there is the risk not only of financial loss but also of an accident causing injury or death.

Second-hand components or assemblies obtained from a car breaker can be a good buy in some circumstances, but this sort of purchase is best made by the experienced DIY mechanic.

Vehicle identification numbers

Modifications are a continuing and unpublicised process in vehicle manufacture, quite apart from major model changes. Spare parts manuals and lists are compiled upon a numerical basis, the individual vehicle identification numbers being essential to correct identification of the component concerned.

When ordering spare parts, always give as much information as possible. Quote the vehicle model, year of manufacture, vehicle identification number, body and engine numbers as appropriate.

The *vehicle identification plate* is located on the passenger's side stepwell, just inside the door **(see illustration)**. In addition to many other details, it carries the Vehicle Identification Number (VIN),

The vehicle identification plate is located on the passenger's side stepwell, just inside the door

0-10 Buying spare parts and vehicle identification numbers

On later vehicles, the vehicle identification number is also on the facia on the passenger's side, and can be viewed through the windscreen

maximum vehicle weight information, and codes for interior trim and body colours.

The *Vehicle Identification Number* is given on the vehicle identification plate. On later vehicles, it is also located on the facia on the passenger's side, and can be viewed through the windscreen **(see illustration)**.

The *body number and paint code numbers* are located on the vehicle identification plate.

The *engine number* is located on the front left-hand side of the cylinder block above the sump flange on normally-aspirated engines, and on the rear right-hand side of the cylinder block above the sump flange, and on the front end of the cylinder head, on Turbo models **(see illustration)**.

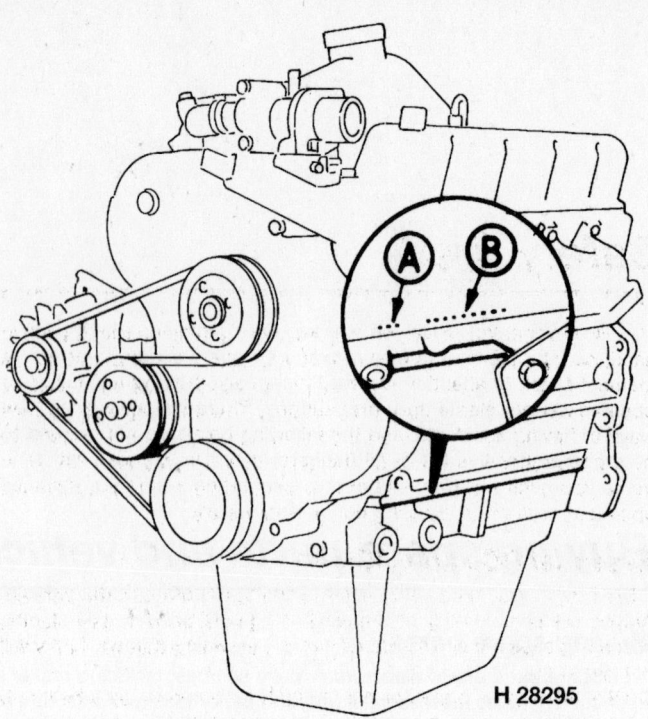

Engine number location on normally-aspirated engines
A   Engine code   *B   Engine number*

Safety first!

However enthusiastic you may be about getting on with the job in hand, do take the time to ensure that your safety is not put at risk. A moment's lack of attention can result in an accident, as can failure to observe certain elementary precautions. There will always be new ways of having accidents, and the following points do not pretend to be a comprehensive list of all dangers; they are intended rather to make you aware of the risks and to encourage a safety-conscious approach to all work you carry out on your vehicle.

Essential DOs and DON'Ts

DON'T rely on a single jack when working underneath the vehicle. Always use reliable additional means of support, such as axle stands, securely placed under a structural part of the vehicle that you know will not give way.

DON'T attempt to loosen or tighten high-torque nuts (eg wheel hub nuts) while the vehicle is on a jack; it may be pulled off.

DON'T start the engine without first ascertaining that the transmission is in neutral (or "Park" where applicable) and the handbrake applied.

DON'T suddenly remove the filler cap from a hot cooling system - cover it with a cloth and release the pressure gradually first, or you may get scalded by escaping coolant.

DON'T attempt to drain oil, automatic transmission fluid, or coolant until you are sure it has cooled sufficiently to avoid scalding you.

DON'T grasp any part of the engine, exhaust or catalytic converter (where applicable) without first ascertaining that it is sufficiently cool to avoid burning you.

DON'T allow brake fluid or antifreeze to contact vehicle paintwork.

DON'T syphon toxic liquids such as fuel, brake fluid or antifreeze by mouth, or allow them to remain on your skin.

DON'T inhale dust - it may be injurious to health (see *Asbestos* below).

DON'T allow any spilt oil or grease to remain on the floor - wipe it up straight away, before someone slips on it.

DON'T use ill-fitting spanners or other tools which may slip and cause injury.

DON'T attempt to lift a heavy component which may be beyond your capability - get assistance.

DON'T rush to finish a job, or take unverified short cuts.

DON'T allow children or animals in or around an unattended vehicle.

DON'T park vehicles with catalytic converters over combustible materials such as dry grass, oily rags, etc if the engine has recently been run. As catalytic converters reach extremely high temperatures, any such materials in close proximity may ignite.

DON'T run vehicles with catalytic converters without the exhaust system heat shields fitted.

DO wear eye protection when using power tools such as an electric drill, sander, bench grinder etc, and when working under the vehicle.

DO use a barrier cream on your hands prior to undertaking dirty jobs - it will protect your skin from infection, as well as making the dirt easier to remove afterwards; but make sure your hands aren't left slippery. Note that long-term contact with used engine oil can be a health hazard.

DO keep loose clothing (cuffs, tie etc) and long hair well out of the way of moving mechanical parts.

DO remove rings, wristwatch etc, before working on the vehicle - especially the electrical system.

DO ensure that any lifting tackle or jacking equipment used has a safe working load rating adequate for the job, and is used precisely as recommended by the equipment manufacturer.

DO keep your work area tidy - it is only too easy to fall over articles left lying around.

DO get someone to check periodically that all is well when working alone on the vehicle.

DO carry out work in a logical sequence, and check that everything is correctly assembled and tightened afterwards.

DO remember that your vehicle's safety affects that of yourself and others. If in doubt on any point, get specialist advice.

IF, in spite of following these precautions, you are unfortunate enough to injure yourself, seek medical attention as soon as possible.

Asbestos

Certain friction, insulating, sealing, and other products - such as brake linings, brake bands, clutch linings, gaskets, etc - contain asbestos. *Extreme care must be taken to avoid inhalation of dust from such products, since it is hazardous to health.* If in doubt, assume that they *do* contain asbestos.

Fire

Remember at all times that fuel is highly flammable. Never smoke, or have any kind of naked flame around, when working on the vehicle. But the risk does not end there - a spark caused by an electrical short-circuit, by two metal surfaces contacting each other, by careless use of tools, or even by static electricity built up in your body under certain conditions, can ignite fuel vapour, which in a confined space is highly explosive.

Whenever possible disconnect the battery earth terminal before working on any part of the fuel or electrical system, and never risk spilling fuel on to a hot engine or exhaust. Catalytic converters run at extremely high temperatures, and consequently can be an additional fire hazard. Observe the precautions outlined elsewhere in this section.

It is recommended that a fire extinguisher of a type suitable for fuel and electrical fires is kept handy in the garage or workplace at all times. Never try to extinguish a fuel or electrical fire with water. If a vehicle fire does occur, take note of the remarks below about hydrofluoric acid.

Note: *Any reference to a "torch" appearing in this manual should always be taken to mean a hand-held battery-operated electric lamp or flashlight. It does NOT mean a welding/gas torch or blowlamp.*

Hydrofluoric acid

Hydrofluoric acid is extremely corrosive. It is formed when certain types of synthetic rubber, which may be found in O-rings, oil seals, brake hydraulic system seals, fuel hoses etc, are exposed to temperatures above 400°C. The obvious circumstance in which this could happen on a vehicle is in the case of a fire. The rubber does not burn, but changes into a charred or sticky substance which contains the acid. *Once formed, the acid remains dangerous for years. If it gets onto the skin, it may be necessary to amputate the limb concerned.*

When dealing with a vehicle which has suffered a fire, or with components salvaged from such a vehicle, always wear protective gloves, and discard them carefully after use. Bear this in mind if obtaining components from a breaker.

Fumes

Certain fumes are highly toxic, and can quickly cause unconsciousness and even death if inhaled to any extent, especially if inhalation takes place through a lighted cigarette or pipe. Fuel vapour comes into this category, as do the vapours from certain solvents such as trichloroethylene. Any draining or pouring of such volatile fluids should be done in a well-ventilated area.

When using cleaning fluids and solvents, read the instructions carefully. Never use materials from unmarked containers - they may give off poisonous vapours.

Never run the engine of a motor vehicle in an enclosed space such as a garage. Exhaust fumes contain carbon monoxide which is extremely poisonous; if you need to run the engine, always do so in the open air, or at least have the rear of the vehicle outside the workplace. Although Diesel engines have greatly-reduced carbon monoxide emissions, the above precautions should still be observed.

If you are fortunate enough to have the use of an inspection pit, never drain or pour fuel, and never run the engine, while the vehicle is standing over it; the fumes, being heavier than air, will concentrate in the pit, with possibly lethal results.

The battery

Batteries which are sealed for life require special precautions, which are normally outlined on a label attached to the battery. Such precautions are primarily related to situations involving battery charging and jump starting from another vehicle.

With a conventional battery, never cause a spark, or allow a naked light, in close proximity to it. It will normally be giving off a certain amount of hydrogen gas, which is highly explosive.

Whenever possible, disconnect the battery earth terminal before working on the fuel or electrical systems.

If possible, loosen the filler plugs or cover when charging the battery from an external source. Do not charge at an excessive rate, or the battery may burst. Special care should be taken with the use of high-charge-rate boost chargers, to prevent the battery from overheating.

Take care when topping-up and when carrying the battery. The acid electrolyte, even when diluted, is very corrosive, and should not be allowed to contact clothing, eyes or skin.

Always wear eye protection when cleaning the battery, to prevent the caustic deposits from entering your eyes.

The vehicle electrical system

Take care when making alterations or repairs to the vehicle wiring. Electrical faults are the commonest cause of vehicle fires. Make sure that any accessories are wired correctly, using an appropriately-rated fuse and wire of adequate current-carrying capacity. When possible, avoid the use of "piggy-back" or self-splicing connectors to power additional electrical equipment from existing feeds; make up a new feed with its own fuse instead.

When considering the current which a new circuit will have to handle, do not overlook the switch, especially when planning to use an existing switch to control additional components - for instance, if spotlights are to be fed via the main lighting switch. For preference, a relay should be used to switch heavy currents. If in doubt, consult an auto electrical specialist.

Any wire which passes through a body panel or bulkhead must be protected from chafing with a grommet or similar device. A wire which is allowed to chafe bare against the bodywork will cause a short-circuit and possibly a fire.

Mains electricity and electrical equipment

When using an electric power tool, inspection light, diagnostic equipment etc., which works from the mains, always ensure that the appliance is correctly connected to its plug and that, where necessary, it is properly earthed. Do not use such appliances in damp conditions and, again, beware of creating a spark or applying excessive heat in the vicinity of fuel or fuel vapour. Also ensure that the appliances meet the relevant national safety standards.

Diesel fuel

Diesel injection pumps supply fuel at very high pressure. Extreme care must be taken when working on the fuel injectors and fuel pipes. It is advisable to place an absorbent cloth around the union before slackening a fuel pipe. *Never expose the hands, face or any other part of the body to injector spray; the high working pressure can penetrate the skin, with potentially fatal results.* Injector test rigs produce similarly high pressures, and must be treated with the same respect.

Diesel fuel is more irritating to the skin than petrol. It is also harmful to the eyes. Besides the use of a barrier cream to protect the hands, consider using lightweight disposable gloves when fuel spillage is inevitable. Change out of fuel-soaked clothing as soon as possible.

Spilt diesel fuel does not evaporate like petrol. Clear up spillages promptly, to avoid accidents caused by slippery patches on the workshop floor. Note also that diesel attacks tarmac surfaces: if working at the roadside or in a drive, put down newspaper or a plastic sheet if fuel spillage is expected.

Jacking and vehicle support

The jack provided with the vehicle is designed primarily for emergency wheel changing, and its use for servicing and overhaul work on the vehicle is best avoided. Instead, a more substantial workshop jack (trolley jack or similar) should be used. Whichever type is employed, it is essential that additional safety support is provided by means of axle stands designed for this purpose. Never use makeshift means such as wooden blocks or piles of house bricks, as these can easily topple or, in the case of bricks, disintegrate under the weight of the vehicle. Further information on the correct positioning of the jack and axle stands is provided in the *"Jacking, towing and wheel changing"* section.

If removal of the wheels is not required, the use of drive-on ramps is recommended. Caution should be exercised to ensure that they are correctly aligned with the wheels, and that the vehicle is not driven too far along them so that it promptly falls off the other ends, or tips the ramps.

General repair procedures

Whenever servicing, repair or overhaul work is carried out on the vehicle or its components, it is necessary to observe the following procedures and instructions. This will assist in carrying out the operation efficiently and to a professional standard of workmanship.

Joint mating faces and gaskets

When separating components at their mating faces, never insert screwdrivers or similar implements into the joint between the faces in order to prise them apart. This can cause severe damage which results in oil leaks, coolant leaks, etc upon reassembly. Separation is usually achieved by tapping along the joint with a soft-faced hammer in order to break the seal. However, note that this method may not be suitable where dowels are used for component location.

Where a gasket is used between the mating faces of two components, ensure that it is renewed on reassembly, and fit it dry unless otherwise stated in the repair procedure. Make sure that the mating faces are clean and dry, with all traces of old gasket removed. When cleaning a joint face, use a tool which is not likely to score or damage the face, and remove any burrs or nicks with an oilstone or fine file.

Make sure that tapped holes are cleaned with a pipe cleaner, and keep them free of jointing compound, if this is being used, unless specifically instructed otherwise.

Ensure that all orifices, channels or pipes are clear, and blow through them, preferably using compressed air.

Oil seals

Oil seals can be removed by levering them out with a wide flat-bladed screwdriver or similar implement. Alternatively, a number of self-tapping screws may be screwed into the seal, and these used as a purchase for pliers or some similar device in order to pull the seal free.

Whenever an oil seal is removed from its working location, either individually or as part of an assembly, it should be renewed.

The very fine sealing lip of the seal is easily damaged, and will not seal if the surface it contacts is not completely clean and free from scratches, nicks or grooves. If the original sealing surface of the component cannot be restored, and the manufacturer has not made provision for slight relocation of the seal relative to the sealing surface, the component should be renewed.

Protect the lips of the seal from any surface which may damage them in the course of fitting. Use tape or a conical sleeve where possible. Lubricate the seal lips with oil before fitting and, on dual-lipped seals, fill the space between the lips with grease.

Unless otherwise stated, oil seals must be fitted with their sealing lips toward the lubricant to be sealed.

Use a tubular drift or block of wood of the appropriate size to install the seal and, if the seal housing is shouldered, drive the seal down to the shoulder. If the seal housing is unshouldered, the seal should be fitted with its face flush with the housing top face (unless otherwise instructed).

Screw threads and fastenings

Seized nuts, bolts and screws are quite a common occurrence where corrosion has set in, and the use of penetrating oil or releasing fluid will often overcome this problem if the offending item is soaked for a while before attempting to release it. The use of an impact driver may also provide a means of releasing such stubborn fastening devices, when used in conjunction with the appropriate screwdriver bit or socket. If none of these methods works, it may be necessary to resort to the careful application of heat, or the use of a hacksaw or nut splitter device.

Studs are usually removed by locking two nuts together on the threaded part, and then using a spanner on the lower nut to unscrew the stud. Studs or bolts which have broken off below the surface of the component in which they are mounted can sometimes be removed using a proprietary stud extractor. Always ensure that a blind tapped hole is completely free from oil, grease, water or other fluid before installing the bolt or stud. Failure to do this could cause the housing to crack, due to the hydraulic action of the bolt or stud as it is screwed in.

When tightening a castellated nut to accept a split pin, tighten the nut to the specified torque, where applicable, and then tighten further to the next split pin hole. Never slacken the nut to align the split pin hole, unless stated in the repair procedure.

When checking or retightening a nut or bolt to a specified torque setting, slacken the nut or bolt by a quarter of a turn, and then retighten to the specified setting. However, this should not be attempted where angular tightening has been used.

For some screw fastenings, notably cylinder head bolts or nuts, torque wrench settings are no longer specified for the latter stages of tightening, "angle-tightening" being called up instead. Typically, a fairly low torque wrench setting will be applied to the bolts/nuts in the correct sequence, followed by one or more stages of tightening through specified angles.

Locknuts, locktabs and washers

Any fastening which will rotate against a component or housing in the course of tightening should always have a washer between it and the relevant component or housing.

Spring or split washers should always be renewed when they are used to lock a critical component such as a big-end bearing retaining bolt or nut. Locktabs which are folded over to retain a nut or bolt should always be renewed.

Self-locking nuts can be reused in non-critical areas, providing resistance can be felt when the locking portion passes over the bolt or stud thread. However, it should be noted that self-locking stiffnuts tend to lose their effectiveness after long periods of use, and in such cases should be renewed as a matter of course.

Split pins must always be replaced with new ones of the correct size for the hole.

When thread-locking compound is found on the threads of a fastener which is to be re-used, it should be cleaned off with a wire brush and solvent, and fresh compound applied on reassembly.

Special tools

Some repair procedures in this manual entail the use of special tools such as a press, two or three-legged pullers, spring compressors etc. Wherever possible, suitable readily-available alternatives to the manufacturer's special tools are described, and are shown in use. In some instances, where no alternative is possible, it has been necessary to resort to the use of a manufacturer's tool, and this has been done for reasons of safety as well as the efficient completion of the repair operation. Unless you are highly skilled and have a thorough understanding of the procedures described, never attempt to bypass the use of any special tool when the procedure described specifies its use. Not only is there a very great risk of personal injury, but expensive damage could be caused to the components involved.

Fuel injection system

Cleanliness is vital for reliable operation and long life of the fuel injection system components. Always clean around fuel system unions before disconnecting them, and plug or cap open unions to keep dirt and moisture out. (Fingers cut from discarded rubber or plastic gloves, secured with rubber bands or cable ties, are ideal for this.) Avoid using compressed air for cleaning in the vicinity of open fuel system unions, as there is a risk of dirt being blown into them.

Environmental considerations

When disposing of used engine oil, brake fluid, antifreeze etc., give due consideration to any detrimental environmental effects. Do not, for instance, pour any of the above liquids down drains into the general sewage system or onto the ground to soak away. Many local council refuse tips provide a facility for waste oil disposal, as do some garages. If none of these facilities are available, consult your local Environmental Health Department for further advice.

With the universal tightening-up of legislation regarding the emission of environmentally-harmful substances from motor vehicles, most current vehicles have tamperproof devices fitted to the main adjustment points of the fuel system. These devices are primarily designed to prevent unqualified persons from adjusting the fuel/air mixture (with the chance of a consequent increase in toxic emissions). If such devices are encountered during servicing or overhaul, they should, wherever possible, be renewed or refitted in accordance with the vehicle manufacturer's requirements or with current legislation.

Tools and working facilities

Introduction

A selection of good tools is a fundamental requirement for anyone contemplating the maintenance and repair of a motor vehicle. For the owner who does not possess any, their purchase will prove a considerable expense, offsetting some of the savings made by doing-it-yourself. However, provided that the tools purchased meet the relevant national safety standards and are of good quality, they will last for many years and prove an extremely worthwhile investment.

To help the average owner to decide which tools are needed to carry out the various tasks detailed in this manual, we have compiled three lists of tools under the following headings: *Maintenance and minor repair*, *Repair and overhaul*, and *Special*. Newcomers to practical mechanics should start off with the *Maintenance and minor repair* tool kit and confine themselves to the simpler jobs around the vehicle. Then, as confidence and experience grow, more difficult tasks can be undertaken, with extra tools being purchased as, and when, they are needed. In this way, a *Maintenance and minor repair* tool kit can be built up into a *Repair and overhaul* tool kit over a considerable period of time without any major cash outlays. The experienced do-it-yourselfer will have a tool kit good enough for most repair and overhaul procedures, and will add tools from the *Special* category when it is felt that the expense is justified by the amount of use to which these tools will be put.

Maintenance and minor repair tool kit

The tools given in this list should be considered as a minimum requirement if routine maintenance, servicing and minor repair operations are to be undertaken. We recommend the purchase of combination spanners (ring one end, open-ended the other); although more expensive than open-ended ones, they do give the advantages of both types of spanner.

Combination spanners:
  Metric - 8, 9, 10, 11, 12, 13, 14, 15, 16, 17, 19, 22, 21, 24 & 26 mm
Adjustable spanner - 35 mm jaw (approx)
Engine sump/gearbox drain plug key
Set of feeler blades
Brake bleed nipple spanner
Screwdrivers:
  Flat blade - approx 100 mm long x 6 mm dia
  Cross blade - approx 100 mm long x 6 mm dia
Combination pliers
Hacksaw (junior)
Tyre pump
Tyre pressure gauge
Oil can
Oil filter removal tool
Fine emery cloth
Wire brush (small)
Funnel (medium size)

Repair and overhaul tool kit

These tools are virtually essential for anyone undertaking any major repairs to a motor vehicle, and are additional to those given in the *Maintenance and minor repair* list. Included in this list is a comprehensive set of sockets. Although these are expensive, they will be found invaluable as they are so versatile - particularly if various drives are included in the set. We recommend the half-inch square-drive type, as this can be used with most proprietary torque wrenches. If you cannot afford a socket set, even bought piecemeal, then inexpensive tubular box spanners are a useful alternative.

The tools in this list will occasionally need to be supplemented by tools from the *Special* list.

Sockets (or box spanners) to cover range in previous list
Reversible ratchet drive (for use with sockets) **(see illustration)**
Extension piece, 250 mm (for use with sockets)
Universal joint (for use with sockets)
Torque wrench (for use with sockets)

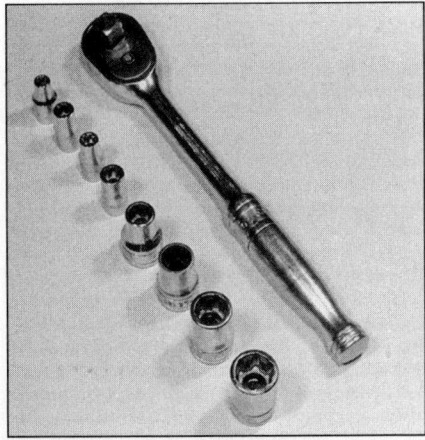
Sockets and reversible ratchet drive

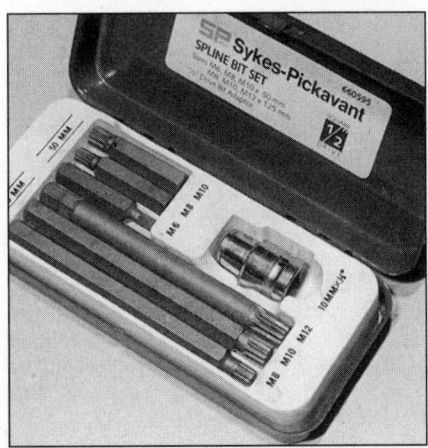
Spline bit set

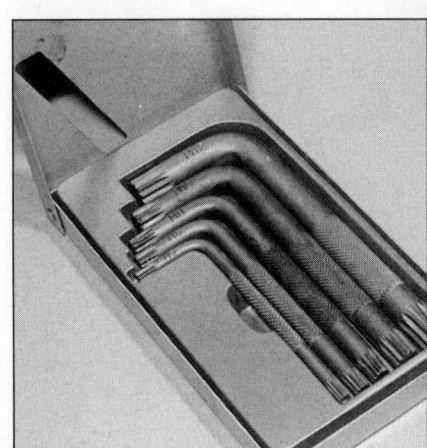
Spline key set

Tools and working facilities

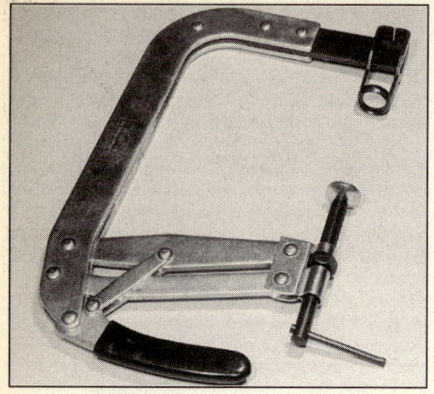
Valve spring compressor

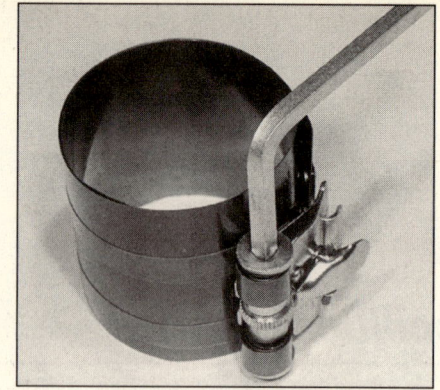
Piston ring compressor

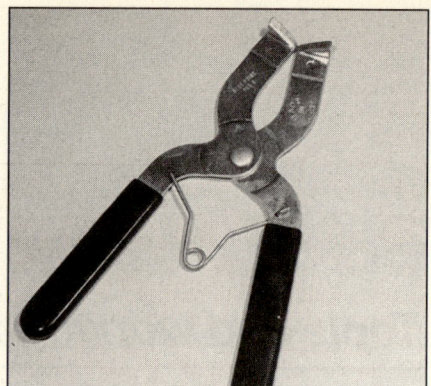
Piston ring removal/installation tool

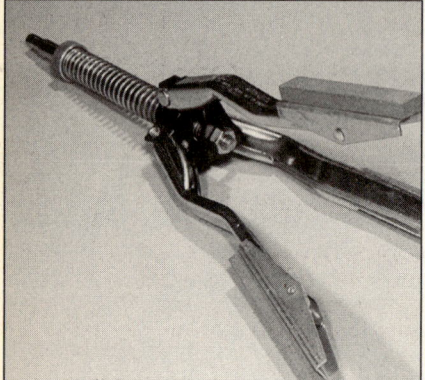
Cylinder bore hone

Three-legged hub and bearing puller

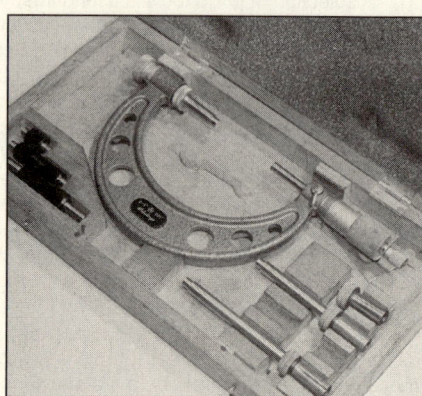
Micrometer set

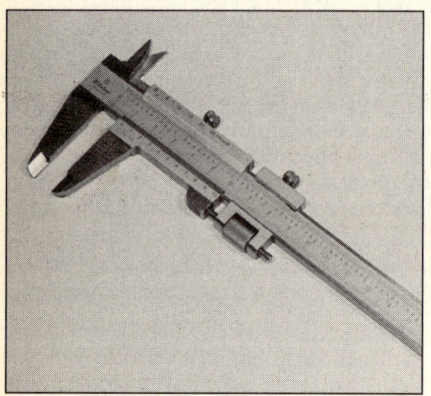
Vernier calipers

Dial test indicator and magnetic stand

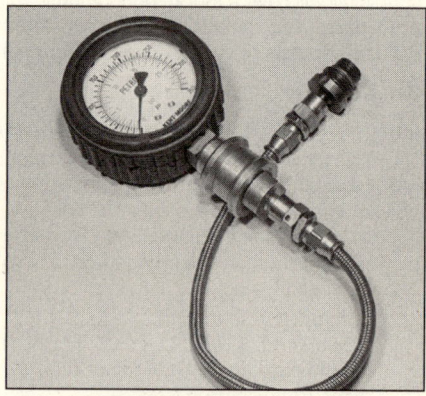
Cylinder compression gauge

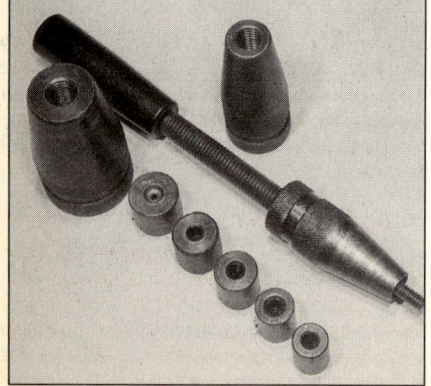
Clutch plate alignment set

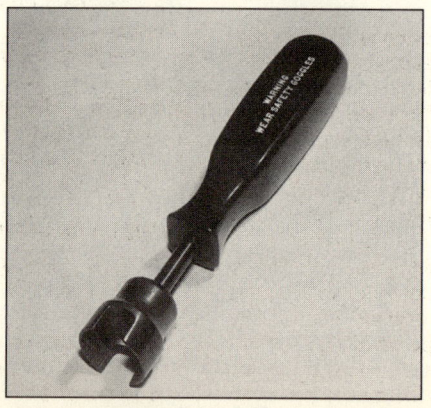
Brake shoe steady spring cup removal tool

Bush and bearing removal/installation set

Tools and working facilities

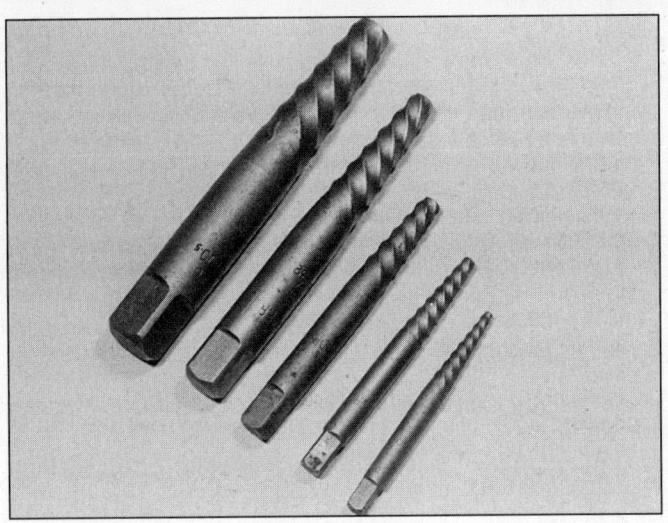

Stud extractor set

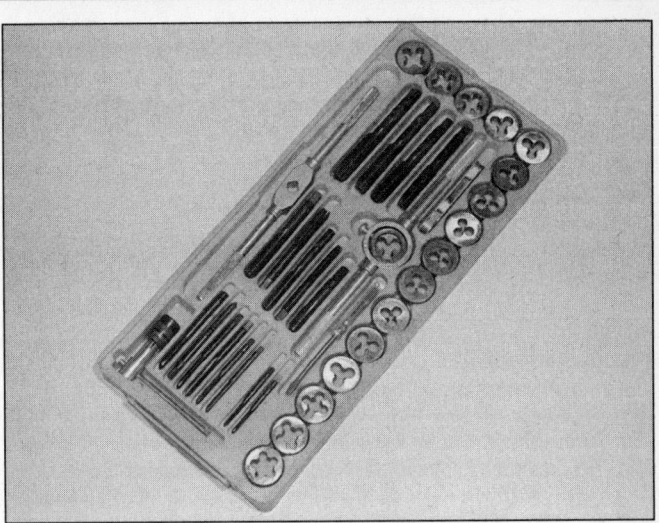

Tap and die set

Fuel injector removal socket (27 mm)
Self-locking grips
Ball pein hammer
Soft-faced mallet (plastic/aluminium or rubber)
Screwdrivers:
  Flat blade - long & sturdy, short (chubby), and narrow
  electrician's) types
  Cross blade - Long & sturdy, and short (chubby) types
Pliers:
  Long-nosed
  Side cutters (electrician's)
  Circlip (internal and external)
Cold chisel - 25 mm
Scriber
Scraper
Centre-punch
Pin punch
Hacksaw
Brake hose clamp
Brake bleeding kit
Selection of twist drills
Steel rule/straight-edge
Allen keys (inc. splined/Torx type) **(see illustrations)**
Selection of files
Wire brush
Axle stands
Jack (strong trolley or hydraulic type)
Light with extension lead

Special tools

The tools in this list are those which are not used regularly, are expensive to buy, or which need to be used in accordance with their manufacturers' instructions. Unless relatively difficult mechanical jobs are undertaken frequently, it will not be economic to buy many of these tools. Where this is the case, you could consider clubbing together with friends (or joining a motorists' club) to make a joint purchase, or borrowing the tools against a deposit from a local garage or tool hire specialist. It is worth noting that many of the larger DIY superstores now carry a large range of special tools for hire at modest rates.

The following list contains only those tools and instruments freely available to the public, and not those special tools produced by the vehicle manufacturer specifically for its dealer network. You will find occasional references to these manufacturer's special tools in the text of this manual. Generally, an alternative method of doing the job without the vehicle manufacturer's special tool is given. However, sometimes there is no alternative to using them. Where this is the case

and the relevant tool cannot be bought or borrowed, you will have to entrust the work to a franchised garage.

Valve spring compressor **(see illustration)**
Valve grinding tool
Piston ring compressor **(see illustration)**
Piston ring removal/installation tool **(see illustration)**
Cylinder bore hone **(see illustration)**
Balljoint separator
Coil spring compressors (where applicable)
Two/three-legged hub and bearing puller **(see illustration)**
Impact screwdriver
Micrometer and/or vernier calipers **(see illustrations)**
Dial test indicator **(see illustration)**
Tachometer
Universal electrical multi-meter
Cylinder compression gauge (suitable for Diesel engines) **(see illustration)**
Clutch plate alignment set **(see illustration)**
Brake shoe steady spring cup removal tool **(see illustration)**
Bush and bearing removal/installation set **(see illustration)**
Stud extractors **(see illustration)**
Tap and die set **(see illustration)**
Lifting tackle
Trolley jack

Buying tools

For practically all tools, a tool factor is the best source, since he will have a very comprehensive range compared with the average garage or accessory shop. Having said that, accessory shops often offer excellent quality tools at discount prices, so it pays to shop around.

Remember, you don't have to buy the most expensive items on the shelf, but it is always advisable to steer clear of the very cheap tools. There are plenty of good tools around at reasonable prices, but always aim to purchase items which meet the relevant national safety standards. If in doubt, ask the proprietor or manager of the shop for advice before making a purchase.

Care and maintenance of tools

Having purchased a reasonable tool kit, it is necessary to keep the tools in a clean and serviceable condition. After use, always wipe off any dirt, grease and metal particles using a clean, dry cloth, before putting the tools away. Never leave them lying around after they have been used. A simple tool rack on the garage or workshop wall for items such as screwdrivers and pliers is a good idea. Store all normal spanners and sockets in a metal box. Any measuring instruments, gauges, meters, etc, must be carefully stored where they cannot be damaged or become rusty.

Take a little care when tools are used. Hammer heads inevitably become marked, and screwdrivers lose the keen edge on their blades from time to time. A little timely attention with emery cloth or a file will soon restore items like this to a good serviceable finish.

Working facilities

Not to be forgotten when discussing tools is the workshop itself. If anything more than routine maintenance is to be carried out, some form of suitable working area becomes essential.

It is appreciated that many an owner-mechanic is forced by circumstances to remove an engine or similar item without the benefit of a garage or workshop. Having done this, any repairs should always be done under the cover of a roof.

Wherever possible, any dismantling should be done on a clean, flat workbench or table at a suitable working height.

Any workbench needs a vice; one with a jaw opening of 100 mm is suitable for most jobs. As mentioned previously, some clean dry storage space is also required for tools, as well as for any lubricants, cleaning fluids, touch-up paints and so on, which become necessary.

Another item which may be required, and which has a much more general usage, is an electric drill with a chuck capacity of at least 8 mm. This, together with a good range of twist drills, is virtually essential for fitting accessories.

Last, but not least, always keep a supply of old newspapers and clean, lint-free rags available, and try to keep any working area as clean as possible.

Spanner jaw gap and bolt size comparison table

Jaw gap - in (mm)	Spanner size	Bolt size
0.197 (5.00)	5 mm	M 2.5
0.216 (5.50)	5.5 mm	M 3
0.218 (5.53)	7/32 in AF	
0.236 (6.00)	6 mm	M 3.5
0.250 (6.35)	1/4 in AF	
0.275 (7.00)	7 mm	M 4
0.281 (7.14)	9/32 in AF	
0.312 (7.92)	5/16 in AF	
0.315 (8.00)	8 mm	M 5
0.343 (8.71)	11/32 in AF	
0.375 (9.52)	3/8 in AF	
0.394 (10.00)	10 mm	M 6
0.406 (10.32)	13/32 in AF	
0.433 (11.00)	11 mm	M 7
0.437 (11.09)	7/16 in AF	1/4 in SAE
0.468 (11.88)	15/32 in AF	
0.500 (12.70)	1/2 in AF	5/16 in SAE
0.512 (13.00)	13 mm	M 8
0.562 (14.27)	9/16 in AF	3/8 in SAE
0.593 (15.06)	19/32 in AF	
0.625 (15.87)	5/8 in AF	7/16 in SAE
0.669 (17.00)	17 mm	M 10
0.687 (17.44)	11/16 in AF	
0.709 (19.00)	19 mm	M 12
0.750 (19.05)	3/4 in AF	1/2 in SAE
0.781 (19.83)	25/32 in AF	
0.812 (20.62)	13/16 in AF	
0.866 (22.00)	22 mm	M 14
0.875 (22.25)	7/8 in AF	9/16 in SAE
0.937 (23.79)	15/16 in AF	5/8 in SAE
0.945 (24.00)	24 mm	M 16
0.968 (24.58)	31/32 in AF	
1.000 (25.40)	1 in AF	11/16 in SAE
1.062 (26.97)	1 1/16 in AF	3/4 in SAE
1.063 (27.00)	27 mm	M 18
1.125 (28.57)	1 1/8 in AF	
1.182 (30.00)	30 mm	M 20
1.187 (30.14)	1 3/16 in AF	
1.250 (31.75)	1 1/4 in AF	7/8 in SAE
1.260 (32.00)	32 mm	M 22
1.312 (33.32)	1 5/16 in AF	
1.375 (34.92)	1 3/8 in AF	
1.418 (36.00)	36 mm	M 24
1.437 (36.49)	1 7/16 in AF	1 in SAE
1.500 (38.10)	1 1/2 in AF	
1.615 (41.00)	41 mm	M 27

Booster battery (jump) starting

When jump-starting using a booster battery, observe the following precautions.
a) *Before connecting the booster battery, make sure that the ignition is switched off.*
b) *Ensure that all electrical equipment (lights, heater, wipers etc) is switched off.*
c) *Make sure that the booster battery is the same voltage as the discharged one in the vehicle.*
d) *If the vehicle is being jump-started from the battery in another vehicle, the two vehicles MUST NOT TOUCH each other.*
e) *Make sure that the transmission is in Neutral (manual transmission) or Park (automatic transmission).*

Connect one jump lead between the positive (+) terminals of the two batteries. Connect the other jump lead first to the negative (-) terminal of the booster battery, and then to a good earthing point on the vehicle to be started, such as a bolt or bracket on the engine block, at least 45 cm from the battery if possible **(see illustration)**. Make sure that the jump leads will not come into contact with the fan, drivebelts or other moving parts of the engine.

Start the engine using the booster battery, then with the engine running at idle speed, disconnect the jump leads in the reverse order of connection.

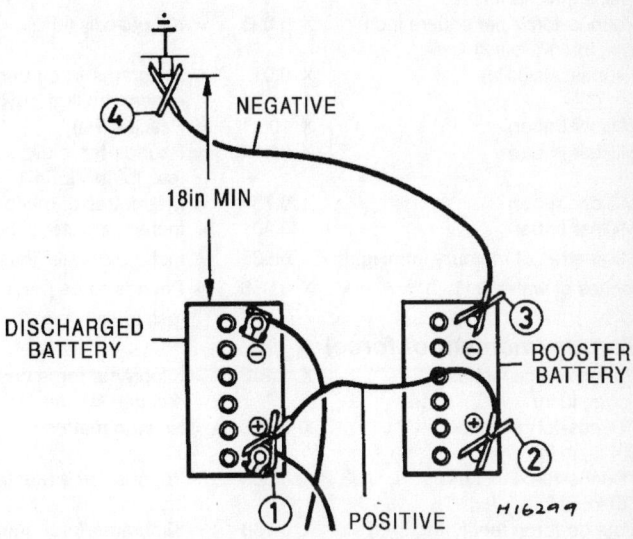

Jump start lead connections for negative-earth vehicles - connect leads in order shown

Radio/cassette unit anti-theft system

On later vehicles, the radio/cassette unit fitted as standard equipment by Ford is with a built-in security code, to deter thieves. If the power source to the unit is cut, the anti-theft system will activate. Even if the power source is immediately reconnected, the radio/cassette unit will not function until the correct security code has been entered. Therefore, if you do not know the correct security code for the radio/cassette unit, **do not** disconnect either of the battery terminals, or remove the radio/cassette unit from the vehicle.

To enter the correct security code, follow the instructions provided with the radio/cassette player handbook.

If an incorrect code is entered, the unit will become locked, and cannot be operated.

If this happens, or if the security code is lost or forgotten, seek the advice of your Ford dealer.

Conversion factors

Length (distance)
Inches (in)	X 25.4	= Millimetres (mm)	X 0.0394	= Inches (in)
Feet (ft)	X 0.305	= Metres (m)	X 3.281	= Feet (ft)
Miles	X 1.609	= Kilometres (km)	X 0.621	= Miles

Volume (capacity)
Cubic inches (cu in; in^3)	X 16.387	= Cubic centimetres (cc; cm^3)	X 0.061	= Cubic inches (cu in; in^3)
Imperial pints (Imp pt)	X 0.568	= Litres (l)	X 1.76	= Imperial pints (Imp pt)
Imperial quarts (Imp qt)	X 1.137	= Litres (l)	X 0.88	= Imperial quarts (Imp qt)
Imperial quarts (Imp qt)	X 1.201	= US quarts (US qt)	X 0.833	= Imperial quarts (Imp qt)
US quarts (US qt)	X 0.946	= Litres (l)	X 1.057	= US quarts (US qt)
Imperial gallons (Imp gal)	X 4.546	= Litres (l)	X 0.22	= Imperial gallons (Imp gal)
Imperial gallons (Imp gal)	X 1.201	= US gallons (US gal)	X 0.833	= Imperial gallons (Imp gal)
US gallons (US gal)	X 3.785	= Litres (l)	X 0.264	= US gallons (US gal)

Mass (weight)
Ounces (oz)	X 28.35	= Grams (g)	X 0.035	= Ounces (oz)
Pounds (lb)	X 0.454	= Kilograms (kg)	X 2.205	= Pounds (lb)

Force
Ounces-force (ozf; oz)	X 0.278	= Newtons (N)	X 3.6	= Ounces-force (ozf; oz)
Pounds-force (lbf; lb)	X 4.448	= Newtons (N)	X 0.225	= Pounds-force (lbf; lb)
Newtons (N)	X 0.1	= Kilograms-force (kgf; kg)	X 9.81	= Newtons (N)

Pressure
Pounds-force per square inch (psi; lbf/in^2; lb/in^2)	X 0.070	= Kilograms-force per square centimetre (kgf/cm^2; kg/cm^2)	X 14.223	= Pounds-force per square inch (psi; lbf/in^2; lb/in^2)
Pounds-force per square inch (psi; lbf/in^2; lb/in^2)	X 0.068	= Atmospheres (atm)	X 14.696	= Pounds-force per square inch (psi; lbf/in^2; lb/in^2)
Pounds-force per square inch (psi; lbf/in^2; lb/in^2)	X 0.069	= Bars	X 14.5	= Pounds-force per square inch (psi; lbf/in^2; lb/in^2)
Pounds-force per square inch (psi; lbf/in^2; lb/in^2)	X 6.895	= Kilopascals (kPa)	X 0.145	= Pounds-force per square inch (psi; lbf/in^2; lb/in^2)
Kilopascals (kPa)	X 0.01	= Kilograms-force per square centimetre (kgf/cm^2; kg/cm^2)	X 98.1	= Kilopascals (kPa)
Millibar (mbar)	X 100	= Pascals (Pa)	X 0.01	= Millibar (mbar)
Millibar (mbar)	X 0.0145	= Pounds-force per square inch (psi; lbf/in^2; lb/in^2)	X 68.947	= Millibar (mbar)
Millibar (mbar)	X 0.75	= Millimetres of mercury (mmHg)	X 1.333	= Millibar (mbar)
Millibar (mbar)	X 0.401	= Inches of water (inH$_2$O)	X 2.491	= Millibar (mbar)
Millimetres of mercury (mmHg)	X 0.535	= Inches of water (inH$_2$O)	X 1.868	= Millimetres of mercury (mmHg)
Inches of water (inH$_2$O)	X 0.036	= Pounds-force per square inch (psi; lbf/in^2; lb/in^2)	X 27.68	= Inches of water (inH$_2$O)

Torque (moment of force)
Pounds-force inches (lbf in; lb in)	X 1.152	= Kilograms-force centimetre (kgf cm; kg cm)	X 0.868	= Pounds-force inches (lbf in; lb in)
Pounds-force inches (lbf in; lb in)	X 0.113	= Newton metres (Nm)	X 8.85	= Pounds-force inches (lbf in; lb in)
Pounds-force inches (lbf in; lb in)	X 0.083	= Pounds-force feet (lbf ft; lb ft)	X 12	= Pounds-force inches (lbf in; lb in)
Pounds-force feet (lbf ft; lb ft)	X 0.138	= Kilograms-force metres (kgf m; kg m)	X 7.233	= Pounds-force feet (lbf ft; lb ft)
Pounds-force feet (lbf ft; lb ft)	X 1.356	= Newton metres (Nm)	X 0.738	= Pounds-force feet (lbf ft; lb ft)
Newton metres (Nm)	X 0.102	= Kilograms-force metres (kgf m; kg m)	X 9.804	= Newton metres (Nm)

Power
Horsepower (hp)	X 745.7	= Watts (W)	X 0.0013	= Horsepower (hp)

Velocity (speed)
Miles per hour (miles/hr; mph)	X 1.609	= Kilometres per hour (km/hr; kph)	X 0.621	= Miles per hour (miles/hr; mph)

Fuel consumption*
Miles per gallon, Imperial (mpg)	X 0.354	= Kilometres per litre (km/l)	X 2.825	= Miles per gallon, Imperial (mpg)
Miles per gallon, US (mpg)	X 0.425	= Kilometres per litre (km/l)	X 2.352	= Miles per gallon, US (mpg)

Temperature
Degrees Fahrenheit = (°C x 1.8) + 32   Degrees Celsius (Degrees Centigrade; °C) = (°F - 32) x 0.56

It is common practice to convert from miles per gallon (mpg) to litres/100 kilometres (l/100km), where mpg (Imperial) x l/100 km = 282 and mpg (US) x l/100 km = 235

Fault diagnosis

Contents

	Section
Engine	1

Engine fails to rotate when attempting to start
Starter motor turns engine slowly
Starter motor spins without turning engine
Starter motor noisy or excessively-rough in engagement
Engine rotates but will not start
Engine fires but will not run
Engine difficult to start when cold
Engine difficult to start when hot
Engine idles erratically
Engine misfires at idle speed
Engine misfires throughout the driving speed range
Engine stalls
Engine lacks power
Oil pressure warning light illuminated with engine running
Engine runs-on after switching off
Engine noises

Cooling system 2

Overheating
Overcooling
External coolant leakage
Internal coolant leakage
Corrosion

Fuel and exhaust systems 3

Excessive fuel consumption
Fuel leakage and/or fuel odour
Excessive noise or fumes from exhaust system

Clutch 4

Pedal travels to floor - no pressure or very little resistance
Clutch fails to disengage (unable to select gears)
Clutch slips (engine speed increases with no increase in vehicle speed)
Judder as clutch is engaged
Noise when depressing or releasing clutch pedal

Manual transmission 5

Noisy in neutral with engine running
Noisy in one particular gear
Difficulty engaging gears
Jumps out of gear
Vibration
Lubricant leaks

Automatic transmission 6

Fluid leakage
Transmission fluid brown, or has burned smell
General gear selection problems
Transmission will not downshift (kickdown) with accelerator fully depressed
Engine will not start in any gear, or starts in gears other than Park or Neutral
Transmission slips, shifts roughly, is noisy, or has no drive in forward or reverse gears

Propeller shaft 7

Vibration when accelerating or decelerating
Noise (grinding or high-pitched squeak) when moving slowly
Noise (knocking or clicking) when accelerating or decelerating

Rear axle 8

Roughness or rumble from rear of vehicle (perhaps less with handbrake slightly applied)
Noise (high-pitched whine) increasing with roadspeed
Noise (knocking or clicking) when accelerating or decelerating
Lubricant leaks

Braking system 9

Vehicle pulls to one side under braking
Noise (grinding or high-pitched squeal) when brakes applied
Excessive brake pedal travel
Brake pedal feels spongy when depressed
Excessive brake pedal effort required to stop vehicle
Judder felt through brake pedal or steering wheel when braking
Brakes binding
Rear wheels locking under normal braking

Suspension and steering systems 10

Vehicle pulls to one side
Wheel wobble and vibration
Excessive pitching and/or rolling around corners or during braking
Wandering or general instability
Excessively-stiff steering
Excessive play in steering
Lack of power assistance
Tyre wear excessive

Electrical system 11

Battery will not hold a charge for more than a few days
Alternator (no-charge) warning light remains illuminated with engine running
Alternator (no-charge) warning light fails to come on
Lights inoperative
Instrument readings inaccurate or erratic
Horn inoperative, or unsatisfactory in operation
Windscreen/tailgate wipers inoperative, or unsatisfactory in operation
Windscreen/tailgate washers inoperative, or unsatisfactory in operation
Electric windows inoperative, or unsatisfactory in operation
Central locking system inoperative, or unsatisfactory in operation

Fault diagnosis

Introduction

The vehicle owner who does his or her own maintenance according to the recommended service schedules should not have to use this section of the manual very often. Modern component reliability is such that, provided those items subject to wear or deterioration are inspected or renewed at the specified intervals, sudden failure is comparatively rare. Faults do not usually just happen as a result of sudden failure, but develop over a period of time. Major mechanical failures in particular are usually preceded by characteristic symptoms over hundreds or even thousands of miles. Those components which do occasionally fail without warning are often small and easily carried in the vehicle (eg bulbs).

With any fault finding, the first step is to decide where to begin investigations. Sometimes this is obvious, but on other occasions a little detective work will be necessary. The owner who makes half a dozen haphazard adjustments or replacements may be successful in curing a fault (or its symptoms), but will be none the wiser if the fault recurs, and ultimately may have spent more time and money than was necessary. A calm and logical approach will be found to be more satisfactory in the long run. Always take into account any warning signs or abnormalities that may have been noticed in the period preceding the fault - power loss, high or low gauge readings, unusual smells, etc - and remember that failure of certain components such as fuses may only be pointers to some underlying fault.

The pages which follow provide an easy reference guide to the more common problems which may occur during the operation of the vehicle. These problems and their possible causes are grouped under headings denoting various components or systems, such as Engine, Cooling system, etc. The Chapter and/or Section which deals with the problem is also shown in brackets. Whatever the fault, certain basic principles apply. These are as follows:

Verify the fault. This is simply a matter of being sure that you know what the symptoms are before starting work. This is particularly important if you are investigating a fault for someone else, who may not have described it very accurately.

Don't overlook the obvious. For example, if the vehicle won't start, is there fuel in the tank? (Don't take anyone else's word on this particular point, and don't trust the fuel gauge either!) If an electrical fault is indicated, look for loose or broken wires before digging out the test gear.

Cure the disease, not the symptom. Substituting a flat battery with a fully-charged one will get you off the hard shoulder, but if the underlying cause is not attended to, the new battery will go the same way.

Don't take anything for granted. Particularly, don't forget that a "new" component may itself be defective (especially if it's been rattling around in the boot for months), and don't leave components out of a fault diagnosis sequence just because they are new or recently fitted. When you do finally diagnose a difficult fault, you'll probably realise that all the evidence was there from the start.

1 Engine

Engine fails to rotate when attempting to start

- Battery terminal connections loose or corroded (Chapter 1).
- Battery discharged or faulty (Chapter 5).
- Broken, loose or disconnected wiring in the starting circuit (Chapter 5).
- Defective starter solenoid or switch (Chapter 5).
- Defective starter motor (Chapter 5).
- Starter pinion or flywheel ring gear teeth loose or broken (Chapter 5 or Chapter 2A).
- Engine earth strap broken or disconnected (Chapter 5).
- Automatic transmission not in Park/Neutral position or starter inhibitor switch faulty (Chapter 7B).

Starter motor turns engine slowly

- Partially-discharged battery (recharge, or use jump leads) (Chapter 5).
- Battery terminals loose or corroded (Chapter 1).
- Battery earth to body defective (Chapter 5).
- Engine earth strap loose (Chapter 5).
- Starter motor (or solenoid) wiring loose (Chapter 5).
- Starter motor internal fault (Chapter 5).

Starter motor spins without turning engine

- Defective starter motor (Chapter 5).
- Starter motor mounting bolts loose (Chapter 5).

Starter motor noisy or excessively-rough in engagement

- Starter pinion or flywheel ring gear teeth loose or broken (Chapter 5 or Chapter 2A).
- Starter motor mounting bolts loose or missing (Chapter 5).
- Starter motor internal components worn or damaged (Chapter 5).

Engine rotates but will not start

- Fuel tank empty.
- Battery discharged (engine rotates slowly) (Chapter 5).
- Battery terminal connections loose or corroded (Chapter 1).
- Air in fuel (Chapter 4).
- Wax formed in fuel (in very cold weather).
- Faulty stop solenoid (Chapter 4).
- Low cylinder compressions (Chapter 2A).
- Fuel system or preheating system fault (Chapters 4 and 5).
- Major mechanical failure (eg camshaft drive) (Chapter 2A).
- Fault in anti-theft system (Chapter 12).

Engine fires but will not run

- Preheating system fault (Chapter 5).
- Air in fuel (Chapter 4).
- Wax formed in fuel (in very cold weather).
- Other fuel system fault (Chapter 4).

Engine difficult to start when cold

- Battery discharged (Chapter 5).
- Battery terminal connections loose or corroded (Chapter 1).
- Air in fuel (Chapter 4).
- Air filter element dirty or clogged (Chapter 1).
- Wax formed in fuel (in very cold weather).
- Preheating system fault (Chapter 5).
- Other fuel system fault (Chapter 4).
- Low cylinder compressions (Chapter 2A).

Engine difficult to start when hot

- Battery discharged (Chapter 5).
- Battery terminal connections loose or corroded (Chapter 1).
- Air filter element dirty or clogged (Chapter 1).
- Air in fuel (Chapter 4).
- Low cylinder compressions (Chapter 2A).

Engine idles erratically

- Incorrectly-adjusted idle speed (Chapter 1).
- Air filter element clogged (Chapter 1).
- Incorrectly-adjusted valve clearances (Chapter 2A).
- Uneven or low cylinder compressions (Chapter 2A).
- Camshaft lobes worn (Chapter 2A).
- Timing belt incorrectly tensioned (Chapter 2A).
- Incorrect fuel injection pump timing (Chapter 4).

Engine misfires at idle speed

- Air in fuel (Chapter 4).
- Wax formed in fuel (in very cold weather).

Fault diagnosis

- Other fuel system fault (Chapter 4).
- Incorrectly-adjusted valve clearances (Chapter 2A).
- Uneven or low cylinder compressions (Chapter 2A).
- Disconnected, leaking or perished crankcase ventilation hoses (Chapters 1 and 4).
- Incorrect fuel injection pump timing (Chapter 4).

Engine misfires throughout the driving speed range
- Fuel filter choked (Chapter 1).
- Fuel tank vent blocked or fuel pipes restricted (Chapter 4).
- Uneven or low cylinder compressions (Chapter 2A).
- Incorrect fuel injection pump timing (Chapter 4).

Engine stalls
- Incorrectly-adjusted idle speed (Chapter 1).
- Fuel filter choked (Chapter 1).
- Fuel tank vent blocked or fuel pipes restricted (Chapter 4).

Engine lacks power
- Air in fuel (Chapter 4).
- Incorrect fuel injection pump timing (Chapter 4).
- Timing belt incorrectly fitted or tensioned (Chapter 2A).
- Fuel filter choked (Chapter 1).
- Uneven or low cylinder compressions (Chapter 2A).
- Brakes binding (Chapters 1 and 9).
- Clutch slipping (Chapter 6).
- Automatic transmission fluid level incorrect (Chapter 1).

Oil pressure warning light illuminated with engine running
- Low oil level or incorrect oil grade (Chapter 1).
- Faulty oil pressure switch (Chapter 5).
- Worn engine bearings and/or oil pump (Chapter 2B).
- High engine operating temperature (Chapter 3).
- Oil pressure relief valve defective (Chapter 2B).
- Oil pick-up strainer clogged (Chapter 2B).

Note: *Low oil pressure in a high-mileage engine at tickover is not necessarily a cause for concern. Sudden pressure loss at speed is far more significant. In any event, check the warning light sender before condemning the engine.*

Engine runs-on after switching off
- Faulty stop solenoid (Chapter 4).

Engine noises
Note: *To inexperienced ears, the Diesel engine can sound alarming even when there is nothing wrong with it, so it may be prudent to have an unusual noise expertly diagnosed before making renewals or repairs.*

Whistling or wheezing noises
- Leaking manifold gasket (Chapter 4).
- Leaking vacuum hose (Chapters 1 and 4).
- Blowing cylinder head gasket (Chapter 2A).

Tapping or rattling noises
- Incorrect valve clearances (Chapter 2A).
- Worn valve gear or camshaft (Chapter 2A).
- Broken piston ring (ticking noise) (Chapter 2B).
- Ancillary component fault (water pump, alternator etc) (Chapters 3 and 5).

Knocking or thumping noises
- Air in fuel (Chapter 4).
- Worn drivebelt (Chapter 1 and Chapter 2A).
- Fuel injector(s) leaking or sticking (Chapter 4).
- Worn big-end bearings (regular heavy knocking, perhaps less under load) (Chapter 2B).
- Worn main bearings (rumbling and knocking, perhaps worsening under load) (Chapter 2B).
- Piston slap (most noticeable when cold) (Chapter 2B).
- Ancillary component fault (alternator, water pump etc) (Chapters 3 and 5).

2 Cooling system

Overheating
- Insufficient coolant in system (Chapter 1).
- Thermostat faulty (Chapter 3).
- Radiator core blocked, or grille restricted (Chapter 3).
- Cooling fan viscous coupling faulty (Chapter 3).
- Pressure cap faulty (Chapter 3).
- Timing belt worn, or incorrectly adjusted (Chapter 2A).
- Inaccurate temperature gauge sender unit (Chapter 3).
- Air-lock in cooling system (Chapter 1).

Overcooling
- Thermostat faulty (Chapter 3).
- Inaccurate temperature gauge sender unit (Chapter 3).

External coolant leakage
- Deteriorated or damaged hoses or hose clips (Chapter 1).
- Radiator core or heater matrix leaking (Chapter 3).
- Pressure cap faulty (Chapter 3).
- Water pump seal leaking (Chapter 3).
- Boiling due to overheating (Chapter 3).
- Core plug leaking (Chapter 2B).

Internal coolant leakage
- Leaking cylinder head gasket (Chapter 2A).
- Cracked cylinder head or cylinder bore (Chapter 2A or B).

Corrosion
- Infrequent draining and flushing (Chapter 1).
- Incorrect antifreeze mixture or inappropriate antifreeze type (Chapter 1).

3 Fuel and exhaust systems

Excessive fuel consumption
- Air filter element dirty or clogged (Chapter 1).
- Preheating system fault (Chapter 5).
- Incorrect idle speed (Chapter 1).
- Incorrect fuel injection pump timing (Chapter 4).
- Brakes binding (Chapter 9).
- Tyres under-inflated (Chapter 1).

Fuel leakage and/or fuel odour
- Damaged fuel tank, pipes or connections (Chapters 1 and 4).

Excessive noise or fumes from exhaust system
- Leaking exhaust system or manifold joints (Chapter 4).
- Leaking, corroded or damaged silencers or pipe (Chapter 4).
- Broken mountings causing body or suspension contact (Chapter 4).

4 Clutch

Pedal travels to floor - no pressure or very little resistance
- Broken clutch cable (Chapter 6).

Fault diagnosis

- Faulty automatic adjustment mechanism (Chapter 6).
- Broken clutch release bearing or fork (Chapter 6).
- Broken diaphragm spring in clutch pressure plate (Chapter 6).

Clutch fails to disengage (unable to select gears)
- Faulty automatic adjustment mechanism (Chapter 6).
- Clutch disc sticking on transmission input shaft splines (Chapter 6).
- Clutch disc sticking to flywheel or pressure plate (Chapter 6).
- Faulty pressure plate assembly (Chapter 6).
- Transmission input shaft seized in crankshaft spigot bearing (Chapter 2A).
- Clutch release mechanism worn or incorrectly assembled (Chapter 6).

Clutch slips (engine speed increases with no increase in vehicle speed)
- Faulty automatic adjustment mechanism (Chapter 6).
- Clutch disc linings excessively worn (Chapter 6).
- Clutch disc linings contaminated with oil or grease (Chapter 6).
- Faulty pressure plate or weak diaphragm spring (Chapter 6).

Judder as clutch is engaged
- Clutch disc linings contaminated with oil or grease (Chapter 6).
- Clutch disc linings excessively worn (Chapter 6).
- Clutch cable sticking or frayed (Chapter 6).
- Faulty or distorted pressure plate or diaphragm spring (Chapter 6).
- Worn or loose engine or transmission mountings (Chapter 2A).
- Clutch disc hub or transmission input shaft splines worn (Chapter 6).

Noise when depressing or releasing clutch pedal
- Faulty automatic adjustment mechanism (Chapter 6).
- Worn clutch release bearing (Chapter 6).
- Worn or dry clutch pedal bushes (Chapter 6).
- Faulty pressure plate assembly (Chapter 6).
- Pressure plate diaphragm spring broken (Chapter 6).
- Broken clutch disc cushioning springs (Chapter 6).

5 Manual transmission

Noisy in neutral with engine running
- Input shaft bearings worn (noise apparent with clutch pedal released but not when depressed) (Chapter 7A).*
- Clutch release bearing worn (noise apparent with clutch pedal depressed, possibly less when released) (Chapter 6).

Noisy in one particular gear
- Worn, damaged or chipped gear teeth (Chapter 7A).*

Difficulty engaging gears
- Clutch fault (Chapter 6).
- Worn or damaged gear selectors (Chapter 7A).*
- Worn synchroniser units (Chapter 7A).*

Jumps out of gear
- Worn synchroniser units (Chapter 7A).*
- Worn selector forks (Chapter 7A).*

Vibration
- Lack of oil (Chapter 1).
- Worn bearings (Chapter 7A).*

Lubricant leaks
- Leaking oil seal (Chapter 7A).
- Leaking housing joint (Chapter 7A).*

*Although the corrective action necessary to remedy the symptoms described is beyond the scope of the home mechanic, the above information should be helpful in isolating the cause of the condition, so that the owner can communicate clearly with a professional mechanic.

6 Automatic transmission

Note: *Due to the complexity of the automatic transmission, it is difficult for the home mechanic to properly diagnose and service this unit. For problems other than the following, the vehicle should be taken to a dealer service department or automatic transmission specialist. Do not be too hasty in removing the transmission if a fault is suspected, as most of the testing is carried out with the unit still fitted.*

Fluid leakage
- Automatic transmission fluid is usually dark in colour. Fluid leaks should not be confused with engine oil, which can easily be blown onto the transmission by airflow.
- To determine the source of a leak, first remove all built-up dirt and grime from the transmission housing and surrounding areas using a degreasing agent, or by steam-cleaning. Drive the vehicle at low speed, so airflow will not blow the leak far from its source. Raise and support the vehicle, and determine where the leak is coming from. The following are common areas of leakage:
  a) Oil pan (Chapter 1 and Chapter 7B).
  b) Dipstick tube (Chapter 1 and Chapter 7B).
  c) Transmission-to-fluid cooler pipes/unions (Chapter 7B).

Transmission fluid brown, or has burned smell
- Transmission fluid level low, or fluid in need of renewal (Chapter 1).

General gear selection problems
- Chapter 7B deals with checking and adjusting the selector cable on automatic transmissions. The following are common problems which may be caused by a poorly-adjusted cable:
  a) Engine starting in gears other than Park or Neutral.
  b) Indicator panel indicating a gear other than the one actually being used.
  c) Vehicle moves when in Park or Neutral.
  d) Poor gear shift quality or erratic gear changes.
- Refer to Chapter 7B for the selector cable adjustment procedure.

Transmission will not downshift (kickdown) with accelerator pedal fully depressed
- Low transmission fluid level (Chapter 1).
- Incorrect downshift cable adjustment (Chapter 7B).
- Incorrect selector cable adjustment (Chapter 7B).

Engine will not start in any gear, or starts in gears other than Park or Neutral
- Incorrect starter/inhibitor switch adjustment (Chapter 7B).
- Incorrect selector cable adjustment (Chapter 7B).

Transmission slips, shifts roughly, is noisy, or has no drive in forward or reverse gears
- There are many probable causes for the above problems, but the home mechanic should be concerned with only one possibility - fluid level. Before taking the vehicle to a dealer or transmission specialist, check the fluid level and condition of the fluid as described in Chapter 1. Correct the fluid level as necessary, or change the fluid and filter if needed. If the problem persists, professional help will be necessary.

Fault diagnosis 0-25

7 Propeller shaft

Vibration when accelerating or decelerating
- Propeller shaft out of balance or incorrectly fitted (Chapter 8).
- Propeller shaft flange bolts loose (Chapter 8).
- Lack of lubrication at sliding spline joint (Chapter 1 and Chapter 8).
- Excessive wear in universal joints (Chapter 8).

Noise (grinding or high-pitched squeak) when moving slowly
- Excessive wear in universal joints (Chapter 8).
- Excessive wear in centre bearing (Chapter 8).

Noise (knocking or clicking) when accelerating or decelerating
- Propeller shaft flange bolts loose (Chapter 8).
- Lack of lubrication at sliding spline joint (Chapter 1 and Chapter 8).
- Excessive wear in universal joints (Chapter 8).

8 Rear axle

Roughness or rumble from rear of vehicle (perhaps less with handbrake slightly applied)
- Rear hub bearings worn (Chapter 8).

Noise (high-pitched whine) increasing with road speed
- Differential crownwheel and pinion gear teeth worn (Chapter 8).
- Incorrect crownwheel and pinion mesh (Chapter 8).
- Differential bearings worn (Chapter 8).

Noise (knocking or clicking) when accelerating or decelerating
- Worn halfshaft splines (Chapter 8).
- Differential pinion flange bolts loose (Chapter 8).
- Incorrect crownwheel and pinion mesh (Chapter 8).
- Loose rear spring U-bolts (Chapter 8).
- Roadwheel nuts loose (Chapter 1, and Chapter 10).

Lubricant leaks
- Leaking oil seal (Chapter 8).
- Leaking differential housing or cover joint (Chapter 8).

9 Braking system

Note: *Before assuming that a brake problem exists, make sure that the tyres are in good condition and correctly inflated, the front wheel alignment is correct, and the vehicle is not loaded with weight in an unequal manner. Apart from checking the condition of all pipe and hose connections, any faults occurring on the anti-lock braking system (where fitted) should be referred to a Ford dealer for diagnosis.*

Vehicle pulls to one side under braking
- Worn, defective, damaged or contaminated front or rear brake pads/shoes on one side (Chapter 9).
- Seized or partially-seized front or rear brake caliper/wheel cylinder piston (Chapter 9).
- A mixture of brake pad/shoe lining materials fitted between sides (Chapter 9).
- Brake caliper mounting bolts loose (Chapter 9).
- Rear brake backplate mounting bolts loose (Chapter 9).
- Worn or damaged steering or suspension components (Chapter 10).

Noise (grinding or high-pitched squeal) when brakes applied
- Brake pad or shoe friction lining material worn down to metal backing (Chapter 9).
- Excessive corrosion of brake disc or drum. (May be apparent after the vehicle has been standing for some time (Chapter 9).

Excessive brake pedal travel
- Inoperative rear brake self-adjust mechanism (Chapter 9).
- Faulty master cylinder (Chapter 9).
- Air in hydraulic system (Chapter 9).
- Faulty vacuum servo unit (Chapter 9).
- Faulty brake vacuum pump (Chapter 9).

Brake pedal feels spongy when depressed
- Air in hydraulic system (Chapter 9).
- Deteriorated flexible rubber brake hoses (Chapter 9).
- Master cylinder mounting nuts loose (Chapter 9).
- Faulty master cylinder (Chapter 9).

Excessive brake pedal effort required to stop vehicle
- Faulty vacuum servo unit (Chapter 9).
- Disconnected, damaged or insecure brake servo vacuum hose (Chapters 1 and 9).
- Faulty brake vacuum pump (Chapter 9).
- Primary or secondary hydraulic circuit failure (Chapter 9).
- Seized brake caliper or wheel cylinder piston(s) (Chapter 9).
- Brake pads or brake shoes incorrectly fitted (Chapter 9).
- Incorrect grade of brake pads or brake shoes fitted (Chapter 9).
- Brake pads or brake shoe linings contaminated (Chapter 9).

Judder felt through brake pedal or steering wheel when braking
- Excessive run-out or distortion of front discs or rear drums (Chapter 9).
- Brake pad or brake shoe linings worn (Chapter 9).
- Brake caliper or rear brake backplate mounting bolts loose (Chapter 9).
- Wear in suspension or steering components or mountings (Chapter 10).

Brakes binding
- Seized brake caliper or wheel cylinder piston(s) (Chapter 9).
- Incorrectly-adjusted handbrake mechanism or linkage (Chapter 9).
- Faulty master cylinder (Chapter 9).

Rear wheels locking under normal braking
- Rear brake shoe linings contaminated (Chapter 9).
- Faulty brake pressure control valve - where fitted (Chapter 9).
- Faulty or incorrectly adjusted load apportioning valve - where fitted (Chapter 9).

10 Suspension and steering systems

Note: *Before diagnosing suspension or steering faults, be sure that the trouble is not due to incorrect tyre pressures, mixtures of tyre types or binding brakes.*

Vehicle pulls to one side
- Defective tyre (Chapter 1).
- Excessive wear in suspension or steering components (Chapter 10).

0-26   Fault diagnosis

- Incorrect front wheel alignment (Chapter 10).
- Accident damage to steering or suspension components (Chapter 10).

Wheel wobble and vibration

- Front roadwheels out-of-balance (vibration felt mainly through the steering wheel) (Chapter 10).
- Rear roadwheels out-of-balance (vibration felt throughout the vehicle) (Chapter 10).
- Roadwheels damaged or distorted (Chapter 1).
- Faulty or damaged tyre (Chapter 1).
- Worn steering or suspension joints, bushes or components (Chapter 10).
- Wheel nuts loose (Chapter 10).

Excessive pitching and/or rolling around corners or during braking

- Defective shock absorbers (Chapter 10).
- Broken or weak coil/leaf spring and/or suspension component (Chapter 10).
- Worn or damaged anti-roll bar or mountings - where fitted (Chapter 10).

Wandering or general instability

- Incorrect front wheel alignment (Chapter 10).
- Worn steering or suspension joints, bushes or components (Chapter 10).
- Roadwheels out-of-balance (Chapter 10).
- Faulty or damaged tyre (Chapter 1).
- Wheel nuts loose (Chapter 10).
- Defective shock absorbers (Chapter 10).

Excessively-stiff steering

- Lack of steering gear lubricant - possibly due to split rubber gaiter (Chapter 10).
- Seized track-rod end balljoint or suspension balljoint (Chapter 10).
- Broken or incorrectly-adjusted power steering pump drivebelt (Chapter 1).
- Incorrect front wheel alignment (Chapter 10).
- Steering column bent or damaged (Chapter 10).

Excessive play in steering

- Worn steering column universal joint(s) or intermediate coupling (Chapter 10).
- Worn steering track-rod end balljoints (Chapter 10).
- Worn rack-and-pinion steering gear (Chapter 10).
- Incorrectly adjusted worm and nut steering gear (Chapter 10).
- Worn steering or suspension joints, bushes or components (Chapter 10).

Lack of power assistance

- Broken or incorrectly-adjusted power steering pump drivebelt (Chapter 1).
- Incorrect power steering fluid level (Chapter 1).
- Restriction in power steering fluid hoses (Chapter 1).
- Faulty power steering pump (Chapter 10).
- Faulty steering gear (Chapter 10).

Tyre wear excessive

Tyres worn on inside or outside edges

- Tyres under-inflated (wear on both edges) (Chapter 1).
- Incorrect camber or castor angles (wear on one edge only) (Chapter 10).
- Worn steering or suspension joints, bushes or components (Chapter 10).
- Excessively-hard cornering.
- Accident damage.

Tyre treads exhibit feathered edges

- Incorrect toe setting (Chapter 10).

Tyres worn in centre of tread

- Tyres over-inflated (Chapter 1).

Tyres worn on inside and outside edges

- Tyres under-inflated (Chapter 1).

Tyres worn unevenly

- Tyres out-of-balance (Chapter 1).
- Excessive wheel or tyre run-out (Chapter 1).
- Worn shock absorbers (Chapter 10).
- Faulty tyre (Chapter 1).

11 Electrical system

Note: *For problems associated with the starting system, refer to the faults listed under "Engine" earlier in this Section.*

Battery will not hold a charge for more than a few days

- Battery defective internally (Chapter 5).
- Battery electrolyte level low - where applicable (Chapter 1).
- Battery terminal connections loose or corroded (Chapter 1).
- Alternator drivebelt worn or incorrectly adjusted (Chapter 1).
- Alternator not charging at correct output (Chapter 5).
- Alternator or voltage regulator faulty (Chapter 5).
- Short-circuit causing continual battery drain (Chapter 5).

Alternator (no-charge) warning light remains illuminated with engine running

- Alternator drivebelt broken, worn, or incorrectly adjusted (Chapter 1).
- Alternator brushes worn, sticking, or dirty (Chapter 5).
- Alternator brush springs weak or broken (Chapter 5).
- Internal fault in alternator or voltage regulator (Chapter 5).
- Broken, disconnected, or loose wiring in charging circuit (Chapter 5).

Alternator (no-charge) warning light fails to come on

- Warning light bulb blown (Chapter 12).
- Broken, disconnected, or loose wiring in warning light circuit (Chapter 12).
- Alternator faulty (Chapter 5).

Lights inoperative

- Bulb blown (Chapter 12).
- Corrosion of bulb or bulbholder contacts (Chapter 12).
- Blown fuse (Chapter 12).
- Faulty relay (Chapter 12).
- Broken, loose, or disconnected wiring (Chapter 12).
- Faulty switch (Chapter 12).

Instrument readings inaccurate or erratic

Instrument readings increase with engine speed

- Faulty voltage regulator (Chapter 12).

Fuel or temperature gauges give no reading

- Faulty gauge sender unit (Chapters 3 or 4).
- Wiring open-circuit (Chapter 5).
- Faulty gauge (Chapter 12).

Fault diagnosis

Fuel or temperature gauges give continuous maximum reading
- Faulty gauge sender unit (Chapters 3 or 4).
- Wiring short-circuit (Chapter 5).
- Faulty gauge (Chapter 12).

Horn inoperative, or unsatisfactory in operation

Horn operates all the time
- Horn push either earthed or stuck down (Chapter 12).
- Horn cable-to-horn push earthed (Chapter 12).

Horn fails to operate
- Blown fuse (Chapter 12).
- Cable or cable connections loose, broken or disconnected (Chapter 12).
- Faulty horn (Chapter 12).

Horn emits intermittent or unsatisfactory sound
- Cable connections loose (Chapter 12).
- Horn mountings loose (Chapter 12).
- Faulty horn (Chapter 12).

Windscreen/tailgate wipers inoperative, or unsatisfactory in operation

Wipers fail to operate, or operate very slowly
- Wiper blades stuck to screen, or linkage seized or binding (Chapter 1 or Chapter 12).
- Blown fuse (Chapter 12).
- Cable or cable connections loose, broken or disconnected (Chapter 12).
- Faulty relay (Chapter 12).
- Faulty wiper motor (Chapter 12).

Wiper blades sweep over too large or too small an area of the glass
- Wiper arms incorrectly positioned on spindles (Chapter 12).
- Excessive wear of wiper linkage (Chapter 12).
- Wiper motor or linkage mountings loose or insecure (Chapter 12).

Wiper blades fail to clean the glass effectively
- Wiper blade rubbers worn or perished (Chapter 1).
- Wiper arm tension springs broken or arm pivots seized (Chapter 12).
- Insufficient windscreen washer additive to adequately remove road film (Chapter 1).

Windscreen/tailgate washers inoperative, or unsatisfactory in operation

One or more washer jets inoperative
- Blocked washer jet (Chapter 12).
- Disconnected, kinked or restricted fluid hose (Chapter 12).
- Insufficient fluid in washer reservoir (Chapter 1).

Washer pump fails to operate
- Broken or disconnected wiring or connections (Chapter 12).
- Blown fuse (Chapter 12).
- Faulty washer switch (Chapter 12).
- Faulty washer pump (Chapter 12).

Washer pump runs for some time before fluid is emitted from jets
- Faulty one-way valve in fluid supply hose (Chapter 12).

Electric windows inoperative, or unsatisfactory in operation

Window glass will only move in one direction
- Faulty switch (Chapter 11).

Window glass slow to move
- Regulator seized or damaged, or in need of lubrication (Chapter 11).
- Door internal components or trim fouling regulator (Chapter 11).
- Faulty motor (Chapter 11).

Window glass fails to move
- Blown fuse (Chapter 12).
- Faulty relay (Chapter 12).
- Broken or disconnected wiring or connections (Chapter 12).
- Faulty motor (Chapter 11).

Central locking system inoperative, or unsatisfactory in operation

Complete system failure
- Blown fuse (Chapter 12).
- Faulty relay (Chapter 12).
- Broken or disconnected wiring or connections (Chapter 12).

Latch locks but will not unlock, or unlocks but will not lock
- Faulty master switch (Chapter 11).
- Broken or disconnected latch operating rods or levers (Chapter 11).
- Faulty relay (Chapter 12).

One solenoid/motor fails to operate
- Broken or disconnected wiring or connections (Chapter 12).
- Faulty solenoid/motor (Chapter 11).
- Broken, binding or disconnected latch operating rods or levers (Chapter 11).
- Fault in door latch (Chapter 11).

MOT test checks

Introduction

Motor vehicle testing has been compulsory in Great Britain since 1960, when the Motor Vehicle (Tests) Regulations were first introduced. At that time, testing was only applicable to vehicles ten years old or older, and the test itself only covered lighting equipment, braking systems and steering gear. Current vehicle testing is far more extensive and, in the case of private vehicles, is now an annual inspection commencing three years after the date of first registration. Test standards are becoming increasingly stringent; for details of changes, consult the latest edition of the MOT Inspection Manual (available from HMSO or bookshops).

This section is intended as a guide to getting your vehicle through the MOT test. It lists all the relevant testable items, how to check them yourself, and what is likely to cause the vehicle to fail. Obviously, it will not be possible to examine the vehicle to the same standard as the professional MOT tester, who will be highly experienced in this work and will have all the necessary equipment available. However, working through the following checks will provide a good indication as to the condition of the vehicle, and will enable you to identify any problem areas before submitting the vehicle for the test. Where a component is found to need repair or renewal, reference should be made to the appropriate Chapter in the manual, where further information will be found.

The following checks have been sub-divided into four categories, as follows:

a) *Checks carried out from the driver's seat.*
b) *Checks carried out with the vehicle on the ground.*
c) *Checks carried out with the vehicle raised and with the wheels free to rotate.*
d) *Exhaust emission checks.*

In most cases, the help of an assistant will be necessary to carry out these checks thoroughly.

Checks carried out from the driver's seat

Handbrake

Test the operation of the handbrake by pulling on the lever until the handbrake is in the normal fully-applied position. Ensure that the travel of the lever (the number of clicks of the ratchet) is not excessive before full resistance of the braking mechanism is felt. If so, this would indicate incorrect adjustment of the rear brakes, or incorrectly-adjusted handbrake cables.

With the handbrake fully applied, tap the lever sideways, and make sure that it does not release, which would indicate wear in the ratchet and pawl. Release the handbrake, and move the lever from side to side to check for excessive wear in the pivot bearing. Check the security of the lever mountings, and make sure that there is no corrosion of any part of the body structure within 30 cm of the lever mounting. If the lever mountings cannot be readily seen from inside the vehicle, carry out this check later when working underneath.

Footbrake

Check that the brake pedal is sound, without visible defects such as excessive wear of the pivot bushes, or a broken or damaged pedal pad. Check also for signs of fluid leaks on the pedal, floor or carpets, which would indicate failed seals in the brake master cylinder.

Depress the brake pedal slowly at first, then rapidly until sustained pressure can be held. Maintain this pressure, and check that the pedal does not creep down to the floor, which would again indicate problems with the master cylinder. Release the pedal, wait a few seconds, then depress it once until firm resistance is felt. Check that this resistance occurs near the top of the pedal travel. If the pedal travels nearly to the floor before firm resistance is felt, this would indicate incorrect brake adjustment, resulting in "insufficient reserve travel" of the footbrake. If firm resistance cannot be felt, ie the pedal feels spongy, this would indicate that air is present in the hydraulic system, which will necessitate complete bleeding of the system.

Check that the servo unit is operating correctly by depressing the brake pedal several times to exhaust the vacuum. Keep the pedal depressed, and start the engine. As soon as the engine starts, the brake pedal resistance will be felt to alter. If this is not the case, there may be a leak from the brake servo vacuum hose, or the servo unit itself may be faulty.

Steering wheel and column

Examine the steering wheel for fractures or looseness of the hub, spokes or rim. Move the steering wheel from side to side and then up and down, in relation to the steering column. Check that the steering wheel is not loose on the column, indicating wear in the column splines or a loose steering wheel retaining nut. Continue moving the steering wheel as before, but also turn it slightly from left to right. Check that there is no abnormal movement of the steering wheel, indicating excessive wear in the column upper support bearing, universal joint(s) or flexible coupling.

Windscreen and mirrors

The windscreen must be free of cracks or other damage which will seriously interfere with the driver's field of view, or which will prevent the windscreen wipers from operating properly. Small stone chips are acceptable. Any stickers, dangling toys or similar items must also be clear of the field of view.

Rear view mirrors must be secure, intact and capable of being adjusted. The nearside (passenger side) door mirror is not included in the test unless the interior mirror cannot be used - for instance, in the case of a van with blacked-out rear windows.

MOT test checks

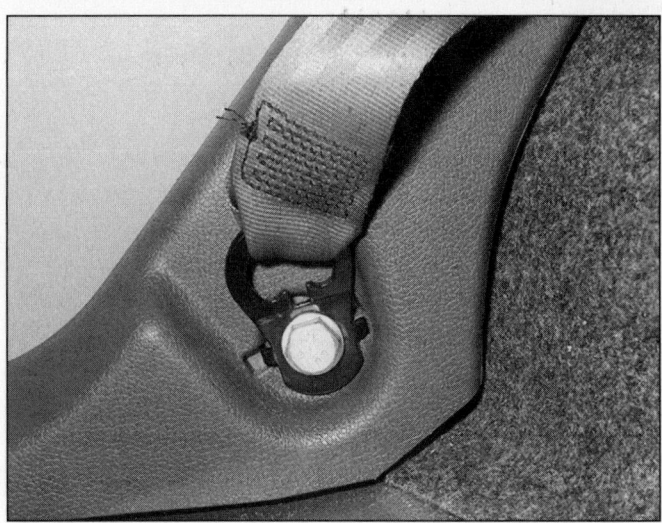

Check the security of all seat belt mountings

Seat belts and seats

Note: *The following checks are applicable to all seat belts, front and rear. Front seat belts must be of a type that will restrain the upper part of the body; lap belts are not acceptable. Various combinations of seat belt types are acceptable at the rear.*

Carefully examine the seat belt webbing for cuts, or any signs of serious fraying or deterioration. If the seat belt is of the retractable type, pull the belt all the way out, and examine the full extent of the webbing.

Fasten and unfasten the belt, ensuring that the locking mechanism holds securely and releases properly when intended. If the belt is of the retractable type, check also that the retracting mechanism operates correctly when the belt is released.

Check the security of all seat belt mountings and attachments which are accessible, without removing any trim or other components, from inside the vehicle **(see illustration)**. Any serious corrosion, fracture or distortion of the body structure within 30 cm of any mounting point will cause the vehicle to fail. Certain anchorages will not be accessible or even visible from inside the vehicle; in this instance, further checks should be carried out later, when working underneath. If any part of the seat belt mechanism is attached to the front seat, then the seat mountings are treated as anchorages, and must also comply as above.

The front seats themselves must be securely attached so that they cannot move unexpectedly, and the backrests must lock in the upright position.

Doors

Both front doors must be able to be opened and closed from outside and inside, and must latch securely when closed. In the case of a Pick-up, the tailgate must be securely attached and capable of being securely fastened.

Electrical equipment

Switch on the ignition and operate the horn. The horn must operate and produce a clear sound audible to other road users. Note that a gong, siren or two-tone horn fitted as an alternative to the manufacturer's original equipment is not acceptable.

Check the operation of the windscreen washers and wipers. The washers must operate with adequate flow and pressure, and with the jets adjusted so that the liquid strikes the windscreen near the top of the glass.

Operate the windscreen wipers in conjunction with the washers, and check that the blades cover their designed sweep of the windscreen without smearing. The blades must effectively clean the glass so that the driver has an adequate view of the road ahead, and to the front nearside and offside of the vehicle. If the screen smears or does not clean adequately, it is advisable to renew the wiper blades before the MOT test.

Depress the footbrake with the ignition switched on, and have your assistant check that both rear stop-lights operate, and are extinguished when the footbrake is released. If one stop-light fails to operate, it is likely that a bulb has blown or there is a poor electrical contact at, or near, the bulbholder. If both stop-lights fail to operate, check for a blown fuse, faulty stop-light switch, or possibly two blown bulbs. If the lights stay on when the brake pedal is released, it is possible that the switch is at fault.

Checks carried out with the vehicle on the ground

Vehicle identification

Front and rear number plates must be in good condition, securely fitted and easily read. Letters and numbers must be correctly spaced, with the gap between the group of numbers and the group of letters at least double the gap between adjacent numbers and letters.

The vehicle identification number on the plate in the passenger's stepwell must be legible. It will be checked during the test as part of the measures taken to prevent the fraudulent acquisition of certificates.

Electrical equipment

Switch on the sidelights, and check that both front and rear sidelights and the number plate lights are illuminated, and that the lenses and reflectors are secure and undamaged. This is particularly important at the rear, where a cracked or damaged lens would allow a white light to show to the rear, which is unacceptable. Note in addition that any lens that is excessively dirty, either inside or out, such that the light intensity is reduced, could also constitute a fail.

Switch on the headlights, and check that both dipped beam and main beam units are operating correctly and at the same light intensity. If either headlight shows signs of dimness, this is usually attributable to a poor earth connection or severely-corroded internal reflector. Inspect the headlight lenses for cracks or stone damage. Any damage to the headlight lens will normally constitute a fail, but this is very much down to the tester's discretion. Bear in mind that with all light units, they must operate correctly when first switched on. It is not acceptable to tap a light unit to make it operate.

The headlights must not only be aligned so as not to dazzle other road users when switched to dipped beam, but also so as to provide adequate illumination of the road. This can only be accurately checked using optical beam-setting equipment, so if you have any doubts about the headlight alignment, it is advisable to have this professionally checked and if necessary reset, before the MOT test.

With the ignition switched on, operate the direction indicators, and check that they show amber lights to the front and to the rear, that they flash at the rate of between one and two flashes per second, and that the "tell-tale" on the instrument panel also functions. Operation of the sidelights and stop-lights must not affect the indicators - if it does, the cause is usually a bad earth at the rear light cluster. Similarly check the operation of the hazard warning lights, which must work with the ignition on and off. Examine the lenses for cracks or damage as described previously.

Check the operation of the rear foglight(s). The test only concerns itself with the statutorily-required foglight, which is the one on the offside. The light must be secure, and emit a steady red light. The warning light on the instrument panel or in the switch must also work.

Footbrake

From within the engine compartment, examine the brake pipes for signs of leaks, corrosion, insecurity, chafing or other damage, and check the master cylinder and servo unit for leaks, security of their mountings or excessive corrosion in the vicinity of the mountings. The master cylinder reservoir must be secure; if it is of the translucent type, the fluid level must be between the upper and lower level markings.

Turn the steering as necessary so that the right-hand front brake flexible hose can be examined. Inspect the hose carefully for any sign of cracks or deterioration of the rubber. This will be most noticeable if the hose is bent in half, and is particularly common where the rubber portion enters the metal end fitting. Turn the steering onto full-left then full-right lock, and ensure that the hose does not contact the wheel, tyre, or any part of the steering or suspension mechanism. While your assistant depresses the brake pedal firmly, check the hose for any bulges or fluid leaks under pressure. Now repeat these checks on the left-hand front hose. Should any damage or deterioration be noticed, renew the hose.

Steering mechanism and suspension

Have your assistant turn the steering wheel from side to side slightly, up to the point where the steering gear just begins to transmit this movement to the roadwheels. Check for excessive free play between the steering wheel and the steering gear, which would indicate wear in the steering column joints, wear or insecurity of the steering column-to-steering gear coupling, or insecurity, incorrect adjustment, or wear in the steering gear itself. Generally speaking, free play greater than 1.3 cm for vehicles with rack-and-pinion type steering (or 7.6 cm for vehicles with steering box mechanisms), should be considered excessive.

Have your assistant turn the steering wheel more vigorously in each direction, up to the point where the roadwheels just begin to turn. As this is done, carry out a complete examination of all the steering joints, linkages, fittings and attachments. Any component that shows signs of wear, damage, distortion, or insecurity should be renewed or attended to accordingly. On vehicles with power steering, also check that the power steering pump is secure, that the pump drivebelt is in satisfactory condition and correctly adjusted, that there are no fluid leaks or damaged hoses, and that the system operates correctly. Additional checks can be carried out later with the vehicle raised, when there will be greater working clearance underneath.

Check that the vehicle is standing level and at approximately the correct ride height. Ensure that there is sufficient clearance between the suspension components and the bump stops to allow full suspension travel over bumps.

Shock absorbers

Depress each corner of the vehicle in turn, and then release it. If the shock absorbers are in good condition, the corner of the vehicle will rise and then settle in its normal position. If there is no noticeable damping effect from the shock absorber, and the vehicle continues to rise and fall, then the shock absorber is defective and the vehicle will fail. A shock absorber which has seized will also cause the vehicle to fail.

Exhaust system

Start the engine, and with your assistant holding a rag over the tailpipe, check the entire system for leaks, which will appear as a rhythmic fluffing or hissing sound at the source of the leak. Check the effectiveness of the silencer, ensuring that the noise produced is of a level to be expected from a vehicle of similar type. Providing that the system is structurally sound, it is acceptable to cure a leak using a proprietary exhaust system repair kit or similar method.

Checks carried out with the vehicle raised and with the wheels free to rotate

Apply the handbrake, then jack up the front and rear of the vehicle, and securely support it on axle stands positioned at suitable load-bearing points under the vehicle structure. Position the stands clear of the suspension assemblies, ensuring that the wheels are clear of the ground, and that the steering can be turned onto full-right and full-left lock.

Steering mechanism

Examine the steering rack rubber gaiters for signs of splits, lubricant leakage, or insecurity of the retaining clips. If power steering is fitted, check for signs of deterioration, damage, chafing or leakage of

Shake the roadwheel vigorously to check for excess play in the wheel bearings and suspension components

the fluid hoses, pipes or connections. Also check for excessive stiffness or binding of the steering, a missing split pin or locking device, or any severe corrosion of the body structure within 30 cm of any steering component attachment point.

Have your assistant turn the steering onto full-left then full-right lock. Check that the steering turns smoothly, without undue tightness or roughness. Also check that no part of the steering mechanism, including a wheel or tyre, fouls any brake flexible or rigid hose or pipe, or any part of the body structure.

On vehicles with four-wheel steering, similar considerations apply to the rear wheel steering linkages. However, it is permissible for a rear wheel steering system to be inoperative, provided that the rear wheels are secured in the straight-ahead position, and that the front wheel steering system is operating effectively.

Front and rear suspension and wheel bearings

Starting at the front right-hand side of the vehicle, grasp the roadwheel at the 3 o'clock and 9 o'clock positions, and shake it vigorously. Check for any free play at the wheel bearings, suspension balljoints, or suspension mountings, pivots and attachments. Check also for any serious deterioration of the rubber or metal casing of any mounting bushes, or any distortion, deformation or severe corrosion of any components. Look for missing split pins, tab washers or other locking devices on any mounting or attachment, or any severe corrosion of the vehicle structure within 30 cm of any suspension component attachment point.

If any excess free play is suspected at a component pivot point, this can be confirmed by using a large screwdriver or similar tool, and levering between the mounting and the component attachment. This will confirm whether the wear is in the pivot bush, its retaining bolt or in the mounting itself (the bolt holes can often become elongated).

Now grasp the wheel at the 12 o'clock and 6 o'clock positions **(see illustration)**, shake it vigorously and repeat the previous inspection. Rotate the wheel, checking for roughness or tightness of the front wheel bearing such that imminent failure of the bearing is indicated.

Carry out all the above checks at the other front wheel, and then at both rear wheels.

Roadsprings and shock absorbers

On vehicles with strut type suspension units, examine the strut assembly for signs of serious fluid leakage, corrosion or severe pitting of the piston rod, or damage to the casing. Check also for security of the mounting points.

If coil springs are fitted, check that the spring ends locate correctly in their spring seats, that there is no severe corrosion of the spring, and that it is not cracked, broken, or in any way damaged.

MOT test checks

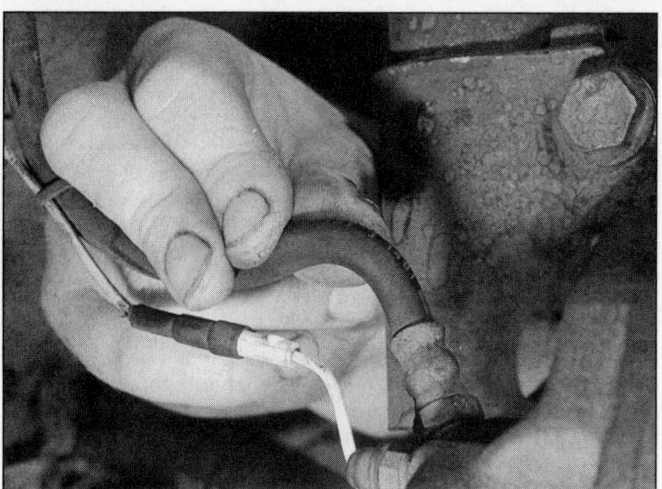
Check the braking system pipes and hoses for signs of damage or deterioration

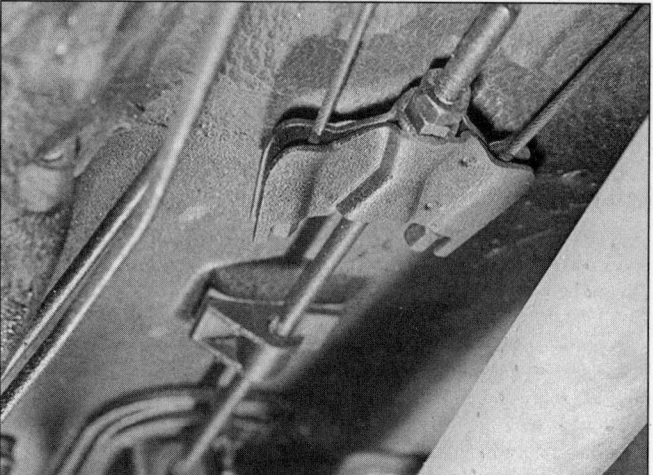
Inspect the handbrake cables under the rear of the vehicle

If the vehicle is fitted with leaf springs, check that all leaves are intact, that the axle is securely attached to each spring, and that there is no wear or deterioration of the spring eye mountings, bushes, or shackles.

The same general checks apply to vehicles fitted with other suspension types, such as torsion bars, hydraulic displacer units, etc. In all cases, ensure that all mountings and attachments are secure, that there are no signs of excessive wear, corrosion, cracking, deformation or damage to any component or bush, and that there are no fluid leaks or damaged hoses or pipes (hydraulic types).

Inspect the shock absorbers for signs of serious fluid leakage. (Slight seepage of fluid is normal for some types of shock absorber, and is not a reason for failing.) Check for excessive wear of the mounting bushes or attachments, or damage to the body of the unit.

Driveshafts

With the steering turned onto full-lock, rotate each front wheel in turn, and inspect the constant velocity joint gaiters for splits or damage. Also check that the gaiter is securely attached to its respective housings by clips or other methods of retention.

Continue turning the wheel, and check that each driveshaft is straight, with no sign of damage.

Braking system

If possible, without dismantling, check for wear of the brake pads and the condition of the discs. Ensure that the friction lining material has not worn excessively, and that the discs are not fractured, pitted, scored or worn excessively.

Carefully examine all the rigid brake pipes underneath the vehicle, and the flexible hoses at the rear (see illustration). Look for signs of excessive corrosion, chafing, or insecurity of the pipes, and for signs of bulging under pressure, chafing, splits or deterioration of the flexible hoses.

Look for signs of hydraulic fluid leaks at the brake calipers or on the brake backplates, indicating failed hydraulic seals in the components concerned.

Slowly spin each wheel, while your assistant depresses the footbrake then releases it. Ensure that each brake is operating, and that the wheel is free to rotate when the pedal is released. It is not possible to test brake efficiency without special equipment, but (traffic and local conditions permitting) a road test can be carried out to check that the vehicle pulls up in a straight line.

Examine the handbrake mechanism, and check for signs of frayed or broken cables, excessive corrosion, or wear or insecurity of the linkage. Have your assistant operate the handbrake, while you check that the mechanism works on each relevant wheel, and releases fully, without binding (see illustration).

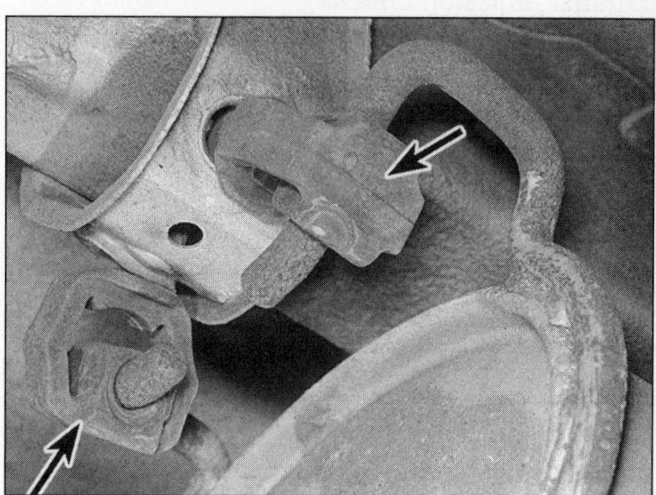
Check the condition of the exhaust system, paying particular attention to the mountings (arrowed)

Fuel and exhaust systems

Inspect the fuel tank, fuel pipes, hoses and unions (including the unions at the pump, filter, injectors and injection pump). All components must be secure, and free from leaks. The fuel filler cap must also be secure and of an appropriate type.

Examine the exhaust system over its entire length, checking for any damaged, broken or missing mountings, security of the pipe retaining clamps, and condition of the system with regard to rust and corrosion (see illustration).

Wheels and tyres

Carefully examine each tyre in turn, on both the inner and outer walls and over the whole of the tread area. Look for signs of cuts, tears, lumps, bulges, and for separation of the tread and exposure of the ply or cord due to wear or other damage. Check also that the tyre bead is correctly seated on the wheel rim, and that the tyre valve is sound and properly seated. Spin the wheel, and check that it is not excessively distorted or damaged, particularly at the bead rim.

Check that the tyres are of the correct size for the vehicle, and that they are of the same size and type on each axle. (Having a "space-saver" spare tyre in use is not acceptable.) The tyres should also be inflated to the specified pressures.

Using a suitable gauge, check the tyre tread depth. The current legal requirement states that the tread pattern must be visible over the whole tread area, and must be of a minimum depth of 1.6 mm over at least three-quarters of the tread width. It is acceptable for some wear of the inside or outside edges of the tyre to be apparent, but this wear must be in one even circumferential band, and the tread must be visible. Any excessive wear of this nature may indicate incorrect front wheel alignment, which should be checked before the tyre becomes excessively worn. See the appropriate Chapters for further information on tyre wear patterns and front wheel alignment.

Body corrosion

Check the condition of the entire vehicle structure for signs of corrosion in any load-bearing areas. For the purpose of the MOT test, all chassis box sections, side sills, crossmembers, pillars, suspension, steering, braking system and seat belt mountings and anchorages should all be considered as load-bearing areas. As a general guide, any corrosion which has seriously reduced the metal thickness of a load-bearing area to weaken it, is likely to cause the vehicle to fail. Should corrosion of this nature be encountered, professional repairs are likely to be needed.

Body damage or corrosion which causes sharp or otherwise dangerous edges to be exposed will also cause the vehicle to fail.

Exhaust emission checks

Have the engine at normal operating temperature, and make sure that the preliminary conditions for checking idle speed (injection system in good order, air filter element clean, etc) have been met.

Before any measurements are carried out, raise the engine speed to around 2500 rpm, and hold it at this speed for 10 seconds. Allow the engine speed to return to idle, and watch for smoke emissions from the exhaust tailpipe. If the idle speed is obviously much too high, or if dense blue or black smoke comes from the tailpipe for more than 5 seconds, the vehicle will fail. As a rule of thumb, blue smoke signifies oil being burnt (worn valve stem oil seals, valve guides, piston rings or bores) while black smoke signifies unburnt fuel (dirty air cleaner element, injection timing incorrect, injector(s) leaking or sticking, or other fuel injection system fault).

The only emission check currently specified for Diesel engines is for smoke. (CO and HC emission checks as carried out on petrol engines are not significant for Diesels.)

Smoke testing

In principle, the testing station should measure exhaust smoke using suitable testing equipment. At the time of writing, the free acceleration smoke test introduced at the beginning of 1993 had been abandoned. The test involves accelerating the engine several times to its maximum unloaded speed; a number of vehicles suffered serious damage during the test because of timing belt failure.

For the time being, the old situation has been restored, in that the MOT tester decides by visual inspection and by experience (the "calibrated eyeball") whether smoke emission is excessive. Some more precise test will probably be introduced in due course. Consult an MOT testing station for details of the latest regulations.

Note: *If the free acceleration smoke test is reintroduced, it is of the utmost importance that the engine timing belt be in good condition before the test is carried out.*

Chapter 1
Routine maintenance and servicing

Contents

	Section		Section
Air cleaner element renewal	36	Handbrake linkage lubrication and adjustment check	26
Air conditioning system check	19	Idle speed and anti-stall speed check and adjustment	35
Automatic transmission fluid level check	34	Introduction	1
Automatic transmission linkage lubrication	25	Load-apportioning valve check and adjustment	31
Battery check, maintenance and charging	8	Manual transmission oil level check	22
Brake check	16	Overdrive slipjoint and propeller shaft lubrication	24
Brake fluid renewal	40	Power steering fluid level check	5
Clutch cable lubrication	23	Propeller shaft universal joint and centre bearing check	27
Coolant renewal	39	Purge preheating system flame plug fuel reservoir	43
Door and bonnet check and lubrication	20	Rear axle oil level check	30
Drivebelt check and renewal	10	Road test	33
Electrical system check	7	Roadwheel nut tightness check	32
Engine compartment wiring check	17	Seat belt check	9
Engine oil and filter change	12	Steering kingpin and bush lubrication - beam axle models	21
Engine oil filler cap check and cleaning	13	Steering, suspension and roadwheel check	15
Exhaust system check	29	Timing belt renewal	42
Fluid level checks	3	Tyre and tyre pressure checks	4
Ford Transit Diesel maintenance schedule	1	Underbody and fuel/brake line check	28
Front wheel alignment check	41	Underbonnet check for fluid leaks and hose condition	11
Front wheel bearing adjustment	38	Valve clearance adjustment	18
Fuel filter draining	14	Windscreen/tailgate washer system and wiper blade check	6
Fuel filter renewal	37		

Specifications

Engine
Oil filter type:
- Up to 1989 .... Champion E103
- 1989 on .... Champion type not available

Cooling system
Coolant protection at standard 50% antifreeze/water mixture ratio:
- Slush point .... -25°C (-13°F)
- Solidifying point .... -30°C (-22°F)

Coolant specific gravity at standard 50% antifreeze/water mixture ratio
and 15°C/59°F - with no other additives in coolant 1.061

Fuel system
Idle speed:
- Normally-aspirated engines .... 800 to 850 rpm
- Turbocharged engines* .... 800 to 900 rpm

Air filter element type:
- Engines with circular air cleaner mounted on engine .... Champion W184
- Engines with square air cleaner mounted on engine .... Champion type not available
- Engines with air cleaner mounted at side of engine .... Champion U634

Fuel filter .... Champion L209

*Note: *The idle speed cannot be adjusted on turbocharged engines controlled by the Lucas EPIC engine management system, as this is a function of the system's electronic control unit.*

Braking system
- Minimum front brake pad lining thickness .... 1.5 mm
- Minimum rear brake shoe lining thickness .... 1.0 mm

Chapter 1 Routine maintenance and servicing

Tyre pressures (up to 1992 model year)

Vehicle type / tyre size	Pressures - bar (psi) Front	Rear
80 Van or Combi / 185 R14 Rein	2.8 (41)	2.9 (42)
100 Van or Combi / 185 R14C 6PR	3.0 (43)	3.4 (50)
100 Bus / 185 R14C 6PR	2.9 (42)	2.9 (42)
115 Bus / 195 R14C 6PR	2.7 (39)	3.0 (44)
120 all models / 195 R14C 6PR	2.7 (39)	3.7 (54)
100L Van, Combi, Chassis Cab / 195 R14C 8PR	2.8 (40)	4.1 (59)
130 all models / 185 R14 Rein	2.7 (39)	2.3 (33)
130 all models / 185 R14C 6PR	2.9 (42)	2.5 (36)
160 all models / 185 R14 Rein	2.7 (39)	2.7 (39)
160 all models / 185 R14C 6PR	2.9 (42)	2.9 (42)
190 Van, Combi, Chassis Cab / 185 R14C 6PR	3.1 (45)	3.2 (47)

Tyre pressures (1992 to 1995 model years)

Vehicle type / tyre size	Pressures - bar (psi) Front	Rear
80S Van or Combi / 185 R14 Rein	3.4 (50)	2.8 (41)
80S Van or Combi / 185 R14C 8PR	3.4 (50)	3.1 (46)
100S Van or Combi / 185 R14C 6PR/8PR	3.4 (50)	3.6 (53)
120S Van, Combi, Chassis Cab / 195 R14C 6PR/8PR	3.4 (50)	3.6 (53)
150S Van, Combi / 215/70 R15C 8PR	2.7 (40)	4.2 (62)
150S Chassis Cab / 225/70 R15C 6PR	2.1 (31)	3.6 (53)
100 L (non-turbo) Van, Combi Chassis Cab / 195 R14C 6PR	3.3 (49)	3.6 (53)
100 L (turbo) Van, Combi, Chassis Cab / 225/70 R14C 6PR	2.6 (38)	2.8 (41)
150L Van, Combi, Chassis Cab / 225/70 R15C 6PR	2.8 (41)	3.6 (53)
190 L Van, Combi, Chassis Cab / 225/70 R15C 8PR	2.8 (41)	4.3 (63)
190 Twin-wheel Chassis Cab / 185 R15C 6PR	3.8 (56)	2.6 (38)
190EF Twin-wheel Chassis Cab / 185 R15C 6PR	3.3 (49)	3.2 (47)
9-seat Bus / 185 R14C 6PR	3.4 (50)	3.1 (46)
9-seat Bus / 185 R14C 8PR	3.4 (50)	3.6 (53)
12-seat Bus / 195 R14C 6PR/8PR	3.4 (50)	3.0 (44)
13-seat Bus / 195 R14C 6PR/8PR	3.4 (50)	3.6 (53)
LCY Bus / 225/70 R15C 6PR	2.8 (41)	3.6 (53)

Tyre pressures (1995 model year onwards)

Vehicle type / tyre size	Pressures - bar (psi) Front	Rear
80S Van or Combi / 185 R14 Rein	2.3 (34)	2.8 (41)
80S Van or Combi / 195 R14C 6PR	2.5 (37)	2.6 (38)
100S Van or Combi / 185 R14 6PR	3.0 (44)	3.5 (51)
100S Van or Combi / 195 R14C 6PR	3.8 (41)	3.2 (47)
120S Van, Combi, Chassis Cab / 195 R14C 6PR	2.8 (42)	3.6 (53)
150S Van, Combi / 215/70 R15 8PR	2.7 (40)	4.2 (62)
150S Chassis Cab / 225/70 R15 6PR	2.2 (32)	3.6 (53)
100 L Van, Combi Chassis Cab / 195 R14C 6PR	3.3 (49)	3.6 (53)
150 L Van, Combi, Chassis Cab / 225/70 R15 6PR	2.8 (41)	3.6 (53)
190 L Van, Combi, Chassis Cab / 225/70 R15 8PR	2.8 (41)	4.5 (66)
190 Twin-wheel Chassis Cab / 185 R15C 6PR	3.8 (56)	3.2 (47)
190EF Twin-wheel Chassis Cab / 185 R15C 6PR	3.8 (56)	3.2 (47)
9-seat Bus / 205/70 R14 Rein	2.4 (35)	2.3 (34)
12-seat Bus / 205/70 R14 Rein	2.4 (35)	2.7 (40)
15-seat Bus / 225/70 R15 6PR	2.8 (41)	3.6 (53)

Note: *Pressures apply only to original equipment tyres, and may vary if any other make or type is fitted; check with the tyre manufacturer or supplier for correct pressures if necessary.*

Wiper blades

Windscreen	Champion X-5503
Tailgate	Champion type not available

Torque wrench settings

	Nm	lbf ft
Engine oil drain plug	20 to 27	15 to 20
Manual transmission filler/level plug	23 to 32	17 to 24
Manual transmission drain plug	23 to 32	17 to 24
Roadwheel nuts:		
Five-stud wheels	85	63
Six-stud wheels	168	124
Seat belt mounting bolts	38 to 53	28 to 39

Lubricants, fluids and capacities

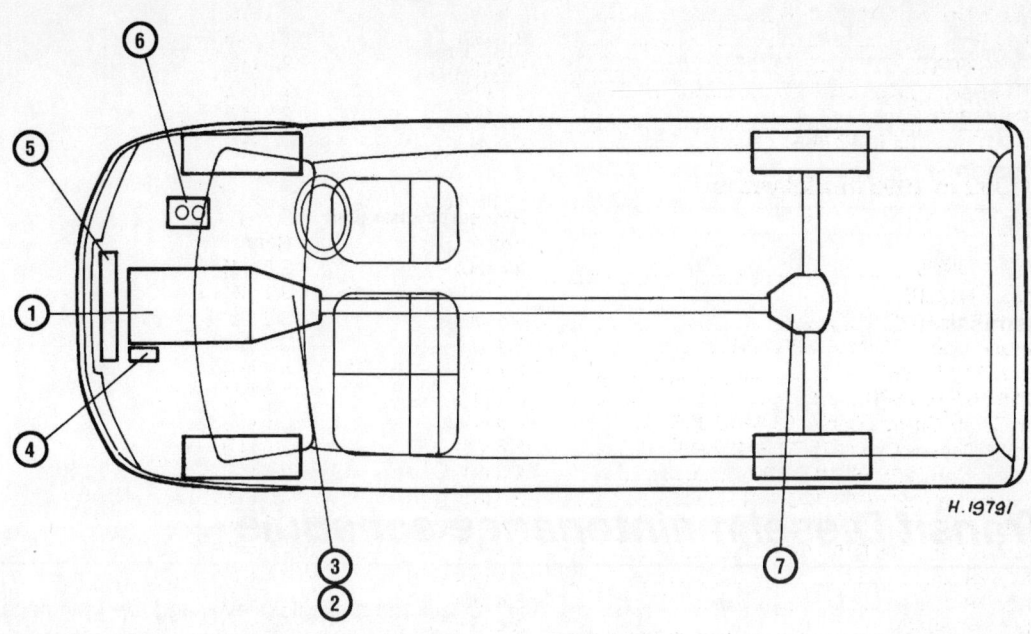

Lubricants and fluids

Component or system	Lubricant type/specification	Duckhams recommendation
1 Engine	Multigrade engine oil to specification API SG/CD or better, viscosity range 5W/50 to 10W/30	Duckhams Diesel, QS, QXR, Hypergrade Plus, or Hypergrade

2 Manual transmission:
   4-speed
   5-speed
	
	SAE 80 EP gear oil to Ford specification SQM2C-9008-A
	SAE 80 EP gear oil to Ford specification ESD-M2C 175-A and ESD-M2C 186-A
		
		Duckhams Hypoid 80W/90
		Duckhams Hypoid 75W/90S

3 Automatic transmission	Transmission fluid to Ford specification SQM-2C-9010-A or ESP-M2C-166-H	Duckhams Uni-Matic
4 Power steering	Transmission fluid to Ford specification ESP-M2C-166-H	Duckhams Uni-Matic
5 Cooling system	Soft water, and ethylene glycol-based antifreeze suitable for use in mixed-metal cooling systems) to Ford specification ESD-M97B-49-A	Duckhams Universal Antifreeze andSummer Coolant
6 Braking system	Hydraulic fluid to Ford specification ESD-M6C-57-A, Super DOT 4 or equivalent	Duckhams Universal Brake and Clutch Fluid
7 Rear axle	SAE 90 EP Hypoid gear oil to Ford specification SQM-2C-9002-AA or 9003-AA	Duckhams Hypoid 80W/90S
Wheel hub bearing grease (front and rear)	Grease to Ford specification SAM-1C-9111A	Duckhams LB10 or LBM10

Capacities

Engine oil
At oil and filter change:
- Normally-aspirated engines .... 6.15 litres
- Turbocharged engines .... 6.25 litres

Difference between dipstick minimum and maximum level notches ...... 0.5 to 1.0 litre

Cooling system
Normally-aspirated engines... 11.5 litres
Turbocharged engines.. 12.0 litres

Fuel tank .... 55.0 litres

Manual transmission
Type G .... 1.98 litres
Type G with overdrive.. 2.5 litres
Type N .... 1.5 litres
MT75 .... 1.25

Automatic transmission .... 8.2 litres

1 Ford Transit Diesel maintenance schedule

General

The manufacturer's recommended maintenance schedule for these vehicles is as described below - note that the schedule starts from the vehicle's date of registration. These are the minimum maintenance intervals recommended by the factory for Transits driven daily, but subjected only to "normal" use. If you wish to keep your vehicle in peak condition at all times, you may wish to perform some of these procedures even more often. Because frequent maintenance enhances the efficiency, performance and resale value of your vehicle, we encourage you to do so. If your usage is not "normal", shorter intervals are also recommended - the most important examples of these are noted in the schedule. These shorter intervals apply particularly if you drive in dusty areas, tow a trailer, sit with the engine idling or drive at low speeds for extended periods (ie, in heavy traffic), or drive for short distances (less than four miles) in below-freezing temperatures.

When your vehicle is new, it should be serviced by a Ford dealer service department to protect the factory warranty. In many cases, the initial maintenance check is done at no cost to the owner. Note that this first free service (carried out by the selling dealer 1500 miles or 3 months after delivery), although an important check for a new vehicle, is not part of the regular maintenance schedule, and is therefore not mentioned here.

It should be noted that for the 1992 model year, the service time/mileage intervals for normally-aspirated models were extended by the manufacturer from an interim service every 6000 miles/6 months, followed by a standard service every 12 000 miles/12 months, to one annual service at 10 000 mile/12 month intervals. As the following service schedule is based on the earlier 6000 mile/6 month intervals, owners of later models may wish to extend their maintenance periods slightly from those shown.

Daily, when refuelling, or before any long journey

Check the engine oil level, and top-up if necessary (Section 3)

Check the brake fluid level, and top-up if necessary (Section 3). If repeated topping-up is required, check the system for leaks or damage at the earliest possible opportunity (Sections 11 and 28)

Check the windscreen/tailgate washer fluid level, and top-up if necessary (Section 3)

Check the tyre pressures, including the spare (Section 4)

Visually check the tyres for excessive tread wear, or damage (Section 4)

Check the operation of all (exterior and interior) lights and the horn, wipers and windscreen/tailgate washer system (Sections 6 and 7). Renew any blown bulbs (Chapter 12), and clean the lenses of all exterior lights

Monthly

Repeat all the daily checks, then carry out the following:

Check the coolant level, and top-up if necessary (Section 3)

Check the battery electrolyte level, where applicable (Section 3)

Check the power steering fluid level (where applicable) and top-up if necessary (Section 5)

Visually check all reservoirs, hoses and pipes for leakage (Section 11)

Check the operation of the air conditioning system (where fitted) (Section 19)

Check the operation of the handbrake (Section 26)

Check the aim of the windscreen/tailgate/headlight washer jets, correcting them if required (Section 6)

Check the condition of the wiper blades, renewing them if worn or no longer effective - note that the manufacturer recommends renewing the blades annually as a safety precaution, irrespective of their apparent condition (Section 6)

Chapter 1 Routine maintenance and servicing

Interim service - every 6000 miles or 6 months, whichever occurs first

Repeat all the monthly checks, then carry out the following:
- Check the electrical system (Section 7)
- Check the battery (Section 8)
- Check the seat belts (Section 9)
- Check the drivebelts (Section 10)
- Check under the bonnet for fluid leaks and hose condition (Section 11)
- Change the engine oil and filter (Section 12)
- Clean the engine oil filler cap (Section 13)
- Drain the fuel filter (Section 14)
- Check the steering, suspension and roadwheels (Section 15)
- Check the braking system (Section 16)

Note: *If the vehicle is used regularly for very short journeys (less than 10 miles), or for stop/start driving, the oil and filter should be renewed between services. Seek the advice of a local Ford dealer if in doubt on this point.*

Standard service - every 12 000 miles or 12 months, whichever occurs first

Carry out all operations listed above, plus the following:
- Check the condition of all engine compartment wiring (Section 17)
- Check the valve clearance adjustment (Section 18)
- Check the condition of all air conditioning components (where fitted) (Section 19)
- Check the doors and bonnet, and lubricate the hinges and locks (Section 20)
- Lubricate the steering kingpins and bushes (beam axle models) (Section 21)
- Check the manual transmission oil level (Section 22)
- Lubricate the clutch cable (Section 23)
- Lubricate the overdrive slipjoint and propeller shaft sliding spline (Section 24)
- Lubricate the automatic transmission linkage (Section 25)
- Lubricate the handbrake linkage, and check the handbrake adjustment (Section 26)
- Check the propeller shaft and centre bearing for wear (Section 27)
- Check the underbody and all fuel and brake lines (Section 28)
- Check the exhaust system (Section 29)
- Check the rear axle oil level (Section 30)
- Adjust the load-apportioning valve (Section 31)
- Check the security of all roadwheel nuts (Section 32)
- Road test (Section 33)
- Check the automatic transmission fluid level (Section 34)
- Check and adjust the engine idle speed and anti-stall speed (Section 35)

Extended service - every 24 000 miles or 2 years, whichever occurs first

Carry out all operations listed above, plus the following:
- Renew the air cleaner filter element (Section 36). Note that this task must be carried out at more frequent intervals if the vehicle is used in dusty or polluted conditions
- Renew the fuel filter (Section 37)
- Check/adjust the front wheel bearings (Section 38)

Every 36 000 miles or 3 years, whichever occurs first

Carry out all operations listed above, plus the following:
- Renew the coolant (Section 39)
- Renew the brake fluid (Section 40)
- Check the front wheel alignment (Section 41)

Every 48 000 miles

- Renew the timing belt (Section 42)

Annually, at the beginning of Winter

- Purge the pre-heating system flame plug fuel reservoir (where fitted) (Section 43)

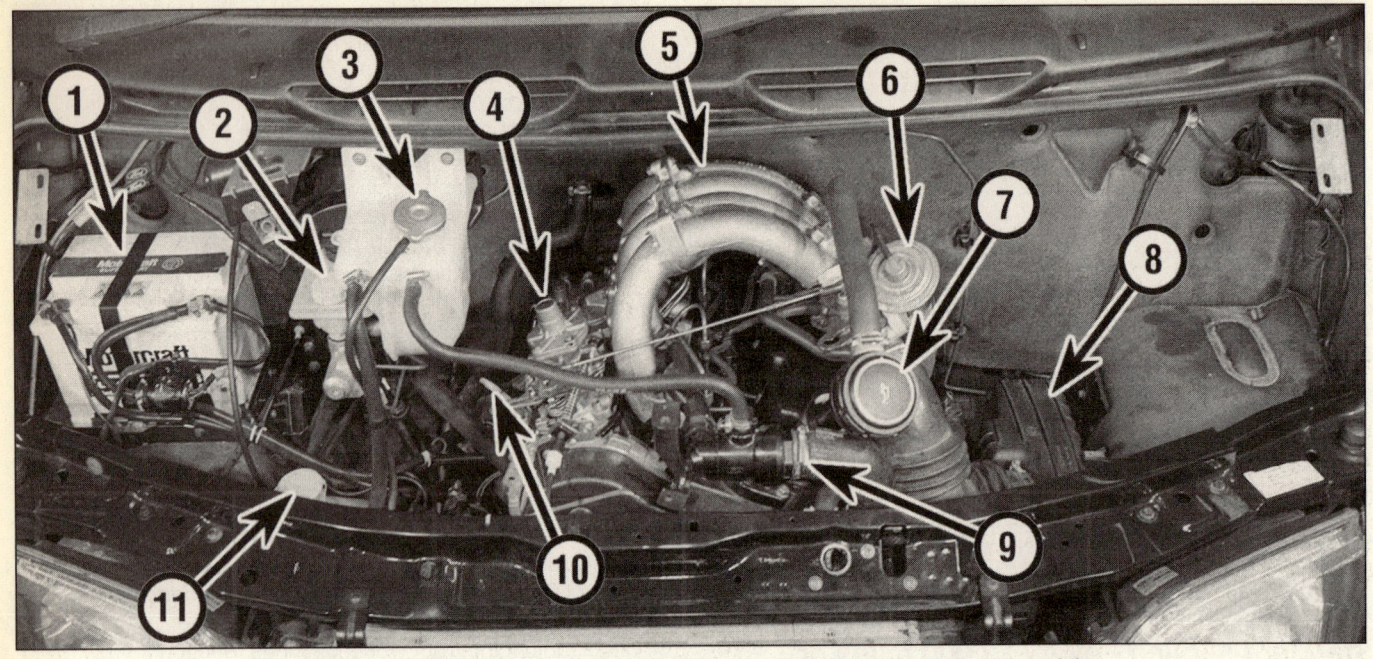

1-6 Chapter 1 Routine maintenance and servicing

Engine compartment component locations on a 1992 normally-aspirated model

1. Battery
2. Brake fluid reservoir
3. Coolant expansion tank
4. Fuel injection pump
5. Inlet manifold (two-piece type)
6. EGR valve
7. Oil filler cap
8. Air cleaner unit
9. Thermostat housing
10. Engine oil dipstick
11. Windscreen washer reservoir

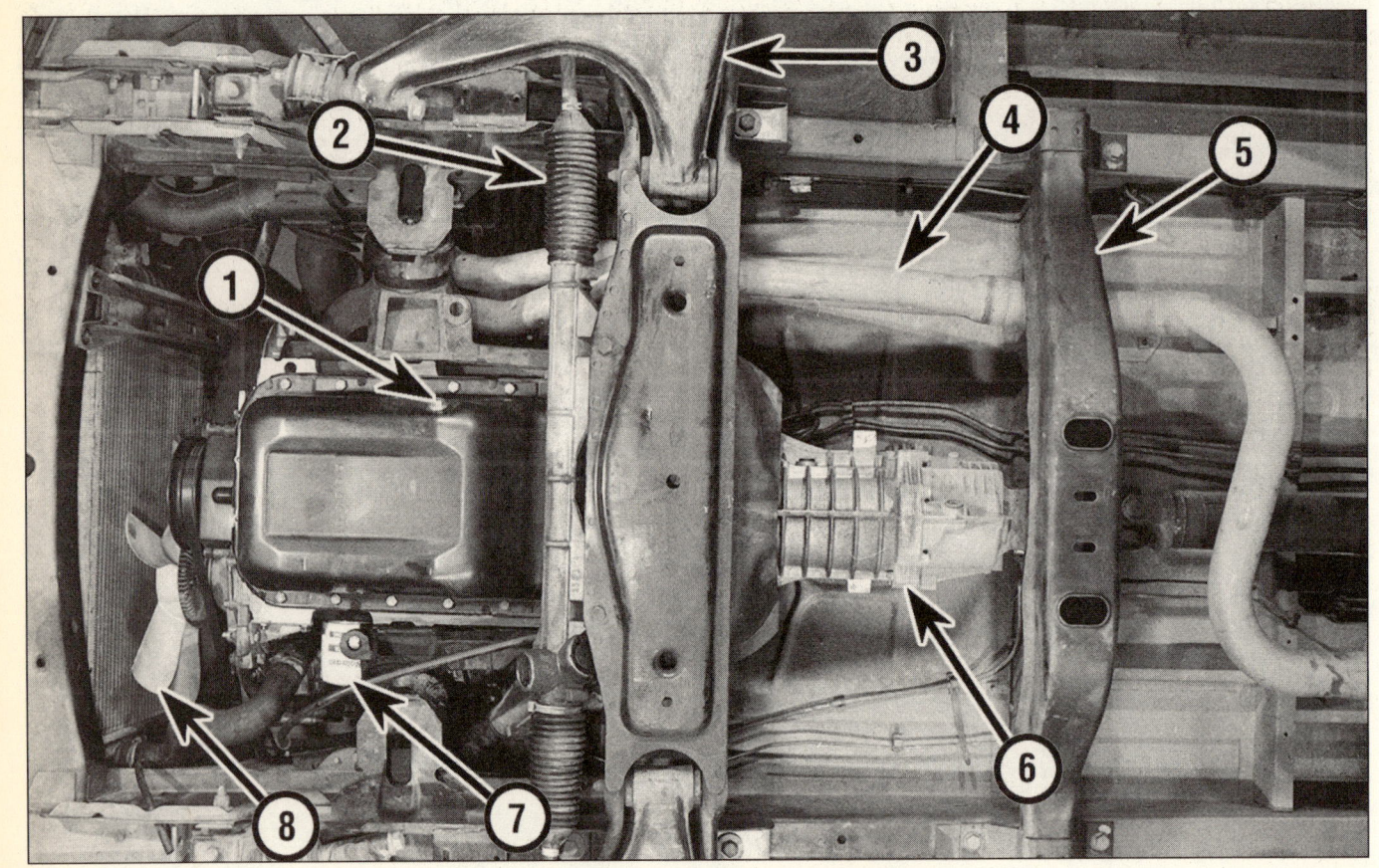

Underside view at front of a 1992 short-wheelbase Van

1. Engine oil drain plug
2. Steering rack rubber gaiter
3. Suspension lower arm
4. Exhaust pipe
5. Transmission crossmember
6. Transmission assembly
7. Oil filter
8. Cooling fan

Chapter 1 Routine maintenance and servicing

Underside view at rear of a 1992 short-wheelbase Van

1. Fuel tank
2. Handbrake cable
3. Load-apportioning valve
4. Spare wheel carrier
5. Exhaust pipe rear section
6. Rear axle
7. Pinion flange and propeller shaft universal joint
8. Handbrake cable compensator

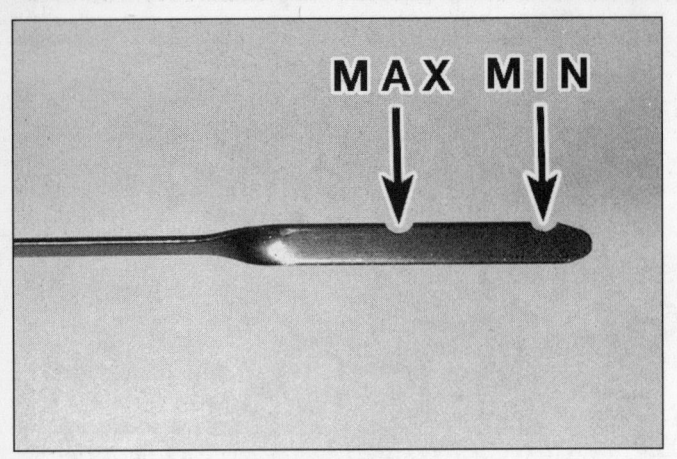

3.4 Maximum and minimum level markings on the engine oil dipstick

3.6 Topping-up the engine oil

2 Introduction

This Chapter is designed to help the home mechanic maintain the Ford Transit Diesel for peak performance, economy, safety and long life.

On the following pages is a master maintenance schedule, followed by Sections dealing specifically with each item on the schedule. Visual checks, adjustments, component replacement and other helpful items are included. Refer to the accompanying illustrations of the engine compartment and the underside of the vehicle for the location of various components.

Servicing your Transit in accordance with the mileage/time maintenance schedule and the following Sections will provide it with a planned maintenance programme, which should result in a long and reliable service life. This is a comprehensive plan, so maintaining some items but not others at the specified service intervals will not produce the same results.

As you service your Transit, you will discover that many of the procedures can - and should - be grouped together, because of the nature of the particular procedure you're performing, or because of the close proximity to one another of two otherwise-unrelated components.

For example, if the vehicle is raised for any reason, you should inspect the exhaust, suspension, steering and fuel systems while you're under the vehicle. When you're checking the tyres, it makes good sense to check the brakes and wheel bearings, especially if the roadwheels have already been removed.

Finally, let's suppose you have to borrow or hire a torque wrench. Even if you only need to tighten the wheel nuts, you might as well check the torque of as many critical fasteners as time allows.

The first step of this maintenance programme is to prepare yourself before the actual work begins. Read through all the Sections which are relevant to the procedures you're planning to carry out, then make a list of, and gather together, all the parts and tools you will need to do the job. If it looks as if you might run into problems during a particular segment of some procedure, seek advice from your local parts man or dealer service department.

3 Fluid level checks (Daily/Monthly)

General

1 Fluids are an essential part of the lubrication, cooling, braking and other systems. Because these fluids gradually become depleted and/or contaminated during normal operation of the vehicle, they must be periodically replenished. See *"Lubricants, fluids and capacities"* at the beginning of this Chapter before adding fluid to any of the following components. **Note:** *The vehicle must be on level ground before fluid levels can be checked.*

Engine oil

2 The engine oil level is checked with a dipstick located on the right-hand side of the engine; it can be identified by its yellow/black plastic grip. The dipstick protrudes through a metal tube, from which it extends down into the sump at the bottom of the engine.
3 The oil level should be checked before the vehicle is driven, or about 5 minutes after the engine has been switched off. If the level is checked immediately after driving the vehicle, some of the oil will remain in the engine upper components, producing an inaccurate dipstick reading.
4 Pull the dipstick from the tube, and wipe all the oil from the end with a clean rag or paper towel; note the dipstick's maximum and minimum levels, indicated by marks or notches **(see illustration)**. Insert the clean dipstick all the way back into its metal tube, and pull it out again. Observe the oil on the end of the dipstick; its level should be between these two notches.
5 Do not allow the level to drop below the minimum level notch, or oil starvation may cause engine damage. Conversely, overfilling the engine (adding oil above the maximum level notch) may cause oil-fouled spark plugs, oil leaks or oil seal failures.
6 The push-fit oil filler cap is located on the front end of the cylinder head rocker cover; remove it to add oil. When topping-up, use only the correct grade and type of oil, as given in the Specifications Section of this Chapter; use a funnel to prevent spills **(see illustration)**. It takes approximately 0.5 to 1.0 litre of oil to raise the level from the dipstick's minimum level notch to its maximum level notch. After adding the oil, refit the filler cap, start the engine, and allow it to idle while the oil is redistributed around the engine. While you are waiting, look carefully for any oil leaks, particularly around the oil filter or drain plug. Stop the engine; check the oil level again, after the oil has had enough time to drain from the upper block and cylinder head galleries.
7 Checking the oil level is an important preventive maintenance step. A continually-dropping oil level indicates oil leakage through damaged seals and from loose connections, or oil consumption past worn piston rings or valve guides. If the oil looks milky in colour, or has water droplets in it, the cylinder head gasket may be blown - the engine's compression pressure should be checked immediately (see Chapter 2A). The condition of the oil should also be checked. Each time you check the oil level, slide your thumb and index finger up the dipstick before wiping off the oil. If you see small dirt or metal particles clinging to the dipstick, the oil should be changed (Section 11).

Coolant

Warning: *Do not allow antifreeze to come in contact with your skin, or with the painted surfaces of the vehicle. Flush contaminated areas immediately with plenty of water. Don't store new coolant, or leave old coolant lying around, where it's accessible to children or pets - they're attracted by its sweet smell. Ingestion of even a small amount of coolant can be fatal! Wipe up garage-floor and drip-pan spills*

Chapter 1 Routine maintenance and servicing

3.10 Coolant expansion tank maximum and minimum level markings

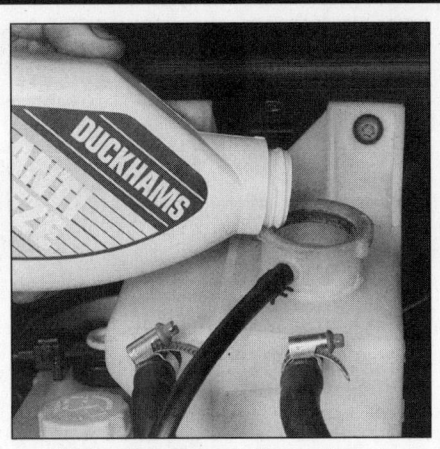

3.13 Topping-up the coolant expansion tank

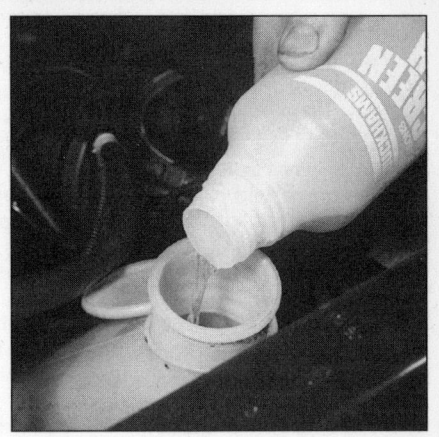

3.17 Topping-up the windscreen washer reservoir

immediately. Keep antifreeze containers covered, and repair cooling system leaks as soon as they're noticed.

8   All vehicles covered by this manual have a sealed, pressurised cooling system. A translucent plastic expansion tank, located on the engine compartment bulkhead, is connected by hoses to the main cooling system. As the coolant heats up during engine operation, surplus coolant passes through the connecting hose into the expansion tank; a connection to the radiator bottom hose union allows coolant to circulate through the tank and back to the water pump, thus purging any air from the system. As the engine cools, the coolant is automatically drawn back into the cooling system's main components, to maintain the correct level.

9   While the coolant level must be checked regularly, remember therefore that it will vary with the temperature of the engine. When the engine is cold, the coolant level should be between the "MAX" and "MIN" level lines on the tank, but once the engine has warmed up, the level may rise to above the "MAX" level line.

10   For an accurate check of the coolant level, the engine must be cold. The level must be between the "MAX" and "MIN" level lines on the tank **(see illustration)**. If it is below the "MIN" level line, the coolant must be topped-up as follows.

11   First prepare a sufficient quantity of coolant mixture, using clean, soft water and antifreeze of the recommended type, in the specified mixture ratio. Mix equal quantities of water and antifreeze to produce the 50/50 mixture ratio specified when topping-up. If only a small amount of coolant is required to bring the system up to the proper level, plain water can be used, but repeatedly doing this will dilute the antifreeze/water solution in the system, reducing the protection it should provide against freezing and corrosion. To maintain the specified antifreeze/water ratio, it is essential to top-up the coolant level with the correct mixture, as described here. Use only ethylene/glycol type antifreeze, and *do not* use supplementary inhibitors or additives. **Warning:** *Never remove the expansion tank filler cap when the engine is running, or has just been switched off, as the cooling system will be pressurised, and the coolant may be extremely hot - the consequent escaping steam and scalding coolant could cause serious injury.*

12   If topping-up is necessary, wait until the system has cooled completely (or at least 10 minutes after switching off the engine, if lack of time means it is absolutely necessary to top-up while the engine may still be warm). Wrap a thick cloth around the expansion tank filler cap, and unscrew it slowly by one full turn. If any hissing is heard as steam escapes, wait until the hissing ceases, indicating that pressure is released, then slowly unscrew the filler cap until it can be removed. If more hissing sounds are heard, wait until they have stopped before unscrewing the filler cap completely. At all times, keep your face, hands and other exposed skin well away from the filler opening.

13   When the filler cap has been removed, add coolant to bring the level up to the "MAX" level line **(see illustration)**. Refit the cap, tightening it securely.

14   With this type of cooling system, the addition of coolant should only be necessary at very infrequent intervals. If topping-up is regularly required, or if the coolant level drops within a short time after replenishment, there may be a leak in the system. Inspect the radiator, hoses, expansion tank filler cap, radiator drain plug and water pump. If no leak is evident, have the filler cap and the entire system pressure-tested by your dealer or suitably-equipped garage; this will usually show up a small leak not otherwise visible. If significant leakage is found at any time, use an antifreeze hydrometer to check the concentration of antifreeze remaining in the coolant.

15   Coolant hydrometers are available at most automotive accessory shops. If the specific gravity of a sample taken from the expansion tank (when the engine is switched off and fully cooled down) is less than that specified, the coolant mixture strength has fallen below the minimum. If this is found, either the coolant strength must be restored, either by adding neat antifreeze or by draining and flushing the system, then refilling it with fresh coolant mixture of the correct ratio.

16   When checking the coolant level, always note its condition; it should be relatively clear. If it is brown or rust-coloured, the system should be drained, flushed and refilled. If antifreeze has been used which does not meet Ford's specification, its corrosion inhibitors will lose their effectiveness with time; such coolant must be renewed regularly, even if it appears to be in good condition, usually at the intervals suggested at the beginning of Section 2 of this Chapter.

Windscreen/tailgate and headlight washer fluid

17   Fluid for the windscreen (and, where applicable, the headlight washer system) is stored in a plastic reservoir, which is located at either the right-hand or left-hand front corner of the engine compartment. The reservoir for the tailgate washer system is located on the rear trim panel, on the right-hand side. In milder climates, plain water can be used to top-up the reservoir, but the reservoir should be kept no more than two-thirds full, to allow for expansion should the water freeze. In colder climates, the use of a specially-formulated windscreen washer fluid additive, available at your dealer or any car accessory shop, will help lower the freezing point of the fluid. *Do not* use regular (engine) antifreeze - it will damage the vehicle's paintwork. On all reservoirs, remove the plastic cap and top-up as necessary **(see illustration)**.

Battery electrolyte

18   On models not fitted with a sealed battery (see Section 8), check the electrolyte level of all the battery cells. The level must be approximately 10 mm above the plates; this may be shown by maximum and minimum level lines marked on the battery's casing. If the level is low, use a coin to release the filler/vent cap, and add distilled water. Install and securely retighten the cap. **Caution:** *Overfilling the cells may cause electrolyte to spill over during periods of heavy charging, causing corrosion or damage. Refer also to the warning at the beginning of Section 9.* On earlier vehicles fitted with two batteries, don't forget to check/top-up both of them.

1•10 Chapter 1 Routine maintenance and servicing

Brake fluid

19 The brake fluid reservoir is located on the top of the brake master cylinder, which is attached to the front of the vacuum servo unit. The "MAX" and "MIN" marks are indicated on the side of the translucent reservoir, and the fluid level should be maintained between these marks at all times **(see illustration)**.

20 The brake fluid inside the reservoir is readily visible. With the vehicle on level ground, the level should normally be on or just below the "MAX" mark.

21 Progressive wear of the brake pads and brake shoe linings causes the level of the brake fluid to gradually fall; however, when the brake pads are renewed, the original level of the fluid is restored. It is not therefore necessary to top-up the level to compensate for this minimal drop, but the level must never be allowed to fall below the minimum mark.

22 If topping-up is necessary, first wipe the area around the filler cap with a clean rag before removing the cap. When adding fluid, pour it carefully into the reservoir, to avoid spilling it on surrounding painted surfaces **(see illustration)**. Be sure to use only the specified hydraulic fluid (see *"Lubricants, fluids and capacities"* at the start of this Chapter), since mixing different types of fluid can cause damage to the system. **Warning:** *Brake hydraulic fluid can harm your eyes and damage painted surfaces, so use extreme caution when handling and pouring it. Wash off spills immediately with plenty of water. Do not use fluid that has been standing open for some time, as it absorbs moisture from the air. Excess moisture content can cause corrosion and a dangerous loss of braking effectiveness.*

23 When adding fluid, it is a good idea to inspect the reservoir for contamination. The system should be drained and refilled if deposits, dirt particles or contamination are seen in the fluid.

24 After filling the reservoir to the correct level, make sure that the cap is refitted securely, to avoid leaks and the entry of foreign matter.

25 If the reservoir requires repeated replenishing to maintain the correct level, this is an indication of an hydraulic leak somewhere in the system, which should be investigated immediately.

Power steering fluid

26 See Section 5 of this Chapter.

4 Tyre and tyre pressure checks (Daily)

1 Periodic inspection of the tyres may spare you from the inconvenience of being stranded with a flat tyre. It can also provide you with vital information regarding possible problems in the steering and suspension systems before major damage occurs.

2 The original tyres on this vehicle are with tread wear indicator (TWI) bands, which will appear when the tread depth reaches approximately 1.6 mm. Most tyres have a mark around the tyre at regular intervals to indicate the location of the tread wear indicators, the mark being TWI, an arrow, or the tyre manufacturer's symbol. Tread wear can also be monitored with a simple inexpensive device known as a tread depth indicator gauge **(see illustration)**.

3 Ensure that tyre pressures are checked regularly and maintained correctly (see the Specifications at the beginning of this Chapter for pressures). Checking should be carried out with the tyres cold, and *not* immediately after the vehicle has been in use. If the pressures are checked with the tyres hot, an apparently-high reading will be obtained, owing to heat expansion. *Under no circumstances* should an attempt be made to reduce the pressures to the quoted cold reading in this instance, or effective under-inflation will result. Most garage forecourts have a pressure line which combines a gauge to check and adjust the tyre pressures, but they may vary in accuracy, due to general misuse and abuse. It therefore pays to carry a good-quality tyre pressure gauge in the vehicle, to make the regular checks required and to ensure pressure accuracy **(see illustration)**.

4 Note any abnormal tread wear **(see illustration)**. Tread pattern irregularities such as feathering, flat spots, and more wear on one side than the other, are indications of front wheel alignment and/or balance problems. If any of these conditions are noted, they should be rectified as soon as possible.

5 Under-inflation will cause overheating of the tyre, owing to excessive flexing of the casing, and the tread will not sit correctly on the road surface. This will cause a consequent loss of adhesion and excessive wear, not to mention the danger of sudden tyre failure due to heat build-up.

6 Over-inflation will cause rapid wear of the centre part of the tyre

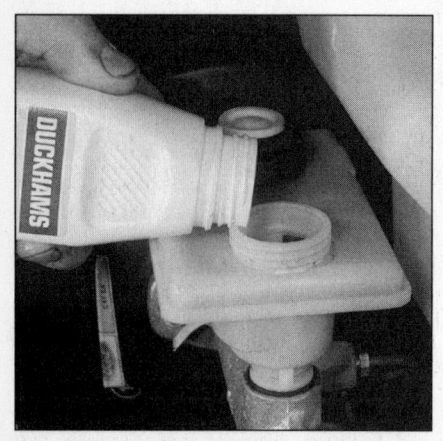

3.19 Brake fluid maximum and minimum level markings on the side of the reservoir

3.22 Topping-up the brake fluid

4.2 Check the tyre tread depth with a tread depth indicator gauge

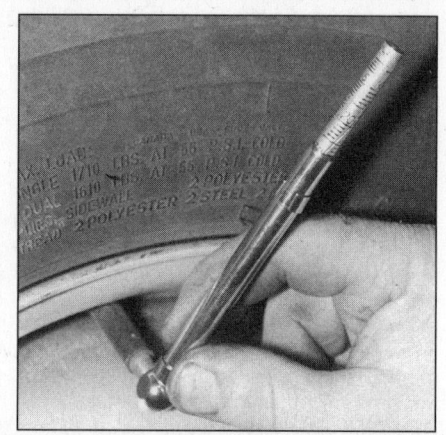

4.3 Use a reliable pressure gauge to check the tyre pressures when the tyres are cold

Chapter 1 Routine maintenance and servicing

Condition	Probable cause	Corrective action	Condition	Probable cause	Corrective action
Shoulder wear	• Underinflation (wear on both sides) • Incorrect wheel camber (wear on one side) • Hard cornering	• Check and adjust pressure • Repair or renew suspension parts • Reduce speed	Toe wear (Feathered edge)	• Incorrect toe setting	• Adjust front wheel alignment
Centre wear	• Overinflation	• Measure and adjust pressure	Uneven wear	• Incorrect camber or castor • Malfunctioning suspension • Unbalanced wheel • Out-of-round brake disc/drum	• Repair or renew suspension parts • Repair or renew suspension parts • Balance tyres • Machine or renew disc/drum

4.4 Tyre tread wear patterns and causes

tread, coupled with reduced adhesion, harder ride, and the danger of damage occurring in the tyre casing.

7 Regularly check the tyres for damage in the form of cuts or bulges, especially in the sidewalls. Remove any nails or stones embedded in the tread, before they penetrate the tyre to cause deflation. If removal of a nail reveals that the tyre has been punctured, refit the nail, so that its point of penetration is marked. Then immediately change the wheel, and have the tyre repaired by a tyre dealer. Do not drive on a tyre in such a condition. If in any doubt as to the possible consequences of any damage found, consult your local tyre dealer for advice.

8 General tyre wear is influenced to a large degree by driving style - harsh braking and acceleration, or fast cornering, will all produce more rapid tyre wear. Interchanging of tyres may result in more even wear; however, if this is completely effective, the added expense is incurred of replacing a complete set of tyres at once, which may prove financially-restrictive for many owners.

9 Front tyres may wear unevenly as a result of wheel misalignment. The front wheels should always be correctly aligned according to the settings specified by the vehicle manufacturer.

10 Don't forget to check the spare tyre for condition and pressure.

11 Legal restrictions apply to many aspects of tyre fitting and usage. In the UK, this information is contained in the Motor Vehicle Construction and Use Regulations. It is suggested that a copy of these regulations is obtained from your local police, if in doubt as to current legal requirements with regard to tyre type and condition, minimum tread depth, etc.

5 Power steering fluid level check (Monthly)

1 The power steering fluid reservoir is located on the front left-hand side of the engine compartment.

2 For the fluid level check, the power steering system should be at its normal operating temperature, so it is best to carry out the check after a run.

3 Position the vehicle on level ground, with the front wheels pointing straight ahead, and switch off the engine.

4 There are two different types of reservoirs fitted to Diesel-powered Transits (see illustration). The reservoirs will be marked either "MAX HOT", "MAX COLD" and "MIN", or just "MAX" and "MIN". Check that the fluid level is up to the "MAX HOT" or "MAX" mark on the reservoir when the engine is warm.

5 If topping-up is required, first use a clean rag to wipe the filler cap and the surrounding area, to prevent foreign matter from entering the system. Unscrew and remove the filler cap.

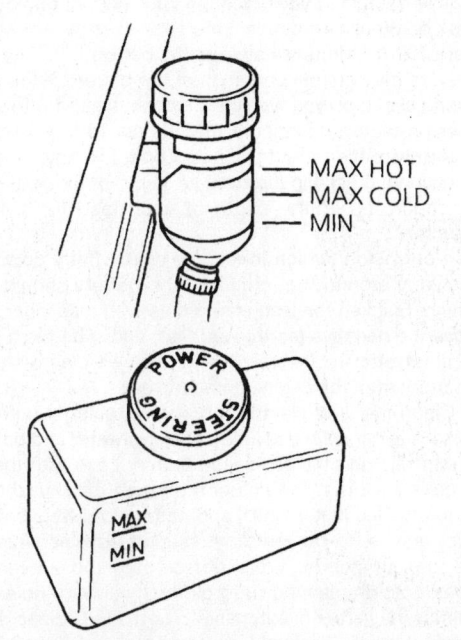

5.4 Power steering fluid reservoir markings on the two different types of reservoirs

1•12 Chapter 1 Routine maintenance and servicing

6 Top-up the level to the "MAX HOT" or "MAX" mark, using the grade of fluid specified at the beginning of this Chapter. Be careful not to introduce dirt into the system, and do not overfill. The need for frequent topping-up indicates a leak, which should be investigated.
7 Refit the filler cap.

6 Windscreen/tailgate washer system and wiper blade check (Daily/Monthly)

1 The windscreen wiper and blade assembly should be inspected at the specified intervals for damage, loose components, and cracked or worn blade elements.
2 Road film can build up on the wiper blades and affect their efficiency, so they should be washed regularly with a mild detergent solution.
3 The action of the wiping mechanism can loosen bolts, nuts and fasteners, so they should be checked and tightened, as necessary, at the same time as the wiper blades are checked.
4 If the wiper blade elements are cracked, worn or warped, or no longer clean adequately, they should be replaced with new ones.
5 Lift the wiper arm and blade away from the glass.
6 To remove the windscreen wiper blade, release the catch on the arm, then turn the blade through 90° and withdraw the blade from the end of the arm (see illustration).
7 To remove the tailgate wiper blade, push the wiper blade forward, and at the same time depress it against the spring pressure, then withdraw it from the end of the arm.
8 If the metal part of the wiper blade is in good condition, it may be possible to renew the rubber insert separately. The insert can be obtained from some car accessory shops and, according to type, it may need to be cut to the correct length before sliding into the clips.
9 Refit the wiper blade assembly using a reversal of the removal procedure, making sure that it fully engages with the spring clip.
10 Check that the washer jets direct the fluid onto the upper part of the windscreen/tailgate/rear window/headlight, and if necessary adjust the small sphere on the jet with a pin.

7 Electrical system check (every 6000 miles or 6 months)

1 Check the operation of all external lights and indicators (front and rear).
2 Check for satisfactory operation of the instrument panel, its illumination and warning lights, the switches and their illumination lights.
3 Check the horn(s) for satisfactory operation.
4 Check all other electrical equipment for satisfactory operation.
5 Check all electrical wiring in the engine compartment for correct routing, and for any signs of physical or heat-damage or chafing.

8 Battery check, maintenance and charging (every 6000 miles or 6 months)

Warning: *Certain precautions must be followed when checking and servicing the battery. Hydrogen gas, which is highly flammable, is always present in the battery cells, so keep lighted tobacco and all other open flames and sparks away from the battery. The electrolyte inside the battery is actually dilute sulphuric acid, which will cause injury if splashed on your skin or in your eyes. It will also ruin clothes and painted surfaces. When disconnecting the battery, always detach the negative (earth) lead first and connect it last!*

General

1 A routine preventive maintenance programme for the battery in your vehicle is the only way to ensure quick and reliable starts.
2 There are also several precautions that should be taken whenever battery maintenance is performed. Before servicing the battery, always turn the engine and all accessories off, and disconnect the lead from the negative terminal of the battery. Refer to the section

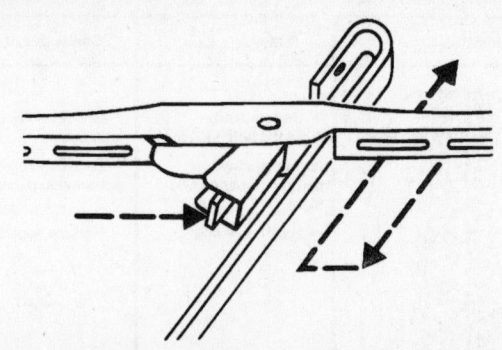

6.6 To remove the windscreen wiper blade, release the catch on the arm, then turn the blade through 90°

8.6 Battery attachments showing negative terminal (arrowed)

"Radio/cassette unit anti-theft system - precaution" at the beginning of this manual before disconnecting the battery.
3 The battery produces hydrogen gas, which is both flammable and explosive. Never create a spark, smoke, or light a match around the battery. Always charge the battery in a well-ventilated area.
4 Electrolyte contains poisonous and corrosive sulphuric acid. Do not allow it to get in your eyes, on your skin, or on your clothes. Never ingest it. Wear protective safety glasses when working near the battery. Keep children away from the battery.
5 Note the external condition of the battery. If the positive terminal and lead clamp on your vehicle's battery is fitted with a plastic cover or rubber protector, make sure that it's not torn or damaged. It should completely cover the terminal. Look for any corroded or loose connections, cracks in the case or cover, or loose hold-down clamps. Also check the entire length of each lead for cracks and frayed conductors.
6 If corrosion (which looks like white, fluffy deposits) is evident, particularly around the terminals, the battery should be removed for cleaning. Slacken the lead clamp nuts with a spanner, being careful to remove the negative (earth) lead first, and slide them off the terminals (see illustration). Unscrew the hold-down clamp/strap, and remove the battery from the engine compartment.
7 Clean the lead clamps thoroughly, using a soft wire brush or a terminal cleaner, with a solution of warm water and baking soda. Wash the terminals and the top of the battery case with the same solution, but make sure that the solution doesn't get into the battery. When cleaning the leads, terminals and battery top, wear safety goggles and rubber gloves, to prevent any solution from coming in contact with your eyes or hands. Wear old clothes too - even when diluted, sulphuric acid splashed onto clothes will burn holes in them. If the terminals have been extensively corroded, clean them up with a terminal cleaner. Thoroughly wash all cleaned areas with plain water.
8 Make sure that the battery tray is in good condition, and that the hold-down clamps are secure. If the battery is removed from the tray,

Chapter 1 Routine maintenance and servicing 1•13

CRACKS RUNNING ACROSS "V" PORTIONS OF BELT

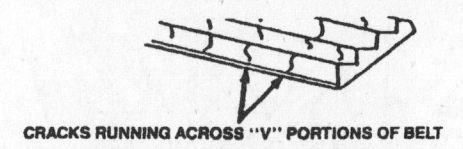

ACCEPTABLE

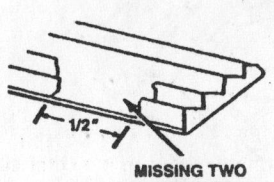

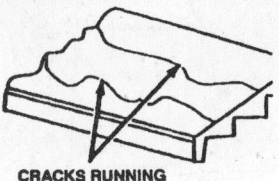

MISSING TWO OR MORE ADJACENT RIBS 1/2" OR LONGER

CRACKS RUNNING PARALLEL TO "V" PORTIONS OF BELT

UNACCEPTABLE

10.4 Check the drivebelt for signs of wear like these. Very small cracks across the drivebelt ribs are acceptable. If the cracks are deep, or if the drivebelt looks worn or damaged in any other way, renew it. This is the "polyvee" type belt, but the checks on the V-belt type are the same

10.7a Check the drivebelt deflection as shown

make sure no parts remain in the bottom of the tray when the battery is refitted.
9 Information on removing and installing the battery can be found in Chapter 5. Information on jump starting can be found at the front of this manual. For more detailed battery checking procedures, refer to the Haynes *"Automobile Electrical and Electronic Systems Manual"*.

Cleaning
10 Corrosion on the hold-down components, battery case and surrounding areas can be removed with a solution of water and baking soda. Thoroughly rinse all cleaned areas with plain water.
11 Any metal parts of the vehicle damaged by corrosion should be covered with a zinc-based primer, then painted.

Charging
Warning: *When batteries are being charged, hydrogen gas, which is very explosive and flammable, is produced. Do not smoke, or allow open flames, near a charging or a recently-charged battery. Wear eye protection when near the battery during charging. Also, make sure the charger is unplugged before connecting or disconnecting the battery from the charger.*
12 Slow-rate charging is the best way to restore a battery that's discharged to the point where it will not start the engine. It's also a good way to maintain the battery charge in a vehicle that's only driven

a few miles between starts. Maintaining the battery charge is particularly important in Winter, when the battery must work harder to start the engine, and electrical accessories that drain the battery are in greater use.
13 It's best to use a one- or two-amp battery charger (sometimes called a "trickle" charger). They are the safest, and put the least strain on the battery. They are also the least expensive. For a faster charge, you can use a higher-amperage charger, but don't use one rated more than 1/10th the amp/hour rating of the battery (ie no more than 5 amps, typically). Rapid boost charges that claim to restore the power of the battery in one to two hours are hardest on the battery, and can damage batteries which are not in good condition. This type of charging should only be used in emergency situations.
14 The average time necessary to charge a battery should be listed in the instructions that come with the charger. As a general rule, a trickle charger will charge a battery in 12 to 16 hours.

9 Seat belt check (every 6000 miles or 6 months)

1 Check the seat belts for satisfactory operation and condition. Inspect the webbing for fraying and cuts. Check that they retract smoothly and without binding into their reels.
2 Check that the seat belt mounting bolts are tight, and if necessary tighten them to the specified torque wrench setting.

10 Drivebelt check and renewal (every 6000 miles or 6 months)

General
1 The drivebelt is of the flat, multi-ribbed (or "polyvee") type. The drivebelt is located on the front of the engine, and drives the alternator, water pump and cooling fan. An additional drivebelt is used on models with power steering, or power steering and air conditioning. This belt is mounted in front of the main drivebelt, and is also driven from the crankshaft pulley.
2 The good condition and proper tension of the drivebelt is critical to the operation of the engine. Because of their composition and the high stresses to which they are subjected, drivebelts stretch and deteriorate as they get older. They must, therefore, be regularly inspected.

Check
3 With the engine switched off, open and support the bonnet, then locate the drivebelt on the front of the engine. If the engine has recently been running, be very careful, and wear protective gloves to minimise the risk of burning your hands on hot components.
4 Using an inspection light or a small electric torch, and rotating the engine when necessary with a spanner applied to the crankshaft pulley bolt, check the whole length of the drivebelt for cracks, separation of the rubber, and torn or worn ribs **(see illustration)**. Also check for fraying and glazing, which gives the drivebelt a shiny appearance. Both sides of the drivebelt should be inspected, which means you will have to twist the drivebelt to check the underside. Use your fingers to feel the drivebelt where you can't see it. If you are in any doubt as to the condition of the drivebelt, renew it (go to paragraph 13).

Drivebelt tension
5 Ford technicians use a special tension gauge for checking drivebelt adjustment, but for DIY purposes, checking the belt tension using firm finger pressure gives a good indication of correct adjustment. This is done midway between the pulleys on the longest run of the belt.
6 If adjustment is necessary, proceed as follows according to belt type.

Water pump/alternator drivebelt
7 Apply firm finger pressure midway between the pulleys on the longest run of the belt, and look for a deflection of 2.5 mm (i.e. a total drivebelt "swing" of approximately 5.0 mm) **(see illustration)**. If adjustment is required, loosen off the alternator mounting and

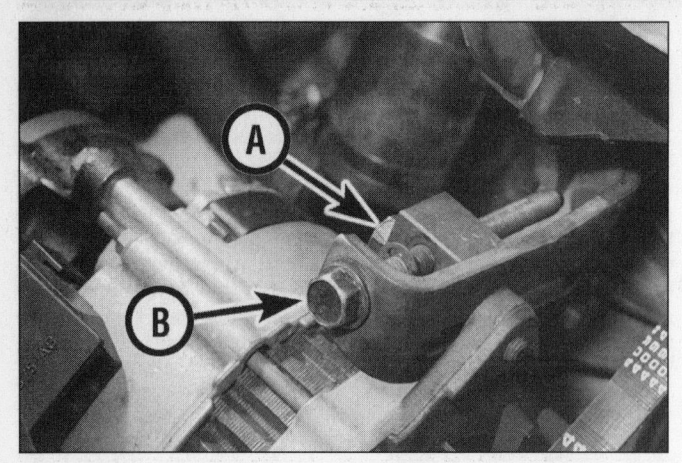

1-14　　Chapter 1　Routine maintenance and servicing

10.7b Alternator adjustment arm attachment bolt (A) and adjuster bolt (B)

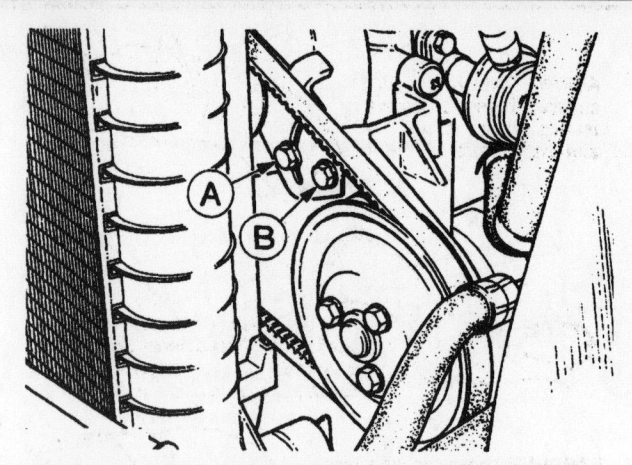

10.9 Power steering pump drivebelt and adjuster bolt (A) and pivot bolt (B)

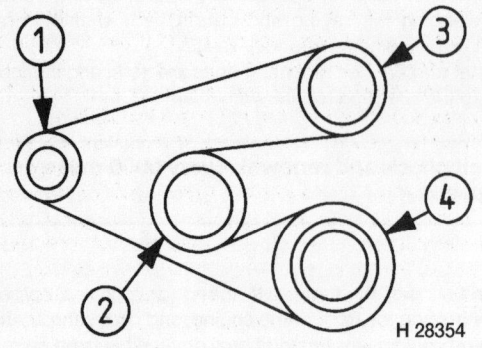

10.13a Alternator/water pump drivebelt arrangement on the pulleys

1　Alternator
2　Fan pulley
3　Water pump pulley
4　Crankshaft pulley

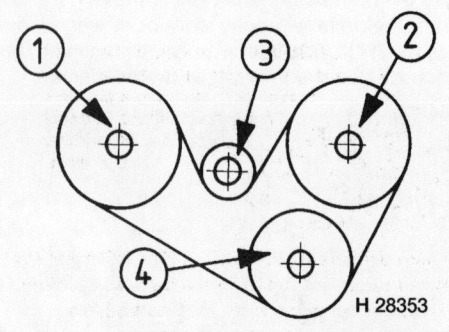

10.13b Power steering and air conditioning drivebelt arrangement on the pulleys

1　Crankshaft pulley
2　Power steering pump pulley
3　Automatic adjuster pulley
4　Air conditioning compressor pulley

adjustment bolts, and turn the adjuster bolt on the adjustment arm as required to provide the correct drive belt tension, then retighten the bolts to secure **(see illustration)**.

8　Run the engine for about five minutes, then recheck the tension.

Power steering pump auxiliary drivebelt (vehicles without air conditioning)

9　Apply firm finger pressure midway between the pulleys on the longest run of the belt, and look for a deflection of 2.0 mm (i.e. a total drivebelt "swing" of 4.0 mm). If adjustment is required, loosen off the pump mounting bracket pivot bolt and adjustment bolt, pivot the pump and bracket as required to provide the correct drivebelt tension, then retighten the bolts to secure **(see illustration)**.

10　Run the engine for about five minutes, then recheck the tension.

Power steering pump auxiliary drivebelt (vehicles with air conditioning)

11　The auxiliary drivebelt fitted to later vehicles with power steering and air conditioning is tensioned by an automatic tensioner; regular checks are not required, and manual "adjustment" is not possible.

12　If you suspect that the drivebelt is slipping and/or running slack, or that the tensioner is otherwise faulty, it must be renewed. To do this, remove the drivebelt as described below, then unbolt and remove the tensioner. On fitting the new tensioner, ensure it is aligned correctly on its mountings, and tightened securely.

Renewal

13　The routing of the water pump/alternator drivebelt and the power steering/air conditioning drivebelts around the pulleys is as shown **(see illustrations)**.

14　If the existing drivebelt is to be refitted, mark it, or note the maker's markings on its flat surface, so that it can be installed the same way round.

15　To renew the water pump/alternator drivebelt, the auxiliary drivebelt(s) must be removed first.

16　To remove the belt(s), slacken the belt tension fully as described above according to type. Where an automatic adjuster is fitted, use a spanner on the tensioner pulley bolt, and move the tensioner to release the belt tension. Slip the belt off the pulleys.

17　Check all the pulleys, ensuring that their grooves are clean, and removing all traces of oil and grease.

18　If the original drivebelt is being refitted, use the marks or notes made on removal, to ensure that it is installed to run in the same direction as it was previously. To fit the drivebelt, arrange it on the grooved pulleys so that it is centred in their grooves (ie not overlapping their raised sides), and so that it is routed correctly.

19　Using a spanner applied to the crankshaft pulley bolt, rotate the crankshaft through at least two full turns clockwise to settle the drivebelt on the pulleys, then check that the drivebelt is properly installed. With the belt in position, adjust the tension as previously described.

11　Underbonnet check for fluid leaks and hose condition (every 6000 miles or 6 months)

Caution: *Renewal of air conditioning hoses must be left to a dealer service department or air conditioning specialist who has the equipment to depressurise the system safely.* **Never** *remove air conditioning components or hoses until the system has been depressurised.*

Chapter 1 Routine maintenance and servicing

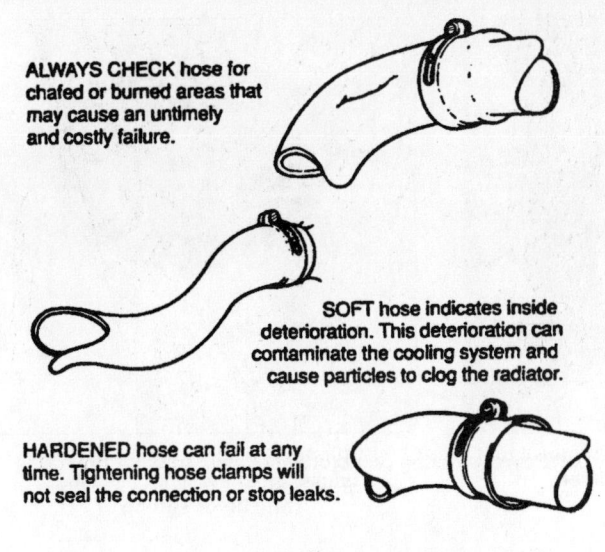

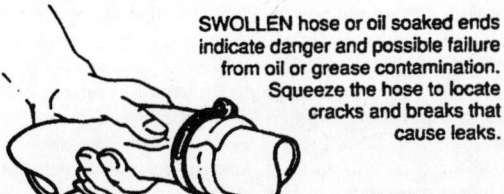

ALWAYS CHECK hose for chafed or burned areas that may cause an untimely and costly failure.

SOFT hose indicates inside deterioration. This deterioration can contaminate the cooling system and cause particles to clog the radiator.

HARDENED hose can fail at any time. Tightening hose clamps will not seal the connection or stop leaks.

SWOLLEN hose or oil soaked ends indicate danger and possible failure from oil or grease contamination. Squeeze the hose to locate cracks and breaks that cause leaks.

11.2 Hoses, like drivebelts, have a habit of failing at the worst possible time - to prevent the inconvenience of a blown hose, inspect them carefully as shown here

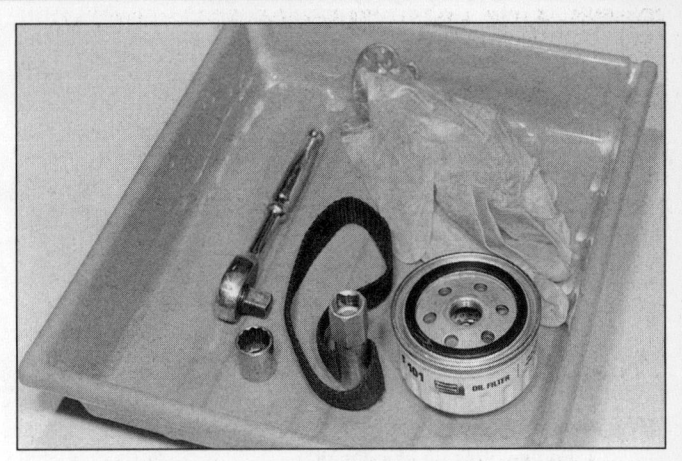

12.2 Tools and materials required for engine oil and filter renewal

General

1 High temperatures in the engine compartment can cause the deterioration of the rubber and plastic hoses used for engine, accessory and emission systems operation. Periodic inspection should be made for cracks, loose clamps, material hardening and leaks.
2 Carefully check the large top and bottom radiator hoses, along with the other smaller-diameter cooling system hoses and metal pipes; do not forget the heater hoses/pipes which run from the engine to the bulkhead. Inspect each hose along its entire length, replacing any that is cracked, swollen or shows signs of deterioration. Cracks may become more apparent if the hose is squeezed **(see illustration)**.
3 Make sure that all hose connections are tight. A leak in the cooling system will usually show up as white- or rust-coloured deposits on the areas adjoining the leak; if the spring clamps that are used to secure the hoses in this system appear to be slackening, they should be renewed to prevent the possibility of leaks.
4 Some other hoses are secured to their fittings with clamps. Where clamps are used, check to be sure they haven't lost their tension, allowing the hose to leak. If clamps aren't used, make sure the hose has not expanded and/or hardened where it slips over the fitting, allowing it to leak.
5 Check all fluid reservoirs, filler caps, drain plugs and fittings etc, looking for any signs of leakage of oil, transmission and/or brake hydraulic fluid, coolant and power steering fluid. If the vehicle is regularly parked in the same place, close inspection of the ground underneath it will soon show any leaks; ignore the puddle of water which will be left if the air conditioning system is in use. As soon as a leak is detected, its source must be traced and rectified. Where oil has been leaking for some time, it is usually necessary to use a steam cleaner, pressure washer or similar, to clean away the accumulated dirt, so that the exact source of the leak can be identified.

Vacuum hoses

6 It's quite common for vacuum hoses, especially those in the emissions system, to be colour-coded, or to be identified by coloured stripes moulded into them. Various systems require hoses with different wall thicknesses, collapse resistance and temperature resistance. When renewing hoses, be sure the new ones are made of the same material.
7 Often the only effective way to check a hose is to remove it completely from the vehicle. If more than one hose is removed, be sure to label the hoses and fittings to ensure correct installation.
8 When checking vacuum hoses, be sure to include any plastic T-fittings in the check. Inspect the fittings for cracks, and check the hose where it fits over the fitting for distortion, which could cause leakage.
9 A small piece of vacuum hose (quarter-inch inside diameter) can be used as a stethoscope to detect vacuum leaks. Hold one end of the hose to your ear, and probe around vacuum hoses and fittings, listening for the "hissing" sound characteristic of a vacuum leak. **Warning:** *When probing with the vacuum hose stethoscope, be very careful not to come into contact with moving engine components such as the drivebelt or radiator cooling fan, etc.*

Fuel hoses

10 Check all fuel hoses for deterioration and chafing. Check especially for cracks in areas where the hose bends, and also just before fittings, such as where a hose attaches to the fuel filter.
11 High-quality fuel line, usually identified by the word "Fluoro-elastomer" printed on the hose, should be used for fuel line renewal. Never, under any circumstances, use unreinforced vacuum line, clear plastic tubing or water hose for fuel lines.
12 Spring-type clamps are commonly used on fuel lines. These clamps often lose their tension over a period of time, and can be "sprung" during removal. Replace all spring-type clamps with screw clamps whenever a hose is replaced.

Metal lines

13 Sections of metal piping are often used for fuel line between the fuel filter and the engine. Check carefully to be sure the piping has not been bent or crimped, and that cracks have not started in the line.
14 If a section of metal fuel line must be renewed, only seamless steel piping should be used, since copper and aluminium piping don't have the strength necessary to withstand normal engine vibration.
15 Check the metal brake lines where they enter the master cylinder and ABS hydraulic unit (if used) for cracks in the lines, or loose fittings. Any sign of brake fluid leakage calls for an immediate and thorough inspection of the brake system.

12 Engine oil and filter change (every 6000 miles or 6 months)

1 Frequent oil changes are the best preventive maintenance the home mechanic can give the engine, because ageing oil becomes diluted and contaminated, which leads to premature engine wear.
2 Make sure that you have all the necessary tools before you begin this procedure **(see illustration)**. You should also have plenty of rags

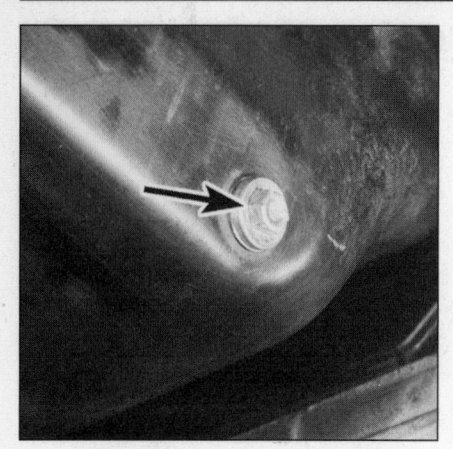

1•16 Chapter 1 Routine maintenance and servicing

12.7 Engine oil drain plug location

12.9 Using a chain wrench removal tool to unscrew the oil filter

12.10 Apply a light coating of clean engine oil to the filter's sealing ring before fitting

or newspapers handy, for mopping up any spills. To avoid any possibility of scalding, and to protect yourself from possible skin irritants and other harmful contaminants in used engine oils, it is advisable to wear gloves when carrying out this work.

3 Access to the underside of the vehicle is greatly improved if the vehicle can be lifted on a hoist, driven onto ramps, or supported by axle stands. **Warning:** *Do not work under a vehicle which is supported only by an hydraulic or scissors-type jack, or by bricks, blocks of wood, etc.*

4 If this is your first oil change, get under the vehicle, and familiarise yourself with the position of the engine oil drain plug in the sump. The engine and exhaust components will be warm during the actual work, so try to anticipate any potential problems while the engine and accessories are cool.

5 The oil should preferably be changed when the engine is still warm, just after a run (the needle on the temperature gauge should be in the "Normal" sector of the gauge); warm oil and sludge will flow out more easily. Park the vehicle on firm, level ground, apply the handbrake firmly, then select 1st or reverse gear (manual transmission) or the "P" position (automatic transmission). Open the bonnet and remove the engine oil filler cap from the cylinder head rocker cover, then remove the oil level dipstick from its tube (see Section 3).

6 There's a lot of room to work underneath a Transit, but if you think you need extra clearance, raise the front of the vehicle, and support it securely on axle stands. **Warning:** *To avoid personal injury, never get beneath the vehicle when it is supported by only by a jack. The jack provided with your vehicle is designed solely for raising the vehicle to remove and refit the roadwheels. Always use axle stands to support the vehicle when it becomes necessary to place your body underneath the vehicle.*

7 Being careful not to touch the hot exhaust components, place the drain pan under the drain plug, and unscrew the plug **(see illustration)**. If possible, try to keep the plug pressed into the sump while unscrewing it by hand the last couple of turns. As the plug releases from the threads, move it away sharply, so the stream of oil issuing from the sump runs into the pan, not up your sleeve! Allow the oil to drain into the drain pan. Check the condition of the plug's sealing washer; renew it if worn or damaged.

8 Allow some time for the old oil to drain, noting that it may be necessary to reposition the pan as the oil flow slows to a trickle. When the oil has completely drained, wipe clean the drain plug and its threads in the sump and refit the plug, tightening it to the specified torque wrench setting.

9 Reposition the drain pan under the oil filter then, using a suitable filter removal tool if necessary, unscrew the oil filter from the cylinder block; be prepared for some oil spillage **(see illustration)**. Check the old filter to make sure that the rubber sealing ring hasn't stuck to the engine; if it has, carefully remove it. Withdraw the filter through the wheel arch, taking care to spill as little oil as possible.

10 Using a clean, lint-free rag, wipe clean the cylinder block around the filter mounting. If there are no specific instructions supplied with it, fit a new oil filter as follows. Apply a light coating of clean engine oil to the filter's sealing ring **(see illustration)**. Screw the filter into position on the engine until it seats, then tighten it through a further half- to three-quarters of a turn *only*. Tighten the filter by hand only - do not use any tools.

11 Remove the old oil and all tools from under the vehicle, and if raised, lower it to the ground.

12 Refill the engine with oil, using the correct grade and type of oil, as given in the Specifications Section of this Chapter. Pour in half the specified quantity of oil first, then wait a few minutes for the oil to fall to the sump. Continue adding oil a small quantity at a time, until the level is up to the lower notch on the dipstick. Adding approximately 0.5 to 1.0 litre will raise the level to the dipstick's upper notch.

13 Start the engine. The oil pressure warning light will take a few seconds to go out while the new filter fills with oil; do not race the engine while the light is on. Run the engine for a few minutes, while checking for leaks around the oil filter seal and the drain plug.

14 Switch off the engine, and wait a few minutes for the oil to settle in the sump once more. With the new oil circulated and the filter now completely full, recheck the level on the dipstick, and add more oil as necessary.

15 Dispose of the used engine oil safely, with reference to *"General repair procedures"* in the preliminary Sections of this manual.

13 Engine oil filler cap check and cleaning (every 6000 miles or 6 months)

1 Remove and inspect the cap to ensure that it is in good condition and not blocked up with sludge.

2 Disconnect the hoses at the cap, and clean it if necessary by brushing the inner mesh filter with solvent and blowing through with light pressure from an air line. Renew the cap if it is badly congested.

14 Fuel filter draining (every 6000 miles or 6 months)

1 Disconnect the battery negative lead.

2 To prevent damage from escaping fuel, it's advisable to cover the starter motor with a plastic bag or something similar. Also place a container beneath the filter to collect the escaping fuel.

3 Slacken the drain screw at the bottom of the filter. If fuel does not flow out, also slacken the bleed screw or the fuel inlet connection on the filter head.

4 When fuel, free of water, flows out of the drain screw, tighten the drain screw (and, if slackened, the bleed screw or inlet connection). If a hand-priming pump is fitted to the filter head, operate it until resistance is felt. If a hand-priming pump isn't fitted, the fuel system will

Chapter 1 Routine maintenance and servicing

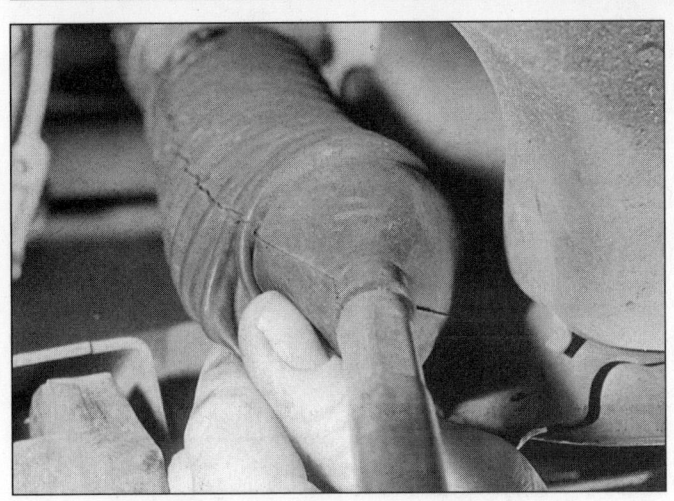

15.2 Visually inspect the steering gear gaiters for splits, chafing or deterioration

15.4 Rocking the roadwheel to check steering/suspension components

self-bleed while the engine is being started.
5 Remove the plastic bag and reconnect the battery.
6 Dispose of the drained fuel and water safely, with reference to *"General repair procedures"* in the preliminary Sections of this manual.

15 Steering, suspension and roadwheel check (every 6000 miles or 6 months)

Front suspension and steering check

1 Apply the handbrake, then raise the front of the vehicle and support it on axle stands.
2 Visually inspect the balljoint dust covers and the steering gear gaiters for splits, chafing or deterioration **(see illustration)**. Any wear of these components will cause loss of lubricant, together with dirt and water entry, resulting in rapid deterioration of the balljoints or steering gear.
3 Check the power-assisted steering fluid hoses (where fitted) for chafing or deterioration, and the pipe and hose unions for fluid leaks. Also check for signs of fluid leakage under pressure from the steering gear rubber gaiters, which would indicate failed fluid seals within the steering gear.
4 Grasp the roadwheel at the 12 o'clock and 6 o'clock positions, and try to rock it **(see illustration)**. Very slight free play may be felt, but if the movement is appreciable, further investigation is necessary to determine the source. Continue rocking the wheel while an assistant depresses the footbrake. If the movement is now eliminated or significantly reduced, it is likely that the hub bearings are at fault. If the free play is still evident with the footbrake depressed, then there is wear in the suspension joints or mountings.
5 Now grasp the wheel at the 9 o'clock and 3 o'clock positions, and try to rock it as before. Any movement felt now may again be caused by wear in the hub bearings or the steering track rod or drag link balljoints. On rack-and-pinion steering systems, if the outer track rod end balljoint is worn, the visual movement will be obvious. If the inner joint is suspect, it can be felt by placing a hand over the rack-and-pinion rubber gaiter, and gripping the track rod. If the wheel is now rocked, movement will be felt at the inner joint if wear has taken place.
6 Using a large screwdriver or flat bar, check for wear in the suspension mounting bushes or kingpins by levering between the relevant suspension component and its attachment point. Some movement is to be expected, but excessive wear should be obvious. Also check the condition of any visible rubber bushes, looking for splits, cracks or contamination of the rubber. Carry out a similar check of the leaf spring eyes where beam axle suspension is fitted.
7 With the vehicle standing on its wheels, have an assistant turn the steering wheel back-and-forth, about an eighth of a turn each way. There should be very little, if any, lost movement between the steering wheel and roadwheels. If this is not the case, closely observe the joints and mountings previously described, but in addition, check the steering column universal joints for wear, and also check the steering gear unit itself.

Rear suspension check

8 Chock the front wheels, then raise the rear of the vehicle and support it on axle stands.
9 Check the rear hub bearings for wear, using the method described for the front hub bearings (paragraph 4).
10 Using a large screwdriver or flat bar, check for wear in the rear spring mounting bushes by levering between the relevant spring eye and its attachment point. Some movement is to be expected, as the mountings are made of rubber, but excessive wear should be obvious. Check the condition of the spring leaves and the shock absorber condition and attachments.

Roadwheel check and balancing

11 Periodically remove the roadwheels, and clean any dirt or mud from the inside and outside surfaces. Examine the wheel rims for signs of rusting, corrosion or other damage. Check for signs of buckling of the rim or other distortion. If apparent, renewal of the wheel is very often the only course of remedial action possible.
12 The balance of each wheel and tyre assembly should be maintained, not only to avoid excessive tyre wear, but also to avoid wear in the steering and suspension components. Wheel imbalance is normally signified by vibration through the vehicle's bodyshell, although in many cases it is particularly noticeable through the steering wheel. Conversely, it should be noted that wear or damage in suspension or steering components may cause excessive tyre wear. Out-of-round or out-of-true tyres, damaged wheels and wheel bearing wear/maladjustment also fall into this category. Balancing will not usually cure vibration caused by such wear.
13 Wheel balancing may be carried out with the wheel either on or off the vehicle. If balanced on the vehicle, ensure that the wheel-to-hub relationship is marked in some way prior to subsequent wheel removal, so that it may be refitted in its original position.

16 Brake check (every 6000 miles or 6 months)

Note: *For detailed photographs of the brake system, refer to Chapter 9.*
1 The work described in this Section should be carried out at the specified intervals, or whenever a defect is suspected in the braking

system. Any of the following symptoms could indicate a potential brake system defect:

a) *The vehicle pulls to one side when the brake pedal is depressed.*
b) *The brakes make scraping or dragging noises when applied.*
c) *Brake pedal travel is excessive.*
d) *The brake fluid requires repeated topping-up.*

2 A thorough inspection should be made to confirm the thickness of the linings, as follows.

Front disc brakes

3 Apply the handbrake, then jack up the front of the vehicle and support it on axle stands.
4 For better access to the brake calipers, remove the wheels.
5 Look through the inspection window in the caliper, and check that the thickness of the friction lining material on each of the pads is not less than the recommended minimum thickness given in the Specifications. **Note:** *Bear in mind that the lining material is normally bonded to a metal backing plate.*
6 If it is difficult to determine the exact thickness of the pad linings, or if you are at all concerned about the condition of the pads, then remove them from the calipers for further inspection (refer to Chapter 9).
7 Check the other brake caliper in the same way.
8 If any one of the brake pads has worn down to, or below, the specified limit, *all four* pads must be renewed as a set.
9 Measure the thickness of the discs with a micrometer, if available, to make sure that they still have service life remaining. If any disc is thinner than the specified minimum thickness, renew it (refer to Chapter 9). In any case, check the general condition of the discs. Look for excessive scoring and discolouration caused by overheating. If these conditions exist, remove the relevant disc and have it resurfaced or renewed (refer to Chapter 9).
10 Before refitting the wheels, check all brake lines and hoses (refer to Chapter 9). In particular, check the flexible hoses in the vicinity of the calipers, where they are subjected to most movement. Bend them between the fingers (but do not actually bend them double, or the casing may be damaged) and check that this does not reveal previously-hidden cracks, cuts or splits.

Rear drum brakes

11 Chock the front wheels, then jack up the rear of the vehicle and support on axle stands.
12 For better access, remove the rear wheels.
13 To check the brake shoe lining thickness without removing the brake drums, prise the rubber plugs from the backplates, and use an electric torch to inspect the linings of the leading brake shoes. Check that the thickness of the lining material on the brake shoes is not less than the minimum given in the Specifications.
14 If it is difficult to determine the exact thickness of the brake shoe linings, or if you are at all concerned about the condition of the shoes, then remove the rear drums for a more comprehensive inspection (refer to Chapter 9).
15 With the drum removed, check the shoe return and hold-down springs for correct installation, and check the wheel cylinders for leakage of brake fluid. Check the friction surface of the brake drums for scoring and discoloration. If excessive, the drum should be resurfaced or renewed.
16 Before refitting the wheels, check all brake lines and hoses (refer to Chapter 9). On completion, apply the handbrake and check that the rear wheels are locked. The handbrake also requires periodic adjustment; if its travel seems excessive, refer to Section 26.

17 Engine compartment wiring check (every 12 000 miles or 12 months)

1 With the vehicle parked on level ground, apply the handbrake firmly and open the bonnet. Using an inspection light or a small electric torch, check all visible wiring within and beneath the engine compartment.

2 What you are looking for is wiring that is obviously damaged by chafing against sharp edges, or against moving suspension/transmission components and/or the drivebelt, by being trapped or crushed between carelessly-refitted components, or melted by being forced into contact with the hot engine castings, coolant pipes, etc. In almost all cases, damage of this sort is caused in the first instance by incorrect routing on reassembly after previous work has been carried out.
3 Depending on the extent of the problem, damaged wiring may be repaired by rejoining the break or splicing-in a new length of wire, using solder to ensure a good connection, and remaking the insulation with adhesive insulating tape or heat-shrink tubing, as appropriate. If the damage is extensive, given the implications for the vehicle's future reliability, the best long-term answer may well be to renew that entire section of the loom, however expensive this may appear.
4 When the actual damage has been repaired, ensure that the wiring loom is refitted correctly. Route the wiring so that it is clear of other components, is not stretched or kinked, and is secured out of harm's way using the plastic clips, guides and ties provided.
5 Check all electrical connectors, ensuring that they are clean, securely fastened, and that each is locked by its plastic tabs or wire clip, as appropriate. If any connector shows external signs of corrosion (accumulations of white or green deposits, or streaks of "rust"), or if any is thought to be dirty, it must be unplugged and cleaned using electrical contact cleaner. If the connector pins are severely corroded, the connector must be renewed; note that this may mean the renewal of that entire section of the loom - see your local Ford dealer for details.
6 If the cleaner completely removes the corrosion to leave the connector in a satisfactory condition, it would be wise to pack the connector with a suitable material which will exclude dirt and moisture, preventing the corrosion from occurring again; a Ford dealer may be able to recommend a suitable product.
7 Check the condition of the battery connections - remake the connections or renew the leads if a fault is found. Use the same techniques to ensure that all earth points in the engine compartment provide good electrical contact through clean, metal-to-metal joints, and that all are securely fastened. (In addition to the earth connections at the cylinder block and/or starter motor, there are others in various places, so check carefully).

18 Valve clearance adjustment (every 12 000 miles or 12 months)

Refer to Chapter 2A.

19 Air conditioning system check (Monthly/every 12 000 miles or 12 months)

Warning: *The air conditioning system is under high pressure.* **Do not** *loosen any fittings or remove any components until after the system has been discharged. Air conditioning refrigerant must be properly discharged into an approved type of container, at a dealer service department or an automotive air conditioning repair facility capable of handling the refrigerant safely. Always wear eye protection when disconnecting air conditioning system fittings.*

1 The following maintenance checks should be performed on a regular basis, to ensure that the air conditioner continues to operate at peak efficiency:

a) *Check the auxiliary drivebelt. If it's worn or deteriorated, renew it (see Section 10).*
b) *Check the system hoses. Look for cracks, bubbles, hard spots and deterioration. Inspect the hoses and all fittings for oil bubbles and seepage. If there's any evidence of wear, damage or leaks, renew the hose(s).*

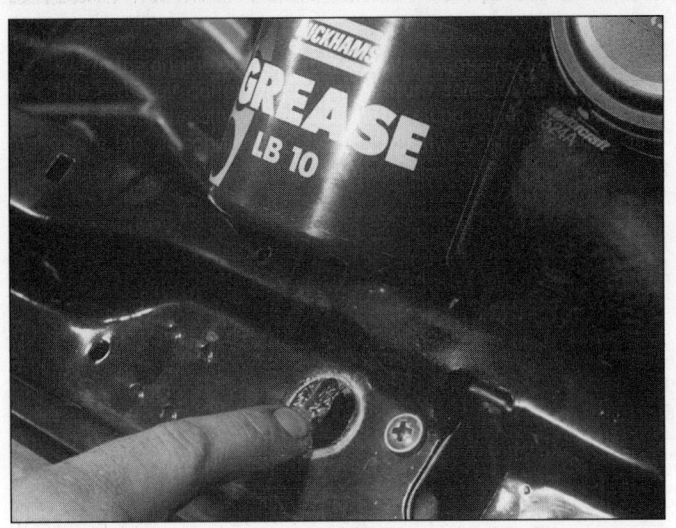

Chapter 1 Routine maintenance and servicing

20.2 Lubricate the locks and bonnet catch with a little grease

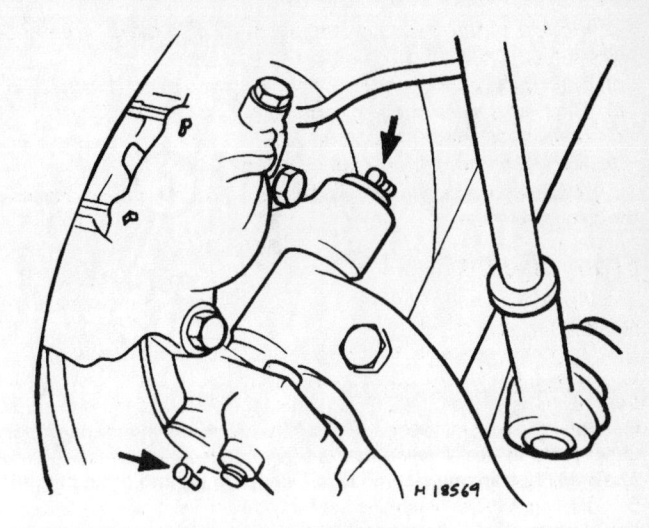

21.2 Kingpin upper and lower grease nipple locations (arrowed) on beam axle models

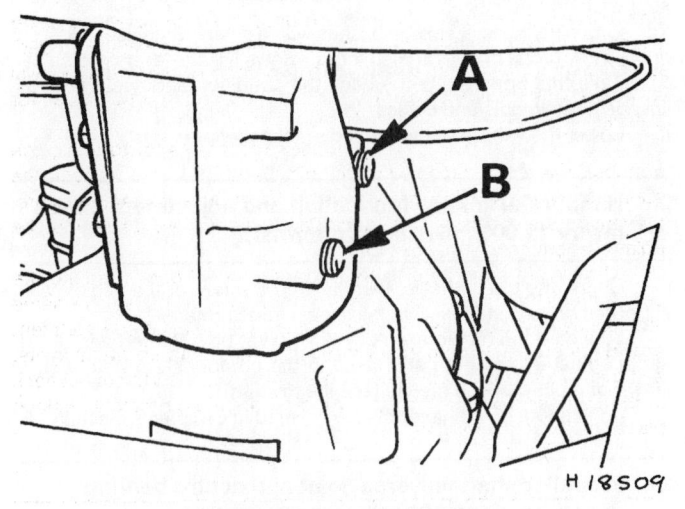

22.1a Type G transmission oil level/filler plug (A) and drain plug (B)

c) Inspect the condenser fins for leaves, insects and other debris. Use a "fin comb" or compressed air to clean the condenser. **Warning:** *Wear eye protection when using compressed air!*
d) Check that the drain tube from the front of the evaporator is clear - note that it is normal to have clear fluid (water) dripping from this while the system is in operation, to the extent that quite a large puddle can be left under the vehicle when it is parked.

2 It's a good idea to operate the system for about 30 minutes at least once a month, particularly during the Winter. Long-term non-use can cause hardening, and subsequent failure, of the seals.
3 Because of the complexity of the air conditioning system, and the special equipment necessary to service it, in-depth fault diagnosis and repairs are not included in this manual. For more complete information on the air conditioning system, refer to the Haynes *"Automotive Heating and Air Conditioning Manual"*.
4 The most common cause of poor cooling is simply a low system refrigerant charge. If a noticeable drop in cool air output occurs, the following quick check will help you determine if the refrigerant level is low.
5 Warm the engine up to normal operating temperature.
6 Place the air conditioning temperature selector at the coldest setting, and put the blower at the highest setting. Open the doors - to make sure the air conditioning system doesn't cycle off as soon as it cools the passenger compartment.
7 With the compressor engaged - the clutch will make an audible click, and the centre of the clutch will rotate - feel the inlet and outlet pipes at the compressor. One side should be cold, and one hot. If there's no perceptible difference between the two pipes, there's something wrong with the compressor or the system. It might be a low charge - it might be something else. Take the vehicle to a dealer service department or an automotive air conditioning specialist.

20 Door and bonnet check and lubrication (every 12 000 miles or 12 months)

1 Check that the doors, bonnet and tailgate close securely. Check that the bonnet safety catch operates correctly. Check the operation of the door check straps.
2 Lubricate the hinges, door check straps, the striker plates and the bonnet catch sparingly with a little oil or grease **(see illustration)**.

21 Steering kingpin and bush lubrication - beam axle models (every 12 000 miles or 12 months)

1 Apply the handbrake, then jack up the front of the vehicle and support it on axle stands so that the wheels are free to rotate.
2 Clean all around the two grease nipples on the upper and lower kingpin caps on the stub axle **(see illustration)**.
3 Using a grease gun filled with good-quality grease, apply the grease gun nozzle to the nipple, and push it firmly home.
4 Operate the grease gun until grease can be seen to appear at the kingpin bushes.
5 Repeat the procedure on the other side, then lower the vehicle to the ground.

22 Manual transmission oil level check (every 12 000 miles or 12 months)

1 The manual transmission does not have a dipstick. To check the oil level, raise the vehicle and support it securely on axle stands, making sure that the vehicle remains level. On the side of the transmission housing, you will see the filler/level plug. Unscrew and remove it. If the lubricant level is correct, the oil should be up to the lower edge of the hole **(see illustrations)**.

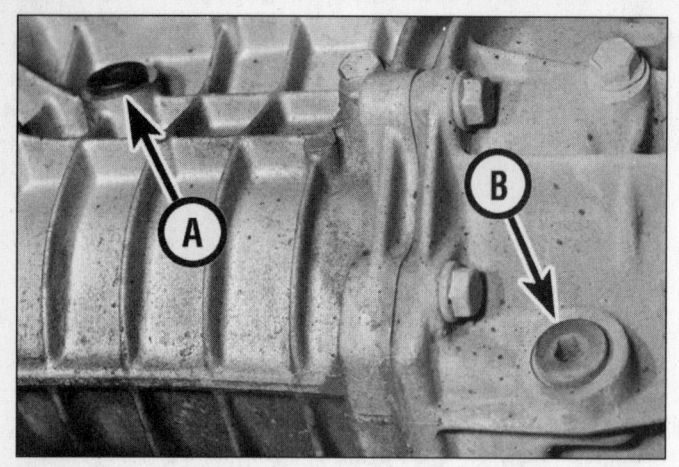

1-20 Chapter 1 Routine maintenance and servicing

22.1b MT75 transmission oil level/filler plug (A) and drain plug (B)

2   If the transmission needs more lubricant (if the oil level is not up to the hole), use a syringe, or a plastic bottle and tube, to add more. Stop filling the transmission when the lubricant begins to run out of the hole. Make sure that you refer to *"Lubricants, fluids and capacities"* at the beginning of this Chapter for the correct grade of lubricant to use, according to transmission type.
3   Refit the filler/level plug, and tighten it to the specified torque wrench setting. Drive the vehicle a short distance, then check for leaks.
4   A need for regular topping-up can only be due to a leak, which should be found and rectified without delay.
5   The type G and MT75 transmissions also incorporate a drain plug, so although renewal of the transmission oil is not a service operation, it's often useful to be able to drain the units to renew the oil after a high mileage, or if a repair or overhaul operation is being carried out. Unfortunately this isn't possible on the Type N transmission, as no drain plug is provided.
6   To drain the transmission, place a large bowl beneath the drain plug, located at the bottom or lower side of the casing, then unscrew the plug and allow the oil to drain. On completion, refit the plug then fill the transmission as previously described.

23 Clutch cable lubrication (every 12 000 miles or 12 months)

1   Apply the handbrake, then jack up the front of the vehicle and support it on axle stands.
2   Pull back the protective rubber boot over the cable end fitting at the transmission end.
3   Lubricate the cable and its location in the clutch release lever with multi-purpose grease **(see illustration)**.
4   Refit the rubber boot and lower the vehicle to the ground.

24 Overdrive slipjoint and propeller shaft lubrication (every 12 000 miles or 12 months)

1   Apply the handbrake, then jack up the front of the vehicle and support it on axle stands.
2   Clean around the grease nipples on the propeller shaft at the sliding (slip) joints **(see illustration)**.
3   Using a grease gun filled with good-quality grease and applied firmly to the nipple, give the gun a few strokes to lubricate the sliding internal splines.
4   Lower the vehicle to the ground on completion.

25 Automatic transmission linkage lubrication (every 12 000 miles or 12 months)

1   Apply the handbrake, then jack up the front of the vehicle and support it on axle stands.
2   Lubricate the shift linkage bushes with a smear of grease, and also apply a few drops of engine oil to the kickdown linkage levers and cable.
3   Take this opportunity to check the condition and security of all linkage attachments and cables.
4   Lower the vehicle to the ground on completion.

26 Handbrake linkage lubrication and adjustment check (every 12 000 miles or 12 months)

1   Chock the front wheels, then jack up the rear of the vehicle and support it on axle stands with the wheels free to rotate.
2   Lubricate the handbrake relay lever pivot bolt, the threads of the cable adjuster, and the cable itself in the compensator unit, with a smear of multi-purpose grease **(see illustration)**.
3   Adjustment of the handbrake is covered in Chapter 9, Section 14.

27 Propeller shaft universal joint and centre bearing check (every 12 000 miles or 12 months)

1   Ideally, the vehicle should be raised at the front and rear, and securely supported on axle stands with the rear wheels free to rotate.
2   Check around the rubber portion of the centre bearing for any signs of cracks, oil contamination or deformation of the rubber (see

23.3 Lubricate the clutch cable and its location in the release lever with multi-purpose grease

24.2 Propeller shaft grease nipple (arrowed)

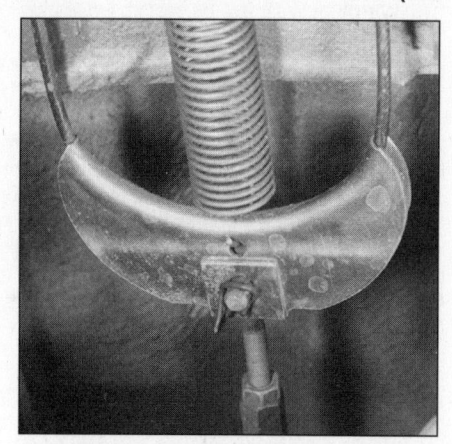

26.2 Lubricate the threads of the handbrake adjuster, and the cable itself in the compensator unit, with a smear of multi-purpose grease

Chapter 1 Routine maintenance and servicing

27.2 Check the rubber portion of the propeller shaft centre bearing for signs of cracks, oil contamination or deformation

27.3 Check the condition of the propeller shaft universal joints

29.2 Check the exhaust system rubber mountings, ensuring that any replacements are of the correct type

illustration). If any of these conditions are apparent, the centre bearing should be renewed as described in Chapter 8.
3 At the same time, check the condition of the universal joints by holding the propeller shaft in one hand and the transmission or rear axle flange in the other **(see illustration)**. Try to twist the two components in opposite directions, and look for any movement in the universal joint spiders. Repeat this check at the centre bearing, and in all other areas where the individual parts of the propeller shaft or universal joints connect. If any wear is evident, refer to Chapter 8 for repair procedures. If grating or squeaking noises have been heard from below the vehicle, or if there is any sign of rust-coloured deposits around the universal joint spiders, this indicates an advanced state of wear, and should be seen to immediately.

28 Underbody and fuel/brake line check (every 12 000 miles or 12 months)

1 With the vehicle raised and supported on axle stands or over an inspection pit, thoroughly inspect the underbody and wheel arches for signs of damage and corrosion. In particular, examine the bottom of the side sills, and any concealed areas where mud can collect. Where corrosion and rust is evident, press and tap firmly on the panel with a screwdriver, and check for any serious corrosion which would necessitate repairs. If the panel is not seriously corroded, clean away the rust, and apply a new coating of underseal. Refer to Chapter 11 for more details of body repairs.
2 At the same time, inspect the PVC-coated lower body panels for stone damage and general condition.

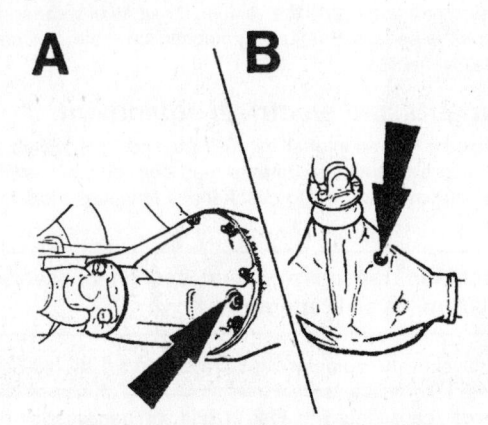

30.2 Rear axle oil level/filler plug locations

A "H" axle B "G" axle

3 Inspect all of the fuel and brake lines on the underbody for damage, rust, corrosion and leakage. Also make sure that they are correctly supported in their clips. Where applicable, check the PVC coating on the lines for damage.

29 Exhaust system check (every 12 000 miles or 12 months)

1 With the engine cold (at least three hours after the vehicle has been driven), check the complete exhaust system, from its starting point at the engine to the end of the tailpipe. Ideally, this should be done on a hoist, where unrestricted access is available; if a hoist is not available, raise and support the vehicle on axle stands.
2 Check the pipes and connections for evidence of leaks, severe corrosion, or damage. Make sure that all brackets and rubber mountings are in good condition, and tight; if any of the mountings are to be renewed, ensure that the replacements are of the correct type **(see illustration)**. Leakage at any of the joints or in other parts of the system will usually show up as a black sooty stain in the vicinity of the leak. Holts Flexiwrap and Holts Gun Gum exhaust repair systems can be used for effective repairs to exhaust pipes and silencer boxes, including ends and bends. Holts Flexiwrap is an MOT-approved permanent exhaust repair. Holts Firegum is suitable for the assembly of all exhaust system joints. **Note:** *Exhaust sealants should not be used on any part of the exhaust system upstream of the catalytic converter (where fitted) - even if the sealant does not contain additives harmful to the converter, pieces of it may break off and foul the element, causing local overheating.*
3 At the same time, inspect the underside of the body for holes, corrosion, open seams, etc. which may allow exhaust gases to enter the vehicle. Seal all body openings with silicone or body putty.
4 Rattles and other noises can often be traced to the exhaust system, especially the rubber mountings. Try to move the system, silencer(s) and catalytic converter. If any components can touch the body or suspension parts, secure the exhaust system with new mountings.

30 Rear axle oil level check (every 12 000 miles or 12 months)

1 Ideally, the vehicle should be standing on its wheels for this check, but if this is a problem (and you can't squeeze underneath) either raise it at the front and rear and support it on axle stands, or use a hoist or inspection pit.
2 Wipe all around the filler/level plug on the rear axle, then unscrew the plug **(see illustration)**. It is permissible for the oil level to be as much as 6 mm below the plug orifice, but no more. The best way to

1•22 Chapter 1 Routine maintenance and servicing

check the level is to use a "dipstick" made up from a bent piece of wire. Put the wire in the hole (but don't drop it in) and check the level.
3 If the axle needs more lubricant, use a syringe, or a plastic bottle and tube, to add more. Stop filling the axle when the lubricant begins to run out of the hole. Make sure that you refer to *"Lubricants, fluids and capacities"* at the beginning of this Chapter for the correct grade of lubricant to use.
4 Refit the filler/level plug, and tighten it securely.
5 A need for regular topping-up can only be due to a leak, which should be found and rectified without delay.

31 Load-apportioning valve check and adjustment (every 12 000 miles or 12 months)

1 The function of this device is to restrict brake fluid pressure to the rear wheels, according to vehicle loading. The load-apportioning valve is only fitted to certain models, and differs in design according to vehicle type and model year.
2 The LAV unit is mounted on the chassis in front of the rear axle, and is operated by a lever and load-sensing spring interconnected between the valve and the axle.
3 Adjustment of the valve requires the use of specialised equipment, and reference to several graphs depending on the vehicle body type, and this should therefore be entrusted to a Ford dealer.

32 Roadwheel nut tightness check (every 12 000 miles or 12 months)

Note: *Vehicles with six-stud wheels have **left-hand thread** wheel nuts (these unscrew **clockwise**) on the left-hand side up to the 1992 model year. From 1992 onwards, conventional right-hand thread nuts are used on both sides.*
1 Apply the handbrake.
2 Where applicable, remove the wheel covers, using the flat end of the wheelbrace supplied in the tool kit, or a screwdriver.
3 Check that the roadwheel nuts are tightened to the specified torque wrench setting **(see illustration)**.
4 Refit the wheel covers.

33 Road test (every 12 000 miles or 12 months)

Check the operation and performance of the braking system

1 Make sure that the vehicle does not pull to one side when braking, and that the wheels do not lock prematurely when braking hard.
2 Check that there is no vibration through the steering when braking.
3 Check that the handbrake operates correctly, without excessive movement of the lever, and that it holds the vehicle stationary on a slope.
4 With the engine switched off, test the operation of the brake servo unit as follows. Depress the footbrake four or five times to exhaust the vacuum, then start the engine. As the engine starts, there should be a noticeable "give" in the brake pedal as vacuum builds up. Allow the engine to run for at least two minutes, and then switch it off. If the brake pedal is now depressed again, it should be possible to detect a hiss from the servo as the pedal is depressed. After about four or five applications, no further hissing should be heard, and the pedal should feel considerably harder.

Steering and suspension

5 Check for any abnormalities in the steering, suspension, handling or road "feel".

32.3 Check that the roadwheel nuts are tightened to the specified torque

6 Drive the vehicle, and check that there are no unusual vibrations or noises.
7 Check that the steering feels positive, with no excessive sloppiness or roughness, and check for any suspension noises when cornering and driving over bumps.

Drivetrain

8 Check the performance of the engine, transmission and rear axle.
9 Check that the engine starts correctly, both when cold and when hot.
10 Listen for any unusual noises from the engine and transmission.
11 Make sure that the engine runs smoothly when idling, and that there is no hesitation when accelerating.
12 On manual transmission models, check that all gears can be engaged smoothly without noise, and that the gear lever action is not abnormally vague or "notchy".
13 On automatic transmission models, make sure that the drive seems smooth, without jerks or engine speed "flare-ups". Check that all the gear positions can be selected with the vehicle at rest. If any problems are found, they should be referred to a Ford dealer.

Clutch

14 Check that the clutch pedal moves smoothly and easily through its full travel, and that the clutch itself functions correctly, with no trace of slip or drag. If the movement is uneven or stiff in places, check that the cable is routed correctly, with no sharp turns.
15 Inspect both ends of the clutch inner cable, both at the transmission end and inside the vehicle, for signs of wear and fraying.
16 Check the pedal self-adjusting mechanism - refer to Chapter 6 for more details if necessary.

Instruments and electrical equipment

17 Check the operation of all instruments and electrical equipment.
18 Make sure that all instruments read correctly, and switch on all electrical equipment in turn, to check that it functions properly.

34 Automatic transmission fluid level check (every 12 000 miles or 12 months)

1 The level of the automatic transmission fluid should be carefully maintained. Low fluid level can lead to slipping or loss of drive, while overfilling can cause foaming, loss of fluid and transmission damage.
2 The transmission fluid level should only be checked when the transmission is hot (at its normal operating temperature). If the vehicle has just been driven over at least 10 miles (15 miles in a cold climate),

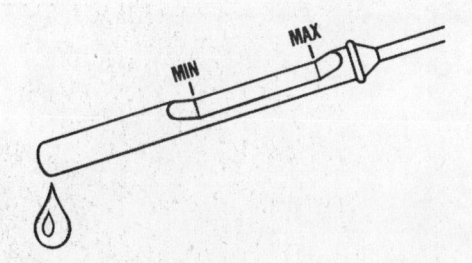

Chapter 1 Routine maintenance and servicing

34.6 Automatic transmission fluid level dipstick markings

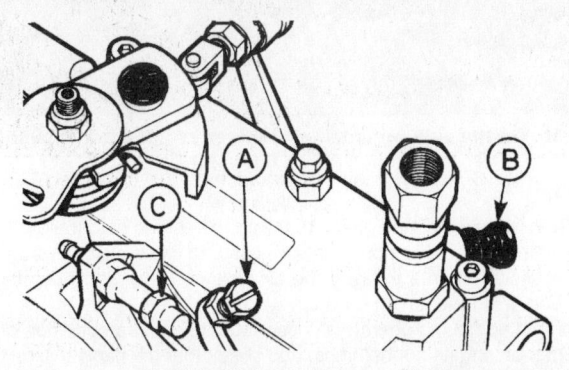

35.5b Lucas/CAV fuel injection pump adjustment points

- A Idle speed adjustment screw
- B Anti-stall adjustment screw (under cap)
- C Maximum speed adjustment screw (under cap)

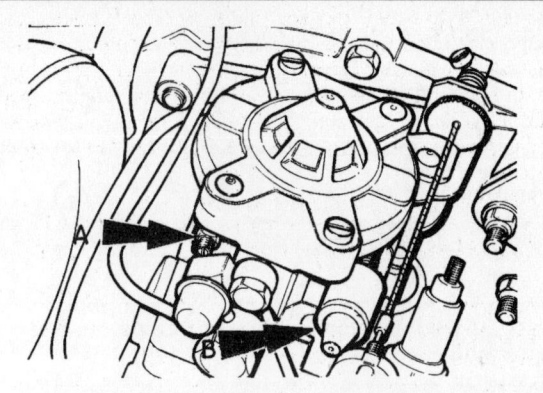

35.5a Bosch fuel injection pump adjustment points

- A Idle speed adjustment screw
- B Maximum speed adjustment screw (under cap)

and the fluid temperature is 160 to 175°F, the transmission is hot. **Caution:** *If the vehicle has just been driven for a long time at high speed, or in city traffic in hot weather, or if it has been pulling a trailer, an accurate fluid level reading cannot be obtained. In these circumstances, allow the fluid to cool down for about 30 minutes.*

3 Park the vehicle on level ground, apply the handbrake, and start the engine. While the engine is idling, depress the brake pedal and move the selector lever through all the gear ranges three times, beginning and ending in "P".

4 Allow the engine to idle for one minute, then (with the engine still idling) remove the dipstick from its tube. Note the condition and colour of the fluid on the dipstick.

5 Wipe the fluid from the dipstick with a clean rag, and re-insert it into the filler tube until the cap seats.

6 Pull the dipstick out again, and note the fluid level. The level should be between the "MIN" and "MAX" marks **(see illustration)**. If the level is on the "MIN" mark, stop the engine, and add the specified automatic transmission fluid through the dipstick tube, using a clean funnel if necessary. It is important not to introduce dirt into the transmission when topping-up.

7 Add the fluid a little at a time, and keep checking the level as previously described until it is correct.

8 The need for regular topping-up of the transmission fluid indicates a leak, which should be found and rectified without delay.

9 The condition of the fluid should also be checked along with the level. If the fluid at the end of the dipstick is black or a dark reddish-brown colour, or if it has a burned smell, the fluid should be changed. If you are in doubt about the condition of the fluid, purchase some new fluid, and compare the two for colour and smell.

35 Idle speed and anti-stall speed check and adjustment (every 12 000 miles or 12 months)

Note: *On turbocharged engines with the Lucas EPIC engine management system, all injection pump parameters are controlled by the system electronic control unit, and adjustments are not possible.*

The following adjustments are applicable to normally-aspirated engines, and earlier turbocharged engines without engine management systems. Note also that in general, this is not a routine service operation, and should only require attention at this service interval if the settings are believed to be incorrect.

1 The usual type of tachometer (rev counter), which works from ignition system pulses, cannot be used on Diesel engine. If it is not felt that adjusting the idle speed "by ear" is satisfactory, one of the following alternatives may be used:

a) Purchase or hire an appropriate tachometer.
b) Delegate the job to a Ford dealer or other specialist.
c) Timing light (strobe) operated by a petrol engine running at the desired speed. If the timing light is pointed at a mark on the crankshaft pulley, the mark will appear stationary when the two engines are running at the same speed.

2 Before making adjustments, warm-up the engine to the normal operating temperature. Make sure that the accelerator cable is correctly adjusted (see Chapter 4).

Idle speed checking and adjustment

3 Make sure that, with the accelerator pedal released, the accelerator lever on the fuel injection pump is resting against its stop.

4 On engines with a fast idle thermostatic sensor, ensure that the sensor cable is correctly adjusted as described in Chapter 4, Section 5.

5 Allow the engine to idle, and check the speed. If adjustment is necessary, turn the idle speed adjustment screw until it is correct **(see illustrations)**.

Anti-stall speed checking and adjustment

6 On models with a Lucas/CAV fuel injection pump, accelerate the engine and allow it to return to idle. If it shows a tendency to stall, or is slow to decelerate, adjust the anti-stall setting as follows.

7 Remove the tamperproof cap or seal from the anti-stall screw. Slacken the screw locknut, give the screw a quarter-turn clockwise, then repeat the deceleration check and observe the effect. Continue to adjust the anti-stall screw until deceleration and idling are satisfactory, then tighten the locknut and fit a new tamperproof seal. **Note:** *If the engine speed rises when the anti-stall screw is turned, this suggests a fault in the pump. Consult a Lucas/CAV agent or other specialist.*

36 Air cleaner element renewal (every 24 000 miles or 2 years)

1 The air cleaner filter element is located in the air cleaner assembly mounted either on top of the inlet manifold, or on the left-hand side of the engine compartment. Undo the retaining screws and/or release the clips, and lift the air cleaner cover. Lift out the element, and wipe out the housing **(see illustrations)**. Check that no foreign matter is visible, either in the air inlet or in the air inlet ducting.

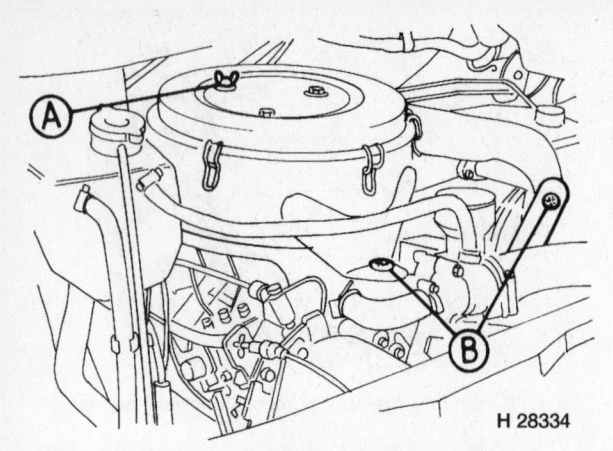

1-24 Chapter 1 Routine maintenance and servicing

36.1a Circular type air cleaner assembly as fitted to certain normally-aspirated engines

A Centre retaining bolt
B Support bracket retaining bolts

36.1b On the side-mounted air cleaner, release the retaining catches (three arrowed)...

2 If carrying out a routine service, the element must be renewed regardless of its apparent condition.

3 If you are checking the element for any other reason, inspect its lower surface; if it is oily or very dirty, renew the element. If it is only moderately dusty, it can be re-used by blowing it clean from the upper to the lower surface with compressed air. **Warning:** *Wear eye protection when using compressed air!* Because it is a pleated-paper type filter, it cannot be washed or re-oiled. If it cannot be cleaned satisfactorily with compressed air (or by brushing) discard and renew it. **Caution:** *Never drive the vehicle with the air cleaner filter element removed. Excessive engine wear could result.*

4 Refitting is the reverse of the removal procedure. Ensure that the element and cover are securely seated, so that unfiltered air cannot enter the engine.

Air cleaner temperature control system check

5 Certain early engines were fitted with an air cleaner assembly incorporating an inlet air temperature control system.

6 On these units, the air cleaner has two sources of air, one direct from the outside of the engine compartment, and the other from a shroud on the exhaust manifold. When the ambient air temperature is below a predetermined level, a flap valve admits air heated by the exhaust manifold shroud; as the ambient temperature rises, the flap opens to admit more cool air, until eventually it is fully open.

7 The system check must be made when the engine is cold. Disconnect the main inlet air duct, and check that the flap to the hot-air inlet is closed (ie open to the passage of cold air).

8 Start the engine, and check that with the engine cold (below 12°C) and at idling speed, the hot-air inlet is open, to allow warm air from the exhaust manifold area to enter the air cleaner. If the flap operates as described, it is functioning correctly.

9 If the flap fails to operate as described, check the condition of the vacuum pipe and its connections, and check that the flap valve has not seized. If these are in order, either the temperature sensor or vacuum actuator is faulty, and a new air cleaner assembly must be obtained. Refit the main air duct on completion.

37 Fuel filter renewal (every 24 000 miles or 2 years)

1 Drain the fuel filter as described in Section 14.

2 Slacken the wing nut on the filter securing clamp as far as possible, then remove the old filter **(see illustrations)**. Make sure that the old seal comes away with the filter.

3 If the original filter contains a water-in-fuel sensor, this should be transferred to the new filter prior to fitting **(see illustration)**.

4 Smear a little clean fuel onto the sealing ring of the new filter. Insert the filter into the filter head, using a pushing and twisting action to seat it.

5 Tighten the securing clamp wing nut, holding the filter in place until it is gripped. Do not overtighten the wing nut, or the filter may be distorted and will leak.

6 If a hand-priming pump is fitted to the filter head, operate it until resistance is felt. When no priming pump is fitted, prime the system by cranking the engine in ten-second bursts until it starts. If any difficulties are experienced, refer to Chapter 4, Section 2.

7 Run the engine and check that there are no leaks around the filter.

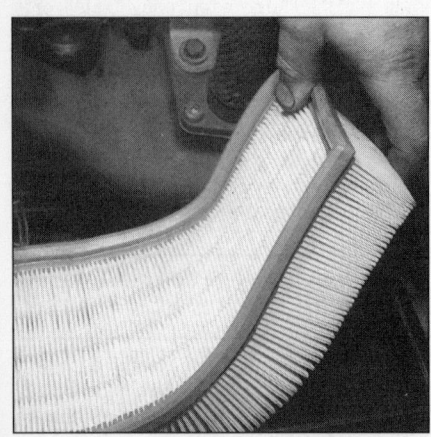

36.1c ...and lift out the element

37.2a Slacken the wing nut on the fuel filter securing clamp (arrowed)...

37.2b ...then remove the old filter

Chapter 1 Routine maintenance and servicing

37.3 If the original fuel filter contains a water-in-fuel sensor, the components shown should be transferred to the new filter

38 Front wheel bearing adjustment (every 24 000 miles or 2 years)

Refer to Chapter 10, Section 2, or 12 according to front suspension type.

39 Coolant renewal (every 36 000 miles or 3 years)

Note: *If the antifreeze used is Ford's own, or of similar quality, the coolant may remain in the system for a maximum of four years (or even longer with the latest-specification antifreeze). If the vehicle's history is unknown, if antifreeze of lesser quality is known to be in the system, or simply if you prefer to follow conventional servicing intervals, the coolant should be changed periodically (typically, every 3 years) as described here.*

Warning: *Do not allow antifreeze to come in contact with your skin, or with the painted surfaces of the vehicle. Flush contaminated areas immediately with plenty of water. Don't store new coolant, or leave old coolant lying around, where it's accessible to children or pets - they're attracted by its sweet smell. Ingestion of even a small amount of coolant can be fatal! Wipe up garage-floor and drip-pan spills immediately. Keep antifreeze containers covered, and repair cooling system leaks as soon as they're noticed.*

Warning: *Never remove the expansion tank filler cap when the engine is running, or has just been switched off, as the cooling system will be hot, and the consequent escaping steam and scalding coolant could cause serious injury.*

Coolant draining

Warning: *Wait until the engine is COLD before starting this procedure.*
1 To drain the system, first remove the expansion tank filler cap (see Section 3).
2 If the additional working clearance is required, apply the handbrake, then raise the front of the vehicle and support it securely on axle stands.
3 Where fitted, remove the engine undershield, then place a large drain tray underneath, and unscrew the radiator drain tap **(see illustration)**. Direct as much of the escaping coolant as possible into the tray.
4 When the radiator has drained, move the tray to the left-hand side of the engine, and unscrew the cylinder block drain plug located just to the rear of the engine mounting bracket.

System flushing

5 With time, the cooling system may gradually lose its efficiency, as the radiator core becomes choked with rust, scale deposits from the water, and other sediment. To minimise this, as well as using only good-quality antifreeze and clean soft water, the system should be

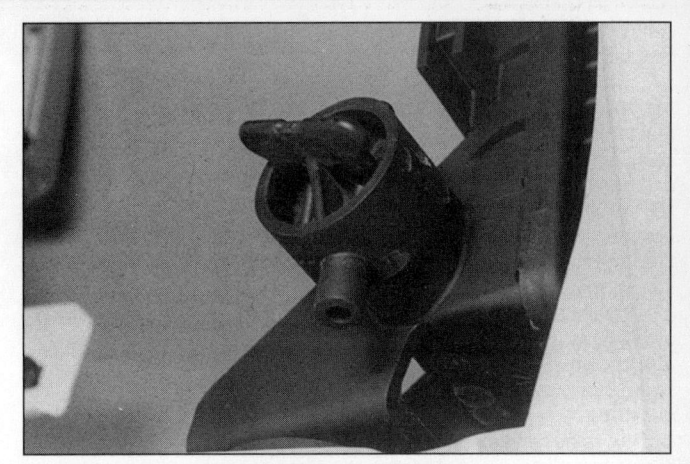

39.3 Radiator drain tap

flushed as follows whenever any part of it is disturbed, and/or when the coolant is renewed.
6 With the coolant drained, refit the drain plugs and refill the system with fresh water. Refit the expansion tank filler cap, start the engine and warm it up to normal operating temperature, then stop it and (after allowing it to cool down completely) drain the system again. Repeat as necessary until only clean water can be seen to emerge, then refill finally with the specified coolant mixture.
7 If only clean, soft water and good-quality antifreeze (even if not to Ford's specification) has been used, and the coolant has been renewed at the suggested intervals, the above procedure will be sufficient to keep clean the system for a considerable length of time. If, however, the system has been neglected, a more thorough operation will be required, as follows.
8 First drain the coolant, then disconnect the radiator top and bottom hoses. Insert a garden hose into the top hose, and allow water to circulate through the radiator until it runs clean from the bottom outlet.
9 To flush the engine, insert the garden hose into the thermostat water outlet, and allow water to circulate until it runs clear from the bottom hose. If, after a reasonable period, the water still does not run clear, the radiator should be flushed with a good proprietary cleaning agent, such as Holts Radflush or Holts Speedflush.
10 In severe cases of contamination, reverse-flushing of the radiator may be necessary. To do this, remove the radiator (Chapter 3), invert it, and insert the garden hose into the bottom outlet. Continue flushing until clear water runs from the top hose outlet. A similar procedure can be used to flush the heater matrix.
11 The use of chemical cleaners should be necessary only as a last resort. Normally, regular renewal of the coolant will prevent excessive contamination of the system.

Coolant filling

12 With the cooling system drained and flushed, ensure that all disturbed hose unions are correctly secured, and that the radiator and cylinder block drain plugs are securely tightened. Refit the engine undershield, if it was removed for access. If it was raised, lower the vehicle to the ground.
13 Prepare a sufficient quantity of the specified coolant mixture (see below); allow for a surplus, so as to have a reserve supply for topping-up.
14 Slowly fill the system through the expansion tank; since the tank is the highest point in the system, all the air in the system should be displaced into the tank by the rising liquid. Slow pouring reduces the possibility of air being trapped and forming air-locks.
15 Continue filling until the coolant level reaches the expansion tank "MAX" level line, then cover the filler opening to prevent coolant splashing out.
16 Start the engine, and run it at idle speed until it has warmed-up to normal operating temperature; watch the temperature gauge to check for signs of overheating. If the level in the expansion tank drops signifi-

cantly, top-up to the "MAX" level line, to minimise the amount of air circulating in the system.

17 Stop the engine, allow it to cool down *completely* (overnight, if possible), then uncover the expansion tank filler opening, and top-up the tank to the "MAX" level line. Refit the filler cap, tightening it securely, and wash off any spilt coolant from the engine compartment and bodywork.

18 After refilling, always check carefully all components of the system (but especially any unions disturbed during draining and flushing) for signs of coolant leaks. Fresh antifreeze has a searching action, which will rapidly expose any weak points in the system.

19 **Note:** *If, after draining and refilling the system, symptoms of overheating are found which did not occur previously, then the fault is almost certainly due to trapped air at some point in the system, causing an air-lock and restricting the flow of coolant; usually, the air is trapped because the system was refilled too quickly. In some cases, air-locks can be released by tapping or squeezing the various hoses. If the problem persists, stop the engine and allow it to cool down completely, before unscrewing the expansion tank filler cap or disconnecting hoses to bleed out the trapped air.*

Antifreeze mixture

20 If the antifreeze used is not to Ford's specification, it should always be renewed at the suggested intervals. This is necessary not only to maintain the antifreeze properties, but also to prevent the corrosion which would otherwise occur as the corrosion inhibitors become progressively less effective. Always use an ethylene glycol-based antifreeze which is suitable for use in mixed-metal cooling systems.

21 If the antifreeze used is to Ford's specification, the levels of protection it affords are indicated in the Specifications Section of this Chapter. To give the recommended *standard* mixture ratio for this antifreeze, 50% (by volume) of antifreeze must be mixed with 50% of clean, soft water; if you are using any other type of antifreeze, follow its manufacturer's instructions to achieve the correct ratio. It is best to make up slightly more than the system's specified capacity, so that a supply is available for subsequent topping-up.

22 Before adding antifreeze, the cooling system should be completely drained, preferably flushed, and all hoses checked for condition and security. As noted earlier, fresh antifreeze will rapidly find any weaknesses in the system.

23 After filling with antifreeze, a label should be attached to the expansion tank, stating the type and concentration of antifreeze used, and the date installed. Any subsequent topping-up should be made with the same type and concentration of antifreeze.

24 Do not use engine antifreeze in the windscreen/tailgate washer system, as it will damage the vehicle's paintwork. A screen wash additive such as Turtle Wax High Tech Screen Wash should be added to the washer system, in its maker's recommended quantities.

General cooling system checks

25 The engine should be cold for the cooling system checks, so perform the following procedure before driving the vehicle, or after it has been shut off for at least three hours.

26 Remove the expansion tank filler cap (see Section 3), and clean it thoroughly inside and out with a rag. Also clean the filler neck on the expansion tank. The presence of rust or corrosion in the filler neck indicates that the coolant should be changed. The coolant inside the expansion tank should be relatively clean and transparent. If it is rust-coloured, drain and flush the system, and refill with a fresh coolant mixture.

27 Carefully check the radiator hoses and heater hoses along their entire length; renew any hose which is cracked, swollen or deteriorated.

28 Inspect all other cooling system components (joint faces, etc.) for leaks. A leak in the cooling system will usually show up as white- or rust-coloured deposits on the area adjoining the leak. Where any problems of this nature are found on system components, renew the component or gasket with reference to Chapter 3.

29 Clean the front of the radiator with a soft brush to remove all insects, leaves, etc, embedded in the radiator fins. Be careful not to damage the radiator fins, or cut your fingers on them.

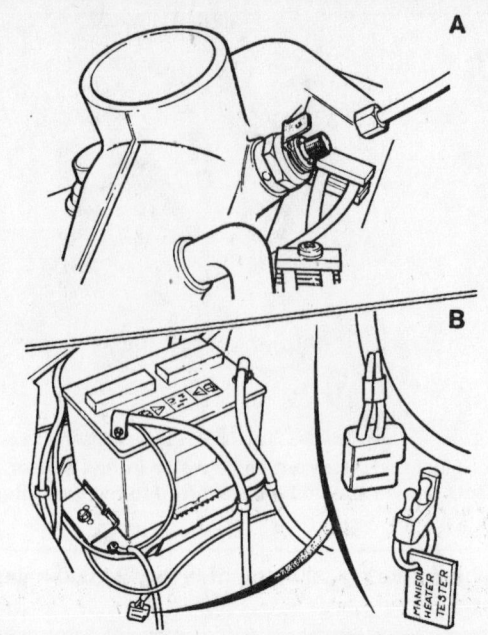

43.2 Purging the preheating system flame plug fuel reservoir

A Disconnect the fuel supply pipe
B Bridge the test connector terminals

40 Brake fluid renewal (every 36 000 miles or 3 years)

The procedure is similar to that for the bleeding of the hydraulic system as described in Chapter 9, except that the brake fluid reservoir should be emptied by syphoning, and allowance should be made for the old fluid to be removed from the circuit when bleeding a section of the circuit.

41 Front wheel alignment check (every 36 000 miles or 3 years)

Refer to Chapter 10, Section 36.

42 Timing belt renewal (every 48 000 miles)

Refer to Chapter 2A, Section 7.

43 Purge preheating system flame plug fuel reservoir (annually, at the beginning of Winter)

1 On models fitted with the optional preheating system, the fuel reservoir should be purged of summer-grade fuel at the beginning of Winter. If this is not done, the fuel in the reservoir may suffer from waxing when cold weather begins.

2 Disconnect the fuel supply pipe from the flame plug, and place the end of the pipe in a suitable container **(see illustration)**.

3 Locate the preheating system test connector below the battery tray. Bridge the connector terminals using an insulated wire link with two male connectors.

4 Switch the ignition on for 25 seconds. (The preheating warning light will come on for 5 seconds, then go out again.) Switch off the ignition momentarily, then switch on again for a further 25 seconds. Switch off again.

5 Dispose of the fuel which has flowed into the container. Reconnect the fuel supply pipe, and remove the test connector bridging wire. **Note:** *If the bridging wire is not removed, the preheating system will operate every time the engine is started, whether it is needed or not.*

Chapter 2 Part A:
In-vehicle engine repair procedures

Contents

	Section
Alternator/water pump drivebelt check, adjustment and renewal	See Chapter 1
Compression and leakdown tests - description and interpretation	3
Crankshaft oil seals - renewal	15
Cylinder head - removal and refitting	11
Cylinder head and valve components - cleaning and inspection	See Chapter 2B
Cylinder head rocker cover - removal and refitting	5
Cylinder head rocker gear - removal, inspection and refitting	10
Engine oil and filter change	See Chapter 1
Engine oil cooler - removal and refitting	18
Engine oil filler cap check and cleaning	See Chapter 1
Engine oil level check	See Chapter 1
Engine overhaul - general information	See Chapter 2B
Engine mountings - inspection and renewal	17
Engine/transmission - removal and refitting	See Chapter 2B
Flywheel - removal, inspection and refitting	16
General engine checks	See Chapter 1
General information	1
Oil pump - dismantling, inspection and reassembly	14
Oil pump - removal and refitting	13
Repair operations possible with the engine in the vehicle	2
Sump - removal and refitting	12
Timing belt - removal, inspection, refitting and tensioning	7
Timing belt cover - removal and refitting	6
Timing belt sprockets and tensioner - removal and refitting	8
Top Dead Centre (TDC) for No 1 piston - locating	4
Valve clearances - checking and adjustment	9
Water pump - removal and refitting	See Chapter 3

Specifications

General
Engine type	Four-cylinder, in-line overhead valve
Capacity	2496 cc
Bore	93.67 mm
Stroke	90.54 mm
Compression ratio:	
Normally-aspirated engines	19:1
Turbocharged engines	18.3:1
Compression pressure at cranking speed	33.8 bars
Approximate pressure difference between cylinders	2.07 bars
Firing order	1-2-4-3 (No 1 cylinder at timing belt end)
Direction of crankshaft rotation	Clockwise (seen from front of vehicle)

Flywheel
Flywheel run-out (maximum)	0.130 mm at a radius of 120 mm from centre

Valves
Valve clearance (warm or cold):	
Inlet	0.20 mm
Exhaust	0.38 mm

Lubrication

Engine oil type/specification	See "Lubricants, fluids and capacities"
Engine oil capacity	See "Lubricants, fluids and capacities"
Oil pressure:	
Idling	1.0 bar
Normal operation	2.7 to 4.8 bars
Oil pump clearances:	
Drivegear backlash	0.05 to 0.33 mm
Outer rotor-to-body:	
Hobourn Eaton pump	0.110 to 0.237 mm
Moto Fides pump	0.130 to 0.310 mm
All pumps from 1992 onwards	0.13 to 0.30 mm
Inner rotor-to-outer rotor:	
Hobourn Eaton pump	0.052 mm maximum
Moto Fides pump	0.100 mm maximum
All pumps from 1992 onwards	0.150 mm maximum
Rotor endfloat:	
Hobourn Eaton pump	0.017 to 0.237 mm
Moto Fides pump	0.017 to 0.098 mm
All pumps from 1992 onwards	0.01 to 0.09 mm

Torque wrench settings

	Nm	lbf ft
Camshaft sprocket bolt:		
Stage 1	8 to 12	6 to 9
Stage 2	Angle-tighten a further 60°	
Crankshaft pulley/sprocket bolt:		
M14 bolt	140 to 185	103 to 137
M24 bolt	312 to 346	230 to 255
Cylinder head bolts:		
Stage 1	70	52
Stage 2	70	52
Stage 3	Angle-tighten a further 90°	
Fan pulley bolts	9 to 12	7 to 9
Flywheel bolts:		
Pre-1992 model year	59 to 67	43 to 49
1992 model year onwards:		
Stage 1	18 to 23	13 to 17
Stage 2	Angle-tighten a further 25 to 30°	
Fuel injection pump sprocket bolts	22 to 27	16 to 20
Oil cooler retaining bolt	60 to 70	44 to 52
Oil pump housing bolts	20 to 25	15 to 18
Oil pump-to-intermediate plate bolts	17 to 21	12 to 15
Rear oil seal carrier bolts	17 to 21	12 to 15
Rocker cover bolts:		
Stage 1	6 to 8	4 to 6
Stage 2	6 to 8	4 to 6
Rocker gear pedestals to cylinder head:		
M8 bolts	26 to 32	19 to 24
M10 bolts	63 to 69	46 to 51
Rocker gear pedestals to shaft	11 to 14	8 to 10
Sump bolts:		
Pre-1989 model year with divided gasket:		
Normally-aspirated engines	16 to 20	12 to 15
Turbocharged engines	12 to 16	9 to 12
1989 model year onwards with one-piece gasket	12 to 16	9 to 12
Sump drain plug	20 to 27	15 to 20
Timing belt cover bolts	5 to 9	3.5 to 6.6
Timing belt tensioner roller bolt	51 to 64	38 to 47
Timing belt tensioner sliding arm bolt	21 to 26	15 to 19
Water pump pulley bolts	9 to 12	7 to 9

Note: *Refer to Part B of this Chapter for remaining torque wrench settings.*

Chapter 2 Part A: In-vehicle engine repair procedures

1 General information

How to use this Chapter

This Part of Chapter 2 is devoted to repair procedures possible while the engine is still installed in the vehicle, and includes only the Specifications relevant to those procedures. Since these procedures are based on the assumption that the engine is installed in the vehicle, if the engine has been removed from the vehicle and mounted on a stand, some of the preliminary dismantling steps outlined will not apply.

Information concerning engine/transmission removal and refitting, and engine overhaul, can be found in Part B of this Chapter, which also includes the Specifications relevant to those procedures.

Engine description

The engine is an overhead valve, water-cooled, four cylinder in-line, direct-injection Diesel **(see illustration)**. It is mounted longitudinally at the front of the vehicle, together with the transmission, to form a combined power unit.

The crankshaft is supported in five shell-type main bearings. The connecting rod big-end bearings are also split shell-type, and are attached to the pistons by fully-floating gudgeon pins. Each piston is fitted with two compression rings and one oil control ring.

The camshaft, which runs on bearings within the cylinder block, is belt-driven from the crankshaft, and operates the valves via pushrods and rocker arms. The valves are each closed by a single valve spring, and operate in guides integral in the cylinder head.

The oil pump is mounted at the front of the engine, within a housing forming part of the engine intermediate plate. The pump incorporates a full-flow oil filter, and is also belt-driven from the crankshaft. On later engines, a fuel lift pump is also driven from the camshaft, via an eccentric lobe.

2 Repair operations possible with the engine in the vehicle

The following major repair operations can be accomplished without removing the engine from the vehicle:

a) Compression pressure and leakdown tests.
b) Cylinder head rocker cover - removal and refitting.
c) Valve clearances - adjustment.
d) Timing belt - removal and refitting.
e) Rocker shaft assembly - removal and refitting.
f) Cylinder head - removal and refitting.
g) Cylinder head and pistons - decarbonising.
h) Crankshaft oil seals - renewal.
i) Oil filter renewal.
j) Oil pump - removal and refitting.
k) Sump - removal and refitting.
l) Piston/connecting rod assemblies - removal and refitting.
m) Flywheel - removal, inspection and refitting.
n) Engine mountings - removal and refitting.

Clean the engine compartment and the exterior of the engine with some type of degreaser before any work is done. It will make the job

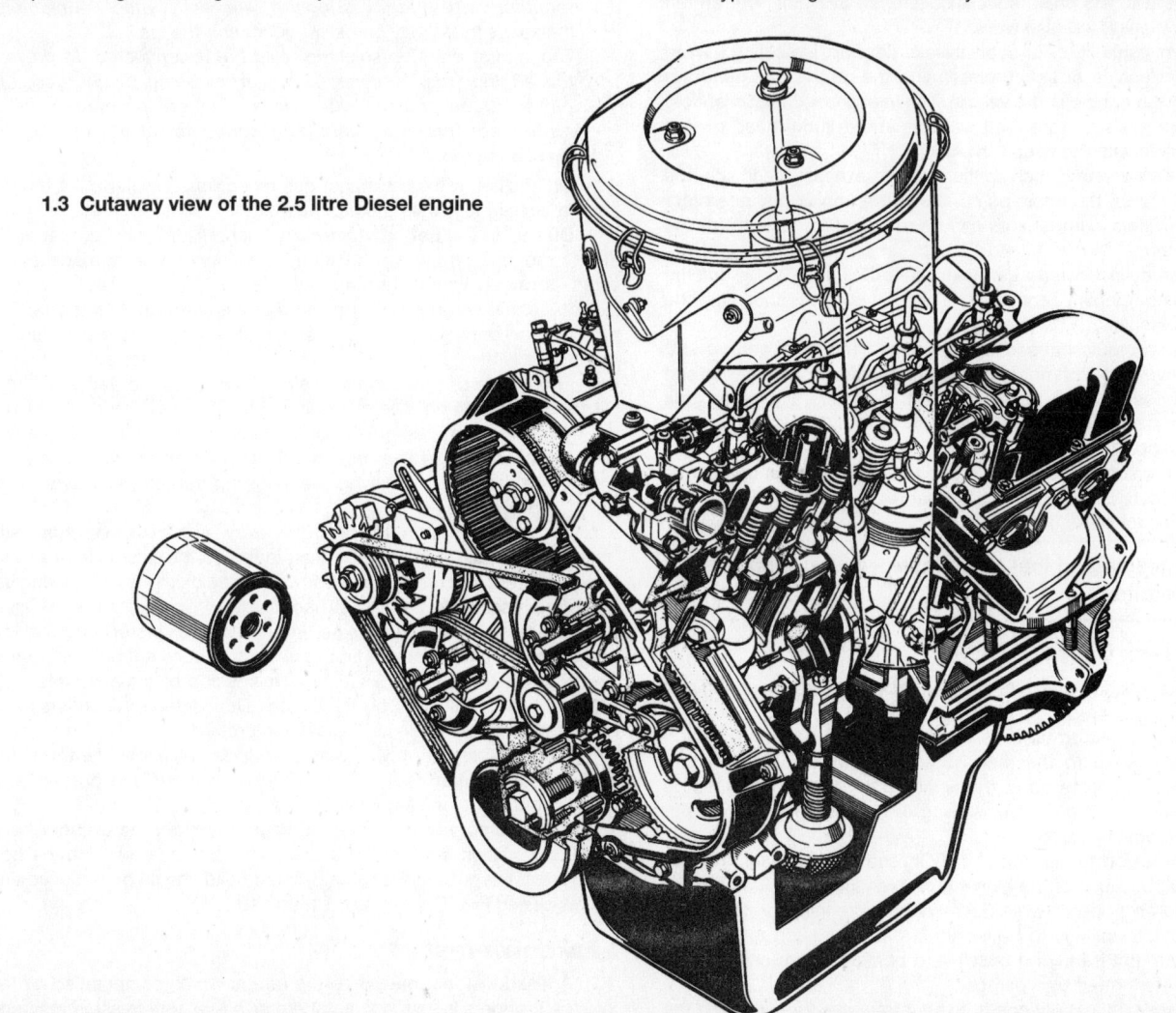

1.3 Cutaway view of the 2.5 litre Diesel engine

3.2 Performing a compression test

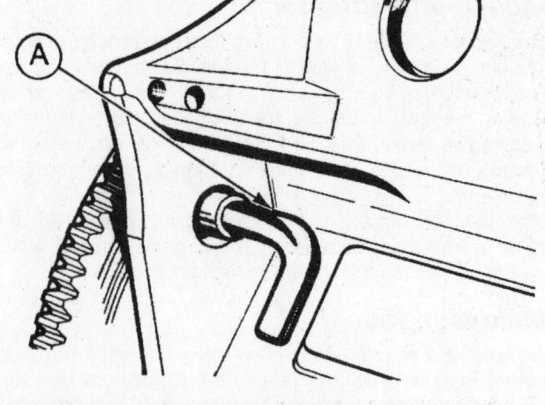

4.6 Crankshaft timing peg (A) engaged with the hole in the cylinder block and flywheel

easier, and will help to keep dirt out of the internal areas of the engine (it is especially important to keep dirt out of the fuel injection system).

Depending on the components involved, it may be helpful to remove the bonnet, to improve access to the engine as repairs are performed (refer to Chapter 11 if necessary). Cover the wings to prevent damage to the paint; special covers are available, but an old bedspread or blanket will also work.

If vacuum, exhaust, oil or coolant leaks develop, indicating a need for component/gasket or seal replacement, the repairs can generally be made with the engine in the vehicle. The inlet and exhaust manifold gaskets, sump gasket, crankshaft oil seals and cylinder head gasket are all accessible with the engine in place.

Exterior components such as the inlet and exhaust manifolds, the sump, the oil pump, the water pump, the starter motor, the alternator and the fuel system components can be removed for repair with the engine in place.

Since the cylinder head can be removed without lifting out the engine, valve component servicing can also be accomplished with the engine in the vehicle.

In extreme cases caused by a lack of necessary equipment, repair or renewal of piston rings, pistons, connecting rods and big-end bearings is possible with the engine in the vehicle. However, this practice is not recommended, because of the cleaning and preparation work that must be done to the components involved, and because of the amount of preliminary dismantling work required - these operations are therefore covered in Part B of this Chapter.

3 Compression and leakdown tests - description and interpretation

Compression test

Note: *A compression tester specifically designed for Diesel engines must be used for this test.*

1 When engine performance is down, or if misfiring occurs which cannot be attributed to the fuel system, a compression test can provide diagnostic clues as to the engine's condition. If the test is performed regularly, it can give warning of trouble before any other symptoms become apparent.

2 A compression tester specifically intended for Diesel engines must be used, because of the higher pressures involved. The tester is connected to an adapter which screws into the injector hole **(see illustration)**. It is unlikely to be worthwhile buying such a tester for occasional use, but it may be possible to borrow or hire one - if not, have the test performed by a garage.

3 Unless specific instructions to the contrary are supplied with the tester, observe the following points:

a) *The battery must be in a good state of charge, the air filter must be clean, the valve clearances must be correctly adjusted, and the engine should be at normal operating temperature.*
b) *All the injectors should be removed before starting the test, together with their respective washers (where applicable) otherwise these may be blown out during the test.*
c) *The lead at the stop solenoid must be disconnected, to prevent the engine from running or fuel from being discharged. On turbocharged engines with Lucas EPIC engine management, disconnect the large multi-plug connector at the rear of the injection pump.*

4 On engines with an exhaust gas recirculation system, the throttle should be held fully open during the test.

5 Due to the variety of testers available, and the fluctuation in starter motor speed when cranking the engine, different readings are often obtained when carrying out the compression test. For this reason, actual compression pressure figures are not as important as the balance between cylinders, and that is what this test is mainly concerned with.

6 The cause of poor compression is less easy to establish on a Diesel engine than on a petrol engine. The effect of introducing oil into the cylinders ("wet" testing) is not conclusive, because there is a risk that the oil will sit in the recesses in the piston crown, instead of passing to the rings. However, the following can be used as a rough guide to diagnosis.

7 All cylinders should produce very similar pressures; any difference greater than that specified indicates the existence of a fault. Note that the compression should build up quickly in a healthy engine; low compression on the first stroke, followed by gradually-increasing pressure on successive strokes, indicates worn piston rings. A low compression reading on the first stroke which does not build up during successive strokes indicates leaking valves or a blown head gasket (a cracked head could also be the cause). Deposits on the underside of the valve heads can also cause low compression.

8 A low reading from two adjacent cylinders is almost certainly due to the head gasket having blown between them; the presence of coolant in the engine oil will confirm this.

9 If the compression reading is unusually high, the cylinder head surfaces, valves and pistons are probably coated with carbon deposits. If this is the cause, the cylinder head should be removed and decarbonised (see Chapter 2B, Section 10).

Leakdown test

10 A leakdown test measures the rate at which compressed air fed into the cylinders is lost. It is an alternative to a compression test, and

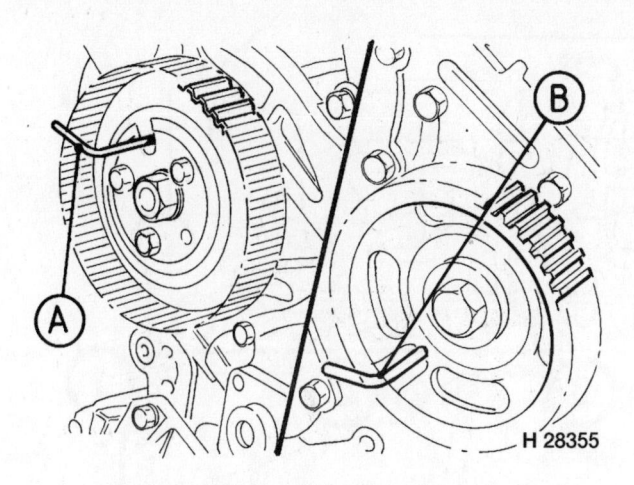

Chapter 2 Part A: In-vehicle engine repair procedures

4.7 Injection pump sprocket timing peg (A) and camshaft sprocket timing peg (B) engaged with their respective locating holes

5.7 Undo the nine bolts, and lift the rocker cover off the cylinder head

in many ways it is better, since the escaping air provides easy identification of where pressure loss is occurring (piston rings, valves or head gasket).
11 The equipment needed for leakdown testing is unlikely to be available to the home mechanic. If poor compression is suspected, have the test performed by a suitably-equipped garage.

4 Top Dead Centre (TDC) for No 1 piston - locating

Note: *To carry out this procedure, two drill bits, dowel rods or proprietary timing pins, of appropriate diameters will be needed. Refer to Chapter 4, Section 8 for the sizes required, and additional information.*

1 Top dead centre (TDC) is the highest point in the cylinder that each piston reaches as the crankshaft turns. Each piston reaches its TDC position at the end of its compression stroke, and then again at the end of its exhaust stroke. For the purpose of engine timing, TDC refers to the position of No 1 piston at the end of its compression stroke. On the engines covered by this manual, No 1 piston is at the timing belt end of the engine.
2 Remove the timing belt cover as described in Section 6.
3 Remove the large rubber bung from the front of the crankshaft pulley.
4 Remove the plastic plug from the crankshaft timing peg insertion hole at the rear of the engine just above the starter motor. On turbocharged engines with the Lucas EPIC system, the crankshaft position/speed sensor is located over the crankshaft peg insertion hole. Disconnect the wiring multi-plug, undo the retaining bolt, and remove the sensor. Recover the shim, if fitted, behind the sensor.
5 Turn the engine, using a spanner on the crankshaft pulley bolt, until the U-shaped cut-out in the injection pump sprocket is located just before the 12 o'clock position.
6 Insert the crankshaft timing peg into its hole, apply gentle pressure to the peg, and slowly turn the engine back and forth slightly until the peg engages with the hole in the flywheel **(see illustration)**.
7 Fit the injection pump timing peg through the U-shaped cut-out, and into the drilling behind it **(see illustration)**.
8 Using the camshaft timing peg, lock the camshaft sprocket by inserting the peg through the hole in the sprocket, and into the drilling behind it
9 The crankshaft, camshaft and injection pump are now "locked" in position, with No 1 piston at TDC.
10 If the engine is to be left in this state for a long period of time, it is a good idea to place suitable warning notices inside the vehicle, and in

the engine compartment. This will reduce the possibility of the engine being accidentally cranked on the starter motor, which is likely to cause damage with the locking tools in place.

5 Cylinder head rocker cover - removal and refitting

Note: *A new rocker cover gasket must be used on refitting.*

Removal

1 Disconnect the battery negative lead.
2 According to engine type, refer to Chapter 4, Section 3 and remove the air cleaner assembly (or the air inlet hose to the inlet manifold or throttle housing) as necessary.
3 On engines with exhaust gas recirculation, detach the EGR connecting hose or pipe at the EGR valve and, if necessary for access, at the exhaust manifold, collecting the steel washer(s) at the flange joint(s). Undo the support bracket bolt (where fitted), and remove the pipe/hose.
4 On later turbocharged engines with an EGR charge cooler mounted on the top of the engine, disconnect the air inlet pipe cooler and turbocharger ends, and remove the pipe.
5 On engines with a two-piece inlet manifold over the top of the engine, undo the bolt securing the throttle housing to the exhaust manifold support bracket. Disconnect the throttle actuating lever at the throttle housing and fuel injection pump. Undo the nuts and bolts, and separate the manifold upper section from the lower section. Recover the gasket between the two halves.
6 Disconnect any remaining hoses or pipes as necessary, if they are likely to impede access to the rocker cover.
7 Undo the nine bolts, and lift the rocker cover off the cylinder head **(see illustration)**. Recover and discard the gasket.

Refitting

8 Refitting is a reversal of removal, bearing in mind the following points:
   a) *If a cork gasket was originally fitted, clean off all traces of old gasket from the rocker cover and cylinder head mating faces.*
   b) *Place the rocker cover in position with a new gasket, then refit and tighten the retaining bolts progressively to the specified torque in the sequence shown* **(see illustration)**.
   c) *On engines with a two-piece inlet manifold, use a new gasket, and tighten the bolts to the specified torque (see Chapter 4).*
   d) *Refit the remainder of the disturbed components with reference to Chapter 4, where necessary.*

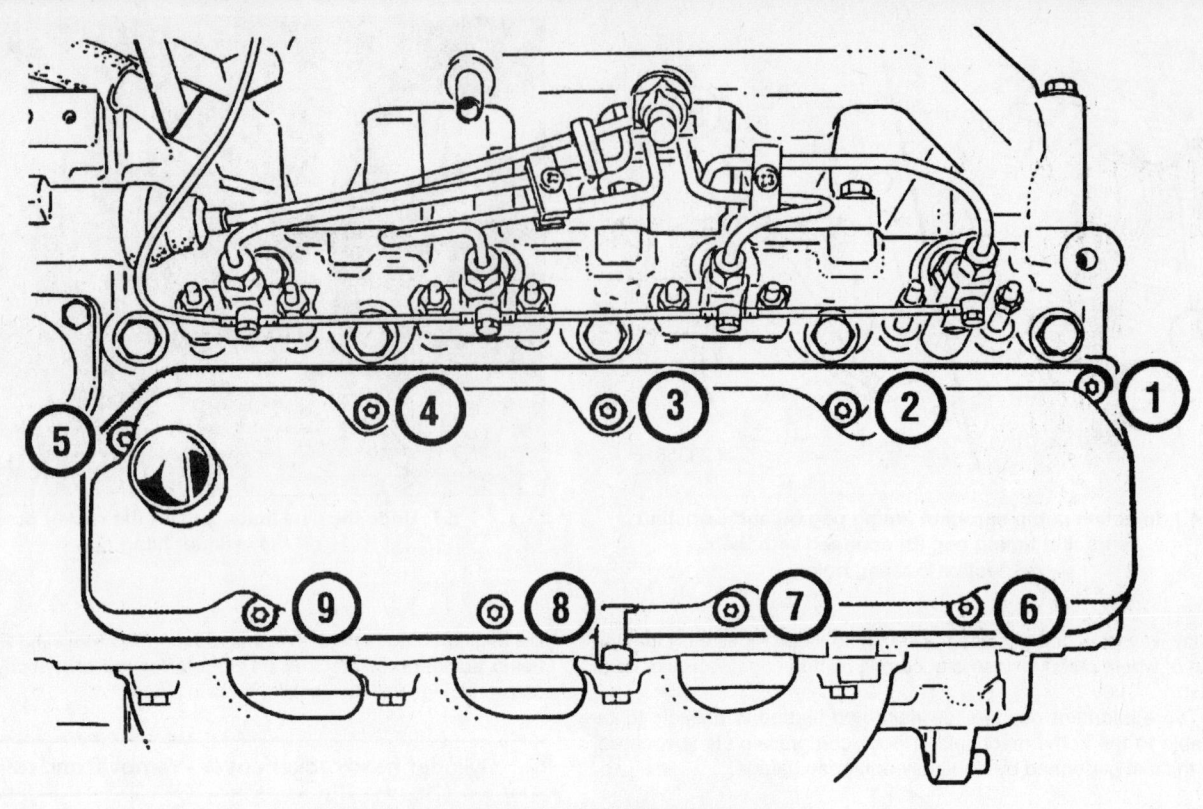

2A-6 Chapter 2 Part A: In-vehicle engine repair procedures

5.8 Rocker cover retaining bolt tightening sequence

6.4a Undo the four bolts and remove the water pump pulley ...

6.4b ... and the fan pulley

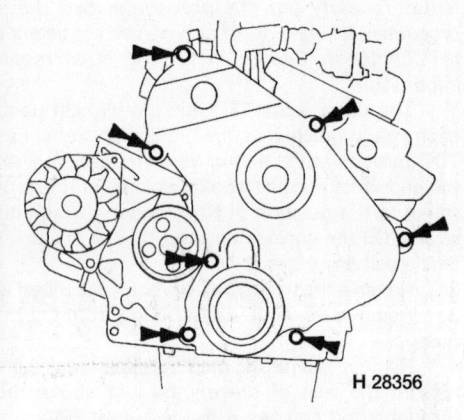

6.5a Undo the timing belt cover securing bolts (arrowed) ...

6 Timing belt cover - removal and refitting

Removal

1 Remove the radiator as described in Chapter 3, Section 4.
2 Remove the viscous cooling fan clutch as described in Chapter 3, Section 5.
3 Remove the alternator/water pump drivebelt as described in Chapter 1, Section 9.
4 Undo the four bolts each, and remove the water pump pulley and fan pulley (see illustrations).
5 Undo the seven Torx bolts securing the timing belt cover to the engine (see illustration). To facilitate removal of the cover over the crankshaft pulley, slacken the two small bolts just above the crankshaft pulley, and push the splash guard upwards to the extent of the elongated bolt slots (see illustration).
6 Pivot the lower portion of the timing belt cover downwards, then manipulate the cover around the crankshaft pulley and off the engine (see illustrations).

Refitting

7 Locate the cover in position, and refit the seven retaining bolts tightened to the specified torque.
8 Slide the splash guard down to its original position, and tighten the two small bolts.
9 Refit the water pump and fan pulleys, and tighten the bolts to the specified torque.
10 Refit the drivebelt as described in Chapter 1, and the fan clutch and radiator as described in Chapter 3.

Chapter 2 Part A: In-vehicle engine repair procedures

6.5b ... slacken the two small bolts just above the crankshaft pulley (arrowed), and push the splash guard upwards

6.6a Pivot the lower portion of the timing belt cover downwards ...

6.6b ... and manipulate the cover around the crankshaft pulley

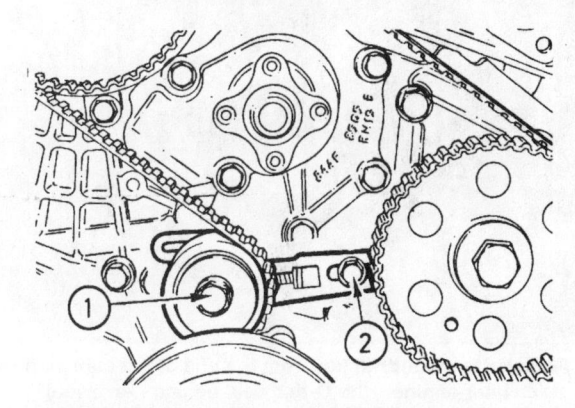

7.7 Timing belt tensioner roller retaining bolt (1) and sliding arm retaining bolt (2)

7.8 Removing the timing belt from the sprockets

7 Timing belt - removal, inspection, refitting and tensioning

General

1 The timing belt drives the camshaft and fuel injection pump from a toothed sprocket on the front of the crankshaft. If the belt slips or breaks in service, the pistons are likely to hit the valve heads, resulting in expensive damage.

2 The timing belt should be renewed at the specified intervals, or earlier if it is contaminated with oil, or at all noisy in operation (a "scraping" noise due to uneven wear).

3 If the timing belt is to be removed, it is a wise precaution to check the condition of the water pump at the same time (check for signs of coolant leakage). This may avoid the need to remove the timing belt again at a later stage, should the water pump fail.

Removal

4 Disconnect the battery negative lead.
5 Remove the timing belt cover as described in Section 6.
6 Set No 1 piston to TDC, then lock the crankshaft, camshaft and injection pump sprockets in position as described in Section 4.
7 Slacken the timing belt tensioner roller and sliding arm retaining bolts, then push the tensioner back (using a lever if necessary) to release the tension on the belt **(see illustration)**. Hold the tensioner in this position, and retighten the retaining bolts.

8 Mark the timing belt with an arrow to indicate its running direction, if it is to be re-used. Remove the timing belt from the sprockets **(see illustration)**.

Inspection

9 Inspect the belt for cracks, fraying, and damage to the teeth. Pay particular attention to the roots of the teeth. If any damage is evident, or if the belt is contaminated with oil, fuel or coolant, it must be renewed (and any leak rectified).

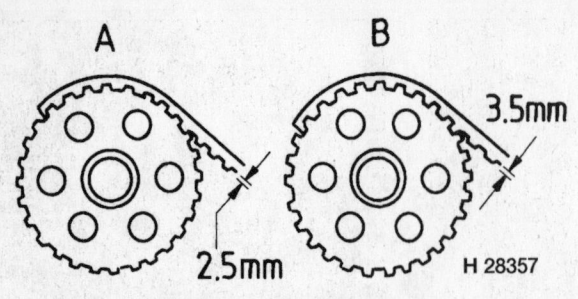

2A-8 Chapter 2 Part A: In-vehicle engine repair procedures

7.10 Timing belt tooth details

A Pre-1992 model year
B 1992 model year onwards

8.5 Recover the Woodruff key from the end of the camshaft (and on later engines, the O-ring seal behind - arrowed)

7.14 Feed the timing belt over the sprockets, keeping it taut

8.8 Hold the camshaft sprocket with a forked tool, and tighten the bolts to the Stage 2 setting using an angular torque setting gauge

10 If the new timing belt is being renewed, ensure that the correct type is obtained, according to vehicle model year. Pre-1992 model year vehicles use a timing belt with a 2.5 mm tooth depth. From 1992 onwards, the tooth depth was increased to 3.5 mm **(see illustration)**.

Refitting

11 Ensure that No 1 piston is still at TDC, and the three timing pegs are still inserted.
12 Slacken the four injection pump sprocket retaining bolts, and turn the sprocket so that the bolts are in the centre of their elongated slots.
13 Locate the timing belt over the crankshaft sprocket, making sure that the direction-of-rotation arrow is facing the correct way.
14 Hold the belt in place on the crankshaft sprocket, then feed it over the camshaft sprocket and injection pump sprocket, keeping it taut **(see illustration)**. If necessary, turn the injection pump sprocket, within the limits of the bolt holes, to aid fitting.
15 Pull the belt down and around the tensioner, then slacken the tensioner retaining bolts and allow the tensioner to spring back. Tighten the bolts again securely.
16 Tighten the injection pump sprocket retaining bolts to the specified torque.
17 Remove the three timing pegs, and rotate the crankshaft by 1-and-7/8 turns in the clockwise direction.
18 Slacken the two timing belt tensioner retaining bolts once more, then press down firmly on the timing belt in the centre of its longest run to actuate the tensioner. Retighten the tensioner bolts to the specified torque.
19 Turn the crankshaft 1/8 of a turn clockwise until the crankshaft timing peg can again be inserted.
20 Check that the injection pump timing peg can be inserted; if not, slacken the injection pump sprocket retaining bolts, and tap the bolts one way or the other slightly until the timing peg goes in. Now tighten

the bolts to the specified torque.
21 Remove all three timing pegs, and refit the plastic plug in the crankshaft peg hole. On engines with a crankshaft position sensor, refit the sensor and spacing shim, if fitted.
22 Refit the timing belt cover as described in Section 6, then reconnect the battery

8 Timing belt sprockets and tensioner - removal and refitting

Camshaft sprocket

Removal

1 Remove the timing belt as described in Section 7.
2 Remove the timing peg from the camshaft sprocket - this must not be used to hold the sprocket as the retaining bolt is undone. Do not rotate the sprocket, otherwise piston-to-valve contact may occur.
3 Make up a forked tool, with two bolts at the ends of the forks to engage in the slots of the camshaft sprocket **(see illustration 8.8)**.
4 Hold the sprocket stationary using the tool, then undo the sprocket retaining nut and withdraw sprocket from the end of the camshaft.
5 Recover the Woodruff key from the end of the camshaft (together with, on later engines, the O-ring seal) **(see illustration)**.
6 Prior to refitting, inspect the head of the sprocket retaining bolt. The bolt can only be used a maximum of six times, and should have centre-

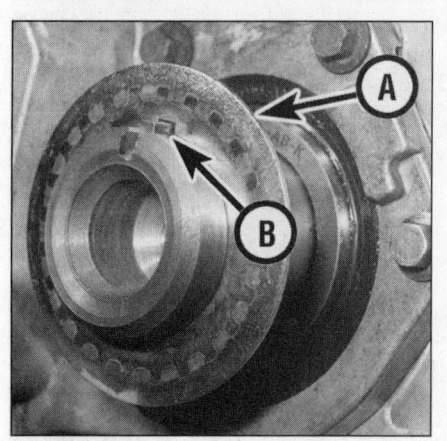

Chapter 2 Part A: In-vehicle engine repair procedures

8.14 Remove the timing belt guide plate (A) from behind the crankshaft pulley/sprocket - note Woodruff key (B)

8.16 Lay the timing belt in position, and slide on the crankshaft pulley

8.21 Withdraw the injection pump retaining plate and sprocket

8.27 Spring and spring cap on the rear of the timing belt tensioner plate

punch marks on its head for every time it has been removed. If in any doubt about the history of the engine, it is a wise precaution to renew the bolt - if previously removed, the marking of the bolt may have been overlooked. Note also that the O-ring seal fitted to the end of the camshaft (from the 1989 model year onwards) must also be renewed.

Refitting

7 Position the new O-ring seal (where fitted) over the end of the camshaft, and locate the Woodruff key in the camshaft slot. On early engines without an O-ring on the camshaft, apply sealing compound to the camshaft sprocket hub at the front and rear. Locate the sprocket in position on the camshaft.

8 Refit the retaining bolt, tighten it to the specified Stage 1 torque setting, then tighten further through the specified angle of rotation. Prevent the sprocket from rotating using the forked tool and where possible, use an angular torque setting gauge attachment tool for accurate Stage 2 tightening **(see illustration)**.

9 Re-insert the timing peg to lock the camshaft sprocket.

10 Refit the timing belt as described in Section 7.

Crankshaft pulley/sprocket

Removal

11 Remove the large rubber bung from the centre of the crankshaft pulley.

12 On manual transmission vehicles, engage top gear and apply the handbrake fully. Enlist the help of an assistant to firmly apply the brakes, then using a suitable socket, slacken the crankshaft pulley retaining bolt. Alternatively (and necessarily on vehicles with automatic transmission) remove the starter motor as described in Chapter 5, and lock the flywheel ring gear teeth with a large screwdriver or other suitable tool while the bolt is unscrewed.

13 Remove the timing belt as described in Section 7.

14 Remove the previously-slackened crankshaft pulley retaining bolt, then withdraw the pulley/sprocket assembly from the crankshaft. If it is tight, use two-legged puller to draw it off. Remove the timing belt guide plate from behind the pulley, and also remove the Woodruff key if it is loose **(see illustration)**.

Refitting

15 Refit the Woodruff key (if removed) into the crankshaft slot, then slide on the timing belt guide plate.

16 Lay the timing belt in position on the engine, making sure that the direction-of-rotation arrow is facing the correct way. Now slide on the crankshaft pulley, engage the timing belt in the sprocket teeth, and push the pulley fully home **(see illustration)**.

17 Refit the pulley retaining bolt, and tighten it just snugly at this stage. Final tightening is easier after the rest of the components have been refitted.

18 Ensure that the crankshaft timing peg is in place, then refit the timing belt as described in Section 7.

19 Lock the crankshaft using the same method as for removal, then tighten the crankshaft pulley retaining bolt to the specified torque. Refit the bung to the centre of the pulley.

Fuel injection pump sprocket

Removal

20 Remove the timing belt as described in Section 7.

21 Remove the timing peg from the fuel injection pump sprocket, then undo the four sprocket bolts. Withdraw the retaining plate and sprocket **(see illustration)**.

Refitting

22 Place the sprocket on the injection pump hub, followed by the retaining plate. Ensure that the word "FRONT" on the plate is visible.

23 Refit the four retaining bolts, and tighten them finger-tight at this stage.

24 Locate the injection pump timing peg through the U-shaped cut-out and into the drilling behind.

25 Refit the timing belt as described in Section 7.

Timing belt tensioner

Removal

26 Remove the timing belt as described in Section 7.

27 Undo the two tensioner retaining bolts, and withdraw the tensioner assembly. Take care not to lose the spring and spring cap on the rear of the tensioner plate **(see illustration)**.

2A

9.3 Checking/adjusting the valve clearances using a feeler blade (A) and ring spanner (B)

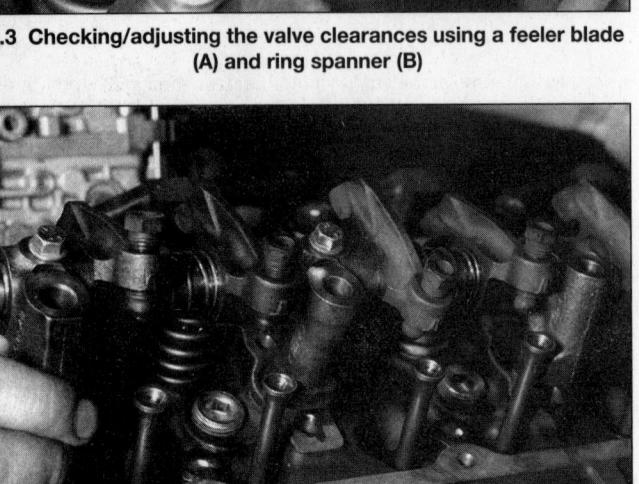

10.2a Unscrew the retaining bolts . . .

10.2b . . . and lift the rocker gear assembly from the cylinder head

Refitting

28 Prior to refitting, smear the rear contact surface of the tensioner plate with high-melting-point grease.
29 Position the spring and spring cap on the rear of the tensioner, then place the assembly in position.
30 Refit the two retaining bolts, then push the tensioner away from the camshaft sprocket against the pressure of the spring, and tighten the bolts.
31 Refit the timing belt as described in Section 7.

9 Valve clearances - checking and adjustment

1 Remove the cylinder head rocker cover as described in Section 5.
2 Remove the rubber bung from the front of the crankshaft pulley. Turn the crankshaft clockwise, using a spanner on the crankshaft pulley bolt, until the first two valves listed in the table below are fully open. In this position, check the clearance of the first two valves specified in the list.

Valves fully open	Valves to adjust
1 and 6	4 (In) and 7 (Ex)
2 and 3	5 (Ex) and 8 (In)
4 and 7	1 (Ex) and 6 (In)
5 and 8	2 (In) and 3 (Ex)

3 The clearances for the inlet and exhaust valves differ (see *"Specifications"*). Use a feeler blade of the appropriate thickness to check each clearance between the end of the valve stem and the rocker arm **(see illustration)**. The gauge should be an firm sliding fit (not slack, but not tight) between the valve and rocker arm. Where adjustment is necessary, turn the adjuster bolt as required with a ring spanner to set the clearance to that specified. The adjuster bolts are of stiff-thread type, and require no locking nut.
4 When the clearance is correct for the first pair of valves, rotate the crankshaft clockwise again until the next pair of valves listed are fully open. Check/adjust the second pair of valves listed, then repeat the procedure until all are done.
5 On completion, refit the rubber bung to the crankshaft pulley, then refit the rocker cover as described in Section 5.

10 Cylinder head rocker gear - removal, inspection and refitting

Removal

1 Remove the rocker cover as described in Section 5.
2 Unscrew the five M10 and eight M8 retaining bolts, and lift the rocker gear assembly from the cylinder head **(see illustrations)**.
3 Lift the valve caps off the valves, placing them in numbered trays so that they can be refitted to their original valves on reassembly **(see illustration)**.
4 Lift out the pushrods. Keep them in the correct order of fitting by inserting them in a piece of card, numbering them 1 to 8 from the front of the cylinder head **(see illustrations)**.

Inspection

5 To dismantle the rocker shaft unit, undo the support pedestal retaining bolts, then slide off the pedestals, rocker arms and coil springs from the shaft, but take care to keep them in their original order of fitting **(see illustrations)**.
6 Clean the respective components, and inspect them for signs of excessive wear or damage. Check that the oil lubrication holes in the shaft are clean.
7 Check the rocker shaft and rocker arm pads which bear on the valve caps for wear and scoring, and check each rocker arm on the shaft for excessive wear. Renew any components as necessary.
8 Lubricate the rocker arms and shaft with clean engine oil prior to reassembling **(see illustration)**.
9 Refit the pedestals, springs and rocker arms in their original position, ensuring correct orientation **(see illustration)**.

Chapter 2 Part A: In-vehicle engine repair procedures

10.3 Lift the valve caps off the valves

10.4a Lift out the pushrods . . .

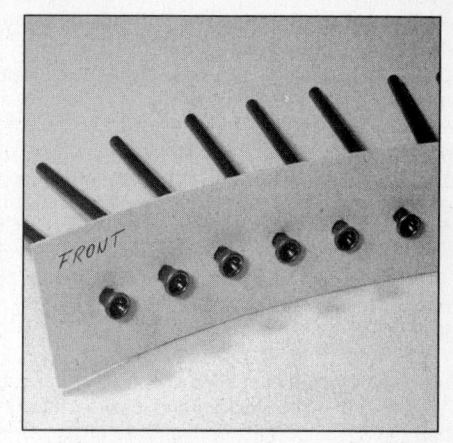

10.4b . . . and insert them in order in a suitably-marked piece of card

10.5a Slide off the rocker arms, pedestals . . .

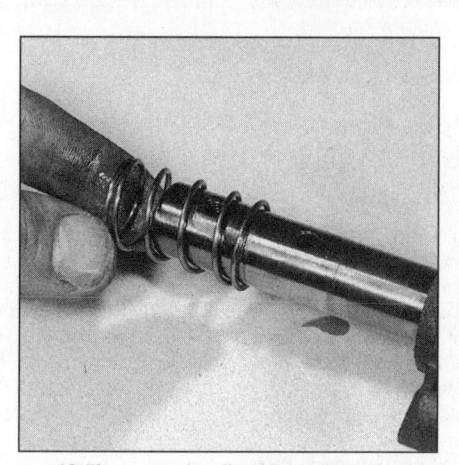

10.5b . . . and coil springs from the rocker shaft

10.8 Lubricate the rocker arms and shaft with clean engine oil prior to reassembling

Refitting

10 Lubricate the pushrods, and place them in their original locations.
11 Lay the valve caps over each valve, then lower the rocker gear assembly into place. As the rocker gear is refitted, engage each rocker arm ball stud into the cup of its respective pushrod.
12 Refit the bolts and progressively tighten them to the specified torque, tightening the M10 bolts first.
13 Adjust the valve clearances as described in Section 9, then refit the rocker cover as described in Section 5.

11 Cylinder head - removal and refitting

Note: *This is an involved procedure, and it is suggested that the Section is read thoroughly before starting work. To aid refitting, always label disconnected hoses, wiring connectors, vacuum pipes and fuel lines clearly before removal, so that they can be correctly reassembled. Masking tape and/or a touch-up paint applicator work well for marking items. Take instant photos, or sketch the locations of components and brackets if necessary. A new cylinder head gasket must be used on refitting.*

10.9 Assembled rocker gear, showing correct orientation of the components

Removal

1 Disconnect the battery negative lead.
2 Refer to Chapter 1 and drain the cooling system.
3 Refer to Section 5 and remove the cylinder head rocker cover.
4 Remove the inlet manifold as described in Chapter 4.
5 Remove the exhaust manifold (complete with turbocharger, on engines so equipped) as described in Chapter 4.
6 Disconnect the hoses from the thermostat housing.
7 Disconnect the heater hose from the front face of the cylinder head, and release it from the support clips/brackets.
8 Disconnect the wiring multi-plug(s) from the thermostat housing. On early engines, disconnect the fast idle thermostatic sensor cable from the fuel injection pump.

Chapter 2 Part A: In-vehicle engine repair procedures

9 Remove the clamps from the injector pipes, then unscrew the pipe unions at the injectors and fuel injection pump **(see illustration)**. Use a second spanner to counterhold the injector if necessary as the pipe union is undone. Plug or cap the open unions.

10 Carefully remove the injector pipes from the engine, taking care not to bend or distort them as they are removed.

11 Detach the leak-off pipe between the injectors and injection pump, and the leak-off hoses between the injectors.

12 Remove the fuel injectors as described in Chapter 4.

13 Refer to Section 10 and remove the rocker gear and pushrods.

14 The front cylinder head retaining bolt may be inaccessible, due to the proximity of the temperature gauge sender unit. If so, remove the sender unit.

15 Ensure that all pipes, hoses and fuel lines likely to impede removal of the cylinder head are either disconnected, or moved clear.

16 Progressively unscrew and loosen off the cylinder head retaining bolts in the sequence shown **(see illustration)**. When they are all loosened off, remove the bolts, then lift clear the cylinder head and remove the gasket. Whilst the gasket must always be renewed, it should be noted that the cylinder head retaining bolts may be re-used, but only three times. They should be marked accordingly with a punch or paint mark. If there is any doubt as to how many times the bolts have been used, they must be renewed.

17 To dismantle/overhaul the cylinder head, refer to Part B of this Chapter. It is normal for the cylinder head to be decarbonised and the valves reground whenever the head is removed.

Refitting

18 Prior to refitting the cylinder head, clean all carbon deposits, dirt and any traces of the old cylinder head gasket from the mating faces of both the head and the cylinder block. Do not allow any dirt to drop into the cylinder bores, oil passages or waterways; if it does, remove it. Clean the threads of the cylinder head bolts (unless new bolts are being fitted) and clean out the bolt holes in the block. Note that screwing a bolt into an oil- or water-filled hole could cause the block to fracture, due to hydraulic pressure.

19 Check that the new cylinder head gasket is the same type as the original, then locate the gasket onto the top face of the cylinder block and over the dowels **(see illustration)**.

20 Lower the cylinder head carefully into position, then insert the retaining bolts and hand-tighten them **(see illustration)**.

21 Tightening of the cylinder head bolts must done in three stages, and in the correct sequence. First tighten all of the bolts in the sequence shown to the Stage 1 setting, then again in sequence to the Stage 2 setting. When all of the bolts are tightened to the Stage 2 setting, further tighten each bolt (in sequence) through the specified angle of rotation (Stage 3). Where possible, use an angular torque setting gauge attachment tool for accurate Stage 3 tightening **(see illustrations)**. Centre-punch or otherwise mark each of the bolt heads when all are tight - see paragraph 16.

22 Refer to Section 10 and refit the rocker gear and pushrods.

23 Adjust the valve clearances as described in Section 9.

24 Refit the fuel injectors as described in Chapter 4.

25 Attach the leak-off pipe between the injectors and injection pump, and the leak-off hoses between the injectors. Use new copper washers on the banjo unions (where applicable).

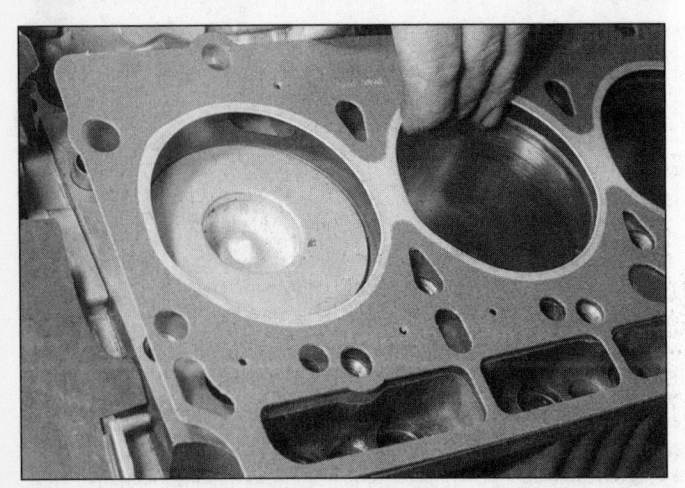

11.9 Remove the injector pipes (A) and leak-off hoses (B)

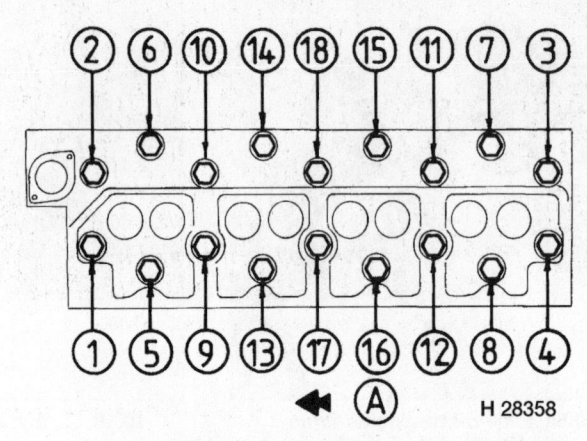

11.16 Cylinder head bolt slackening sequence

A   Front of engine

11.19 Locate the cylinder head gasket over the dowels

11.20 Lower the cylinder head carefully into position

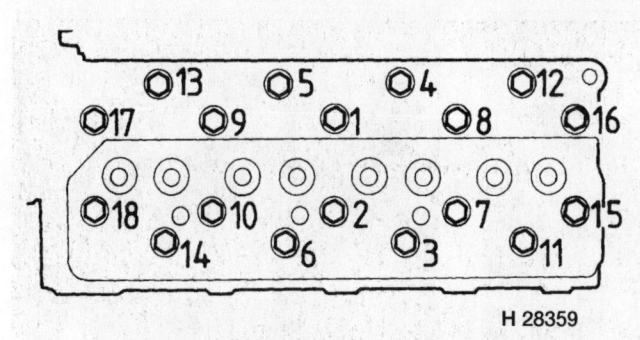

Chapter 2 Part A: In-vehicle engine repair procedures 2A-13

11.21a Cylinder head bolt tightening sequence

11.21b Tighten the cylinder head bolts initially with a torque wrench . . .

26 Carefully locate the injector pipes in position on the engine, taking care not to bend or distort them as they are refitted.
27 Remove the blanking caps used to cover the open unions, then screw the pipe unions to the injectors and fuel injection pump. Use a second spanner to counterhold the injector if necessary as the pipe unions are fully tightened.
28 Reconnect the wiring multi-plug(s) to the thermostat housing. On early engines, connect the fast idle thermostatic sensor cable to the fuel injection pump, and adjust the cable as described in Chapter 4.
29 Reconnect the heater hose to the front face of the cylinder head, and locate it in the support clips/brackets.
30 Reconnect all the hoses at the thermostat housing.
31 Refit the inlet and exhaust manifolds as described in Chapter 4.

32 Refit the cylinder head rocker cover as described in Section 5.
33 Refer to Chapter 1 and refill the cooling system.
34 Reconnect the battery negative lead on completion.
35 When the engine is restarted, check for any sign of fuel, oil and/or coolant leakages from the various cylinder head joints.

12 Sump - removal and refitting

Note: A new sump gasket will be required for refitting.

Removal

1 Disconnect the battery negative lead.
2 Apply the handbrake, then jack up the front of the vehicle and support it securely on axle stands.
3 Refer Chapter 1 and drain the engine oil. Refit the sump drain plug.
4 On vehicles with rack-and-pinion steering gear, undo the two nuts and bolts securing the steering gear to the crossmember, and move the steering gear unit forwards as far as possible.
5 Where fitted, undo the two bolts and remove the clutch housing front cover.
6 On turbocharged engines, disconnect the turbocharger oil return pipe union on the side of the sump.
7 Undo the two socket-headed bolts at the rear of the sump, using a suitable socket and universal joint (clearance is minimal).
8 Undo the remaining two socket-headed bolts at the front of the sump.
9 Undo the remaining sixteen hexagon-headed bolts, remove the reinforcing plates (where separate from the sump) then prise free and lower the sump. If the sump is stuck tight to the engine, cut around the flange gasket with a sharp knife, then lightly tap and prise it free. Keep the sump upright as it is lowered, to prevent spillage of any remaining oil in it. Also be prepared for oil drips from the crankcase once the sump is removed.
10 Remove any dirt and old gasket from the contact faces of the sump and crankcase, and wash the sump out thoroughly before refitting. Check that the mating faces of the sump are not distorted. Check that the oil pick-up strainer is clear, cleaning it if necessary.

Refitting

11 On early engines with a divided sump gasket, apply sealing compound to both sides of the gasket, particularly around the dovetail joints and end pieces, then locate the gasket on the sump.
12 On later engines with a one-piece rubber gasket, apply sealing compound to the areas where the rear oil seal carrier and the engine intermediate plate contact the cylinder block **(see illustration)**. Apply sealer to the sump and cylinder block, then locate the gasket in position, with the locating tabs pointing downwards (ie away from the cylinder block) **(see illustration)**.

11.21c . . . then through the specified angle of rotation using an angular torque setting gauge attachment

12.12a Area where sealing compound should be applied on engines with a one-piece rubber sump gasket

12.12b Locate the gasket in position, with the locating tabs pointing downwards (away from the cylinder block)

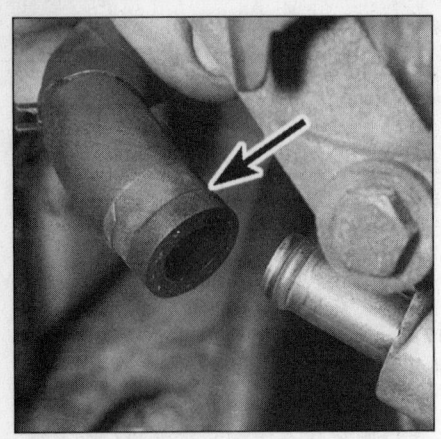

2A-14 Chapter 2 Part A: In-vehicle engine repair procedures

13.2 Detach the oil return hose (arrowed) from the oil pump housing

13.4 Withdraw the oil pump housing from the engine intermediate plate

13.5a Extract the Woodruff key from the slot in the crankshaft . . .

13.5b . . . then withdraw the oil pump drivegear

13.6 Turn the oil pump auxiliary gear so that the pump retaining bolts are accessible through the cut-outs

13.7a Withdraw the oil pump assembly . . .

13 Fit the sump into position, and locate the reinforcing plates and retaining bolts. Initially tighten the bolts all finger-tight, then further tighten them to the specified torque in a diagonal sequence.
14 On turbocharged engines, reconnect the oil return pipe union to the side of the sump.
15 Where fitted, refit the clutch housing front cover.
16 On vehicles with rack-and-pinion steering gear, refit the steering gear to the crossmember, and secure with the two nuts and bolts tightened to the specified torque (see Chapter 10).
17 Check that the oil drain plug is fitted and tightened to the specified torque, then lower the vehicle to the ground.
18 Refill the engine with the correct type and quantity of oil, as described in Chapter 1.
19 Reconnect the battery, start the engine and check for leaks.

13 Oil pump - removal and refitting

Note: *New gaskets, oil seals and O-ring seals will be required for refitting.*

Removal

1 Remove the crankshaft pulley/sprocket and timing belt tensioner as described in Section 8.
2 Disconnect the high-pressure oil pipe from the rear of the vacuum pump (at the rear of the alternator) and detach the oil return hose from the oil pump housing **(see illustration)**.
3 Undo the alternator mounting and adjustment bolts, and remove the alternator and adjustment arm.
4 Undo the oil pump housing retaining bolts in the reverse sequence to that shown **(see illustration 13.20)**. Note the positions of the longer bolts, then withdraw the housing from the engine intermediate plate **(see illustration)**.
5 Extract the Woodruff key from the slot in the crankshaft, then withdraw the oil pump drivegear **(see illustrations)**.
6 Turn the oil pump auxiliary gear so that the pump retaining bolts are accessible through the cut-outs in auxiliary gear **(see illustration)**.
7 Using a socket and extension bar, undo the Torx retaining bolts, and withdraw the oil pump assembly from the engine intermediate plate. Recover the two O-ring seals from the pump location in the cylinder block **(see illustrations)**.
8 Thoroughly clean all the components, and remove all traces of old gasket from the mating faces.
9 Before refitting, renew the crankshaft front oil seal in the oil pump housing, as described in Section 15. Obtain a new gasket for the oil pump housing, and two new O-rings for the oil channel seal.

Refitting

10 Clean the O-ring locations in the cylinder block, and place the two new O-rings in the oil channel recesses in the cylinder block **(see illustration 13.7b)**.
11 Fill the oil pump with clean engine oil **(see illustration)**. Locate the pump in position in the intermediate plate, and turn it as necessary to line up the bolt holes.
12 Insert the pump retaining bolts, and tighten them to the specified torque **(see illustration)**.

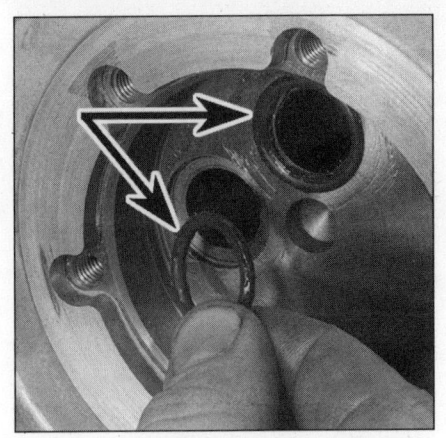

Chapter 2 Part A: In-vehicle engine repair procedures

13.7b ... and recover the two O-ring seals (arrowed)

13.11 Fill the oil pump with clean engine oil prior to fitting

13.12 Tighten the pump retaining bolts to the specified torque

13.13a Apply sealing compound to the inner surface of the oil pump drivegear ...

13.13b ... then fit the gear to the crankshaft, with the oil seal track facing outwards

13.16 Locate the new oil pump housing gasket in position on the intermediate plate

13   Apply sealing compound to the inner surface of the oil pump drivegear that faces the engine. Fit the gear to the crankshaft, with the oil seal track facing outwards (see illustrations).
14   Using feeler blades, measure the backlash of the oil pump gears at four equi-distant points. If the backlash is outside the limits given in the Specifications, renew the drivegear. If, even with a new drivegear, the backlash is still excessive, renew the complete oil pump assembly.
15   Refit the Woodruff key to the slot in the crankshaft.
16   Locate the new oil pump housing gasket in position on the intermediate plate (see illustration).
17   The new oil seal fitted to the oil pump housing should have been supplied with a plastic sleeve, to protect the lip of the oil seal when refitting the housing. If a sleeve was not supplied, make up a suitable alternative from a paper drinking cup or similar.
18   Liberally lubricate the oil seal lip, then insert the protective sleeve into the oil seal from the rear, so that it will be pushed out by the oil pump drivegear as the housing is fitted.
19   Fit the oil pump housing, and collect the protective sleeve as the oil seal lip rides up over the pump drivegear. Insert the retaining bolts in their correct locations as noted during removal, and tighten them finger-tight only at this stage.
20   It is now necessary to ensure that the oil seal is exactly centred over the drivegear. Ideally, Ford special tools 21-101, or 21-149 should be used to do this. In practice, however, there is so little movement of the housing within the constraints of the retaining bolt holes, that centralisation can be judged visually. When the housing is centred, tighten the retaining bolts to the specified torque in the order shown (see illustration).

13.20 Tighten the housing retaining bolts in the order shown

21   Refit the alternator and adjustment arm.
22   Reconnect the high-pressure oil pipe to the rear of the vacuum pump, and the oil return hose to the oil pump housing.
23   Refit the timing belt tensioner and the crankshaft pulley/sprocket as described in Section 8.

2A-16 Chapter 2 Part A: In-vehicle engine repair procedures

14.2a Undo the retaining screw (arrowed) . . .

14.2b . . . and remove the rear cover plate from the oil pump body

14.5a Check the clearances between the pump body and the outer rotor . . .

14.5b . . . the inner-to-outer rotor clearance . . .

14.5c . . . and the rotor endfloat

14.8 Ensure that the oil pump rear cover retaining screw passes through into the hole in the mounting plate (arrowed)

14 Oil pump - dismantling, inspection and reassembly

Note: *Oil pump components are not available separately. If as a result of the following inspection the pump is found to be worn, a complete new oil pump must be obtained.*

Dismantling

1 Remove the oil pump from the engine as described in Section 13.
2 To inspect the oil pump components for excessive wear, undo the retaining screw and remove the rear cover plate from the pump body **(see illustrations)**.
3 Wipe the exterior of the pump housing clean.

Inspection

4 Inspect the rotors and inner body of the pump for signs of severe scoring or excessive wear, which if evident will necessitate renewal of the pump unit.
5 Using feeler blades, check the clearances between the pump body and the outer rotor, the inner-to-outer rotor clearance, and the amount of rotor endfloat **(see illustrations)**.
6 If the clearances measured are outside the specified maximum clearances, the pump unit must be renewed.

Reassembly

7 Lubricate the pump thoroughly with clean engine oil, then refit the rear cover plate to the pump body.
8 Align the retaining screw holes, and refit the screw. Ensure that the screw passes through into the hole in the mounting plate **(see illustration)**.

15 Crankshaft oil seals - renewal

Front oil seal

Removal

1 Remove the oil pump housing as described in paragraphs 1 to 4 inclusive of Section 13.
2 Note and record the fitted depth of the oil seal, in relation to the outer face of the oil pump housing.
3 Support the housing on blocks of wood, and drive out the old seal using a small punch **(see illustration)**.
4 Clean the housing thoroughly, and remove all traces of old gasket from the mating surfaces. Similarly clean the mating face of the engine intermediate plate. Obtain a new oil seal and new oil pump housing gasket.

Refitting

5 Locate the new seal in the housing bore, with the open side of the seal towards the inside (engine side of the housing).
6 Squarely tap the new seal into place, using the old seal as a guide and mandrel. Ensure that the new seal is fitted to the same depth as noted during removal.
7 The new oil seal should have been supplied with a plastic sleeve, to protect the oil seal lip as it engages over the oil pump housing. Retain this sleeve for use when refitting.
8 Refit the oil pump housing as described in paragraphs 16 to 23 inclusive of Section 13.

Chapter 2 Part A: In-vehicle engine repair procedures

2A-17

15.3 Drive out the old crankshaft front oil seal using a small punch

15.13 Undo the four bolts, and remove the rear oil seal carrier

15.14 Remove the old oil seal from the carrier

15.16 Crankshaft rear oil seal, protective plastic sleeve and carrier

15.18 Tap the new seal fully home until it contacts the shoulder in the carrier

15.19 Place the plastic sleeve in position from the inside

Rear oil seal

Removal

9   Remove the flywheel as described in Section 16.
10   One of two possible methods may be used to renew the rear oil seal, depending on the tools available.
11   If Ford tools 21-151 and 21-102 (up to the 1989 model year) or 21-102-03 (1989 model year onwards) are available, these tools can be used to extract the old seal from the carrier, and to fit the new seal. Use the instructions provided with the tools, if this method is being used.
12   If the special tools are not available, it will be necessary to remove the sump as described in Section 12, then proceed as follows.
13   Undo the four bolts, and remove the oil seal carrier from the rear face of the cylinder block **(see illustration)**.
14   Support the carrier on blocks of wood, and drive out the old seal using a small punch **(see illustration)**.
15   Clean the housing thoroughly, and remove all traces of old gasket from the mating surfaces. Similarly clean the mating face of the cylinder block, and the surface of the crankshaft on which the oil seal lip bears. Obtain a new oil seal and new oil seal carrier gasket.

Refitting

16   The new oil seal should have been supplied with a plastic sleeve, to protect the oil seal lip as it engages over the crankshaft. Retain this sleeve for use when refitting **(see illustration)**.
17   Locate the oil seal in position in the carrier, with the open side of the seal toward the engine.
18   Using a block of wood, tap the seal fully home until it contacts the shoulder in the carrier **(see illustration)**.
19   Lubricate the lips of the oil seal, and place the plastic sleeve in

15.20 Refit the oil seal carrier, using a new gasket

position from the inside **(see illustration)**.
20   Position the new carrier gasket in place on the cylinder block, and refit the oil seal carrier; collect the plastic sleeve that will be pushed out as the carrier is fitted **(see illustration)**. Insert the bolts, and tighten them finger-tight only.
21   Align the lower face of the oil seal carrier with the lower face of the cylinder block, and tighten the bolts to the specified torque.
22   Refit the sump as described in Section 12, and the flywheel as described in Section 16.

2A-18 Chapter 2 Part A: In-vehicle engine repair procedures

16.3 A home-made tool (arrowed) can be used to prevent the flywheel/crankshaft from rotating as the bolts are removed

16.7 Locate the flywheel onto the crankshaft, engaging the locating dowel

16.8 Tighten the bolts progressively in pairs, in a diagonal sequence to the specified torque

16.9 Check the flywheel run-out using a dial gauge fixture

16 Flywheel - removal, inspection and refitting

Removal

1 Access to the flywheel can be gained either by removing the transmission as described in Chapter 7A or 7B as applicable, or by removing the engine as described in Part B of this Chapter.
2 On manual transmission vehicles, remove the clutch assembly as described in Chapter 6.
3 Unscrew the eight retaining bolts, and remove the flywheel from the rear end flange of the crankshaft. A tool similar to that shown can be fitted to prevent the flywheel/crankshaft from rotating as the bolts are removed, and later during refitting **(see illustration)**.

Inspection

4 Inspect the starter ring gear on the flywheel for any broken or excessively-worn teeth. If evident, the ring gear must be renewed, but due to the removal and refitting method required, this is a task best entrusted to a Ford dealer or a competent garage.
5 The clutch friction surface on the flywheel must be carefully inspected for grooving or hairline cracks (caused by overheating). If these conditions are evident, it may be possible to have the flywheel surface-ground to renovate it, providing that the balance is not upset. Regrinding is a task for an automotive engineer. If surface-grinding is not possible, the flywheel must be renewed.

6 Carefully inspect the heads of the retaining bolts for punch marks. The bolts may be used a maximum of six times, and should (theoretically) be marked with a centre-punch each time they are removed. If five punch marks are visible, or if there is any doubt about the condition of the bolts, they should be renewed.

Refitting

7 Check that the mating faces of the flywheel and the crankshaft are clean before refitting. Locate the flywheel onto the crankshaft, engaging the locating dowel, and insert the bolts **(see illustration)**.
8 Tighten the bolts progressively in pairs, in a diagonal sequence, to the specified torque. Note that from the 1992 model year onwards, the bolts are tightened initially to the Stage 1 setting given in the Specifications, then through the specified angle of rotation (Stage 2). Where possible, use an angular torque setting gauge attachment tool for accurate Stage 2 tightening **(see illustration)**. Centre-punch or otherwise mark the bolt heads after fitting - see paragraph 6.
9 With the flywheel in position, it is advisable to check the run-out using a dial gauge fixture as shown **(see illustration)**. If the run-out exceeds the maximum figure given in the Specifications, remove the flywheel again and check the mating faces for damage. If the mating faces appear sound, the flywheel must be renewed.
10 On manual transmission vehicles, refit the clutch assembly as described in Chapter 6, then refit the engine or transmission as applicable.

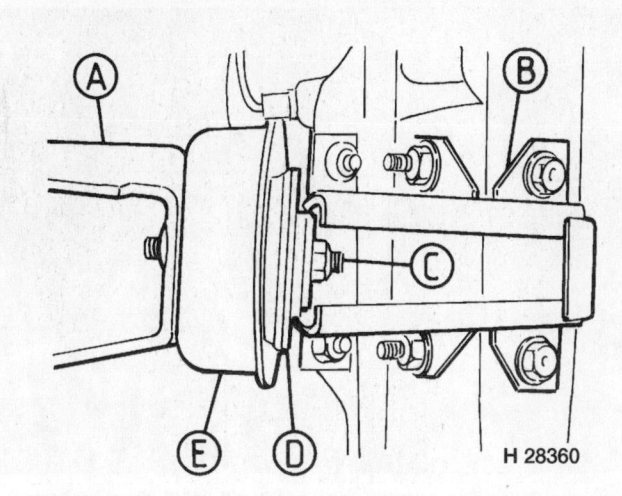

Chapter 2 Part A: In-vehicle engine repair procedures

17.8a Engine mounting components fitted to pre-1992 model year vehicles

- A Engine bracket
- B Chassis side member
- C Rubber mounting retaining nut
- D Rubber mounting
- E Supporting cup

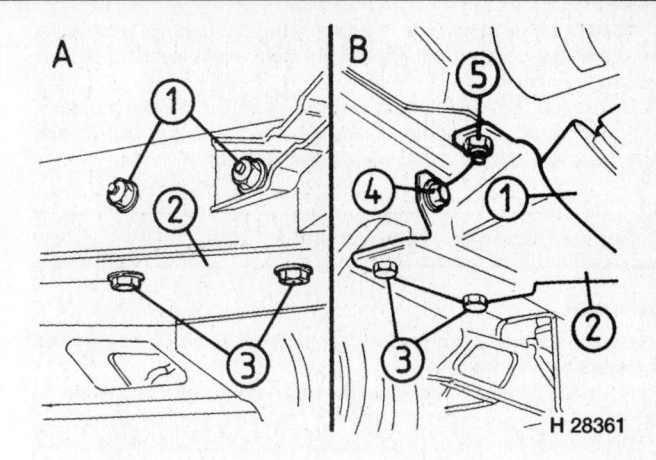

17.8b Engine mounting components fitted from 1992 to 1995 model year vehicles

- A   View of outside chassis side member
- B   View of inside chassis side member
- A1 Through-bolts
- B1 Supporting cap
- 2   Engine bracket
- 3   Engine bracket lower retaining bolts
- 4   Engine bracket side retaining bolts
- 5   Engine bracket upper retaining bolts

17.8c Engine rubber mounting and bracket as used from the 1995 model year onwards

17.8d 1995 model year onwards rubber mounting-to-engine bracket retaining nut . . .

17 Engine mountings - inspection and renewal

Inspection

1 The engine mountings seldom require attention, but broken or deteriorated mountings should be renewed immediately, or the added strain placed on the driveline components may cause damage or wear.
2 During the check, the engine must be raised slightly, to remove its weight from the mountings.
3 Apply the handbrake, then raise the front of the vehicle, and support it securely on axle stands. Position a jack under the sump, with a large block of wood between the jack head and the sump, then carefully raise the engine just enough to take the weight off the mountings.
4 Check the mountings to see if the rubber is cracked, hardened or separated from the metal components. Sometimes the rubber will split right down the centre.
5 Check for relative movement between each mounting's brackets and the engine or body (use a large screwdriver or lever to attempt to move the mountings). If movement is noted, lower the engine and check-tighten the mounting fasteners.

Renewal

6 The engine mountings can be removed once the weight of the engine is supported by one of the following alternative methods.
7 Either support the weight of the assembly from underneath, using a jack and a suitable piece of wood between the jack saddle and the sump (to prevent damage), or from above by attaching a hoist to the engine. Where the air cleaner assembly is mounted on top of the engine, this should be removed, to provide suitable clearance to raise the engine. Also remove the engine undershield, where fitted.
8 Once the weight of the engine is suitably supported, any of the mountings can be unbolted and removed. The accompanying illustrations show the mountings and their attachments, and should be used for reference (see illustrations). As the mountings are disconnected and removed, note the location and orientation of the fixings and any associated fittings.

9 Refitting of all mountings is a reversal of the removal procedure. Ensure that the original sequence of washers and associated fittings are correctly located.
10 Do not fully tighten the mounting fixings until all of the mountings are in position. Check that the mounting rubbers do not twist or distort as the mounting bolts and nuts are tightened securely.

19 Engine oil cooler - removal and refitting

Removal

1 Certain turbocharged engines are fitted with an oil cooler, which is mounted behind the oil filter.
2 Refer to Chapter 1 and drain the engine oil, then remove the oil filter.
3 Disconnect the two hose connections from the outlet stubs on the oil cooler.
4 Unscrew the oil cooler centre retaining bolt, then withdraw the oil cooler and recover the gasket.

Refitting

5 Clean the mating surfaces of the cylinder block and oil cooler.
6 Locate a new gasket in position, then fit the cooler into the guide on the cylinder block.
7 Refit and tighten the retaining bolt to the specified torque.
8 Reconnect the oil cooler hoses, then fit a new oil filter, and fill the engine with oil as described in Chapter 1.

17.8e ... and rubber mounting-to-chassis bracket retaining nut (viewed from below)

Chapter 2 Part B:
Engine removal and general engine overhaul procedures

Contents

Section		Section	
Camshaft and tappets - removal, inspection and refitting	12	Engine overhaul - general information	2
Crankshaft - inspection	17	Engine overhaul - reassembly sequence	19
Crankshaft - refitting and main bearing running clearance check	21	Engine removal - methods and precautions	3
Crankshaft - removal	14	Engine (turbocharged) - removal and refitting	5
Cylinder block/crankcase - cleaning and inspection	15	Engine (turbocharged) and transmission - removal and refitting	7
Cylinder head - dismantling	9	General information	1
Cylinder head - reassembly	11	Main and big-end bearings - inspection	18
Cylinder head and valve components - cleaning and inspection	10	Piston/connecting rod assemblies - inspection	16
Engine - initial start-up after overhaul	23	Piston/connecting rod assemblies - refitting and big-end bearing running clearance check	22
Engine (normally-aspirated) - removal and refitting	4	Piston/connecting rod assemblies - removal	13
Engine (normally-aspirated) and transmission - removal and refitting	6	Piston rings - refitting	20
Engine overhaul - dismantling sequence	8		

Specifications

Cylinder head
Valve seat angle:
  Inlet .... 30° to 30° 30'
  Exhaust .... 45° to 45° 30'
Valve guide internal diameter (inlet and exhaust) .... 8.982 to 9.013 mm

Valves - general

	Inlet	Exhaust
Valve head diameter	41.90 to 42.10 mm	36.20 to 36.40 mm
Valve stem diameter	8.941 to 8.966 mm	8.923 to 8.948 mm
Valve seat angle	29° 30' to 30°	44° 30' to 45°
Valve spring free length (inlet and exhaust)	51 mm	

Pushrods and rocker gear
Rocker shaft diameter .... 18.87 to 18.90 mm
Rocker arm-to-shaft clearance .... 0.02 to 0.08 mm
Tappet stem diameter .... 17.745 to 17.488 mm
Pushrod length .... 153.87 to 154.87 mm

Cylinder block
Cylinder bore diameter:
  Class 1 .... 93.648 to 93.660 mm
  Class 2 .... 93.660 to 93.672 mm
  Class 3 .... 93.672 to 93.684 mm
  Class 4 .... 93.684 to 93.696 mm

Pistons and piston rings

Piston diameter (Mahle pistons):
- Class 1 .... 93.508 to 93.520 mm
- Class 2 .... 93.520 to 93.532 mm
- Class 3 .... 93.532 to 93.544 mm
- Class 4 .... 93.544 to 93.556 mm

Piston diameter (H & G pistons):
- Class 1 .... 93.621 to 93.633 mm
- Class 2 .... 93.633 to 93.645 mm
- Class 3 .... 93.645 to 93.657 mm
- Class 4 .... 93.657 to 93.669 mm

Piston oversizes .... 0.65 mm, 1.00 mm

Piston-to-cylinder bore clearance:
- With Mahle pistons .... 0.021 to 0.059 mm
- With H & G pistons .... 0.015 to 0.039 mm

Gudgeon pin bore diameter:
- With Mahle pistons .... 43.5 mm
- With H & G pistons .... 81.5 mm

Piston protrusion over block face at TDC:
- Production .... 0.301 to 0.503 mm
- Service .... 0.211 to 0.503 mm

Gudgeon pin clearance in piston .... 0.002 to 0.010 mm

Piston ring end gaps (nominal):
- Compression rings .... 0.40 to 0.65 mm
- Oil control ring .... 0.38 to 1.14 mm

Piston ring-to-groove clearance (nominal):
- Upper compression ring .... 0.14 to 0.17 mm
- Second compression ring .... 0.06 to 0.095 mm
- Oil control ring .... 0.02 to 0.055 mm

Crankshaft and bearings

Main bearing journal diameter:

Rear:
- Size 1 .... 76.980 to 77.000 mm
- Size 2 .... 76.730 to 76.750 mm

Others:
- Size 1 .... 69.980 to 70.000 mm
- Size 2 .... 69.730 to 69.750 mm

Regrind undersizes (nominal):

Rear:
- Size 3 .... 76.490 to 76.500 mm
- Size 4 .... 76.240 to 76.250 mm

Others:
- Size 3 .... 69.490 to 69.500 mm
- Size 4 .... 69.240 to 69.250 mm

Main bearing journal-to-shell running clearance:
- Journals 1 to 4 .... 0.052 to 0.090 mm
- Journal 5 .... 0.056 to 0.094 mm

Crankpin (big-end) bearing journal diameter:
- Size 1 .... 60.000 to 59.980 mm
- Size 2 .... 59.750 to 59.730 mm

Regrind undersizes .... 0.25, 0.50 and 0.75 mm below nominal journal
Crankpin (big-end) bearing journal-to-shell running clearance .... 0.030 to 0.095 mm
Crankshaft endfloat .... 0.075 to 0.325 mm

Connecting rods

Gudgeon pin bush bore diameter .... 29.010 to 29.032 mm
Gudgeon pin clearance in bush .... 0.006 to 0.026 mm

Camshaft

Cam lift:
- Inlet .... 7.3 mm
- Exhaust .... 7.6 mm

Bearing journal diameter .... 55.966 to 55.941 mm
Bearing journal running clearance .... 0.072 to 0.116 mm
Camshaft endfloat .... 0.10 to 0.25 mm

Flywheel

Flywheel run-out (maximum) .... 0.130 mm at a radius of 120 mm from centre

Chapter 2 Part B: Engine removal and general engine overhaul procedures

Torque wrench settings	Nm	lbf ft
Camshaft rear plate	20 to 25	15 to 18
Camshaft thrust plate	20 to 25	15 to 18
Crankpin (big-end) bearing cap bolts:		
Stage 1	47 to 65	35 to 48
Stage 2	65 to 72	48 to 53
Engine intermediate plate:		
Bolts 1 to 8	32 to 40	24 to 30
Bolt 9	20 to 25	15 to 18
Main bearing cap bolts:		
Pre-1992 model year:		
Stage 1 - all bolts	110 to 126	81 to 93
Stage 2 - centre bearing cap	140 to 155	103 to 114
Stage 2 - all other caps	126 to 140	93 to 103
1992 model year onwards:		
Stage 1 - all bolts	78 to 90	58 to 66
Stage 2 - all bolts	160 to 180	118 to 133
Oil pressure relief valve	52 to 58	38 to 43
Oil pick-up pipe	16 to 20	12 to 15

Note: *Refer to Part A of this Chapter for remaining torque wrench settings.*

1 General information

How to use this Chapter

This Part of Chapter 2 is devoted to engine removal and refitting, to those repair procedures requiring the removal of the engine from the vehicle, and to the overhaul of engine components. It includes only the Specifications relevant to those procedures. Refer to Part A for additional Specifications, if required.

General information

The information ranges from advice concerning preparation for an overhaul and the purchase of replacement parts, to detailed step-by-step procedures covering removal and installation of internal engine components and the inspection of parts.

The following Sections have been written based on the assumption that the engine has been removed from the vehicle. For information concerning in-vehicle engine repair, as well as removal and installation of the external components necessary for the overhaul, see Part A of this Chapter, and Section 8 of this Part.

2 Engine overhaul - general information

It's not always easy to determine when, or if, an engine should be completely overhauled, as a number of factors must be considered.

High mileage is not necessarily an indication that an overhaul is needed, while low mileage doesn't preclude the need for an overhaul. Frequency of servicing is probably the most important consideration. An engine that's had regular and frequent oil and filter changes, as well as other required maintenance, will most likely give many thousands of miles of reliable service. Conversely, a neglected engine may require an overhaul very early in its life.

Excessive oil consumption is an indication that piston rings, valve seals and/or valve guides are in need of attention. Make sure that oil leaks aren't responsible before deciding that the rings and/or guides are worn. Perform a cylinder compression test or leakdown test to determine the extent of the work required.

Loss of power, rough running, knocking or metallic engine noises, excessive valve train noise and high fuel consumption rates may also point to the need for an overhaul, especially if they're all present at the same time. If a full service doesn't remedy the situation, major mechanical work is the only solution.

An engine overhaul involves restoring all internal parts to the specification of a new engine. **Note:** *Always check first what replacement parts are available before planning any overhaul operation. Ford dealers, or a good engine reconditioning specialist/automotive parts supplier may be able to suggest alternatives which will enable you to overcome the lack of replacement parts if there is a problem.*

During an overhaul, it is usual to renew the piston rings, and to rebore and/or hone the cylinder bores; where the rebore is done by an automotive machine shop, new oversize pistons and rings will also be installed - all these operations, of course, assume the availability of suitable replacement parts. The main and big-end bearings are generally renewed and, if necessary, the crankshaft may be reground to restore the journals. Generally, the valves are serviced as well, since they're usually in less-than-perfect condition at this point. While the engine is being overhauled, other components, such as the starter and alternator, can be renewed as well, or rebuilt, if the necessary parts can be found. The end result should be an as-new engine that will give many trouble-free miles. **Note:** *Critical cooling system components such as the hoses, drivebelt, thermostat and water pump MUST be replaced with new parts when an engine is overhauled. The radiator should be checked carefully, to ensure that it isn't clogged or leaking (see Chapter 3). Also, as a general rule, the oil pump should be renewed when an engine is rebuilt.*

Before beginning the engine overhaul, read through the entire procedure, to familiarise yourself with the scope and requirements of the job. Overhauling an engine isn't difficult, but it is time-consuming. Plan on the vehicle being off the road for a minimum of two weeks, especially if parts must be taken to an automotive machine shop for repair or reconditioning. Check on availability of parts, and make sure that any necessary special tools and equipment are obtained in advance. Most work can be done with typical hand tools, although a number of precision measuring tools are required, for inspecting parts to determine if they must be replaced. Often, an automotive machine shop will handle the inspection of parts, and will offer advice concerning reconditioning and replacement. **Note:** *Always wait until the engine has been completely dismantled, and all components, especially the cylinder block/crankcase, have been inspected, before deciding what service and repair operations must be performed by an automotive machine shop. Since the block's condition will be the major factor to consider when determining whether to overhaul the original engine or buy a rebuilt one, never purchase parts or have machine work done on other components until the cylinder block/crankcase has been thoroughly inspected.* As a general rule, time is the primary cost of an overhaul, so it doesn't pay to install worn or sub-standard parts.

As a final note, to ensure maximum life and minimum trouble from a rebuilt engine, everything must be assembled with care, in a spotlessly-clean environment.

2B-4 Chapter 2 Part B: Engine removal and general engine overhaul procedures

3 Engine removal - methods and precautions

If you've decided that an engine must be removed for overhaul or major repair work, several preliminary steps should be taken.

Locating a suitable place to work is extremely important. Adequate work space, along with storage space for the vehicle, will be needed. If a workshop or garage isn't available, at the very least, a flat, level, clean work surface made of concrete or asphalt is required.

Cleaning the engine compartment and engine/transmission before beginning the removal procedure will help keep tools clean and organised.

To remove the engine, or engine and transmission, an engine hoist or A-frame will be necessary. Make sure the equipment is rated in excess of the combined weight of the unit being removed. Bear in mind that a Diesel engine weighs considerably more than an equivalent-size petrol unit. Safety is of primary importance, considering the potential hazards involved in removing the engine/transmission from the vehicle.

If this is the first time you have removed an engine, a helper should ideally be available. Advice and aid from someone more experienced would also be helpful. There are many instances when one person cannot simultaneously perform all of the operations required when removing the engine from the vehicle.

Plan the operation ahead of time. Arrange for, or obtain, all of the tools and equipment you'll need, prior to beginning the job. Some of the equipment necessary to perform removal and installation safely and with relative ease, and which may have to be hired or borrowed, includes (in addition to the engine hoist) a heavy-duty trolley jack, a strong pair of axle stands, some wooden blocks, and an engine dolly (a low, wheeled platform capable of taking the weight of the engine/transmission, so that it can be moved easily when on the ground). A complete set of spanners and sockets (as described in the front of this manual) will obviously be needed, together with plenty of rags and cleaning solvent for mopping-up spilled oil, coolant and fuel. If the hoist is to be hired, make sure that you arrange for it in advance, and perform all of the operations possible without it beforehand. This will save you money and time.

Plan for the vehicle to be out of use for quite a while. A machine shop will be required to perform some of the work which the do-it-yourselfer can't accomplish without special equipment. These establishments often have a busy schedule, so it would be a good idea to consult them before removing the engine, to accurately estimate the amount of time required to rebuild or repair components that may need work.

Always be extremely careful when removing and installing the engine/transmission. Serious injury can result from careless actions. By planning ahead and taking your time, the job (although a major task) can be accomplished successfully.

4 Engine (normally-aspirated) - removal and refitting

Note: *Read through the entire Section, as well as reading the advice in Section 3, before beginning this procedure. In this procedure, the engine is removed separately from the transmission, and is lifted upwards and out of the engine compartment.*

Removal

1 Disconnect the battery negative lead.
2 Refer to Chapter 1 for details, and drain the engine coolant and engine oil. Refit the drain plug to the sump on completion, to prevent the leakage of any oil remaining in the engine.
3 Refer to Chapter 11 for details, and remove the bonnet. Position it out of the way, in a safe place where it will not get damaged.
4 Refer to Chapter 4 for details, and remove the air cleaner unit.
5 Release the retaining clips and detach the coolant hoses from the thermostat housing, the bottom hose from the radiator to the water pump, and the heater hoses at the bulkhead and engine connections. Allow for coolant spillage as the hoses are detached, note their routing, then position them out of the way.
6 With all the hoses disconnected, undo the two screws and remove the cooling system expansion tank.
7 Refer to Chapter 11 and remove the front grille and front bumper.
8 Refer to Chapter 3 and remove the radiator, together with the upper support crossmember.
9 On engines with exhaust gas recirculation, remove the inlet manifold as described in Chapter 4, to provide increased clearance when lifting the engine upwards and out of the engine compartment,
10 Undo the retaining nuts, and separate the exhaust downpipe from the manifold flange.
11 On vehicles with power steering, refer to Chapter 1 and remove the power steering pump drivebelt. Detach the power steering pump mounting bracket from the cylinder block, and move the pump assembly to one side, clear of the engine.
12 On vehicles with air conditioning, refer to Chapter 1 and remove the air conditioning compressor drivebelt, release the compressor from the engine, and position it to one side. **Do not** disconnect any of the air conditioning system hoses.
13 Disconnect the accelerator cable from the injection pump and from the support bracket.
14 Disconnect the fuel feed pipes at the fuel filter, and the fuel return pipe at the fuel injection pump. Recover the banjo union washers (where applicable), and plug or cap all open unions.
15 Where applicable, disconnect the fuel supply hose from the fuel pump. Where quick-release couplings are used on the fuel hoses, release the protruding locking lugs on the union, by squeezing them together and carefully pulling the coupling apart. Use rag to soak up any spilt fuel. Plug the hose to prevent the ingress of dirt and fuel spillage.
16 According to alternator type, either disconnect the wiring multi-plug or remove the plastic cover, undo the terminal nuts and disconnect the alternator wires, noting their locations.
17 Undo the union nut, and detach the vacuum pipe from the rear of the brake servo vacuum pump on the alternator.
18 Noting their locations, disconnect the wiring connectors from the following (where fitted) **(see illustration)**:

a) *Coolant temperature gauge sender unit.*
b) *Oil pressure switch.*
c) *Cylinder block earth lead.*
d) *Fuel filter water separator.*
e) *Injection pump stop solenoid.*
f) *Injection pump cold start device.*

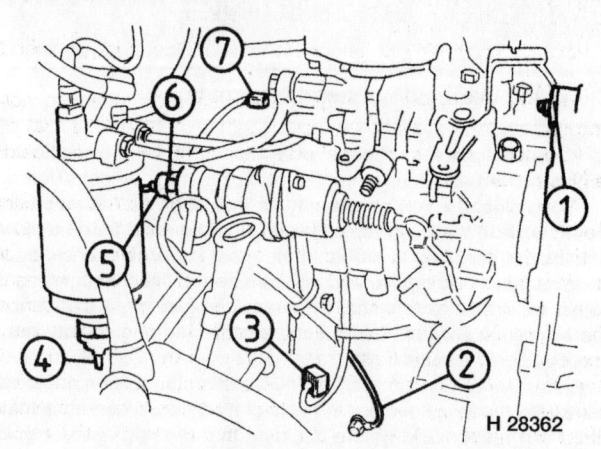

4.18 Disconnect the wiring connectors from the following components

1	*Coolant temperature gauge sender unit*	5	*Injection pump cold start device*
2	*Cylinder block earth lead*	6	*Injection pump cold start accelerator (Bosch pumps)*
3	*Oil pressure switch*	7	*Injection pump stop solenoid*
4	*Fuel filter water separator*		

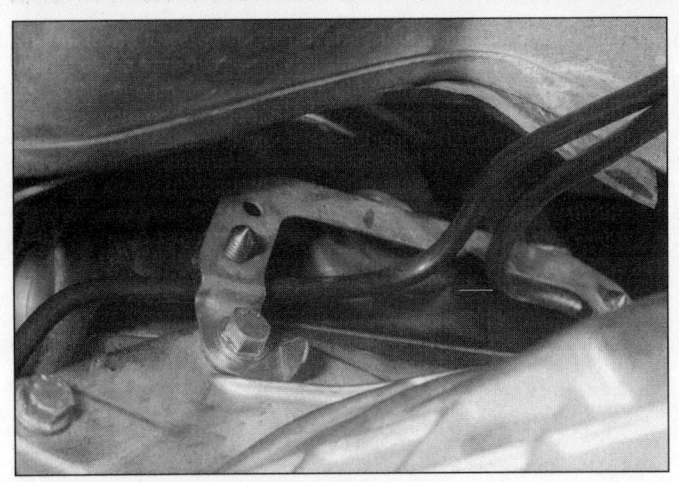

Chapter 2 Part B: Engine removal and general engine overhaul procedures

4.30 Release the fuel pipe clips from the pipe support bracket at the top of the transmission

4.32 Engine unit removal

19 Remove the starter motor as described in Chapter 5.
20 Apply the handbrake, then raise the front of the vehicle and support it on axle stands.
21 From under the vehicle, detach the clutch release lever rubber boot from the side of the clutch housing, and slide it up the cable.
22 Slip the inner cable out of the slot on the release lever, and free the outer cable from the clutch housing. Slide the rubber boot off the cable.
23 Where fitted, undo the two bolts and remove the clutch housing lower cover.
24 On vehicles fitted with the MT75 manual transmission, disconnect the wires at the reversing light switch on the transmission.
25 On automatic transmission models, unbolt and detach the engine/transmission brace. Working through the starter motor aperture, unscrew the four torque converter-to-driveplate nuts. The engine can be turned by means of a spanner on the crankshaft pulley bolt to bring the torque converter nuts into an accessible position.
26 Undo the lower nut and washer from both engine mountings.
27 Undo the lower engine-to-clutch housing bolts which are accessible from underneath, then lower the vehicle to the ground.
28 Attach a suitable hoist to the engine. If possible, fabricate lifting eyes to connect the hoist to the engine, but make sure that they are strong enough, and connect them to the front and rear of the engine at diagonally-opposite points.
29 Position a suitable jack under the transmission, and just take the unit's weight.
30 Unscrew the remaining engine-to-transmission retaining bolts, noting that on later models, the upper bolts also retain the fuel pipe support bracket. Release the fuel pipe clips from the support bracket (see illustration).
31 Check around the engine to ensure that all of the relevant fixings and attachments are disconnected and out of the way for the removal.
32 Enlist the aid of an assistant, then move the engine forwards and away from the transmission, whilst simultaneously raising it. When the engine is separated from the transmission, carefully guide it up and out of the engine compartment (see illustration). Do not allow the weight of the engine to hang on the transmission input shaft at any point during the removal (or refitting) of the engine. On automatic transmission models, ensure that the torque converter remains in place on the transmission. When the engine sump is clear of the vehicle, swing the power unit out of the way, and lower it onto a trolley (if available). Unless a mobile hoist is being used, it will be necessary to move the vehicle rearwards and out of the way in order to allow the engine to be lowered for removal. In this instance, ensure that the weight of the transmission is well supported as the vehicle is moved.
33 While the engine is removed, check the mountings; renew them if they are worn or damaged. Similarly, check the condition of all coolant and vacuum hoses and pipes (see Chapter 1). Components that are normally hidden can now be checked properly, and should be renewed if there is any doubt at all about their condition. Also, take the opportunity to overhaul the clutch components (see Chapter 6). It is regarded by many as good working practice to renew the clutch assembly as a matter of course, whenever major engine overhaul work is carried out. Check also the condition of all components (such as the transmission oil seals) disturbed on removal, and renew any that are damaged or worn.

Refitting

34 Refitting is in general, a reversal of the removal procedure, but the following special points should be noted.
35 Before coupling the engine to the transmission, apply a thin smear of high-melting-point grease onto the transmission input shaft splines. If the clutch has been removed, ensure that the clutch disc is centralised.
36 Tighten all fixings to their recommended torque wrench settings.
37 With the engine in position on its mountings, check that an equal clearance exists on both sides between the lower edge of the rubber mounting and the lower edge of the chassis-mounted bracket.
38 Check that the mating faces are clean, then reconnect the exhaust downpipe, using a new exhaust downpipe-to-manifold gasket and self-locking nuts.
39 Ensure that all wiring connections are correctly and securely made.
40 Remove the temporary plugs or caps from the fuel lines before reconnecting them correctly and securely.
41 Reconnect and adjust the accelerator cable as described in Chapter 4. The refitting details for the inlet manifold and air cleaner unit are also given in that Chapter.
42 Renew any coolant hoses (and/or retaining clips) that are not in good condition.
43 Refer to Chapter 6 for details on reconnecting the clutch cable.
44 On vehicles with power steering and/or air conditioning, refit and adjust the drivebelt(s) as described in Chapter 1.
45 When the engine is fully refitted, check that the various hoses are connected, and then top-up the engine oil and coolant levels as described in Chapter 1.
46 When engine refitting is completed, refer to Section 23 for the engine start-up procedures.

5 Engine (turbocharged) - removal and refitting

Note: *Read through the entire Section, as well as reading the advice in Section 3, before beginning this procedure. In this procedure, the engine is removed separately from the transmission and is lifted upwards and out of the engine compartment.*

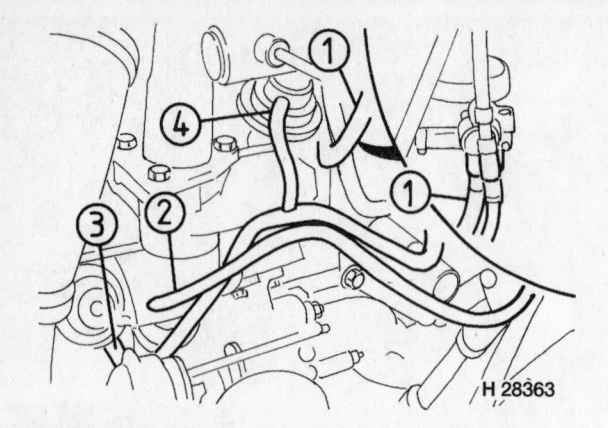

2B-6 Chapter 2 Part B: Engine removal and general engine overhaul procedures

5.10 Disconnect the vacuum hoses at the following locations

1. Vacuum flow controller to vacuum pump
2. Throttle housing to manifold absolute pressure sensor
3. Turbocharger wastegate to vacuum flow controller
4. Exhaust gas recirculation valve to vacuum flow controller

Removal

1 Disconnect the battery negative lead.
2 Refer to Chapter 1 for details, and drain the engine coolant and engine oil. Refit the drain plug to the sump on completion, to prevent the leakage of any oil remaining in the engine.
3 Refer to Chapter 11 for details, and remove the bonnet. Position it out of the way, in a safe place where it will not get damaged.
4 Refer to Chapter 4 for details, and remove the air cleaner unit.
5 Release the retaining clips and detach the coolant hoses from the thermostat housing, the bottom hose from the radiator to the water pump, and the heater hoses at the bulkhead and engine connections. Allow for coolant spillage as the hoses are detached, note their routing, then position them out of the way.
6 With all the hoses disconnected, undo the two screws and remove the cooling system expansion tank.
7 Refer to Chapter 11 and remove the front grille and front bumper.
8 Refer to Chapter 3 and remove the radiator, together with the upper support crossmember.
9 Detach the air inlet pipe from the turbocharger flange, and from the inlet manifold. Recover the gasket at the turbocharger end.
10 Disconnect the vacuum hoses at the following locations (see illustration):

a) Vacuum flow controller to vacuum pump.
b) Throttle housing to manifold absolute pressure sensor.
c) Turbocharger wastegate to vacuum flow controller.
d) Exhaust gas recirculation valve to vacuum flow controller.

11 On vehicles with power steering, refer to Chapter 1 and remove the power steering pump drivebelt. Detach the power steering pump mounting bracket from the cylinder block, and move the pump assembly to one side, clear of the engine.
12 On vehicles with air conditioning, refer to Chapter 1 and remove the air conditioning compressor drivebelt. Release the compressor from the engine, and position it to one side. **Do not** disconnect any of the air conditioning system hoses.
13 On 1995 model year vehicles onwards with an exhaust gas recirculation charge cooler, remove the charge cooler as described in Chapter 4.
14 Disconnect the fuel feed pipes at the fuel filter, and the fuel return pipe at the fuel injection pump. Plug or cap all open unions.
15 Where applicable, disconnect the fuel supply hose from the fuel pump. Where quick-release couplings are used on the fuel hoses, release the protruding locking lugs on the union, by squeezing them together and carefully pulling the coupling apart. Use rag to soak up any spilt fuel. Plug the hose, to prevent fuel spillage and the ingress of dirt.
16 According to alternator type, either disconnect the wiring multi-

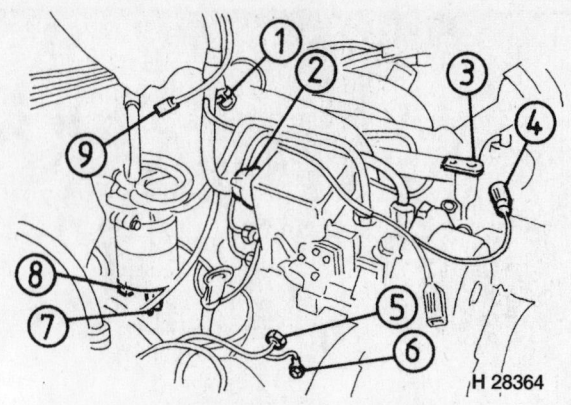

5.18 Disconnect the wiring connectors from the following locations

1. Cable bracket on inlet manifold
2. EPIC wiring multi-plug on injection pump
3. Coolant temperature gauge sender unit
4. Coolant temperature sensor
5. Oil pressure switch
6. Cylinder block earth lead
7. Fuel filter water separator
8. Crankshaft position/speed sensor
9. Preheating system flame plug (where fitted)

plug, or remove the plastic cover, undo the terminal nuts and disconnect the alternator wires, noting their locations.
17 Undo the union nut, and detach the vacuum pipe from the rear of the brake servo vacuum pump on the alternator.
18 Noting their locations, disconnect the wiring connectors from the following (see illustration):

a) Coolant temperature gauge sender unit.
b) Coolant temperature sensor.
c) Oil pressure switch.
d) Cylinder block earth lead.
e) Fuel filter water separator.
f) EPIC wiring multi-plug on injection pump.
g) Crankshaft position/speed sensor.
h) Preheating system flame plug (where fitted).
i) Exhaust gas recirculation valve.

19 Remove the starter motor as described in Chapter 5.
20 Apply the handbrake, then raise the front of the vehicle and support it on axle stands.
21 On 1995 model year vehicles onwards, undo the two nuts and bolts securing the steering gear to the crossmember, then pull the unit forwards and down as far as possible.
22 Disconnect the exhaust downpipe at the manifold and front flange of the silencer. Remove the pipe, and recover the flange gaskets.
23 From under the vehicle, detach the clutch release lever rubber boot from the side of the clutch housing, and slide it up the cable.
24 Slip the inner cable out of the slot on the release lever, and free the outer cable from the clutch housing. Slide the rubber boot off the cable.
25 Where fitted, undo the two bolts and remove the clutch housing lower cover.
26 On vehicles fitted with the MT75 manual transmission, disconnect the wires at the reversing light switch on the transmission.
27 Undo the lower nut and washer from both engine mountings.
28 Undo the lower engine-to-clutch housing bolts which are accessible from underneath, then lower the vehicle to the ground.
29 Attach a suitable hoist to the engine. If possible, fabricate lifting eyes to connect the hoist to the engine, but make sure that they are strong enough, and connect them to the front and rear of the engine at diagonally-opposite points.
30 Position a suitable jack under the transmission, and just take the unit's weight.

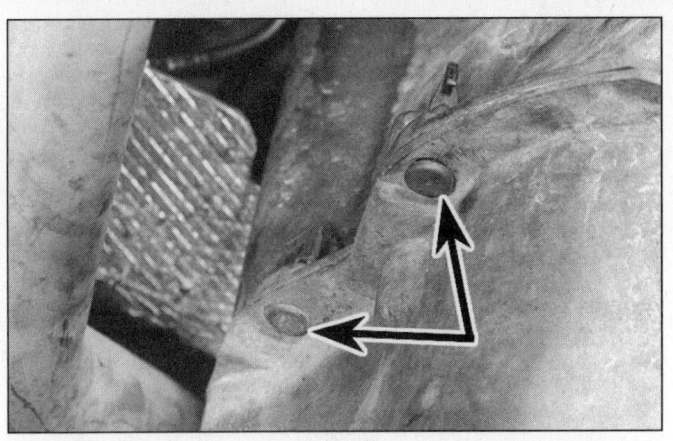

Chapter 2 Part B: Engine removal and general engine overhaul procedures 2B-7

6.6 Where fitted, release the fasteners (arrowed) and remove the two-piece cover assembly fitted around the clutch housing

31 Unscrew the remaining engine-to-transmission retaining bolts, noting that on later models, the upper bolts also retain the fuel pipe support bracket. Release the fuel pipe clips from the support bracket.
32 Check around the engine to ensure that all of the relevant fixings and attachments are disconnected and out of the way for the removal.
33 Enlist the aid of an assistant, then move the engine forwards and away from the transmission, whilst simultaneously raising it. When the engine is separated from the transmission, carefully guide it up and out of the engine compartment. Do not allow the weight of the engine to hang on the transmission input shaft at any point during the removal (or refitting) of the engine. When the engine sump is clear of the vehicle, swing the power unit out of the way, and lower it onto a trolley (if available). Unless a mobile hoist is being used, it will be necessary to move the vehicle rearwards and out of the way, in order to allow the engine to be lowered for removal. In this instance, ensure that the weight of the transmission is well supported as the vehicle is moved.
34 While the engine is removed, check the mountings; renew them if they are worn or damaged. Similarly, check the condition of all coolant and vacuum hoses and pipes (see Chapter 1). Components that are normally hidden can now be checked properly, and should be renewed if there is any doubt at all about their condition. Also, take the opportunity to overhaul the clutch components (see Chapter 6). It is regarded by many as good working practice to renew the clutch assembly as a matter of course, whenever major engine overhaul work is carried out. Check also the condition of all components (such as the transmission oil seals) disturbed on removal, and renew any that are damaged or worn.

Refitting

35 Refitting is in general a reverse of the removal procedure. Refer to paragraphs 34 to 46 in Section 4 for additional information and special points.

6 Engine (normally-aspirated) and transmission - removal and refitting

Note: *Read through the entire Section, as well as reading the advice in Section 3, before beginning this procedure. The engine and transmission are removed as a unit, lifted upwards and out of the engine compartment, then separated outside the vehicle.*

Removal

1 Refer to Section 4, and carry out the operations described in paragraphs 1 to 18 inclusive.
2 Disconnect the wiring at the starter motor, noting the cable positions.
3 Apply the handbrake, then raise the front of the vehicle and support it on axle stands.

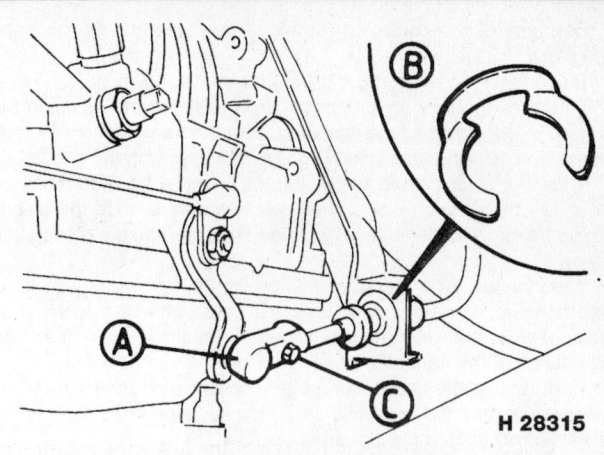

6.21 Selector cable attachments at the transmission
- A Cable ball stud end fitting
- B Cable retaining C-clip
- C Cable adjuster screw

Manual transmission models

4 Detach the clutch release lever rubber boot from the side of the clutch housing, and slide it up the cable.
5 Slip the inner cable out of the slot on the release lever, and free the outer cable from the clutch housing. Slide the rubber boot off the cable.
6 Where fitted, release the fasteners and remove the lower engine cover, and the two-piece cover assembly fitted around the clutch housing **(see illustration)**.
7 Refer to Chapter 7A, and remove the gearshift lever assembly, according to transmission type.
8 Disconnect the wires at the reversing light switch on the transmission.
9 On type G and MT75 transmissions, place a suitable container beneath the drain plug, and drain the transmission oil. Refit the drain plug on completion.
10 Remove the propeller shaft as described in Chapter 8.
11 Undo the retaining bolt, and remove the speedometer drive cable retaining plate. Withdraw the speedometer cable from the transmission, and position it out of the way.
12 If an electronic tachograph is fitted, detach its lead and position it out of the way.
13 Unbolt and detach the lower cover plate(s) from the clutch housing.
14 Release the fuel pipes from the clips on the support bracket located at the top of the clutch housing. Where applicable, also disconnect the engine earth cable if it is attached to one of the clutch housing bolts.
15 Position a trolley jack under the transmission to support it.
16 Undo the single centre bolt (type G and type N transmissions), or the two nuts (MT75 transmission) securing the transmission mounting to the transmission case. Undo the two bolts each side, and remove the transmission crossmember from under the vehicle.

Automatic transmission models

17 Refer to Chapter 8 and remove the propeller shaft.
18 Disconnect the exhaust front downpipe from the exhaust manifold and silencer, and withdraw it from beneath the vehicle.
19 Disconnect the speedometer cable from the rear of the transmission. Where applicable, disconnect the wiring from the electronic tachograph.
20 From inside the cab area, move the gear selector lever to the "N" position.
21 From under the vehicle, prise the selector cable end fitting from the ball stud on the transmission selector lever **(see illustration)**. Undo the two bolts, and move the selector cable bracket, complete with cable, to one side.

2B-8 Chapter 2 Part B: Engine removal and general engine overhaul procedures

22 Disconnect the wiring to the kickdown solenoid at the cable connector.
23 Disconnect the wiring from the starter inhibitor switch.
24 Withdraw the fluid level dipstick, then unscrew the retaining bolt and remove the dipstick tube assembly from the transmission. Plug the transmission opening after removing the tube assembly.
25 Wipe the area around the fluid cooler connections to the right-hand side of the transmission, then unscrew and remove the unions. Plug the transmission openings and pipe ends, and tie the pipes out of the way.
26 Take the weight of the transmission with a trolley jack positioned beneath the transmission sump; to prevent damage to the sump, place a block of wood between the jack and sump, but make sure that there is no chance of the transmission slipping in subsequent operations.
27 Undo the single bolt securing the transmission mounting to the crossmember, and the two bolts each side securing the crossmember to the underbody. Remove the crossmember.

All models

28 Attach a suitable hoist to the engine. If possible, fabricate lifting eyes to connect the hoist to the engine, but make sure that they are strong enough, and connect them to the front and rear of the engine at diagonally-opposite points.
29 Check around the engine and transmission, ensuring that all of the relevant fixings and attachments are disconnected and out of the way for the removal.
30 Raise the engine slightly to take the weight off the mountings, then remove the engine mounting brackets from the cylinder block each side.
31 Enlist the aid of an assistant, then move the engine and transmission forwards, whilst simultaneously raising it. Carefully guide it up and out of the engine compartment. When the assembly is clear of the vehicle, swing it out of the way, and lower it onto a trolley (if available). Unless a mobile hoist is being used, it will be necessary to move the vehicle rearwards and out of the way, in order to allow the engine and transmission to be lowered for removal.
32 While removed, check the engine and transmission mountings; renew them if they are worn or damaged. Similarly, check the condition of all coolant and vacuum hoses and pipes (see Chapter 1). Components that are normally hidden can now be checked properly, and should be renewed if there is any doubt at all about their condition.

Engine and transmission separation and reconnection

Separation

33 On manual transmission models, undo the two bolts and remove the clutch housing lower cover, where fitted.
34 Undo the bolts and remove the starter motor.
35 On automatic transmission models, unbolt and detach the engine/transmission brace. Working through the starter motor aperture, unscrew the four torque converter-to-driveplate nuts. The engine can be turned by means of a spanner on the crankshaft pulley bolt to bring the torque converter nuts into an accessible position.
36 Undo all the clutch/torque converter housing bolts securing the engine to the transmission.
37 With the engine well supported, withdraw the transmission rearwards off the locating dowels, taking care not allow the weight of the engine to hang on the transmission input shaft. On automatic transmission models, ensure that the torque converter remains in place on the transmission. It is advisable to attach a bracket to the front face of the converter housing, to retain the torque converter in place while the transmission is separated.
38 Move the transmission clear of the engine, and position it out of the way.

Reconnection

39 Before reconnecting the manual transmission to the engine, apply a thin smear of high-melting-point grease onto the transmission input shaft splines. If the clutch has been removed, ensure that the clutch disc is centralised.
40 With the torque converter in position on the transmission and engaged with the oil pump drivegear, ensure that the distance between the converter flange end face and the converter housing flange is at least 21 mm. Maintain a slight rearward tilt to the transmission when refitting, to prevent the torque converter falling out forwards. As the transmission is fitted, guide the threaded studs of the torque converter through the holes in the driveplate. When the transmission is fully mated with the engine, check that the converter rotates freely, then insert the converter housing-to-engine flange bolts.
41 Refit the remainder of the components, and tighten all fixings to their specified torque wrench settings.

Refitting

42 Refitting is in general, a reversal of the removal procedure, but the following special points should be noted.
43 Tighten all fixings to their specified torque wrench settings.
44 With the engine in position on its mountings, check that an equal clearance exists on both sides between the lower edge of the rubber mounting and the lower edge of the chassis-mounted bracket.
45 Check that the mating faces are clean, then reconnect the exhaust downpipe, using a new exhaust downpipe-to-manifold gasket and self-locking nuts.
46 Ensure that all wiring connections are correctly and securely made.
47 Remove the temporary plugs or caps from the fuel lines before reconnecting them correctly and securely.
48 Reconnect and adjust the accelerator cable as described in Chapter 4. The refitting details for the air cleaner unit are also given in that Chapter.
49 Renew any coolant hoses (and/or retaining clips) that are not in good condition.
50 Refer to Chapter 6 for details on reconnecting the clutch cable.
51 On vehicles with power steering and/or air conditioning, refit and adjust the drivebelt(s) as described in Chapter 1.
52 Refit the propeller shaft as described in Chapter 8.
53 On automatic transmission models, adjust the downshift cable and selector cable as described in Chapter 7B.
54 When the engine is fully refitted, check that the various hoses are connected and then top-up the engine oil, transmission fluid and coolant levels as described in Chapter 1.
55 When engine refitting is completed, refer to Section 23 for the engine start-up procedures.

7 Engine (turbocharged) and transmission - removal and refitting

Note: Read through the entire Section, as well as reading the advice in Section 3, before beginning this procedure. The engine and transmission are removed as a unit, lifted upwards and out of the engine compartment, then separated outside the vehicle.

Removal

1 Refer to Section 5, and carry out the operations described in paragraphs 1 to 18 inclusive.
2 Disconnect the wiring at the starter motor, noting the cable positions.
3 Apply the handbrake, then raise the front of the vehicle and support it on axle stands.
4 Refer to Section 6, and carry out the operations described in paragraphs 4 to 16 and 28 to 32.
5 With the engine and transmission assembly removed from the vehicle, separation and reconnection can be carried out as described in the applicable paragraphs of Section 6.

Refitting

6 Refer to Section 6, paragraphs 42 to 55, ignoring any references to automatic transmission models.

Chapter 2 Part B: Engine removal and general engine overhaul procedures 2B-9

9.4 Fit the valve spring compressor to the first valve and spring to be removed

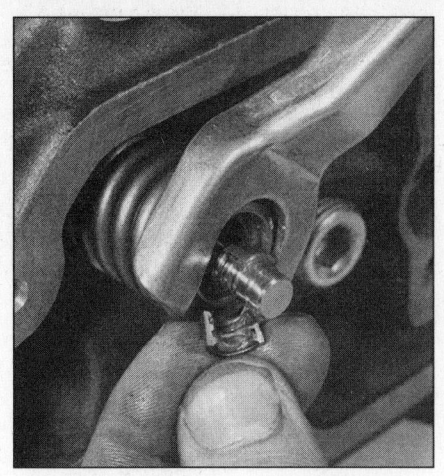

9.5 Wind in the compressor so that the valve collets can be extracted

9.6a Loosen off the compressor and remove the retainer . . .

8 Engine overhaul - dismantling sequence

1 The engine dismantling and reassembly tasks are made easier if the engine is mounted on a portable engine stand. These stands can be hired from a tool hire shop. Depending on the type of stand used, some external components may have to be removed first, to allow the stand fixing plates/bolts to be attached.

2 If a stand is not available, it is possible to dismantle the engine with it suitably supported on a strong workbench or on the floor. Be careful not to tip or drop the engine when working without a stand.

3 If a reconditioned engine is to be fitted, all external components of the original engine must be removed, in order to transfer them to the replacement unit (just as they will if you are doing a complete engine rebuild). Depending on the source of the reconditioned engine, these components will include some or all of the following.
   a) Alternator and mounting brackets.
   b) Timing belt and sprockets.
   c) Water pump.
   d) Oil pump and housing.
   e) Engine intermediate plate.
   f) Thermostat and housing.
   g) Injection system components.
   h) Inlet and exhaust manifolds.
   i) Oil filter.
   j) Fuel pump (where fitted).
   k) Engine mountings.
   l) Flywheel.

Note: *When removing the external components from the engine, pay close attention to details that may be helpful or important during refitting. Note the fitted positions of gaskets, seals, washers, bolts and other small items.*

4 If you are obtaining a "short" engine (which consists of the engine cylinder block, crankshaft, pistons and connecting rods all assembled), the cylinder head, rocker gear and sump will have to be removed also.

5 If a complete overhaul is planned, the engine can be dismantled and the internal components removed in the following order:
   a) Timing belt, tensioner and sprockets.
   b) Water pump.
   c) Fuel injection pump.
   d) Oil pump and housing.
   e) Inlet and exhaust manifolds (if not removed as part of the engine removal procedures).
   f) Cylinder head.
   g) Intermediate plate.
   h) Flywheel.
   i) Camshaft and tappets.
   j) Sump.
   k) Pistons (with connecting rods).
   l) Crankshaft.

6 Before starting the dismantling and overhaul procedures, make sure that you have all of the correct tools for the jobs to tackled. Refer to the introductory pages at the start of this manual for further information.

9 Cylinder head - dismantling

Note: *New and reconditioned cylinder heads are available from the manufacturers, and from engine overhaul specialists. Due to the fact that some specialist tools are required for the dismantling and inspection procedures, it may be more practical and economical for the home mechanic to purchase a reconditioned head, rather than to dismantle, inspect and recondition the original head.*

1 Remove any remaining hose attachments, support brackets or allied components, then undo the retaining bolts and lift off the inlet manifold (if not already removed as part of the cylinder head removal procedure). Remove the inlet manifold-to-cylinder head gasket.

2 If still in position, undo the retaining bolts and lift off the exhaust manifold from the cylinder head (again removing any associated components first).

3 Undo the bolts and remove the thermostat housing, recovering the gasket.

4 To remove the valve springs and valves from the cylinder head, a standard valve spring compressor will required. Fit the spring compressor to the first valve and spring to be removed **(see illustration)**. Assuming that all of the valves and springs are to be removed, start by compressing the No 1 valve (nearest the timing cover end) spring. Take care not to damage the valve stem with the compressor, and do not over-compress the spring, or the valve stem may bend. When tightening the compressor, it may be found that the spring retainer does not release, and the collets are then difficult to remove. In this instance, remove the compressor, then press a piece of tube (or a socket of suitable diameter) so that it does not interfere with the removal of the collets, against the retainer's outer rim. Tap the tube (or socket) with a hammer to unsettle the components.

5 Refit the compressor, and wind it in to enable the collets to be extracted **(see illustration)**.

6 Loosen off the compressor, and remove the retainer and spring **(see illustrations)**. Withdraw the valve from the cylinder head.

7 Repeat the removal procedure with each of the remaining seven valve assemblies in turn. As they are removed, keep the individual valves in their respective order of fitting by placing them in a piece of card which has holes punched in it, numbered 1 to 8 (from the timing

2B-10 Chapter 2 Part B: Engine removal and general engine overhaul procedures

9.6b ... and valve spring

9.7 Place the valve components in a separate labelled bag

9.8 Extract the valve stem oil seal cups using a pair of pliers

10.6 Use a straight edge and feeler blade to check that the cylinder head gasket surface is not distorted

10.12 Measure the valve stem diameter at several points, using a micrometer

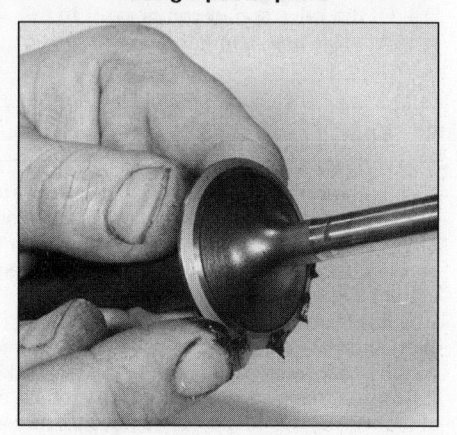

10.15a Smear a trace of valve-grinding compound on the valve seat face ...

cover end) and group their springs, collets and retainers in a similar manner. Alternatively, place each assembly in a separate labelled bag **(see illustration)**.

8   When all the valves have been removed, extract the valve stem oil seal cups using a pair of pliers **(see illustration)**.

10 Cylinder head and valve components - cleaning and inspection

Note: *Always check first what replacement parts are available before planning any overhaul operation. A Ford dealer, or a good engine reconditioning specialist/automotive parts supplier, may be able to suggest alternatives which will enable you to overcome the lack of replacement parts if there is a problem.*

1   Thorough cleaning of the cylinder head and valve components, followed by a detailed inspection, will enable you to decide how much valve service work must be carried out during the engine overhaul.
Note: *If the engine has been severely overheated, it is best to assume that the cylinder head is warped, and to check carefully for signs of this.*

Cleaning

2   Scrape away all traces of old gasket material, carbon and sealing compound from the cylinder head, then wash the head thoroughly with paraffin or a suitable solvent.
3   Scrape off any heavy carbon deposits that may have formed on the valves.
4   Use a power-operated wire brush to remove deposits from the valve heads and stems.

Inspection

Note: *Be sure to perform all the following inspection procedures before concluding that the services of a machine shop or engine overhaul specialist are required. Make a list of all items that require attention.*

Cylinder head

5   Inspect the head very carefully for cracks, evidence of coolant leakage, and other damage. If cracks are found, a new cylinder head should be obtained.
6   Use a straight edge and feeler blade to check that the cylinder head gasket surface is not distorted **(see illustration)**. If it is, it may be possible to re-surface it. No actual figures are provided by the manufacturer for allowable distortion but as a rough guide, anything in excess of 0.15 mm, measured over the full length, must be considered excessive.
7   Examine the valve seats in each of the combustion chambers. If they are severely pitted, cracked or burned, then they will need to be renewed or re-cut by an engine overhaul specialist. If they are only slightly pitted, this can be removed by grinding-in the valve heads and seats with fine valve-grinding compound, as described below.
8   If the valve guides are worn, indicated by a side-to-side motion of the valve, new guides must be fitted. Measure the diameter of the existing valve stems (see below) and the bore of the guides, then calculate the clearance, and compare the result with the specified value; if the clearance is excessive, renew the valves or guides as necessary.
9   The renewal of valve guides is best carried out by an engine overhaul specialist.
10   If the valve seats are to be re-cut, this must be done *only after* the guides have been renewed.

Chapter 2 Part B: Engine removal and general engine overhaul procedures   2B-11

10.15b ... then with a semi-rotary action, grind the valve head to its seat

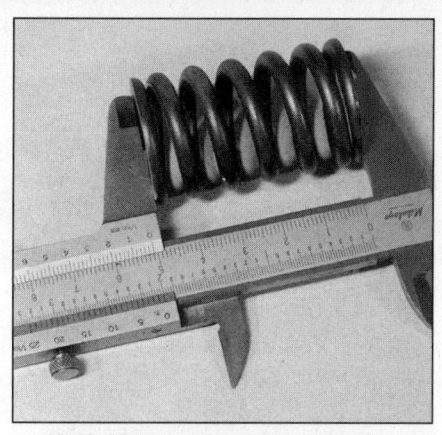

10.18 Measure the valve spring free length using vernier calipers

10.19 Check each valve spring for squareness

11.2a Place the new valve stem oil seal cups over each valve guide ...

11.2b ... and push them fully into place using a deep socket of suitable diameter

11.3 Lubricate each valve stem before refitting

Valves

11   Examine the head of each valve for pitting, burning, cracks and general wear, and check the valve stem for scoring and wear ridges. Rotate the valve, and check for any obvious indication that it is bent. Look for pits and excessive wear on the tip of each valve stem. Renew any valve that shows any such signs of wear or damage.

12   If the valve appears satisfactory at this stage, measure the valve stem diameter at several points, using a micrometer **(see illustration)**. Any significant difference in the readings obtained indicates wear of the valve stem. Should any of these conditions be apparent, the valve(s) must be renewed.

13   If the valves are in satisfactory condition, they should be ground (lapped) into their respective seats, to ensure a smooth gas-tight seal. If the seat is only lightly pitted, or if it has been re-cut, fine grinding compound *only* should be used to produce the required finish. Coarse valve-grinding compound should *not* be used unless a seat is badly burned or deeply pitted; if this is the case, the cylinder head and valves should be inspected by an expert, to decide whether seat re-cutting, or even the renewal of the valve or seat insert, is required.

14   Valve grinding is carried out as follows. Place the cylinder head upside-down on a bench, with a block of wood at each end to give clearance for the valve stems.

15   Smear a trace of (the appropriate grade of) valve-grinding compound on the seat face, and press a suction grinding tool onto the valve head. With a semi-rotary action, grind the valve head to its seat, lifting the valve occasionally to redistribute the grinding compound **(see illustrations)**. A light spring placed under the valve head will greatly ease this operation.

16   If coarse grinding compound is being used, work only until a dull, matt even surface is produced on both the valve seat and the valve, then wipe off the used compound, and repeat the process with fine compound. When a smooth unbroken ring of light grey matt finish is produced on both the valve and seat, the grinding operation is complete. *Do not* grind in the valves any further than absolutely necessary, or the seat will be prematurely sunk into the cylinder head.

17   When all the valves have been ground-in, carefully wash off *all* traces of grinding compound, using paraffin or a suitable solvent, before reassembly of the cylinder head.

Valve components

18   Examine the valve springs for signs of damage and discoloration, and also measure their free length using vernier calipers **(see illustration)**.

19   Stand each spring on a flat surface, and check it for squareness **(see illustration)**. If any of the springs are damaged, distorted, or have lost their tension, obtain a complete set of new springs.

20   Check the spring seats and collets for obvious wear and cracks. Any questionable parts should be renewed, as extensive damage will occur if they fail during engine operation. Any damaged or excessively-worn parts must be renewed; the valve stem oil seals must be renewed as a matter of course whenever they are disturbed.

21   Check the rocker gear components as described in earlier Part A of this Chapter.

11 Cylinder head - reassembly

1   Before reassembling the cylinder head, first ensure that it is perfectly clean, and that no traces of grinding paste are left in the head, nor on the valves and guides. Use compressed air, if available, to blow out all the oil holes and passages.

2   Commence reassembly of the cylinder head by placing the new valve stem oil seal cups over each valve guide, pushing them fully into place using a deep socket of suitable diameter **(see illustrations)**.

3   Lubricate each valve stem before refitting **(see illustration)**.

2B-12 Chapter 2 Part B: Engine removal and general engine overhaul procedures

11.4a Apply a little grease to the split collets . . .

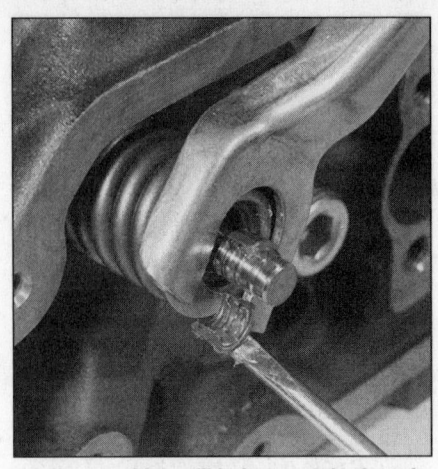

11.4b . . . which will help to retain them in position on the valve

12.6 Detach the hoses at the coolant pipe behind the engine intermediate plate

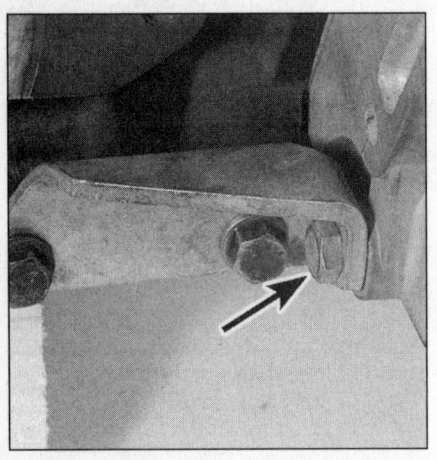

12.7a Undo the intermediate plate lower support bracket bolt (arrowed)

12.7b Withdraw the intermediate plate from the front of the cylinder block . . .

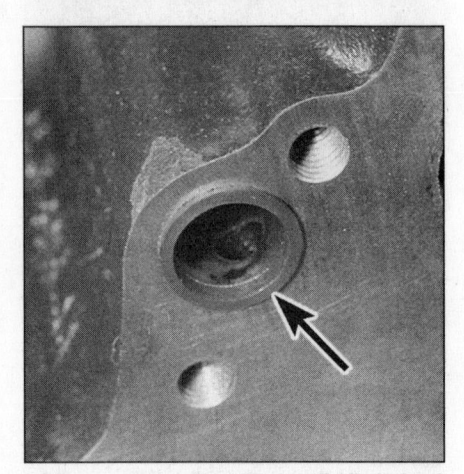

12.7c . . . and collect the small oil channel seal (arrowed) from behind

4 Insert the first valve into its guide, then locate the valve spring and its retainer over the valve stem, and engage the valve spring compressor. Compress the spring and retainer just enough to allow the split collets to be inserted in the location groove in the valve stem, noting that a little grease applied to the collet groove will help retain them in position **(see illustrations)**. Holding the collets in position, slowly release and remove the valve spring compressor.

5 Repeat the operation on the remaining valves, ensuring that each valve is fitted in its appropriate location.

6 On completion, support the cylinder head on a suitable piece of wood, and lightly strike the end of each valve stem in turn with a plastic- or copper-faced hammer. This will fractionally open the valve, and seat the valve components.

12 Camshaft and tappets - removal, inspection and refitting

Removal

1 Remove the timing belt and the timing belt sprockets and tensioner as described in Part A, Sections 7 and 8.
2 Remove the cylinder head as described in Part A, Section 10.
3 Remove the sump as described in Part A, Section 12.
4 Remove the oil pump as described in Part A, Section 14.
5 Remove the water pump as described in Chapter 3, and the fuel injection pump, and (where fitted) the fuel pump, as described in Chapter 4.

6 Detach the hoses at the coolant pipe behind the engine intermediate plate **(see illustration)**. Undo the retaining bracket bolt, and remove the coolant pipe.
7 Undo the intermediate plate lower support bracket bolt, and the bolts securing the intermediate plate to the cylinder block **(see illustration)**. Withdraw the intermediate plate from the front of the cylinder block, and collect the small oil channel seal from behind **(see illustrations)**.
8 Withdraw the O-ring (where fitted) and spacer sleeve from the front of the camshaft.
9 Invert the engine so that it is supported on its cylinder head face (on a clean work area). This is necessary to make all of the tappets slide to the top of their stroke, thus allowing the camshaft to be withdrawn. Rotate the camshaft through a full turn, to ensure that all of the tappets slide up their bores, clear of the camshaft.
10 Undo the two bolts, and remove the camshaft front thrust plate **(see illustration)**.
11 Carefully withdraw the camshaft from the cylinder block, taking care not to damage the bearing bushes **(see illustration)**.
12 Extract each tappet in turn **(see illustration)**. Keep them in order of fitting by inserting them in a card with eight holes in it, numbered 1 to 8 (from the timing belt end of the engine). A valve grinding tool will be found to be useful for the removal of tappets.

Inspection

13 Examine the camshaft bearing journals and lobes for damage or excessive wear **(see illustration)**. If evident, the camshaft must be renewed.

Chapter 2 Part B: Engine removal and general engine overhaul procedures   2B-13

12.10 Undo the two bolts, and remove the camshaft front thrust plate

12.11 Withdraw the camshaft from the cylinder block . . .

12.12 . . . and extract each tappet in turn, keeping them in order

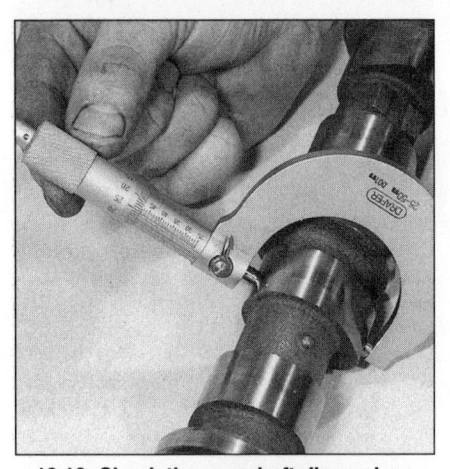

12.13 Check the camshaft dimensions with a micrometer

12.20 Note and record the fitted depth of the intermediate plate oil seal

12.21 Drive out the old seal using a small punch

14 Examine the camshaft bearing internal diameters for signs of damage or excessive wear. If evident, the bearings must be renewed by a Ford dealer or engine overhaul specialist.

15 Measure the thickness of the camshaft thrust plate, and the depth of the shoulder on the camshaft spacer sleeve. The difference between the two measurements is the camshaft endfloat. If this value is outside the limits given in the Specifications, renew the thrust plate and spacer ring.

16 It is seldom that the tappets wear excessively in their bores, but it is likely that after a high mileage, the cam lobe contact surfaces will show signs of depression or grooving.

17 Where this condition is evident, renew the tappets. Grinding out the grooves and wear marks will reduce the thickness of the surface hardening, and accelerate further wear.

18 Thoroughly clean all traces of old gasket from the cylinder block and intermediate plate.

19 Prior to refitting, it is advisable to renew the oil seal in the intermediate plate as follows.

20 Note and record the fitted depth of the oil seal in relation to the outer face of the intermediate plate **(see illustration)**.

21 Support the plate on blocks of wood, and drive out the old seal using a small punch **(see illustration)**.

22 Locate the new seal in the intermediate plate bore, with the open side of the seal towards the inside (engine side of the plate) **(see illustration)**.

23 Squarely tap the new seal into place, using the old seal as a guide and mandrel. Ensure that the new seal is fitted to the same depth as noted during removal.

24 The new oil seal should have been supplied with a plastic sleeve,

12.22 Locate the new seal in the intermediate plate bore, with the open side of the seal towards the inside

to protect the oil seal lip as it engages over the oil pump housing. Retain this sleeve for use when refitting.

Refitting

25 To refit the tappets and the camshaft, it is essential that the crankcase is inverted.

26 Lubricate the tappets and their bores, then insert each tappet fully

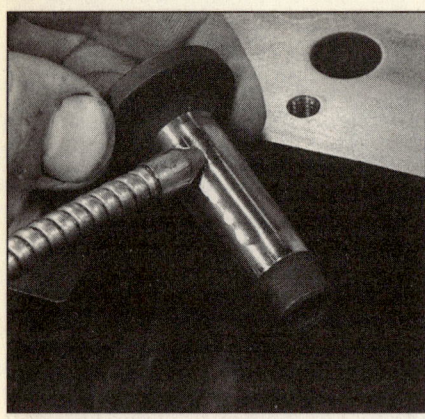

2B-14 Chapter 2 Part B: Engine removal and general engine overhaul procedures

12.26 Lubricate the tappets and their bores in the cylinder block

12.27a Make sure that the steel ball is in place in the end of the camshaft . . .

12.27b . . . then insert the camshaft into the crankcase

12.29 Locate a new gasket in position on the intermediate plate

12.32 Liberally lubricate the oil seal lip, then insert the protective sleeve into the oil seal from the rear

12.35a Lubricate and insert the camshaft sprocket spacer sleeve . . .

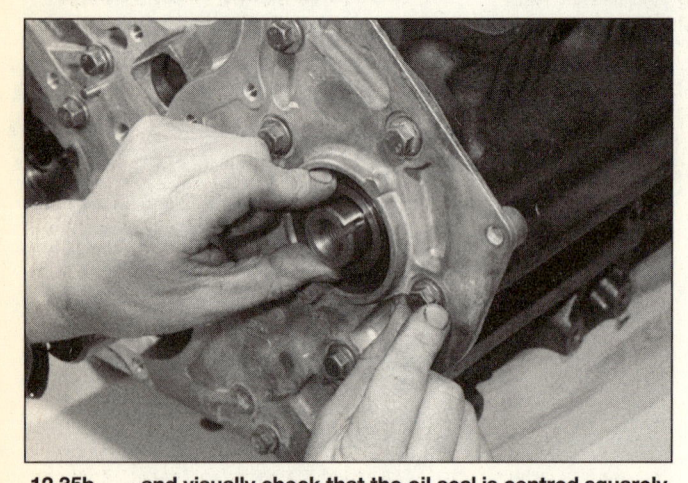

12.35b . . . and visually check that the oil seal is centred squarely over the sleeve

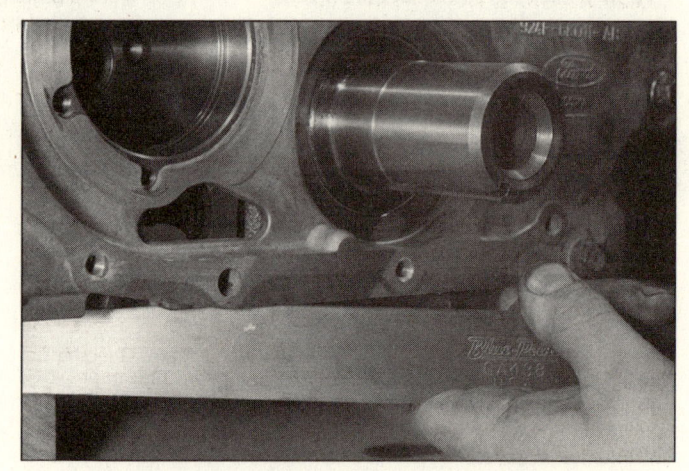

12.35c At the same time, check that the intermediate plate and cylinder block lower faces are perfectly flush, using a straight edge

into its original bore in the cylinder block **(see illustration)**.
27 Make sure that the steel ball is in place in the end of the camshaft, then lubricate the camshaft bearings, camshaft and thrust plate. Insert the camshaft into the crankcase from the timing belt end **(see illustrations)**.
28 Fit the thrust plate with the two oil groves facing outwards, and tighten the retaining bolts to the specified torque setting. Check that the camshaft is able to rotate freely.
29 Locate a new gasket in position on the intermediate plate **(see**

illustration).
30 Place a new oil channel seal into the recess in the cylinder block face **(see illustration 12.7b)**.
31 The new oil seal fitted to the intermediate plate should have been supplied with a plastic sleeve, to protect the lip of the oil seal when refitting the housing. If a sleeve was not supplied, make up a suitable alternative from a paper drinking cup or similar.
32 Liberally lubricate the oil seal lip, then insert the protective sleeve into the oil seal from the rear, so that it will be pushed out by the

Chapter 2 Part B: Engine removal and general engine overhaul procedures   2B-15

12.35d Tighten the retaining bolts in the sequence shown

13.2a Undo the two bolts, and remove the oil pick-up pipe and strainer

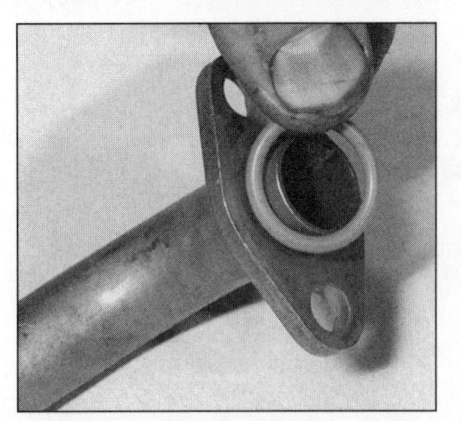

13.2b Recover the O-ring seal from the end of the strainer

13.7 Remove the big-end bearing cap and shell

13.8 Push the connecting rod/piston assembly out through the top of the engine

camshaft as the intermediate plate is fitted **(see illustration)**.

33 Fit the plate, and collect the protective sleeve as it is pushed out. Insert the retaining bolts, and tighten them finger-tight only at this stage.

34 It is now necessary to ensure that the oil seal is exactly centred over the camshaft. Ideally, Ford special tools 21-159 should be used to do this. However, in practice, there is so little movement of the intermediate plate within the constraints of the retaining bolt holes, that centralisation can be achieved without the special tool as follows.

35 Lubricate and insert the camshaft sprocket spacer sleeve, and visually check that the oil seal is centred squarely over the sleeve. At the same time, check that the intermediate plate and cylinder block lower faces are perfectly flush, using a straight edge. When all is correct, tighten the retaining bolts to the specified torque in the sequence shown **(see illustrations)**. Note that the torque setting for bolt No 9 is not the same as for the others.

36 Refit the intermediate plate lower support bracket bolt.

37 Locate a new O-ring seal (where fitted) over the front of the camshaft, and push it up against the spacer sleeve.

38 Refit the coolant pipe and hoses.

39 Refit the remainder of the removed components with reference to the relevant Sections and Chapters.

13 Piston/connecting rod assemblies - removal

Note: *Always check first what replacement parts are available before planning any overhaul operation. A Ford dealer, or a good engine reconditioning specialist/automotive parts supplier, may be able to suggest alternatives which will enable you to overcome the lack of replacement parts if there is a problem.*

1 Remove the cylinder head as described in Part A, Section 11.

2 Remove the sump as described in Part A, Section 12, then undo the two bolts and remove the oil pick-up pipe and strainer. Recover the O-ring seal from the end of the strainer **(see illustrations)**.

3 Temporarily refit the crankshaft pulley, so that the crankshaft can be rotated - remove the crankshaft timing peg if still in place.

4 Check that the connecting rod big-end caps have adjacent matching numbers. If no marks can be seen, make your own before disturbing any of the components, so that you can be certain of refitting each piston/connecting rod assembly the right way round, to its correct (original) bore, with the cap also the right way round.

5 Use your fingernail to feel if a ridge has formed at the upper limit of ring travel (about a quarter-inch down from the top of each cylinder). If carbon deposits or cylinder wear have produced ridges, they must be completely removed with a special tool. Follow the manufacturer's instructions provided with the tool. Failure to remove the ridges before attempting to remove the piston/connecting rod assemblies may result in piston ring breakage.

6 Turn the crankshaft until two of the connecting rods are in their lowest position.

7 Slacken the big-end bearing cap nuts half a turn at a time, until they can be removed by hand. Remove the cap and bearing shell **(see illustration)**. Don't drop the shell out of the cap.

8 Remove the upper bearing shell, and push the connecting rod/piston assembly out through the top of the engine **(see**

2B-16 Chapter 2 Part B: Engine removal and general engine overhaul procedures

14.1 Checking the crankshaft endfloat using a dial test indicator

14.3 Alternatively, feeler gauges can be used to check the endfloat

14.4 The main bearing caps should have marks to indicate their respective fitted positions in the block, and arrow marks pointing towards the timing belt end of the engine

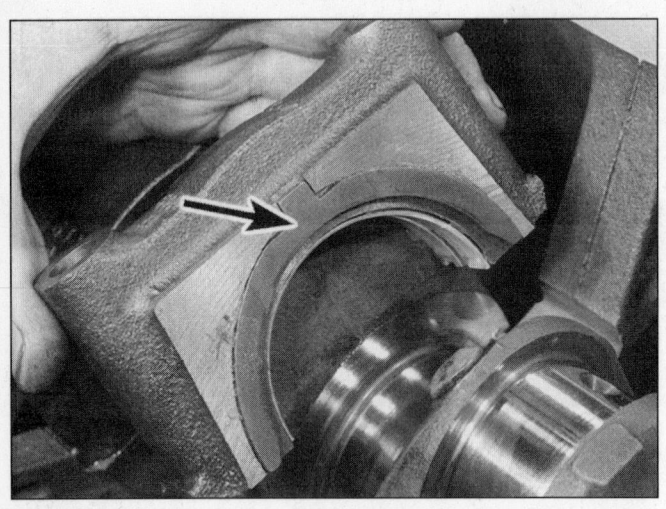

14.5 Unscrew the retaining bolts and remove the main bearing caps, collecting the lower thrustwashers from the centre cap

15.1a Remove the camshaft rear plate . . .

illustration). Use a wooden hammer handle to push on the connecting rod's bearing recess. If resistance is felt, double-check that all of the ridge was removed from the cylinder.

9 Repeat the procedure for the remaining cylinders.

10 After removal, reassemble the big-end bearing caps and shells on their respective connecting rods, and refit the nuts finger-tight. Leaving the old shells in place until reassembly will help prevent the bearing recesses from being accidentally nicked or gouged. New shells should be used on reassembly.

14 Crankshaft - removal

Note: *The crankshaft can be removed only after the engine has been removed from the vehicle. It is assumed that the transmission, flywheel, timing belt, cylinder head, sump, oil pump, engine intermediate plate, oil pick-up pipe and strainer, and piston/connecting rod assemblies, have already been removed. The crankshaft rear oil seal carrier must be unbolted from the cylinder block before proceeding with crankshaft removal.*

1 Before the crankshaft is removed, check the endfloat. Mount a DTI (Dial Test Indicator, or dial gauge) with the stem in line with the crankshaft and just touching the crankshaft **(see illustration)**.

2 Push the crankshaft fully away from the gauge, and zero it. Next, lever the crankshaft towards the gauge as far as possible, and check the reading obtained. The distance that the crankshaft moved is its endfloat; if it is greater than specified, check the crankshaft thrust surfaces for wear. If no wear is evident, new thrustwashers should correct the endfloat.

3 If no dial gauge is available, feeler blades can be used. Gently lever or push the crankshaft all the way towards the right-hand end of the engine. Slip feeler blades between the crankshaft and the main bearing incorporating the thrustwashers to determine the clearance **(see illustration)**.

4 Check that the main bearing caps have marks to indicate their respective fitted positions in the block. They also have arrow marks pointing towards the timing belt end of the engine to indicate correct orientation **(see illustration)**.

5 Unscrew the retaining bolts, and remove the main bearing caps. Collect the lower thrustwashers from the centre cap as it is removed **(see illustration)**. If the caps are reluctant to separate from the block face, lightly tap them free using a plastic- or copper-faced hammer. If the bearing shells are likely to be used again, keep them with their bearing caps for safekeeping. However, unless the engine is known to be of low mileage, it is recommended that they be renewed.

6 Lift the crankshaft out from the crankcase, then extract the upper bearing shells and side thrustwashers. Keep them with their respective caps for correct repositioning if they are to be used again.

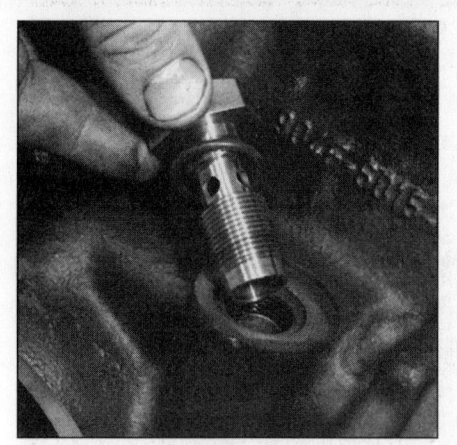

Chapter 2 Part B: Engine removal and general engine overhaul procedures 2B-17

15.1b ... and the oil pressure relief valve cap and O-ring ...

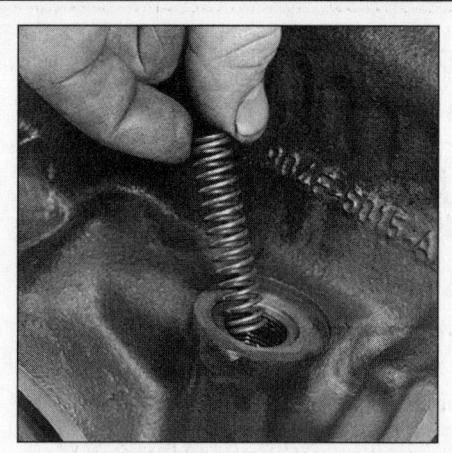

15.1c ... relief valve spring ...

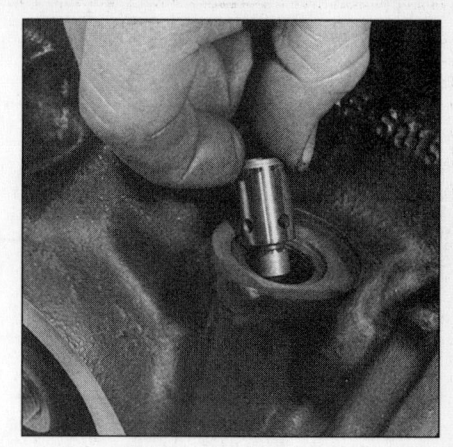

15.1d ... and plunger

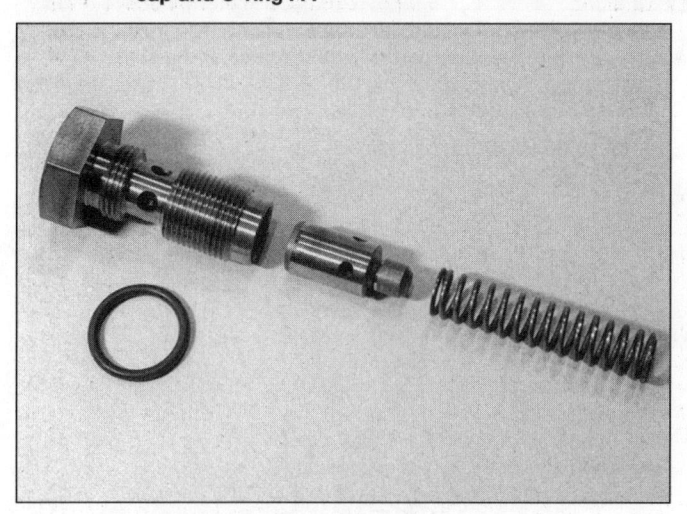

15.1e Oil pressure relief valve components

15.6 Clean all threaded holes in the cylinder block using the correct-size tap

7   Remove the crankshaft oil seals from the oil pump housing and the rear oil seal carrier.

15 Cylinder block/crankcase - cleaning and inspection

Note: *Always check first what replacement parts are available before planning any overhaul operation. A Ford dealer, or a good engine reconditioning specialist/automotive parts supplier, may be able to suggest alternatives which will enable you to overcome the lack of replacement parts if there is a problem.*

Cleaning

1   Prior to cleaning, remove all internal and external components and senders as previously described. Additionally, if the cylinder block is to be sent away for machining operations, remove the camshaft rear plate and the oil pressure relief valve cap, O-ring, spring and plunger **(see illustrations)**.

2   Inspect all the cylinder block core plugs for any sign of corrosion or deterioration. If this is apparent, they should all be renewed. Drill a small hole in the centre of each core plug, and pull them out with a car bodywork dent puller or similar tool. **Caution:** *The core plugs (also known as freeze or soft plugs) may be difficult or impossible to retrieve if they are driven into the block coolant passages.*

3   If any of the castings are extremely dirty, all should be steam-cleaned.

4   After the castings are returned from steam-cleaning, clean all oil holes and oil galleries one more time. Flush all internal passages with warm water until the water runs clear, then dry thoroughly, and apply a light film of oil to all machined surfaces, to prevent rusting. If you have access to compressed air, use it to speed the drying process, and to blow out all the oil holes and galleries. **Warning:** *Wear eye protection when using compressed air!*

5   If the castings are not very dirty, you can do an adequate cleaning job with hot soapy water (as hot as you can stand!) and a stiff brush. Take plenty of time, and do a thorough job. Regardless of the cleaning method used, be sure to clean all oil holes and galleries very thoroughly, and to dry all components completely; protect the machined surfaces as described above, to prevent rusting.

6   All threaded holes must be clean and dry, to ensure accurate torque readings during reassembly. Run the proper-size tap into each of the holes, to remove rust, corrosion, thread sealant or sludge, and to restore damaged threads **(see illustration)**. If possible, use compressed air to clear the holes of debris produced by this operation; a good alternative is to inject aerosol-applied water-dispersant lubricant into each hole, using the long spout usually supplied. **Warning:** *Wear eye protection when cleaning out these holes in this way, and be sure to dry out any excess liquid left in the holes.*

7   When all inspection and repair procedures are complete (see below) and the block is ready for reassembly, apply suitable sealant to the new core plugs, and insert them into the holes in the block. Make sure they are driven in straight and seated properly, or leakage could result. Special tools are available for this purpose, but a large socket with an outside diameter that will just slip into the core plug, used with an extension and hammer, will work just as well.

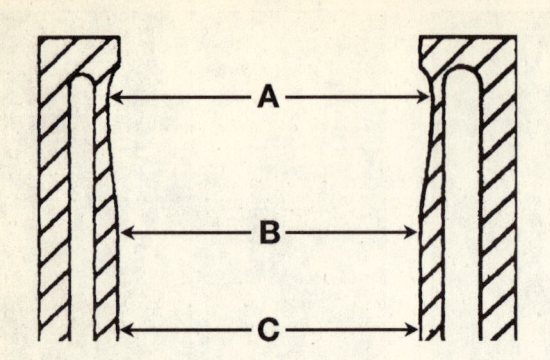

2B-18   Chapter 2 Part B: Engine removal and general engine overhaul procedures

15.12 Measure the diameter of each cylinder just under the wear ridge (A), at the centre (B) and at the bottom (C)

8   Refit all other external components removed, referring to the relevant Chapter of this manual for further details where required. Refit the main bearing caps, and tighten the bolts finger-tight. Also refit the camshaft rear plate using a new gasket, and the oil pressure relief valve cap, O-ring, spring and plunger.
9   If the engine is not going to be reassembled right away, cover it with a large plastic bag to keep it clean; protect the machined surfaces as described above, to prevent rusting.

Inspection

10   Visually check the castings for cracks and corrosion. Look for stripped threads in the threaded holes. If there has been any history of internal coolant leakage, it may be worthwhile having an engine overhaul specialist check the cylinder block/crankcase for cracks with special equipment. If defects are found, have them repaired, if possible, or renew the assembly.
11   Check each cylinder bore for scuffing and scoring.
12   Noting that the cylinder bores must be measured with all the crankshaft main bearing caps bolted in place (without the crankshaft and bearing shells), to the specified torque wrench settings, measure the diameter of each cylinder at the top (just under the ridge area), centre and bottom of the cylinder bore, parallel to the crankshaft axis. Next, measure each cylinder's diameter at the same three locations across the crankshaft axis **(see illustration)**. Note the measurements obtained.
13   Measure the piston diameter at right-angles to the gudgeon pin axis, just above the bottom of the skirt; again, note the results **(see illustration)**.
14   If it is wished to obtain the piston-to-bore clearance, measure the bore and piston skirt as described above, and subtract the skirt diameter from the bore measurement. If the precision measuring tools shown are not available, the condition of the pistons and bores can be assessed, though not quite as accurately, by using feeler blades as follows. Select a feeler blade of thickness equal to the specified piston-to-bore clearance, and slip it into the cylinder along with the matching piston. The piston must be positioned exactly as it normally would be. The feeler blade must be between the piston and cylinder on one of the thrust faces (at right-angles to the gudgeon pin bore). The piston should slip through the cylinder (with the feeler blade in place) with moderate pressure; if it falls through or slides through easily, the clearance is excessive, and a new piston will be required. If the piston binds at the lower end of the cylinder, and is loose toward the top, the cylinder is tapered. If tight spots are encountered as the piston/feeler blade is rotated in the cylinder, the cylinder is out-of-round (oval).
15   Repeat these procedures for the remaining pistons and cylinder bores.
16   Compare the results with the Specifications at the beginning of this Chapter; if any measurement is beyond the dimensions specified, or if any bore measurement is significantly different from the others (indicating that the bore is tapered or oval), the piston or bore is excessively-worn.
17   If any of the cylinder bores are badly scuffed or scored, or if they

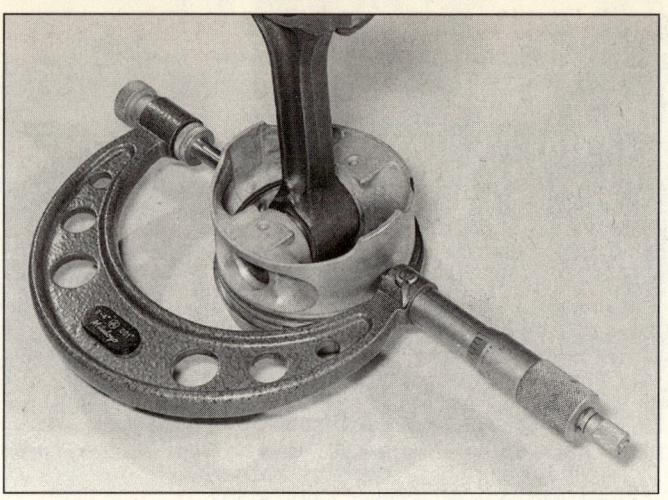

15.13 Measure the piston skirt diameter at right-angles to the gudgeon pin axis, just above the base of the skirt

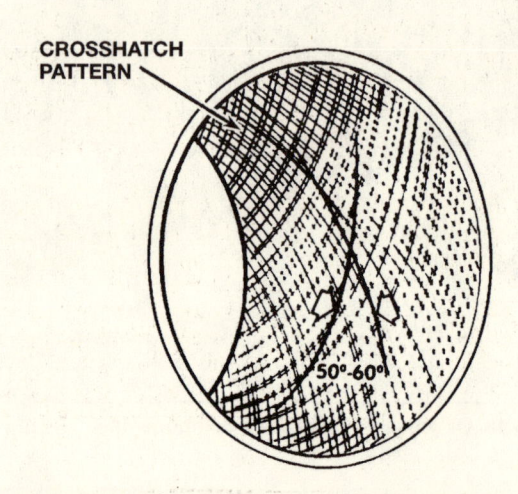

15.20 The honed cylinder bore should have a smooth cross-hatch pattern with the lines intersecting at approximately a 60° angle

are excessively-worn, out-of-round or tapered, the usual course of action would be to have the cylinder block/crankcase rebored, and to fit new, oversized, pistons on reassembly. See a Ford dealer or engine reconditioning specialist for advice.
18   If the bores are in reasonably good condition and not worn excessively, then it may only be necessary to renew the piston rings.
19   If this is the case, the bores should be honed, to allow the new rings to bed in correctly and provide the best possible seal; before honing the bores, refit the main bearing caps (without the bearing shells), and tighten the bolts to the specified torque wrench setting.
Note: *If you don't have the tools, or don't want to tackle the honing operation, most engine reconditioning specialists will do it for a reasonable fee.*
20   Two types of cylinder hones are commonly available - the flex hone or "bottle-brush" type, and the more traditional surfacing hone with spring-loaded stones. Both will do the job and are used with a power drill, but for the less-experienced mechanic, the "bottle-brush" hone will probably be easier to use. You will also need some paraffin or honing oil, and rags. Proceed as follows:

a) *Mount the hone in the drill, compress the stones, and slip it into the first bore. Be sure to wear safety goggles or a face shield!*
b) *Lubricate the bore with plenty of honing oil, switch on the drill, and move the hone up and down the bore, at a pace that will produce a fine cross-hatch pattern on the cylinder walls. Ideally,*

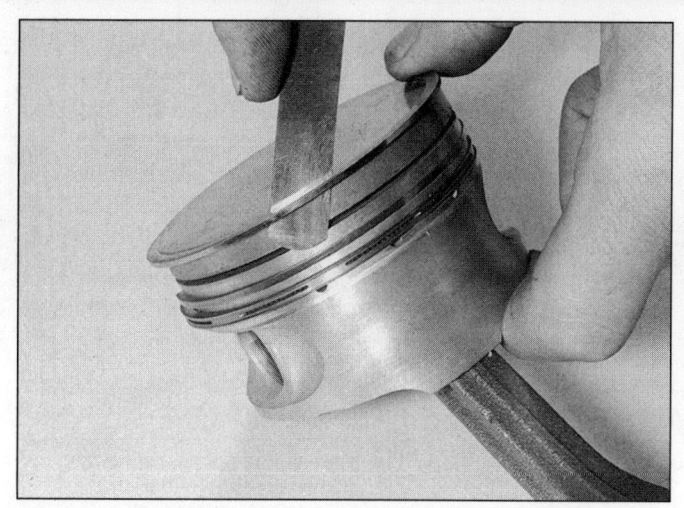

Chapter 2 Part B: Engine removal and general engine overhaul procedures

16.2 The use of old feeler blades will be helpful in preventing the piston rings dropping into empty grooves during removal

the cross-hatch lines should intersect at approximately a 60° angle **(see illustration)**. *Be sure to use plenty of lubricant, and don't take off any more material than is absolutely necessary to produce the desired finish.* **Note:** *Piston ring manufacturers may specify a different crosshatch angle - read and follow any instructions included with the new rings.*

c) *Don't withdraw the hone from the bore while it's running. Instead, switch off the drill, and continue moving the hone up and down the bore until it comes to a complete stop, then compress the stones and withdraw the hone. If you're using a "bottle-brush" hone, switch off the drill, then turn the chuck in the normal direction of rotation while withdrawing the hone from the bore.*

d) *Wipe the oil out of the bore, and repeat the procedure for the remaining cylinders.*

e) *When all the cylinder bores are honed, chamfer the top edges of the bores with a small file, so the rings won't catch when the pistons are installed. Be very careful not to nick the cylinder walls with the end of the file.*

f) *The entire cylinder block/crankcase must be washed very thoroughly with warm, soapy water, to remove all traces of the abrasive grit produced during the honing operation.* **Note:** *The bores can be considered clean when a lint-free white cloth - dampened with clean engine oil - used to wipe them out doesn't pick up any more honing residue, which will show up as grey areas on the cloth. Be sure to run a brush through all oil holes and galleries, and flush them with running water.*

g) *When the cylinder block/crankcase is completely clean, rinse it thoroughly and dry it, then lightly oil all exposed machined surfaces, to prevent rusting.*

21 The cylinder block/crankcase should now be completely clean and dry, with all components checked for wear or damage, and repaired or overhauled as necessary. Refit as many ancillary components as possible, for safekeeping (see paragraphs 7 and 8 above). If reassembly is not to start immediately, cover the block with a large plastic bag to keep it clean, and protect the machined surfaces as described above to prevent rusting.

16 Piston/connecting rod assemblies - inspection

Note: *Always check first what replacement parts are available before planning any overhaul operation; refer to Section 1 of this Part. A Ford dealer, or a good engine reconditioning specialist/automotive parts supplier may be able to suggest alternatives which will enable you to overcome the lack of replacement parts.*

1 Before the inspection process can be carried out, the piston/connecting rod assemblies must be cleaned, and the original piston rings removed from the pistons. The rings should have smooth, polished working surfaces, with no dull or carbon-coated sections (showing that the ring is not sealing correctly against the bore wall, so allowing combustion gases to blow by) and no traces of wear on their top and bottom surfaces. The end gaps should be clear of carbon, but not polished (indicating a too-small end gap), and all the rings (including the elements of the oil control ring) should be free to rotate in their grooves, but without excessive up-and-down movement. If the rings appear to be in good condition, they are probably fit for further use; check the end gaps (in an unworn part of the bore) as described in Section 20. If any of the rings appears to be worn or damaged, or has an end gap significantly different from the specified value, the usual course of action is to renew all of them as a set. **Note:** *While it is usual always to renew piston rings when an engine is overhauled, this of course assumes that rings are available separately - if not, it follows that great care must be taken not to break or damage any of the rings during the following procedures, and to ensure that each ring is marked on removal so that it is refitted* **only** *the original way up, and* **only** *to the same groove.*

2 Using a piston ring installation tool, carefully remove the rings from the pistons. If such a tool is not available, the rings can be removed by hand, expanding them over the top of the pistons. The use of two or three old feeler blades will be helpful in preventing the rings dropping into empty grooves **(see illustration)**. Be careful not to nick or gouge the pistons in the process, and mark or label each ring as it is removed, so that its original top surface can be identified on reassembly, and so that it can be returned to its original groove. Take care also with your hands - piston rings are sharp!

3 Scrape all traces of carbon from the top of the piston. A hand-held wire brush or a piece of fine emery cloth can be used, once the majority of the deposits have been scraped away. *Do not*, under any circumstances, use a wire brush mounted in a drill motor to remove deposits from the pistons - the piston material is soft, and may be eroded away by the wire brush.

4 Use a piston ring groove-cleaning tool to remove carbon deposits from the ring grooves. If a tool isn't available, but replacement rings have been found, a piece broken off the old ring will do the job. Be very careful to remove only the carbon deposits - don't remove any metal, and do not nick or scratch the sides of the ring grooves. Protect your fingers - piston rings are sharp!

5 Once the deposits have been removed, clean the piston/rod assemblies with solvent, and dry them with compressed air (if available). Make sure that the oil return holes in the back sides of the ring grooves are clear.

6 If the pistons and cylinder walls aren't damaged or worn excessively - refer to Section 15 for details of inspection and measurement procedures - and if the cylinder block/crankcase has not been rebored, new pistons won't be necessary. Normal piston wear appears as even vertical wear on the piston thrust surfaces, and slight looseness of the top ring in its groove.

7 Carefully inspect each piston for cracks around the skirt, at the pin bosses, and at the ring lands (between the ring grooves).

8 Look for scoring and scuffing on the thrust faces of the skirt, holes in the piston crown, and burned areas at the edge of the crown. If the skirt is scored or scuffed, the engine may have been suffering from overheating and/or abnormal combustion, which caused excessively-high operating temperatures. The cooling and lubrication systems should be checked thoroughly.

9 Corrosion of the piston, in the form of small pits, indicates that coolant is leaking into the combustion chamber and/or the crankcase. Again, the cause must be corrected, or the problem may persist in the rebuilt engine.

10 If renewing pistons without reboring, make sure that the correct class is obtained. Information on cylinder bore diameter, main bearing journal diameter and big-end journal diameter for an original engine is provided on a plate attached to the lower right-hand corner of the cylinder block. The advice of a Ford dealer or engine reconditioning specialist is also helpful in obtaining the correct new components.

11 To separate the piston from its connecting rod, extract the circlips

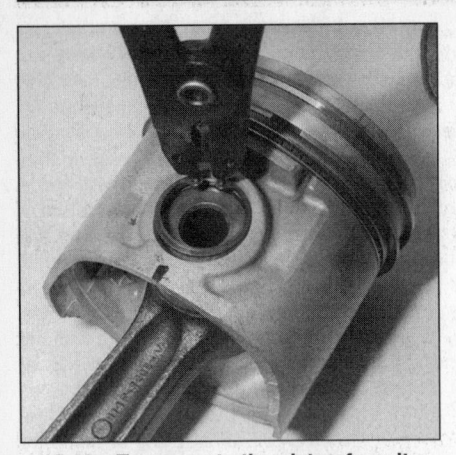

2B-20 Chapter 2 Part B: Engine removal and general engine overhaul procedures

16.11a To separate the piston from its connecting rod, extract the circlips . . .

16.11b . . . and push out the gudgeon pins

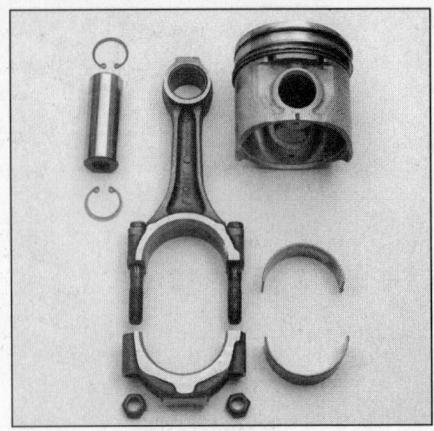

16.11c Keep all the piston/connecting rod components together and correctly identified

and push out the gudgeon pins. Identify the piston and rod, and the fitted direction of each, to ensure correct reassembly **(see illustrations)**.

12 Wear between the gudgeon pin and the connecting rod small-end bush can be cured by renewing both the rod and the bush. Bush renewal, however, is a specialist job; press facilities are required, and the new bush must be reamed accurately.

13 New gudgeon pins and circlips are supplied when purchasing new pistons. The connecting rods themselves should not be in need of renewal, unless seizure or some other major mechanical failure has occurred. Check the alignment of the connecting rods visually, and if the rods are not straight, take them to a specialist for a more detailed check.

14 Where applicable, reassemble the pistons and rods. Make sure that the pistons are fitted the right way round as noted during removal. Oil the gudgeon pins before fitting them. When assembled, the piston should pivot freely on the rod.

15 Measure the piston diameters, and check that they are within the limits for the corresponding bore diameters. If the piston-to-bore clearance is excessive, the block will have to be rebored, and new pistons and rings fitted.

17 Crankshaft - inspection

Note: *Always check first what replacement parts are available before planning any overhaul operation; refer to Section 1 of this Part. A Ford dealer, or a good engine reconditioning specialist/automotive parts supplier, may be able to suggest alternatives which will enable you to overcome the lack of replacement parts.*

1 Clean the crankshaft, and dry it with compressed air if available. **Warning:** *Wear eye protection when using compressed air!* Be sure to clean the oil holes with a pipe cleaner or similar probe.

2 Check the main and crankpin (big-end) bearing journals for uneven wear, scoring, pitting and cracking.

3 Rub a penny across each journal several times. If a journal picks up copper from the penny, it is too rough.

4 Remove all burrs from the crankshaft oil holes with a stone, file or scraper.

5 Using a micrometer, measure the diameter of the main bearing and crankpin (big-end) journals, and compare the results with the Specifications at the beginning of this Chapter **(see illustration)**.

6 By measuring the diameter at a number of points around each journal's circumference, you will be able to determine whether or not the journal is out-of-round. Take the measurement at each end of the journal, near the webs, to determine if the journal is tapered.

7 If the crankshaft journals are damaged, tapered, out-of-round, or worn beyond the limits specified in this Chapter, the crankshaft must be taken to an engine overhaul specialist, who will regrind it, and who

17.5 Using a micrometer, measure the diameter of the crankshaft journals

can supply the necessary undersize bearing shells.

8 Check the oil seal journals at each end of the crankshaft for wear and damage. If either seal has worn an excessive groove in its journal, consult an engine overhaul specialist, who will be able to advise whether a repair is possible, or whether a new crankshaft is necessary.

18 Main and big-end bearings - inspection

Note: *Always check first what replacement parts are available before planning any overhaul operation; refer to Section 1 of this Part. A Ford dealer, or a good engine reconditioning specialist/automotive parts supplier, may be able to suggest alternatives which will enable you to overcome the lack of replacement parts.*

1 Even though the main and big-end bearing shells should be renewed during the engine overhaul, the old shells should be retained for close examination, as they may reveal valuable information about the condition of the engine **(see illustration)**.

2 Bearing failure occurs because of lack of lubrication, the presence of dirt or other foreign particles, overloading the engine, and corrosion. Regardless of the cause of bearing failure, it must be corrected before the engine is reassembled, to prevent it from happening again.

3 When examining the bearing shells, remove them from the cylinder block/crankcase and main bearing caps, and from the connecting rods and the big-end bearing caps, then lay them out on a clean surface in the same general position as their location in the engine. This will enable you to match any bearing problems with the corresponding crankshaft journal. *Do not* touch any shell's bearing

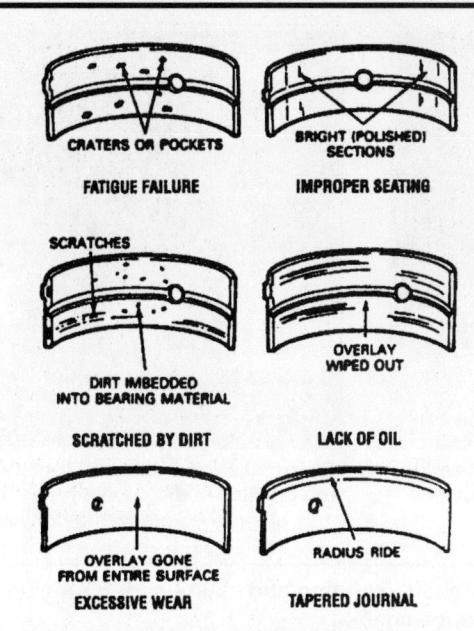

Chapter 2 Part B: Engine removal and general engine overhaul procedures

18.1 When inspecting the main and big-end bearings, look for these problems

surface with your fingers while checking it, or the delicate surface may be scratched.

4 Dirt or other foreign matter gets into the engine in a variety of ways. It may be left in the engine during assembly, or it may pass through filters or the crankcase ventilation system. It may get into the oil, and from there into the bearings. Metal chips from machining operations and normal engine wear are often present. Abrasives are sometimes left in engine components after reconditioning, especially when parts are not thoroughly cleaned using the proper cleaning methods. Whatever the source, these foreign objects often end up embedded in the soft bearing material, and are easily recognised. Large particles will not embed in the material, and will score or gouge the shell and journal. The best prevention for this cause of bearing failure is to clean all parts thoroughly, and to keep everything spotlessly-clean during engine assembly. Frequent and regular engine oil and filter changes are also recommended.

5 Lack of lubrication (or lubrication breakdown) has a number of inter-related causes. Excessive heat (which thins the oil), overloading (which squeezes the oil from the bearing face) and oil leakage (from excessive bearing clearances, worn oil pump or high engine speeds) all contribute to lubrication breakdown. Blocked oil passages, which usually are the result of misaligned oil holes in a bearing shell, will also starve a bearing of oil, and destroy it. When lack of lubrication is the cause of bearing failure, the bearing material is wiped or extruded from the shell's steel backing. Temperatures may increase to the point where the steel backing turns blue from overheating.

6 Driving habits can have a definite effect on bearing life. Full-throttle, low-speed operation (labouring the engine) puts very high loads on bearings, which tends to squeeze out the oil film. These loads cause the shells to flex, which produces fine cracks in the bearing face (fatigue failure). Eventually, the bearing material will loosen in pieces, and tear away from the steel backing. Short-distance driving leads to corrosion of bearings, because insufficient engine heat is produced to drive off condensed water and corrosive gases. These products collect in the engine oil, forming acid and sludge. As the oil is carried to the engine bearings, the acid attacks and corrodes the bearing material.

7 Incorrect shell refitting during engine assembly will lead to bearing failure as well. Tight-fitting shells leave insufficient bearing running clearance, and will result in oil starvation. Dirt or foreign particles trapped behind a bearing shell result in high spots on the bearing, which lead to failure. *Do not* touch any shell's bearing surface with your fingers during reassembly; there is a risk of scratching the delicate surface, or of depositing particles of dirt on it.

20.3 Measure the piston ring end gap using feeler gauges

19 Engine overhaul - reassembly sequence

1 Before reassembly begins, ensure that all new parts have been obtained, and that all necessary tools are available. Read through the entire procedure, to familiarise yourself with the work involved, and to ensure that all items necessary for reassembly of the engine are at hand. In addition to all normal tools and materials, jointing and thread-locking compound will be needed during engine reassembly. For general-purpose applications, it is recommended that Loctite 275 setting sealer or Hylomar PL32M non-setting sealer be used for joints where required, and Loctite 270 for stud and bolt thread-locking. These are recommended by and obtained from Ford dealers. In all other cases, provided the relevant mating surfaces are clean and flat, new gaskets will be sufficient to ensure joints are oil-tight. *Do not* use any kind of silicone-based sealant on any part of the fuel system or inlet manifold, and *never* use exhaust sealants upstream of the catalytic converter (where fitted).

2 In order to save time and avoid problems, engine reassembly can be carried out in the following order (as applicable).

  a) *Crankshaft and main bearings.*
  b) *Tappets and camshaft.*
  c) *Pistons and connecting rods.*
  d) *Oil pump and housing.*
  e) *Water pump.*
  f) *Sump.*
  g) *Flywheel.*
  h) *Cylinder head.*
  i) *Timing sprockets and belt.*
  j) *Engine external components.*

3 Ensure that everything is clean prior to reassembly. As mentioned previously, dirt and metal particles can quickly destroy bearings and result in major engine damage. Use clean engine oil to lubricate during reassembly.

20 Piston rings - refitting

1 Before installing new piston rings, check the end gaps. Lay out each piston set with a piston/connecting rod assembly, and keep them together as a matched set from now on.

2 Insert the top compression ring into the first cylinder, and square it up with the cylinder walls by pushing it in with the top of the piston.

3 To measure the end gap, slip feeler blades between the ends of the ring, until a gauge equal to the gap width is found **(see illustration)**. The feeler blade should slide between the ring ends with a slight amount of drag. Compare the measurement to the value given

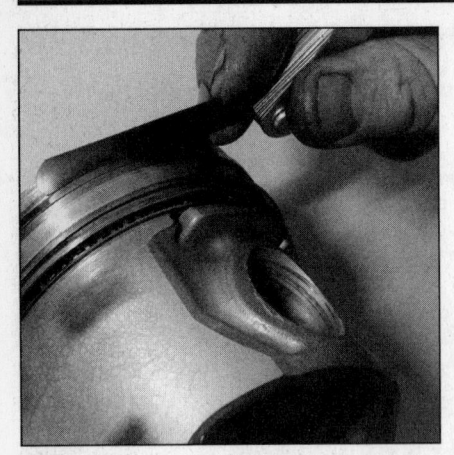

2B-22 Chapter 2 Part B: Engine removal and general engine overhaul procedures

20.10 Measuring the piston ring-to-groove clearance

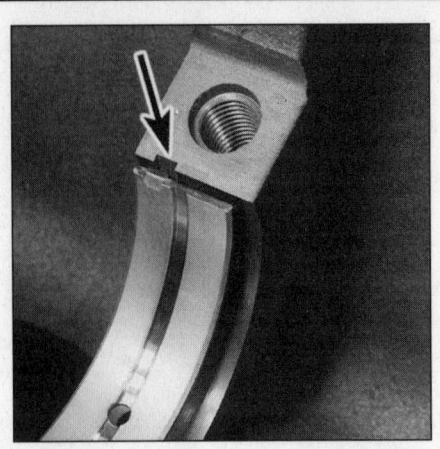

21.4 Make sure the tab on each bearing shell fits into the notch in the block or cap (arrowed)

21.5 Place the crankshaft thrustwashers into position in the crankcase so that their oil grooves are facing outwards

in the Specifications Section of this Chapter; if the gap is larger or smaller than specified, double-check to make sure you have the correct rings before proceeding. If you are assessing the condition of used rings, have the cylinder bores checked and measured by a Ford dealer or similar engine reconditioning specialist, so that you can be sure of exactly which component is worn, and seek advice as to the best course of action to take.

4 If the end gap is still too small, it must be opened up by careful filing of the ring ends using a fine file. If it is too large, this is not as serious, unless the specified limit is exceeded, in which case very careful checking is required of the dimensions of all components, as well as of the new parts.

5 Repeat the procedure for each ring that will be installed in the first cylinder, and for each ring in the remaining cylinders. Remember to keep rings, pistons and cylinders matched up.

6 Refit the piston rings as follows. Where the original rings are being refitted, use the marks or notes made on removal, to ensure that each ring is refitted to its original groove and the same way up. New rings generally have their top surfaces identified by markings (often an indication of size, such as "STD", or the word "TOP") - the rings must be fitted with such markings uppermost. **Note:** *Always follow the instructions printed on the ring package or box - different manufacturers may require different approaches. Do not mix up the top and second compression rings, as they usually have different cross-sections.*

7 The oil control ring (lowest one on the piston) is usually installed first. It is composed of three separate elements. Slip the spacer/expander into the groove. If an anti-rotation tang is used, make sure that it is inserted into the drilled hole in the ring groove. Next, install the lower side rail. Don't use a piston ring installation tool on the oil ring side rails, as they may be damaged. Instead, place one end of the side rail into the groove between the spacer/expander and the ring land, hold it firmly in place, and slide a finger around the piston while pushing the rail into the groove. Next, install the upper side rail in the same manner.

8 After the three oil ring components have been installed, check that both the upper and lower side rails can be turned smoothly in the ring groove.

9 The second compression (middle) ring is installed next, followed by the top compression ring - ensure that their marks are uppermost, and be careful not to confuse them. Don't expand either ring any more than necessary to slide it over the top of the piston.

10 With the rings in position, measure the ring-to-groove clearance using feeler blades, and ensure that the clearances are as specified **(see illustration)**.

11 When all of the rings are fitted to each piston, arrange them so that the gap in the oil control ring is on the thrust side of the piston, and the compression ring gaps located on opposite sides of the piston, in line with the gudgeon pin.

21 Crankshaft - refitting and main bearing running clearance check

Note: *New bolts will be required when refitting the crankshaft main bearing caps.*

1 It is assumed at this point that the cylinder block/crankcase and crankshaft have been cleaned, inspected and repaired or reconditioned as necessary. Position the engine upside-down.

2 Remove the main bearing cap bolts, and lift out the caps. Lay the caps out in the proper order, to ensure correct installation.

3 If they're still in place, remove the old bearing shells from the block and the main bearing caps. Wipe the bearing recesses of the block and caps with a clean, lint-free cloth. They must be kept spotlessly-clean!

Main bearing running clearance check

Note: *"Plastigage" bearing clearance checking material, available from Ford dealers or engine reconditioning specialists, will be required for this check.*

4 Wipe clean the main bearing shell seats in the crankcase, and clean the backs of the bearing shells. Insert the respective upper shells (dry) into position in the crankcase. Where the old main bearings are being refitted, ensure that they are located in their original positions. Make sure the tab on each bearing shell fits into the notch in the block or cap **(see illustration)**. **Caution:** *Don't hammer the shells into place, and don't nick or gouge the bearing faces. No lubrication should be used at this time.*

5 Place the crankshaft thrustwashers into position in the crankcase so that their oil grooves are facing outwards (away from the central web) **(see illustration)**.

6 Clean the bearing surfaces of the shells in the block, and the crankshaft main bearing journals with a clean, lint-free cloth. Check or clean the oil holes in the crankshaft, as any dirt here can go only one way - straight through the new bearings.

7 Once you're certain the crankshaft is clean, carefully lay it in position in the main bearings. Trim several pieces of the appropriate-size Plastigage (they must be slightly shorter than the width of the main bearings), and place one piece on each crankshaft main bearing journal, parallel with the crankshaft centre-line **(see illustration)**.

8 Clean the bearing surfaces of the cap shells, and install the caps in their respective positions (don't mix them up) with the arrows pointing to the timing belt end of the engine. Don't disturb the Plastigage. Use the old bolts to secure the bearing caps for this check, and save the new ones for final refitting.

9 Working on one cap at a time, from the centre main bearing outwards (and ensuring that each cap is tightened down squarely and evenly onto the block), tighten the main bearing cap bolts to the specified torque wrench setting. Don't rotate the crankshaft at any

Chapter 2 Part B: Engine removal and general engine overhaul procedures 2B-23

21.7 Lay the Plastigage strips (arrowed) on the main bearing journals, parallel to the crankshaft centre-line

21.11 Compare the width of the crushed Plastigage to the scale on the envelope to determine the main bearing running clearance (always take the measurement at the widest point of the Plastigage). Be sure to use the correct scale; imperial and metric scales are included

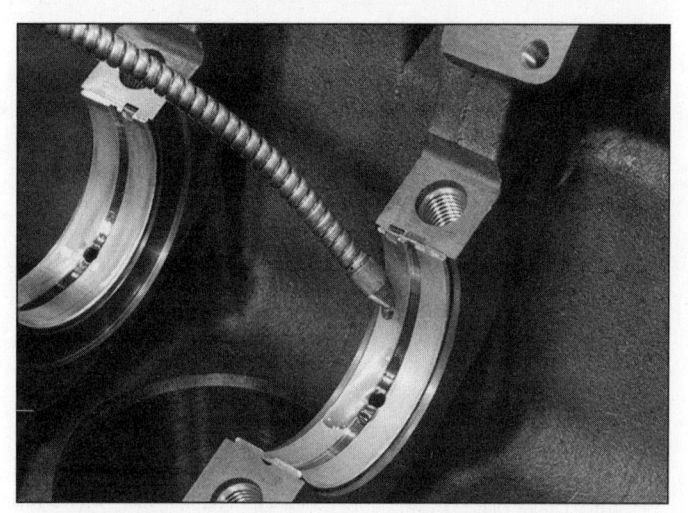

21.14 Apply clean engine oil to each bearing shell surface

time during this operation!

10 Remove the bolts, and carefully lift off the main bearing caps. Keep them in order. Don't disturb the Plastigage or rotate the crankshaft. If any of the main bearing caps are difficult to remove, tap them gently from side-to-side with a soft-faced mallet to loosen them.

11 Compare the width of the crushed Plastigage on each journal with the scale printed on the Plastigage envelope to obtain the main bearing running clearance **(see illustration)**. Check the Specifications to make sure that the clearance is correct.

12 If the clearance is not as specified, seek the advice of a Ford dealer or similar engine reconditioning specialist - if the crankshaft journals are in good condition, it may be possible simply to renew the shells to achieve the correct clearance. If this is not possible, the crankshaft must be reground by a specialist who can supply the necessary undersized shells. First though, make sure that no dirt or oil was between the bearing shells and the caps or block when the clearance was measured. If the Plastigage is noticeably wider at one end than the other, the journal may be tapered (see Section 17).

13 Carefully scrape all traces of the Plastigage material off the main bearing journals and the bearing surfaces. Be very careful not to scratch the bearing - use your fingernail or the edge of a credit card.

Final refitting

14 Carefully lift the crankshaft out of the engine. Clean the bearing surfaces of the shells in the block, then apply clean engine oil to each surface **(see illustration)**. Coat the thrustwasher surfaces as well.

15 Make sure the crankshaft journals are clean, then lay the crankshaft back in place in the block. Clean the bearing surfaces of the shells in the caps, then lubricate them. Install the caps in their respective positions, with the arrows pointing to the timing belt end of the engine.

16 Working on one cap at a time, from the centre main bearing outwards (and ensuring that each cap is tightened down squarely and evenly onto the block), tighten the new main bearing cap bolts to the specified torque wrench setting in the stages given in the Specifications.

17 Rotate the crankshaft a number of times by hand, to check for any obvious binding.

18 Check the crankshaft endfloat (see Section 14). It should be correct if the crankshaft thrust faces aren't worn or damaged.

22 Piston/connecting rod assemblies - refitting and big-end bearing running clearance check

1 Before refitting the piston/connecting rod assemblies, the cylinder bores must be perfectly clean, the top edge of each cylinder must be chamfered, and the crankshaft must be in place.

2 Remove the big-end bearing cap from No 1 cylinder connecting rod (refer to the marks noted or made on removal). Remove the original bearing shells, and wipe the bearing recesses of the connecting rod and cap with a clean, lint-free cloth. They must be kept spotlessly-clean!

Big-end bearing running clearance check

Note: *"Plastigage" bearing clearance checking material, available from Ford dealers or engine reconditioning specialists, will be required for this check.*

3 Clean the back of the new upper bearing shell, fit it to the connecting rod, then fit the other shell of the bearing set to the big-end bearing cap. Make sure the tab on each shell fits into the notch in the rod or cap recess. **Caution:** *Don't hammer the shells into place, and don't nick or gouge the bearing face. Don't lubricate the bearing at this time.*

4 It's critically important that all mating surfaces of the bearing components are perfectly clean and oil-free when they're assembled.

5 Position the piston ring gaps as described in Section 20, lubricate the piston and rings with clean engine oil, and attach a piston ring compressor to the piston. Leave the skirt protruding about a quarter-inch, to guide the piston into the cylinder bore. The rings must be compressed until they're flush with the piston.

6 Rotate the crankshaft until No 1 crankpin (big-end) journal is at

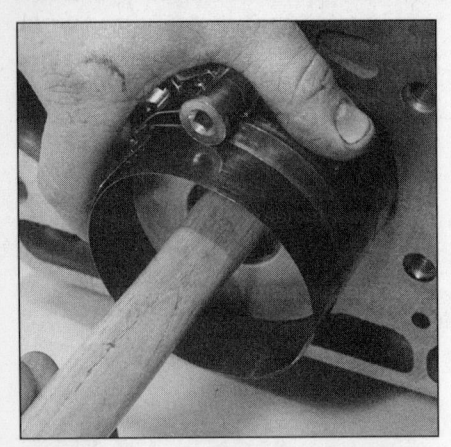

22.9 Gently tap on the top of the piston with the end of a wooden hammer handle while guiding the connecting rod onto the crankpin

22.17 Tighten the big-end cap nuts to the specified torque

22.19 Check the protrusion of each piston above the cylinder block face using a dial test indicator and stand

BDC (Bottom Dead Centre), and apply a coat of engine oil to the cylinder walls.

7 Arrange the No 1 piston/connecting rod assembly so that it is correctly orientated as noted during removal. Gently insert the assembly into the No 1 cylinder bore, and rest the bottom edge of the ring compressor on the engine block.

8 Tap the top edge of the ring compressor to make sure it's contacting the block around its entire circumference.

9 Gently tap on the top of the piston with the end of a wooden hammer handle **(see illustration)**, while guiding the connecting rod's big-end onto the crankpin. The piston rings may try to pop out of the ring compressor just before entering the cylinder bore, so keep some pressure on the ring compressor. Work slowly, and if any resistance is felt as the piston enters the cylinder, stop immediately. Find out what's binding, and fix it before proceeding. *Do not*, for any reason, force the piston into the cylinder - you might break a ring and/or the piston.

10 To check the big-end bearing running clearance, cut a piece of the appropriate-size Plastigage slightly shorter than the width of the connecting rod bearing, and lay it in place on the No 1 crankpin (big-end) journal, parallel with the crankshaft centre-line **(see illustration 21.7)**.

11 Clean the connecting rod-to-cap mating surfaces, and refit the big-end bearing cap. Tighten the cap nuts evenly to the specified torque, in two stages. Don't rotate the crankshaft at any time during this operation!

12 Unscrew the nuts and detach the cap, being very careful not to disturb the Plastigage.

13 Compare the width of the crushed Plastigage to the scale printed on the Plastigage envelope, to obtain the running clearance **(see illustration 21.11)**. Compare it to the Specifications, to make sure the clearance is correct.

14 If the clearance is not as specified, seek the advice of a Ford dealer or similar engine reconditioning specialist - if the crankshaft journals are in good condition, it may be possible simply to renew the shells to achieve the correct clearance. If this is not possible, the crankshaft must be reground by a specialist, who can also supply the necessary undersized shells. First though, make sure that no dirt or oil was trapped between the bearing shells and the connecting rod or cap when the clearance was measured. Also, recheck the crankpin diameter. If the Plastigage was wider at one end than the other, the crankpin journal may be tapered (see Section 17).

15 Carefully scrape all traces of the Plastigage material off the journal and the bearing surface. Be very careful not to scratch the bearing - use your fingernail or the edge of a credit card.

Final piston/connecting rod refitting

16 Make sure that the bearing surfaces are perfectly clean, then apply a uniform layer of clean molybdenum disulphide-based grease, engine assembly lubricant, or clean engine oil, to both of them. You'll have to push the piston into the cylinder to expose the bearing surface of the shell in the connecting rod.

17 Slide the connecting rod back into place on the crankpin (big-end) journal, refit the big-end bearing cap, and then tighten the nuts as described above **(see illustration)**.

18 Repeat the entire procedure for the remaining piston/connecting rod assemblies.

19 Once all the piston/connecting rod assemblies are installed, check the protrusion of each piston above the cylinder block face using a dial test indicator and stand **(see illustration)**. Zero the DTI on the block face, then bring each piston in turn up to the TDC position. Move the DTI probe over the piston, and check the deflection of the needle on the scale. This is the piston protrusion. If any of the assemblies are outside the limits given in the Specifications, change the connecting rod of the offending cylinder with a rod of suitable length. Connecting rods are available in four lengths, identified as 1A, 2A, 3A and 4A; 1A is the shortest, 4A the longest.

20 After all the piston/connecting rod assemblies have been properly installed, rotate the crankshaft a number of times by hand, to check for any obvious binding.

23 Engine - initial start-up after overhaul

1 With the engine refitted in the vehicle, double-check the engine oil and coolant levels.

2 Make a final check that everything has been reconnected, and that there are no tools or rags left in the engine compartment.

3 With the stop solenoid disconnected, or on later turbocharged engines, with the injection pump multi-plug disconnected, turn the engine on the starter until the oil pressure warning light goes out. Reconnect the wiring.

4 Refer to Chapter 4 and bleed the fuel system. The engine will start during the bleeding operation.

5 While the engine is idling, check for fuel, coolant and oil leaks. Don't be alarmed if there are some odd smells and smoke from parts getting hot and burning off oil deposits.

6 Keep the engine idling until hot water is felt circulating through the top hose, check that it idles reasonably smoothly and at the usual speed, then switch it off.

7 After a few minutes, recheck the oil and coolant levels, and top-up as necessary (Chapter 1).

8 If new components such as pistons, rings or crankshaft bearings have been fitted, the engine must be run-in for the first 500 miles (800 km). Do not operate the engine at full-throttle, or allow it to labour in any gear during this period. It is recommended that the oil and filter be changed at the end of this period.

Chapter 3
Cooling, heating and ventilation systems

Contents

	Section
Air conditioning compressor drivebelt check, adjustment and renewal	See Chapter 1
Air conditioning system check	See Chapter 1
Air conditioning system components - removal and refitting	13
Air conditioning system - general information and precautions	12
Alternator/water pump drivebelt check, adjustment and renewal	See Chapter 1
Antifreeze mixture	See Chapter 1
Coolant level check	See Chapter 1
Coolant temperature gauge sender unit - testing, removal and refitting	6
Cooling system checks (coolant leaks, hose condition)	See Chapter 1

	Section
Cooling system expansion tank - removal and refitting	3
Cooling system hoses - disconnection and renewal	2
Cooling system servicing (draining, flushing and refilling)	See Chapter 1
General information and precautions	1
Heating and ventilation systems - general information	9
Heater/ventilation components - removal and refitting	10
Heater/ventilation vents - removal and refitting	11
Radiator - removal, inspection and refitting	4
Thermostat - removal, testing and refitting	7
Viscous cooling fan clutch - removal and refitting	5
Water pump - removal and refitting	8

Specifications

General

System type	Pressurised, front-mounted radiator, viscous cooling fan and belt-driven water pump
System pressure	1.0 bar

Thermostat

Type	Wax
Opening temperature	82 to 85°C
Fully-open temperature	96 to 99°C

Torque wrench settings

	Nm	lbf ft
Fan blades to clutch unit	9 to 11	7 to 8
Radiator to front crossmember	6 to 8	4 to 6
Thermostat housing cover bolts	17 to 20	12 to 15
Viscous clutch to pulley shaft	40 to 50	30 to 37
Water pump retaining bolts:		
M10	40 to 51	30 to 38
M8	11 to 15	8 to 11

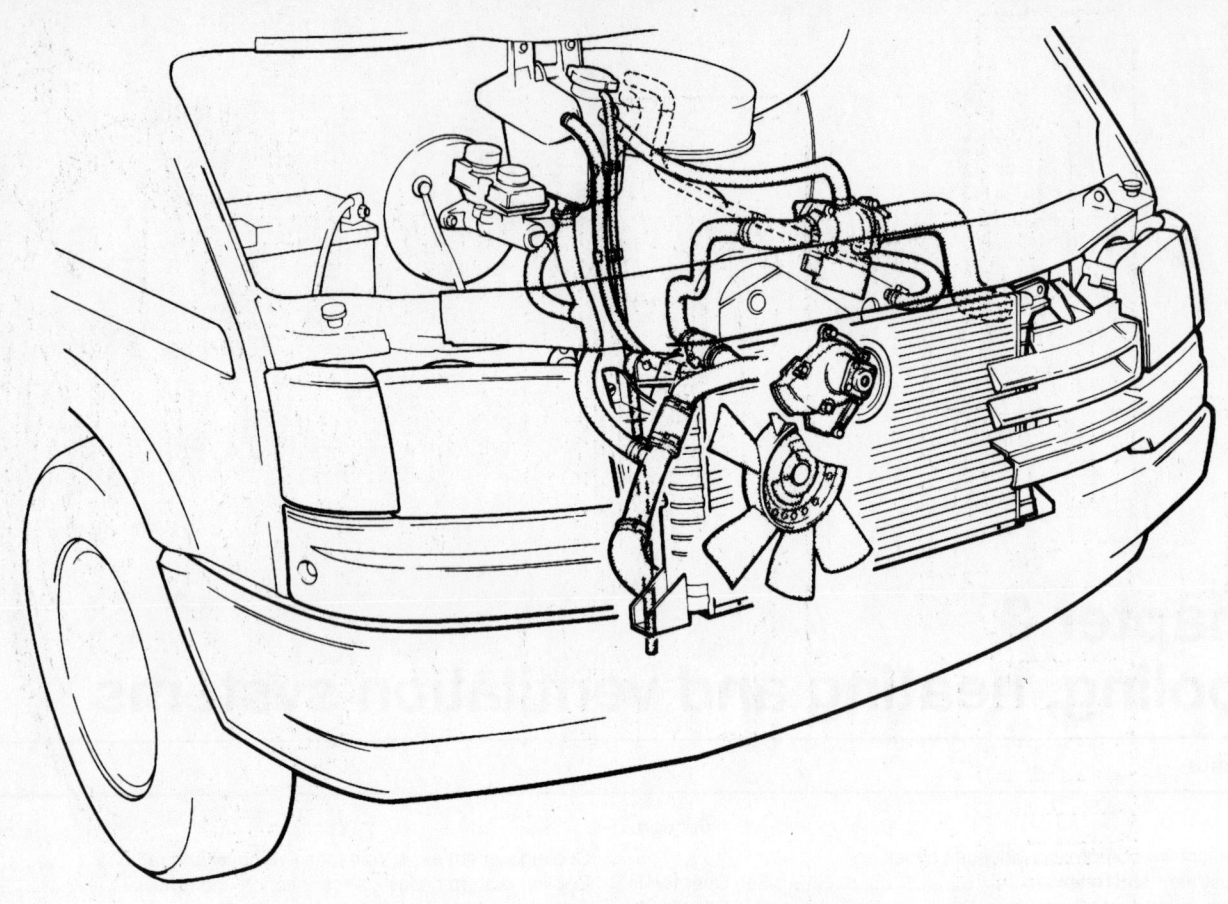

Chapter 3 Cooling, heating and ventilation systems

1.1 General layout of the cooling system components

1 General information and precautions

General information

The cooling system is of pressurised type, and includes a front-mounted crossflow radiator, belt-driven water pump, temperature-conscious thermo-viscous fan, wax-type thermostat, and an expansion tank **(see illustration)**.

The radiator matrix is of aluminium construction, and the end tanks are plastic.

The thermostat is located in a housing at the front of the cylinder head, and its purpose is to ensure rapid engine warm-up by restricting the flow of coolant to the radiator when cold, and also to assist in regulating the normal operating temperature of the engine.

The expansion tank incorporates a pressure cap, which effectively pressurises the cooling system as the coolant temperature rises, thereby increasing the boiling point of the coolant. The tank also has a further degas function. Any accumulation of air bubbles in the coolant, in particular in the thermostat housing and the radiator, is returned to the tank and released in the air space, thus maintaining the efficiency of the coolant.

The system functions as follows. Cold water in the bottom of the radiator circulates through the bottom hose to the water pump, where the pump impeller pushes the water through the passages within the cylinder block and cylinder head. After cooling the cylinder bores, combustion surfaces, and valve seats, the water reaches the underside of the thermostat, which is initially closed. Because the thermostat is closed, circulation continues through the cylinder block, cylinder head and heater matrix, returning to the water pump. When the coolant reaches the predetermined temperature, the thermostat opens and hot water passes through the top hose to the top of the radiator. As the water circulates through the radiator, it is cooled by the passage of air past the radiator when the vehicle is in forward motion, supplemented by the action of the cooling fan. Having reached the bottom of the radiator, the water is now cooled, and the cycle is repeated.

The thermo-viscous fan is controlled by the temperature of air behind the radiator. When the air temperature reaches a predetermined level, a bi-metallic coil starts to open a valve within the unit, and silicon fluid is fed through a system of vanes. Half of the vanes are driven directly by the water pump/alternator drivebelt, and the remaining half are connected to the fan blades. The vanes are arranged so that drive is transmitted to the fan blades in relation to the drag or viscosity of the fluid, and this in turn depends on ambient temperature and engine speed. The fan is therefore only operated when required, and compared with direct-drive type fans, represents a considerable improvement in fuel economy, drivebelt wear and fan noise **(see illustration)**.

The heating and ventilation system operates in conjunction with the cooling system, coolant being circulated through the heater matrix (housed within the heater unit) then flowing back to the engine cooling circuit.

An electric blower motor, also housed in the heater unit, assists when required in supplying hot or cool air as necessary to the vehicle interior and windscreen demister vents.

Precautions

Warning: *DO NOT attempt to remove the expansion tank filler cap, or to disturb any part of the cooling system, while it or the engine is hot, as there is a very great risk of scalding. If the expansion tank filler cap must be removed before the engine and radiator have fully cooled*

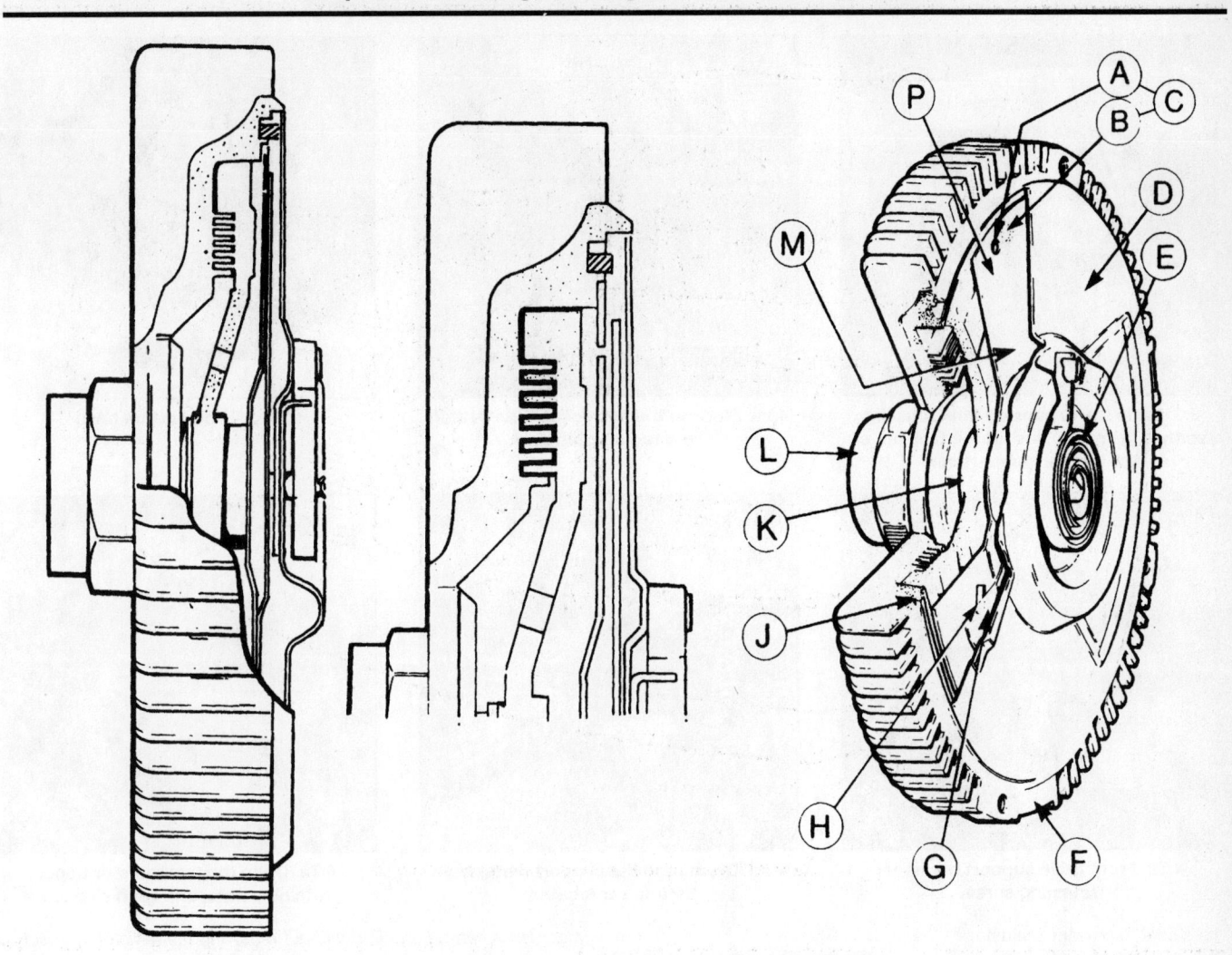

Chapter 3 Cooling, heating and ventilation systems

1.6 Cutaway diagram of the thermo-viscous fan assembly

Left-hand diagram - fluid location at rest
Centre diagram - fluid circuit for drive

- A Discharge port
- B Weir
- C Ram pump
- D Front casing
- E Bi-metallic coil
- F Main casing
- G Control valve
- H Intake port
- J Seal
- K Rotor
- L Drive shaft
- M Fluid reservoir
- P Pump plate

down (even though this is not recommended) the pressure in the cooling system must first be released. Cover the cap with a thick layer of cloth, to avoid scalding, and slowly unscrew the filler cap until a hissing sound can be heard. When the hissing has stopped, showing that pressure is released, slowly unscrew the filler cap further until it can be removed; if more hissing sounds are heard, wait until they have stopped before unscrewing the cap completely. At all times, keep well away from the filler opening.

Warning: *Do not allow antifreeze to come in contact with your skin, or with the painted surfaces of the vehicle. Rinse off spills immediately with plenty of water. Never leave antifreeze lying around in an open container, or in a puddle in the driveway or on the garage floor. Children and pets are attracted by its sweet smell, but antifreeze is fatal if ingested.*

Warning: *Refer to Section 12 for precautions to be observed when working on vehicles with air conditioning.*

2 Cooling system hoses - disconnection and renewal

Note: *Refer to the warnings given in Section 1 of this Chapter before starting work.*

1 If the checks described in Chapter 1 reveal a faulty hose, it must be renewed as follows.

2 First drain the cooling system (see Chapter 1); if the antifreeze is not due for renewal, the drained coolant may be re-used, if it is collected in a clean container.

3 To disconnect any hose, use a pair of pliers to release the spring clamps (or a screwdriver to slacken screw-type clamps), then move them along the hose clear of the union. Carefully work the hose off its stubs. The hoses can be removed with relative ease when new - on an older vehicle, they may have stuck.

4 If a hose proves stubborn, try to release it by rotating it on its unions before attempting to work it off. Gently prise the end of the hose with a blunt instrument (such as a flat-bladed screwdriver), but do not apply too much force, and take care not to damage the pipe stubs or hoses. Note in particular that the radiator hose unions are fragile; do not use excessive force when attempting to remove the hoses. If all else fails, cut the hose with a sharp knife, then slit it so that it can be peeled off in two pieces. While expensive, this is preferable to buying a new radiator. Check first, however, that a new hose is readily available.

5 When refitting a hose, first slide the clamps onto the hose, then work the hose onto its unions. If the hose is stiff, use soap (or washing-up liquid) as a lubricant, or soften it by soaking it in boiling water, but

3•4 Chapter 3 Cooling, heating and ventilation systems

3.3 Undo the expansion tank retaining screws (arrowed) and lift the tank out of the engine compartment

4.2a Slacken the hose clips then detach the radiator top . . .

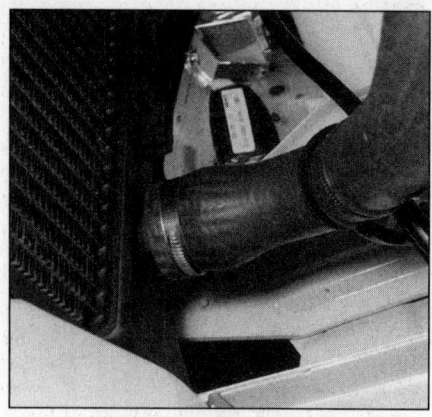

4.2b . . . and bottom hoses

4.5a Front grille support bar upper retaining screw

4.5b Disengage the support bar(s) from their lower location

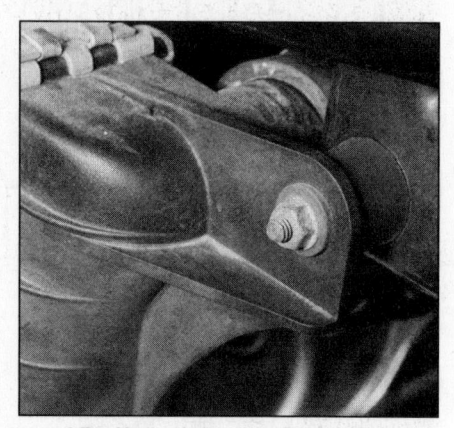

4.7a Undo the two radiator upper retaining nuts, one each side . . .

take care to prevent scalding.
6   Work each hose end fully onto its union, then check that the hose is settled correctly and is properly routed. Slide each clip along the hose until it is behind the union flared end, before tightening it securely.
7   Refill the system with coolant (see Chapter 1).
8   Check carefully for leaks as soon as possible after disturbing any part of the cooling system.

3   Cooling system expansion tank - removal and refitting

Note: *Refer to the warnings given in Section 1 of this Chapter before starting work.*

Removal
1   Drain the cooling system as described in Chapter 1.
2   Release the hose clips and disconnect the hoses at the expansion tank, noting their correct locations for refitting.
3   Undo the retaining screws, and lift the tank out of the engine compartment **(see illustration)**.

Refitting
4   Refitting is a reversal of removal. Refill the cooling system as described in Chapter 1 on completion.

4   Radiator - removal, inspection and refitting

Note: *Refer to the warnings given in Section 1 of this Chapter before starting work. If the radiator is being removed to cure a leak, note that minor leaks can be repaired without removing the radiator, by using a proprietary sealing compound such as Holts Radweld.*

Removal

Pre-1995 model year vehicles
1   Drain the cooling system as described in Chapter 1.
2   Slacken the hose clips, then detach the top and bottom hoses at the radiator **(see illustrations)**.
3   Slacken the clip and detach the expansion tank hose from the radiator.
4   On turbocharged engines, undo the four screws and remove the fan shroud.
5   Remove the front grille together with the support bar(s) by undoing the two screws (one at each end), and the fasteners along the top and in the aperture above the number plate. Disengage the support bar(s) from their lower location, and withdraw the grille **(see illustrations)**. Where fitted, disconnect the headlight washer hoses as the grille is withdrawn.
6   Where applicable, disconnect the automatic transmission fluid cooler pipe connections. Plug the disconnected unions, to prevent fluid loss and dirt ingress.
7   Undo the two radiator upper retaining nuts, one each side, and lift the radiator forwards and upwards out of the lower mounting bushes **(see illustrations)**.

1995 model year vehicles onwards
8   Drain the cooling system as described in Chapter 1.
9   Slacken the hose clips, then detach the radiator bottom hose and, where fitted, the lower automatic transmission fluid cooler pipe connection. Plug the disconnected fluid cooler union, to prevent fluid loss and dirt ingress.

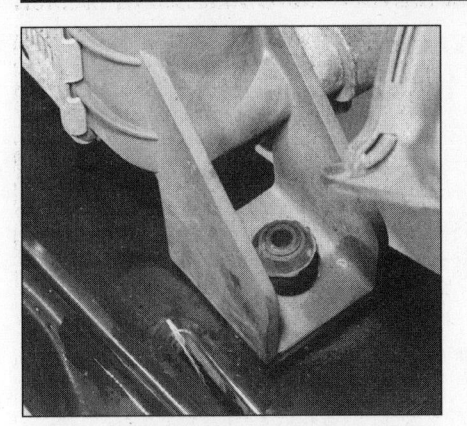

Chapter 3 Cooling, heating and ventilation systems

4.7b ... and lift the radiator out of the lower mounting bushes

4.14 Undo the two bolts each side, and remove the upper crossmember

5.1 A 32 mm open-end spanner will be required to unscrew the fan clutch unit

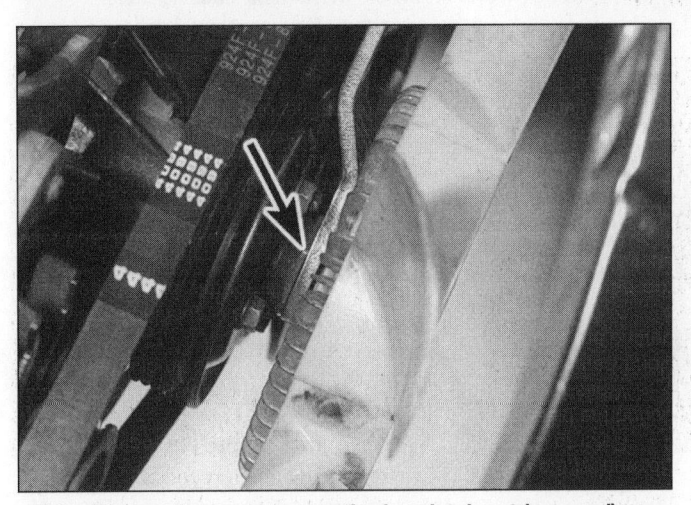

5.2a Engage the spanner over the fan clutch nut (arrowed) ...

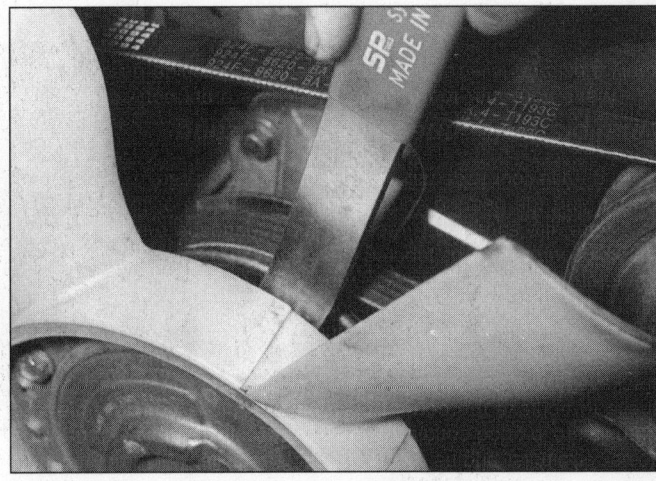

5.2b ... and unscrew the unit from the pulley shaft

10 Undo the fan shroud bolts and the radiator support bar securing bolts.
11 Undo the two bolts at the top, and two at the extreme sides, and remove the radiator grille. Where fitted, disconnect the headlight washer hoses as the grille is withdrawn.
12 Undo the two radiator upper mounting nuts, one each side.
13 Remove the plastic guard, then disconnect the bonnet release cable from the lock and upper crossmember.
14 Undo the two bolts each side, and remove the upper crossmember **(see illustration)**.
15 Slacken the hose clips, then detach the radiator top hose, expansion tank hose and, where fitted, the upper automatic transmission fluid cooler pipe connection. Plug the disconnected fluid cooler union, to prevent fluid loss and dirt ingress.
16 On vehicles with air conditioning, disconnect the electric cooling fan wiring multi-plug, and release the cable from the radiator. Remove the radiator side shields, then separate the air conditioning radiator from the cooling system radiator by sliding it upwards out of its retaining brackets. Take care not to stretch the hoses excessively.
17 Detach the lower fan shroud, and withdraw it from under the vehicle.
18 Lift the radiator upwards and out of the lower mounting bushes.

Inspection

19 The radiator should be flushed through whilst removed, as it can be inverted and reverse-flushed. Clean the exterior of dead flies and dirt with a water jet from a garden hose.
20 Due to the nature of its construction, radiator repairs should be left to a specialist. However in an emergency, minor leaks from the radiator may be cured by using a radiator sealant such as Holts Radweld with the radiator *in situ*.

Refitting

All models

21 Refitting is a reversal of removal, noting the following points:
  a) *Examine and renew any clips and hoses which have deteriorated.*
  b) *Renew the radiator lower mounting bushes if they are in poor condition. Ensure that the radiator engages with the bushes fully as it is fitted.*
  c) *Refill the cooling system as described in Chapter 1.*
  d) *Where automatic transmission is fitted, top-up the transmission fluid as described in Chapter 1.*

5 Viscous cooling fan clutch - removal and refitting

Removal

1 A 32 mm open-end spanner will be required to unscrew the fan clutch unit from the pulley hub. The spanner will need to be 5 mm in section, and cranked as shown to allow it to engage over the flats of the retaining nut. Spanners designed for this purpose are readily available from DIY parts retailers **(see illustration)**. Note that unlike the viscous fan clutch unit fitted to most Ford vehicles, the unit fitted to the Transit Diesel has a conventional right-hand thread, and is unscrewed in the normal way.
2 Engage the spanner over the fan clutch nut, and unscrew the unit from the pulley shaft **(see illustrations)**. To stop the pulley from

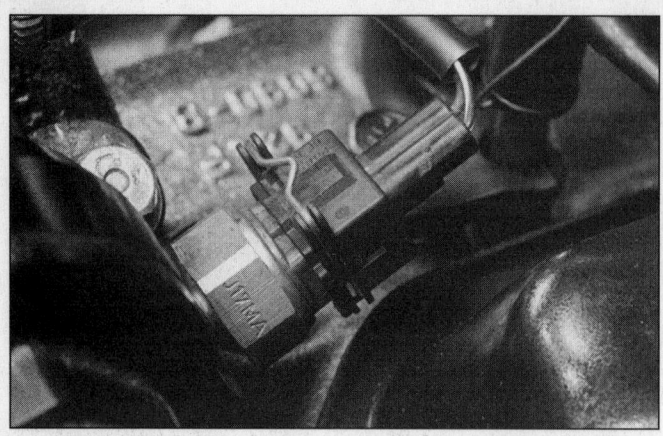

3-6 Chapter 3 Cooling, heating and ventilation systems

6.7 Unplug the electrical connector from the sender unit

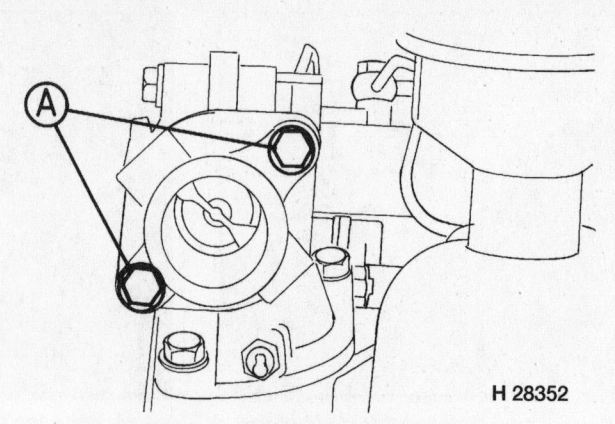

7.4 On early models, undo the two bolts (A) and lift off the thermostat housing cover

7.5a On later models, unscrew the thermostat housing cover using suitable grips ...

7.5b ... Lift out the thermostat ...

7.5c ... and remove the sealing ring

rotating as the fan clutch is loosened, hold it with the aid of a strap wrench or similar. If necessary, tap the spanner to free the clutch unit.
3 On removal, the fan blades can be separated from the clutch unit by undoing the four retaining bolts.

Refitting
4 Refitting is a reversal of removal.

6 Coolant temperature gauge sender unit - testing, removal and refitting

Testing
1 If the coolant temperature gauge is inoperative, check the fuses first (see Chapter 12).
2 If the gauge indicates Hot at any time, consult the *"Fault diagnosis"* section at the front of this manual, to assist in tracing possible cooling system faults.
3 If the gauge indicates Hot shortly after the engine is started from cold, unplug the coolant temperature sender's electrical connector. The sender is located below the radiator top hose connection in the thermostat housing on early vehicles, or at the rear of the thermostat housing on later vehicles. If the gauge reading now drops, renew the sender. If the reading remains high, the wire to the gauge may be shorted to earth, or the gauge is faulty.
4 If the gauge fails to indicate after the engine has been warmed up (approximately 10 minutes) and the fuses are known to be sound, switch off the engine. Unplug the sender's electrical connector, and use a jumper wire to ground the connector to a clean earth point (bare metal) on the engine. Switch on the ignition without starting the engine.

If the gauge now indicates Hot, renew the sender.
5 If the gauge still does not work, the circuit may be open, or the gauge may be faulty. See Chapter 12 for additional information.

Removal
6 Partially drain the cooling system of about 2.5 litres of coolant (see Chapter 1).
7 Unplug the electrical connector from the sender unit **(see illustration)**.
8 Unscrew the sender and withdraw it.

Refitting
9 Clean as thoroughly as possible the sender unit location, then apply a light coat of sealant to the sender's threads. Screw in the sender, tighten it securely and plug in its electrical connector.
10 Top-up the cooling system (see Chapter 1) and run the engine. Check for leaks and proper gauge operation.

7 Thermostat - removal, testing and refitting

Note: *Refer to the warnings given in Section 1 of this Chapter before starting work.*

Removal
1 Disconnect the battery negative lead.
2 Drain the cooling system (see Chapter 1).
3 Loosen the clip and disconnect the radiator top hose from the thermostat housing.
4 On early models, undo the two bolts, then lift off the thermostat

Chapter 3 Cooling, heating and ventilation systems

3-7

7.11 Method of checking thermostat opening temperature

housing cover and withdraw the thermostat from the cover **(see illustration)**

5 On later models, unscrew the thermostat housing cover using suitable grips on the flats of the cover. Lift out the thermostat, and remove the sealing ring from its periphery **(see illustrations)**.

Testing

General check

6 Before assuming the thermostat is to blame for a cooling system problem, check the coolant level, drivebelt tension and condition (see Chapter 1) and temperature gauge operation.

7 If the engine seems to be taking a long time to warm up (based on heater output or temperature gauge operation), the thermostat is probably stuck open. Renew the thermostat.

8 If the engine runs hot, use your hand to check the temperature of the radiator top hose. If the hose isn't hot, but the engine is, the thermostat is probably stuck closed, preventing the coolant inside the engine from escaping to the radiator - renew the thermostat. **Caution:** *Don't drive the vehicle without a thermostat. The lack of a thermostat will slow warm-up time. Also, on models with an engine management system, the system's ECU will then stay in warm-up mode for longer than necessary, causing emissions and fuel economy to suffer.*

9 If the radiator top hose is hot, it means that the coolant is flowing and the thermostat is open. Consult the *"Fault diagnosis"* section at the front of this manual to assist in tracing possible cooling system faults.

Thermostat test

10 If the thermostat remains in the open position at room temperature, it is faulty, and must be renewed as a matter of course.

11 To test it fully, suspend the (closed) thermostat on a length of string in a container of cold water, with a thermometer beside it; ensure that neither touches the side of the container **(see illustration)**.

12 Heat the water, and check the temperature at which the thermostat begins to open; compare this value with that specified. It's difficult to check the fully-open temperature, because this occurs very near the boiling point of water at normal atmospheric pressure. If the temperature at which the thermostat began to open was as specified, then it is most likely that the thermostat's OK. Remove the thermostat and allow it to cool down; check that it closes fully.

13 If the thermostat does not open and close as described, if it sticks in either position, or if it does not open at the specified temperature, it must be renewed.

Refitting

14 Refitting is a reversal of removal. Clean the mating surfaces carefully, and renew the thermostat's seal or housing gasket, as applicable.

15 Refill the cooling system (see Chapter 1).

8.6 Undo the six bolts (arrowed) and remove the water pump

16 Start the engine and allow it to reach normal operating temperature, then check for leaks and proper thermostat operation.

8 Water pump - removal and refitting

Note: *Refer to the warnings given in Section 1 of this Chapter before starting work.*

Removal

1 Disconnect the battery negative lead.
2 Remove the radiator as described in Section 4.
3 Remove the viscous cooling fan clutch as described in Section 5.
4 Remove the alternator/water pump drivebelt as described in Chapter 1, Section 9.
5 Remove the timing belt cover as described in Chapter 2A, Section 6.
6 Undo the six bolts and remove the water pump from the engine front adapter plate **(see illustration)**. Note the positions of the retaining bolts, as they are of different sizes.
7 No provision is made for the repair of the water pump, and therefore if it is noisy or defective in any way, it must be renewed.

Refitting

8 Clean the engine adapter plate and water pump mating faces. Ensure that the mating faces are clean and dry.
9 Using a new gasket, position the water pump on the adapter plate. Insert the retaining bolts in their originally-noted positions, and tighten them progressively, in a diagonal sequence to the specified torque.
10 Refit the timing belt cover, drivebelt, fan clutch and radiator as described in the relevant Sections and Chapters of this manual.
11 Refill the cooling system, reconnect the battery, then run the engine and check for leaks.

9 Heating and ventilation systems - general information

The heating system consists of a blower fan and heater matrix (radiator) located in the heater unit, with hoses connecting the heater matrix to the engine cooling system. Hot engine coolant is circulated through the heater matrix. When the heater temperature control on the facia is operated, a flap door opens to expose the heater box to the passenger compartment. When the blower control is operated, the blower fan forces air through the unit according to the setting selected.

The blower fan speed is controlled by a rotary switch on the

3•8 Chapter 3 Cooling, heating and ventilation systems

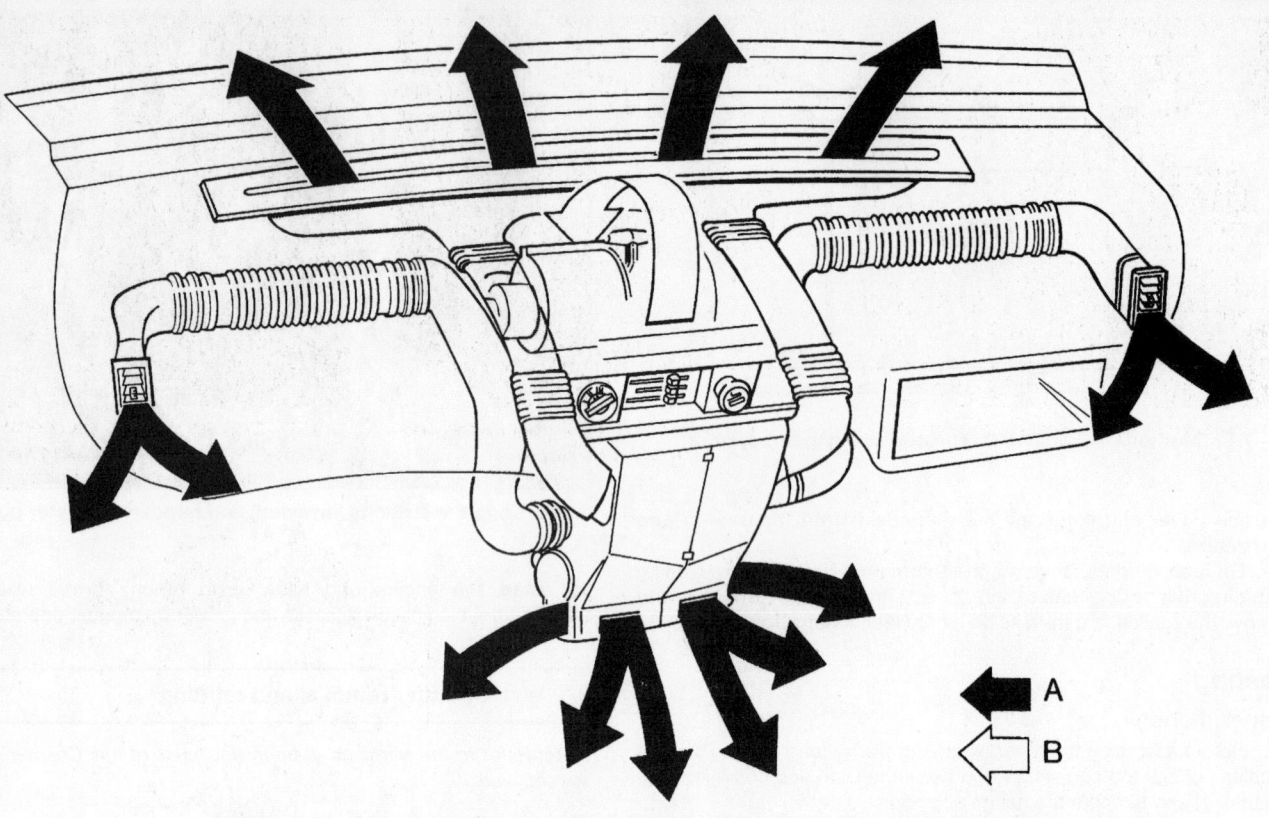

9.2 Heating and fresh air ventilation system layout. Cold/warm air (A), recirculated air (B)

heater control panel on all models. On early models, sliding levers control the temperature, recirculation and distribution of air within the passenger compartment. Altering the position of these controls allows fresh air or recirculated air to be directed through the interior vents or windscreen demister vents as required **(see illustration)**. On later models, rotary switches instead of sliding levers are used for all the controls.

10 Heater/ventilation components - removal and refitting

Heater assembly - pre-1995 model year vehicles

Removal
1 Disconnect the battery negative lead.
2 Drain the cooling system as described in Chapter 1.
3 Loosen off the retaining clips, and detach the heater flow and return hoses at the bulkhead connections **(see illustration)**.
4 Working inside the vehicle, undo the four retaining screws and withdraw the heater control panel. As it is withdrawn, detach the wiring connectors and bulbholders from the fan motor switch and the cigarette lighter units **(see illustration)**. Remove the ashtray.
5 Disconnect the heater flap control panel by undoing the two retaining nuts from the positions shown **(see illustrations)**.
6 Detach the heater unit demister and ventilation hoses **(see illustration)**.
7 Unscrew and remove the four heater unit-to-bulkhead retaining screws, and then carefully withdraw the heater assembly from the vehicle. As the unit is withdrawn, disconnect the fan motor wiring connections.

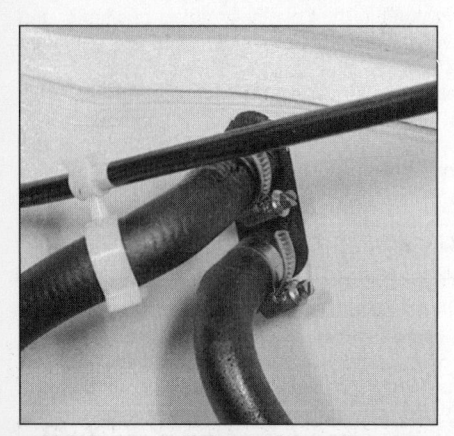

10.3 Loosen off the retaining clips and detach the heater flow and return hoses

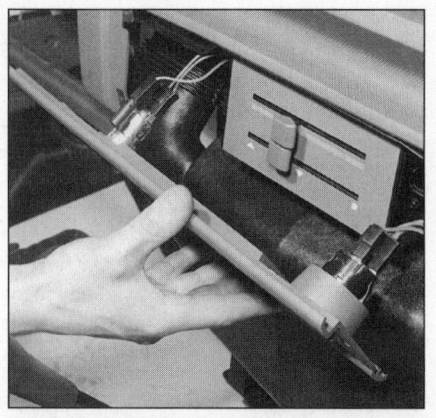

10.4 Undo the four retaining screws and withdraw the heater control panel

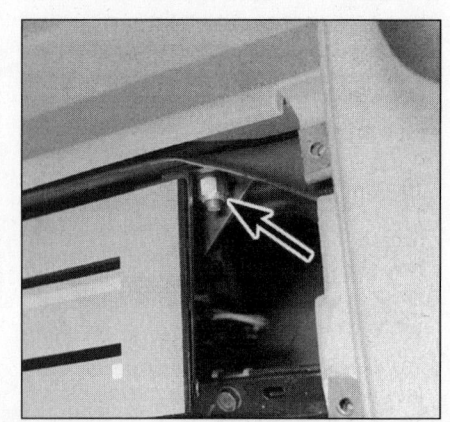

10.5a Disconnect the heater flap control panel by undoing the retaining nut (arrowed) each side . . .

Chapter 3 Cooling, heating and ventilation systems

10.5b ... then withdraw the panel

10.6 Detach the heater unit demister and ventilation hoses

10.11 On later models, disconnect the quick-release couplings (arrowed) and detach the heater hoses

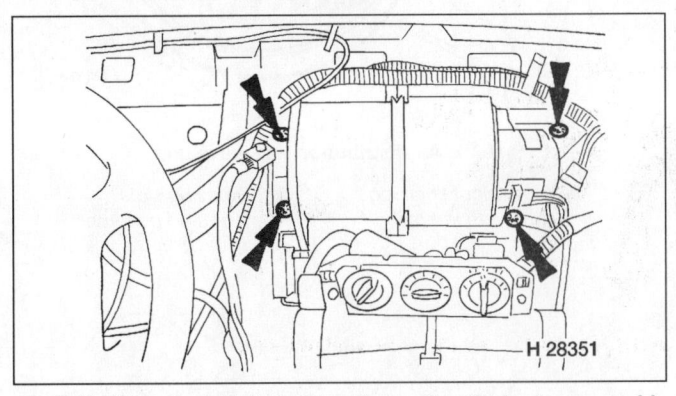

10.13 Undo the four bolts (arrowed) securing the heater assembly to the bulkhead

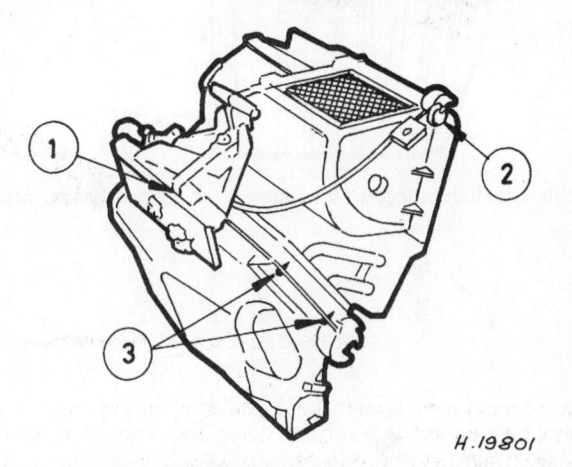

10.17 Heater unit showing control (1) air flap assembly (2) and casing retaining screws (3)

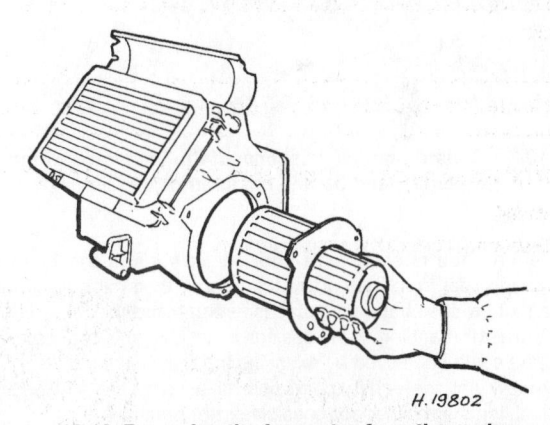

10.18 Removing the fan motor from the casing

Refitting

8 Refitting is a reversal of the removal procedure, but note the following points:
  a) When refitting the heater flap control panel, position the control levers 2 mm from their end stops, and fit the control cable sheath securing clips. Each flap should be at the end of its travel.
  b) Ensure that the wiring connectors are securely attached to the fan motor switch and the cigarette lighter.
  c) Check that the heater hose connections are securely made, then refill the cooling system as described in Chapter 1.
  d) When the engine is restarted, operate the heater and ventilation system to check for satisfactory operation, and also check for any signs of coolant leaks from the system.

Heater assembly - 1995 model year vehicles onwards

Removal

9 Disconnect the battery negative lead.
10 Drain the cooling system as described in Chapter 1.
11 From within the engine compartment, disconnect the quick-release couplings and detach the heater hoses from the heater radiator **(see illustration)**. To do this, compress the collar of the plastic insert, and pull off the hose using angled pointed pliers. Take care not to lose the seals.
12 Remove the facia as described in Chapter 11, Section 29.
13 Undo the four bolts securing the heater assembly to the bulkhead **(see illustration)**.
14 Pull the assembly forwards and remove it from inside the cab.

Refitting

15 Refitting is a reversal of removal.

Heater matrix, blower motor and controls - pre 1995 model year vehicles

Removal

16 With the heater assembly removed from the car, detach the heater control cables from the heater unit, and remove the control cables and panel.
17 Undo the eight retaining screws, and separate the upper casing from the lower casing **(see illustration)**.
18 To remove the fan motor, unscrew the three securing screws, and then withdraw the unit from the casing **(see illustration)**.

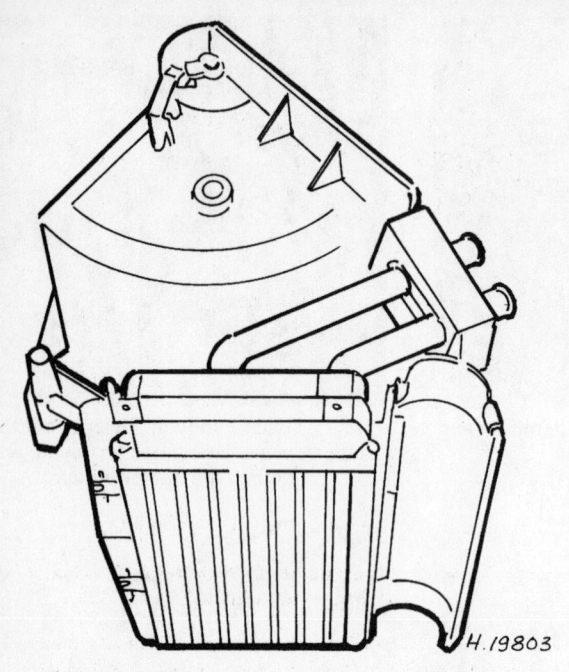

3-10 Chapter 3 Cooling, heating and ventilation systems

10.19 Carefully withdraw the matrix from the heater unit casing

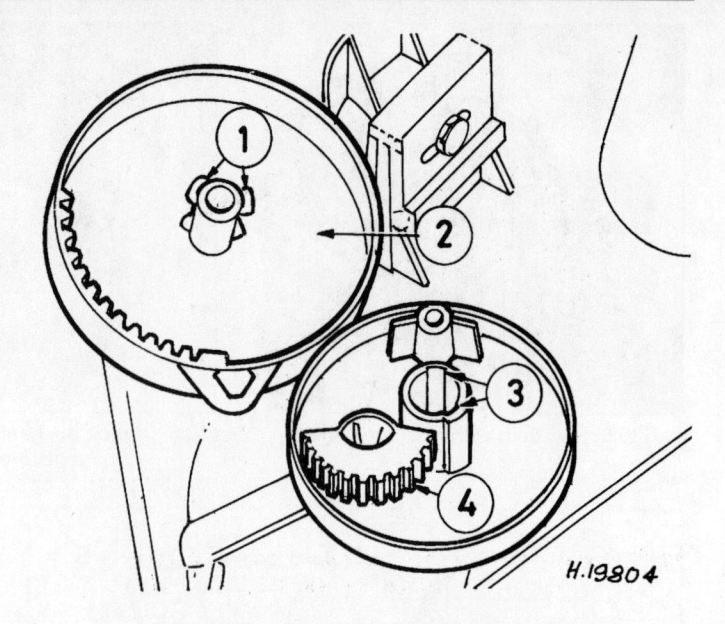

10.22 Air distribution flap valve unit

1 Actuator spigot shaft lugs
2 Actuator (with internal teeth)
3 Housing slots
4 Toothed quadrant

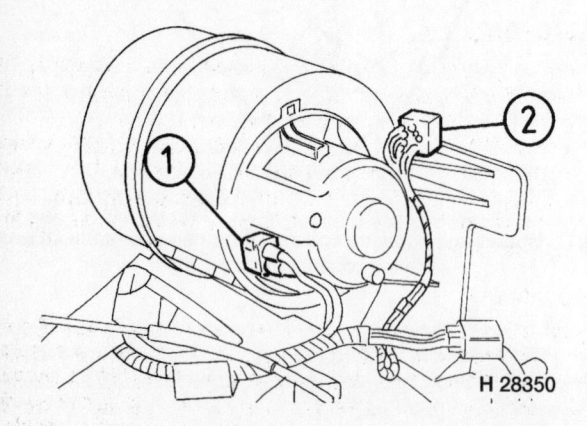

10.24 On later models, disconnect the fan motor wiring multi-plug (1) and detach the fan motor resistor (2)

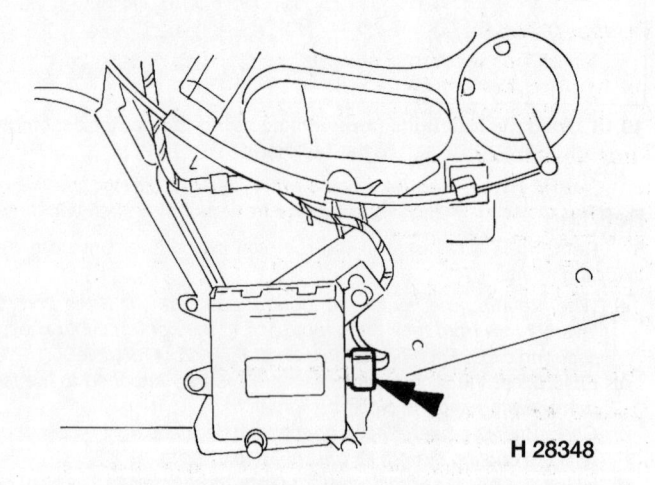

10.25 Disconnect the wiring multi-plug (arrowed) from the air recirculation valve control motor

19 Remove the coolant pipe support screw and the foam seal. Remove the seal from the end of the matrix, then carefully withdraw the matrix from the heater unit case **(see illustration)**.
20 Further dismantling of the casings is unlikely to be necessary, but if required can be achieved by releasing the retaining clips.
21 Renew any defective components as necessary. Repairs to individual items are either not possible or not practical.

Refitting

22 Reassemble in the reverse order of dismantling. If the flap valve control quadrant was dismantled, fit the quadrant, then locate the actuator and align the spigot shaft lugs with the casing slots, (rotating slightly to secure in position) **(see illustration)**.
23 When reassembling the casing halves, use a new foam seal. Also fit a new seal to the matrix when installing it.

Heater matrix, blower motor and controls - 1995 model year vehicles onwards

Removal

24 With the heater assembly removed from the car, disconnect the fan motor wiring multi-plug, and detach the fan motor resistor from the side of the heater casing **(see illustration)**.
25 Disconnect the wiring multi-plug from the air recirculation valve control motor **(see illustration)**.
26 Release the heater control outer cables on each side of the casing by springing back the clips. Disconnect the inner cables from the adjusting levers, and remove the control unit assembly.
27 Pull up the fan motor retaining tab, then turn the motor anti-clockwise and remove it from the casing.
28 Undo the three screws on the side of the casing **(see illustration)**, and remove the heater matrix cover panel. Carefully lift out the matrix from the heater casing.
29 Undo the three screws and withdraw the air recirculation valve control motor.

Refitting

30 Reassemble in the reverse order of dismantling.

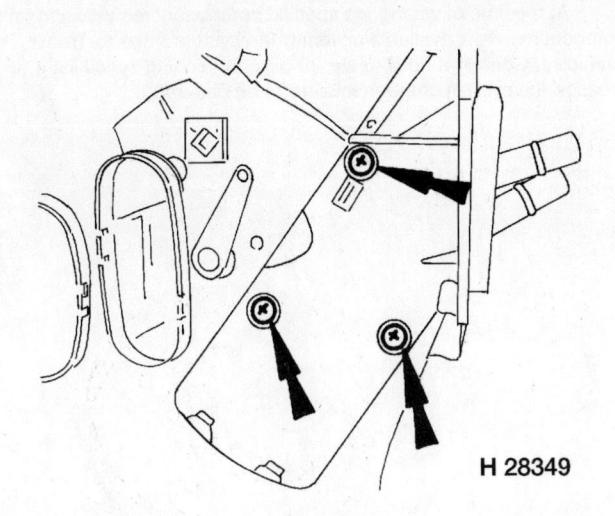

Chapter 3 Cooling, heating and ventilation systems

10.28 Undo the three matrix cover panel screws (arrowed) on the side of the casing

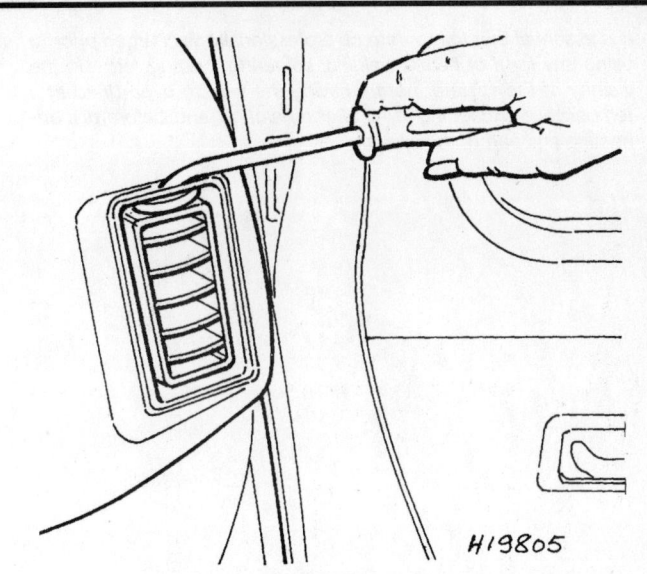

11.3 Carefully prise free the face vent nozzle grille using a screwdriver

11 Heater/ventilation vents - removal and refitting

Pre-1995 model year vehicles

Demister hose

1 Detach the hose from the nozzle and the heater casing by simply pulling it free, then withdraw it.
2 Refit the demister hose by fitting it to the demister nozzle first.

Face vent nozzle

3 Carefully prise free the nozzle grille, using a screwdriver as a lever. Prise at the top and bottom edges to ease it free, then withdraw the nozzle (**see illustration**).
4 To refit the nozzle unit, align it correctly in its aperture, then carefully press it into position so that it is felt to engage with the adapter.

1995 model year vehicles onwards

Centre vent nozzle

5 Disconnect the battery negative lead.
6 Remove the screws, and withdraw the upper and lower shrouds from the steering column.
7 Remove the crosshead screws, and withdraw the multi-function switch assembly from the steering column.
8 Disconnect the wiring multi-plug, and remove the switch assembly.
9 Undo the four screws, and withdraw the instrument panel surround.
10 Undo the two screws, and withdraw the radio/clock surround from the facia. Disconnect the wiring multi-plugs, and remove the surround.
11 Disconnect the vent nozzle from the heater housing, and remove the nozzle.
12 Release the three retaining clips, and remove the vent nozzle from the radio/clock surround.
13 Refitting is a reversal of removal.

Side vent nozzle (driver's side)

14 Proceed as described in paragraphs 5 to 9 above.
15 Undo the two screws securing the switch/vent panel, and withdraw the panel.
16 Refitting is a reversal of removal.

12 Air conditioning system - general information and precautions

General information

The air conditioning system consists of a condenser, an evaporator, a compressor, a dehydrator, additional electric cooling fans, and the plumbing connecting all of the above components.

A blower fan forces the warmer air of the passenger compartment through the evaporator core (rather like a radiator in reverse), transferring the heat from the air to the refrigerant. The liquid refrigerant boils off into low-pressure vapour, taking the heat with it when it leaves the evaporator.

Precautions

Warning: *The air conditioning system is under high pressure. Do not loosen any fittings or remove any components until after the system has been discharged. Air conditioning refrigerant should be properly discharged into an approved type of container, at a dealer service department or an automotive air conditioning repair facility capable of handling the refrigerant safely. Always wear eye protection when disconnecting air conditioning system fittings.*

When an air conditioning system is fitted, it is necessary to observe the following special precautions whenever dealing with any part of the system, its associated components, and any items which necessitate disconnection of the system:

a) *The refrigerant used is a very dangerous substance. It must not be allowed into contact with the skin or eyes, or there is a risk of frostbite. It must also not be discharged in an enclosed space, as there is a risk of suffocation. The refrigerant is heavier than air, and so must never be discharged over a pit.*

b) *The refrigerant must not be allowed to come in contact with a naked flame, otherwise a poisonous gas will be created - under certain circumstances, this can form an explosive mixture with air. For similar reasons, smoking in the presence of refrigerant is highly dangerous, particularly if the vapour is inhaled through a lighted cigarette.*

c) *Never discharge the system to the atmosphere - R134a refrigerant is not an ozone-depleting ChloroFluoroCarbon (CFC), but is instead a hydrofluorocarbon, which causes environmental damage by contributing to the "greenhouse effect" if released into the atmosphere.*

d) *If for any reason the system must be disconnected, entrust this task to your Ford dealer or a refrigeration engineer.*

e) *It is essential that the system be professionally discharged prior to using any form of heat - welding, soldering, brazing, etc - in the vicinity of the system, before having the vehicle oven-dried at a temperature exceeding 70ºC after repainting, and before disconnecting any part of the system.*

At the time of writing, no specific component removal and refitting procedures were available covering the system fitted to Transit Diesel vehicles. Consult a Ford dealer or air conditioning specialist if for any reason the system components are to be disturbed.

Chapter 4
Fuel, exhaust and emissions control systems

Contents

	Section		Section
Accelerator cable - removal, refitting and adjustment	13	Fuel pump - removal and refitting	17
Accelerator pedal - removal and refitting	14	Fuel system - priming and bleeding	2
Air cleaner assembly - removal and refitting	3	Fuel tank - removal, repair and refitting	16
Air cleaner element renewal	See Chapter 1	General information and precautions	1
Air cleaner thermostatic control system check	See Chapter 1	Idle speed and anti-stall speed - checking and adjustment	See Chapter 1
Emission control systems - general information	24	Information sensors (Lucas EPIC system) - general information, testing, removal and refitting	27
Emission control systems - testing and component renewal	25		
Exhaust manifold - removal and refitting	19	Injection timing - checking and adjustment methods	8
Exhaust system - general information and component renewal	23	Injection timing - checking and adjustment	9
Fast idle thermostatic sensor - removal, refitting and adjustment	5	Inlet manifold - removal and refitting	18
		Lucas Electronic Programmed Injection Control (EPIC) system - description and precautions	26
Fuel filter assembly - removal and refitting	12		
Fuel filter renewal	See Chapter 1	Maximum speed - checking and adjustment	4
Fuel filter water draining	See Chapter 1	Stop solenoid - description, removal and refitting	6
Fuel gauge sender unit - removal and refitting	15	Turbocharger - description and precautions	20
Fuel injection pump - removal and refitting	7	Turbocharger - examination and renovation	22
Fuel injectors - testing, removal and refitting	10	Turbocharger - removal and refitting	21
Fuel injector delivery pipes - removal and refitting	11		

Specifications

General

System type:
- Normally-aspirated engines .... Centrally-mounted fuel tank, distributor fuel injection pump, direct injection. Exhaust gas recirculation fitted to certain engines
- Turbocharged engines .... Centrally-mounted fuel tank, distributor fuel injection pump, direct injection. Lucas EPIC engine management system on later engines, exhaust gas recirculation on all engines
- Firing order .... 1-2-4-3 (No 1 cylinder at timing belt end)
- Fuel tank capacity .... 68 litres

Maximum speed

No load:
- Bosch injection pump .... 4320 to 4560 rpm
- Lucas/CAV injection pump .... 4280 to 4480 rpm
- Full load .... 4000 rpm

Chapter 4 Fuel, exhaust and emissions control systems

Injection pump
Type.. Bosch or Lucas/CAV
Direction of rotation .... Clockwise, viewed from sprocket end
Static timing... 11° BTDC (using timing pegs - see text)

Injectors
Type:
    Pre-1989 model year... Bosch or Lucas/CAV, 4-hole
    1989 model year onwards... Bosch or Lucas/CAV, 5-hole "Stanadyne" type
Opening pressure:
    Pre-1989 model year:
        Bosch.. 250 bars
        Lucas/CAV... 260 bars
    1989 model year onwards:
        New... 275 bars
        Used... 241 bars

Turbocharger
Type.. Garrett or KKK
Boost pressure (full load)... 0.61 to 0.71 bars

Torque wrench settings

	Nm	lbf/ft
Air intake pipe to turbocharger	20 to 25	14 to 18
EGR connecting hose to valve and manifold	20 to 25	14 to 18
EGR valve to throttle housing:		
Normally-aspirated engines	20 to 25	14 to 18
Turbocharged engines	15 to 20	11 to 14
Exhaust manifold to cylinder head	40 to 57	30 to 42
Exhaust system flange nuts and bolts	40	30
Fast idle thermostatic sensor to thermostat housing	15 to 20	11 to 14
Fuel filter assembly to manifold	15 to 21	11 to 15
Fuel injector clamp bolts (Stanadyne injectors)	37 to 42	27 to 31
Fuel injector clamp nuts (pre-1989 model year)	12 to 15	9 to 11
Fuel injector delivery pipe unions	18 to 20	13 to 14
Fuel pump heat shield	20 to 25	14 to 18
Fuel pump to cylinder block	20 to 25	14 to 18
Injection pump front mounting nuts and bolts	21 to 26	15 to 19
Injection pump rear support bracket	21 to 26	15 to 19
Injection pump sprocket bolts	22 to 27	16 to 20
Inlet manifold to cylinder head	20 to 25	14 to 18
Throttle housing to exhaust manifold	20 to 25	14 to 18
Throttle housing to inlet manifold	20 to 25	14 to 18
Turbocharger exhaust downpipe elbow bolts	20 to 25	14 to 18
Turbocharger oil return pipe bolts	20 to 28	14 to 21
Turbocharger oil supply pipe	8 to 12	6 to 9
Turbocharger support bracket bolts	20 to 25	14 to 18
Turbocharger to exhaust manifold	20 to 25	14 to 18
Two-piece inlet manifold upper part to lower part	20 to 25	14 to 18

1 General information and precautions

General information

The fuel system consists of a centre-mounted fuel tank, a mechanical fuel pump (later models only), a fuel filter with integral water separator, a fuel injection pump, injectors and associated components. A turbocharger is fitted to certain engines, as is an exhaust system catalytic converter and exhaust gas recirculation (EGR) system.

Fuel is drawn from the fuel tank by the fuel injection pump, or by a mechanical fuel lift pump on later models. Before reaching the injection pump, the fuel passes through a fuel filter, where foreign matter and water are removed. Excess fuel lubricates the moving components of the pump, and is then returned to the tank. A stop solenoid cuts the fuel supply to the injection pump rotor when the ignition is switched off.

The fuel injection pump is driven at half-crankshaft speed by the timing belt. The high pressure required to inject the fuel into the compressed air in the combustion chambers is achieved by a cam plate acting on a single piston on the Bosch pump, or by two opposed pistons forced together by rollers running in a cam ring on the Lucas/CAV pump. The fuel passes through a central rotor with a single outlet drilling which aligns with ports leading to the injector pipes.

Fuel metering is controlled by a centrifugal governor, which reacts to accelerator pedal position and engine speed. The governor is linked to a metering valve, which increases or decreases the amount of fuel delivered at each pumping stroke. On turbocharged models, a separate device also increases fuel delivery with increasing boost pressure.

Basic injection timing is determined when the pump is fitted. When the engine is running, it is varied automatically to suit the prevailing engine speed by a mechanism which turns the cam plate or ring.

On later turbocharged engines with the Lucas EPIC engine

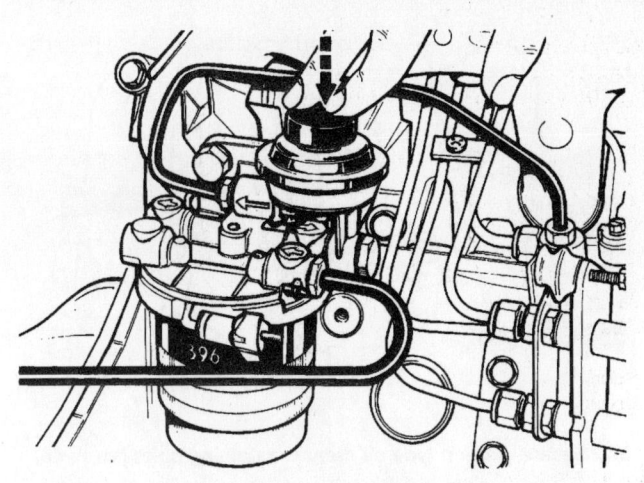

Chapter 4 Fuel, exhaust and emissions control systems

2.3 Hand-operated priming pump on the Lucas/CAV injection system

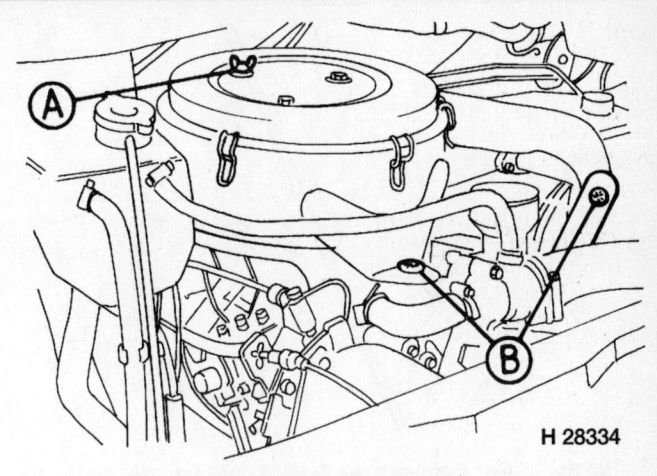

3.1a Circular type air cleaner assembly as fitted to certain normally-aspirated engines
- A Centre retaining bolt or wing nut
- B Support bracket retaining bolts

management system (see below), the fuel injection pump is electronically controlled, and precise fuel metering is achieved by the system's electronic control unit.

The four fuel injectors produce a homogeneous spray of fuel into the cylinder head. The injectors are calibrated to open and close at critical pressures, to provide efficient and even combustion. Each injector needle is lubricated by fuel, which accumulates in the spring chamber, and is channelled to the injection pump return hose by leak-off pipes.

Bosch or Lucas/CAV fuel system components may be fitted, depending on model. Components from the latter manufacturer may be marked either "CAV", "Roto-Diesel" or "Con-Diesel", depending on their date and place of manufacture. With the exception of the fuel filter assembly, replacement components must be of the same make as those originally fitted.

On certain models, a thermostatic sensor in the cooling system operates a fast idle lever on the injection pump to increase the idle speed when the engine is cold.

From the 1992 model year onwards, turbocharged engines are fitted with the Lucas Electronic Programmed Injection Control (EPIC) engine management system. Further details of this system are given in Section 26.

Provided that the specified maintenance is carried out, the fuel injection equipment will give long and trouble-free service. The injection pump itself may well outlast the engine. The main potential cause of damage to the injection pump and injectors is dirt or water in the fuel.

Servicing of the injection pump and injectors is very limited for the home mechanic, and any dismantling or adjustment other than that described in this Chapter must be entrusted to a Ford dealer or fuel injection specialist.

Precautions

Warning: *It is necessary to take certain precautions when working on the fuel system components, particularly the fuel injectors. Before carrying out any operations on the fuel system, refer to the precautions given in "Safety first!" at the beginning of this manual, and to any additional warning notes at the start of the relevant Sections.*

2 Fuel system - priming and bleeding

1 After disconnecting part of the fuel supply system or running out of fuel, it will be necessary to prime the system, and bleed off any air which may have entered the system components.
2 Vehicles fitted with the Lucas/CAV injection system may have a hand-operated priming pump, located on the fuel filter assembly.

Vehicles with the Bosch, or later type Lucas/CAV, system do not normally need priming, as these systems are theoretically self-bleeding. In some instances however, depending on the extent to which the fuel system has been disconnected, priming of the high-pressure circuit may be necessary.
3 If working on the Lucas/CAV system with a hand-operated priming pump, operate the priming pump plunger slowly for approximately 15 to 20 strokes or until resistance is felt, indicating that air has been expelled from the fuel injection pump **(see illustration)**. It should be possible to hear the fuel circulating through the pump when the all the air has been expelled.
4 On all systems, crank the engine on the starter motor in ten-second bursts until it starts. If the engine refuses to start, air may have reached the injectors, in which case the high-pressure circuit must be bled, as follows.
5 Place wads of clean rag around the fuel pipe unions at the injectors to absorb spilt fuel, then slacken the fuel pipe unions.
6 Crank the engine on the starter motor until fuel emerges from the unions, then stop cranking the engine and tighten the unions. Mop up any spilt fuel.
7 Start the engine with the accelerator pedal fully depressed. Additional cranking may be necessary to finally bleed the system before the engine starts.

3 Air cleaner assembly - removal and refitting

Note: *A variety of air cleaner types have been fitted to Transit Diesel engines since the start of production, and all differ according to engine power output, year of manufacture and type of injection equipment fitted, or induction layout. The following procedures apply to the units most likely to be encountered, but some differences may be noticed on certain models.*

Normally-aspirated engines

Removal

1 If the air cleaner assembly is of circular shape and mounted over the top of the engine, detach the air cleaner inlet hose from the inlet duct and, where fitted, from the vacuum pipe at the brake servo vacuum hose T-piece connector. Undo the centre retaining bolt on top of the air cleaner, and the support bracket retaining bolts at the front **(see illustrations)**. Lift the unit off the engine; where fitted, detach the warm-air supply hose. Where an exhaust gas recirculation system is fitted, remove the air cleaner complete with oil filler cap and breather hose.

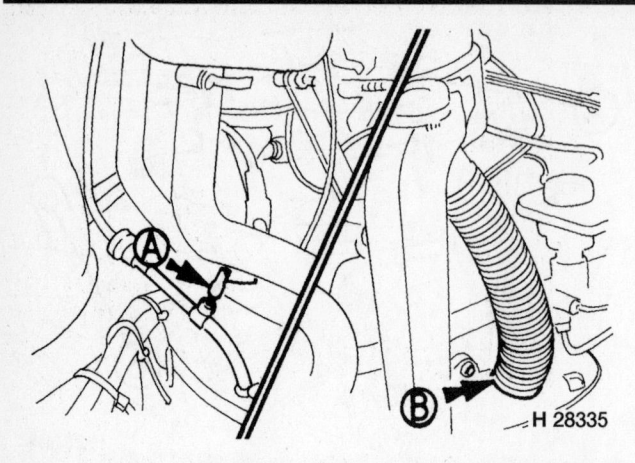

4-4 Chapter 4 Fuel, exhaust and emissions control systems

3.1b Air cleaner vacuum hose T-piece connector (A) and warm-air supply hose (B)

3.2 Square section type air cleaner retaining bolts (arrowed)

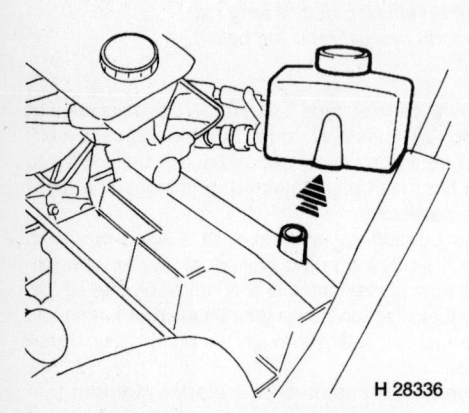

3.3a Remove the power steering pump reservoir (where fitted) from the side-mounted air cleaner assembly

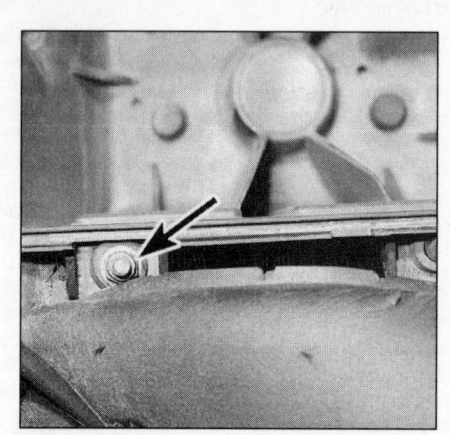

3.3b Undo the retaining bolt (arrowed) . . .

3.3c . . . and pull the air cleaner upwards to disengage it from the locating lugs (element and cover shown removed for clarity)

2 If the air cleaner is of square section shape and mounted over the top of the engine, slacken the hose clip and detach the inlet hose from the throttle housing. Lift off the engine oil filler/vent cap, then undo the three bolts securing the air cleaner assembly to the engine **(see illustration)**. Lift the unit up and remove it, complete with filler/vent cap and hose, from the engine.

3 If the air cleaner assembly is mounted at the side of the engine, lift out the power steering reservoir (where applicable) from the side of the air cleaner, and place it to one side. On some versions, the reservoir is retained with one bolt. Slacken the hose clip(s) or remove the two screws, and detach the cold-air inlet duct and/or inlet hose. Disconnect any remaining vacuum hoses, noting their locations. Undo the lower retaining nut, then pull the air cleaner upwards to disengage it from the locating lugs **(see illustrations)**.

Refitting
4 In all cases, refitting is a reversal of removal.

Turbocharged engines
Removal
5 If the air cleaner is mounted over the top of the engine, disconnect the inlet air temperature sensor wiring multi-plug (where fitted) from the side of the air cleaner assembly, and release the clip securing the air inlet hose to the turbocharger. Disconnect the cold-air inlet duct, and undo the three air cleaner assembly retaining bolts **(see illustration 3.2)**. Pull off the oil filler cap, and remove the air cleaner assembly, complete with oil filler cap and turbocharger inlet hose.

6 If the air cleaner assembly is mounted at the side of the engine, lift out the power steering reservoir (where applicable) from the side of the air cleaner, and place it to one side. On some versions, the reservoir is retained with one bolt. Disconnect the inlet air temperature sensor wiring multi-plug (where fitted) from the side of the air cleaner assembly, and release the clip securing the air inlet hose to the turbocharger. Disconnect any remaining vacuum hoses, noting their locations. Undo the lower retaining nut, then pull the air cleaner upwards to disengage it from the locating lugs.

Refitting
7 In all cases, refitting is a reversal of removal.

4 Maximum speed - checking and adjustment

Caution: *The maximum speed adjustment screw is only fitted to certain versions of fuel injection pump, and is sealed by the manufacturers at the factory, using paint or a locking wire and lead seal. There is no reason why it should require adjustment. Do not disturb the screw if the vehicle is still within the warranty period, otherwise the warranty will be invalidated. This adjustment requires the use of a tachometer - refer to Chapter 1, Section 36 for alternative methods. In all cases, the advice of a Ford dealer or Diesel injection specialist should be sought before carrying out the following procedures.*

1 Run the engine to normal operating temperature.
2 Have an assistant fully depress the accelerator pedal, and check that the maximum engine speed is as given in the Specifications. Do not keep the engine at maximum speed for more than two or three seconds.

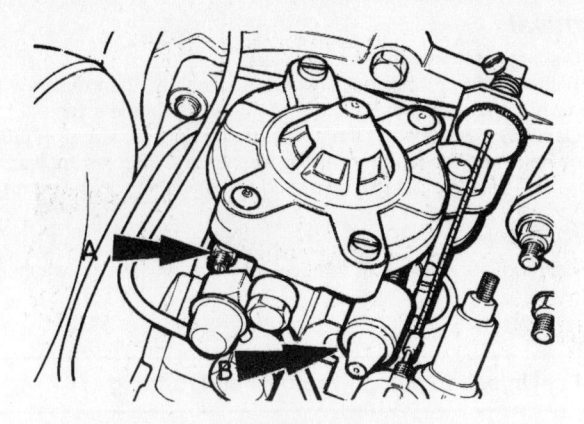

Chapter 4 Fuel, exhaust and emissions control systems

4.3a Bosch fuel injection pump adjustment points
- A Idle speed adjustment screw
- B Maximum speed adjustment screw (under cap)

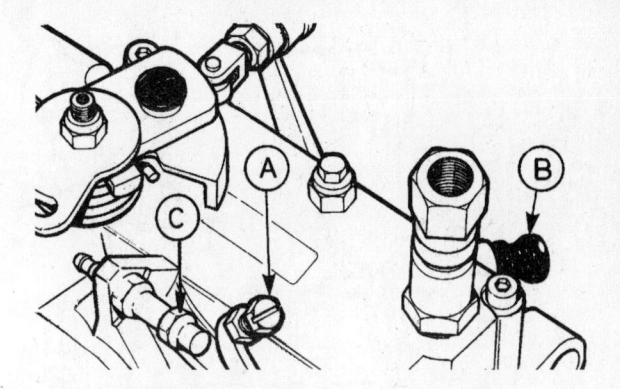

4.3b Lucas/CAV fuel injection pump adjustment points
- A Idle speed adjustment screw
- B Anti-stall adjustment screw (under cap)
- C Maximum speed adjustment screw (under cap)

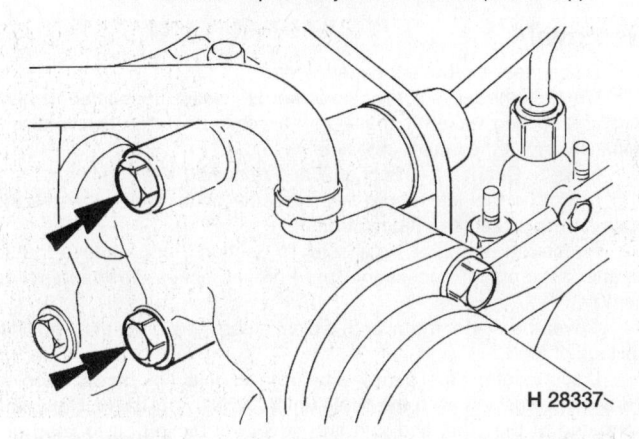

5.5 Thermostatic sensor to thermostat housing retaining bolts (arrowed)

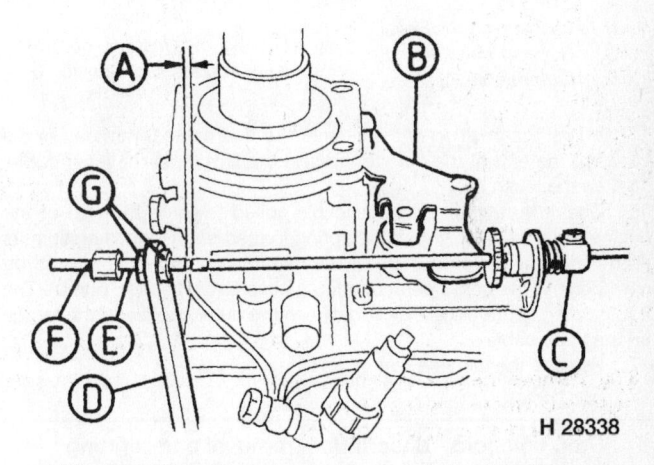

5.14a Fast idle adjustment on the Bosch fuel injection pump
- A 2 to 3 mm gap
- B Fast idle control lever
- C Spring-loaded end fitting
- D Support bracket
- E Adjustment thread
- F Outer cable
- G Locknuts

3   If adjustment is necessary, stop the engine, then loosen the locknut, turn the maximum speed adjustment screw as necessary, and retighten the locknut **(see illustrations)**.
4   Repeat the procedure in paragraph 2 to check the adjustment.
5   Stop the engine and disconnect the tachometer.

5 Fast idle thermostatic sensor - removal, refitting and adjustment

1   On pre-1992 models, a thermostatic sensor in the cooling system operates a fast idle lever on the injection pump to increase the idle speed when the engine is cold. The thermostatic sensor is located in the side of the thermostat housing.
2   On later engines, the thermostatic sensor forms part of the injection pump assembly, and is non-serviceable.

Removal
3   Disconnect the battery negative lead.
4   Drain the cooling system as described in Chapter 1.
5   Undo the two bolts securing the thermostatic sensor assembly to the thermostat housing. Withdraw the sensor assembly and gasket from its location in the housing **(see illustration)**. Note that a new gasket will be required when refitting.
6   Release the outer cable locknuts from the support bracket on the injection pump.
7   Release the inner cable end fitting from the injection pump fast idle lever. On the Bosch injection pump, the inner cable is released by slackening the screw securing the cable to the spring-loaded end fitting.
8   Remove the thermostatic sensor and cable assembly from the engine.

Refitting
9   Thoroughly clean all traces of old gasket from the thermostat housing and sensor mating faces, and place a new gasket in position.
10   Fit the sensor assembly, and secure with the retaining bolts.
11   Refit the inner and outer cable using the reverse of the removal procedure, but leave the outer cable locknuts (and securing screw of the spring-loaded end fitting on Bosch pumps) slack ready for adjustment.
12   Adjust the cable as described in the following paragraphs, then refill the cooling system (see Chapter 1) and reconnect the battery.

Adjustment
13   Move the fast idle control lever on the injection pump to the fast idle position, and temporarily secure it in this position.
14   On the Bosch injection pump, push the spring-loaded cable end fitting hard against the fast idle stop bracket, and tighten the screw to secure the inner cable to the end fitting **(see illustrations)**.

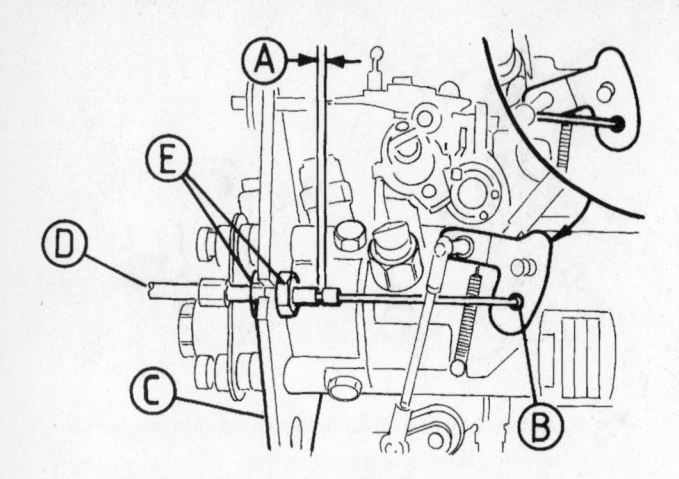

4•6 Chapter 4 Fuel, exhaust and emissions control systems

5.14b Fast idle adjustment on the Lucas/CAV fuel injection pump

- A 2 to 3 mm gap
- B Fast idle control lever
- C Support bracket
- D Outer cable
- E Locknuts

(Inset shows fast idle control lever in normal idle position)

15 Adjust the position of the locknuts so that a 2 to 3 mm gap exists between the end of the outer cable and the ferrule on the inner cable. Tighten the locknuts.
16 Check that, with the outer cable pulled towards the rear of the engine to tension the cable, the spring-loaded end fitting is against its stop (Bosch injection pump), or the fast idle control lever should be hard against the cold operation stop (Lucas/CAV injection pump). The 2 to 3 mm gap should still exist between the outer cable and the ferrule on the inner cable.
17 Release the fast idle control lever.

6 Stop solenoid - description, removal and refitting

Caution: *Be careful not to allow dirt into the injection pump during this procedure.*

Description

1 The stop solenoid is located on the fuel injection pump **(see illustrations)**. Its purpose is to cut the fuel supply when the ignition is switched off. If an open-circuit occurs in the solenoid or supply wiring, it will be impossible to start the engine, as the fuel will not reach the injectors.

Removal

2 Disconnect the battery negative lead.
3 Withdraw the rubber boot (where applicable), then unscrew the terminal nut and disconnect the wire from the top of the solenoid.
4 Carefully clean around the solenoid, then unscrew and withdraw the solenoid, and recover the sealing washer or O-ring (as applicable). Recover the solenoid plunger and spring if they remain in the pump.

Refitting

5 Refitting is a reversal of removal, using a new sealing washer or O-ring.

7 Fuel injection pump - removal and refitting

Caution: *Be careful not to allow dirt into the injection pump or injector pipes during this procedure. New sealing rings should be used on the fuel pipe unions when refitting.*

Removal

1 Disconnect the battery negative lead.
2 On 1995 model year vehicles onwards, release the heater element from the cooling system expansion tank, then undo the two retaining bolts and move the tank to one side.
3 Refer to Chapter 2A, Section 7 and remove the timing belt.
4 Undo the fuel injection pump sprocket bolts, then withdraw the plate and sprocket **(see illustrations)**.
5 According to engine type, refer to Section 3 and remove the air cleaner assembly if necessary, for improved access to the injection pump.
6 Cover the starter motor with a plastic bag, as a precaution against spillage of fuel.
7 Disconnect the fuel supply pipe from the injection pump. Recover the sealing washers from the banjo union, where applicable. Cover the open end of the pipe, and refit and cover the banjo bolt to keep dirt out.
8 Disconnect the main fuel return pipe and where fitted, the injector leak-off return pipe banjo union **(see illustration)**. Recover the sealing washers from the banjo union. Again, cover the open end of the hose and the banjo bolt, to keep dirt out.
9 Disconnect all relevant wiring from the pump. Note that on certain Bosch pumps, this can be achieved by simply disconnecting the wiring connectors at the brackets on the pump. On some pumps, it will be necessary to disconnect the wiring from the individual components (some connections may be protected by rubber covers). On turbocharged models with Lucas EPIC engine management, disconnect the large wiring multi-plug from the socket at the rear of the pump. Cover the opening in the pump after disconnection.

6.1 Stop solenoid (arrowed) on the Bosch fuel injection pump

7.4a Undo the fuel injection pump sprocket bolts . . .

7.4b . . . then withdraw the plate . . .

Chapter 4 Fuel, exhaust and emissions control systems   4-7

7.4c ... and sprocket

7.8 Disconnect the injector leak-off return pipe banjo union (arrowed) from the fuel injection pump

7.10 Cover the open fuel unions using small plastic bags, or fingers cut from rubber gloves

7.11 Disconnect the EGR throttle valve control rod

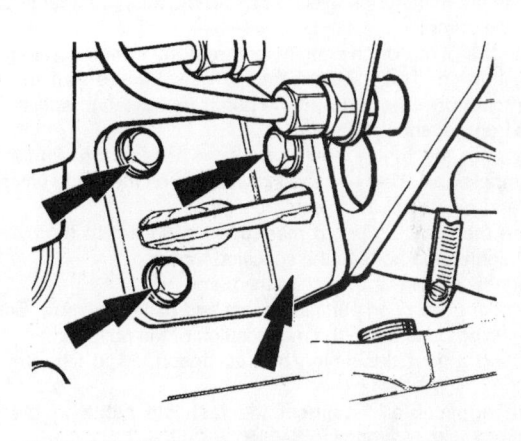

7.13 Undo the injection pump rear support bracket bolts (arrowed)

10 Unscrew the union nuts securing the injector pipes to the fuel injection pump and injectors. Counterhold the unions on the pump, while unscrewing the pipe-to-pump union nuts. Remove the pipes as a set. Cover open unions to keep dirt out, using small plastic bags, or fingers cut from discarded (but clean!) rubber gloves **(see illustration)**.
11 Disconnect the accelerator cable from the fuel injection pump, with reference to Section 13. Where fitted, disconnect the EGR throttle valve control rod **(see illustration)**.
12 Where applicable, disconnect the fast idle cable from the fuel injection pump, with reference to Section 5.
13 Undo the bolts and remove the injection pump rear support bracket **(see illustration)**.
14 Support the injection pump, and undo the front mounting nuts or bolts. Lift the pump up and off the engine **(see illustrations)**.

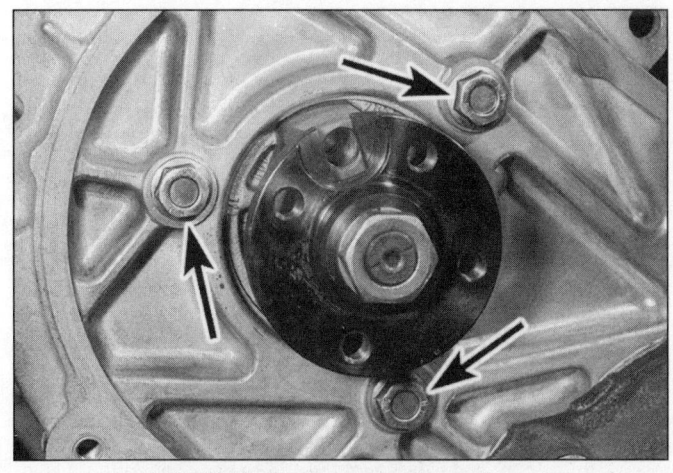

7.14a Undo the front mounting bolts . . .

7.14b . . . and lift the pump up and off the engine

4•8 Chapter 4 Fuel, exhaust and emissions control systems

9.2a Remove the blanking plug from the timing belt cover (arrowed) . . .

9.2b . . . and the rubber bung from the front of the crankshaft pulley

9.5 Insert the crankshaft timing peg (arrowed) into its hole at the rear of the engine

Refitting

15 Commence refitting the injection pump by fitting the rear support bracket to the pump.
16 Locate the pump on the engine and refit the front mounting nuts and bolts, tightened to the specified torque. Ensure that the rear support bracket does not prevent the pump from seating squarely on the engine front mounting flange.
17 Reconnect the fuel supply and return hoses, and tighten the unions, as applicable. Use new sealing washers on the banjo unions.
18 Refit and reconnect the injector fuel pipes.
19 Secure the injection pump rear support bracket to the cylinder block, and tighten the bolts to the specified torque.
20 Reconnect all relevant wiring to the pump.
21 Refit the fuel injection pump sprocket and plate assembly. Ensure that the retaining bolts are in the mid position of the pulley slots.
22 Refit and adjust the timing belt as described in Chapter 2A, Section 7.
23 Where applicable, reconnect the fast idle cable to the fuel injection pump, with reference to Section 5.
24 Reconnect the accelerator cable to the fuel injection pump, with reference to Section 13.
25 Refit the air cleaner, if removed, with reference to Section 3.
26 Reconnect the battery negative lead.
27 Remove the protective plastic bag from the starter motor.
28 Bleed the fuel system as described in Section 2.
29 Start the engine, and check the fuel injection pump adjustments as described in Chapter 1, Section 36.

8 Injection timing - checking and adjustment methods

1 Checking the injection timing is not a routine operation. It is only necessary after the injection pump or timing belt has been disturbed.
2 Injection timing checking is carried out simply by using pegs to lock the crankshaft, camshaft sprocket and injection pump sprocket. For checking, only the crankshaft and injection pump sprocket pegs are needed; for adjustment, the camshaft sprocket peg will be needed as well.
3 The locking pegs are available as Ford special tools, or as complete kits from Diesel injection equipment specialists. Alternatively, rods or drill bits of the correct sizes will suffice. The peg tool numbers and their diameters are as follows:
   Crankshaft: (Ford tool No. 23-020): 13 mm
   Camshaft: (Ford tool No. 21-123): 8 mm
   Injection pump:
   Lucas/CAV and early Bosch: (Ford tool No. 23-019): 6 mm
   Bosch with Stanadyne injectors - 1989 model year onwards: (Ford tool No. 23-029): 9 mm
4 Read through the procedures described in the following Section before starting work, to find out what is involved.

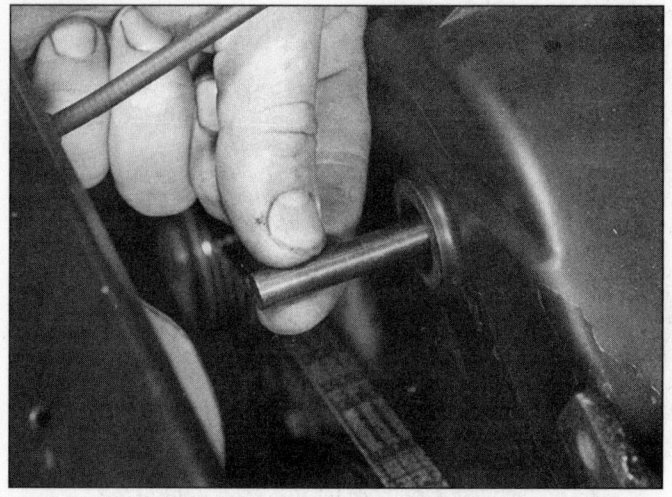

9.6 Fit the injection pump timing peg through the U-shaped cut-out, and into the drilling behind it

9 Injection timing - checking and adjustment

Note: *the timing pegs described in the previous Section will be necessary for the following checks and adjustments. Do not attempt to rotate the engine with any of the pegs in position, and do not use the pegs as a method of preventing engine rotation when slackening or tightening retaining nuts or bolts.*

Checking

1 Disconnect the battery negative lead.
2 Remove the blanking plug from the timing belt cover, and the rubber bung from the front of the crankshaft pulley **(see illustrations)**.
3 Remove the plastic plug from the crankshaft peg insertion hole at the rear of the engine just above the starter motor. On turbocharged engines with the Lucas EPIC system, the crankshaft position/speed sensor is located over the crankshaft peg insertion hole. Disconnect the wiring multi-plug, undo the retaining bolt, and remove the sensor. Recover the shim, if fitted, behind the sensor.
4 Turn the engine, using a spanner on the crankshaft pulley bolt, until the U-shaped cut-out in the injection pump sprocket becomes visible through the hole in the timing belt cover. It may be necessary to use a mirror to accurately observe the sprocket through the timing belt cover hole.
5 Insert the crankshaft timing peg into its hole, apply gentle pressure to the peg, and slowly turn the engine back and forth slightly until the peg engages with the hole in the flywheel **(see illustration)**.

Chapter 4 Fuel, exhaust and emissions control systems

9.10 Lock the camshaft sprocket by inserting the peg through the hole in the sprocket and into the drilling behind it

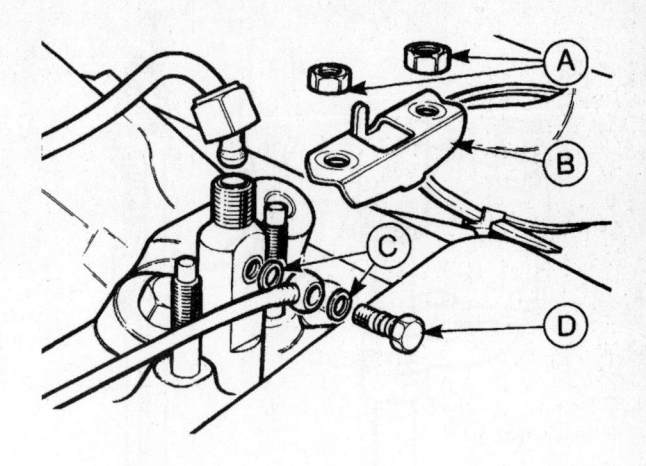

10.7 Fuel injector fittings on pre-1989 model year vehicles

- A Clamp nuts
- B Clamp
- C Banjo union washers
- D Banjo bolt

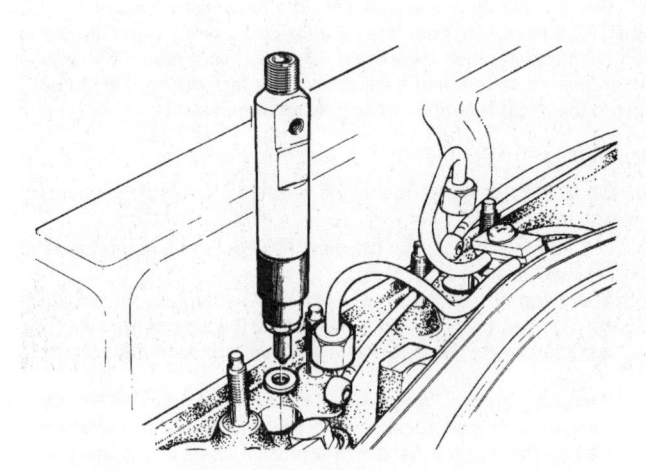

10.9 Pull the injectors out of their locations in the cylinder head

6 With the crankshaft peg inserted, try to fit the injection pump timing peg through the U-shaped cut-out and into the drilling behind it **(see illustration)**. If the peg enters easily, the injection pump timing is correct. Remove the timing pegs, refit the plugs and bungs, and reconnect the battery. On engines with a crankshaft position sensor, refit the sensor and spacing shim, if fitted.
7 If the timing peg will not go in, the injection pump timing must be adjusted as follows.

Adjustment

8 Refer to Chapter 2A and remove the timing belt cover.
9 If not already in place, insert the crankshaft timing peg into its hole as described previously in this Section.
10 Using the camshaft timing peg, lock the camshaft sprocket by inserting the peg through the hole in the sprocket, and into the drilling behind it **(see illustration)**.
11 Slacken the injection pump sprocket retaining bolts, and carefully tap one of the slackened bolts with a soft-faced mallet, in one direction or the other, until the timing peg can be fully inserted. Once the peg is in place, tighten the pump sprocket retaining bolts.
12 If there is insufficient movement allowed by the slots of the pump sprocket to enable the timing peg to be fitted, then it will be necessary to remove the timing belt and reposition it on the sprockets. Refer to the procedures contained in Chapter 2A, Section 7 for removal, refitting and tensioning of the timing belt.
13 On completion, remove the timing pegs, and refit the disturbed components with reference to their relevant Chapters.

10 Fuel injectors - testing, removal and refitting

Warning: *Exercise extreme caution when working on the fuel injectors. Never expose the hands or any part of the body to injector spray, as the high working pressure can cause the fuel to penetrate the skin, with possibly fatal results. You are strongly advised to have any work which involves testing the injectors under pressure carried out by a dealer or fuel injection specialist.*

Testing

1 Injectors do deteriorate with prolonged use, and it is reasonable to expect them to need reconditioning or renewal after 60 000 miles (100 000 km) or so. Accurate testing, overhaul and calibration of the injectors must be left to a specialist. A defective injector which is causing knocking or smoking can be located without dismantling as follows.
2 Run the engine at a fast idle. Slacken each injector union in turn, placing rag around the union to catch spilt fuel, and being careful not to expose the skin to any spray. When the union on the defective injector is slackened, the knocking or smoking will stop.

Removal

Bosch or Lucas/CAV injectors

3 Fuel injectors of either Bosch or Lucas/CAV manufacture are fitted to all engines up to the 1989 model year.
4 Disconnect the battery negative lead.
5 Remove the air cleaner assembly as described in Section 3.
6 Carefully clean around the injectors and injector pipe union nuts.
7 Undo the fuel supply union nuts and the leak-off pipe banjo bolts. Withdraw the pipes from the injectors, and plug or cap the open unions. Recover the two copper washers from each banjo bolt union **(see illustration)**.
8 Unscrew the injector clamp nuts, and remove the clamp from each injector.
9 Pull the injectors out of their locations in the cylinder head **(see illustration)**. If they are tight, use an injector puller. Recover the sealing washers from the injector tips, or from the holes in the cylinder head. Fit protective caps to the injector nozzles while they are removed.

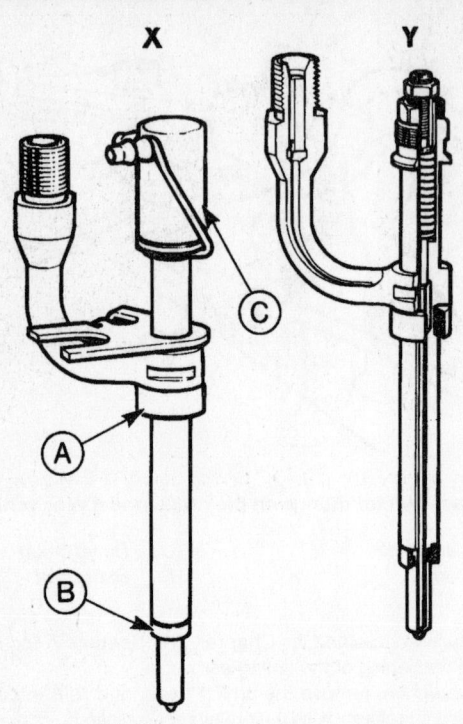

4-10 Chapter 4 Fuel, exhaust and emissions control systems

10.10 Stanadyne "slim-tip" injectors (X) as used from 1989 onwards

A Dust seal
B PTFE seal
C Leak-off cap
Y Cutaway view of injector

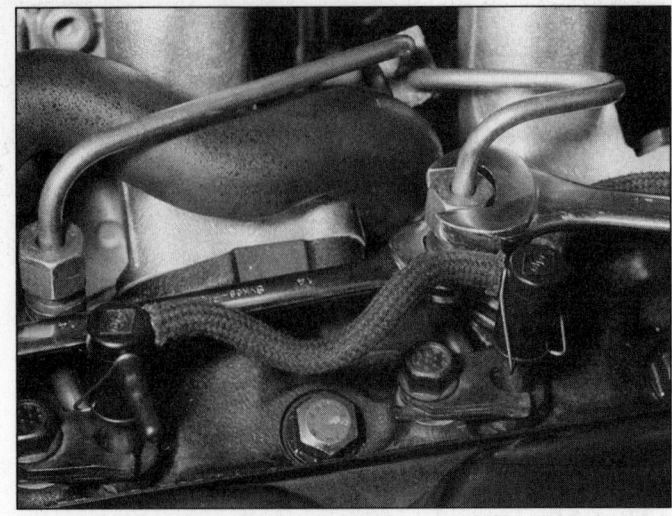

10.14 Unscrew the fuel supply pipe unions from the injectors

Stanadyne "slim-tip" injectors

10 Stanadyne "slim-tip" fuel injectors are fitted to all engines from the 1989 model year onwards **(see illustration)**.
11 Disconnect the battery negative lead.
12 Remove the air cleaner assembly as described in Section 3.
13 Carefully clean around the injectors and injector pipe union nuts.
14 Unscrew the fuel supply pipe unions from the injectors **(see illustration)**. If necessary, use a second spanner to counterhold the injector as the pipe union is undone. Plug or cap the open unions.
15 Carefully pull the fuel leak-off pipes from the injectors **(see illustration)**.
16 Undo the injector clamp bolts and remove the clamp plate assemblies.
17 Pull the injectors out of their locations in the cylinder head. If they are stuck, use Ford removal tool 23-030 or a proprietary injector puller.

Do not try to lever the injectors free **(see illustrations)**.
18 Remove the dust-seal washers from the injector bodies. Remove the PTFE sealing washers from the injector tips by carefully cutting them with a knife, then ease them off using pliers **(see illustrations)**. Obtain new dust-seal and sealing washers for refitting. Fit protective caps to the injector nozzles while they are removed.

Refitting

19 On all injector types, refitting is a reversal of removal, noting the following points:

a) Use new injector sealing washers, PTFE washers and banjo union copper washers, as applicable.
b) If working on the Bosch or Lucas/CAV injectors, note that the injector leak-off pipe connections face towards the rocker cover, and the pointed ends of the injector clamps face the front of the engine.
c) If working on the Stanadyne injectors, fit the new PTFE sealing washers with their recesses facing upwards. Fit the washers by placing them in the handle of tool 23-030, or in a suitably-sized socket or shouldered tube clamped in a vice. Push the injector tip through the washer **(see illustrations)**.
d) Tighten all fastenings and unions to the specified torque. Make sure that the injector pipes are not under strain.
e) Prime the fuel system as described in Section 2, then start the engine and check for fuel leaks.

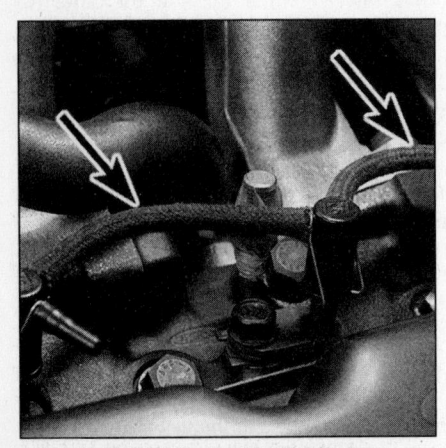

10.15 Pull the fuel leak-off pipes (arrowed) from the injectors

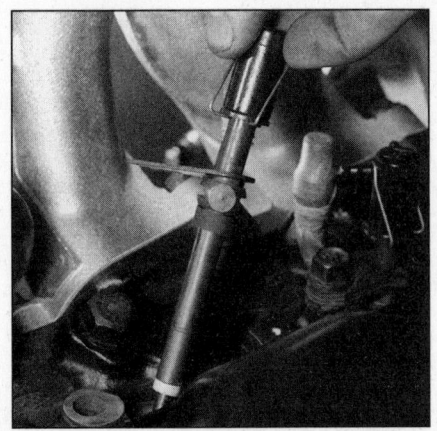

10.17a Pull the injectors out of their locations in the cylinder head . . .

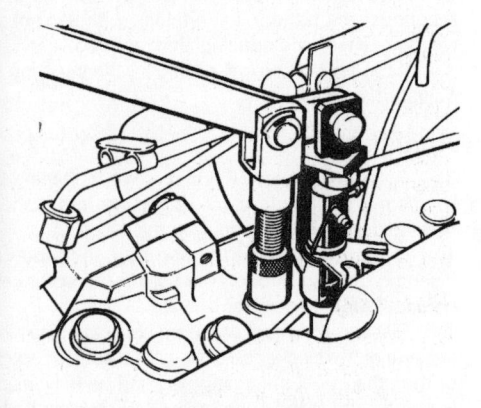

10.17b . . . If they are stuck, use Ford removal tool 23-030 or a proprietary injector puller

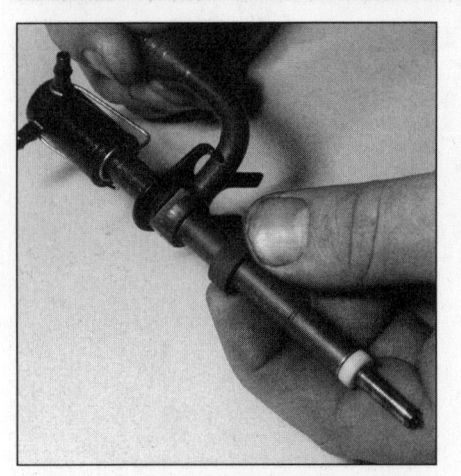

Chapter 4 Fuel, exhaust and emissions control systems

10.18a Remove the dust-seal washers from the injector bodies

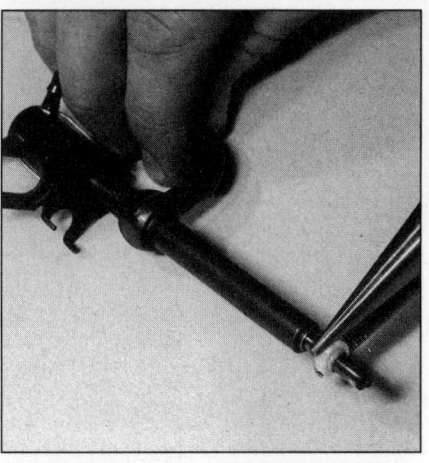

10.18b Remove the PTFE sealing washers from the injector tips

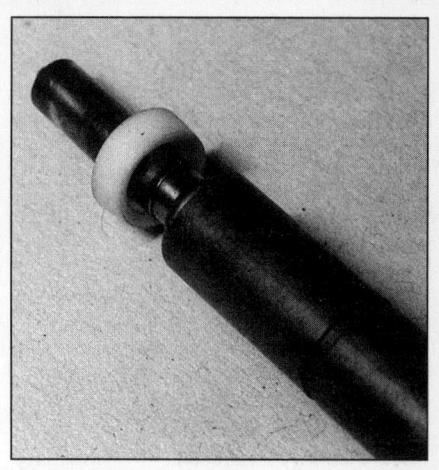

10.19a Fit the new PTFE sealing washers with their recesses facing upwards

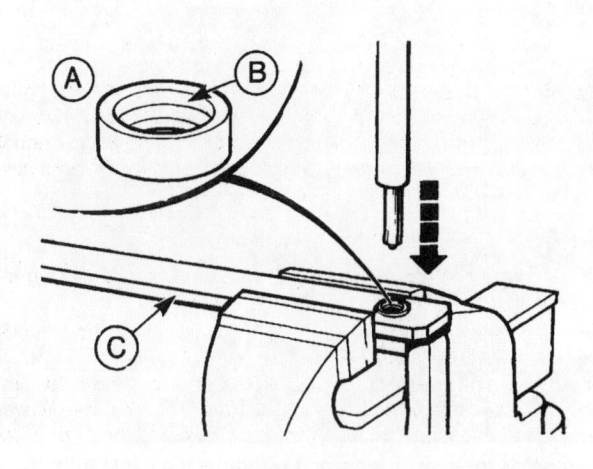

10.19b Correct fitting of Stanadyne injector sealing washers (A)

B Recess   C Fitting tool

11 Fuel injector delivery pipes - removal and refitting

Removal

1 Disconnect the battery negative lead.
2 According to engine type, refer to Section 3 and remove the air cleaner assembly if necessary, for improved access to the injection pump.
3 Cover the starter motor with a plastic bag, as a precaution against spillage of fuel.
4 Remove the clamps from the injector pipes, then unscrew the pipe unions at the injectors and fuel injection pump. Use a second spanner to counterhold the injector if necessary as the pipe union is undone. Plug or cap the open unions.
5 Carefully remove the injector pipes from the engine, taking care not to bend or distort them as they are removed.

Refitting

6 Refitting is a reversal of removal, noting the following points:
  a) Tighten all the pipe unions finger-tight initially, then tighten them fully once they all are connected.
  b) Tighten all unions to the specified torque. Make sure that the injector pipes are not under strain.
  c) Prime the fuel system as described in Section 2, then start the engine and check for fuel leaks.

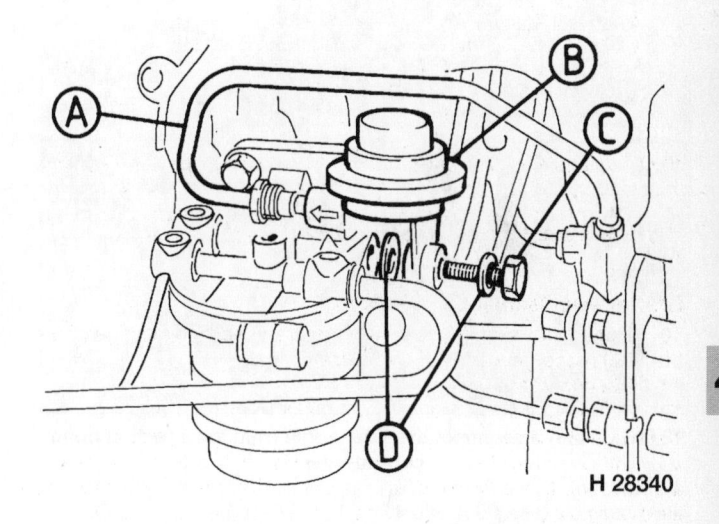

12.4 Details of the Lucas/CAV fuel filter assembly with hand-priming pump

A Fuel feed pipes   C Banjo bolt
B Hand-priming pump   D Sealing washers

12 Fuel filter assembly - removal and refitting

Removal

1 Disconnect the battery negative lead.
2 According to engine type, refer to Section 3 and remove the air cleaner assembly if necessary, for improved access to the filter assembly.
3 Cover the starter motor with a plastic bag, as a precaution against spillage of fuel.
4 On the Lucas/CAV filter assembly with hand-priming pump, unscrew the unions and remove the fuel pipe between the hand-priming pump and the fuel injection pump. Undo the banjo bolt and sealing washers, and remove the hand-priming pump from the filter assembly **(see illustration)**.
5 Unscrew the unions, and remove the fuel pipe between the filter assembly and the fuel injection pump.
6 Unscrew the unions, and remove the fuel supply pipe from the

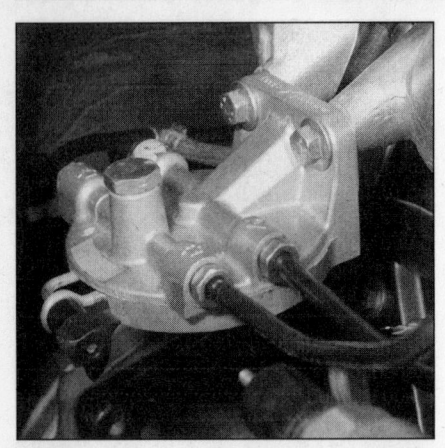

4-12　Chapter 4　Fuel, exhaust and emissions control systems

12.6 Fuel pipe unions and filter mounting bolts on the Bosch fuel filter assembly (shown with element removed)

13.3 Prise off the clip (arrowed) retaining the accelerator cable to the pedal, and unhook the cable

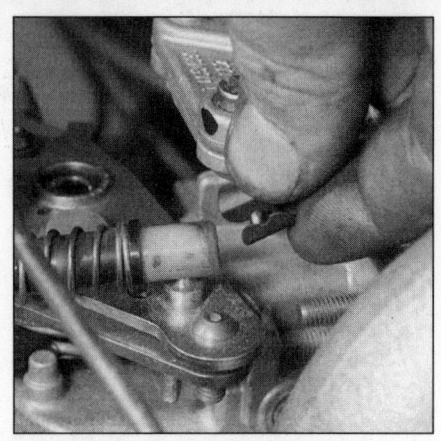

13.6a Extract the retaining clip . . .

13.6b . . . and disconnect the inner cable from the injection pump control lever

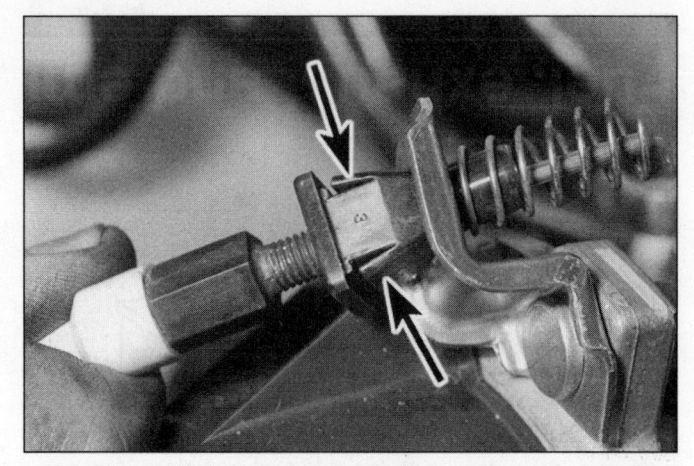

13.8 Depress the plastic legs, and withdraw the cable from the support bracket

filter assembly **(see illustration)**.
7　Where a water-in-fuel sensor is fitted, disconnect the wiring multi-plug from the filter body.
8　Undo the two retaining bolts and remove the filter assembly.

Refitting

9　Refitting is a reversal of removal. Use new sealing washers, and tighten all fastenings and unions to the specified torque.
10　On completion, prime the fuel system as described in Section 2, then start the engine and check for leaks.

13　Accelerator cable - removal, refitting and adjustment

Removal

1　Disconnect the battery negative lead.
2　According to engine type, refer to Section 3 and remove the air cleaner assembly if necessary, for improved access to the fuel injection pump.
3　Prise off the clip retaining the cable to the accelerator pedal, and unhook the cable **(see illustration)**.
4　Working in the engine compartment, release the cable from the bulkhead, and pull it through.
5　Release the cable ties or clips securing the cable to the radiator or front panel.
6　Extract the retaining clip, and disconnect the inner cable from the injection pump control lever **(see illustrations)**.

7　Prise the spring clip from the cable bracket using a screwdriver.
8　Depress the plastic legs, and withdraw the cable from the support bracket **(see illustration)**.
9　Remove the cable from the engine compartment.

Refitting

10　Refitting is a reversal of removal, but ensure that the cable is routed correctly; on completion, adjust the cable as follows.

Adjustment

11　Have an assistant fully depress the accelerator pedal, then check that the injection pump control lever is in the full-throttle position. If not, turn the adjuster on the outer cable as necessary.
12　Release the accelerator pedal, and check that the injection pump control lever returns to the idle position.

14　Accelerator pedal - removal and refitting

Removal

All normally-aspirated engines, and pre-1995 model year turbocharged engines

1　Disconnect the battery negative lead.
2　Prise free the retaining clip, and detach the accelerator cable from the pedal.
3　Pivot the two square-headed pedal bushes through 45°, and detach them. Withdraw the pedal and shaft unit.

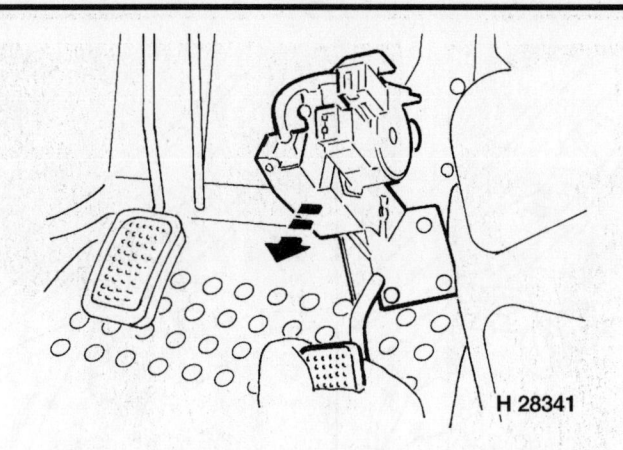

Chapter 4 Fuel, exhaust and emissions control systems

14.8 Withdraw the accelerator pedal and pedal position sensor assembly from inside the vehicle

Turbocharged engines, 1995 model year onwards

4 On later turbocharged engines, the accelerator pedal incorporates the pedal position sensor used by the engine management system (see Section 27).
5 Disconnect the battery negative lead.
6 Disconnect the wiring multi-plugs at the top of the accelerator pedal assembly.
7 From within the engine compartment, undo the retaining nuts securing the pedal assembly to the bulkhead.
8 Withdraw the pedal and sensor assembly from inside the vehicle **(see illustration)**.

Refitting

All models

9 Refitting is a reversal of removal. Where applicable, reconnect the accelerator cable to the pedal, and adjust if necessary as described in Section 13.

15 Fuel gauge sender unit - removal and refitting

Removal

1 Remove the fuel tank as described in Section 16.
2 Unscrew the sender unit from the tank. There is a Ford tool (No. 23-014) which engages with the lugs on the unit, but with patience, a pair of crossed screwdrivers or similar items can be used instead.
3 Remove the sender unit, taking care not to damage the float, nor bend the float arm. Recover the seal **(see illustration)**.
4 A defective sender unit must be renewed; spares are not available. Renew the seal in any case.

Refitting

5 Before refitting the sender unit, examine the condition of the sealing ring, and renew if necessary.
6 Refitting is a reversal of removal.

16 Fuel tank - removal, repair and refitting

Note: *The fuel tank does not incorporate a drain plug, so it is advisable to let the fuel level run down as much as possible prior to removal. Syphon the remaining fuel in the tank using proprietary fuel draining equipment. Refer to the precautions given in "Safety first!" at the start of this manual before proceeding.*

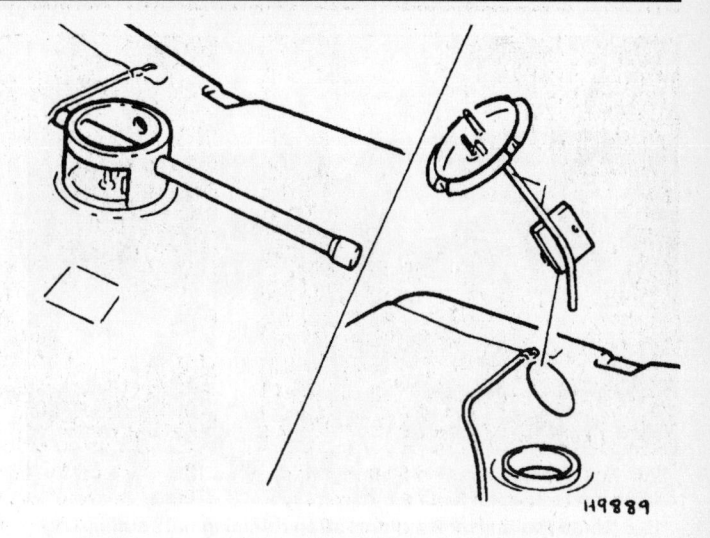

15.3 Remove the fuel gauge sender unit (using the special tool if necessary), taking care not to damage the float, nor bend the float arm

16.5 On early models, release the clips and disconnect the fuel filler hose and vent pipes at the side of the fuel tank

Removal

1 Disconnect the battery negative lead.
2 On 1992 model year onwards vehicles, remove the filler cap, and release the filler neck bezel. On 1992 to 1995 model year vehicles, Ford special tool 23-037 is (theoretically) needed to release and reinsert the bezel into the body aperture, although with patience, it should be possible to do this without the tool. On later models, a simpler method is employed, and the bezel is retained by a single screw; in this case, the special tool is not required.
3 Raise and support the vehicle on axle stands, to allow sufficient working clearance underneath for detaching and removing the tank.
4 Locate a trolley jack or stands under the tank, set at a height which will allow the tank to be partially lowered and supported whilst the upper attachments are disconnected.
5 On early models, release the clips and disconnect the fuel filler hose and vent pipes at the side of the tank **(see illustration)**. On later models, the filler pipe is an integral part of the tank, and is not detachable.
6 Undo the fuel tank support strap retaining nuts sufficiently to allow the straps to be unhooked from the underbody. Note the position

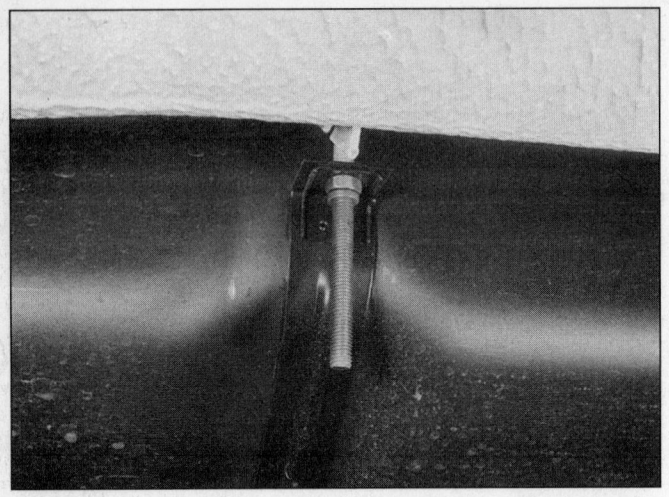

4-14 Chapter 4 Fuel, exhaust and emissions control systems

16.6 Undo the fuel tank support strap retaining nuts sufficiently to allow the straps to be unhooked from the underbody

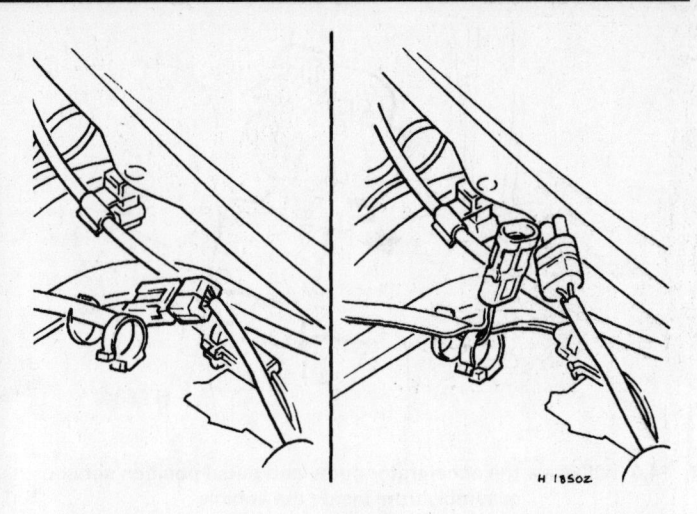

16.7 Disconnect the fuel and electrical connections at the top of the tank

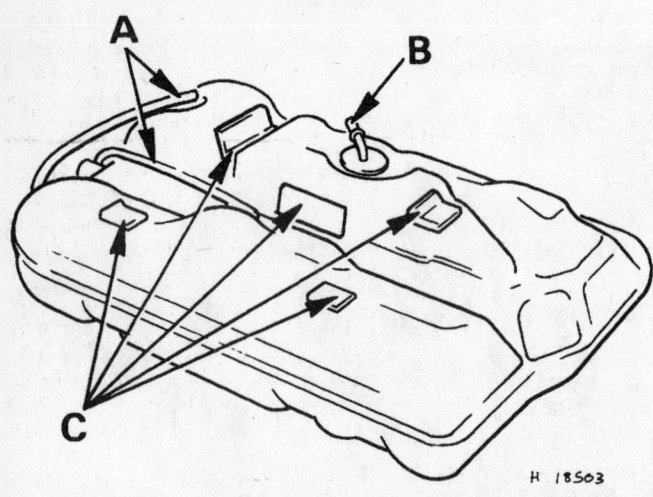

16.11a Fuel tank and fittings - short-wheelbase models

A Vent pipes
B Fuel supply outlet
C Insulation pad locations

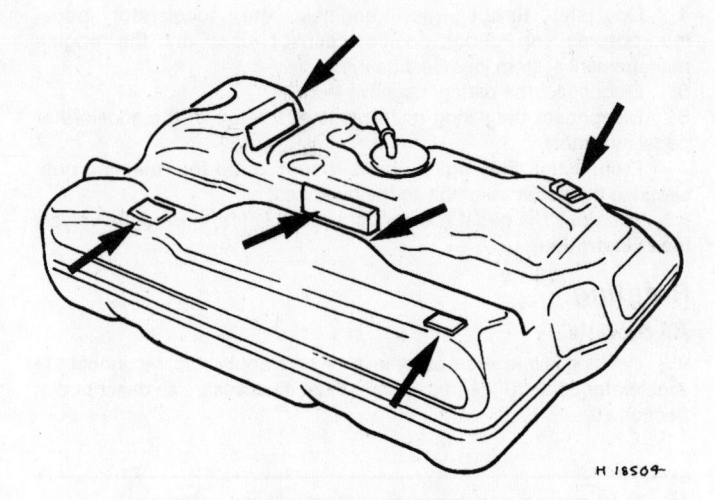

16.11b Fuel tank insulation pad locations (arrowed) on long-wheelbase models

of the nuts relative to the threads on the strap hook bolts before removal, to ensure correct refitting **(see illustration)**.
7 Lower the tank onto the jack or stands, then disconnect the fuel and electrical connections at the top of the tank **(see illustration)**. Note that on later models, the fuel pipe unions incorporate quick-release couplings. Release the protruding locking lugs on each union by squeezing them together and carefully pulling the coupling apart.
8 With all attachments disconnected, lower the tank and remove it from under the vehicle.
9 If the fuel tank is to be renewed, detach the ventilation pipes (where applicable) and remove the fuel gauge sender unit as described in Section 15.

Repair

10 The tank is made of plastic. If it is damaged, it should be renewed. Proprietary repair kits are available, but check that they are suitable for use on plastic tanks. A fuel leak is not just expensive, it is dangerous.

Refitting

11 Refitting is a reversal of the removal procedure, but note the following additional points:

a) Fit a new sender unit seal (if the sender was removed).
b) Replace any crimped type hose clips with screw types.
c) Fit new tank insulation pads into position as shown, where applicable **(see illustrations)**.
d) Tighten the tank retaining strap hook bolt nuts to the positions noted during removal, to ensure that they are not overtightened.
e) Fit new cable clips when securing the fuel line(s).
f) Ensure that the fuel ventilation pipes are routed correctly, according to model.

17 Fuel pump - removal and refitting

Removal

1 Disconnect the battery negative lead.
2 For improved access, undo the two bolts and remove the fuel pump heat shield **(see illustration)**.
3 Disconnect the fuel hoses from the fuel pump, noting their respective connections for refitting. Where quick-release couplings are used on the fuel hoses, release the protruding locking lugs on each union by squeezing them together and carefully pulling the coupling apart. Use rag to soak up any spilt fuel. Where the unions are colour-

Chapter 4 Fuel, exhaust and emissions control systems   4-15

17.2 Fuel pump heat shield and pump

18.2 Remove the air cleaner inlet duct from the inlet manifold

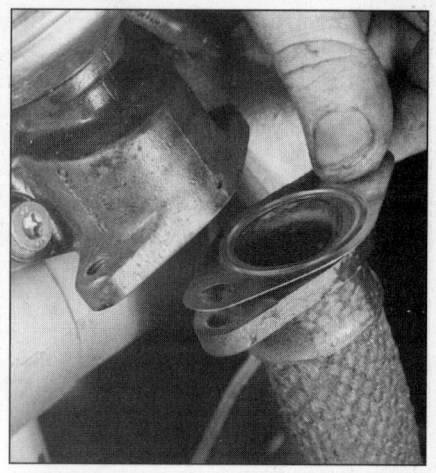

18.5a Disconnect the EGR connecting hose at the throttle housing, and recover the metal gasket . . .

18.5b . . . or on later models, slacken the clamp ring (arrowed) to release the pipe

18.5c Disconnect the throttle actuating lever at the throttle housing

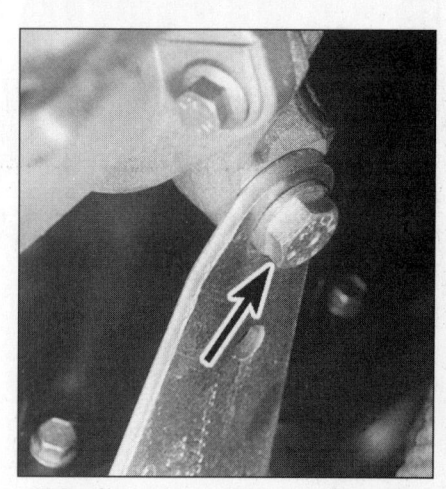

18.8a On engines with a two-piece inlet manifold, undo the bolt (arrowed) securing the manifold to the support bracket

coded, the pipes cannot be confused. Where both unions are the same colour, note carefully which pipe is connected to which, and ensure that they are correctly reconnected on refitting. Plug the hoses, to prevent the ingress of dirt and fuel spillage.
4 Unscrew and remove the retaining nuts, and remove the fuel pump.
5 Recover the O-ring seal from the pump, noting that a new seal will be required for refitting.
6 Thoroughly clean the mating faces on the pump and engine.

Refitting

7 Refit in the reverse order of removal. Be sure to use a new O-ring seal, and tighten the securing bolts/nuts securely. Ensure that the hoses are correctly and securely reconnected. Where quick-release couplings are fitted, press them together until the locking lugs snap into their groove.
8 On completion, prime the fuel system as described in Section 2, then start the engine and check for leaks.

18 Inlet manifold - removal and refitting

Note: *The design of the inlet manifold and its attachments to the engine varies considerably according to model year, engine power*

output, and equipment fitted (EGR system, turbocharger, engine management etc). The following procedures cover removal and refitting of the manifold with the ancillary components still attached. If necessary, these can be removed later by referring to the relevant Chapters and Sections of this manual.

Removal

1 Disconnect the battery negative lead.
2 Remove the air cleaner assembly, or the air cleaner inlet duct from the inlet manifold, according to engine type **(see illustration)**.
3 Where applicable, undo the two bolts securing the fuel filter assembly to the inlet manifold. Ease the filter assembly away from the manifold as far as the fuel pipes will allow.
4 Disconnect the engine breather hose from the manifold.
5 On engines with exhaust gas recirculation, disconnect the EGR connecting hose/pipe at the throttle housing, and recover the metal gasket, where applicable. Disconnect the throttle actuating lever at the throttle housing **(see illustrations)**.
6 On turbocharged engines, slacken the hose clips and disconnect the inlet pipe at the hose connection on the inlet manifold.
7 Mark the locations as an aid to reassembly, then disconnect any remaining hose and electrical connections as necessary.
8 On engines with a two-piece inlet manifold, undo the bolt securing the manifold to the support bracket. Undo the nuts and bolts, and separate the manifold upper section from the lower section.

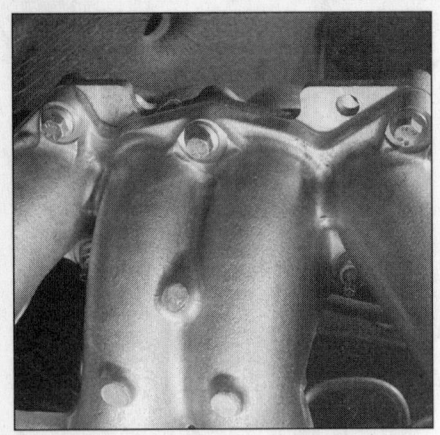

4-16　**Chapter 4　Fuel, exhaust and emissions control systems**

18.8b Undo the nuts and bolts . . .

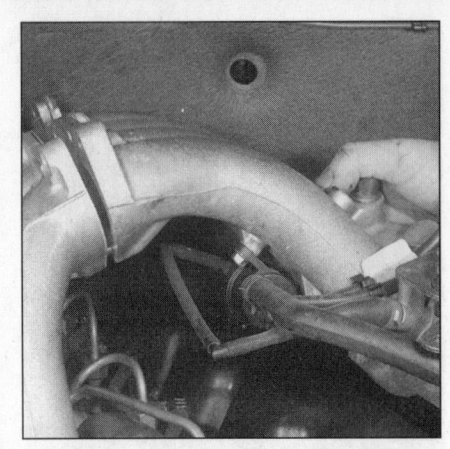

18.8c . . . separate the manifold upper section from the lower section . . .

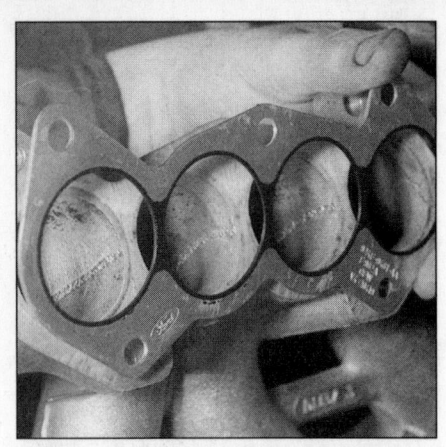

18.8d . . . and recover the gasket between the two halves

18.9 Withdraw the manifold from the cylinder head, and recover the gasket

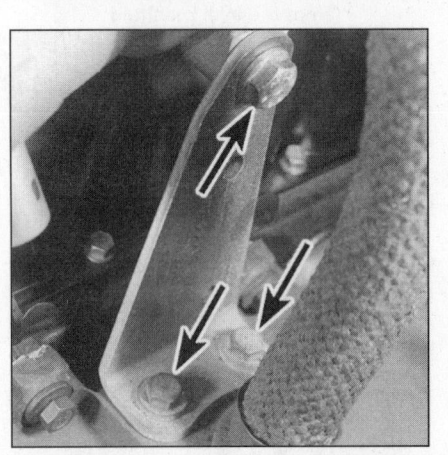

19.5 Undo the bolts (arrowed) securing the support bracket to the exhaust manifold and throttle housing

19.6 Removing the exhaust manifold from the engine

Recover the gasket between the two halves **(see illustrations)**.

9 Undo the nuts and bolts securing the manifold to the cylinder head, then withdraw the manifold and recover the gasket **(see illustration)**.

Refitting

10 Refitting is a reversal of removal. Use new gaskets at the manifold and EGR system joints (as applicable), and tighten all nuts and bolts to the specified torque.

19 Exhaust manifold - removal and refitting

Normally-aspirated engines
Removal
1 Disconnect the battery negative lead.
2 For improved access, remove the air cleaner assembly or the air cleaner inlet duct from the inlet manifold, according to engine type.
3 Apply the handbrake, then raise the front of the vehicle and support it securely on axle stands.
4 Disconnect the exhaust downpipe from the manifold flange. Recover the gasket.
5 On engines with exhaust gas recirculation, disconnect the EGR connecting hose at the throttle housing, and recover the metal gasket. Undo the bolts securing the support bracket to the exhaust manifold and throttle housing, and remove the bracket **(see illustration)**.
6 Undo the bolts securing the exhaust manifold to the cylinder head, and remove the manifold from the engine **(see illustration)**.
7 Thoroughly clean the manifold and cylinder head mating faces prior to refitting.

Refitting
8 Refitting is a reversal of removal. Use suitable heat-resistant jointing compound on the exhaust manifold-to-cylinder head mating face, and tighten the retaining bolts to the specified torque.

Turbocharged engines
9 On turbocharged engines, the exhaust manifold is removed complete with the turbocharger, as described in the Section 21.

20 Turbocharger - description and precautions

Description
1 On turbocharged engines, the turbocharger increases engine efficiency by raising the pressure in the inlet manifold above atmospheric pressure. Instead of the air simply being sucked into the cylinders, it is forced in. Additional fuel is supplied by the injection pump in proportion to the increased air inlet.
2 Energy for the operation of the turbocharger comes from the exhaust gas. The gas flows through a specially-shaped housing (the turbine housing) and in so doing, spins the turbine wheel. The turbine wheel is attached to a shaft, at the end of which is another vaned wheel, known as the compressor wheel. The compressor wheel spins

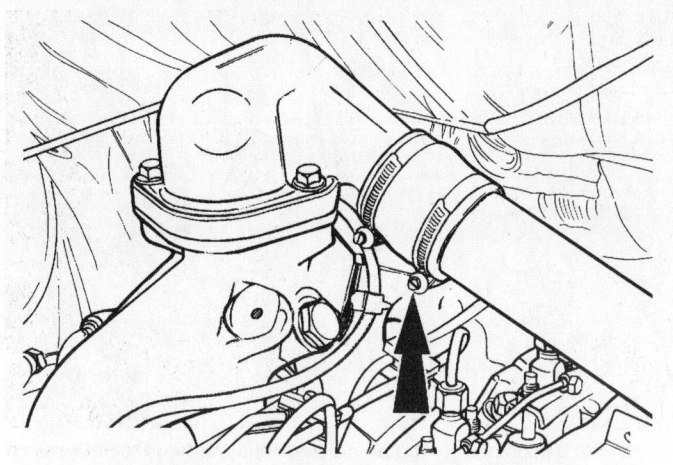

Chapter 4 Fuel, exhaust and emissions control systems

21.3 Slacken the hose clip (arrowed) and disconnect the inlet pipe at the hose connection on the inlet manifold

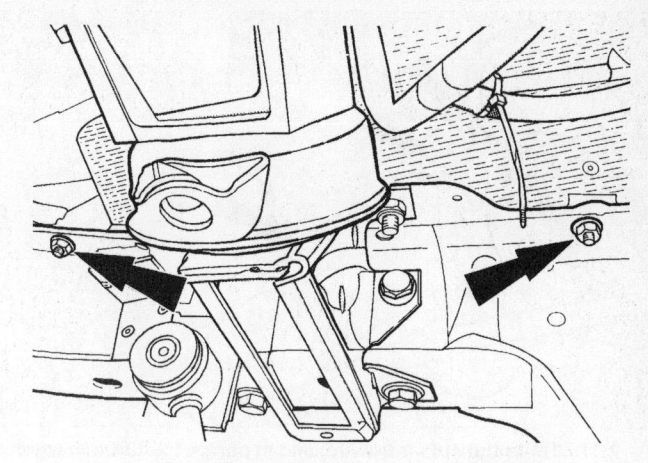

21.4 Undo the heatshield retaining nuts and bolts (lower nuts shown - arrowed)

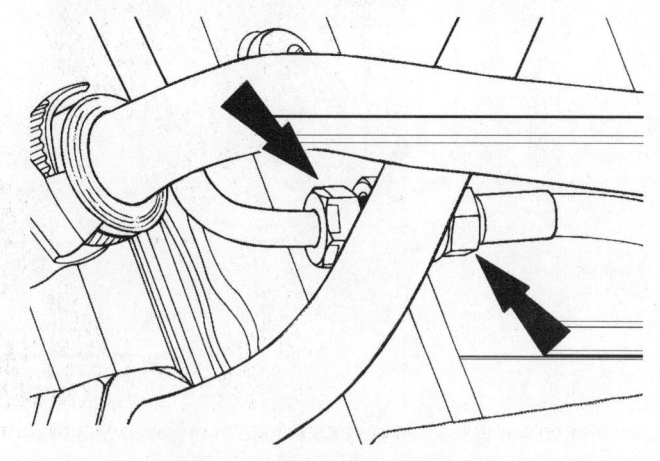

21.8 Disconnect the turbocharger high-pressure oil pipe at the flexible hose coupling (arrowed)

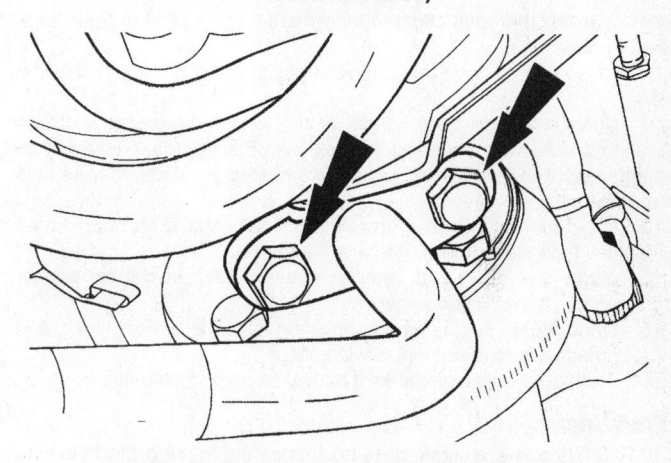

21.9 Undo the two bolts (arrowed) and disconnect the turbocharger oil return pipe at the flange joint

in its own housing, and compresses the inlet air on the way to the inlet manifold.
3 Boost pressure (the pressure in the inlet manifold) is limited by a wastegate, which diverts the exhaust gas away from the turbine wheel in response to a pressure-sensitive actuator.
4 The turbo shaft is pressure-lubricated by an oil feed pipe from the main oil gallery. The shaft "floats" on a cushion of oil. A drain pipe returns the oil to the sump.

Precautions

5 The turbocharger operates at extremely high speeds and temperatures. Certain precautions must be observed, to avoid premature failure of the turbo, or injury to the operator.
6 Do not operate the turbo with any of its parts exposed, or with any of its hoses removed. Foreign objects falling onto the rotating vanes could cause excessive damage, and (if ejected) personal injury.
7 Do not race the engine immediately after start-up, especially if it is cold. Give the oil a few seconds to circulate.
8 Always allow the engine to return to idle speed before switching it off - do not blip the throttle and switch off, as this will leave the turbo spinning without lubrication.
9 Allow the engine to idle for several minutes before switching off after a high-speed run.
10 Observe the recommended intervals for oil and filter changing, and use a reputable oil of the specified quality. Neglect of oil changing, or use of inferior oil, can cause carbon formation on the turbo shaft, leading to subsequent failure.

21 Turbocharger - removal and refitting

Pre-1992 model year vehicles

Removal

1 Disconnect the battery negative lead.
2 Remove the air cleaner assembly as described in Section 3.
3 Undo the bolts, detach the inlet pipe connection at the turbocharger end, and recover the gasket. Slacken the hose clips, and disconnect the inlet pipe at the hose connection on the inlet manifold **(see illustration)**. Release the pipe from the support bracket, and remove it from the engine. Close off the turbocharger inlet using a suitable cap or clean rag.
4 Undo the heatshield retaining nuts and bolts, raise the windscreen/headlight washer reservoir, and remove the heatshield **(see illustration)**.
5 Undo the bolt, and remove the oil breather pipe support bracket attachment from the exhaust manifold.
6 Apply the handbrake, then raise the front of the vehicle and support it securely on axle stands.
7 Disconnect the exhaust downpipe from the turbocharger outlet connection. Recover the gasket.
8 Slacken the union nuts, and disconnect the turbocharger high-pressure oil pipe at the flexible hose coupling **(see illustration)**.
9 Undo the two bolts and disconnect the turbocharger oil return pipe at the flange joint **(see illustration)**. Be prepared for a small quantity of oil to be released from the turbocharger as the flange joint is released.

4-18 Chapter 4 Fuel, exhaust and emissions control systems

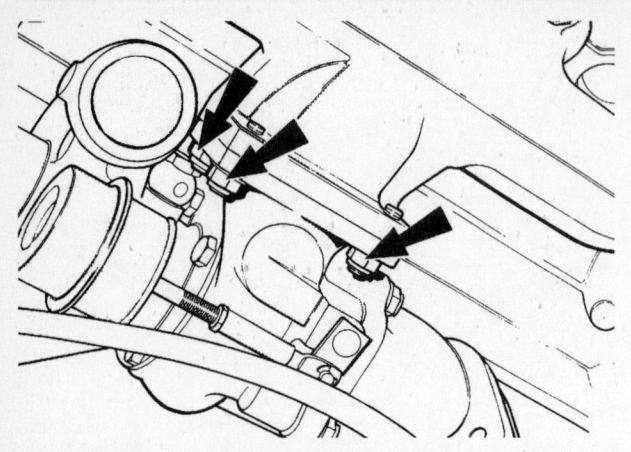

21.13 Undo the nuts (arrowed) and separate the turbocharger from the exhaust manifold

10 Slacken the hose clip securing the oil return pipe to the sump, and remove the pipe.
11 Undo and remove the turbocharger support bracket mounting bolts.
12 Suitably support the weight of the turbocharger and exhaust manifold assembly, then undo the exhaust manifold-to-cylinder head flange nuts. Remove the turbocharger and exhaust manifold assembly from the vehicle.
13 Undo the nuts and separate the turbocharger from the exhaust manifold **(see illustration)**. Recover the gasket.
14 Undo the nuts and remove the exhaust downpipe elbow connection at the turbocharger.
15 Undo the oil supply pipe connection from the turbocharger, and cover the aperture to prevent dirt ingress.
16 Thoroughly clean all the joint mating faces prior to refitting.

Refitting

17 Refitting is a reversal of removal, bearing in mind the following points:
   a) *Use new gaskets at all the flange joints, and new nuts at the turbocharger-to-manifold connection, and at the exhaust downpipe elbow-to-turbocharger connection.*
   b) *Use suitable heat-resistant jointing compound on the exhaust manifold-to-cylinder head mating face.*
   c) *When refitting the turbocharger support bracket, slacken all the mounting bolts, align the bracket to ensure that no strain is evident at the bracket flanges, then tighten the bolts.*
   d) *Use new copper washers when reconnecting the high-pressure oil pipe.*
   e) *Tighten all nuts and bolts to the specified torque.*
   f) *On completion, disconnect the wiring connection at the fuel injection pump stop solenoid. Turn the engine over on the starter motor until the oil pressure warning light is extinguished, then reconnect the stop solenoid and start the engine.*

1992 model year onwards

Removal

18 Disconnect the battery negative lead.
19 Remove the air cleaner assembly as described in Section 3.
20 Undo the bolts, detach the inlet pipe connection at the turbocharger end, and recover the gasket. Slacken the hose clips, and disconnect the inlet pipe at the hose connection on the inlet manifold **(see illustration)**. Release the pipe from the support bracket, and remove it from the engine. Close off the turbocharger inlet using a suitable cap or clean rag.
21 Undo the two bolts, and remove the air cleaner support bracket from the exhaust manifold.
22 Disconnect the EGR valve multi-plug and vacuum hoses, then undo the two Torx bolts and remove the EGR valve **(see illustration)**.

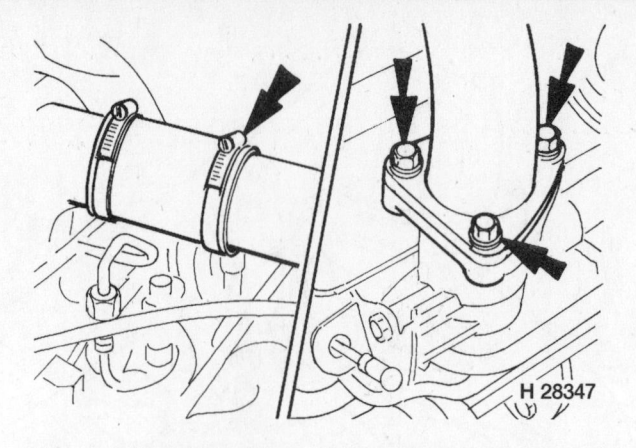

21.20 Detach the inlet pipe connections (arrowed) at the inlet manifold and turbocharger

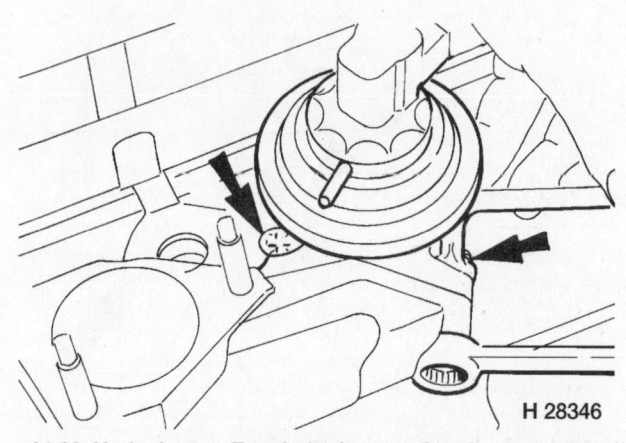

21.22 Undo the two Torx bolts (arrowed) and remove the EGR valve

23 Apply the handbrake, then raise the front of the vehicle and support it securely on axle stands.
24 Undo the four bolts and remove the engine undershield.
25 Remove the EGR throttle body housing.
26 Undo the unions, and disconnect the turbocharger oil feed and return pipes.
27 Undo the two exhaust downpipe support bracket bolts next to the fuel pump heatshield.
28 Undo the three nuts, and separate the exhaust downpipe from the turbocharger outlet flange.
29 Suitably support the weight of the turbocharger and exhaust manifold assembly, then undo the exhaust manifold-to-cylinder head flange nuts and bolts. Remove the turbocharger and exhaust manifold assembly from the vehicle.
30 Undo the nuts, and separate the turbocharger from the exhaust manifold. Recover the gasket.
31 Undo the nuts, and remove the exhaust downpipe elbow connection at the turbocharger.
32 Thoroughly clean all the joint mating faces prior to refitting.

Refitting

33 Refitting is a reversal of removal, bearing in mind the following points:
   a) *Use new gaskets at all the flange joints, and new nuts at the turbocharger-to-manifold connection, and at the exhaust downpipe elbow-to-turbocharger connection.*
   b) *Use suitable heat-resistant jointing compound on the exhaust manifold-to-cylinder head mating face.*
   c) *Tighten all nuts and bolts to the specified torque.*

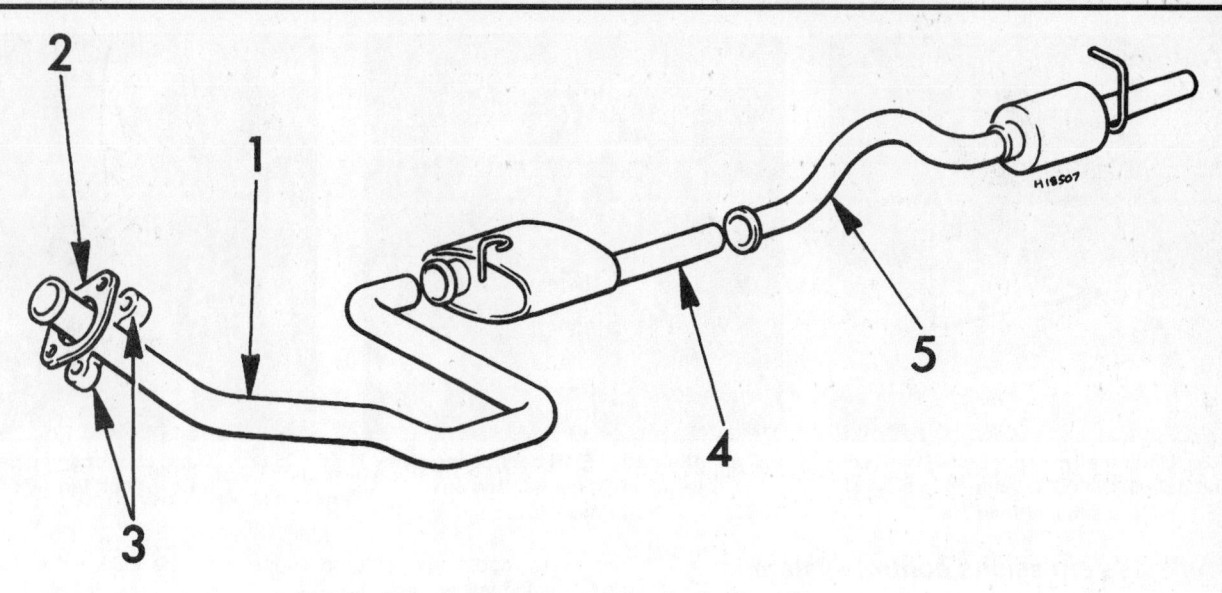

Chapter 4 Fuel, exhaust and emissions control systems

23.1 Typical exhaust system sections and connections

1 Downpipe
2 Flange
3 Flange nuts
4 Intermediate silencer and pipe
5 Rear silencer and pipe

22 Turbocharger - examination and renovation

1 With the turbocharger removed, inspect the housing for cracks or other visible damage.
2 Spin the turbine or the compressor wheel, to verify that the shaft is intact, and to feel for excessive shake or roughness. Some play is normal, since in use, the shaft is "floating" on a film of oil. Check that the wheel vanes are undamaged.
3 If the exhaust or induction passages are oil-contaminated, the turbo shaft oil seals have probably failed.
4 No DIY repair of the turbo is possible. A new unit may be available on an exchange basis.

23 Exhaust system - general information and component renewal

1 The exhaust system consists of multiple sections, and incorporates a catalytic converter on certain models **(see illustration)**.
2 Each part of the original system can be removed independently, although to remove the centre section(s), it is recommended that the complete system is removed, to avoid straining the individual sections.
3 To remove the complete system or part of the system, first jack up the front or rear of the vehicle, as applicable (both, if the complete system is to be removed), and support on axle stands.
4 Unscrew the nuts from the manifold flange, then lower the exhaust downpipe and remove the gasket.
5 Disconnect the mounting rubbers, and lower the complete system from the vehicle.
6 Refitting is a reversal of removal, but clean the flange mating faces, and fit a new gasket. Tighten the flange nuts to the specified torque.
7 The exhaust system sections are secured by U-bolt clamps or by flange joints **(see illustration)**. To separate the sections, undo the flange retaining nuts or the U-bolt nuts, as applicable, then detach the joint. With the U-bolt coupling, the sections are sleeve-jointed, and these will separate by either soaking in penetrating oil, then gripping and pulling them apart, or by cutting them free with a hacksaw, or possibly by prising them free using a suitable screwdriver.
8 On some models, the longer system sections fitted as original equipment on manufacture, are available as two or more separate individual sections as service replacements. In this instance, it is

23.7 Exhaust system flange joint

necessary to obtain the new section, then cut off part of the original long section to accommodate the replacement. Sleeves with U-bolt clamps are provided to connect the new section to the old. Use the original section as a guide to length, then cut it accordingly using a hacksaw.
9 When reconnecting the pipe sections, apply a suitable jointing compound to the joint. Where U-bolt fixings are used, leave fully tightening the joints until after the pipe/system is fully relocated, so that any adjustments to the front and/or rear sections can be made.
10 Where a catalytic converter is fitted, the mounting rubbers are made of a different material than that used on conventional exhausts, to accommodate the intense heat of the catalytic converter. Ensure that the correct mountings are used, according to system type.

24 Emissions control systems - general information

1 Certain engines in the Transit Diesel range are fitted with systems designed to reduce the emissions of harmful by-products of the combustion process into the atmosphere.
2 The following systems may be fitted, according to model.

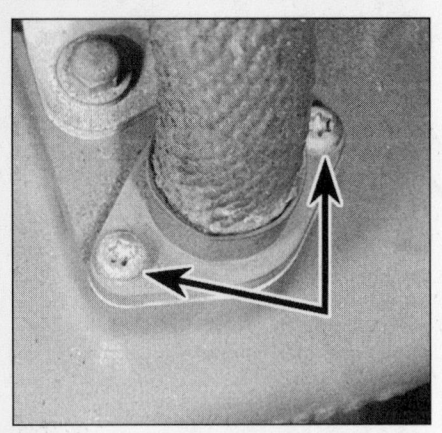

4-20 Chapter 4 Fuel, exhaust and emissions control systems

25.8a Undo the two Torx bolts (arrowed), and detach the EGR connecting hose at the exhaust manifold

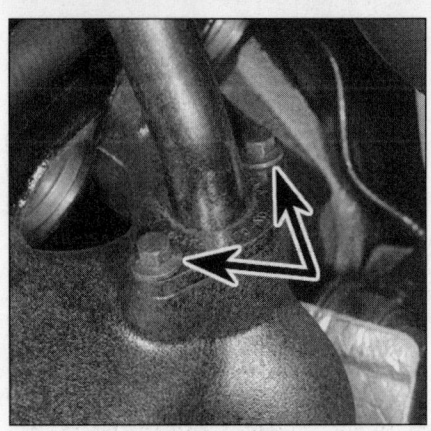

25.8b Alternative EGR connecting pipe-to-manifold connection on later models . . .

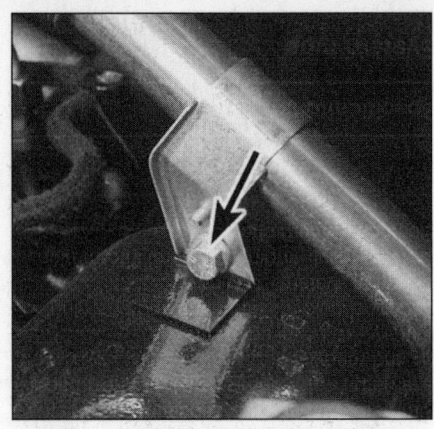

25.8c . . . and connecting pipe support bracket bolt (arrowed)

Crankcase emissions control system

3 A crankcase ventilation system is fitted to all models.

4 Oil fumes and piston blow-by gases (combustion gases which have passed by the piston rings) are drawn from the crankcase and rocker cover through the oil filler cap, into the air inlet tract. The gases are then drawn into the engine for combustion.

Exhaust emissions control system

5 To minimise the level of exhaust gas pollutants released into the atmosphere, a catalytic converter is fitted, located in the exhaust system.

6 The catalytic converter consists of a canister containing a fine mesh impregnated with a catalyst material, over which the exhaust gases pass. The catalyst speeds up the oxidation of harmful carbon monoxide, unburnt hydrocarbons and soot, effectively reducing the quantity of harmful products reaching the atmosphere.

Exhaust gas recirculation system

7 This system is designed to recirculate small quantities of exhaust gas into the inlet tract, and therefore into the combustion process. This reduces the level of oxides of nitrogen present in the final exhaust gas which is released into the atmosphere.

8 The volume of exhaust gas recirculated is controlled by vacuum (supplied from the inlet manifold downstream of the throttle valve) via an EGR valve mounted on the inlet manifold or turbocharger. Before reaching the EGR valve, the vacuum from the manifold passes to a vacuum valve; the purpose of this is to modify the vacuum supplied to the EGR valve according to engine operating conditions.

9 The throttle valve mounted on the inlet manifold allows the ratio of air-to-recirculated exhaust gas to be controlled. The throttle valve also enables the exhaust gases to be drawn into the inlet manifold at idle or under light load. Without the throttle valve, the inlet manifold would be effectively at atmospheric pressure, and the vacuum created by the opening of the engine inlet valves would not be sufficient to cause the exhaust gas to circulate.

10 On turbocharged engines from 1992 onwards, the EGR system operates in conjunction with the Lucas EPIC (Electronic Programmed Injection Control) engine management system. The EGR system is controlled by the EPIC electronic control unit, which receives information on engine operating parameters from an accelerator pedal position sensor, a manifold absolute pressure sensor, a crankshaft position/speed sensor, an engine coolant temperature sensor, and an inlet air temperature sensor.

11 The operating principles of the EGR system fitted to turbocharged engines are essentially the same as on normally-aspirated versions, but before reaching the EGR valve, the vacuum from the manifold passes to a vacuum flow controller mounted on the engine compartment bulkhead. The purpose of the vacuum flow controller is to modify the vacuum supplied to the EGR valve according to information supplied by the electronic control unit.

12 From 1995 model year onwards, certain turbocharged models are fitted with an EGR charge cooler incorporated in the engine coolant circuit.

25 Emissions control systems - testing and component renewal

Crankcase emissions control system components

Testing

1 If the system is thought to be faulty, first check that the hoses are unobstructed. On high-mileage vehicles, particularly those regularly used for short journeys, a jelly-like deposit may be evident inside the crankcase emissions control system hoses or oil filler cap. If excessive deposits are present, the relevant hose(s), or the cap should be removed and cleaned.

2 Periodically inspect the system hoses for security and damage, and renew them as necessary. Note that damaged or loose hoses can cause various engine running problems (erratic idle speed, stalling, etc) which can be difficult to trace.

Component renewal

3 Renewal procedures for the hoses and oil filler cap are self-evident.

Exhaust emissions control system

Testing

4 The system can only be tested accurately using a suitable exhaust gas analyser.

Component renewal

5 The catalytic converter is fitted in the exhaust system between the manifold and centre sections.

6 Removal and refitting are as described for the main exhaust system in Section 23.

Exhaust gas recirculation system

Testing

7 Testing and adjustment of the system should be entrusted to a Ford dealer.

Component renewal

EGR valve - normally-aspirated engines

8 Undo the two Torx bolts or clamp ring, detach the EGR

Chapter 4 Fuel, exhaust and emissions control systems

25.9 Slacken the hose clip, and detach the air inlet hose from the throttle housing

25.11 Disconnect the EGR valve vacuum hose (arrowed)

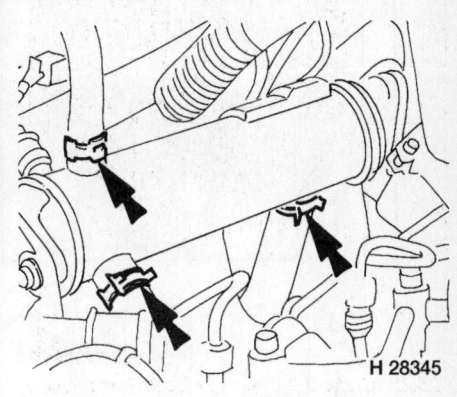

25.25 Release the clips (arrowed) and disconnect the coolant hoses from the EGR charge cooler

connecting hose/pipe at the EGR valve and exhaust manifold, and recover the metal gasket. Where applicable, undo the connecting hose/pipe support bracket bolt **(see illustrations)**.

9 Slacken the hose clip, and detach the air inlet hose from the throttle housing **(see illustration)**.

10 Disconnect the throttle actuating lever from the throttle valve linkage.

11 On engines with a one-piece inlet manifold, disconnect the EGR valve vacuum hose, undo the two throttle housing retaining bolts, and remove the throttle housing, complete with EGR valve, from the inlet manifold **(see illustration)**. Undo the four Torx bolts, and separate the EGR valve and connecting hose from the throttle housing.

12 On engines with a two-piece inlet manifold, undo the bolt securing the manifold to the support bracket. Undo the nuts and bolts, and separate the manifold upper section from the lower section. Recover the gasket between the two halves. Disconnect the EGR valve vacuum hose, then undo the four Torx bolts and separate the EGR valve and connecting hose from the throttle housing.

13 Refitting is a reversal of removal. Use new gaskets at the manifold and EGR valve joints (as applicable), and tighten all nuts and bolts to the specified torque.

EGR valve - turbocharged engines

14 Slacken the hose clips, and disconnect the air inlet pipe at the hose connection on the inlet manifold.

15 Undo the bolts, detach the air inlet pipe connection at the turbocharger end, and recover the gasket. Release the pipe from the support bracket, and remove it from the engine. Close off the turbocharger inlet using a suitable cap or clean rag.

16 Disconnect the EGR valve wiring multi-plug and vacuum hose.

17 Undo the two Torx bolts, and remove the throttle housing complete with EGR valve; undo the remaining two Torx bolts, and separate the valve from the housing.

18 Refitting is a reversal of removal. Use new gaskets as applicable, and tighten all nuts and bolts to the specified torque.

EGR charge cooler - turbocharged engines (1995 model year onwards)

19 Disconnect the battery negative lead.

20 Refer to Chapter 1 and drain the cooling system.

21 Undo the two bolts, disconnect the EGR connecting pipe at the exhaust manifold, and recover the metal gasket.

22 Undo the clamp bolt, and slip off the clamp securing the other end of the EGR connecting pipe to the charge cooler. Remove the pipe.

23 Disconnect the EGR valve wiring multi-plug and vacuum hose.

24 Undo the two Torx bolts, remove the EGR valve, and recover the metal gasket.

25 Release the clips, and disconnect the coolant hoses from the charge cooler **(see illustration)**.

26 Undo the retaining bracket bolts and the flange bolts, and remove the charge cooler.

27 Refitting is a reversal of removal, using new gaskets as applicable.

26 Lucas Electronic Programmed Injection Control (EPIC) system - description and precautions

Description

1 From the 1992 model year onwards, fuel and emissions control systems on turbocharged engines are controlled by the Lucas EPIC engine management system **(see illustration on following page)**.

2 The system provides programmed electronic control of the fuel injection pump, and electronic control of the exhaust gas recirculation system, via the EPIC electronic control module (ECU).

3 For the ECU to assess fuel system requirements under all operating conditions, sensors are provided to monitor accelerator pedal position, manifold absolute pressure, crankshaft speed/position, engine coolant temperature, and inlet air temperature. Operation of the EGR valve is also controlled by the ECU, in conjunction with a vacuum flow controller.

4 A unique feature of this system is the "drive-by-wire" throttle control. Instead of the accelerator cable being connected to the fuel injection pump, as it is in the normal mechanical system, the cable is connected to a pedal position sensor. This sensor sends pedal position signals to the ECU, which in turn controls the fuel injection pump electronically.

Precautions

a) Always disconnect the battery negative lead before removing any of the electronic control system's electrical connectors.
b) When installing a battery, be particularly careful to avoid reversing the positive and negative battery leads.
c) Do not subject any components of the system (especially the ECU) to severe impact during removal or installation.
d) Never attempt to work on the ECU, to test it (with any kind of test equipment), nor to open its cover.
e) If you are inspecting electronic control system components during rainy weather, make sure that water does not enter any part. When washing the engine compartment, do not spray these parts or their electrical connectors with water.

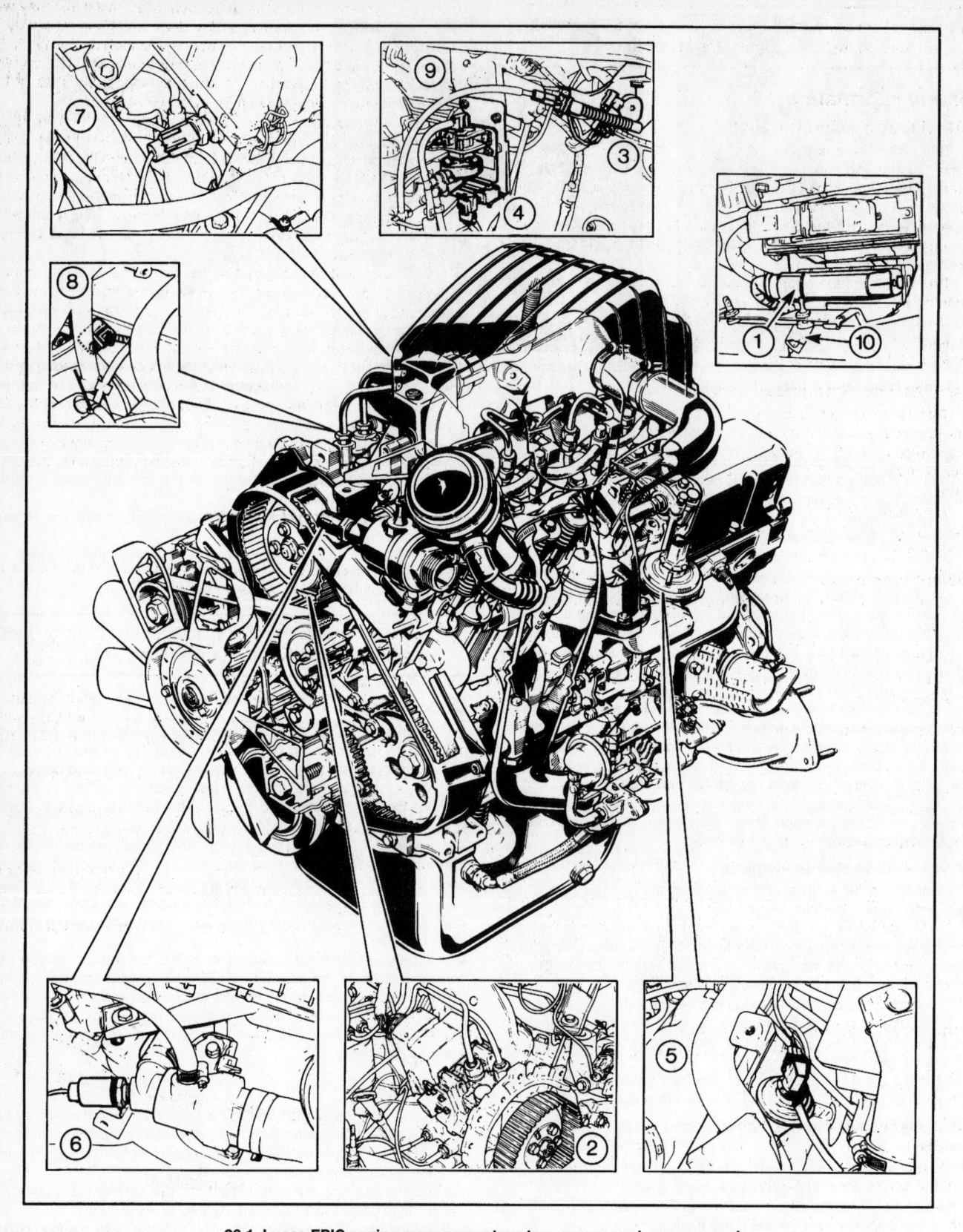

4-22 Chapter 4 Fuel, exhaust and emissions control systems

26.1 Lucas EPIC engine management system component arrangement

1. Electronic control unit
2. Fuel injection pump
3. Accelerator pedal position sensor
4. Manifold absolute pressure sensor
5. Exhaust gas recirculation valve
6. Engine coolant temperature sensor
7. Inlet air temperature sensor
8. Crankshaft position/speed sensor
9. EGR vacuum flow controller
10. Self test connector

Chapter 4 Fuel, exhaust and emissions control systems

27 Information sensors (Lucas EPIC system) - general information, testing, removal and refitting

General information

ECU (Electronic Control Unit)
1 This component is the heart of the entire engine management system, controlling the fuel injection, and the emissions control systems. The ECU receives signals from various sensors, which monitor changing engine operating conditions such as inlet air temperature, coolant temperature, engine speed, accelerator pedal position, etc. These signals are used by the ECU to determine the correct fuel metering by the injection pump.
2 The system is analogous to the central nervous system in the human body - the sensors (nerve endings) constantly relay signals to the ECU (brain), which processes the data and, if necessary, sends out a command to change the operating parameters of the engine (body) by means of the actuators (muscles).

Crankshaft position/speed sensor
3 This is an inductive pulse generator bolted to the cylinder block/crankcase, to scan the ridges between holes machined in the inboard face of the flywheel. As each ridge passes the sensor tip, a signal is generated, which is used by the ECU to determine engine speed.
4 The ridge between one of the holes is missing - this step in the incoming signals is used by the ECU to determine crankshaft (ie, piston) position.

Coolant temperature sensor
5 This component is an NTC (Negative Temperature Coefficient) thermistor - that is, a semi-conductor whose electrical resistance decreases as its temperature increases. It provides the ECU with a constantly-varying (analogue) voltage signal, corresponding to the temperature of the engine coolant. This is used to refine the calculations made by the ECU, when determining fuel metering.

Inlet air temperature sensor
6 This component is also an NTC thermistor - see the previous paragraph - providing the ECU with a signal corresponding to the temperature of air passing into the engine. This is also used to refine fuel metering calculations.

Accelerator pedal position sensor
7 The "drive-by-wire" throttle control information is provided by this sensor. The accelerator cable is connected to the pedal position sensor, which converts accelerator pedal movement into an electrical signal (on later models, the sensor is part of the pedal assembly). After processing this signal (and refining it using information received from the other sensors) the ECU controls the fuel injection pump electronically, so that the correct fuel metering is achieved to obtain the desired road speed.

Manifold absolute pressure sensor
8 The manifold absolute pressure sensor measures inlet manifold vacuum, and supplies this information to the ECU for calculation of engine load at any given throttle position.

EGR vacuum flow controller
9 Before reaching the EGR valve, the vacuum from the inlet manifold passes to a vacuum flow controller mounted on the engine compartment bulkhead. The purpose of the vacuum flow controller is to modify the vacuum supplied to the EGR valve, according to information supplied by the electronic control unit.

Testing
10 The various components of the fuel and emissions control systems are so closely interlinked that diagnosis of a fault in any one component is virtually impossible using traditional methods. Working on simpler systems in the past, the experienced mechanic may well have been able to use personal skill and knowledge immediately to pinpoint the cause of a fault, or quickly to isolate the fault, by elimination; however, with an integrated engine management system, this is not likely to be possible in most instances, because of the number of symptoms that could arise from even a minor fault.
11 So that the causes of faults can be quickly and accurately traced and rectified, the ECU is provided with a built-in self-diagnosis facility, which detects malfunctions in the system's components. When a fault occurs, the ECU identifies the fault, stores a corresponding code in its memory, and (in most cases) runs the system using back-up values pre-programmed ("mapped") into its memory; some form of driveability is thus maintained, to enable the vehicle to be driven to a garage for attention.
12 Any faults that may have occurred are indicated in the form of two- or three-digit codes when the system is connected (via the built-in diagnosis or self-test connectors, as appropriate) to special diagnostic equipment. This points the user in the direction of the faulty circuit, so that further tests can pinpoint the exact location of the fault. Obviously, to be able to interpret these fault codes accurately requires special diagnostic test equipment and an understanding of its use, which puts the diagnostic procedure outside the scope of the DIY enthusiast. Even if one of the following sensors is known to be suspect, accurate testing requires the use of Ford test equipment, and a methodical test procedure. Therefore, testing should be entrusted to a suitably-equipped Ford garage.

Removal and refitting

General
13 Before disconnecting any of these components, always disconnect the battery negative lead first.

ECU (Electronic Control Unit)
Note: *The ECU is FRAGILE. Take care not to drop it, or subject it to any other kind of impact, and do not subject it to extremes of temperature, or allow it to get wet.*
14 On pre-1995 model year vehicles, turn the two retaining catches inside the glove compartment anti-clockwise, push the ECU holding tray slightly forwards, and lower the tray and the ECU **(see illustration)**.
15 Push the ECU retaining bracket inwards to release it from the slot in the tray, and lift the unit upwards off the tray.
16 Pull the wiring multi-plug locking clip outwards to release it, then unhook the other end and disconnect the plug. Remove the ECU.
17 Refitting is a reversal of removal.
18 On later models, undo the two multi-plug rubber boot retaining nuts on the engine compartment bulkhead, pull back the boot, and disconnect the multi-plug.
19 Using a screwdriver and protective pad, prise out the stowage

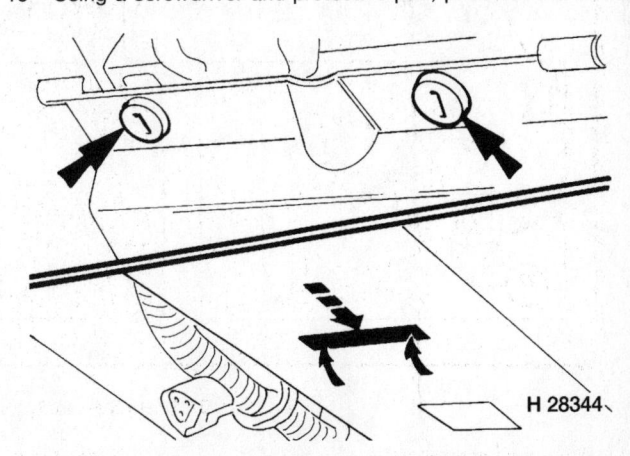

27.14 ECU tray retaining catches (arrowed) and retaining bracket slot

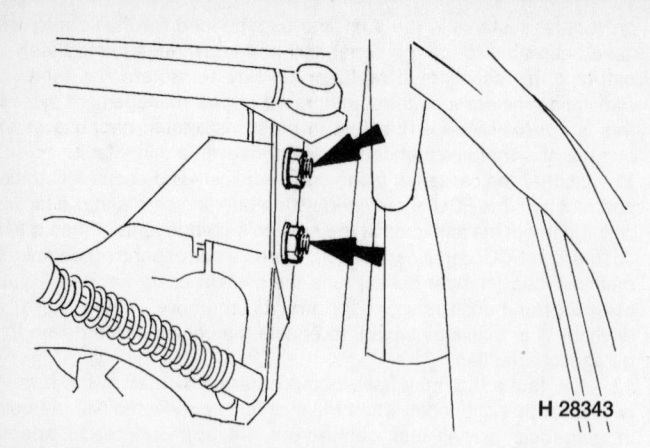

27.32 Undo the two retaining nuts (arrowed) and withdraw the accelerator pedal position sensor mounting bracket assembly

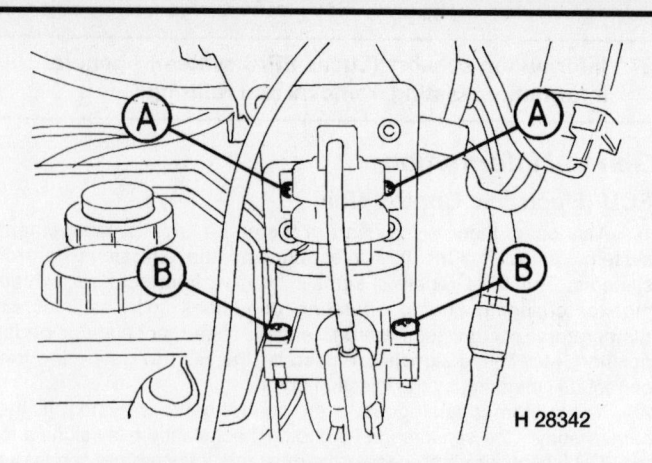

27.37 Manifold absolute pressure sensor retaining screws (B) and EGR vacuum flow controller retaining screws (A)

tray from the top of the facia on the passenger's side.
20 Working through the stowage tray aperture, undo the mounting bracket bolt and remove the ECU.
21 Refitting is a reversal of removal.

Crankshaft position/speed sensor

22 The crankshaft position/speed sensor is located at the rear of the engine, just above the starter motor.
23 Disconnect the wiring multi-plug, then undo the retaining bolt and remove the sensor. Recover the shim, if fitted, behind the sensor.
24 Refitting is a reversal of removal, ensuring that the shim (if fitted) is positioned behind the sensor.

Coolant temperature sensor

25 Drain the cooling system (see Chapter 1).
26 Unplug the electrical connector from the sensor, located on the thermostat housing.
27 Unscrew the sensor and withdraw it.
28 Refitting is a reversal of removal. Apply a light coat of sealant to the sensor's threads prior to installation, and top-up the cooling system (see Chapter 1) on completion.

Inlet air temperature sensor

29 If necessary, remove the air cleaner assembly (Section 3) or air inlet ducting as necessary, to gain access to the sensor.
30 Disconnect the wiring multi-plug, then unscrew the sensor from the air cleaner casing.
31 Refitting is a reversal of removal.

Accelerator pedal position sensor

32 On pre-1995 model year vehicles, undo the two retaining nuts and withdraw the pedal position sensor mounting bracket assembly from its location in the engine compartment (see illustration).
33 Disconnect the accelerator cable from the sensor link stud.
34 Disconnect the wiring multi-plug, then undo the two retaining nuts and withdraw the sensor from the mounting bracket.
35 Refitting is a reversal of removal.
36 On 1995 model year vehicles onwards, the sensor is an integral part of the accelerator pedal assembly, and is removed with it. Refer to Section 14 for details.

Manifold absolute pressure sensor

37 The sensor is located on a bracket attached to the bulkhead at the rear of the engine compartment (see illustration).
38 Undo the mounting bracket bolts, and lower the bracket.
39 Disconnect the wiring multi-plug, and detach the vacuum hose from the base of the sensor.
40 Undo the two retaining screws, and withdraw the sensor from its bracket.
41 Refitting is a reversal of removal.

EGR valve vacuum flow controller

42 The vacuum flow controller is mounted, together with the manifold absolute pressure sensor, on a bracket attached to the bulkhead at the rear of the engine compartment (see illustration 27.37). Removal and refitting procedures are the same as for the MAP sensor described in the previous sub-Section.

Chapter 5 Engine electrical systems

Contents

	Section		Section
Alternator - removal and refitting	5	Engine electrical system - general information and precautions	1
Alternator brushes and regulator - inspection and renewal	6	Ignition switch - removal and refitting	10
Alternator/water pump drivebelt check, adjustment and renewal	See Chapter 1	Oil pressure warning light switch - removal and refitting	11
Battery - removal and refitting	3	Preheating system - description and testing	12
Battery check, maintenance and charging	See Chapter 1	Preheating system flame plug - removal and refitting	13
Charging system - testing	4	Preheating system flame plug fuel reservoir purge	See Chapter 1
Electrical fault-finding - general information	2	Starter motor - brush renewal	9
Electrical system check	See Chapter 1	Starter motor - removal and refitting	8
		Starting system - testing	7

Specifications

System type .... 12-volt, negative earth

Battery
Type .... Lead-acid, low maintenance or "Maintenance Free"
Charge condition:
    Poor .... 12.5 volts
    Normal .... 12.6 volts
    Good .... 12.7 volts

Alternator
Type .... Bosch or Lucas/Magneti-Marelli
Nominal output .... 55 or 70 amps
Regulating voltage (at 4000 rpm engine speed and 3 to 7 amp load) ..... 13.7 to 14.6 volts
Minimum brush length .... 5.0 mm

Starter motor
Type .... Bosch or Lucas/Magneti-Marelli
Minimum brush length .... 10 mm (nominal)

Torque wrench settings
	Nm	lbf ft
Alternator mounting and adjustment nuts and bolts	24	18
Oil pressure warning light switch	13	10
Vacuum pump to alternator	13	10

5-2 Chapter 5 Engine electrical systems

3.2a Battery negative lead connection (arrowed) on batteries with flat terminal posts

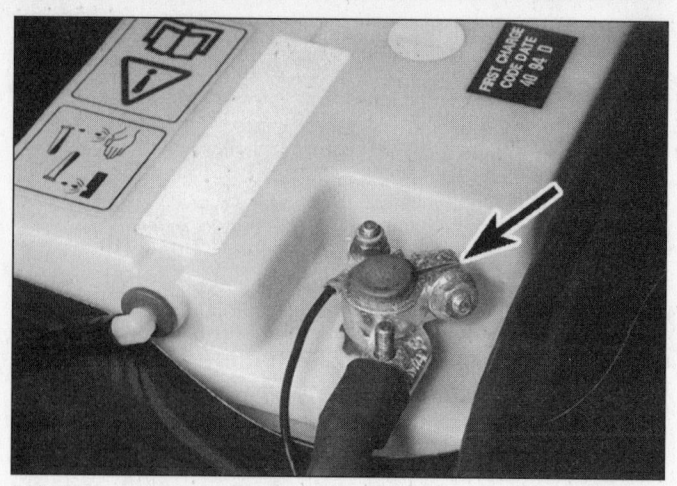

3.2b Battery negative lead connection (arrowed) on later batteries with round terminal posts

1 Engine electrical system - general information and precautions

General information

The engine electrical systems include all charging, starting and pre-heating components. Because of their engine-related functions, these components are covered separately from the body electrical devices such as the lights, the instruments, etc (which are covered in Chapter 12).

The electrical system is of the 12-volt negative earth type.

The battery is of the low-maintenance or "maintenance-free" ("sealed for life") type, and is charged by the alternator which is belt-driven from the crankshaft pulley. A single battery is used on all later models; certain earlier vehicles were fitted with two batteries.

The starter motor is of the pre-engaged type, incorporating an integral solenoid. On starting, the solenoid moves the drive pinion into engagement with the flywheel ring gear before the starter motor is engaged. Once the engine has started, a one-way clutch prevents the motor armature being driven by the engine until the pinion disengages from the flywheel.

Certain models may have a flame-plug type pre-heating system. The electric flame-plug element ignites a small quantity of fuel in the inlet manifold which is drawn into the combustion chambers to assist cold starting.

Further details of the various systems and components are given in the relevant Sections of this Chapter. While some repair procedures are given, the usual course of action is to renew the component concerned. The owner whose interest extends beyond mere component renewal should obtain a copy of the *"Automobile Electrical & Electronic Systems Manual"*, available from the publishers of this manual.

Precautions

It is necessary to take extra care when working on the electrical system, to avoid damage to semi-conductor devices (diodes and transistors), and to avoid the risk of personal injury. In addition to the precautions given in *"Safety first!"* at the beginning of this manual, observe the following when working on the system:

Always remove rings, watches, etc before working on the electrical system. Even with the battery disconnected, capacitive discharge could occur if a component's live terminal is earthed through a metal object. This could cause a shock or nasty burn.

Do not reverse the battery connections. Components such as the alternator, or any other components having semi-conductor circuitry could be irreparably damaged.

If the engine is being started using jump leads and a slave battery, connect the batteries *positive-to-positive* and *negative-to-negative* (see *"Booster battery (jump) starting"*). This also applies when connecting a battery charger.

Never disconnect the battery terminals, the alternator, or any electrical wiring or any test instruments, when the engine is running.

Do not allow the engine to turn the alternator when the alternator is not connected.

Never "test" for alternator output by "flashing" the output lead to earth.

Never use an ohmmeter of the type incorporating a hand-cranked generator for circuit or continuity testing.

Always ensure that the battery negative lead is disconnected when working on the electrical system.

Before using electric-arc welding equipment on the vehicle, disconnect the battery and alternator to protect them from the risk of damage.

The later radio/cassette units fitted as standard equipment by Ford have built-in security codes, to deter thieves. If the power source to the unit is interrupted, the anti-theft system will activate. Even if the power source is immediately reconnected, the radio/cassette unit will not function until the correct security code has been entered. Therefore, if you do not know the correct security code for the radio/cassette unit, *do not* disconnect the negative terminal of the battery, nor remove the radio/cassette unit from the vehicle. Refer to the *"Radio/cassette unit anti-theft system"* Section at the beginning of this manual for further details.

2 Electrical fault-finding - general information

Refer to Chapter 12, Section 2.

3 Battery - removal and refitting

Removal

1 The battery is located in the engine compartment on the right-hand side, or one on either side where twin batteries are fitted.
2 Note the location of the leads, then unscrew the nut and disconnect the negative lead **(see illustrations)**.
3 Lift the plastic cover (if fitted), then unscrew the nut and disconnect the positive lead.
4 Unscrew the clamp bolt (or release the retaining strap) and lift the battery from the platform, taking care not to spill any electrolyte on the bodywork.

Refitting

5 Refitting is a reversal of removal. Refit the leads positive first, negative last.

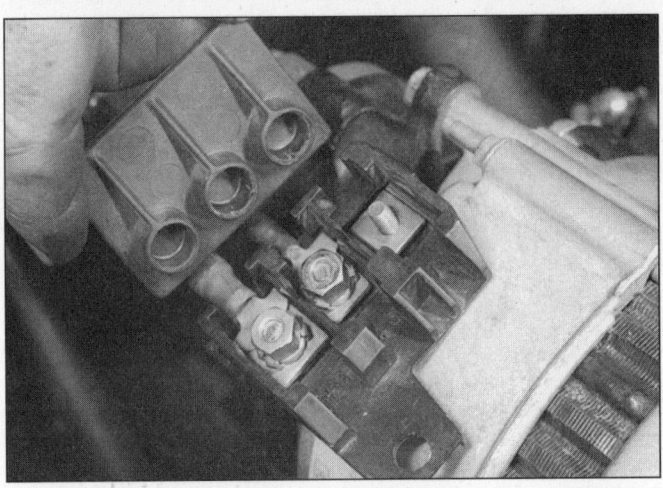

Chapter 5 Engine electrical systems

5.3 Remove the plastic cover, undo the terminal nuts and disconnect the alternator wiring

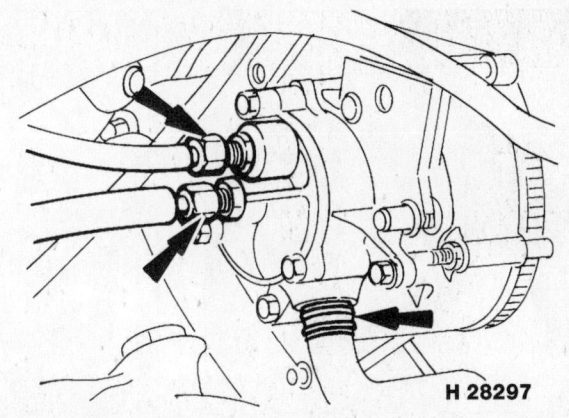

5.4 Detach the oil and vacuum pipes (arrowed) from the rear of the brake servo vacuum pump

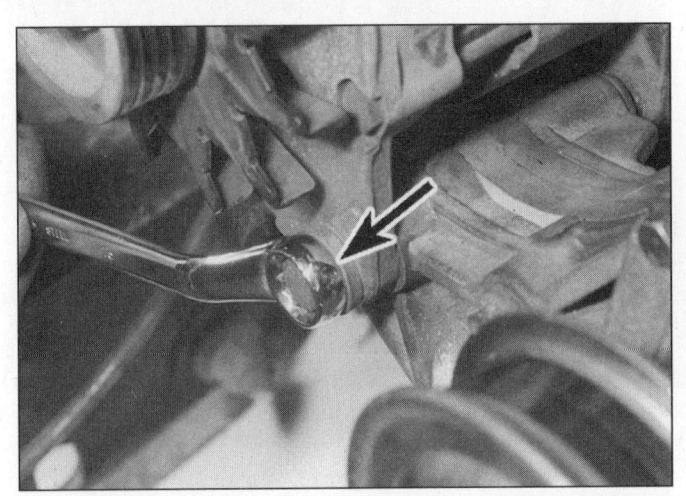

5.5a Unscrew the alternator mounting nut and bolt (arrowed) . . .

5.5b . . . and the adjustment bolt attachment to the adjustment arm

4 Charging system - testing

Note: *Refer to the warnings given in "Safety first!" and in Section 1 of this Chapter before starting work.*

1 If the alternator (no-charge) warning light fails to illuminate when the ignition is switched on, first check the alternator wiring connections for security. If satisfactory, check that the warning light bulb has not blown, and that the bulbholder is secure in its location in the instrument panel. If the light still fails to illuminate, check the continuity of the warning light feed wire from the alternator to the bulbholder. If all is satisfactory, the alternator is at fault, and should be taken to an auto-electrician for testing and repair, or else renewed.

2 If the warning light illuminates when the engine is running, stop the engine and check that the drivebelt is correctly tensioned (see Chapter 1) and that the alternator connections are secure. If all is so far satisfactory, check the alternator brushes and slip rings (see Section 6). If the fault persists, the alternator should be taken to an auto-electrician for testing and repair, or else renewed.

3 If the alternator output is suspect even though the warning light functions correctly, the regulated voltage may be checked as follows.

4 Connect a voltmeter across the battery terminals and start the engine.

5 Increase the engine speed until the voltmeter reading remains steady; the reading should be approximately 12 to 13 volts, and no more than 14 volts.

6 Switch on as many electrical accessories (eg, the headlights, heater blower etc) as possible, and check that the alternator maintains the regulated voltage at around 13.5 to 14.5 volts.

7 If the regulated voltage is not as stated, the fault may be due to worn brushes, weak brush springs, a faulty voltage regulator, a faulty diode, a severed phase winding, or worn or damaged slip rings. The brushes and slip rings may be checked (see Section 6), but if the fault persists, the alternator should be taken to an auto-electrician for testing and repair, or else renewed.

5 Alternator - removal and refitting

Removal

1 Disconnect the battery negative lead.

2 Slacken the alternator/water pump drivebelt tension as described in Chapter 1.

3 According to alternator type, either disconnect the wiring multi-plug or remove the plastic cover, undo the terminal nuts and disconnect the alternator wires, noting their locations **(see illustration)**.

4 Undo the union nuts and slacken the hose clips, then detach the oil and vacuum pipes from the rear of the brake servo vacuum pump **(see illustration)**.

5 Unscrew the alternator mounting and adjustment nuts and bolts, and remove the alternator from the engine **(see illustrations)**.

Refitting

6 Refitting is a reversal of removal. Tension the drivebelt as described in Chapter 1 on completion.

5•4 Chapter 5 Engine electrical systems

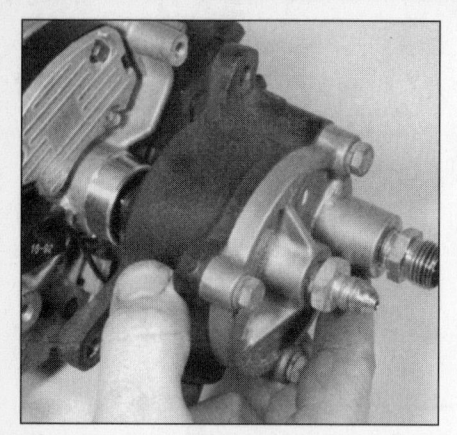

6.2 Remove the vacuum pump from the rear of the alternator

6.3a Remove the screws (arrowed) and withdraw the regulator and brushbox from the rear of the alternator

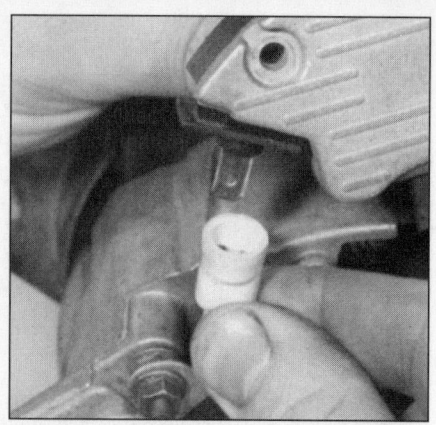

6.3b On the Lucas/Magneti-Marelli unit, disconnect the field connector as the regulator/brushbox assembly is removed

6.4 Measure the protrusion of each brush from the brush holder

8.2a Disconnect the starter motor wiring from the solenoid (arrowed) . . .

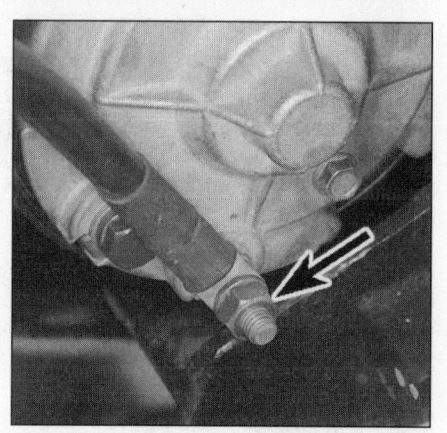

8.2b . . . and where applicable, from the terminal stud on the end cover (arrowed)

6 Alternator brushes and regulator - inspection and renewal

1 Remove the alternator as described in the previous Section.
2 Undo the three bolts, and remove the vacuum pump from the rear of the alternator **(see illustration)**.
3 Remove the screws and withdraw the regulator and brushbox from the rear of the alternator. On the Lucas/Magneti-Marelli unit, disconnect the field connector as the regulator/brushbox assembly is removed **(see illustrations)**.

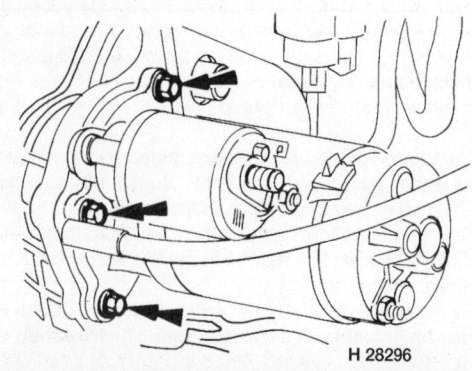

8.3 Unscrew and remove the three starter motor retaining bolts (arrowed) noting that on some motors, the earth cable connection is on one of the bolts

4 Measure the protrusion of each brush from the brush holder, and compare the dimension with the figures given in the Specifications **(see illustration)**. If either brush is worn below the minimum dimension, obtain a new regulator and brushbox assembly.
5 If the original brushes are still serviceable, clean them with a solvent-moistened cloth. Check that the brush spring tension is equal for both brushes, and provides a reasonable pressure. Ensure that the brushes move freely in their holders.
6 Clean the alternator slip-rings with a solvent moistened cloth. Check for signs of scoring, burning or severe pitting on the surface of the slip-rings. It may be possible to have the slip-rings renovated by an electrical specialist.
7 Refit the regulator/brushbox assembly and the vacuum pump, using a reverse of the removal procedure.
8 Refit the alternator as described in the previous Section.

7 Starting system - testing

Note: Refer to the warnings given in "Safety first!" and in Section 1 of this Chapter before starting work.

1 If the starter motor does not turn at all when the switch is operated, make sure that, on automatic transmission models, the selector lever is in Park or Neutral ("P" or "N").
2 Make sure that the battery is fully-charged, and that all leads, both at the battery and starter solenoid terminals, are clean and secure.
3 If the starter motor spins but the engine is not cranking, the overrunning clutch may be slipping, in which case the starter motor must be renewed. (Other possibilities are that the starter motor mounting bolts are very loose, or that teeth are missing from the

Chapter 5 Engine electrical systems

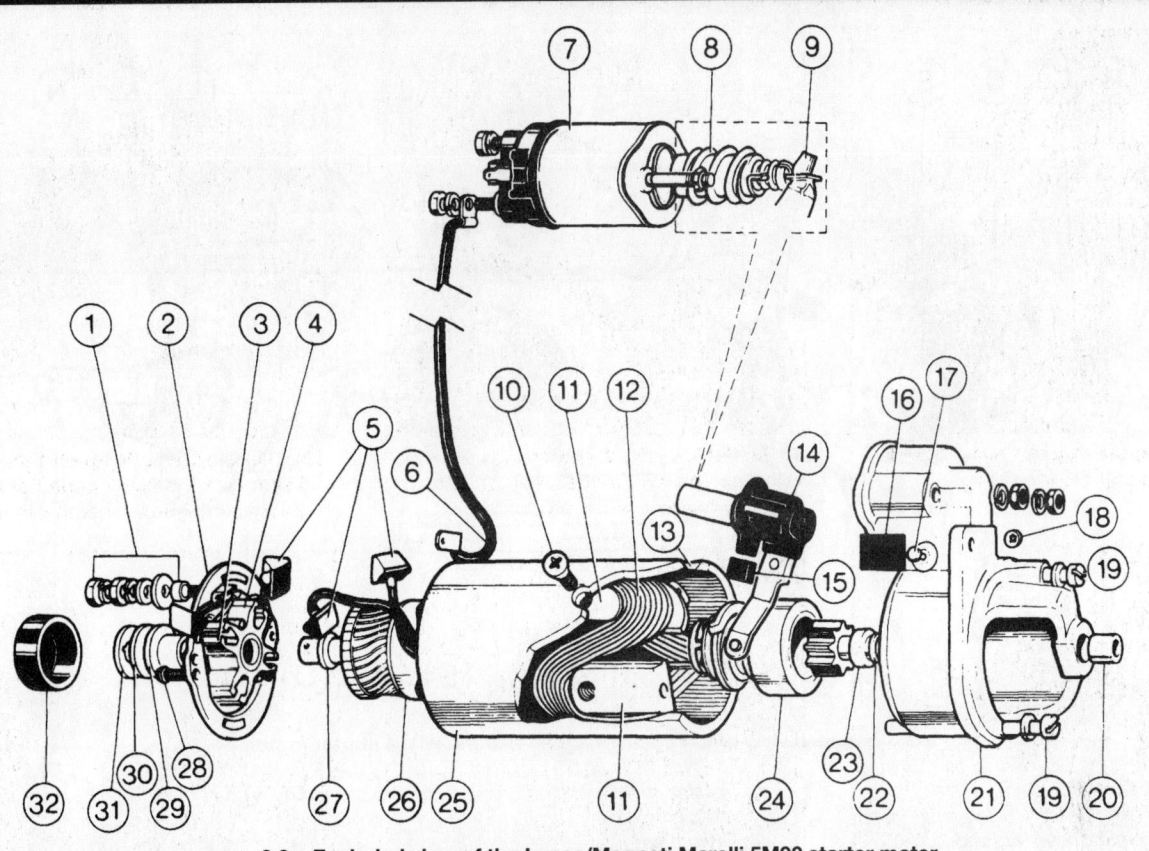

9.0a Exploded view of the Lucas/Magneti Marelli 5M90 starter motor

1 Terminal nuts and washers
2 Commutator end plate
3 Brush holder
4 Brush springs
5 Brushes
6 Connector link, solenoid to starter
7 Solenoid unit
8 Return spring
9 Engagement lever
10 Pole screw
11 Pole shoe
12 Field coils
13 Field to earth connection
14 Rubber seal
15 Rubber dust pad
16 Rubber dust cover
17 Pivot pin
18 Retaining clip
19 Housing retaining screws
20 Bearing bush
21 Drive end housing
22 C-clip
23 Thrust collar
24 Drive assembly
25 Main casing (yoke)
26 Armature
27 Thrustwasher
28 Commutator endplate retaining screws
29 Bearing bush
30 Thrust plate
31 Star clip
32 Dust cover

flywheel/driveplate ring gear.)
4   If, when the switch is actuated, the starter motor does not operate at all but the solenoid clicks, then the problem lies with either the battery, the main solenoid contacts, or the starter motor itself (or the engine is seized).
5   If the solenoid plunger cannot be heard to click when the switch is actuated, the battery is faulty, there is a fault in the circuit, or the solenoid itself is defective.
6   To check the solenoid, connect a fused jumper lead between the battery (+) and the ignition switch terminal (the small terminal) on the solenoid. If the starter motor now operates, the solenoid is satisfactory, and the problem is in the ignition switch, selector lever position sensor (automatic transmission) or in the wiring.
7   If the starter motor still does not operate, remove it (see Section 8). The brushes and commutator may be checked (see Section 9), but if the fault persists, the motor should be renewed, or taken to an auto-electrician for testing and repair.
8   If the starter motor cranks the engine at an abnormally-slow speed, first make sure that the battery is charged, and that all terminal connections are tight. If the engine is partially seized, or has the wrong viscosity oil in it, it will crank slowly.
9   If the engine is known to be sound, and with the correct viscosity oil, but the cranking speed is still slow, the solenoid contacts are burned, the motor is faulty, or there is a poor internal connection.

8 Starter motor - removal and refitting

Removal
1   Disconnect the battery negative lead.
2   Disconnect the starter motor wiring from the solenoid, and where applicable, from the terminal stud on the end cover **(see illustrations)**.
3   Unscrew and remove the three starter motor retaining bolts. Note that on some motors, one of the retaining bolts also secures the earth cable **(see illustration)**. Withdraw the starter motor from the engine.

Refitting
4   Refitting is a reversal of removal, but ensure that the wiring connections are securely made.

9 Starter motor - brush renewal

Note: Brush renewal on the Lucas/Magneti-Marelli M127 type starter motor is described in this Section. However, the procedures for the other starter motor types is similar. Refer to the appropriate illustration for the detail differences between types **(see illustrations)**.

1   Remove the starter motor from the vehicle as described in the previous Section.

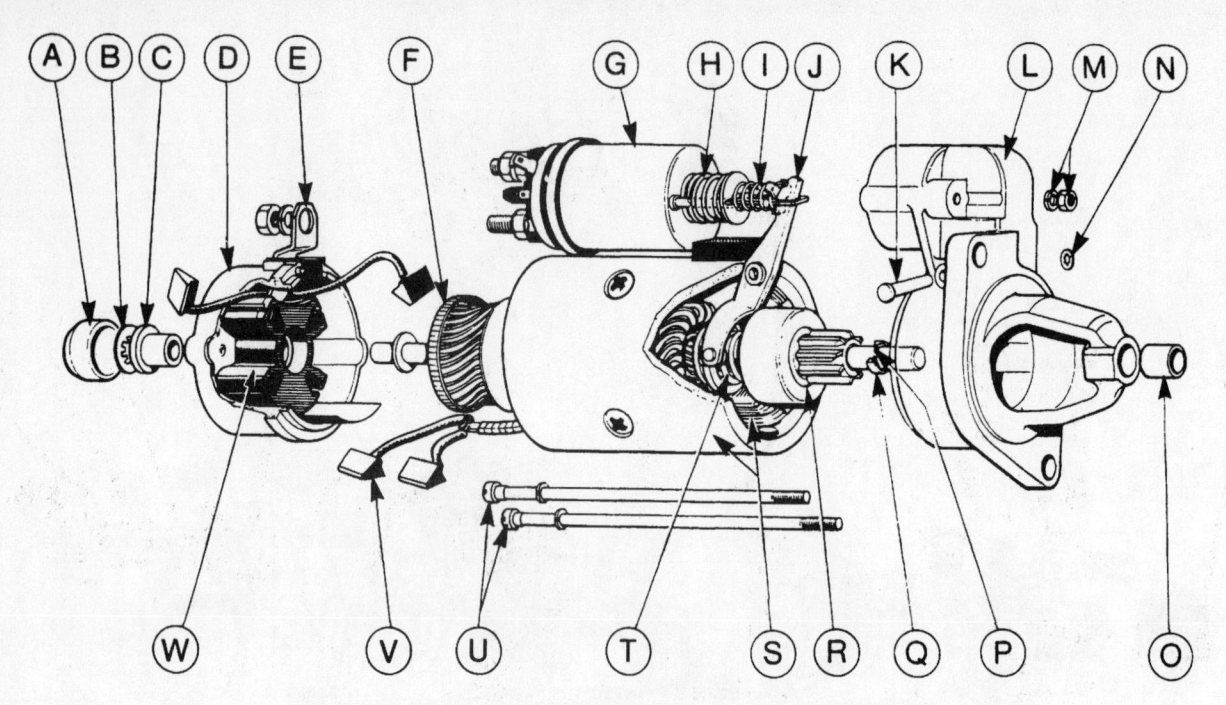

Chapter 5 Engine electrical systems

9.0b Exploded view of the Lucas/Magneti Marelli 2M100 starter motor

A	Rubber cover	I	Lost motion spring	Q	Thrust collar
B	Retainer	J	Actuator lever	R	Pinion gear unit
C	Commutator end housing bush	K	Pivot pin	S	Pole shoe/yoke unit
D	Commutator end housing	L	Drive end bracket	T	Spacer spring
E	Terminal link	M	Solenoid nut/washer	U	Through bolts
F	Armature	N	Clip	V	Brush
G	Solenoid	O	End bracket bush	W	Brush holder
H	Spring	P	C-clips		

9.0c Exploded view of the Lucas/Magneti Marelli M127 starter motor

A Brush holder
B Fibre washer
C Brake shoes and driving peg
D Armature
E Flexible link
F Copper link
G Solenoid
H Return spring
J Seal
K Engagement lever
L Pivot pin
M Drive end bracket
N C-clip
O Bearing bush
P Thrust collar
Q Gasket
R Intermediate bracket
S Seal ring
T Field coils
U Yoke
V Field coil brushes
W Steel thrustwasher
X Bearing bush
Y Seal ring
Z Commutator end cover

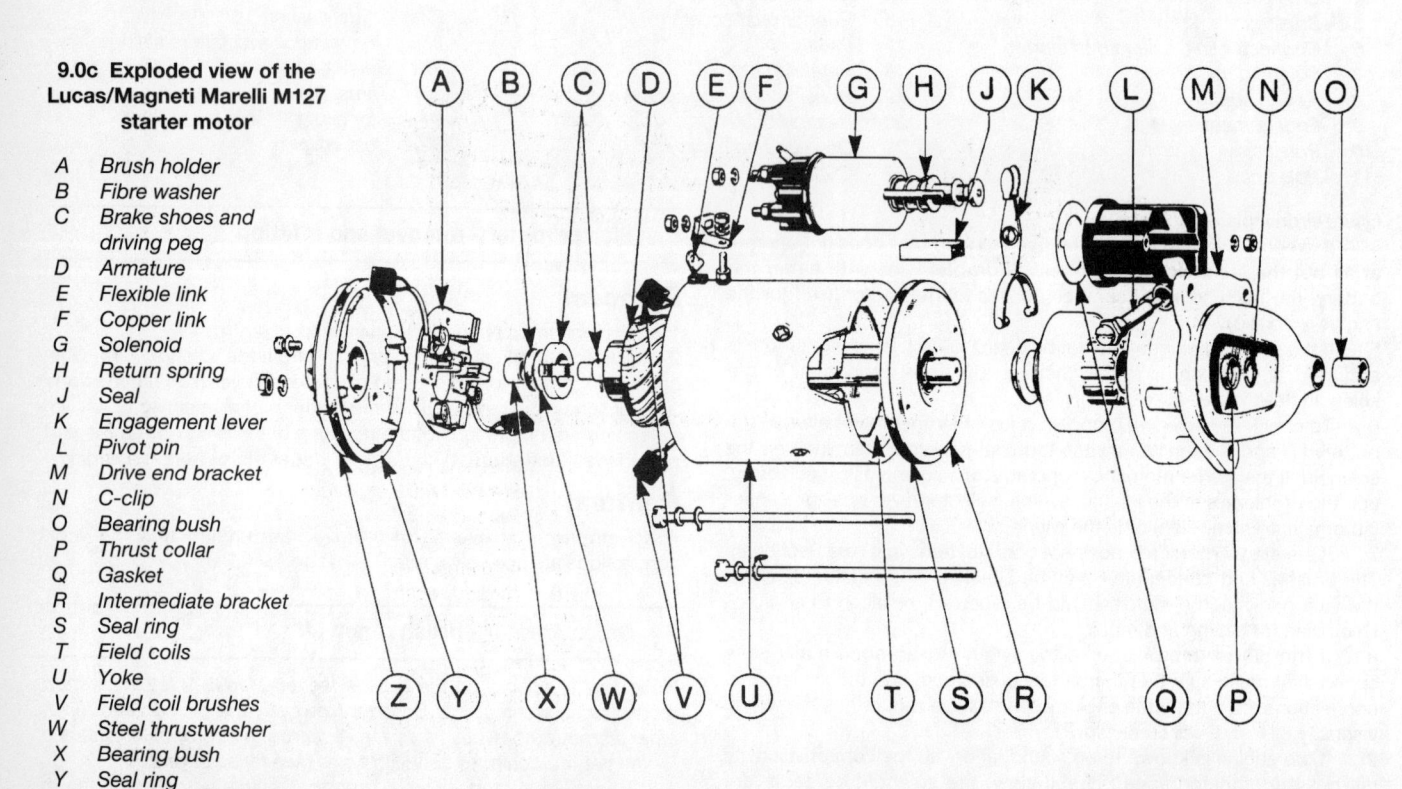

Chapter 5 Engine electrical systems

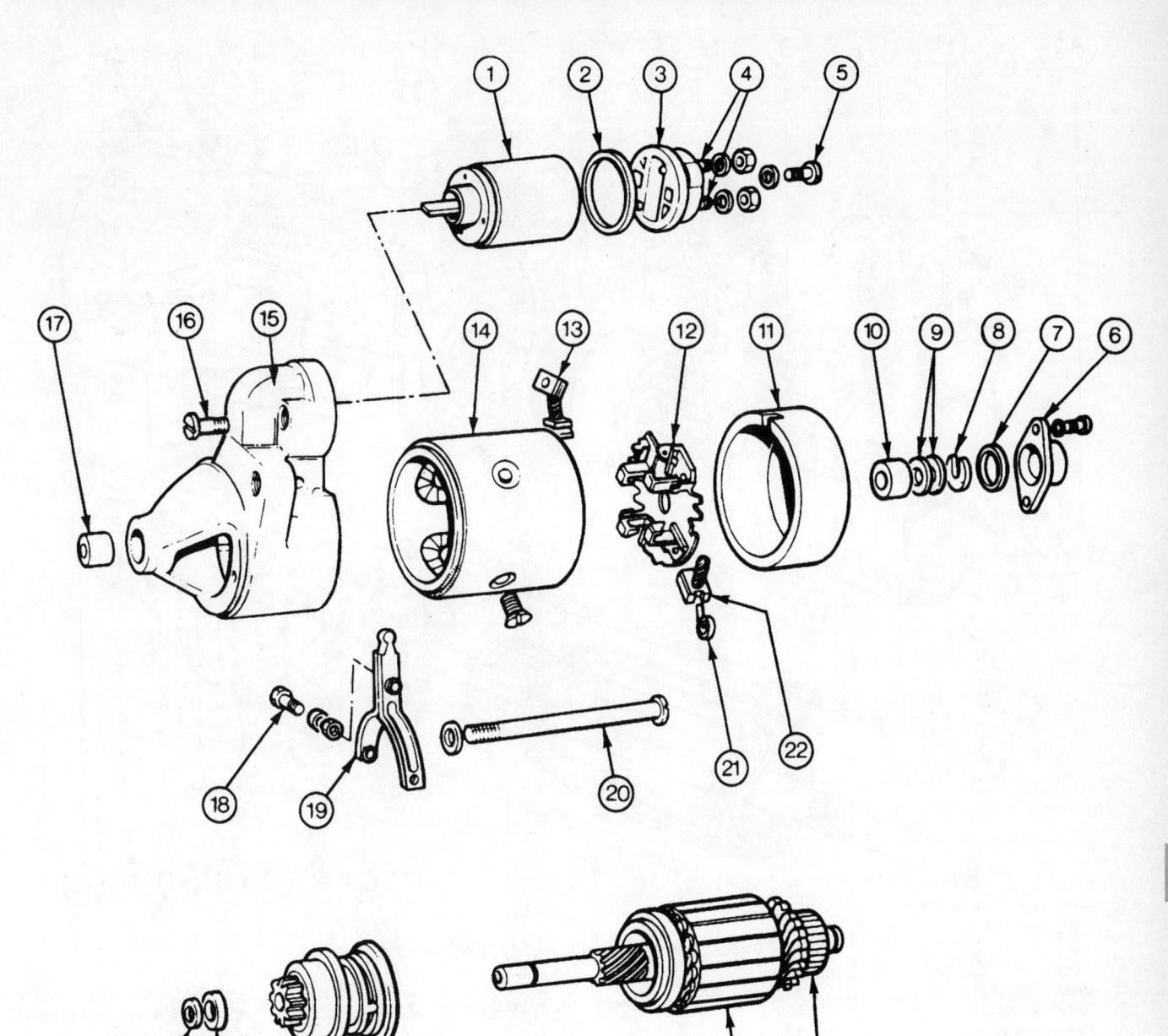

9.0d Exploded view of the Bosch long frame starter motor

1 Solenoid
2 Gasket
3 Switch contacts and cover
4 Terminals
5 Retaining screw
6 End cover
7 Seal
8 C-clip
9 Shim washer
10 Bearing bush
11 Commutator end housing
12 Brushbox assembly
13 Connector link
14 Yoke
15 Drive end housing
16 Solenoid retaining screw
17 Bearing bush
18 Pivot screw
19 Actuating lever
20 Through-bolt
21 Brush spring
22 Brush
23 Commutator
24 Armature
25 Drive pinion assembly
26 Thrust collar
27 C-clip

5-8 Chapter 5 Engine electrical systems

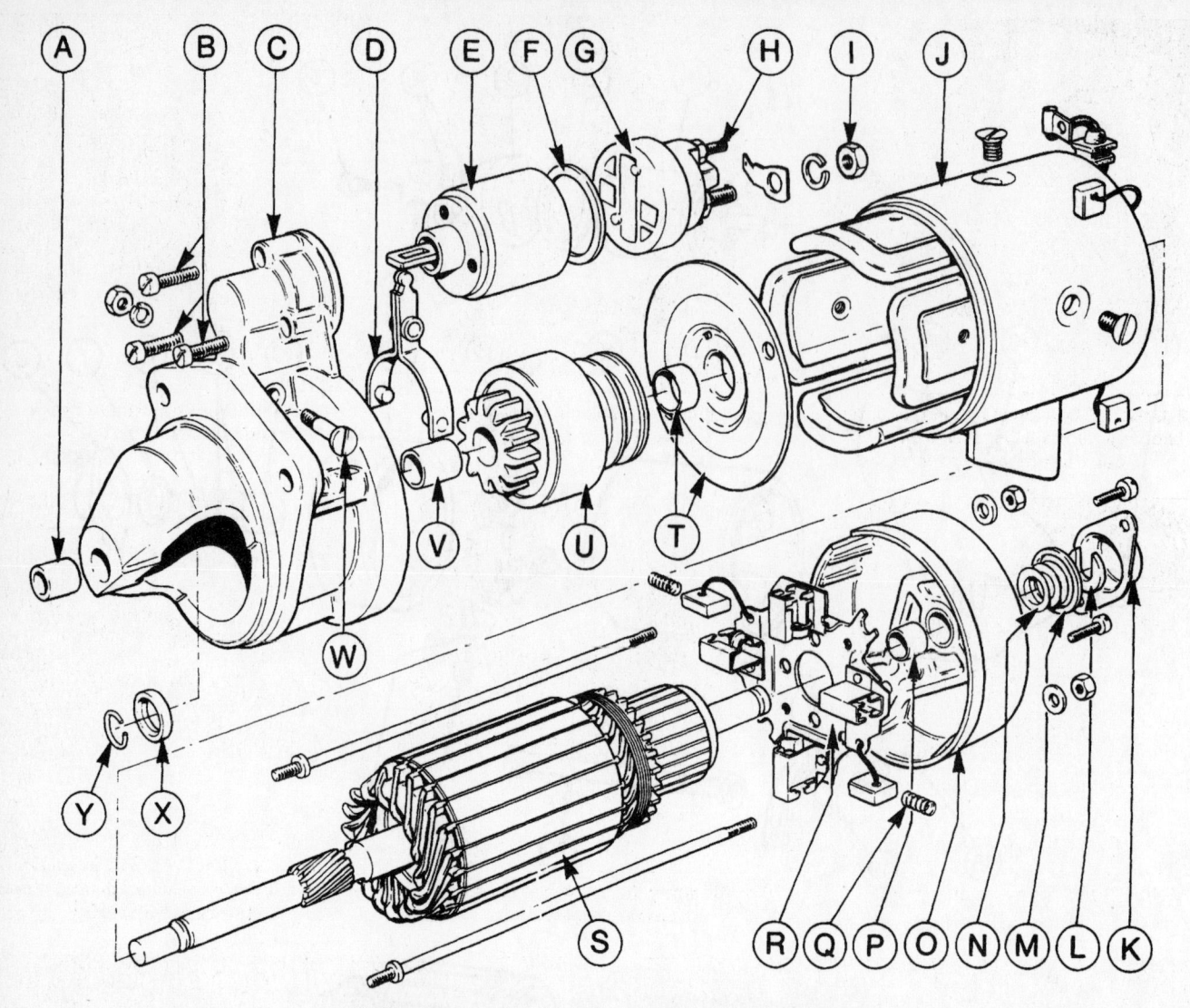

9.0e Exploded view of the Bosch JF (2.7kW) starter motor

A	Bearing bush	H	Main terminals	N	Shims
B	Solenoid screws	I	Nut	O	Commutator end housing
C	Drive end housing	J	Yoke	P	Bearing bush
D	Actuating lever	K	End cover	Q	Brush spring
E	Solenoid	L	C-clip	R	Brushbox
F	Gasket	M	Seal	S	Armature
G	Switch contacts and cover				

T	Centre bearing and plate	W	Pivot screw
U	Drive pinion assembly	X	Thrust collar
V	Bearing bush	Y	C-clip

2 Undo the two small bolts and the two large through-bolts from the commutator end cover **(see illustration)**.
3 Withdraw the commutator end cover from the starter **(see illustration)**.
4 Remove the armature brake shoes and springs, and the two washers, from the end cover **(see illustrations)**.
5 Slip the field coil brushes out of their locations, and withdraw the brush plate assembly from the commutator **(see illustration)**. Withdraw the two remaining brushes from the brush plate assembly after removal.
6 Check the length of the brushes. If any are worn to less than the minimum length given in the Specifications, renew them **(see illustration)**.
7 To renew the field coil brushes, cut the brush lead as near to the conductor as possible, and remove the old brush. Prise the conductor away from the yoke to provide room for soldering, then solder on the new brush lead. Renew the second field coil brush in the same way.
8 To renew the brushes on the brush plate assembly, place a hot soldering iron on the soldered end of the brush lead. As soon as the solder is molten, prise open the connector, remove the old brush lead, and locate the new brush lead. Close the connector, and solder it in place.
9 Clean the commutator with fine glasspaper, then wipe clean with a solvent-moistened cloth.
10 Check the condition of the armature brake shoe driving peg in the armature shaft. If it is damaged or distorted, drive it out with a pin punch, and fit a new peg **(see illustration)**.
11 Check that all four brushes move freely in their holders, and that the springs are undamaged and provide uniform tension.
12 Place the two brush plate brushes in their holders, and engage the springs against the side of the brushes **(see illustration)**. Don't push the brushes in all the way at this time, or it will be difficult to fit the

Chapter 5 Engine electrical systems

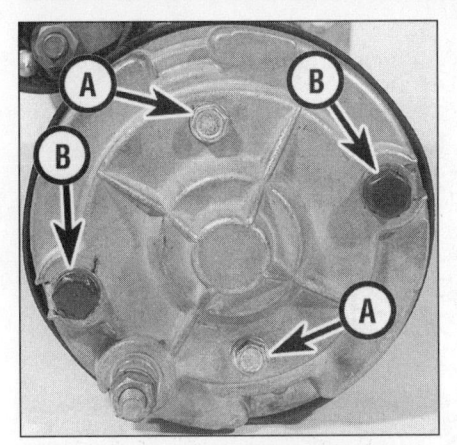

5-9

9.2 Undo the two small bolts (A) and the two large through-bolts (B) from the commutator end cover

9.3 Withdraw the commutator end cover from the starter

9.4a Remove the armature brake shoes and springs . . .

9.4b . . . and the two washers from the end cover

9.5 Withdraw the brush plate assembly from the commutator

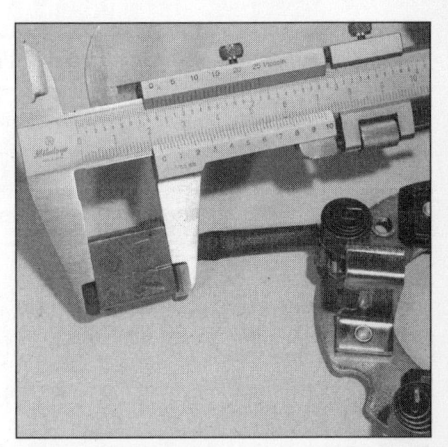

9.6 Measure the brush length and renew the brushes if necessary

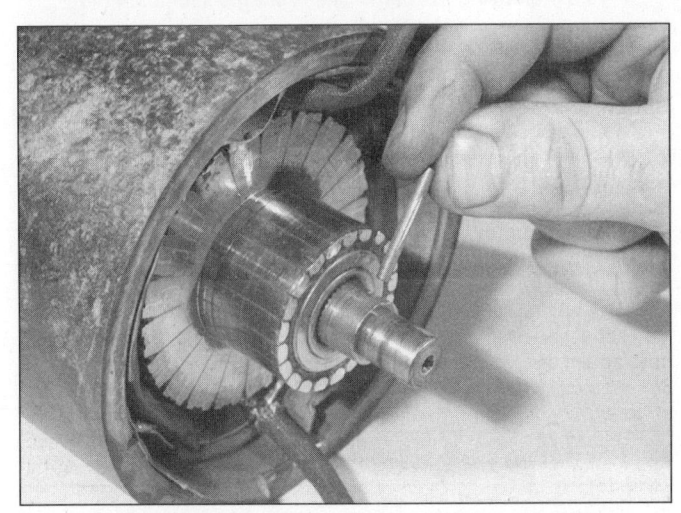

9.10 Renew the armature brake shoe driving peg in the armature shaft if damaged

9.12 Place the two brush plate brushes in their holders, and engage the springs against the side of the brushes to retain them when refitting

brush plate over the commutator.

13 Fit the two field coil brushes to their holders in the same way, then locate the brush plate assembly over the commutator. When in position, push the brush ends towards the commutator until the springs slip into place over the brush ends.

14 Refit the armature brake shoes and springs, and the two washers, to the end cover.

15 Refit the end cover, ensuring that the driving peg on the armature engages in the cut-outs in the brake shoes.

16 Align the bolt holes in the end cover and brush plate assembly, then refit the through-bolts and the two small brush plate retaining bolts.

17 Refit the starter motor as described in Section 8.

5-10 Chapter 5 Engine electrical systems

11.1 Oil pressure warning light switch location (arrowed)

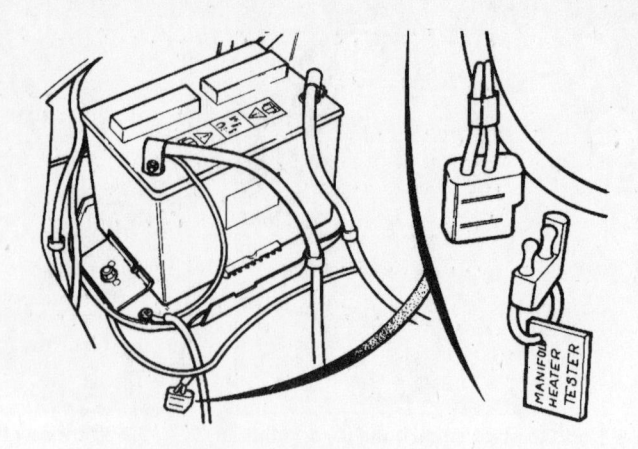

12.2 Preheating system test connector location below the battery tray

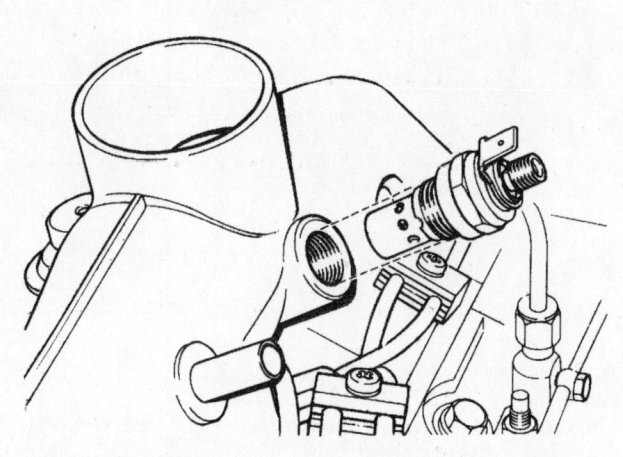

13.3 Removing the flame-plug from the inlet manifold

10 Ignition switch - removal and refitting

The ignition switch removal and refitting procedures are contained in Chapter 12, Section 4.

11 Oil pressure warning light switch - removal and refitting

Removal

1 The oil pressure warning light switch is located on the right-hand side of the cylinder block, below the fuel injection pump **(see illustration)**.
2 Disconnect the wiring from the switch terminal, then unscrew the switch from the cylinder block.

Refitting

3 Refitting is a reversal of removal.

12 Preheating system - description and testing

Description

1 A preheating system is not normally fitted, since the engine will start without preheating at temperatures down to -20°C (-4°F). However, vehicles primarily intended for low temperature operation may be fitted with this option. The system consists of a fuel reservoir, solenoid, control unit and electrically-heated flame-plug. On starting the engine from cold, the solenoid valve allows fuel from the flame-plug reservoir to flow to the flame-plug element located in the inlet manifold. The electric element ignites the fuel, which is then drawn into the combustion chambers to assist starting.

Testing

2 Locate the preheating system test connector below the battery tray. Bridge the connector terminals, using an insulated wire link with two male connectors **(see illustration)**.
3 Have an assistant switch on the ignition; the preheating warning light should illuminate for approximately 5 seconds, and then go out. While the light is lit, and for up to twenty seconds after it goes out, the flame plug should operate. Confirm this by carefully feeling for heat around the plug. **Caution:** *The plug will get very hot.* Switch off the ignition.
4 If the system does not operate, disconnect the fuel pipe from the flame plug, and place the end of the pipe in a small container. Disconnect the electrical connector from the flame plug. Connect a voltmeter or 12-volt test light between the electrical feed and earth.
5 Switch on the ignition again. The voltmeter should read battery voltage, or the test light should come on, while the warning light is on, and for up to twenty seconds after it has gone out. While voltage is present, fuel should flow from the pipe.
6 If no voltage is present at the flame plug electrical feed, there is a fault in the wiring or the control unit. If voltage is present, but fuel does not flow even though the reservoir is full, there is a fault in the wiring to the solenoid valve, or in the valve itself.
7 If voltage and fuel are both present, but the flame plug does not operate, remove the plug and apply 12 volts to its electrical terminal. Earth the body of the plug. The heating element inside the body of the plug should be seen to glow red. **Caution:** *The plug will get very hot.* If the element does not glow, renew the plug.
8 Remove the bridging wire from the test connector on completion.

13 Preheating system flame plug - removal and refitting

Removal

1 Disconnect the battery negative lead.
2 Disconnect the electrical connection at the flame-plug, and unscrew the fuel feed pipe union. Place the end of the fuel pipe in a small container to catch any escaping fuel.
3 Unscrew the flame-plug from the inlet manifold, and remove it **(see illustration)**.

Refitting

4 Refitting is a reversal of removal.

Chapter 6 Clutch

Contents

	Section		Section
Clutch assembly - removal, inspection and refitting.....................	4	Clutch pedal - removal and refitting...	3
Clutch cable - removal and refitting...	2	Clutch release mechanism - removal, inspection and refitting......	5
Clutch cable lubrication... See Chapter 1		General information..	1

Specifications

Type .... Single dry plate with diaphragm spring, cable operation and automatic adjustment

Clutch disc
Diameter .... 242 mm
Lining thickness (new) .... 8.4 mm

Torque wrench settings
	Nm	lbf ft
Clutch cover (pressure plate) to flywheel:		
Type G and N transmissions	16 to 20	12 to 15
MT75 transmission	30	22
Clutch housing to transmission	55 to 65	41 to 48

Chapter 6 Clutch

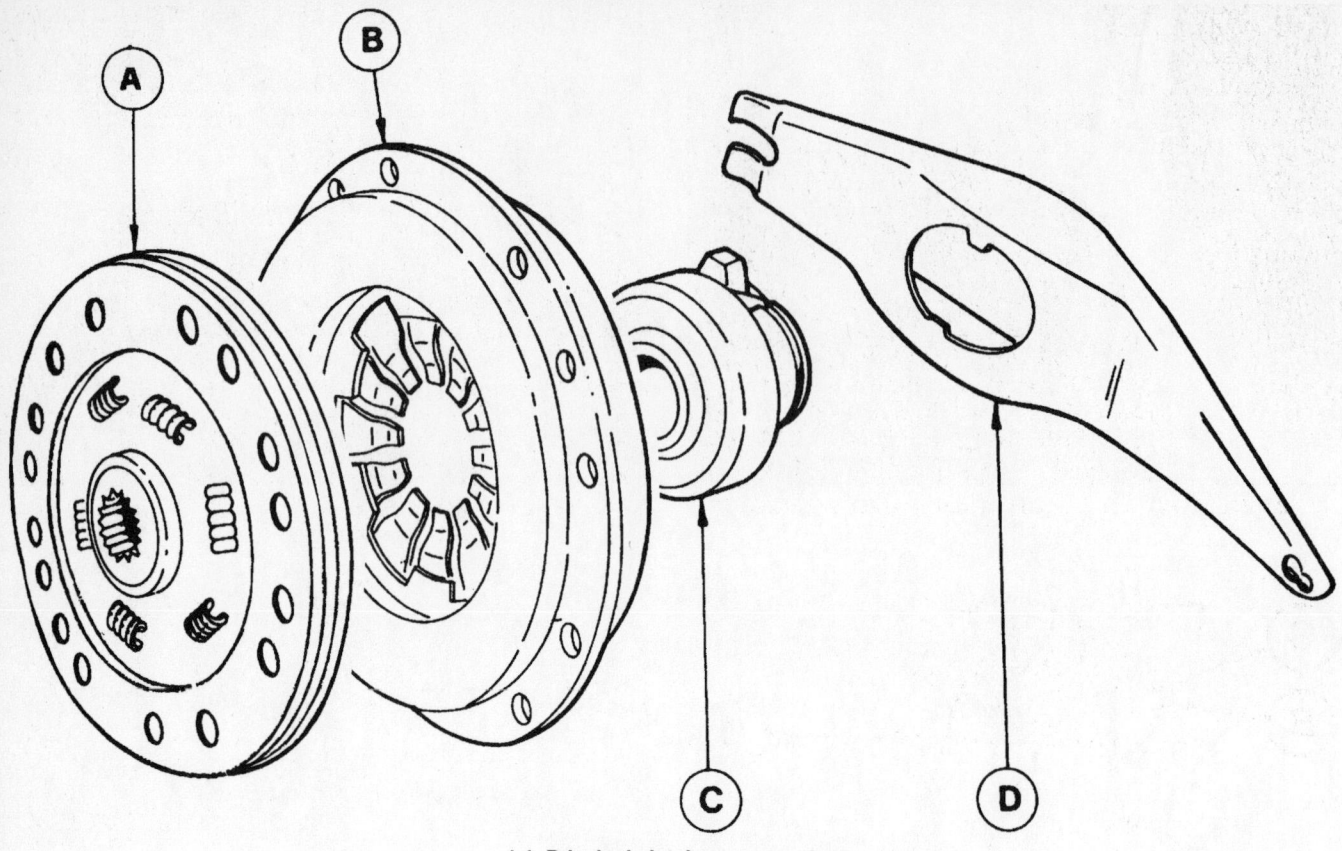

1.1 Principal clutch components

A Clutch disc
B Cover assembly
C Release bearing
D Release lever

1 General information

All manual transmission models have a cable-operated single dry plate diaphragm spring clutch assembly. The unit consists of a steel cover (dowelled and bolted to the rear face of the flywheel), the pressure plate and diaphragm spring **(see illustration)**.

The clutch disc is free to slide along the splines of the transmission input shaft, and is held in position between the flywheel and the pressure plate by the pressure of the diaphragm spring. Friction lining material is riveted to the clutch disc, which has a spring-cushioned hub, to absorb transmission shocks and help ensure a smooth take-up of the drive.

The clutch is actuated by a cable, controlled by the clutch pedal. The clutch release mechanism consists of a release lever and a bearing which is in permanent contact with the fingers of the diaphragm spring. Depressing the clutch pedal actuates the release lever by means of the cable. The lever pushes the release bearing against the diaphragm fingers, so moving the centre of the diaphragm spring inwards. As the centre of the spring is pushed in, the outside of the spring pivots out, so moving the pressure plate backwards and disengaging its grip on the clutch disc.

When the pedal is released, the diaphragm spring forces the pressure plate back into contact with the friction linings on the clutch disc. The disc is now firmly held between the pressure plate and the flywheel, thus transmitting engine power to the transmission.

Wear of the friction material on the clutch disc is automatically compensated for by a self-adjusting mechanism attached to the clutch pedal. The mechanism consists of a toothed segment, a notched pawl and a tension spring. One end of the clutch cable is attached to the segment which is free to pivot on the pedal, but is kept in tension by the spring. As the pedal is depressed, the pawl contacts the segment, thus locking it and allowing the pedal to pull the cable and operate the clutch. As the pedal is released, the tension spring causes the segment to move free of the pawl and rotate slightly, thus taking up any free play that may exist in the cable.

2 Clutch cable - removal and refitting

Removal

1 Check that the handbrake is fully applied, and chock the rear wheels. Raise the front of the vehicle, and support it on axle stands at a height which will allow comfortable working space underneath.
2 Unhook the inner cable from the toothed segment of the automatic adjustment mechanism on the clutch pedal **(see illustration)**.
3 From under the vehicle, detach the clutch release lever rubber boot from the side of the clutch housing, and slide it up the cable **(see illustration)**.
4 Slip the inner cable out of the slot on the release lever, and free the outer cable from the clutch housing. Slide the rubber boot off the cable.
5 Withdraw the cable through the bulkhead, and remove it from the engine compartment side.

Refitting

6 To refit the cable, feed it through the bulkhead and clutch housing, then slide the rubber boot over the cable at the release lever end. Attach the cable to the release lever, and refit the rubber boot.
7 Position a suitable wooden block under the clutch pedal, to raise it fully so that the automatic adjuster pawl is held clear of the toothed segment.

Chapter 6 Clutch

2.2 Clutch cable connection (arrowed) at the pedal end

2.3 Clutch release lever, cable and rubber boot attachments at the transmission end

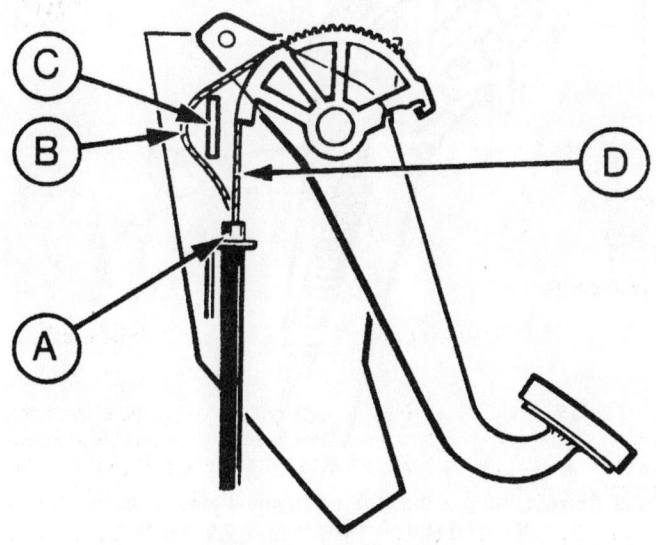

2.8 Clutch cable routing

A Cable abutment
B Incorrect cable route
C Pawl disengagement bracket
D Correct cable route

8 Connect the cable to the toothed segment, ensuring that it is correctly routed **(see illustration)**.
9 Remove the wooden block, and depress the pedal several times to adjust the cable. Lower the vehicle to the ground.

3 Clutch pedal - removal and refitting

Removal

1 Unhook the clutch inner cable from the toothed segment of the automatic adjustment mechanism on the clutch pedal.
2 Prise free the clutch pedal shaft retainer clip, remove the washer, and then withdraw the pedal from the shaft.
3 To dismantle the pedal, extract the two bushes, then withdraw the toothed adjuster segment and the tension spring. Extract the clips, withdraw the pin, and remove the pawl and spring (but note how they are fitted) **(see illustration)**.
4 Renew any worn or damaged parts.

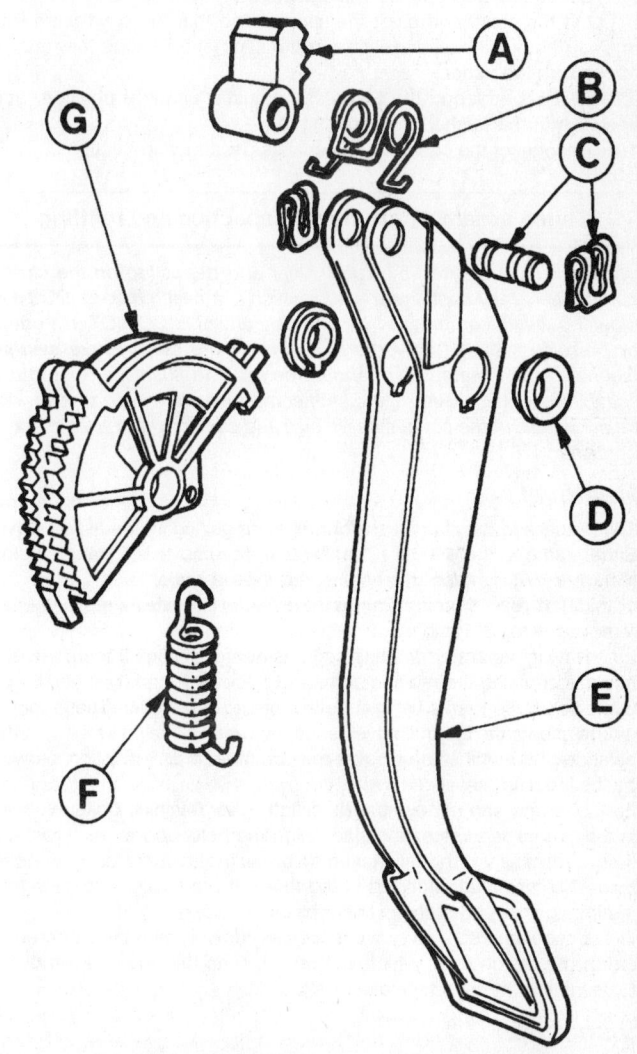

3.3 Exploded view of the clutch pedal and automatic adjuster components

A Pawl
B Spring
C Pawl pin and clip
D Pedal shaft bush
E Clutch pedal
F Toothed segment tension spring
G Toothed segment

6-4 Chapter 6 Clutch

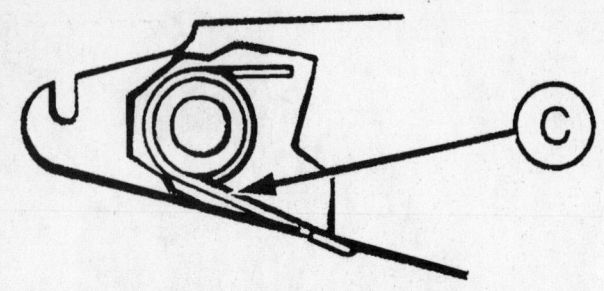

3.5a Correct orientation of the clutch pedal pawl spring (C) - pawl not shown for clarity

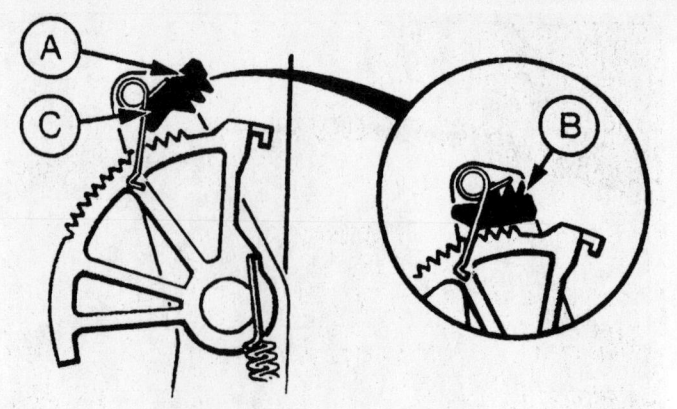

3.5b Clutch pedal pawl orientation

A Correct fitting
B Incorrect fitting
C Pawl

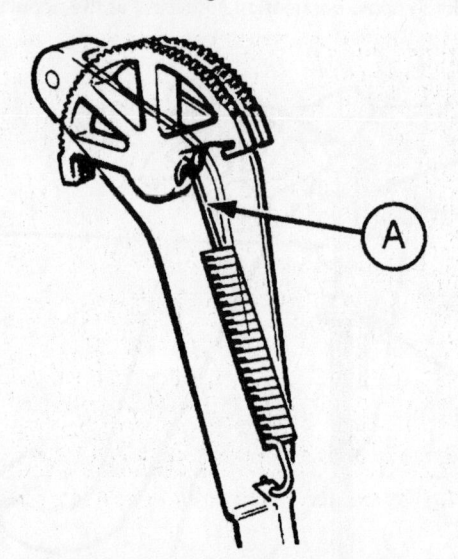

3.6 Correct fitting of the toothed segment tension spring (A) with the long end section towards the segment

Refitting

5 Fit the pawl, spring, pin and retaining clip. Ensure that the spring and pawl are correctly fitted **(see illustrations)**.
6 Engage the toothed segment tension spring to the segment, and the segment to the pedal. Ensure that the spring is fitted with its long end section towards the toothed segment **(see illustration)**.
7 Locate the new bushes in the pedal.
8 Lift the pawl, and pivot the segment so that the pawl teeth rest against the small curved section of the segment. Engage the tension spring with the pedal.
9 Fit the pedal and the automatic adjuster unit into position, and secure with the washer and securing clip.
10 Reconnect the cable to the pedal as described in Section 2.

4 Clutch assembly - removal inspection and refitting

Warning: *Dust created by clutch wear and deposited on the clutch components may contain asbestos, which is a health hazard. DO NOT blow it out with compressed air, or inhale any of it. DO NOT use petrol or petroleum-based solvents to clean off the dust. Brake system cleaner or methylated spirit should be used to flush the dust into a suitable receptacle. After the clutch components are wiped clean with rags, dispose of the contaminated rags and cleaner in a sealed, marked container.*

Removal

1 Access to the clutch assembly may be gained in one of two ways. Either remove the engine (Chapter 2B) or remove the transmission (Chapter 7A). Unless the engine requires a major overhaul or the crankshaft rear oil seal requires renewal, it is easier and quicker to remove the transmission.
2 Having separated the engine/transmission, check if there are any marks identifying the relation of the clutch cover to the flywheel. If not, make your own marks using a dab of paint or a scriber. These marks will be used if the original cover is refitted, and will help to maintain the balance of the unit. A new cover may be fitted in any position allowed by the locating dowels.
3 Unscrew and remove the six clutch cover retaining bolts, working in a diagonal sequence, and slackening the bolts only a few turns at a time. If necessary, the flywheel may be held stationary using a wide-bladed screwdriver, inserted in the teeth of the starter ring gear and resting against part of the cylinder block.
4 Ease the clutch cover off its locating dowels, and be prepared to catch the clutch disc, which will drop out as the cover is removed. Note which way round the disc is fitted.

Inspection

5 The most common problem which occurs in the clutch is wear of the clutch disc. However, all the clutch components should be inspected at this time, particularly if the engine has covered a high mileage. Unless the clutch components are known to be virtually new, it is worth renewing them all as a set (disc, pressure plate and release bearing). Renewing a worn clutch disc by itself is not always satisfactory, especially if the old disc was slipping and causing the pressure plate to overheat.
6 Examine the linings of the clutch disc for wear and loose rivets, and the disc hub and rim for distortion, cracks, broken torsion springs, and worn splines. The surface of the friction linings may be highly glazed, but as long as the friction material pattern can be clearly seen, and the rivet heads are at least 1 mm below the lining surface, this is satisfactory. If there is any sign of oil contamination, indicated by shiny black discoloration, the disc must be renewed, and the source of the contamination traced and rectified. This will be a leaking crankshaft oil seal or transmission input shaft oil seal. The oil seal renewal procedures are given in Chapters 2A and 7A respectively.
7 Check the machined faces of the flywheel and pressure plate. If either is grooved, or heavily scored, renewal is necessary. The pressure plate must also be renewed if any cracks are apparent, or if the diaphragm spring is damaged or its pressure suspect. Pay particular attention to the tips of the spring fingers, where the release bearing acts upon them.
8 With the transmission removed, it is also advisable to check the condition of the release bearing, as described in Section 5. Having got this far, it is almost certainly worth renewing it.

Refitting

9 It is important that no oil or grease is allowed to come into contact with the friction material of the clutch disc, or the pressure plate and flywheel faces. To ensure this, it is advisable to refit the clutch

Chapter 6 Clutch   6-5

4.10 Flywheel side clutch disc marking

4.15 Using a clutch-aligning tool to centralise the clutch disc

4.16 Tighten the cover bolts to the specified torque

5.6 Removing the clutch release bearing

assembly with clean hands, and to wipe down the pressure plate and flywheel faces with a clean dry rag before assembly begins.

10 Begin reassembly by placing the clutch disc against the flywheel, ensuring that it is correctly orientated. It may be marked "flywheel side", but if not, position it with the word "schwungradseite" stamped in the disc face towards the flywheel **(see illustration)**.

11 Place the clutch cover over the dowels. Refit the retaining bolts, and tighten them finger-tight so that the clutch disc is gripped, but can still be moved.

12 The clutch disc must now be centralised so that, when the engine and transmission are mated, the splines of the input shaft will pass through the splines in the centre of the clutch disc hub.

13 Centralisation can be carried out by inserting a round bar through the hole in the centre of the clutch disc, so that the end of the bar rests in the transmission input shaft support bearing in the rear end of the crankshaft. Move the bar sideways or up and down to move the clutch disc in whichever direction is necessary to achieve centralisation.

14 Centralisation can then be checked by removing the bar and viewing the clutch disc hub in relation to the diaphragm spring fingers. When the disc hub appears exactly in the centre of the circle created by the diaphragm spring fingers, the position is correct.

15 An alternative and more accurate method of centralisation is to use a commercially-available clutch-aligning tool obtainable from most accessory shops **(see illustration)**.

16 Once the clutch is centralised, progressively tighten the cover bolts in a diagonal sequence to the torque setting given in the Specifications **(see illustration)**.

17 Ensure that the input shaft splines, clutch disc splines and release bearing guide sleeve are clean. Apply a thin smear of high-melting-point grease to the input shaft splines and the release bearing guide sleeve. Only use a very small amount of grease, otherwise the excess will inevitably find its way onto the friction linings when the vehicle is in use.

18 The engine/transmission can now be refitted by referring to the relevant Chapters of this manual.

5 Clutch release mechanism - removal, inspection and refitting

Removal

1 With the engine and transmission separated to provide access to the clutch, attention can be given to the release mechanism components located in the clutch housing.

Type G transmission

2 If the engine has been removed leaving the transmission still in the vehicle, disconnect the clutch cable at the transmission release lever.

3 Undo the retaining bolts, and separate the clutch housing from the transmission.

4 Disengage the release lever from the fulcrum pin by pulling it sideways, then remove the lever and release bearing from the housing.

5 Extract the retaining circlip, and remove the release bearing from the release lever.

Type N and MT75 transmissions

6 Free the release bearing from the release lever, and withdraw it from the guide sleeve **(see illustration)**.

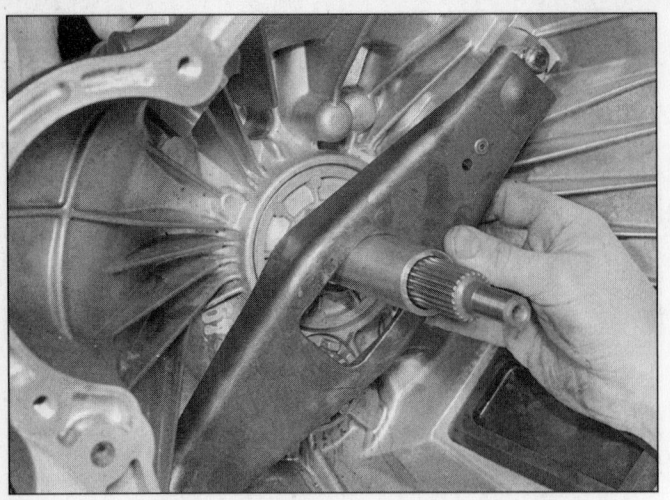

5.7 Withdrawing the clutch release lever from the guide sleeve and input shaft

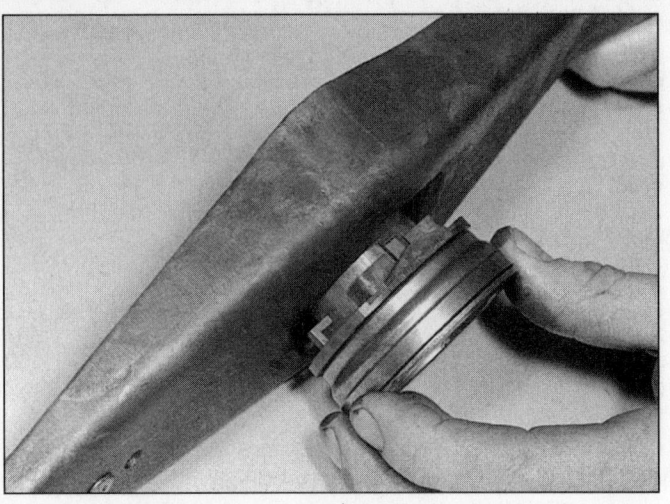

5.11 Release bearing location on the release lever

7 Pull the release lever from the fulcrum pin, then withdraw the lever over the guide sleeve and input shaft **(see illustration)**.

Inspection

8 Check the bearing for smoothness of operation, and renew it if there is any sign of harshness or roughness as the bearing is spun. Do not attempt to dismantle, clean or lubricate the bearing.

9 As mentioned earlier, it is worth renewing the release bearing as a matter of course, unless it is known to be in perfect condition.

10 Check the condition of the release lever, ensuring that it is not bent or distorted.

Refitting

All transmission types

11 Refitting is a reversal of removal. Apply a thin smear of high-melting-point grease to the release bearing guide sleeve and release lever fulcrum pin. Ensure that the bearing is correctly located in the release lever (and secured with the circlip on type G transmissions) and that the release lever forked end engages with the fulcrum pin **(see illustration)**. On type G transmissions, refit the clutch housing, and tighten the retaining bolts to the specified torque.

Chapter 7 Part A: Manual transmission

Contents

	Section		Section
Gear lever - removal and refitting	2	Overdrive solenoid valve - removal and refitting	12
General information	1	Overdrive switch - removal and refitting	10
Manual transmission - removal and refitting	7	Overdrive unit - general information	9
Manual transmission mounting - inspection and renewal	6	Overdrive unit - removal and refitting	13
Manual transmission oil level check	See Chapter 1	Overdrive unit overhaul - general information	14
Manual transmission overhaul - general information	8	Reversing light switch - testing, removal and refitting	4
Oil seals - renewal	3	Speedometer drive pinion - removal and refitting	5
Overdrive inhibitor switch - removal and refitting	11		

Specifications

General
Type.. Four or five forward speeds and reverse. Synchromesh on all forward speeds (and on reverse with MT75 transmission). Overdrive available on type G transmission

Designation:
- Four-speed transmission .... Type G
- Five-speed transmission .... Type N (up to end 1988), MT75 (late 1988 onwards)

Gear ratios
Type G transmission:
- 1st .... 4.06 : 1
- 2nd .... 2.16 : 1
- 3rd .... 1.38 : 1
- 3rd + overdrive .... 1.07 : 1
- 4th .... 1.00 : 1
- 4th + overdrive .... 0.78 : 1
- Reverse .... 4.29 : 1

Type N transmission:
- 1st .... 3.90 : 1
- 2nd .... 2.87 : 1
- 3rd .... 1.38 : 1
- 4th .... 1.00 : 1
- 5th .... 0.81 : 1
- Reverse .... 3.66 : 1

MT75 transmission:

	Close-ratio	Wide-ratio
1st	3.89 : 1	4.17 : 1
2nd	2.08 : 1	2.24 : 1
3rd	1.34 : 1	1.47 : 1
4th	1.00 : 1	1.00 : 1
5th	0.82 : 1	0.82 : 1
Reverse	3.51 : 1	3.76 : 1

Chapter 7 Part A: Manual transmission

Overdrive
Type... Laycock de Normanville, model J
Application... Optional equipment on Type G transmission

Lubrication
Lubricant type/capacity.................................. See "Lubricants, fluids and capacities"

Torque wrench settings

	Nm	lbf ft
Type G and type N transmissions		
Clutch housing to transmission	55 to 65	41 to 48
Oil filler and drain plugs	23 to 32	17 to 23
Overdrive rear housing to overdrive unit	13 to 19	10 to 14
Overdrive unit to transmission intermediate flange	7 to 11	5 to 8
Release bearing guide sleeve to transmission:		
Type G transmission	16 to 21	12 to 15
Type N transmission	9 to 11	6 to 8
Reversing light switch	1 to 2	0.7 to 1.5
Transmission crossmember to floor	40 to 50	30 to 37
Transmission mounting to crossmember	70 to 90	52 to 66
Transmission to engine	30 to 40	22 to 29
MT75 transmission		
Oil filler and drain plugs	35	26
Output shaft flange locknut	200	148
Release bearing guide sleeve to transmission	160	118
Reversing light switch	12	9
Transmission crossmember to floor	50	37
Transmission mounting to crossmember	84	62
Transmission mounting to transmission	50	37
Transmission to engine	35	26

1 General information

The vehicles covered by this manual are fitted with either a 4- or 5-speed manual, or 4-speed automatic transmission. This Part of Chapter 7 contains information on the manual transmission. Service procedures for the automatic transmission are contained in Part B.

Three types of manual transmission are available, namely the type G, type N, and MT75 **(see illustrations)**. An overdrive unit is available as an option on the type G unit. On all models, the transmission is mounted in-line, and to the rear of the engine. A propeller shaft transfers the drive to the rear axle. All transmission types are of constant-mesh design.

Type G and N transmissions

With these types, all forward gear selection is by synchromesh. All forward gears are helical, and the reverse gear is straight-cut.

The clutch housing, selector housing (type G), and the extension housing are all bolted to the main transmission case.

The input shaft and mainshaft are in line, and rotate on ball-bearings. The mainshaft spigot runs in needle-roller bearings, as does the countershaft (layshaft) gear assembly.

The synchronisers are of baulk ring and blocker bar type, and operate in conjunction with tapered cones machined onto the gears. When engaging a gear, the synchroniser sleeve pushes the baulk ring against the tapered gear cone by means of the three spring-tensioned blocker bars. The drag of the baulk ring causes the gear to rotate at the same speed as the synchroniser unit, and at this point, further movement of the sleeve locks the sleeve, baulk ring and gear dog teeth together.

Reverse gear is obtained by moving the reverse idler gear into mesh with the countershaft gear and the spur teeth of the 1st/2nd synchroniser.

With the type G transmission, a three-rail selector mechanism is used, whereby the rails are located in the housing, and move in accordance with the gear lever position. The selector forks are located in position on the rails, and these actuate the gear selection.

On the type N transmission, a single-rail selector mechanism is utilised.

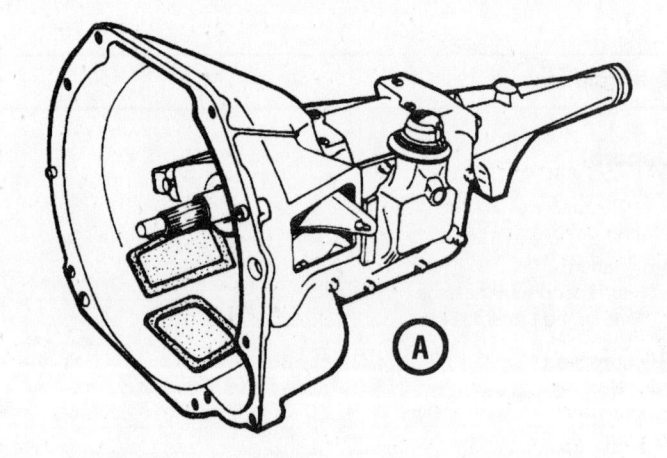

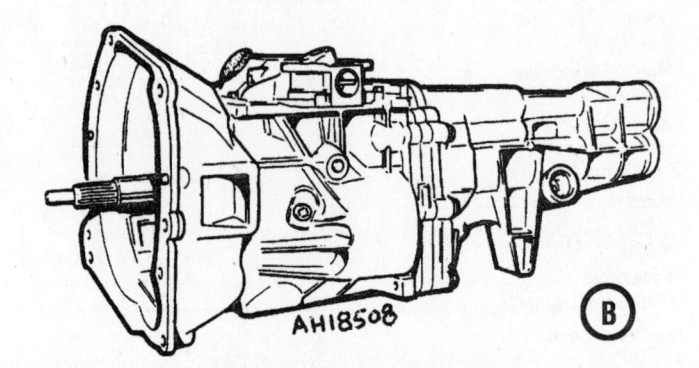

1.2a Type G and N transmissions

A   Type G   B   Type N

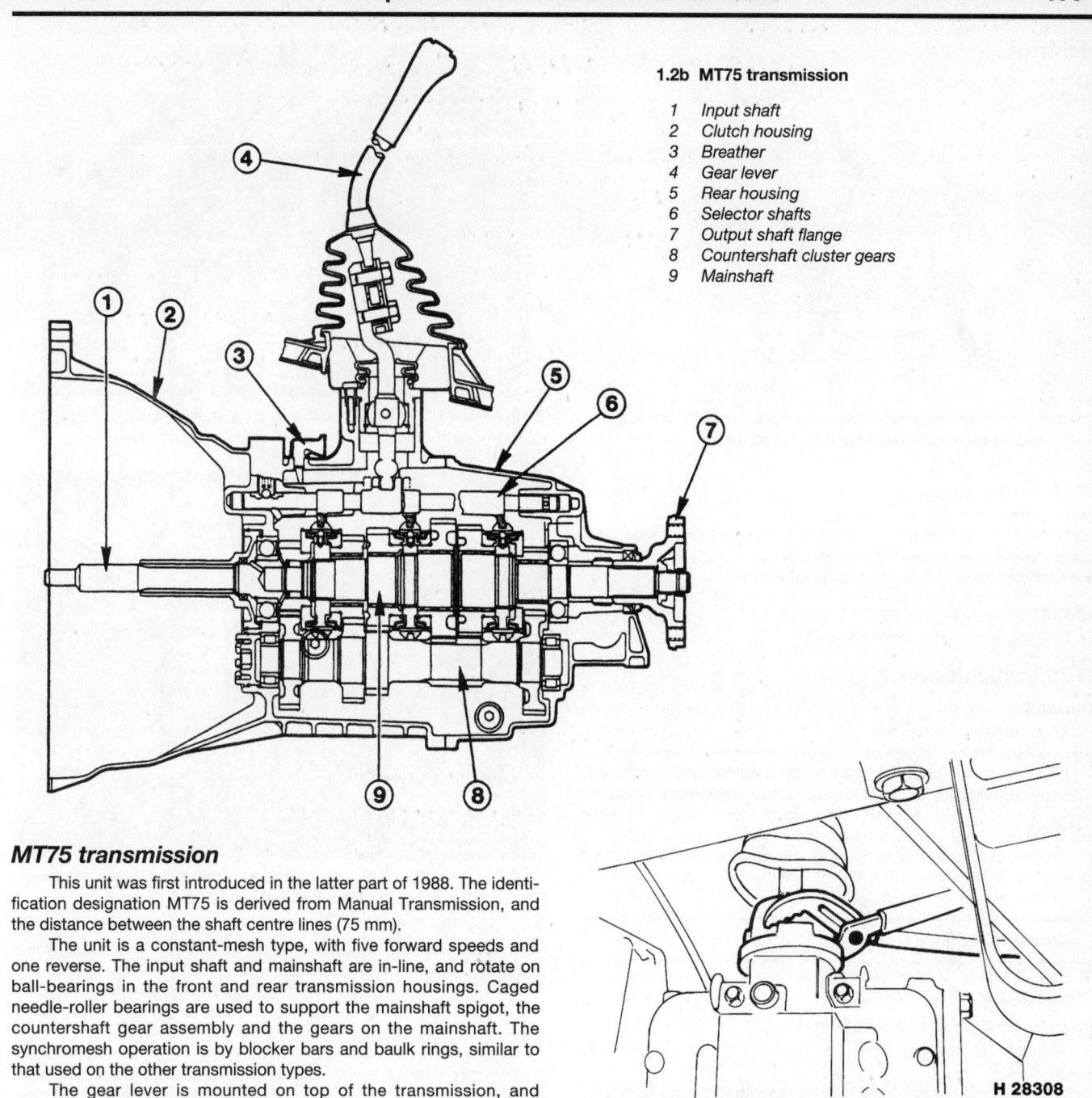

Chapter 7 Part A: Manual transmission

1.2b MT75 transmission

1 Input shaft
2 Clutch housing
3 Breather
4 Gear lever
5 Rear housing
6 Selector shafts
7 Output shaft flange
8 Countershaft cluster gears
9 Mainshaft

MT75 transmission

This unit was first introduced in the latter part of 1988. The identification designation MT75 is derived from Manual Transmission, and the distance between the shaft centre lines (75 mm).

The unit is a constant-mesh type, with five forward speeds and one reverse. The input shaft and mainshaft are in-line, and rotate on ball-bearings in the front and rear transmission housings. Caged needle-roller bearings are used to support the mainshaft spigot, the countershaft gear assembly and the gears on the mainshaft. The synchromesh operation is by blocker bars and baulk rings, similar to that used on the other transmission types.

The gear lever is mounted on top of the transmission, and engages directly with the selector forks.

The transmission case is in two halves, the front half containing the clutch housing, and the rear half which contains the main gear assemblies and the selector units.

2.4 On the type G transmission, unscrew the gear lever plastic retaining cap from the transmission using suitable large grips

2 Gear lever - removal and refitting

Type G transmission

Removal

1 Apply the handbrake, then raise and support the vehicle at the front on axle stands.
2 From inside the cab, undo the screws securing the upper gaiter and cover plate to the floor, and slide the gaiter up the lever.
3 From under the vehicle, unhook the spring from the gear lever and the transmission bracket.
4 Slide the lower gaiter up the lever, then unscrew the gear lever plastic retaining cap from the transmission using suitable large grips **(see illustration)**. Lift the lever out of the transmission, and remove it from under the vehicle.

Refitting

5 Refitting is a reversal of removal.

Type N transmission

Removal

6 Apply the handbrake, then raise and support the vehicle at the front on axle stands.
7 From inside the cab area, unscrew the gear lever knob, then undo the screws securing the upper gaiter and cover plate to the floor. Slide the gaiter and cover plate up and off the gear lever.

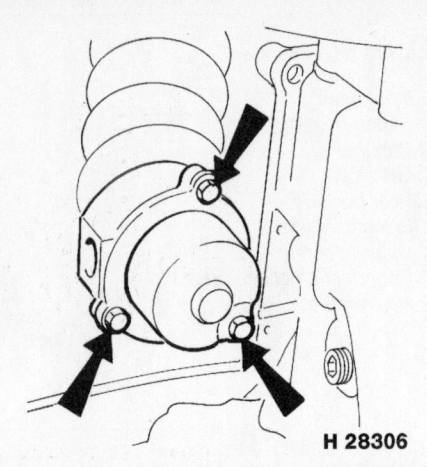

2.9 On the type N transmission, undo the three bolts (arrowed) and withdraw the gear lever from the transmission

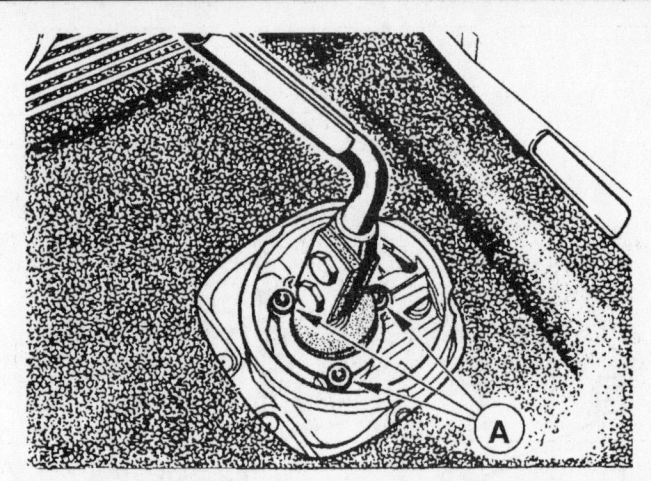

2.12 On the MT75 transmission, undo the three Torx bolts (A) and withdraw the gear lever from the transmission

8 Undo the screws securing the lower gaiter to the transmission selector gate, and withdraw the gaiter upwards and off the lever.
9 From under the vehicle, undo the three bolts securing the gear lever to the selector gate, withdraw the lever from the transmission and remove it from under the vehicle (see illustration).

Refitting
10 Refitting is a reversal of removal.

MT75 transmission

Removal
11 From inside the cab, disengage the rubber gaiter and rubber cover from the floor locating flange, and slide them up the gear lever.
12 Undo the three Torx bolts securing the lever to the transmission, withdraw the lever and remove it from the vehicle (see illustration).

Refitting
13 Refitting is a reversal of removal. Correct location of the gear lever rubber cover is indicated by the words "Top Rear".

3 Oil seals - renewal

Front (input shaft) oil seal

Type G and type N transmissions
1 Remove the transmission from the vehicle as described in Section 7.
2 Thoroughly clean the transmission assembly, paying particular attention to the area inside the clutch housing.
3 On the type N transmission, free the clutch release bearing from the release lever, and withdraw it from the guide sleeve. Pull the release lever from the fulcrum pin, then withdraw the lever from the guide sleeve and input shaft.
4 Unscrew the bolts, and remove the clutch housing from the front of the transmission case (see illustration). On the type G transmission, the housing is removed complete with clutch release bearing and lever.
5 Undo the bolts, and remove the release bearing guide sleeve (see illustration). As no transmission drain plug is provided on the type N transmission, be prepared for some oil spillage as the guide sleeve is removed.
6 Using a screwdriver, prise out the old oil seal from the guide sleeve bore. Fit the new oil seal using a large socket or tube of suitable diameter to drive it home. Ensure that the seal is fitted so that the sealing lip faces the transmission case when installed (see illustrations).

3.4 Unscrew the bolts (arrowed) and remove the clutch housing from the front of the transmission case

7 Clean off all traces of old gasket from the mating faces of the guide sleeve and transmission case.
8 Lubricate the oil seal lip with multi-purpose grease.
9 Wrap some adhesive tape over the splines of the input shaft, to prevent damage to the oil seal when refitting.
10 Using a new gasket, carefully locate the guide sleeve on the transmission case so that the cut-out in the gasket, and the slot in the guide sleeve, align with the oil return port in the transmission case (see illustration).
11 Apply sealing compound to the guide sleeve retaining bolts, refit the bolts and tighten to the specified torque. Remove the protective adhesive tape.
12 Apply a thin smear of high-melting-point grease to the guide sleeve, then refit the clutch housing. Refit and tighten the retaining bolts to the specified torque.
13 On the type N transmission, apply a thin smear of high-melting-point grease to the release lever fulcrum pin, then refit the clutch release bearing and lever.
14 Refit the transmission as described in Section 7.

MT75 transmission
Note: *The following procedure entails the use of Ford special tool 16-040 to remove and refit the input shaft guide sleeve. Ensure that this tool, or a suitable alternative, is available before proceeding.*
15 Remove the transmission from the vehicle as described in Section 7.

Chapter 7 Part A: Manual transmission   7A-5

3.5 Removing the release bearing guide sleeve

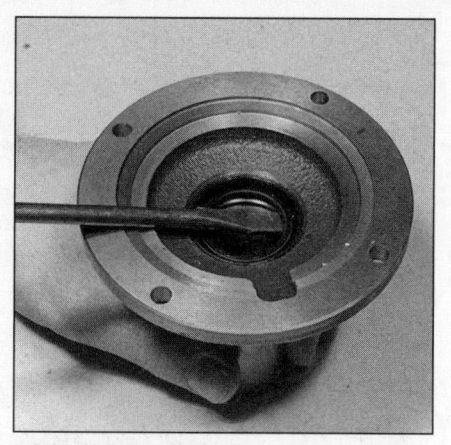

3.6a Using a screwdriver, prise out the old oil seal from the guide sleeve bore

3.6b Fit the new oil seal using a large socket or tube of suitable diameter to drive it home

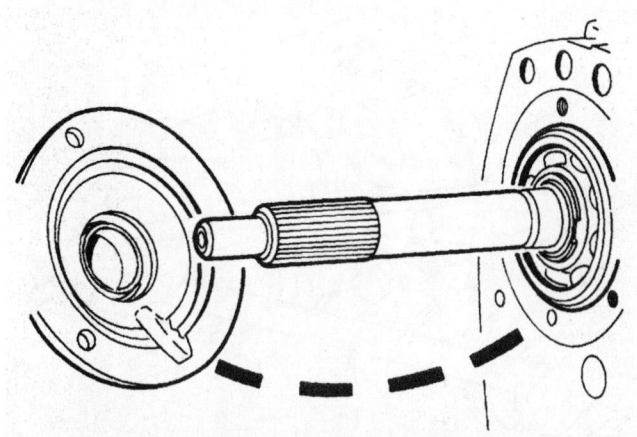

3.10 Locate the guide sleeve on the transmission case so that the cut-out in the gasket, and the slot in the guide sleeve, align with the oil return port in the transmission case

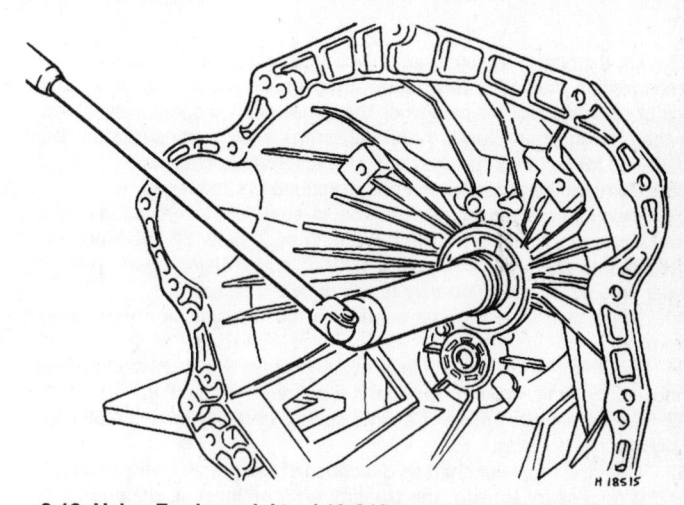

3.19 Using Ford special tool 16-040 to unscrew the input shaft guide sleeve on the MT75 transmission

3.20 MT75 transmission guide sleeve, showing oil seal location and O-ring

from the guide sleeve and input shaft.

19 Using Ford special tool 16-040 or a suitable alternative, unscrew the input shaft guide sleeve, and withdraw it from the transmission **(see illustration)**. Take care not to lose the thrustwasher located behind the guide sleeve.

20 Using a screwdriver, prise out the old oil seal from the guide sleeve bore. Fit the new oil seal using a large socket or tube of suitable diameter to drive it home. Ensure that the seal is fitted so that the sealing lip faces the transmission case when installed. Also renew the large O-ring on the periphery of the guide sleeve **(see illustration)**.

21 Lubricate the oil seal lip and the O-ring with multi-purpose grease.

22 Wrap some adhesive tape over the splines of the input shaft, to prevent damage to the oil seal when refitting.

23 Refit the guide sleeve and thrustwasher, and tighten it to the specified torque using the special tool or an alternative.

24 Apply a thin smear of high-melting-point grease to the guide sleeve and release lever fulcrum pin, then refit the clutch release bearing and lever.

25 Refit the transmission as described in Section 7.

Rear (output shaft) oil seal

Type G and type N transmissions

26 Apply the handbrake, then raise and support the vehicle at the front on axle stands.

16 Thoroughly clean the transmission assembly, paying particular attention to the area inside the clutch housing.

17 Free the clutch release bearing from the release lever, and withdraw it from the guide sleeve.

18 Pull the release lever from the fulcrum pin, then withdraw the lever

7A

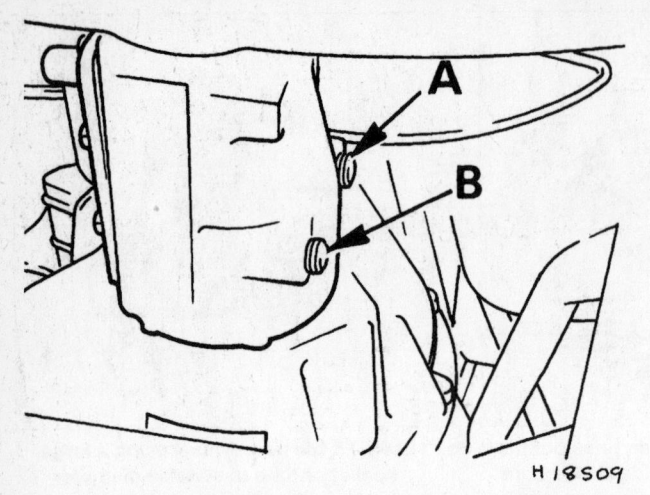

3.27 Type G transmission oil level/filler plug (A) and drain plug (B)

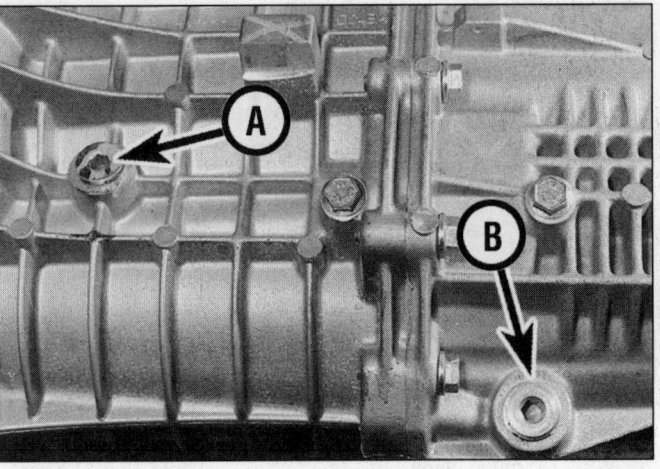

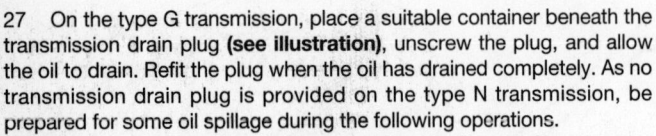

3.35 MT75 transmission oil level/filler plug (A) and drain plug (B)

27 On the type G transmission, place a suitable container beneath the transmission drain plug **(see illustration)**, unscrew the plug, and allow the oil to drain. Refit the plug when the oil has drained completely. As no transmission drain plug is provided on the type N transmission, be prepared for some oil spillage during the following operations.
28 Remove the propeller shaft as described in Chapter 8.
29 Using a screwdriver, prise the old oil seal out of its location in the transmission extension housing. Alternatively, screw two self-tapping screws into the face of the oil seal, 180° apart. Using pliers, pull or lever on each screw alternately to withdraw the oil seal.
30 Wipe clean the oil seal seating in the transmission extension housing.
31 Dip the new oil seal in clean oil, then press it a little way into the housing by hand, making sure that it is square to its seating.
32 Using suitable tubing or a large socket, carefully drive the oil seal fully into the housing.
33 Refit the propeller shaft as described in Chapter 8. Refill, or check and if necessary top-up, the transmission oil level as described in Chapter 1, then lower the vehicle to the ground.

MT75 transmission

Note: *A new output shaft flange locknut, and new propeller shaft coupling flange bolts, will be required when refitting.*
34 Apply the handbrake, then raise and support the vehicle at the front on axle stands.
35 Place a suitable container beneath the transmission drain plug **(see illustration)**, unscrew the plug, and allow the oil to drain. Refit the plug when the oil has drained completely.
36 Mark the relative positions of the propeller shaft and transmission output shaft flange, then unbolt and detach the propeller shaft from the flange. Position the shaft out of the way. Note that new bolts will be required when refitting.
37 Using a bar or suitable forked tool bolted to the output shaft flange holes, hold the flange stationary and unscrew the locknut **(see illustration)**. Note that a new locknut will be required when refitting.
38 Withdraw the output shaft flange using a two- or three-legged puller **(see illustration)**.
39 Using a screwdriver, prise the old oil seal out of its location in the transmission housing. Alternatively, screw two self-tapping screws into the face of the oil seal, 180° apart. Using pliers, pull or lever on each screw alternately to withdraw the oil seal.
40 Wipe clean the oil seal seating in the housing.
41 Dip the new oil seal in clean oil, then press it a little way into the housing by hand, making sure that it is square to its seating.
42 Using suitable tubing or a large socket, carefully drive the oil seal fully into the housing.
43 Lubricate the oil seal lip and the running surface of the output shaft flange, then refit the flange to the output shaft.

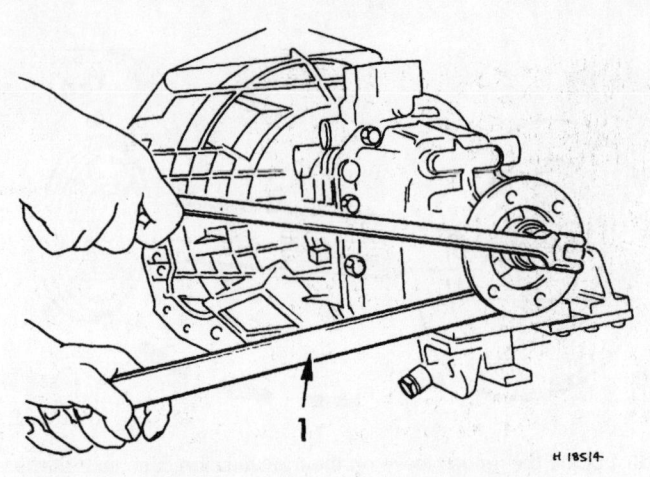

3.37 Using a bar (1) bolted to the output shaft flange to hold it stationary while unscrewing the locknut

44 Fit a new locknut, and tighten it to the specified torque. Whilst tightening the nut, prevent the output shaft flange from turning by holding it as described for removal.
45 Reconnect the propeller shaft, ensuring that the alignment marks correspond. Tighten the new retaining bolts to the specified torque setting (see Chapter 8).
46 Referring to Chapter 1, refill the transmission with oil, then lower the vehicle to the ground.

Overdrive unit output shaft oil seal

47 The procedures for renewal of the overdrive output shaft oil seal are the same as described above for the transmission output shaft oil seal on the MT75 transmission.

Speedometer drive pinion oil seal

48 The procedure is covered in Section 5 of this Chapter.

4 Reversing light switch - testing, removal and refitting

Testing

1 The reversing light circuit is controlled by a plunger-type switch screwed into the side of the transmission casing. If a fault develops in the circuit, first ensure that the circuit fuse has not blown.
2 To test the switch, first apply the handbrake, then raise and support the vehicle at the front on axle stands. Disconnect the switch wiring connector. Use a multi-meter (set to the resistance function) or a

Chapter 7 Part A: Manual transmission

3.38 Withdraw the output shaft flange using a puller

4.4 Reversing light switch location in the MT75 transmission

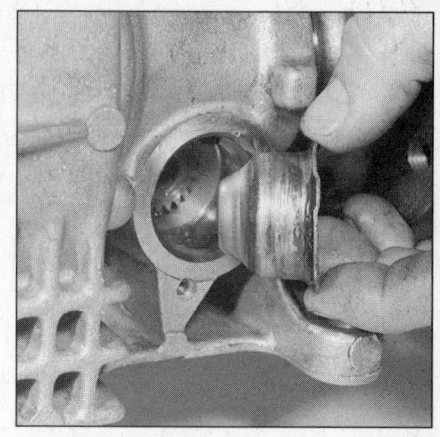

5.3a On the MT75 transmission, prise free the plug from the housing on the opposite side of the speedometer cable aperture...

5.3b ...or on later units, undo the bolt (arrowed) and remove the cover plate...

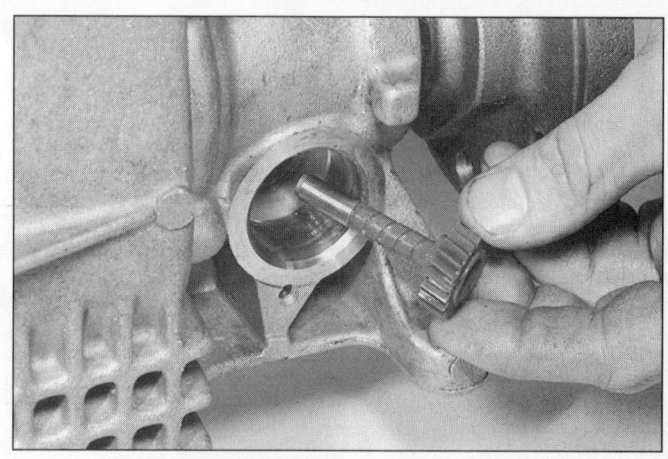

5.3c ...then withdraw the drive pinion from the location port in the side of the transmission

battery-and-bulb test circuit to check that there is continuity between the switch terminals only when reverse gear is selected. If this is not the case, and there are no obvious breaks or other damage to the wires, the switch is faulty and must be renewed.

Removal

3 If not already done, apply the handbrake, then raise and support the vehicle at the front on axle stands.
4 Disconnect the wiring from the reversing light switch, then unscrew the switch from the side of the transmission **(see illustration)**.

Refitting

5 Clean the location in the transmission and the threads of the switch.
6 Insert the switch, and tighten it securely.
7 Reconnect the wiring, ensuring that it is routed clear of the exhaust, and does not catch on the transmission.
8 Check and if necessary, top-up the transmission oil level with reference to Chapter 1, then lower the vehicle to the ground.

5 Speedometer drive pinion - removal and refitting

Removal

1 Apply the handbrake, then raise the vehicle at the front and support it on axle stands.
2 On the type G and type N transmissions, detach the speedometer cable at the transmission end by undoing the retaining plate bolt and pulling the cable clear. The drive pinion and bush assembly can now be withdrawn from the transmission case.
3 On the MT75 unit, detach the speedometer cable at the transmission end by undoing the retaining plate bolt and pulling the cable clear. Prise free the plug from the housing on the opposite side of the cable aperture, or on later models, undo the bolt and remove the cover plate, then withdraw the drive pinion from the location port in the side of the transmission **(see illustrations)**.
4 Allow for a certain amount of oil spillage from the transmission when the pinion is withdrawn.
5 If the pinion itself is badly worn or damaged, it must be renewed. Where fitted, also renew the O-ring seal on the bush assembly if it is in any way damaged.

Refitting

6 Refitting is a reversal of removal, but lubricate the pinion, and clean the area around the location aperture in the housing.
7 Check and if necessary, top-up the transmission oil level with reference to Chapter 1, then lower the vehicle to the ground.

6 Manual transmission mounting - inspection and renewal

Inspection

1 The transmission mounting seldom requires attention, but a broken or deteriorated mounting should be renewed immediately, or

7A-8 Chapter 7 Part A: Manual transmission

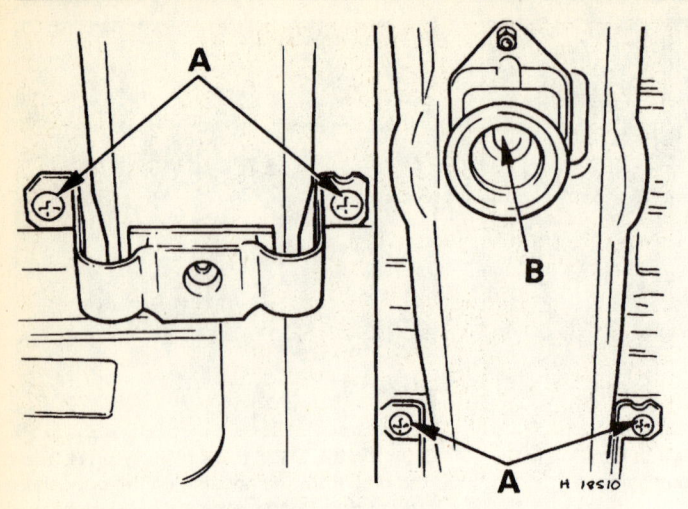

6.7 Transmission mounting and crossmember attachments

A *Crossmember-to-floor fixings*
B *Mounting-to-transmission fixing*

7.8 Release the fasteners (A) on both sides, and remove the two-piece cover assembly fitted around the clutch housing

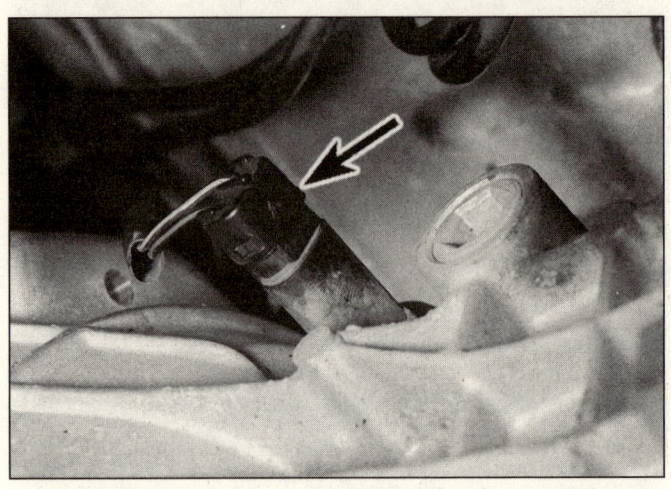

7.11 Detach the reversing light switch lead connector (arrowed)

the added strain placed on the driveline components may cause damage or wear.
2 During the check, the transmission must be raised slightly, to remove its weight from the mounting.
3 Apply the handbrake, then raise the front of the vehicle, and support it securely on axle stands. Position a jack under the transmission, then carefully raise the unit just enough to take the weight off the mounting.
4 Check the mounting to see if the rubber is cracked, hardened, or separated from the metal components. Sometimes the rubber will split right down the centre.
5 If any sign of deterioration is visible, the mounting should be renewed.

Renewal

6 If not already done, apply the handbrake, then raise the front of the vehicle, and support it securely on axle stands. Position a jack under the transmission, then carefully raise the unit just enough to take the weight off the mounting.
7 Undo the single centre bolt (type G and type N transmissions), or the two nuts (MT75 transmission) securing the mounting to the transmission case **(see illustration)**.
8 Undo the two bolts each side and remove the crossmember from under the vehicle, then undo the two nuts or bolts and remove the mounting from the crossmember.
9 Locate the new mounting on the crossmember, and refit the crossmember using the reversal of removal. Note that on some models, the crossmember is asymmetric, and must be fitted with the red paint dot facing the front of the vehicle.
10 Lower the vehicle on completion.

7 Manual transmission - removal and refitting

Note: *The transmission can be removed as a unit with the engine as described in Chapter 2B, then separated from the engine on the bench. However, if work is only necessary on the transmission or clutch unit, it is better to remove the transmission on its own from underneath the vehicle. The latter method is described in this Section. A trolley jack will be required, as will the aid of an assistant during the actual removal (and refitting) procedures.*

Removal

1 Disconnect the battery negative lead.
2 Apply the handbrake, then raise the front of the vehicle and support it securely on axle stands at a height which will provide sufficient working clearance underneath. On type G and MT75 units, place a suitable container beneath the drain plug, and drain the transmission oil. Refit the drain plug on completion.
3 On vehicles with independent front suspension and type G or type N transmissions, it will be necessary to lower the front suspension crossmember to provide sufficient clearance. To do this, first remove both front coil springs as described in Chapter 10. Position a sturdy jack beneath the crossmember, and raise the jack to just take the crossmember weight. Undo the two bolts each side securing the crossmember to the body, then lower the jack and crossmember approximately 100 mm.
4 On engines with an air cleaner assembly mounted directly on the inlet manifold, remove the air cleaner unit as described in Chapter 4.
5 Remove the gear lever as described in Section 2.
6 Remove the starter motor as described in Chapter 5.
7 Remove the propeller shaft as described in Chapter 8.
8 Where fitted, release the fasteners and remove the lower engine cover, and the two-piece cover assembly fitted around the clutch housing **(see illustration)**.
9 Disconnect the exhaust downpipe from the manifold. On later models, it may be beneficial to separate the downpipe at the front pipe flange and remove the downpipe completely, for improved access.
10 Detach the clutch release lever rubber boot from the side of the clutch housing. Slip the inner cable out of the slot on the release lever, and free the outer cable from the clutch housing. Slide the rubber boot off the cable.

Chapter 7 Part A: Manual transmission

7.12a Undo the bolt (arrowed) and remove the speedometer drive cable retaining plate ...

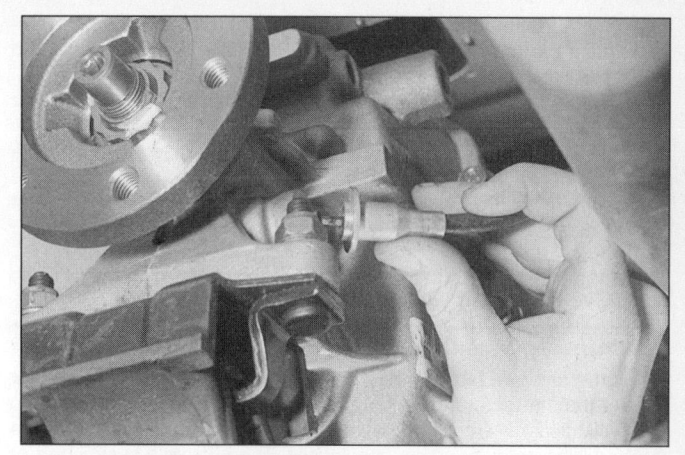

7.12b ... then withdraw the speedometer cable from the transmission

7.16 Undo the two bolts each side (arrowed), and remove the transmission crossmember from under the vehicle

11 Detach the reversing light switch lead connector, and move the lead out of the way **(see illustration)**.
12 Undo the retaining bolt, and remove the speedometer drive cable retaining plate. Withdraw the speedometer cable from the transmission, and position it out of the way **(see illustrations)**.
13 If an electronic tachograph is fitted, detach its lead and position it out of the way.
14 Unbolt and detach the lower cover plate(s) from the clutch housing.
15 Position a trolley jack under the transmission to support it.
16 Undo the single centre bolt (type G and type N transmissions), or the two nuts (MT75 transmission) securing the transmission mounting to the transmission case. Undo the two bolts each side, and remove the transmission crossmember from under the vehicle **(see illustration)**.
17 Unscrew and remove the engine-to-clutch housing retaining bolts, including the single bolt each side securing the engine support braces to the clutch housing. Note that on some models, one bolt also secures the engine earth strap connection or battery positive cable support bracket, and two of the upper bolts retain the fuel pipe bracket.
18 Position a second jack or blocks under the engine sump to support it whilst the transmission is removed. If a jack is used, spread the load at the jack head by placing a large, flat piece of wood between the jack head and the sump.
19 Check that all fixings are fully disconnected and positioned out of the way. Enlist the aid of an assistant to help steady the transmission

as it is withdrawn, then pull it rearwards whilst simultaneously supporting its weight, and detach it from the engine. Where applicable, it may be necessary to initially prise free the clutch housing from the engine location dowels. At no time during its removal (and subsequent refitting), allow the weight of the transmission to rest on the input shaft.
20 When the unit is fully clear of the engine, lower it, and withdraw it from underneath the vehicle.

Refitting

21 Refitting is a reversal of the removal procedure. Before lifting the unit into position, check that the clutch release bearing is correctly positioned, and apply a thin smear of high-melting-point grease to the transmission input shaft.
22 Once the transmission is fully engaged with the engine, insert a couple of retaining bolts, then refit the crossmember/mounting assembly. If working on the MT75 transmission, ensure that the crossmember is fitted with the red marker dot towards the front of the vehicle. Tighten all bolts to the specified torque wrench settings, where given.
23 Refer to the relevant Chapters and Sections of this manual when refitting the clutch cable, propeller shaft, starter motor, gear lever, air cleaner, and where applicable, the front coil springs.
24 On completion, refill/top-up the transmission oil with reference to Chapter 1.

8 Manual transmission overhaul - general information

1 Overhauling a manual transmission is a difficult job for the do-it-yourselfer. It involves the dismantling and reassembly of many small parts. Numerous clearances must be precisely measured and, if necessary, changed with selected spacers and circlips. As a result, if transmission problems arise, while the unit can be removed and refitted by a competent do-it-yourselfer, overhaul should be left to a transmission specialist. Rebuilt transmissions may be available - check with your dealer parts department, motor factors, or transmission specialists. At any rate, the time and money involved in an overhaul is almost sure to exceed the cost of a rebuilt unit.
2 Nevertheless, it's not impossible for an inexperienced mechanic to rebuild a transmission, providing the special tools are available, and the job is done in a deliberate step-by-step manner, so that nothing is overlooked.
3 The tools necessary for an overhaul include: internal and external circlip pliers, a bearing puller, a slide hammer, a set of pin punches, a dial test indicator, and possibly a hydraulic press. In addition, a large, sturdy workbench and a vice or transmission stand will be required.
Note: *The MT75 transmission requires a large number of manufacturer's special tools for overhaul, and it is recommended that any work needed on this unit be left to a specialist.*

7A-10 Chapter 7 Part A: Manual transmission

4   During dismantling of the transmission, make careful notes of how each part comes off, where it fits in relation to other parts, and what holds it in place.

5   Before taking the transmission apart for repair, it will help if you have some idea what area of the transmission is malfunctioning. Certain problems can be closely tied to specific areas in the transmission, which can make component examination and replacement easier. Refer to the *"Fault diagnosis"* section at the front of this manual for information regarding possible sources of trouble.

9 Overdrive unit - general information

Certain Transit models with the G-type transmission also have an overdrive unit as a factory-fitted option. The unit is attached to the rear of the transmission, and takes the form of a hydraulically-operated epicyclic gear. Overdrive operates on third and fourth gears, to provide fast cruising at lower engine revolutions. The overdrive is engaged or disengaged by a driver-operated switch, which controls an electric solenoid mounted on the overdrive unit. A further (inhibitor) switch is included in the electrical circuit, to prevent accidental engagement of overdrive in reverse, first or second gears.

Satisfactory fault diagnosis, repair and/or overhaul of the overdrive unit requires specialist knowledge, factory tools and spotlessly-clean working conditions. For these reasons, it is recommended that the advice of a Ford dealer is sought in the event of any unsatisfactory performance or suspected fault on the unit.

10 Overdrive switch - removal and refitting

Removal

1   Disconnect the battery negative lead.
2   Using a knife blade inserted in the join between the gear lever knob and the knob cover, carefully prise off the cover.
3   Disconnect the switch wiring, and unscrew the switch from the cover.

Refitting

4   Refitting is a reversal of removal.

11 Overdrive inhibitor switch - removal and refitting

Removal

1   Disconnect the battery negative lead.
2   Apply the handbrake, then raise and support the vehicle at the front on axle stands.
3   Disconnect the wiring from the inhibitor switch, then unscrew the switch from the transmission selector housing.

Refitting

4   Clean the location in the transmission, and the threads of the switch.
5   Insert the switch using a new oil seal, and tighten it securely.
6   Reconnect the wiring, ensuring that it is routed clear of the exhaust and does not catch on the transmission.
7   Lower the vehicle to the ground, and reconnect the battery.

12 Overdrive solenoid valve - removal and refitting

Removal

1   Disconnect the battery negative lead.
2   Apply the handbrake, then raise and support the vehicle at the front on axle stands.
3   Support the transmission with a trolley jack, then undo the overdrive mounting retaining bolt and large washer from the crossmember.

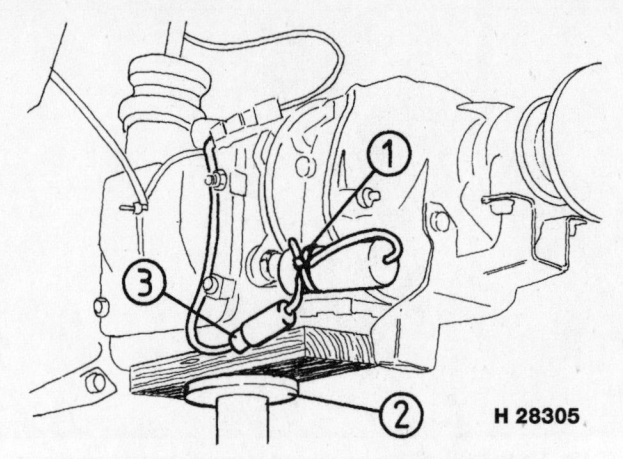

12.6 Overdrive solenoid valve removal

1   Cable tie
2   Support jack
3   Wiring connector

4   Undo the bolt securing the transmission crossmember to the support bracket on the left-hand side.
5   Undo the two bolts securing the transmission crossmember bracket to the body on the right-hand side, and remove the crossmember.
6   Disconnect the solenoid valve wiring, release the cable tie, and unscrew the valve from the overdrive unit **(see illustration)**.

Refitting

7   Refitting is a reversal of removal, but use a new oil seal when refitting the solenoid valve.

13 Overdrive unit - removal and refitting

Warning: *The following procedure requires the rear of the vehicle to be raised and supported on stands, and driven "wheel-free" to facilitate removal of the overdrive unit. As this is a potentially-hazardous operation, take extreme care when doing this, and ensure that the vehicle is safely supported, with the front wheels securely chocked. Refer also to the information contained in "Safety first!" at the beginning of this manual before proceeding.*

Removal

1   If the overdrive unit is still operational, chock the front wheels, then raise the rear of the vehicle and securely support it on axle stands, so that the rear wheels are clear of the ground. Release the handbrake.
2   With due regard for the safety implications of the following procedure, start the engine, engage top gear, and run the vehicle up to approximately 35 mph with the overdrive engaged. Disengage the overdrive, allow the rear wheels to over-run, then depress the clutch and switch off the engine. This procedure releases the load on the splined shaft between the planetary gear carrier and one-way clutch, to facilitate easy removal of the overdrive unit.
3   If the overdrive unit is not operational, it can still be removed, but the additional work described in paragraph 10 will be necessary.
4   Disconnect the battery negative lead.
5   Position a suitable container beneath the transmission drain plug, unscrew the plug, and drain the transmission/overdrive oil. Refit the drain plug on completion.
6   Remove the propeller shaft as described in Chapter 8.
7   Support the transmission with a trolley jack, then undo the overdrive mounting retaining bolt and large washer from the crossmember.
8   Undo the bolt securing the transmission crossmember to the

Chapter 7 Part A: Manual transmission 7A-11

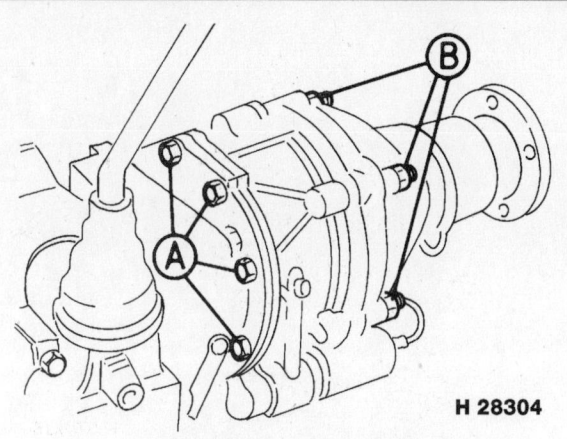

13.13 Overdrive unit attachments

A Overdrive unit-to-transmission intermediate flange retaining nuts (eight in total)
B Overdrive unit rear housing retaining nuts

support bracket on the left-hand side.
9 Undo the two bolts securing the transmission crossmember bracket to the body on the right-hand side, and remove the crossmember.
10 Undo the bolts and remove the mounting bracket from the overdrive unit.
11 Undo the bolt, remove the retaining plate, and withdraw the speedometer cable.
12 Disconnect the solenoid valve wiring, and release the cable-tie.
13 Undo the eight nuts securing the overdrive unit to the transmission intermediate flange **(see illustration)**.
14 Using a soft-faced hammer, tap the overdrive unit rearwards to release it from the intermediate flange, then withdraw the unit from the transmission. If the procedures described in paragraphs 1 and 2 were not carried out due to non-operation of the overdrive, and/or the unit cannot be removed, slacken the six overdrive unit rear housing nuts until they are flush with their studs. This will release the load on the splined shaft between the planetary gear carrier and one-way clutch, and allow removal of the overdrive unit.
15 With the unit removed, clean off all traces of old gasket from the overdrive and transmission intermediate flange mating faces. Tighten the rear housing nuts if it was necessary to slacken them for removal.

Refitting

16 Refit the mounting bracket to the overdrive unit.
17 Using a new gasket, locate the unit on the transmission intermediate flange, and secure with the eight nuts tightened to the specified torque. If the overdrive unit will not fully mate up to the intermediate flange, and stands off by approximately 16 mm, there is a mis-alignment between the one-way clutch splines and the planetary gear carrier. To correct this, remove the unit again, and turn the one-way clutch unit anti-clockwise slightly using a screwdriver. It should now be possible to fit the overdrive unit fully home.
18 Reconnect the solenoid valve wiring and the speedometer cable. Ensure correct routing and security of the wiring.
19 Refit the crossmember, and tighten the bolts to the specified torque.
20 Refit the propeller shaft as described in Chapter 8.
21 Refill/top-up the transmission oil with reference to Chapter 1, then lower the vehicle to the ground and reconnect the battery.

14 Overdrive unit overhaul - general information

In the event of a fault occurring on the overdrive unit, it is first necessary to determine whether it is of an electrical, mechanical or hydraulic nature, and to do this, special test equipment is required. It is therefore essential to have the work carried out by a Ford dealer if an overdrive fault is suspected.

Do not remove the overdrive unit from the vehicle for possible repair before professional fault diagnosis has been carried out, since most tests require the unit to be in the vehicle.

Notes

Chapter 7 Part B: Automatic transmission

Contents

	Section		Section
Automatic transmission - removal and refitting	15	General information	1
Automatic transmission fluid level check	See Chapter 1	Inhibitor switch - removal, refitting and adjustment	7
Automatic transmission linkage lubrication	See Chapter 1	Selector cable - removal, refitting and adjustment	5
Automatic transmission mounting - inspection and renewal	14	Selector mechanism - removal and refitting	6
Automatic transmission overhaul - general information	16	Servo assembly - removal and refitting	10
Brake bands - adjustment	2	Speedometer drive pinion - removal and refitting	13
Downshift (kickdown) cable - adjustment	3	Vacuum diaphragm - removal and refitting	9
Downshift (kickdown) cable - removal and refitting	4	Vacuum governor - checking and adjustment	11
Fluid seals - renewal	8	Vacuum governor - removal and refitting	12

Specifications

General
Type.. Four forward speeds and reverse, epicyclic gear train with hydraulic control and three-element torque converter
Designation... Ford A4LD

Gear ratios
1st.. 2.47 : 1
2nd... 1.47 : 1
3rd.. 1.00 : 1
4th.. 0.75 : 1
Reverse... 2.11 : 1

Vacuum governor test specifications
Vacuum reading - governor control lever at idle position............ 625 ± 40 mbars
Vacuum reading - governor control lever at full-load position..... 0 to 30 mbars

Lubrication
Lubricant type/capacity............................... See "Lubricants, fluids and capacities"

Torque wrench settings

	Nm	lbf ft
Torque converter housing to engine	35	26
Torque converter to driveplate	35	26
Sump pan to transmission:		
With cork gasket	17	13
With polyacrylic gasket	10	7
Downshift cable bracket to transmission	20	15
Starter inhibitor switch	12	9
Oil cooler pipe to connector	23	17
Oil cooler pipe connector to transmission	27	20

Chapter 7 Part B: Automatic transmission

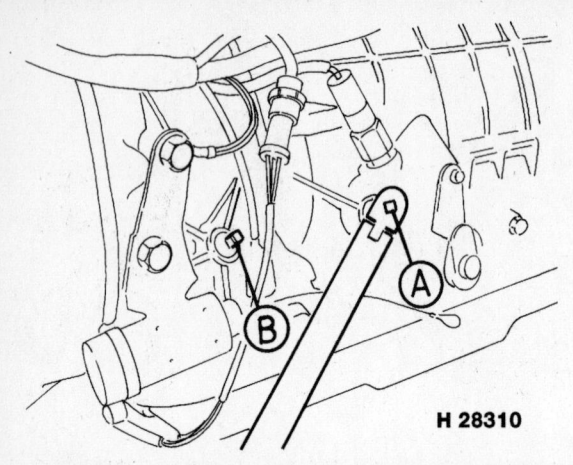

2.3 Brake band adjustment using Ford special tool 17-029

- A Front brake band
- B Centre brake band

3.5 Downshift (kickdown) cable adjustment

- A Kickdown solenoid retaining bolts
- B Transmission kickdown lever
- C Special tool 17-031

1 General information

A four-speed automatic transmission is available as an optional fitting on certain models. The selector lever is centrally located, and incorporates a button in the side of the T-handle. The button must be pressed before the selector can be moved to the "R" (Reverse) position, and to move in and out of the "P" (Park) position. The button must also be depressed when downshifting into "2" and "1".

Forward movement is obtained by selecting "D" (fully automatic shifting) or "1" (low gear lock), "2" (shifting between gears 1 and 2), or "3" (shifting between gears 1 to 3). With the selector lever in "P" (Park), an internal pawl locks the transmission. Reverse gear is engaged by selecting "R".

The system includes a three-element hydrokinetic torque converter which transmits the power from the engine to the transmission; the torque converter is capable of variable torque multiplication, but also incorporates a lock-up clutch. This operates after the shift up to 3rd gear, and remains operative in 4th gear. With the lock-up clutch in operation, torque converter slip is eliminated, thus reducing fuel consumption and engine noise.

The hydraulically-operated epicyclic gearbox responds to both road speed and throttle pedal demand by means of an internal governor and valve control, and the correct gear for the current conditions is therefore automatically selected.

The transmission fluid is cooled by means of a double-tube oil cooler, mounted alongside the radiator.

An inhibitor switch is fitted to the transmission, to prevent inadvertent starting of the engine whilst the selector lever is in any position other than "N" or "P".

Due to the complexity of the automatic transmission, if performance is not up to standard, or overhaul is necessary, it is imperative that this be left to a main agent or specialist, who will have the special equipment and knowledge for fault diagnosis and rectification. The contents of the following Sections are therefore confined to supplying general information and any service information and instructions that can be used by the owner.

Safety note

When the vehicle is parked and left with the engine running, or when any checks and/or adjustments are being carried out, the handbrake **must** be applied, and the selector lever moved to the "P" position.

Do not allow the engine speed to rise above the normal idle speed when the vehicle is stationary with the selector lever in any position other than "P" or "N".

Should it be necessary to tow the vehicle, the selector lever must be moved to the "N" position, but the vehicle must not be towed at speeds in excess of 30 mph, or for distances in excess of 30 miles (50 km). The propeller shaft should be disconnected if these limits are to be exceeded.

2 Brake bands - adjustment

Note: *Ford special tool 17-029 will be required for the following procedure.*

1 Apply the handbrake, then raise the front of the vehicle and support it securely on axle stands.
2 Release the fasteners, and remove the two-piece engine lower soundproofing cover.
3 Slacken the front brake band adjusting screw locknut a few turns **(see illustration)**.
4 Engage the special tool over the brake band adjusting screw, and tighten the screw until the ratchet on the tool jumps a notch.
5 Slacken the adjusting screw by two turns, hold the screw in this position, and tighten the locknut.
6 Slacken the centre brake band adjusting screw locknut a few turns.
7 Engage the special tool over the brake band adjusting screw, and tighten the screw until the ratchet on the tool jumps a notch.
8 Slacken the adjusting screw by two-and-a-half turns, hold the screw in this position, and tighten the locknut.
9 Refit the engine lower cover, and lower the vehicle to the ground.

3 Downshift (kickdown) cable - adjustment

Note: *Ideally, Ford special tool 17-031 should be used for adjustment of the cable on vehicles with a long downshift cable. This tool is simply a forked piece of metal used to impart a slight S-shaped path to the cable during adjustment, and a home-made alternative can easily be fabricated. For adjustment of both the long and short cables, the help of an assistant will be needed.*

Vehicles with long downshift cable

1 Apply the handbrake, then raise the front of the vehicle and support it securely on axle stands.
2 Release the fasteners, and remove the two-piece engine lower soundproofing cover.
3 With the help of an assistant, switch on the ignition (with the selector lever in any position), but do not start the engine. Have your assistant depress the accelerator pedal to the floor, and hold it in that position so that the kickdown solenoid is activated, while you carry out

Chapter 7 Part B: Automatic transmission

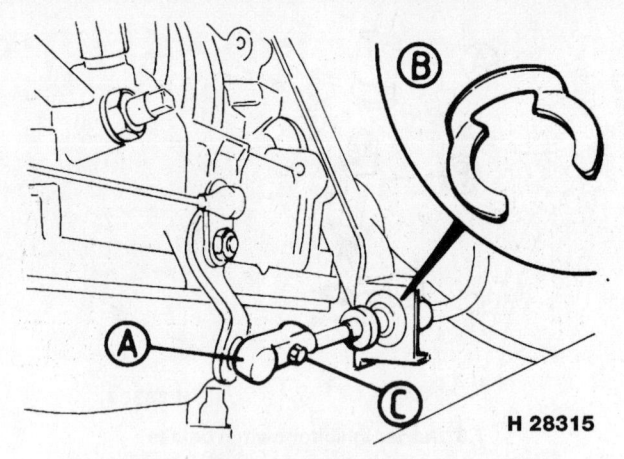

5.4 Selector cable attachments at the transmission

- A Cable ball stud end fitting
- B Cable retaining C-clip
- C Cable adjuster screw

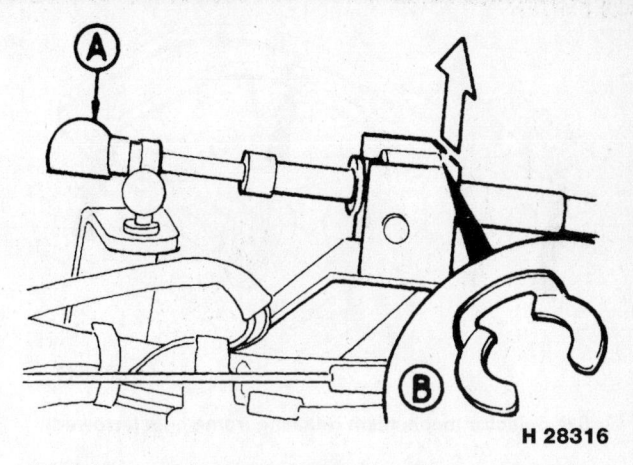

5.6 Selector cable attachments at the selector mechanism

- A Cable ball stud end fitting
- B Cable retaining C-clip

the adjustment from under the vehicle.
4 Move the kickdown lever on the transmission anti-clockwise as far as its stop.
5 Locate the special tool (or the home-made alternative) over the mid-point of the cable **(see illustration)**.
6 Slacken the two kickdown solenoid retaining bolts. Move the solenoid towards the front of the vehicle, until appreciable resistance is encountered and the cable is in tension. If the solenoid is moved too far, the cable will become slack again. If this happens, repeat paragraphs 3 to 6.
7 Hold the solenoid and tighten the two retaining bolts.
8 Remove the special tool, have your assistant release the accelerator pedal, and check that the kickdown lever returns to its initial position. Switch off the ignition.
9 Now check the setting as follows. If the adjustment is correct, the solenoid will pull up and hold the kickdown lever in the correct position for as long as the solenoid is energised (accelerator pedal fully depressed, ignition on). However, it should still be possible to move the kickdown lever by hand anti-clockwise, by a further 0.3 to 0.8 mm up to its actual mechanical stop.
10 If the cable is too tight, the solenoid will energise initially, when the accelerator is fully depressed, but will not hold in the energised position, and the kickdown lever will immediately move back to its initial position. If the setting is marginal, the solenoid will energise and hold initially, but as the solenoid warms up with the vehicle in use, the power of the solenoid holding coil reduces, which will also allow the lever to return to its initial position. Both these conditions may only be obvious during a road test, but if either are apparent, ie the transmission will not stay in the downshift position even though the accelerator pedal is fully depressed, and all other roadspeed and gear position criteria are correct, re-check the adjustment.
11 On completion, refit the engine lower cover, and lower the vehicle to the ground.

Vehicles with short downshift cable

12 Carry out the operations described in paragraphs 1 to 6 above.
13 Move the solenoid back approximately 0.5 mm, so that the tension is just released from the cable (the kickdown lever should still be on its stop in the anti-clockwise direction).
14 Hold the solenoid and tighten the two retaining bolts.
15 Have your assistant release the accelerator pedal, and check that the kickdown lever returns to its initial position. Switch off the ignition.
16 Now check the setting as follows. If the adjustment is correct, the solenoid will pull up and hold the kickdown lever in the correct position for as long as the solenoid is energised (accelerator pedal fully depressed, ignition on). However, it should still be possible to move the kickdown lever by hand anti-clockwise, by a further 0.5 to 1.0 mm up to its actual mechanical stop.
17 If the cable adjustment is incorrect, the conditions described in paragraph 10 above will be encountered, and the adjustment sequence should be repeated.
18 On completion, refit the engine lower cover, and lower the vehicle to the ground.

4 Downshift (kickdown) cable - removal and refitting

Removal

1 Apply the handbrake, then raise the front of the vehicle and support it securely on axle stands.
2 Release the fasteners, and remove the two-piece engine lower soundproofing cover.
3 Undo the retaining nut, and release the cable end from the kickdown lever on the transmission.
4 Disconnect the kickdown solenoid wiring at the connector, then undo the two retaining bolts and remove the kickdown solenoid complete with cable.

Refitting

5 Refitting is a reversal of removal. Adjust the downshift cable as described in the previous Section before refitting the engine soundproofing cover and lowering the vehicle.

5 Selector cable - removal, refitting and adjustment

Removal

1 Move the gear selector lever to the "N" position.
2 Apply the handbrake, then raise the front of the vehicle and support it securely on axle stands.
3 Release the fasteners, and remove the two-piece engine lower soundproofing cover.
4 From under the vehicle, prise the cable end fitting from the ball stud on the transmission selector lever. Extract the retaining C-clip, and withdraw the inner and outer cable from the support bracket **(see illustration)**.
5 From inside the cab, undo the two screws and lift up the gear selector lever cover. Pull the selector illumination bulbholder from the cover, and move the cover clear.
6 Prise the cable end fitting from the gear selector lever ball stud. Extract the retaining C-clip, and withdraw the inner and outer cable from the vehicle **(see illustration)**.

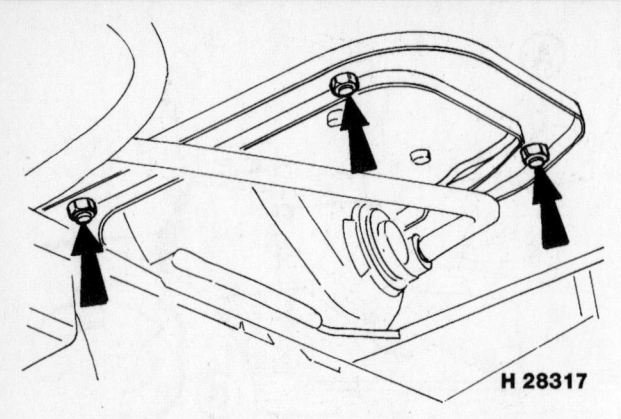

6.5 Selector mechanism retaining frame nuts (arrowed)

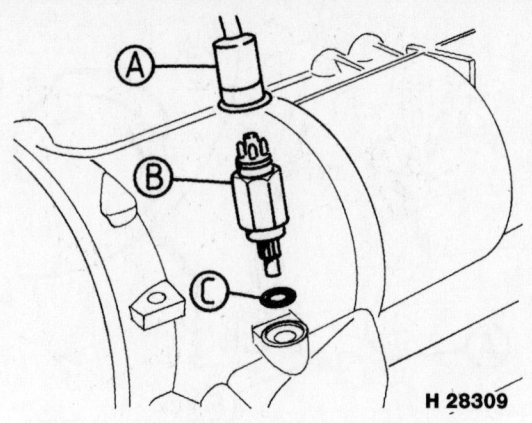

7.3 Starter inhibitor switch details

A Wiring connector
B Inhibitor switch
C O-ring

Refitting and adjustment

7 Ensure that the gear selector lever is still in the "N" position, and locate the cable into place. Secure the outer cable with the C-clip, and push the inner cable end onto the ball stud.
8 Ensure that the transmission selector lever is in the "N" position (two notches from the forward stop, four notches from the rearward stop).
9 Feed the inner and outer cable through the transmission support bracket, and secure the outer cable with the C-clip.
10 Slacken the cable adjuster screw on the inner cable end fitting, then press the inner cable end onto the selector lever ball stud and tighten the adjuster screw.
11 Move the gear selector lever through all the gear positions, ensuring that the engagement is positive.
12 Refit the selector illumination bulbholder and the gear selector lever cover.
13 Refit the engine lower cover, and lower the vehicle to the ground.

6 Selector mechanism - removal and refitting

Removal

1 Apply the handbrake, then raise the front of the vehicle and support it securely on axle stands.
2 Release the fasteners, and remove the two-piece engine lower soundproofing cover.
3 From inside the cab, undo the two screws and lift up the gear selector lever cover. Pull the selector illumination bulbholder from the cover, and move the cover clear.
4 Prise the cable end fitting from the gear selector lever ball stud. Extract the retaining C-clip, and withdraw the inner and outer cable from the selector mechanism.
5 From under the vehicle, undo the four nuts and remove the selector mechanism retaining frame (see illustration).
6 Withdraw the selector mechanism from inside the cab area.

Refitting

7 Refitting is a reversal of removal. On completion, move the gear selector lever through all the gear positions, ensuring that the engagement is positive. If necessary, adjust the cable as described in the previous Section.

7 Inhibitor switch - removal, refitting and adjustment

Removal

1 Apply the handbrake, then raise the front of the vehicle and support it securely on axle stands.
2 Release the fasteners, and remove the two-piece engine lower soundproofing cover.

3 Disconnect the wires to the switch, then unscrew and remove the switch from the transmission (see illustration).
4 Remove the O-ring seal from the switch. This must be renewed.

Refitting and adjustment

5 Locate the new O-ring seal, then screw the switch into the transmission. Correct adjustment is made automatically as the switch is installed.
6 Reconnect the wires to the switch, refit the engine lower cover, and lower the vehicle to the ground.
7 Check that the engine only starts when the selector is set in the "P" or "N" position, and that the reversing light only operates when the selector lever is in the "R" position.

8 Fluid seals - renewal

Rear (output shaft) fluid seal

1 The procedure is the same as that described for the type N manual transmission (refer to Section 3 in Part A of this Chapter).

Speedometer drive pinion fluid seal

2 The procedure is covered in Section 13 of this Chapter.

9 Vacuum diaphragm - removal and refitting

Removal

1 Apply the handbrake, then raise the front of the vehicle and support it securely on axle stands.
2 Release the fasteners, and remove the two-piece engine lower soundproofing cover.
3 Where fitted, release the vacuum hose retaining clip, then pull the hose off the diaphragm stub.
4 Undo the retaining bolt, and withdraw the vacuum diaphragm unit complete with retaining bracket from the side of the transmission. Recover the actuating pin, and take care not to let the throttle valve piston drop out of the transmission when the diaphragm unit is removed (see illustration).
5 Remove the O-ring seal from the diaphragm unit; obtain a new seal for refitting.

Refitting

6 Lubricate the new O-ring, and position it in the groove in the diaphragm unit.
7 Check that the throttle valve piston is free to move in its bore, then insert the actuating pin.

Chapter 7 Part B: Automatic transmission

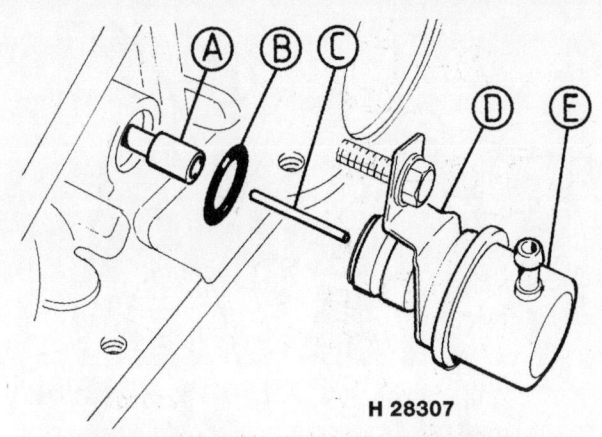

9.4 Vacuum diaphragm components and attachments

A Throttle valve piston
B O-ring
C Actuating pin
D Attachment bracket
E Vacuum diaphragm

11.1 Vacuum governor connection details

A Governor assembly
B Governor control lever
C Venting valve
D Connection to brake servo vacuum pump
E Connection to vacuum diaphragm unit

8   Refit the diaphragm, secure with the retaining bolt, and reconnect the vacuum hose.
9   Refit the engine lower cover, and lower the vehicle to the ground.
10 Check and if necessary, top-up the transmission fluid level with reference to Chapter 1.

10 Servo assembly - removal and refitting

Removal

1   Apply the handbrake, then raise the front of the vehicle and support it securely on axle stands.
2   Release the fasteners, and remove the two-piece engine lower soundproofing cover.
3   Clean the area around the transmission sump pan to transmission casing joint, then undo the eighteen bolts and carefully withdraw the sump pan. As the sump will still be full of transmission fluid, be prepared for spillage (and continuous drips after the sump is removed).
4   Unscrew the servo rear cover, and remove the cover and gasket. Withdraw the servo piston and spring **(see illustration)**.
5   Remove the O-ring seal from the servo piston. Obtain a new O-ring, servo cover gasket and sump pan gasket for refitting.

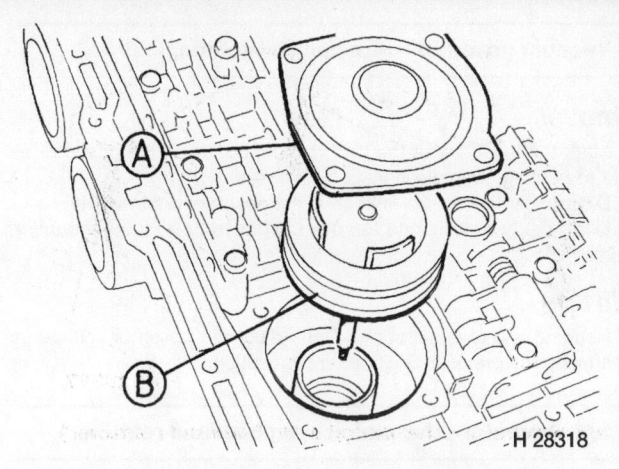

10.4 Servo rear cover (A) and servo piston (B) accessible after removal of the transmission sump pan

6   Empty the fluid from the sump pan, then thoroughly clean the sump, and dry with a lint-free cloth. Ensure that all traces of old gasket are removed from the sump and transmission mating faces.

Refitting

7   Lubricate the new servo piston O-ring in clean transmission fluid, and locate it in position in the piston groove.
8   Insert the piston and spring in the housing, and refit the cover using a new gasket.
9   Locate a new sump pan gasket in position, then refit the sump. Tighten the sump bolts to the specified torque, in two equal stages.
10 Refit the engine lower cover, and lower the vehicle to the ground.
11 Refill the transmission with the specified fluid, with reference to Chapter 1.

11 Vacuum governor - checking and adjustment

Note: *A suitable vacuum gauge will be required for the following adjustments.*

Vacuum check

1   Disconnect the hose from the vacuum diaphragm outlet stub on the governor, and connect a vacuum gauge to the stub **(see illustration)**.
2   With the gear selector lever in the "P" position, start the engine and allow it to idle at the normal idle speed.
3   Check the reading on the vacuum gauge, and compare this with the figures given in the Specifications.
4   Stop the engine, and disconnect the governor-to-fuel injection pump linkage at the governor control lever.
5   Start the engine again, and with the transmission still in the "P" position, turn the governor control lever anti-clockwise as far as the stop.
6   Check the reading on the gauge, and compare this with the full-load figures given in the Specifications.
7   If either of the readings differ significantly from the figures given in the Specifications, the governor must be renewed.
8   Switch off the engine, and remove the vacuum gauge. Reconnect the original hose, and check the control linkage adjustment as follows.

Adjustment

9   Move the throttle linkage on the injection pump to the full-load position, and turn the governor control lever anti-clockwise as far as its stop.
10 Check that the linkage will now engage with the ball stud on the lever. If necessary, adjust the linkage accordingly, then refit it to the governor control lever.

12 Vacuum governor - removal and refitting

Removal
1 Mark the locations of the two vacuum hoses on the governor as an aid to refitting, then disconnect both hoses.
2 Disconnect the control linkage at the governor control lever.
3 Undo the two bolts, and remove the governor from the mounting bracket.

Refitting
4 Refitting is a reversal of removal. Adjust the governor linkage as described in the previous Section on completion.

13 Speedometer drive pinion - removal and refitting

Removal
1 Apply the handbrake, then raise the front of the vehicle and support it securely on axle stands.
2 Undo the bolt securing the speedometer cable retaining plate. Where fitted, disconnect the wiring for the electronic tachograph.
3 Lift off the plate, and withdraw the cable and drive pinion from the transmission.
4 Allow for a certain amount of fluid spillage from the transmission when the drive pinion is withdrawn.
5 Extract the retaining clip, and disconnect the cable from the drive pinion.
6 If the pinion itself is badly worn or damaged, it must be renewed. Where fitted, also renew the O-ring seal on the gear assembly if it is in any way damaged.

Refitting
7 Refitting is a reversal of removal, having lubricated the pinion and cleaned the area around the location aperture in the housing.
8 Lower the vehicle to the ground, then check and if necessary, top-up the transmission fluid with reference to Chapter 1.

14 Automatic transmission mounting - inspection and renewal

The procedure is the same as that for the manual transmission mounting (refer to Chapter 7A, Section 6).

15 Automatic transmission - removal and refitting

Note: *Refer to the previous Sections as necessary for details of the transmission ancillary component connections and attachments.*

Removal
1 Remember that automatic transmission internal faults can only be diagnosed successfully whilst the transmission is still fitted to the vehicle. Therefore, the advice of a Ford dealer or transmission specialist should be sought before removing the unit, unless renewal is the only object.
2 Disconnect the battery negative lead.
3 Apply the handbrake, then raise the front of the vehicle and support it securely on axle stands.
4 Release the fasteners, and remove the two-piece engine lower soundproofing cover.
5 On engines with an air cleaner assembly mounted directly on the inlet manifold, remove the air cleaner unit as described in Chapter 4.
6 Refer to Chapter 8 and remove the propeller shaft.
7 Remove the starter motor as described in Chapter 5.
8 Disconnect the exhaust front downpipe from the exhaust manifold and silencer, and withdraw it from beneath the vehicle.

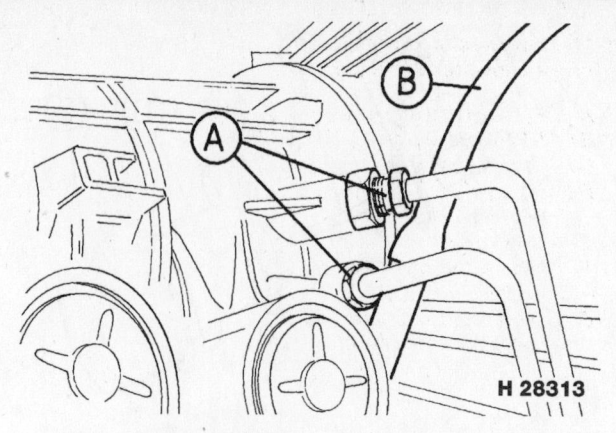

15.16 Transmission fluid cooler pipe connections (A) and fluid filler tube (B)

9 Disconnect the speedometer cable from the rear of the transmission. Where applicable, disconnect the wiring from the electronic tachograph.
10 From inside the cab, move the gear selector lever to the "N" position.
11 From under the vehicle, prise the selector cable end fitting from the ball stud on the transmission selector lever. Undo the two bolts, and move the selector cable bracket, complete with cable, to one side.
12 Disconnect the wiring to the kickdown solenoid at the cable connector.
13 Disconnect the wiring from the starter inhibitor switch.
14 Disconnect the vacuum hose from the vacuum diaphragm.
15 Withdraw the fluid level dipstick, then unscrew the retaining bolt and remove the dipstick tube assembly from the transmission. Plug the transmission opening after removing the tube assembly.
16 Wipe the area around the fluid cooler connections to the right-hand side of the transmission, then unscrew and remove the unions **(see illustration)**. Plug the transmission openings and pipe ends, and tie the pipes out of the way.
17 Working through the starter motor aperture, unscrew and remove the four driveplate-to-torque converter retaining nuts; it will be necessary to rotate the engine with a spanner on the crankshaft pulley bolt to gain access to each of these bolts **(see illustration)**.
18 Unscrew the retaining nut and bolt, and detach the engine-to-transmission braces from the torque converter casing on each side.
19 Undo the two bolts, and remove the adapter plate from the torque converter casing.
20 Take the weight of the transmission with a trolley jack positioned beneath the transmission sump; to prevent damage to the sump, place a block of wood between the jack head and sump, but make sure that there is no chance of the transmission slipping in subsequent operations.
21 Undo the single bolt securing the transmission mounting to the crossmember, and the two bolts each side securing the crossmember to the underbody. Remove the crossmember.
22 Using a further jack and block of wood, support the rear end of the engine beneath the sump.
23 Unscrew and remove the torque converter housing retaining bolts, and carefully withdraw the transmission rearwards to separate the torque converter spigot from the crankshaft adapter. It would be wise to enlist the help of an assistant during this operation, in order to steady the transmission on the trolley jack, and to hold the torque converter in the transmission.
24 Carefully withdraw the transmission from the engine and lower it, for removal from underneath the vehicle. As it is withdrawn, retain the torque converter firmly against the transmission, to prevent it from falling out. If this should happen, allow for considerable fluid spillage as the converter separates from the transmission oil pump. To retain the converter in position once the transmission is removed, locate a suitable retainer bar across the front flange face of the transmission.

Chapter 7 Part B: Automatic transmission

15.17 Transmission driveplate and torque converter attachments

- A Flywheel and ring gear
- B Flexible drive plate
- C Torque converter
- D Driveplate-to-flywheel retaining bolt
- E Captive nut
- F Flywheel-to-crankshaft retaining bolt
- G Driveplate-to-torque converter retaining nut

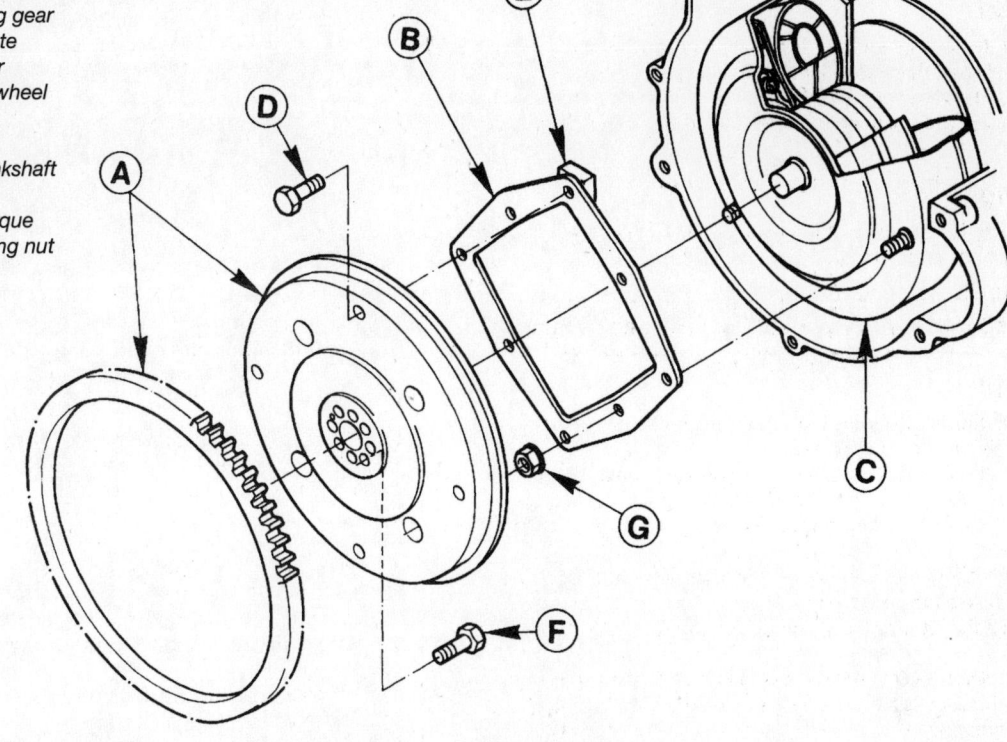

Refitting

25 Refitting the automatic transmission is a reversal of removal, but note the following points:
- a) With the torque converter in position on the transmission and engaged with the oil pump drivegear, ensure that the distance between the converter flange end face and the converter housing flange is at least 21 mm **(see illustration)**.
- b) Maintain a slight rearward tilt to the transmission when refitting to prevent the torque converter falling out forwards.
- c) As the transmission is fitted, guide the threaded studs of the torque converter through the holes in the driveplate.
- d) When the transmission is fully mated with the engine, check that the converter rotates freely, then insert the converter housing-to-engine flange bolts, and tighten to the specified torque.
- e) Adjust the downshift cable and selector cable as described in Sections 4 and 5 respectively.
- f) Refit the starter motor as described in Chapter 5.
- g) Refit the propeller shaft as described in Chapter 8.
- h) Where removed, refit the air cleaner as described in Chapter 4.
- i) On completion, refill the transmission fluid as described in Chapter 1.

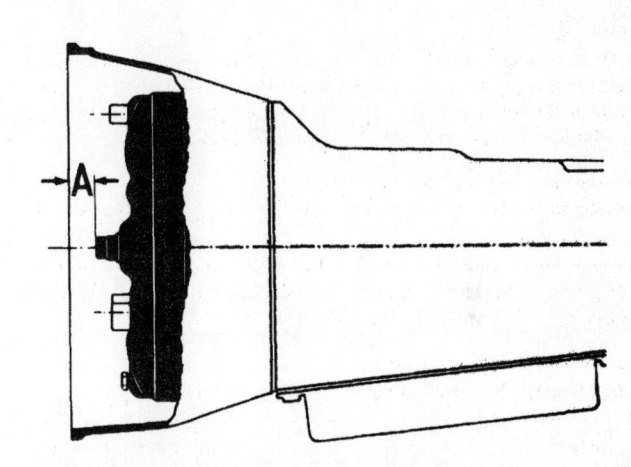

15.25 Torque converter-to-fluid pump drivegear engagement

A = 21 mm minimum

16 Automatic transmission overhaul - general information

In the event of a fault occurring on the transmission, it is first necessary to determine whether it is of an electrical, mechanical or hydraulic nature, and to do this, special test equipment is required. It is therefore essential to have the work carried out by a Ford dealer or transmission specialist if a transmission fault is suspected.

Do not remove the transmission from the vehicle for possible repair before professional fault diagnosis has been carried out, since most tests require the transmission to be in the vehicle.

Notes

Chapter 8
Propeller shaft and rear axle

Contents

	Section		Section
Differential carrier ("H" axle) - removal and refitting	13	Propeller shaft universal joints and centre bearing check	See Chapter 1
Differential unit ("G" axle) - overhaul	14	Rear axle - description	7
Drive pinion oil seal (all axle types) - renewal	12	Rear axle - removal and refitting	8
General information	1	Rear axle halfshaft - removal and refitting	9
Propeller shaft - description	2	Rear axle oil level check	See Chapter 1
Propeller shaft centre bearing - renewal	5	Rear hub and bearing ("H" axle) - removal, overhaul and refitting	10
Propeller shaft rubber "Guibo" joint - removal and refitting	6	Rear hub and bearing ("G" axle) - removal, overhaul and refitting	11
Propeller shaft (three-piece type) - removal and refitting	4		
Propeller shaft (two-piece type) - removal and refitting	3		

Specifications

Propeller shaft
Type .... Two- or three-piece with centre support bearing(s), front, centre and rear universal joints and constant velocity joint or rubber coupling according to model

Rear axle
Type .... Fully floating or three-quarter floating, hypoid
Identification:
   "H" axle .... Type 34
   "G" axle .... Type 51, Type 51A and Type 53
Final drive ratios:
   "H" axle .... 3.9:1, 4.11:1, 4.56:1 or 5.14:1
   "G" axle .... 4.63:1, 5.14:1 or 5.83:1
Hub bearing play - "G" axle .... 0.05 to 0.20 mm
Lubricant type/capacity .... See "Lubricants, fluids and capacities"

Chapter 8 Propeller shaft and rear axle

Torque wrench settings

	Nm	lbf ft
Propeller shaft		
Centre bearing housing to floor	31	23
Propeller shaft-to-rear axle final drive coupling flange	70	52
Propeller shaft-to-transmission coupling flange:		
Transmissions without overdrive	83	61
Transmissions with overdrive	75	55
Universal joint retaining bolt	40	30
Rear axle		
Differential carrier to axle ("H" axle)	62	46
Differential housing rear cover bolts ("G" axle)	38	28
Halfshaft bolts:		
"G" axle (types 51A and 53)	73	54
"G" axle (type 51)	117	86
Hub locknut ("G" axle types 51A and 53)	75	55
Hub nut (see text):		
"H" axle with round, slotted nut	220	162
"H" axle with 50 mm double-hexagon nut	220	162
"H" axle with 2 1/4 inch double-hexagon nut	440	325
"G" axle (types 51A and 53) with locknut and tab washer	85	63
"G" axle (type 51) with 2 1/4 inch double-hexagon nut	540	399
Rear spring-to-axle U-bolts:		
"H" axle	94	69
"G" axle	125	92
Wheel nuts:		
Five-stud wheels	85	63
Six-stud wheels	168	124

1 General information

The information in this Chapter deals with the driveline components from the transmission to the rear wheels. For the purposes of this Chapter, these components are grouped into the two categories, propeller shaft and rear axle. Separate Sections within this Chapter offer general descriptions and checking procedures for each group.

Since many of the procedures covered in this Chapter involve working under the vehicle, make sure that it is securely supported on axle stands placed on firm, level ground.

2 Propeller shaft - description

Drive is transmitted from the transmission to the rear axle by a finely-balanced two- or three-piece tubular propeller shaft, supported at the centre by one (two-piece propeller shaft) or two (three-piece propeller shaft) rubber-mounted bearings **(see illustration)**.

Fitted at the front, centre and rear of the propeller shaft assembly are universal joints, which cater for movement of the rear axle with suspension travel, and slight movement of the power unit on its mountings. On certain models, a rubber "Guibo" joint is used at the front in place of the universal joint. Depending on model and

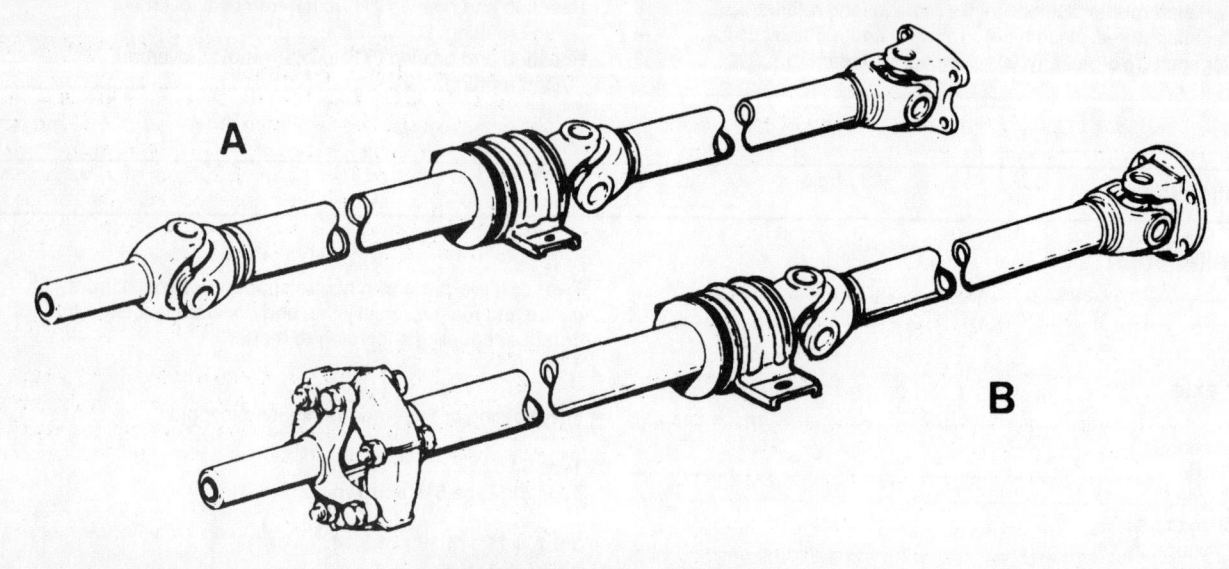

2.1 Typical propeller shaft types

A   Two-piece propeller shaft with standard front universal joint   *B   Two-piece propeller shaft with front rubber Guibo joint*

Chapter 8 Propeller shaft and rear axle

3.3 Propeller shaft rear universal joint and final drive coupling flange bolts

3.4 Propeller shaft front universal joint and transmission coupling flange bolts

3.5 Propeller shaft centre bearing and retaining bolts

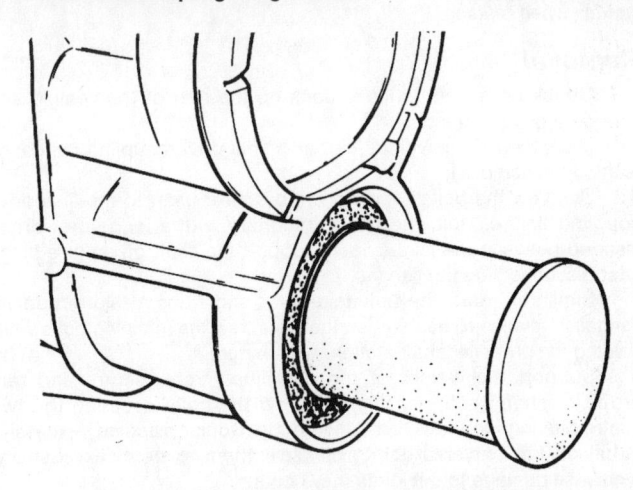

3.6 Using a chamfered plastic cap inserted into the oil seal to prevent any loss of oil/fluid from the transmission

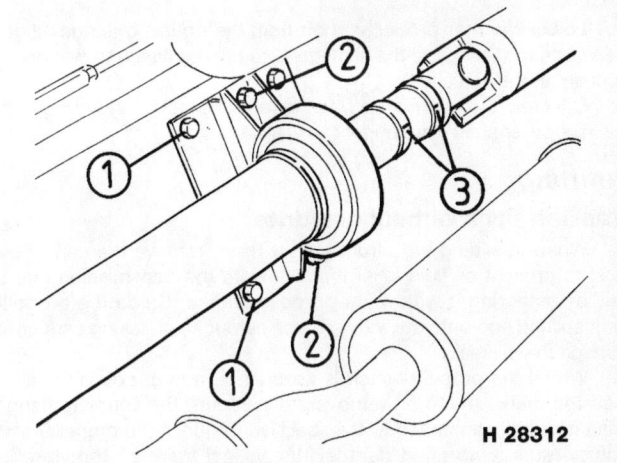

3.9 Propeller shaft centre bearing and sliding spline connection (transmissions with overdrive)

1 Centre bearing support bracket bolts
2 Centre bearing retaining bolts
3 Front-to-rear propeller shaft alignment marks at sliding spline connection

transmission type, a constant velocity joint may be fitted in place of the centre universal joint. The universal joints are of the sealed type and cannot be serviced; however, it is possible to renew the centre bearing and rubber joint.

3 Propeller shaft (two-piece type) - removal and refitting

Note: *New bolts will be required to secure the propeller shaft coupling flange(s) when refitting.*

Removal

Transmissions without overdrive

1 Chock both front wheels. Jack up the rear of the vehicle and support it on axle stands.
2 Mark the rear universal joint and final drive coupling flanges in relation to each other.
3 Unscrew the bolts securing the propeller shaft to the final drive coupling flange **(see illustration)**. Hold the shaft stationary with a long screwdriver inserted between the joint spider. Support the shaft on an axle stand after disconnecting the flanges.
4 If the front of the propeller shaft is secured to the transmission by a coupling flange, mark the universal joint and transmission coupling flanges in relation to each other, then unscrew the retaining bolts while holding the propeller shaft stationary as before **(see illustration)**.
5 Support the weight of the combined front and rear propeller shaft sections, and then unscrew the two centre bearing retaining bolts from the vehicle underbody **(see illustration)**.
6 Lower the propeller shaft from the coupling flanges and the centre bearing mounting, and remove it from the vehicle. If a sliding front joint is used, pull it rearwards to disengage it from the transmission output shaft; to prevent any loss of oil/fluid from the transmission, a chamfered plastic cap can be inserted into the oil seal **(see illustration)**. Alternatively, a plastic bag can be positioned on the transmission, and retained with an elastic band.

Transmissions with overdrive

7 Chock both front wheels. Jack up the rear of the vehicle and support it on axle stands.
8 Mark the front universal joint flange and the overdrive unit output flange in relation to each other, then unscrew the retaining bolts. Hold the propeller shaft stationary with a long screwdriver inserted between the joint spider. Support the shaft on an axle stand after disconnecting the flanges.
9 Mark the position of the rear propeller shaft to the front propeller shaft, at the sliding spline connection just behind the centre bearing **(see illustration)**.
10 Mark the rear universal joint and final drive coupling flanges in relation to each other. Unscrew the retaining bolts while holding the shaft stationary as before.

8-4 Chapter 8 Propeller shaft and rear axle

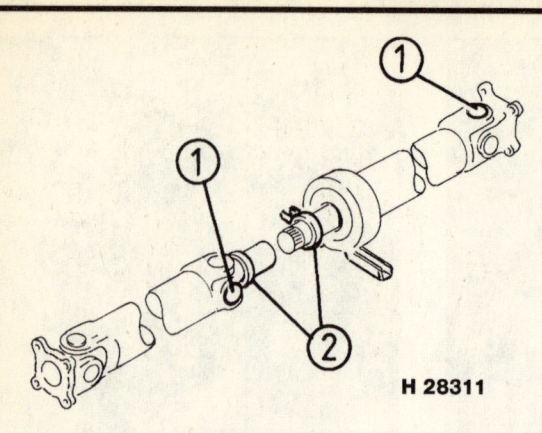

3.22 Front-to-rear propeller shaft universal joint alignment
1 *Universal joint spiders fitted at 90° to each other*
2 *Alignment marks*

11 Lower the rear propeller shaft from the coupling flange, slide it rearwards to disengage the sliding spline connection, and withdraw it from under the vehicle.
12 Unscrew the two centre bearing retaining bolts, and remove the front propeller shaft from under the vehicle.

Refitting

Transmissions without overdrive

13 Where a sliding type front joint is used, remove the cap or bag used to prevent oil/fluid loss, then lubricate the transmission rear oil seal by smearing it with multi-purpose grease. Guide the propeller shaft splined end onto the transmission output shaft, taking care not to damage the oil seal.
14 Where the propeller shaft is secured by a front coupling flange, align the marks made on removal, then secure the coupling flanges using new bolts tightened to the specified torque. If the propeller shaft incorporates a vibration damper, the yellow mark on the vibration damper and the balance weights on the shaft must be aligned.
15 Raise the centre of the propeller shaft, and loosely fit the two centre bearing retaining bolts. Do not tighten the bolts at this stage.
16 Raise the rear of the propeller shaft, align the coupling flange marks made on removal, and secure the flanges using new bolts tightened to the specified torque.
17 On vehicles without a constant velocity joint behind the centre bearing, ensure that the centre bearing is squarely positioned and free of tension, then lower the vehicle to the ground. Tighten the centre bearing retaining bolts to the specified torque with the vehicle standing on its wheels and in an unladen condition.
18 On vehicles with a constant velocity joint behind the centre bearing, ensure that the rear axle is hanging down unsupported. Slide the centre bearing and constant velocity joint as far to the rear as possible, check that the centre bearing rubber insulator is not distorted, then tighten the centre bearing retaining bolts to the specified torque.
19 On vehicles with a splined propeller shaft front connection to the transmission, check and if necessary top-up the transmission oil level as described in Chapter 1.

Transmissions with overdrive

20 Guide the front propeller shaft and centre bearing into position, and loosely fit the two centre bearing retaining bolts. Do not tighten the bolts at this stage.
21 Align the marks on the front universal joint flange and the overdrive unit output flange made during removal, then secure the coupling flanges using new bolts tightened to the specified torque.
22 Liberally lubricate the rear propeller shaft splined end and the splined yoke on the front propeller shaft with multi-purpose grease. Align the marks made during removal, and insert the rear shaft splined end into the yoke. If a new (unmarked) front or rear propeller shaft section is being fitted, make sure that the universal joint spiders are at 90° to each other as shown **(see illustration)**.
23 Raise the rear of the propeller shaft, align the coupling flange marks made on removal, and secure the flanges using new bolts tightened to the specified torque.
24 Check that the centre bearing is squarely positioned and free of tension, then lower the vehicle to the ground. Tighten the centre bearing retaining bolts to the specified torque with the vehicle standing on its wheels and in an unladen condition.
25 On completion, grease the propeller shaft sliding spline at the grease nipple until grease exudes from the breather hole in the end plug of the splined yoke.

4 Propeller shaft (three-piece type) - removal and refitting

Note: *New bolts will be required to secure the propeller shaft coupling flanges when refitting.*

Removal

1 Chock both front wheels. Jack up the rear of the vehicle and support it on axle stands.
2 Mark the rear universal joint and final drive coupling flanges in relation to each other.
3 Unscrew the bolts securing the propeller shaft to the final drive coupling flange. Hold the shaft stationary with a long screwdriver inserted between the joint spider. Support the shaft on an axle stand after disconnecting the flanges.
4 Similarly, mark the universal joint and transmission coupling flanges in relation to each other, then unscrew the retaining bolts while holding the propeller shaft stationary as before.
5 Support the weight of the combined front, centre and rear propeller shaft sections, then unscrew the bolts securing the two centre bearings to the vehicle underbody. Do not place any excessive strain on the universal joints or allow them to bend excessively, otherwise damage to the joints may occur.
6 Lower the propeller shaft, and remove it from under the vehicle.

Refitting

7 Align the marks on the front universal joint flange and the transmission coupling flange made during removal, then secure the coupling flanges using new bolts tightened to the specified torque.
8 Raise the propeller shaft centre section, and loosely fit the retaining bolts to both centre bearings. Do not tighten the bolts at this stage.
9 Raise the propeller shaft rear section, align the coupling flange marks made on removal, and secure the flanges using new bolts tightened to the specified torque.
10 Tighten the retaining bolts securing the two centre bearings to the specified torque, then lower the vehicle to the ground.

5 Propeller shaft centre bearing - renewal

1 Remove the propeller shaft as described in Section 3 or 4, according to type.
2 Prise up the locktab from the universal joint retaining bolt, then loosen off the bolt using a suitable flat ring spanner **(see illustration)**.
3 Extract the U-shaped washer from the bolt head, then insert a screwdriver or metal bar between the bolt head and the universal joint, and lever the two propeller shaft sections apart **(see illustration)**.
4 Remove the housing complete with rubber insulator from the bearing unit.
5 The bearing can now be removed from the propeller shaft using a suitable puller **(see illustration)**.
6 To renew the rubber insulator in the housing, bend open the six metal retaining tongues, and then remove the old insulator. Insert the

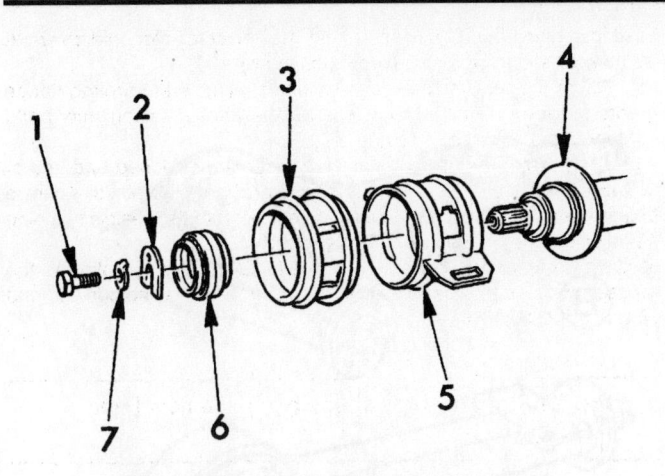

Chapter 8 Propeller shaft and rear axle   8-5

5.2 Propeller shaft centre bearing components

1 Bolt
2 U-shaped washer
3 Rubber insulator
4 Propeller shaft
5 Housing
6 Ball-bearing
7 Locktab

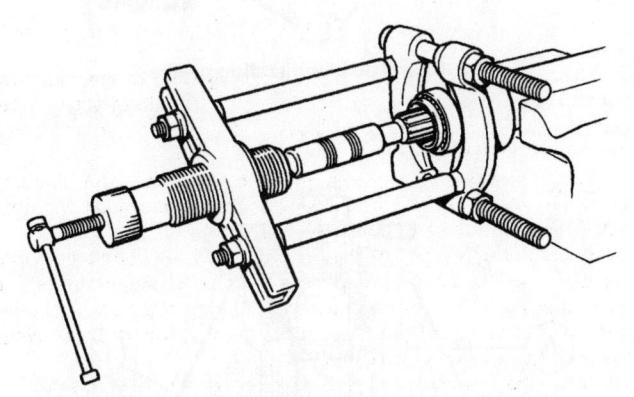

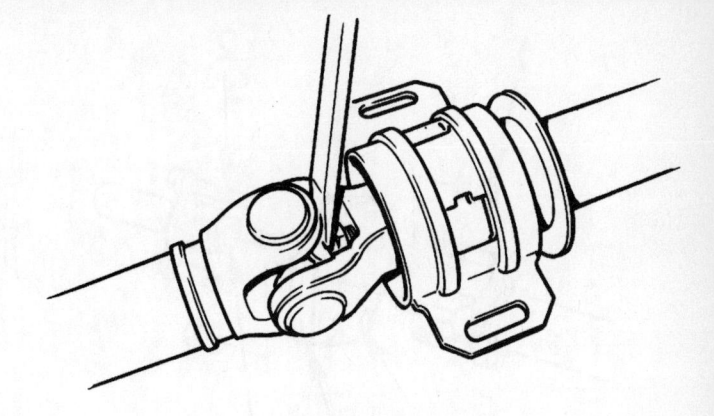

5.3 Levering the two propeller shaft sections apart

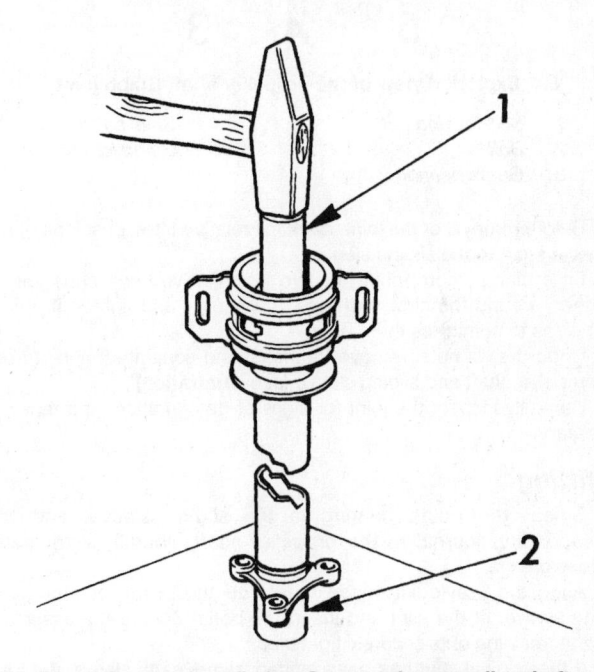

5.5 Remove the bearing from the propeller shaft using a suitable puller

5.8 Centre bearing installation. Support the propeller shaft on a tube (2) and drive the bearing home using a sleeve (1)

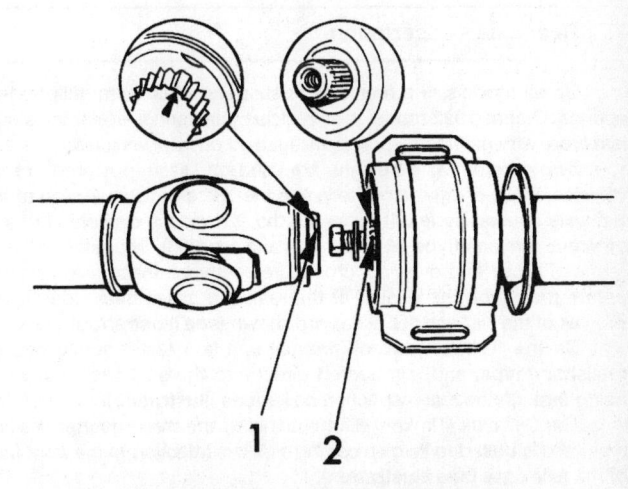

new insulator, together with the ball-bearing, into the housing. Ensure that the insulator engages with the channel in the housing.
7 When the insulator and bearing are fitted, bend back the metal retaining tabs using grips or pliers.
8 Stand the propeller shaft on end, and support it on a tube of suitable diameter. Drive the centre bearing home, using a hammer and tubular sleeve, as far as the stop **(see illustration)**.
9 Refit the bolt, together with a new locktab, but don't tighten the bolt at this stage.
10 Reassemble the universal joint to the shaft, aligning the master spline with the double-width groove, and press them together **(see illustration)**.
11 Slide the U-shaped washer into position with the pegged side towards the bearing, then tighten the universal joint retaining bolt to the specified torque.
12 Use a length of rod or a suitable drift to tap up the locktab and secure the bolt.
13 Refit the propeller shaft as described in Section 3 or 4.

6 Propeller shaft rubber "Guibo" joint - removal and refitting

Removal

1 Remove the propeller shaft as described in Section 3 or 4, depending on type.

5.10 Propeller shaft-to-universal joint alignment

1 Double-width groove   2 Master spline

8•6　Chapter 8　Propeller shaft and rear axle

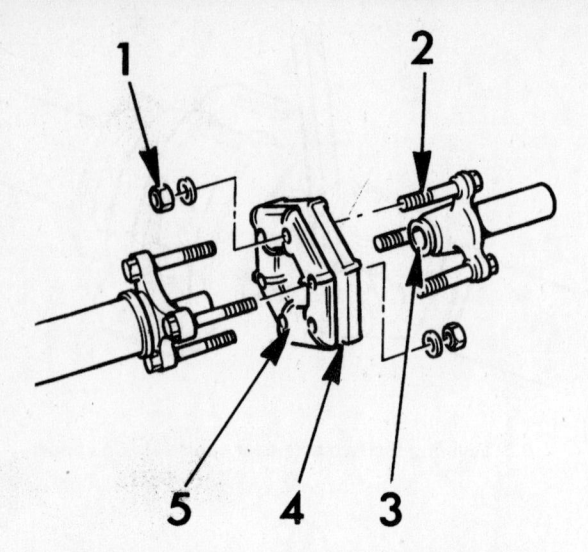

6.4 Exploded view of the propeller shaft Guibo joint

1. Self-locking nut
2. Bolt
3. Guide bearing
4. Steel band
5. Guibo joint

2 Before removal of the joint, mark the relative fitted positions of the propeller shaft to the sliding sleeve.
3 Fit a clamp, comprising of two worm-drive hose clips joined together, around the circumference of the joint, and tighten it until it just begins to compress the rubber.
4 Undo the six nuts, remove the bolts, and separate the joint from the propeller shaft and sliding sleeve **(see illustration)**.
5 Carefully inspect the joint for signs of deterioration, and renew if necessary.

Refitting

6 Smear the guide bearing in the sliding sleeve, and the corresponding journal in the propeller shaft, liberally with multi-purpose grease.
7 Align the previously-made marks on the propeller shaft and sliding sleeve, fit the joint and insert the bolts. Secure the assembly with the retaining nuts securely tightened.
8 If the original joint has been refitted, remove the clamp. If a new joint has been fitted, cut off and discard the metal retaining band.
9 Refit the propeller shaft as described in Section 3 or 4.

7　Rear axle - description

On all models, the rear axle is suspended on semi-elliptic leaf springs. On pre-1992 model year vehicles, the springs are of the single leaf type, with multi-leaf springs being used on later vehicles.
Two different axle designs are used on Diesel-powered Transit vehicles, these being the "H" axle and the "G" axle. One version of the "H" axle is used (type 34), whereas the "G" axle is available in three different versions (type 51, type 51A and type 53). The differences in terms of repair and overhaul procedures between these axle versions centre mainly on the design of the rear hub assemblies. Identifying profiles of the "H" and "G" axles are shown **(see illustration)**.
On the "G" axle, the differential unit is a fully-floating hypoid (Salisbury) type, and is mounted direct into the axle casing, access being through the rear inspection cover **(see illustration)**.
The "H" axle (Timken) differential is of the three-quarter floating type, and is bolted to its own carrier, which is attached to the front face of the axle case **(see illustration)**.
On all axles, the pinion bearing spacer is of the collapsible sleeve type. Special care must be taken when renewing the pinion seal not to overtighten the flange retaining nut, or the sleeve could become

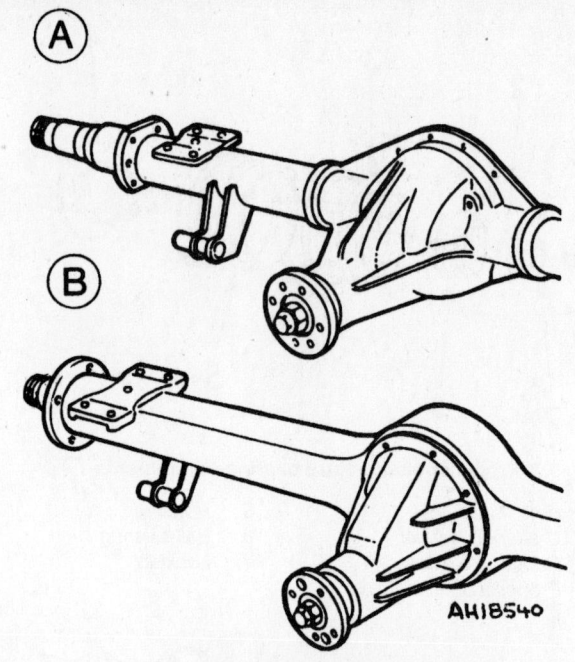

7.2 Rear axle identification profile

A　"G" axle　　　　B　"H" axle

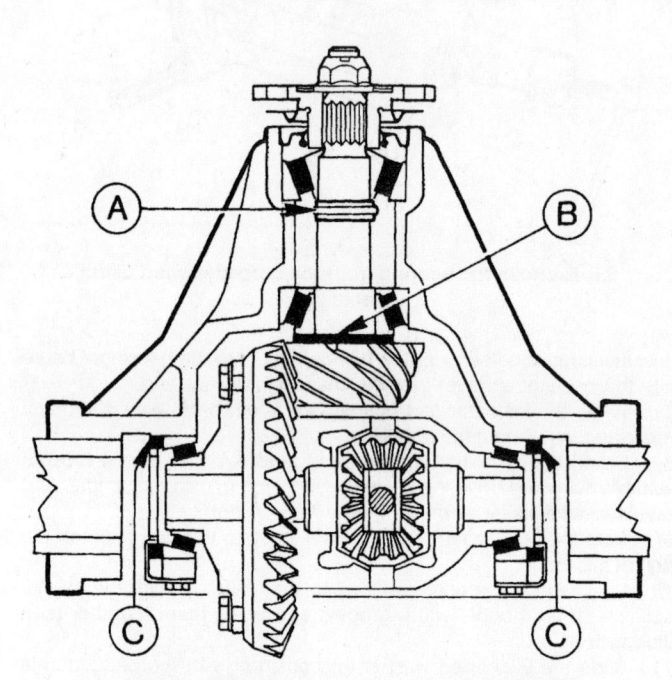

7.3 Sectional view of the "G" axle differential unit

A　Collapsible spacer sleeve
B　Pinion shim
C　Bearing adjusting nuts

distorted and the pinion-to-crownwheel setting be disturbed.
The differential unit runs on taper-roller bearings, the adjustment of which is dependent on type. On the "H" axle, adjustment is made by adjuster nuts in the differential carrier. On the "G" axle, the adjustment is made by adjuster nuts in the axle housing.
The design of the rear wheel hub varies considerably according to axle type and vehicle model year. On the "H" axle, the wheel hub is supported by a double-race ball-bearing **(see illustration)**. The wheel hub of the types 51A and 53 "G" axle is fitted with two taper-roller bearings, the free play of which is set by an adjuster nut which is

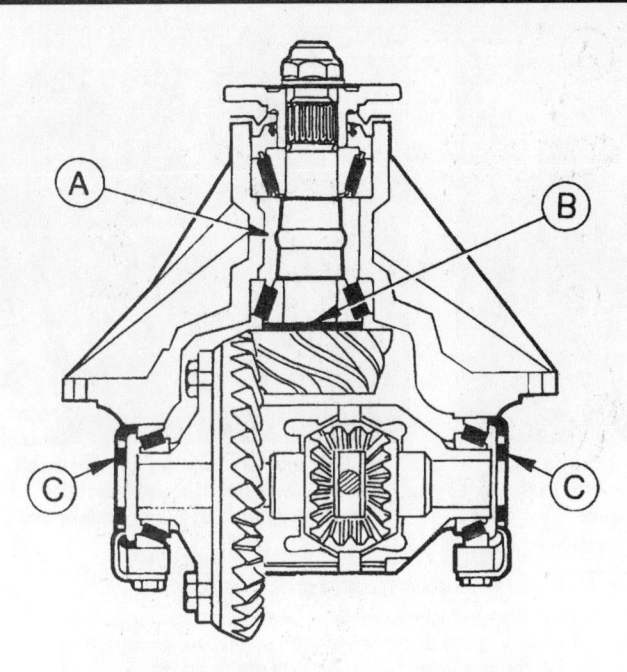

Chapter 8 Propeller shaft and rear axle

7.4 Sectional view of the "H" axle differential unit

A Collapsible spacer sleeve
B Pinion shim
C Bearing adjusting nuts

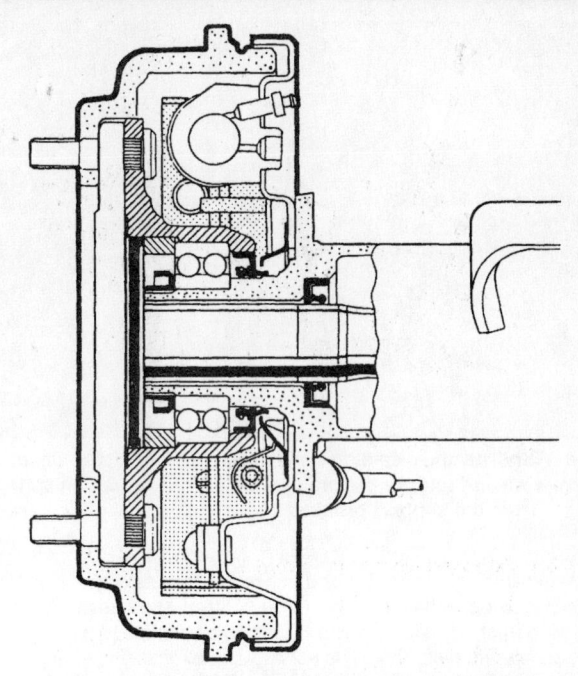

7.7a "H" axle rear wheel hub and bearing assembly

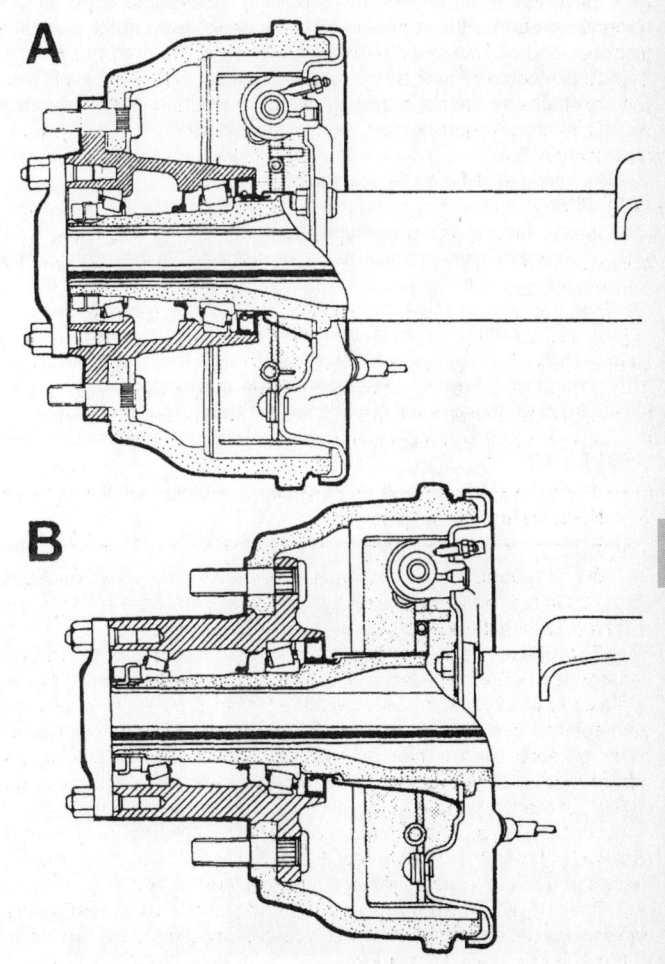

7.7b "G" axle rear wheel hub and bearing assembly

A Type 51A B Type 53

secured by a locktab and locknuts **(see illustration)**. The type 51 "G" axle (which replaced the type 51A unit in 1992) utilises ball-bearings, and is similar in layout to the arrangement used on the "H" axle.

On all axle types, the outer hub bearings are lubricated by the rear axle oil.

8 Rear axle - removal and refitting

Note: *The rear axle removal/refitting details described below are for the removal of the unit on its own. If required, it can be removed together with the roadwheels and rear leaf springs as a combined unit, although this method requires the vehicle to be raised and supported at a greater height (to allow the roadwheels to clear the body during withdrawal of the unit). If the latter method is used, follow the instructions given, but ignore the references to removal of the roadwheels and detaching the springs from the axle. Refer to Chapter 10 for details on detaching the springs from the underbody.*

Removal

1 Ensure that the vehicle is unloaded, then chock the front wheels, remove the wheel trim and slacken the rear wheel nuts. Remember that on pre-1992 model year vehicles with six-stud wheels, the wheel nuts on the left-hand side have a **left-hand thread** - ie they unscrew **clockwise**.

2 Jack up the rear of the vehicle, and support it adequately beneath the underframe side members in front of the rear springs. Support the weight of the rear axle with a trolley jack positioned beneath the differential housing.

3 Unscrew the wheel nuts and remove the rear wheels. On the "H" axle, mark the position of each rear wheel relative to its drum/hub.

4 Mark the pinion and propeller shaft drive flanges so that they can be refitted to their original positions, then unscrew the four bolts and detach the propeller shaft, supporting it on a stand. Note that new flange bolts will be required for refitting.

5 Disconnect the rear brake pipe(s) from the flexible hydraulic brake hose(s), then withdraw the retaining spring clip(s) and release the hose(s) from the support bracket. When disconnected, plug the lines,

8-8　Chapter 8　Propeller shaft and rear axle

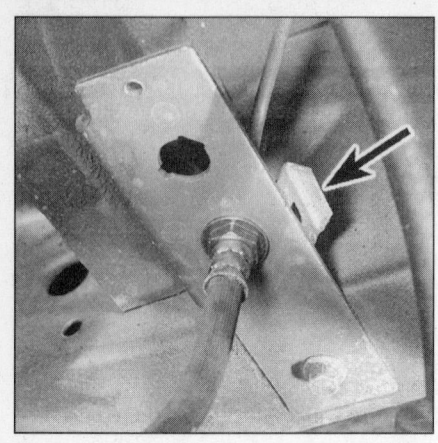

8.5a Withdraw the retaining spring clip (arrowed) and release the brake hose from the support bracket

8.5b On later models, slip the LAV regulating spring out of the slot in the axle bracket (arrowed)

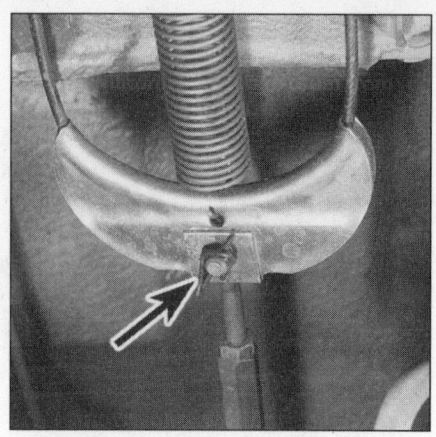

8.6 Extract the retaining clip (arrowed) and clevis pin to disconnect the handbrake cable at the equaliser unit

to prevent the ingress of dirt and excessive fluid leakage. Note that where a load-apportioning valve (LAV) is fitted, the regulating spring must be detached at its top end by removing the clevis pin. Alternatively, on later models, slip the lower end of the regulating spring out of the slot in the axle bracket, after first withdrawing the retaining clip from the top edge of the bracket **(see illustrations)**.

6　Detach the handbrake return spring, then extract the retaining clip and clevis pin to disconnect the handbrake cable at the equaliser unit **(see illustration)**. Release the two outer cable sleeves at the mounting bracket, and also release the exhaust system at the rear, to allow the handbrake cable to clear as the axle is removed.

7　Detach the handbrake cable support brackets from the shock absorber upper mountings or chassis side members.

8　On vehicles equipped with ABS, disconnect the wheel speed sensor wiring at the chassis side member.

9　Undo the retaining nuts and bolts, and detach the rear shock absorbers from the axle **(see illustration)**.

10　Check that the axle unit is securely supported in the centre by the jack. Have an assistant available, to steady the axle each side as it is lowered from the vehicle.

11　Undo the retaining nuts, and remove the spring-to-axle U-bolts and fittings each side **(see illustration)**. Check that the various axle fittings and attachments are disconnected and out of the way, then carefully lower the axle unit and withdraw it from under the vehicle.

Refitting

12　Refitting the axle unit is basically a reversal of the removal procedure, but the following points should be noted:
a) Renew all self-locking nuts and lockwashers during refitting.
b) When raising the axle into position each side, engage the locating hole in the axle over the centre bolt of the spring.
c) Tighten the rear axle U-bolts to their specified torque wrench settings.
d) When reconnecting the propeller shaft to the pinion flange, be sure to align the match marks made during removal, and use new retaining bolts tightened to the specified torque.
e) Refer to Chapter 9 for details on reconnecting the brake system components. Top-up and bleed the brake hydraulic system as also described in Chapter 9.
f) If the axle has been dismantled during removal, top-up the oil level as described in Chapter 1.

9　Rear axle halfshaft - removal and refitting

Removal

"H" axle (type 34)

1　Ensure that the vehicle is unloaded, then chock the front wheels, remove the wheel trim and slacken the rear wheel nuts on the side concerned.

2　Jack up the rear of the vehicle, and support it adequately beneath the underframe side members in front of the rear springs. Support the

8.9 Undo the retaining nuts and bolts, and detach the rear shock absorbers from the axle

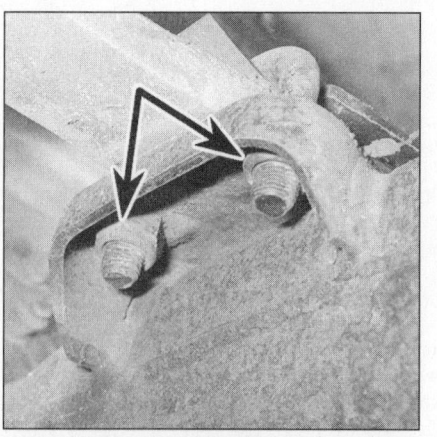

8.11 Undo the retaining nuts (arrowed), and remove the spring-to-axle U-bolts and fittings each side

9.4 Withdraw the brake drum from the hub

Chapter 8 Propeller shaft and rear axle   8-9

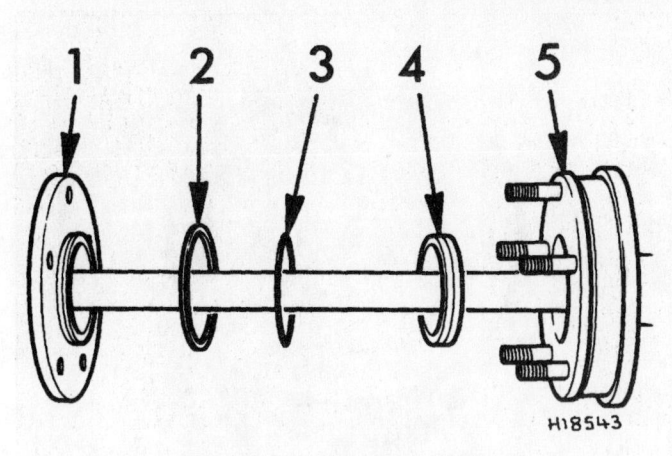

9.5a "H" axle halfshaft and fittings

1 Halfshaft
2 Gasket
3 O-ring seal
4 Spacer ring
5 Hub

weight of the rear axle with a trolley jack positioned beneath the differential housing.

3 Mark the position of the rear wheel relative to its drum/hub, then unscrew the wheel nuts and remove the wheel.

4 Mark the position of the brake drum relative to the hub, then release the handbrake and remove the brake drum **(see illustration)**.

5 Mark the position of the halfshaft in relation to the hub, then release the halfshaft by tapping the flange or carefully easing the flange away from the hub with a screwdriver. Withdraw the halfshaft from the axle housing/hub, taking care not to damage the oil seal within the hub. Be prepared for some oil spillage **(see illustrations)**.

6 Where fitted, recover the gasket and the O-ring oil seal from the flange and if required, extract the spacer ring located in front of the bearing in the axle casing **(see illustration)**.

"G" axle (types 51A and 53)

7 Ensure that the vehicle is unloaded, then chock the front wheels, remove the wheel trim and slacken the rear wheel nuts on the side concerned. Remember that on pre-1992 model year vehicles with six-stud wheels, the wheel nuts on the left-hand side have a **left-hand thread** - ie they unscrew **clockwise**.

8 Jack up the rear of the vehicle, and support it adequately beneath the underframe side members in front of the rear springs. Support the weight of the rear axle with a trolley jack positioned beneath the differential housing.

9 Mark the position of the rear wheel(s) relative to the drum/hub, then unscrew the wheel nuts and remove the rear wheel(s).

10 Unscrew the nuts or bolts securing the halfshaft to the wheel hub.

11 Withdraw the halfshaft from the axle housing/hub, taking care not to damage the oil seal within the hub. Be prepared for some oil spillage.

"G" axle (type 51) - 1992 model year onwards

12 Ensure that the vehicle is unloaded, then chock the front wheels, remove the wheel trim and slacken the rear wheel nuts on the side concerned.

13 Jack up the rear of the vehicle, and support it adequately beneath the underframe side members in front of the rear springs. Support the weight of the rear axle with a trolley jack positioned beneath the differential housing.

14 Mark the position of the rear wheel relative to its drum/hub, then unscrew the wheel nuts and remove the wheel.

15 Mark the position of the brake drum relative to the hub, then release the handbrake and remove the brake drum.

16 Unscrew the bolts securing the halfshaft to the hub.

17 Release the halfshaft by tapping the flange or carefully easing the flange away from the hub with a screwdriver. Withdraw the halfshaft from the axle housing/hub, taking care not to damage the oil seal within the hub. Be prepared for some oil spillage.

18 If required, extract the spacer ring located in front of the bearing in the axle casing.

Refitting

19 Refitting the axle halfshaft is a reversal of the removal procedure, but note the following:

a) Fit the spacer ring in front of the bearing on the "H" axle with its chamfered side facing inwards. The spacer ring may be fitted either way round on the type 51 "G" axle.

b) Clean the mating surfaces of the halfshaft and hub before refitting, and renew the O-ring seal and gasket. On the type 51A and type 53 "G" axle, coat the halfshaft flange with sealer prior to fitting.

c) Align the marks made during removal when fitting the halfshaft, brake drum and roadwheel(s).

d) Check and top-up the rear axle oil level as described in Chapter 1.

10 Rear hub and bearing ("H" axle) - removal, overhaul and refitting

Note: *Various modifications have taken place during the course of production to the method used to retain the rear hub. Read through the entire procedure before starting, and make sure you have the correct tools for the job. Take great care when removing and refitting the hub nuts, as they are tightened to an extremely high torque loading (partic-*

9.5b Carefully ease the halfshaft flange away from the hub with a screwdriver . . .

9.5c . . . then withdraw the halfshaft from the axle housing/hub, taking care not to damage the oil seal within the hub

9.6 Recover the gasket and the O-ring oil seal (arrowed) from the flange

8-10 Chapter 8 Propeller shaft and rear axle

10.2 Extract the spacer ring located in front of the bearing in the axle casing

10.3a Special tool for removing the round slotted type hub nut

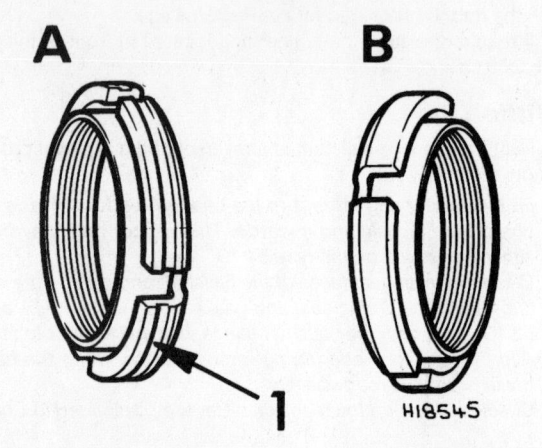

10.3b "H" axle hub nut identification - round slotted type hub nut

A Left-hand thread (left-hand side)
B Right-hand thread (right-hand side)
1 Identification groove (in left-hand nut)

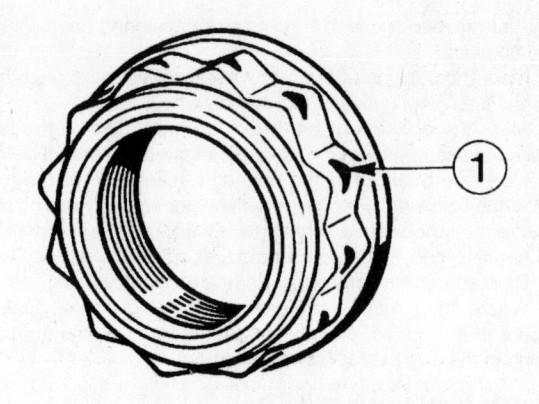

10.5 "H" axle hub nut identification - double-hexagon type
1 Identification groove (in left-hand nut)

ularly on later vehicles). In all cases, new hub nuts must be used when refitting.

Caution: *Due to the extremely high tightening torque of the rear hub nut (particularly on later vehicles), place axle stands beneath the rear axle to supplement the main supports, and take great care when removing and refitting the hub nut. Use only the correct sockets for the type of nut being worked on, and make sure you have a suitable extension bar for removal, and a torque wrench capable of tightening the nut to the correct setting (see Specifications) for refitting. Entrust this work to a dealer or suitably-equipped garage if in doubt about the procedure, or if the required tools are not available.*

Removal

1 Refer to the previous Section and remove the halfshaft on the side concerned.
2 With the halfshaft removed, extract the spacer ring located in front of the bearing in the axle casing **(see illustration)**.

Axles with round, slotted hub nut

3 Lever up the hub nut staking using a screwdriver or thin chisel to prise it clear of the slots, but take care not to damage the threads. Unscrew the hub nut using Ford special tool No 15-077 or similar **(see illustration)**. When removing the hub nut, note that it has a **left-hand**

thread on the left-hand side, and a right-hand thread on the right-hand side. Left-hand threaded nuts can be identified by the marking groove around the periphery of the nut **(see illustration)**. When obtaining a new hub nut for reassembly, only the latest type double-hexagon nut will be supplied by Ford parts stockists, and only this type of nut should be used.
4 Withdraw the hub using Ford special tool No 15-060 (if necessary). A suitable conventional slide hammer may also suffice, if the special Ford tool is not readily available.

Axles with double-hexagon hub nut (pre-1992 model year)

5 A revised double-hexagon type hub nut was introduced for 1989 models, together with a revised removal and refitting procedure. Note that as with the earlier versions, the double-hexagon nut has a **left-hand thread** on the left-hand side, and a conventional right-hand thread on the right-hand side. Left-handed threaded nuts can be identified by the marking groove around the periphery of the nut **(see illustration)**.
6 Using a 3.0 mm drill bit, drill a pilot hole in the staked portion of the hub nut locking tab, then drill out the staking using a 6.0 mm drill bit.
7 Using a 50.0 mm AF socket, and long extension bar, unscrew the hub nut from the axle.
8 Withdraw the hub using Ford special tool No 15-060 (if necessary). A suitable conventional slide hammer may also suffice, if the special Ford tool is not readily available.

Chapter 8 Propeller shaft and rear axle   8-11

10.12a Rear wheel hub and bearing (outboard side)

10.12b Rear wheel hub and oil seal (inboard side)

10.19 Locate the hub assembly onto the axle, and push the hub fully into position

10.20 Screw on the new hub nut . . .

10.21 . . . tighten the nut to the specified torque . . .

10.22 . . . and where applicable, secure the hub nut by staking the locking tab into the axle groove

Axles with double-hexagon hub nut (1992 model year onwards)

9 From the 1992 model year, the double-hexagon type hub nut was further revised. The latest type nut is similar in appearance to the previous version **(see illustration 10.5)**, but the removal and refitting procedures have changed. As before, the nut has a **left-hand thread** for the left-hand side, and a right-hand thread for the right-hand side. A commercially-available 2 1/4 inch AF socket will be required to remove and refit the nut.

10 Using the 2 1/4 inch socket, a sturdy, long extension bar and great care, unscrew the hub nut from the axle.

11 Withdraw the hub using Ford special tool No 15-060 (if necessary). A suitable conventional slide hammer may also suffice, if the special Ford tool is not readily available.

Overhaul

12 Wipe clean all the components, then carefully examine each item for damage and deterioration. Check the bearing for wear by spinning the inner track and checking for any roughness. Similarly, attempt to move the inner track laterally; excessive movement is an indication of wear. Any component which is unserviceable must be renewed **(see illustrations)**.

13 To dismantle the hub, support it on its flange face, not on the studs, and take care not to damage the sensor ring on vehicles fitted with ABS.

14 Drive out the bearing using a suitable drift. Drive or lever out the old oil seal. Thoroughly clean the hub, using a fine file to remove any nicks or burrs caused by removal of the old bearing.

15 To reassemble the hub, first lubricate the bearing with grease, then support the hub with its inner flange facing down.

16 Position the bearing over the hub with its sealed face pointing up.

17 Press the bearing into the hub until it abuts the hub shoulder, using a suitable tubular drift in contact with the bearing outer race. Do not press or drive against the bearing inner race.

18 Invert the hub, and support it on blocks on its outer flange face so that the studs hang free. Press the oil seal into position using a suitable tubular drift.

Refitting

19 With the hub reassembled, lubricate the oil seal lips with grease, then carefully locate the hub assembly onto the axle. Push the hub fully into position, using a soft-faced mallet if necessary to gently tap it into place **(see illustration)**.

20 Screw on the new hub nut, noting the comments made earlier regarding hub nut identification for left- and right-hand sides **(see illustration)**.

21 With the rear axle securely supported, tighten the hub nut to the specified torque, according to nut type **(see illustration)**.

22 On axles with a round slotted hub nut, or 50.0 mm AF double-hexagon hub nut (pre-1992 model year) secure the hub nut by staking the locking tab into the axle groove using a suitable punch **(see illustration)**. On later axles with 2 1/4 inch double-hexagon hub nuts, the hub nut is self-locking, and no staking is required.

23 Fit the spacer ring in position over the bearing, noting that it is fitted with its chamfered side facing inwards.

24 Refit the halfshaft as described in the previous Section.

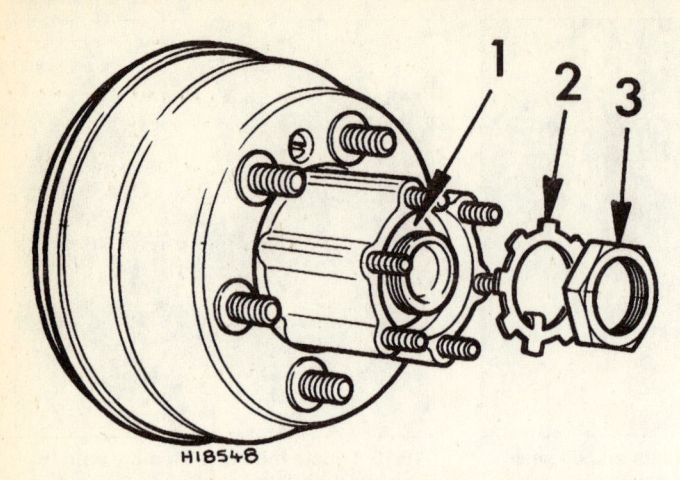

8-12 Chapter 8 Propeller shaft and rear axle

11.2 Types 51A and 53 "G" axle hub nut (1), tab washer (2) and locknut (3)

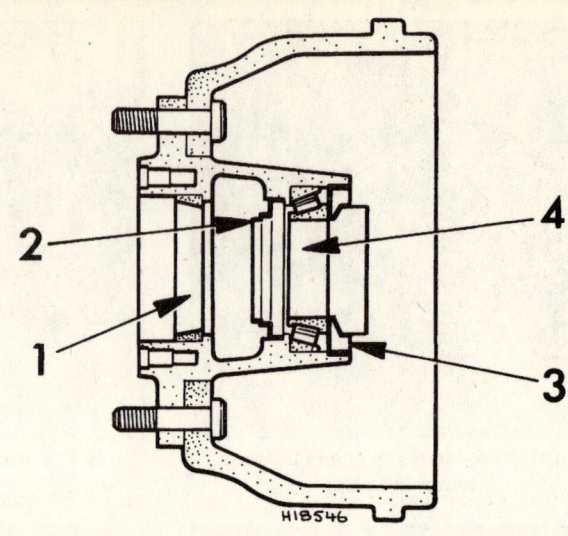

11.9 Sectional view of the hub on types 51A and 53 "G" axle

1 Outer taper-roller bearing cup
2 Outer oil seal
3 Inner oil seal
4 Inner taper-roller bearing cup

11 Rear hub and bearing ("G" axle) - removal, overhaul and refitting

Note: *Various modifications have taken place during the course of production to the method used to retain the rear hub. Read through the entire procedure before starting, and make sure you have the correct tools for the job. Take great care when removing and refitting the hub nuts, as they are tightened to an extremely high torque loading (particularly on later vehicles). In all cases, new hub nuts must be used when refitting.*

Caution: *Due to the extremely high tightening torque of the rear hub nut (particularly on later vehicles), place axle stands beneath the rear axle to supplement the main supports, and take great care when removing and refitting the hub nut. Use only the correct sockets for the type of nut being worked on, and make sure you have a suitable extension bar for removal, and a torque wrench capable of tightening the nut to the correct setting (see Specifications) for refitting. Entrust this work to a dealer or suitably-equipped garage if in doubt about the procedure, or if the required tools are not available.*

Removal

Types 51A and 53

1 Refer to Section 9 and remove the halfshaft on the side concerned.
2 Prise up the tab over the hub locknut, and unscrew the locknut. Remove the tab washer and unscrew the hub nut **(see illustration)**.
3 With the handbrake released, remove the hub and brake drum assembly, collecting the outer bearing race as the hub/drum assembly is withdrawn. On vehicles equipped with ABS, take care to avoid damaging the wheel speed sensor ring.

Type 51 - 1992 model year onwards

4 Refer to Section 9 and remove the halfshaft on the side concerned.
5 With the halfshaft removed, extract the spacer ring located in front of the bearing in the axle casing.
6 The hub is retained by a double-hexagon hub nut, which is tightened to an extremely high torque setting. A commercially-available 2 1/4 inch AF socket will be required to remove and refit the nut. The nut has a **left-hand thread** for the left-hand side, and a right-hand thread for the right-hand side. Left-handed threaded nuts can be identified by the marking groove around the periphery of the nut **(see illustration 10.5)**.
7 Using the 2 1/4 inch socket, a sturdy, long extension bar and great care, unscrew the hub nut from the axle.
8 Withdraw the hub from the axle, taking care not to damage the wheel speed sensor ring on vehicles equipped with ABS.

Overhaul

Types 51A and 53

9 Clean and inspect the hub as described in paragraph 12 of the previous Section **(see illustration)**.
10 To dismantle the hub, support it on its inner and outer flange faces, not on the brake drum or wheel studs, and take care not to damage the sensor ring on vehicles fitted with ABS.
11 Before removing the old oil seals, note and record their position and fitted depth in the hub, as a guide to reassembly. Ford special shouldered tools are available to fit the new seals accurately, but suitable sockets or tubes can be used, provided the correct final fitted position of the seals is known.
12 Using a soft metal drift or tube of suitable diameter, drive out the outer oil seal, the inner taper-roller bearing race, and the inner oil seal.
13 Drive out the inner and outer taper-roller bearing cups.
14 Thoroughly clean the hub, using a fine file to remove any nicks or burrs caused by removal of the bearing cups.
15 To reassemble the hub, support it on its inner face inside the brake drum (not on the drum itself) with the wheel studs uppermost.
16 Press the new outer taper-roller bearing cup into the hub, until it contacts the shoulder in the hub.
17 Turn the hub and drum assembly over, and support it on the hub face with the studs facing down.
18 Press the new inner taper-roller bearing cup into the hub, until it contacts the shoulder in the hub.
19 With the sealing lip facing downwards, press the outer oil seal into the bearing cup, to the fitted position noted during removal.
20 Liberally grease the inner taper-roller bearing, and place it in position in the bearing cup.
21 Press the inner oil seal into the hub to the fitted position as noted during removal.

Type 51 - 1992 model year onwards

22 The overhaul procedure is the same as for the "H" axle described in paragraphs 12 to 18 of Section 10.

Refitting

Types 51A and 53

23 With the hub reassembled, lubricate the inner and outer oil seals and the inner bearing with grease, and refit the hub and drum assembly to the axle.
24 Grease the outer taper-roller bearing, and locate it in the outer

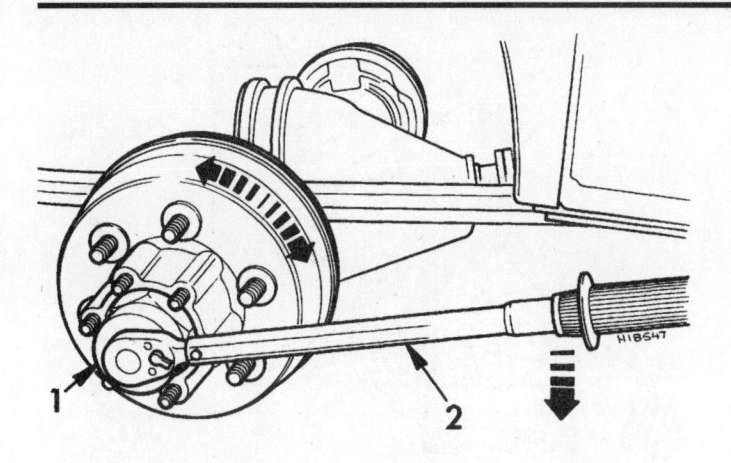

Chapter 8 Propeller shaft and rear axle

11.25 Tightening the hub nut on types 51A and 53 "G" axle

1 Socket   2 Torque wrench

bearing cup in the hub.
25 Screw on the hub nut, and tighten it to the specified torque while rotating the hub/drum assembly in both directions to settle the bearing **(see illustration)**.
26 Back off the hub nut by approximately 180° (half a turn), then fit the tab washer, locating the tab under the hub nut.
27 Screw on the hub locknut, and tighten it to the specified torque.
28 Check the hub bearing play using a suitable dial gauge **(see illustration)**. If necessary, further adjust the hub bearings to comply with the specified play. When the bearing play is satisfactory, bend the tab washer tabs inwards over the hub nut, and outwards over the locknut to secure.
29 Refit the halfshaft as described in Section 9.

Type 51 - 1992 model year onwards

30 With the hub reassembled, lubricate the oil seal lips with grease, then carefully locate the hub assembly onto the axle, using the halfshaft as a guide. Remove the halfshaft again.
31 Screw on the new hub nut, noting the comments made earlier regarding hub nut identification for left- and right-hand sides.
32 With the rear axle securely supported, tighten the hub nut to the specified torque, then fit the spacer ring in front of the bearing.
33 Refit the halfshaft as described in Section 9.

12 Drive pinion oil seal (all axle types) - renewal

Note: *All axle types are fitted with a collapsible spacer sleeve between the pinion shaft taper-roller bearings* **(see illustrations 7.3 and 7.4)**.

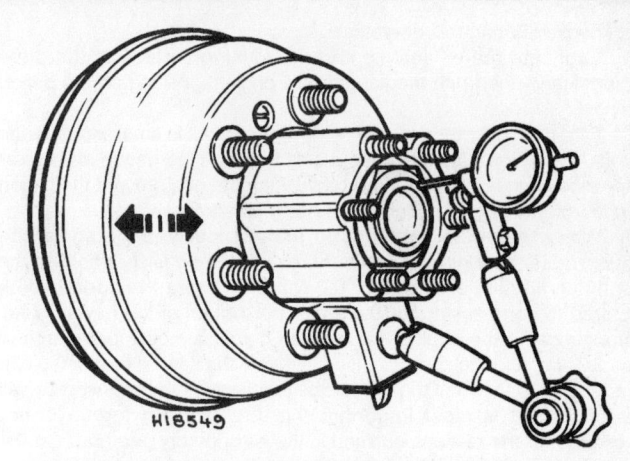

11.28 Checking types 51A and 53 "G" axle hub bearing play, using a dial gauge

Renewal of the drive pinion oil seal should only be attempted by the more experienced DIY mechanic. A pre-load gauge will be needed to measure the pinion turning torque, and a new pinion nut must be fitted on reassembly. No difficulty should be encountered unless the pinion nut is overtightened, in which case removal of the taper-roller bearing to renew the collapsible spacer may present problems.

1 Chock the front wheels, then jack up the rear of the vehicle and support it adequately beneath the underframe side members in front of the rear springs. Support the weight of the rear axle with a trolley jack positioned beneath the differential housing.
2 Remove both rear axle halfshafts as described in Section 9.
3 Mark the relative positions of the propeller shaft and rear axle drive pinion flange, then unbolt and detach the propeller shaft from the flange. Position the shaft out of the way. Note that new bolts will be required when refitting.
4 Using a pre-load gauge, determine the torque required to turn the drive pinion, and note it down **(see illustration)**.
5 Using a bar or suitable forked tool bolted to the pinion flange holes, hold the flange stationary and unscrew the locknut **(see illustration)**. Note that a new locknut will be required when refitting.
6 Mark the position of the pinion flange in relation to the pinion shaft, then remove the flange, using a puller if necessary.
7 Carefully prise free the old oil seal using a blunt screwdriver or similar implement, then clean out the oil seal location in the differential carrier.
8 Locate the new oil seal in the differential carrier, having first greased the mating surfaces of the seal and the carrier. The lips of the oil seal must face inwards.
9 Using a soft metal tube of suitable diameter, carefully drive the new oil seal into the differential carrier recess, until the face of the seal is flush with the carrier. Make sure that the end of the pinion shaft is

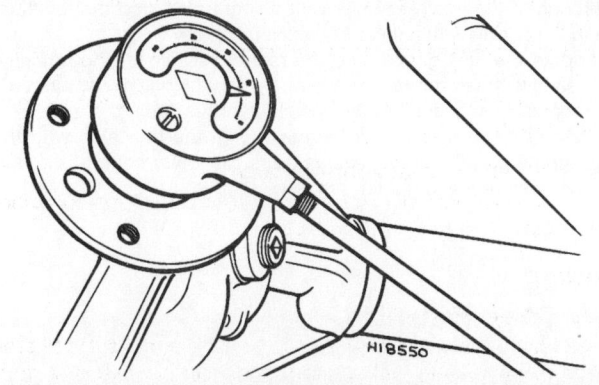

12.4 Using a pre-load gauge to determine the torque required to turn the final drive pinion

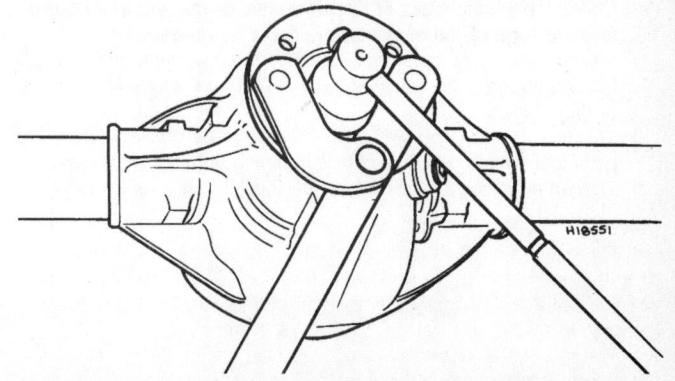

12.5 Forked tool bolted to the drive flange, to hold the flange while the pinion locknut is removed

not knocked during this operation.
10 Lubricate the oil seal lip and the running surface of the drive pinion flange, then refit the flange to its original position on the pinion splines.
11 Fit a new locknut, and progressively tighten it in small increments. Check the pinion turning torque, using the pre-load gauge, at regular intervals during tightening. Whilst tightening the nut, prevent the pinion flange from turning as described in paragraph 5.
12 When the nut is tightened to the previously-recorded torque value, rotate the pinion to settle the bearing, then further tighten the nut by an additional torque of 0.3 Nm, this being the added value required to compensate for the additional friction of the new oil seal. For example, if the original value noted during removal (paragraph 4) was 2.2 Nm, and the compensating value for the new oil seal of 0.3 Nm is added to it, the total turning torque requirement in this instance will be 2.5 Nm. It is most important that the required torque is not exceeded for the reasons outlined in the introductory paragraph at the start of this Section.
13 Reconnect the propeller shaft, ensuring that the alignment marks correspond. Tighten the new retaining bolts to the specified torque wrench setting.
14 Refit the halfshafts as described in Section 9.

13 Differential carrier ("H" axle) - removal and refitting

Note: *On the "H" axle, the differential unit is mounted to the differential carrier, and this is mounted on studs to the front face of the axle casing. The differential unit and carrier assembly can therefore be removed leaving the axle casing still in position in the vehicle, but the halfshafts must first be removed.*

1 Refer to Section 9 and remove both halfshafts.
2 Place a large container beneath the differential carrier, to catch the oil which will drain out.
3 Mark the drive pinion and propeller shaft flanges so that they can be refitted in their original positions, then unscrew the four bolts, detach the shaft, and support it with a stand. Note that new bolts will be required when refitting.
4 Unscrew the eight self-locking nuts which retain the differential carrier to the axle casing, then lift the carrier slightly to allow the oil to drain into the container.
5 Using a trolley jack (or with the aid of an assistant), withdraw the differential carrier off the studs, and remove it from beneath the vehicle **(see illustration)**.
6 Peel the gasket from the axle casing studs; a new gasket will need to be fitted on reassembly.
7 Further dismantling of the differential unit is not recommended. If it is worn or damaged, its overhaul should be entrusted to a dealer with the necessary tools required for this task. Alternatively, obtain an exchange unit.
8 Refitting the differential carrier is a reversal of the removal procedure, but the following points should be noted:
  a) Check the mating faces of the differential carrier and axle housing for burrs, and file them flat; always use a new gasket.
  b) Make sure that the differential carrier is fitted with the pinion to the bottom. Tighten the retaining nuts in diagonal sequence in three or four stages.
  c) The pinion and propeller shaft flanges must be aligned to the previously-made marks, and new retaining bolts must be used.
  d) Tighten all nuts and bolts to the specified torque wrench settings.

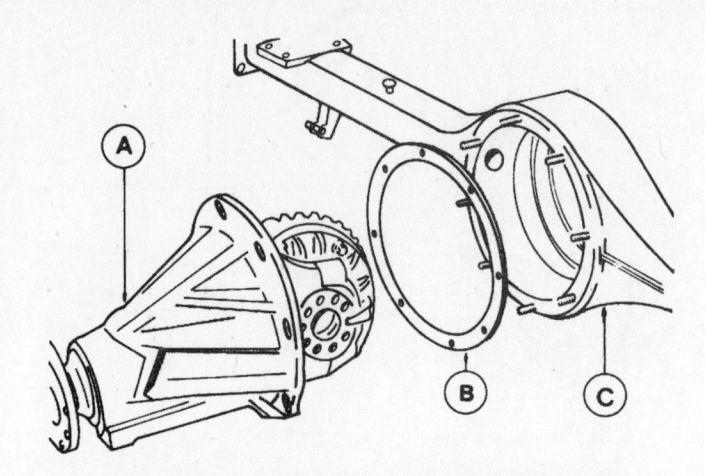

13.5 Removing the differential carrier on the "H" axle

A Differential unit and carrier
B Flange gasket
C Axle casing

  e) Referring to Chapter 1 if necessary, fill the rear axle with the correct grade of oil until the level is up to the lower edge of the filler plug hole, then refit and tighten the plug.
  f) If a new differential unit has been installed, it should be run-in for 500 miles (800 km) to ensure that the new bearings bed-in correctly.

14 Differential unit ("G" axle) - overhaul

1 The design and layout of the "G" axle is such that any attempt to remove the differential unit or pinion assembly from the axle housing will upset their preset meshing.
2 Since special tools and skills are required to set up the crownwheel and pinion mesh, the removal, overhaul and assembly of these differential types is not recommended, and should be entrusted to a dealer.
3 In any case, the current trend is for rear axle components not to be supplied individually, but the complete factory-built unit only to be supplied as a replacement.
4 If required, an inspection of the differential unit can be made to assess for excessive wear or damage to its component parts. To do this, place a large container beneath the differential carrier to catch the oil which will drain out. Unbolt and remove the differential housing rear cover, and allow the oil to drain into the container.
5 Before refitting the rear cover, clean the cover and axle case mating surfaces, and remove the remains of the old gasket. Also clean the threads of the retaining bolts with a wire brush, and the threaded holes in the casing with a suitable cleaning solvent.
6 Locate the new gasket and the rear cover, smear the retaining bolt threads with sealant, and fit them. Tighten the bolts in an alternate and progressive sequence to the specified torque setting.
7 Referring to Chapter 1 if necessary, fill the rear axle with the correct grade of oil until the level is up to the lower edge of the filler plug hole, then refit and tighten the plug.

Chapter 9 Braking system

Contents

	Section
Anti-lock braking system (ABS) - general information	20
Anti-lock braking system components - removal and refitting	21
Brake pedal - removal and refitting	19
Brake pressure control valve - description, removal and refitting	17
Front brake caliper - overhaul	6
Front brake caliper - removal and refitting	5
Front brake disc - inspection, removal and refitting	7
Front brake pads - renewal	4
Front brake pad wear check	See Chapter 1
General information	1
Handbrake - adjustment	14
Handbrake cable - removal and refitting	16
Handbrake lever and primary rod - removal and refitting	15

	Section
Hydraulic fluid level check	See Chapter 1
Hydraulic fluid renewal	See Chapter 1
Hydraulic pipes and hoses - renewal	3
Hydraulic system - bleeding	2
Load-apportioning valve (LAV) - general information	18
Master cylinder - overhaul	11
Master cylinder - removal and refitting	10
Rear brake shoe wear check	See Chapter 1
Rear brake shoes - renewal	8
Rear wheel cylinder - removal, overhaul and refitting	9
Vacuum pump - removal and refitting	13
Vacuum servo unit - testing, removal and refitting	12

Specifications

General

System type .... Dual-circuit hydraulic, vertical or diagonal split with front disc and rear drum brakes. Servo-assistance with vacuum provided by alternator-driven vacuum pump. Cable-operated handbrake acting on rear wheels. Anti-lock braking system optionally available on certain models

Front brakes

Type:
- Vehicles with independent front suspension .... Solid or ventilated disc, with twin-piston sliding calipers
- Vehicles with beam axle front suspension .... Solid disc with two- or four-opposed-piston fixed type calipers

Disc diameter .... 254 or 270 mm, according to model

Disc thickness (new):
- Solid disc .... 14.3 mm
- Ventilated disc .... 24.3 mm

Minimum disc thickness:
- Solid disc .... 12.15 mm
- Ventilated disc .... 22.15 mm

Maximum disc thickness variation .... 0.01 mm
Maximum disc run-out (disc fitted) .... 0.13 mm
Minimum brake pad friction material thickness .... 1.5 mm

Rear brakes

Type .... Drum with leading and trailing shoes and automatic adjusters
Nominal drum diameter:
  Pre-1992 model year:
    "H" axle .... 228.6 mm
    "G" axle .... 254.0 mm
  1992 model year onwards:
    "H" axle .... 254.0 mm
    "G" axle .... 280.0 mm
Maximum drum diameter .... 2.0 mm above nominal diameter
Minimum brake lining thickness .... 1.0 mm

Torque wrench settings

	Nm	lbf ft
ABS hydraulic unit retaining nuts	25	18
Brake caliper anchor bracket bolts	109	80
Brake caliper sliding pin bolts:		
Vehicles with solid brake discs	25	18
Vehicles with ventilated brake discs:		
Lower (short) sliding pin	31	23
Upper (long) sliding pin	50	37
Brake disc-to-hub retaining bolts:		
Independent front suspension	50	37
Beam axle front suspension	70	52
Master cylinder-to-servo unit nuts:		
Standard braking system	15	11
Anti-lock braking system	22	16
Opposed-piston fixed type caliper retaining bolts	109	80
Rear brake backplate to axle	50	37
Roadwheel nuts:		
Five-stud wheels	85	63
Six-stud wheels	168	124
Vacuum pump to alternator	7	5
Vacuum servo unit-to-bulkhead nuts	43	32

1 General information

The braking system is of the diagonally- or vertically-split, dual-circuit hydraulic type, with servo assistance to the front disc brakes and rear drum brakes. With the diagonally-split system, the master cylinder primary circuit feeds the left-hand rear and the right-hand front brake, with the secondary circuit feeding the right-hand rear brake and the left-hand front brake. With the vertically-split system, the master cylinder primary circuit feeds the rear brakes, and the secondary circuit supplies the front brakes. The dual-circuit hydraulic system is a safety feature; in the event of a malfunction somewhere in one of the hydraulic circuits, the other circuit continues to operate, providing at least a reduced braking effort. Under normal circumstances, both brake circuits operate in unison to provide efficient braking.

A vacuum servo unit is fitted between the master cylinder and the bulkhead, its function being to reduce the amount of pedal pressure required to operate the brakes. In the event of the servo unit failing for

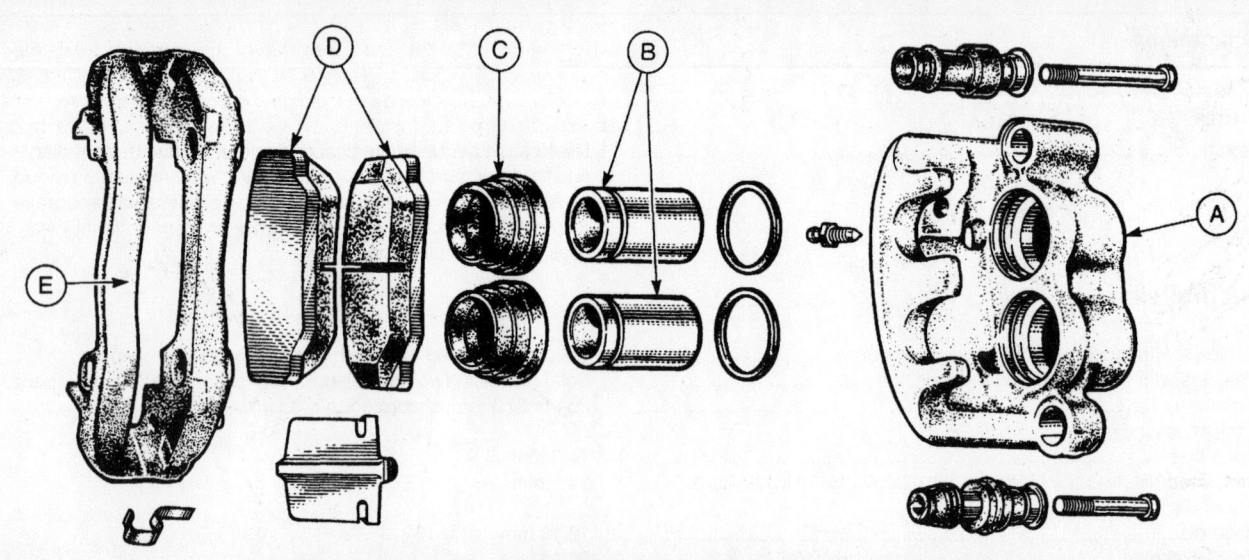

1.4a Exploded view of the early type two-piston sliding pin type brake calipers

A   Caliper piston housing
B   Pistons
C   Dust covers
D   Brake pads
E   Anchor bracket

Chapter 9 Braking system

any reason, the brakes will remain operational, but the pedal effort required to operate them will be noticeably increased. A vacuum pump fitted to, and driven from, the rear of the alternator, provides the necessary vacuum to operate the servo unit.

Depending on model, either brake pressure control valves or a load-apportioning valve (LAV) are incorporated in the rear brake hydraulic circuit. The valve function is to regulate the braking force available at each rear wheel, to reduce the possibility of the rear wheels locking up under heavy braking.

The front brake discs are of the solid type on all pre-1992 models, and of the ventilated type from 1992 onwards. Vehicles with solid front brake discs and independent front suspension are fitted with two-piston sliding pin type brake calipers, whereas vehicles with beam axle front suspension have two- or four-opposed piston fixed type brake calipers **(see illustrations)**. All later models with ventilated front brake discs are fitted with a modified type of two-piston sliding pin type caliper.

The rear drum brakes incorporate leading and trailing shoes, which are actuated by twin-piston wheel cylinders. The rear brakes incorporate a self-adjusting mechanism which automatically adjusts the rear brake shoes, to compensate for wear of the friction linings, whenever the footbrake is operated.

The cable-operated handbrake provides an independent means of rear brake application.

An anti-lock braking system (ABS) is available on some models, and features many of the components in common with the conventional braking system. Further details on the ABS can be found later in this Chapter.

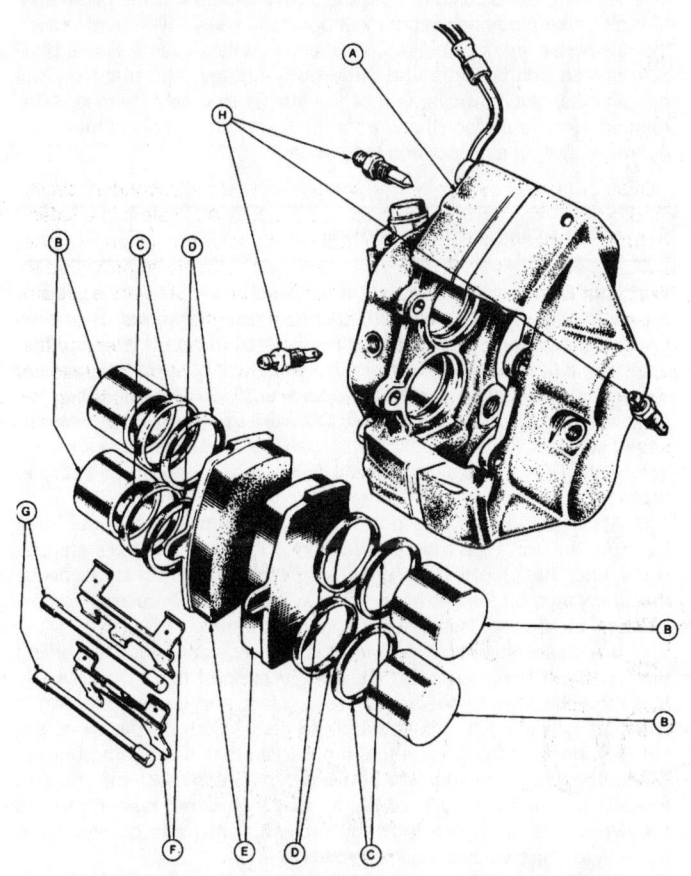

2 Hydraulic system - bleeding

Warning: *Hydraulic fluid is poisonous; wash off immediately and thoroughly in the case of skin contact, and seek immediate medical advice if any fluid is swallowed or gets into the eyes. Certain types of hydraulic fluid are inflammable, and may ignite when allowed into contact with hot components. When servicing any hydraulic system, it is safest to assume that the fluid IS inflammable, and to take precautions against the risk of fire as though it is petrol that is being handled. Hydraulic fluid is also an effective paint stripper, and will attack plastics; if any is spilt, it should be washed off immediately, using copious quantities of clean water. Finally, it is hygroscopic (it absorbs moisture from the air). The more moisture is absorbed by the fluid, the lower its boiling point becomes, leading to a dangerous loss of braking under hard use. Old fluid may be contaminated and unfit for further use. When topping-up or renewing the fluid, always use the recommended type, and ensure that it comes from a freshly-opened sealed container.*

1 If the master cylinder or brake pipes/hoses have been disconnected and reconnected, then the complete system (both circuits) must be bled of air. If a component of one circuit has been disturbed, then only that particular circuit need be bled.

2 If bleeding both circuits on vertically-split systems, bleed the front brakes first, then the rear brakes. On diagonally-split systems, bleed one front brake followed by the diagonally-opposite rear brake, then bleed the other front brake followed by the remaining rear brake.

3 When bleeding the brakes on vehicles with a load-apportioning valve in the rear brake circuit, it is important to note that the vehicle must not be mounted on a "wheel-free" hoist. Instead, it must be standing on its wheels, otherwise the load-apportioning valve will prevent complete bleeding of the system.

4 There are a variety of do-it-yourself brake bleeding kits available from motor accessory shops, and it is recommended that one of these kits is used wherever possible, as they greatly simplify the brake hydraulic circuit bleeding operation. Follow the kit manufacturer's instructions in conjunction with the following procedure.

5 During the bleeding operation, do not allow the brake fluid level in the reservoir to drop below the minimum mark, and only use new fluid for topping-up. *Never re-use fluid bled from the system.*

6 Before starting, check that all rigid pipes and flexible hoses are in good condition, and that all hydraulic unions are tight. Take great care not to allow hydraulic fluid to come into contact with the vehicle paintwork, otherwise the finish will be seriously damaged. Wash off any spilt fluid immediately with cold water.

7 If a brake bleeding kit is not being used, gather together a clean jar, a suitable length of clear plastic or rubber tubing which is a tight fit over the bleed screw, and a new can of the specified brake fluid (see "Lubricants, fluids and capacities" at the beginning of this manual).

8 Clean the area around the bleed nipple on the brake unit to be bled (it is important that no dirt be allowed to enter the hydraulic system) and remove the dust cap **(see illustrations)**. Connect one end

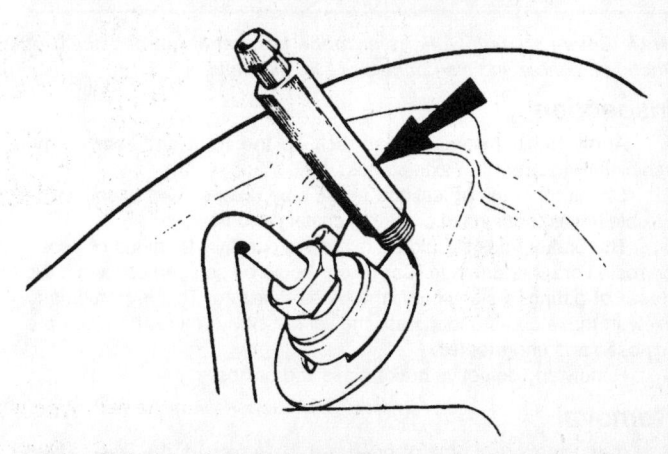

1.4b Exploded view of the four-opposed piston fixed type brake caliper

A	Caliper	E	Brake pads
B	Pistons	F	Anti-rattle clips
C	Seals	G	Pad retainer pins
D	Seal retainers	H	Bleed nipples

2.8a Brake bleed nipple (arrowed) on rear brake wheel cylinder

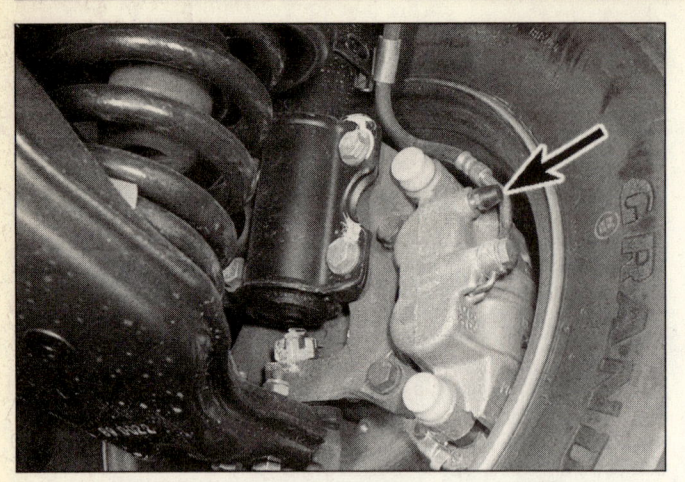

2.8b Brake bleed nipple and dust cap (arrowed) on front brake caliper

of the tubing to the bleed nipple, and immerse the other end in the jar containing sufficient brake fluid to keep the end of the tube submerged. Ensure that the bleed jar is positioned a minimum of 300 mm (12 inches) above the bleed nipple throughout the procedure. The front brake calipers fitted to certain vehicles incorporate multiple bleed nipples. Where these are encountered, connect bleed tubes to all the bleed nipples, and proceed in the manner described, for each one.

9 Open the bleed nipple approximately one turn, and have an assistant depress the brake pedal to the floor. Tighten the bleed nipple at the end of the downstroke, to prevent the expelled air/fluid from being drawn back into the system, then have the assistant release the pedal. Pause briefly at the end of each pedal stroke, to allow the master cylinder to fully recover before depressing the pedal to continue the bleeding process. Continue this procedure until clean brake fluid, free from air bubbles, can be seen flowing into the jar, and then with the pedal in the fully-depressed position, tighten the bleed nipple securely.

10 Remove the tube, refit the dust cap, and repeat this procedure on the other brake in that circuit.

11 Repeat the procedure on the remaining circuit.

12 On vehicles with brake pressure control valves in the rear hydraulic circuit, these should be bled independently, at the valve brake pipe union. With an assistant applying pressure to the brake pedal, carefully slacken the pipe union. When brake fluid appears, retighten the union.

3 Hydraulic pipes and hoses - inspection, removal and refitting

Note: *Before starting work, refer to the warning at the beginning of Section 2 concerning the dangers of hydraulic fluid.*

Inspection

1 Apply the handbrake, then jack up the front and rear of the vehicle, and support on axle stands.

2 Check for signs of leakage at the pipe unions, then examine the flexible hoses for signs of cracking, chafing and fraying.

3 The brake pipes should be examined carefully for signs of dents, corrosion or other damage. Corrosion should be scraped off, and if the depth of pitting is significant, the pipes renewed. This is particularly likely in those areas underneath the vehicle body where the pipes are exposed and unprotected.

4 Renew any defective brake pipes and/or hoses.

Removal

5 If any section of pipe or hose is to be removed, the loss of fluid may be reduced by removing the hydraulic fluid reservoir filler cap, placing a piece of polythene over the filler neck, and securing it with an elastic band. If a section of pipe is to be removed from the master cylinder, the reservoir should be emptied by drawing out the fluid with a syringe. If any brake fluid is spilt onto the bodywork, it must be wiped clean without delay.

6 To remove a section of pipe, secure the adjoining hose union nut with a suitable spanner to prevent it from turning, then unscrew the union nut at the end of the pipe and release it. Repeat the procedure at the other end of the pipe, then release the pipe from the clips attaching it to the body. Where the union nuts are exposed to the full force of the weather, they can sometimes be quite tight. If an open-ended spanner is used, burring of the flats on the nuts is not uncommon, and for this reason, it is preferable to use a split ring spanner which will engage all the flats. If such a spanner is not available, self-locking grips may be used, although this is not recommended.

7 To further minimise the loss of fluid when disconnecting a flexible brake line, clamp the hose as near to the joint to be detached as is possible, using a proprietary brake hose clamp. To remove a flexible hose, first clean the ends of the hose and the surrounding area, then unscrew the union nut(s) from the hose end(s). Recover the spring clip, and withdraw the hose from the serrated mounting in the support bracket.

8 Brake pipes with flared ends and union nuts in place can be obtained individually or in sets from Ford dealers or accessory shops. The pipe is then bent to shape, using the old pipe as a guide, and is ready for fitting to the vehicle.

Refitting

9 Refitting the pipes and hoses is a reversal of removal. Make sure that all brake pipes are securely supported in their clips, and ensure that the hoses are not kinked. Check also that the hoses are clear of all suspension components and underbody fittings, and that they will remain clear during movement of the suspension and steering. After refitting, remove the polythene from the reservoir, and bleed the brake hydraulic system as described in Section 2.

4 Front brake pads - renewal

Warning: *Disc brake pads must be renewed on BOTH front wheels at the same time - NEVER renew the pads on only one wheel, as uneven braking may result. Dust created by wear of the pads may contain asbestos, which is a health hazard. Never blow it out with compressed air, and don't inhale any of it. An approved filtering mask should be worn when working on the brakes. DO NOT use petrol or petroleum-based solvents to clean brake parts. Use brake cleaner or methylated spirit only. DO NOT allow any brake fluid, oil or grease to contact the brake pads or disc.*

1 Apply the handbrake, loosen off the front roadwheel nuts, then jack up the front of the vehicle and support it on axle stands. Remember that on pre-1992 model year vehicles with six-stud wheels, the wheel nuts on the left-hand side have a **left-hand thread** - ie they unscrew **clockwise**. Remove the front roadwheels.

2 Vehicles with independent front suspension are fitted with sliding pin type front brake calipers. The early version of this caliper type is fitted to vehicles with solid front brake discs, and the later version is used on vehicles with ventilated brake discs. Both caliper types are virtually identical in appearance, but certain maintenance and repair procedures vary considerably between types. It is most important to identify the unit being worked on, so that the correct procedures are followed, and to ensure that any replacement parts obtained are suitable for the particular caliper type.

3 All vehicles with beam axle front suspension are fitted with two- or four-opposed piston fixed type calipers.

Sliding pin type caliper

Vehicles with solid brake discs

4 Extract the plastic caps, then undo the two sliding pin bolts securing the caliper piston housing to the anchor bracket. Withdraw

Chapter 9 Braking system

4.4a Extract the plastic caps . . .

4.4b . . . unscrew the upper and lower sliding pin bolts . . .

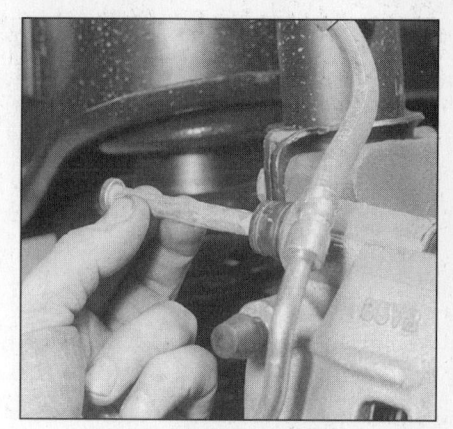

4.4c . . . withdraw the bolts . . .

4.4d . . . then withdraw the caliper piston housing

4.5 Withdrawing the inner and outer brake pads from the anchor bracket

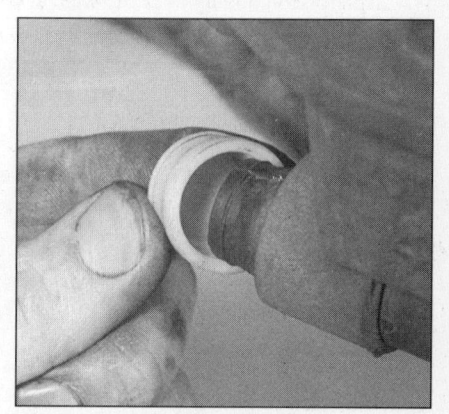

4.15 Prise out the plastic cap from the caliper piston housing lower sliding pin bolt

the piston housing from the brake pads and anchor bracket, and position it to one side, taking care not to stretch the brake hose **(see illustrations)**.

5 Withdraw the inner and outer brake pads from the anchor bracket. If the old pads are likely to be refitted, keep them separated and identified; they are identical, and must be refitted in their original positions **(see illustration)**.

6 Brush the dust and dirt from the housing and pistons, but **do not inhale it, as it is a health hazard**. Inspect the dust covers around the pistons for damage and for evidence of fluid leaks, which if found will necessitate caliper overhaul as described in Section 6.

7 If new brake pads are to be fitted, the caliper pistons will need to be pushed back into their housing bores, to allow for the extra pad thickness. Use a C-clamp or proprietary piston retractor tool to do this, but note that as the pistons are pressed back into their bores, the fluid level in the brake master cylinder reservoir will rise, and possibly overflow. To avoid this possibility, a small quantity of fluid should be syphoned from the reservoir. If any brake fluid is spilt onto the bodywork, hoses or adjacent components in the engine compartment, wipe it clean without delay.

8 Prior to refitting, check that the pads and the disc are clean. If new pads are to be installed, peel the protective backing paper from them. If the old pads are to be refitted, ensure that they are correctly located as noted during their removal.

9 Locate the inner and outer brake pads into position in the caliper anchor bracket.

10 Locate the piston housing in position, and refit the two sliding pin bolts. Tighten the bolts to the specified torque, and refit the plastic caps.

11 Repeat the procedure on the opposite front brake assembly.

12 Before lowering the vehicle, check the that the fluid level in the brake master cylinder reservoir is up to the maximum level mark, and

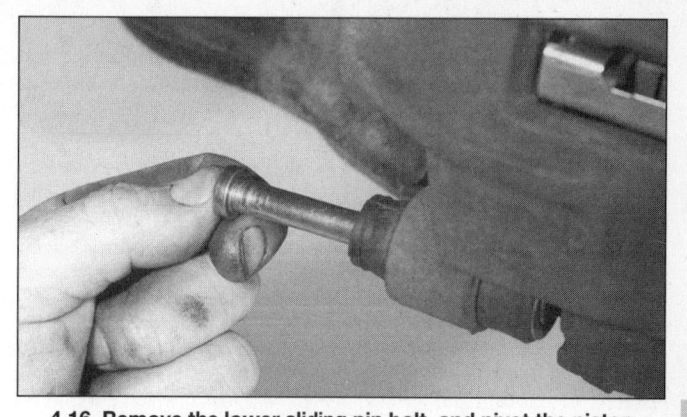

4.16 Remove the lower sliding pin bolt, and pivot the piston housing upwards

top-up with the specified fluid type if required. Depress the brake pedal a few times to position the pads against the disc, then recheck the fluid level in the reservoir, and top-up further if necessary.

13 Refit the roadwheels, then lower the vehicle to the ground. Tighten the roadwheel retaining nuts to the specified torque setting.

14 To allow the new brake pads to bed-in and reach full efficiency, a running-in period of approximately 100 miles or so should be observed if possible before hard use and heavy braking.

Vehicles with ventilated brake discs

15 Using a small screwdriver, prise out the plastic cap from the caliper piston housing lower sliding pin bolt **(see illustration)**.

16 Unscrew the lower sliding pin bolt, and pivot the piston housing upwards for access to the brake pads **(see illustration)**. Tie the

Chapter 9 Braking system

4.18 Pad spring removed from inside the caliper piston housing - photo shows correct orientation for refitting

4.20 Using a piston retractor tool to push the pistons back into their housing bores

4.22 Fit the new pad spring into the caliper piston housing

4.23 Locate the inner and outer brake pads into position in the caliper anchor bracket

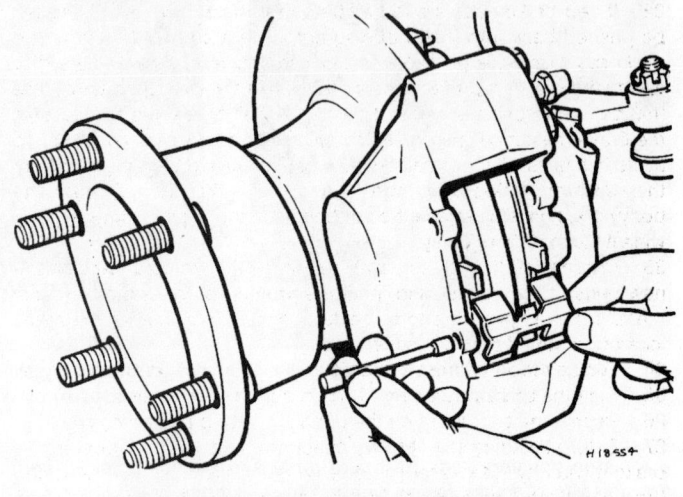

4.29 Removing the brake pad anti-rattle clips and pad retainer pins

housing up in the raised position if necessary, using string or wire.

17 Withdraw the inner and outer brake pads from the anchor bracket. If the old pads are likely to be refitted, keep them separated and identified; they are identical, and must be refitted in their original positions.

18 If new pads are to be fitted, unclip the pad spring from inside the caliper piston housing, using a screwdriver **(see illustration)**.

19 Brush the dust and dirt from the caliper and pistons, but **do not** inhale it, as it is a health hazard. Inspect the dust covers around the pistons for damage and for evidence of fluid leaks, which if found will necessitate caliper overhaul as described in Section 6.

20 If new brake pads are to be fitted, the caliper pistons will need to be pushed back into their housing bores, to allow for the extra pad thickness. Use a C-clamp or proprietary piston retractor tool to do this **(see illustration)**, but note that as the pistons are pressed back into their bores, the fluid level in the brake master cylinder reservoir will rise, and possibly overflow. To avoid this possibility, a small quantity of fluid should be syphoned from the reservoir. If any brake fluid is spilt onto the bodywork, hoses or adjacent components in the engine compartment, wipe it clean without delay.

21 Prior to refitting, check that the pads and the disc are clean. If new pads are to be installed, peel the protective backing paper from them. If the old pads are to be refitted, ensure that they are correctly located as noted during their removal.

22 Clip the new pad spring into the caliper piston housing **(see illustration)**.

23 Locate the inner and outer brake pads into position in the caliper

anchor bracket **(see illustration)**.

24 Lower the piston housing down over the pads, then refit the sliding pin bolt and tighten it to the specified torque. Refit the plastic cap over the pin bolt head.

25 Repeat the procedure on the opposite front brake assembly.

26 Before lowering the vehicle, check the that the fluid level in the brake master cylinder reservoir is up to the maximum level mark, and top-up with the specified fluid type if required. Depress the brake pedal a few times to position the pads against the disc, then recheck the fluid level in the reservoir, and top-up further if necessary.

27 Refit the roadwheels, then lower the vehicle to the ground. Tighten the roadwheel retaining nuts to the specified torque setting.

28 To allow the new brake pads to bed-in and reach full efficiency, a running-in period of approximately 100 miles or so should be observed if possible before hard use and heavy braking.

Opposed-piston fixed type caliper

29 Depress the brake pad anti-rattle clips, simultaneously grip the pad retainer pins, and slide them free. Remove the clips **(see illustration)**.

30 Note the location of each brake pad, then extract the brake pads from the caliper housing, using a pair of long-nosed pliers if they prove difficult to remove **(see illustration)**.

31 Brush the dust and dirt from the caliper and pistons, but **do not** inhale it, as it is a health hazard. Inspect the dust covers around the pistons for damage and for evidence of fluid leaks, which if found will necessitate caliper overhaul as described in Section 6.

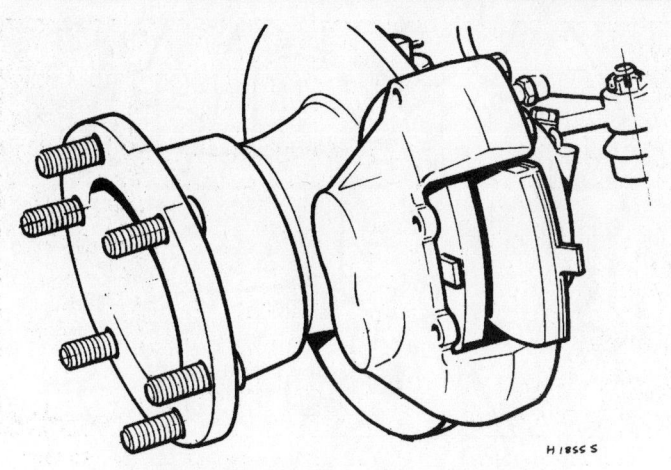

Chapter 9 Braking system

4.30 Removing the brake pads from the caliper

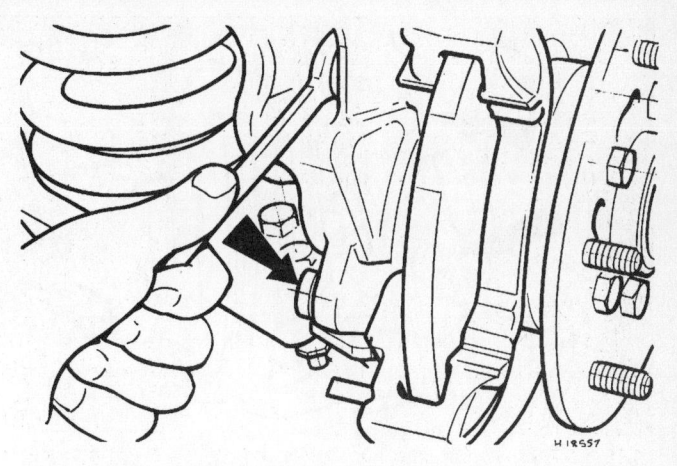

5.5 Undo the two bolts (one arrowed) and remove the caliper anchor bracket

5.9 Brake hose banjo union connection (arrowed) at the brake caliper

32 If new brake pads are to be fitted, the caliper pistons will need to be pushed back into their housing bores, to allow for the extra pad thickness. Use a piston expander, or carefully lever between the disc and pistons with a protected screwdriver or flat bar to do this. Note that as the pistons are pressed back into their bores, the fluid level in the brake master cylinder reservoir will rise, and possibly overflow. To avoid this possibility, a small quantity of fluid should be syphoned from the reservoir, using a syringe. If any brake fluid is spilt onto the bodywork, hoses or adjacent components in the engine compartment, wipe it clean without delay.

33 Prior to refitting, check that the pads and the disc are clean. If new pads are to be installed, peel the protective backing paper from them. If the old pads are to be refitted, ensure that they are correctly located, as noted during their removal.

34 Locate the inner and outer brake pads into position in the caliper

35 Refit the brake pad anti-rattle clips and the pad retainer pins.

36 Repeat the procedure on the opposite front brake assembly.

37 Before lowering the vehicle, check the that the fluid level in the brake master cylinder reservoir is up to the maximum level mark, and top-up with the specified fluid type if required. Depress the brake pedal a few times to position the pads against the disc, then recheck the fluid level in the reservoir, and top-up further if necessary.

38 Refit the roadwheels, then lower the vehicle to the ground. Tighten the roadwheel retaining nuts to the specified torque setting.

39 To allow the new brake pads to bed-in and reach full efficiency, a running-in period of approximately 100 miles or so should be observed if possible before hard use and heavy braking.

5 Front brake caliper - removal and refitting

Note: *Before starting work, refer to the warning at the beginning of Section 2 concerning the dangers of hydraulic fluid, and to the warning at the beginning of Section 4 concerning the dangers of asbestos dust.*

Sliding pin type caliper

Vehicles with solid brake discs

1 Apply the handbrake, loosen off the front roadwheel nuts, then jack up the front of the vehicle and support it on axle stands. Remove the front roadwheels.

2 Clamp the caliper flexible hydraulic brake hose using a proprietary brake hose clamp, to reduce brake fluid loss from the master cylinder.

3 Wipe clean the area around the brake hose banjo union connection at the caliper. Using a socket or ring spanner, unscrew and remove the banjo union bolt, and recover the two copper washers. Cover the banjo union and the orifice in the caliper, to prevent dirt ingress.

4 Remove the front brake pads as described in Section 4.

5 Undo the two bolts securing the caliper anchor bracket to the stub axle, and remove the anchor bracket. Note that the upper bolt will not come fully out, due to the close proximity of the shock absorber, but it will unscrew sufficiently to allow removal of the anchor bracket. **(see illustration).**

6 Refitting is a reversal of the removal sequence. Tighten all retaining bolts to the specified torque and, on completion, release the brake hose clamp and bleed the hydraulic system as described in Section 2. If the flexible hydraulic hose was clamped as described, it should only be necessary to bleed the brake being worked on.

Vehicles with ventilated brake discs

7 Apply the handbrake, loosen off the front roadwheel nuts, then jack up the front of the vehicle and support it on axle stands. Remove the front roadwheels.

8 Clamp the caliper flexible hydraulic brake hose using a proprietary brake hose clamp, to reduce brake fluid loss from the master cylinder.

9 Wipe clean the area around the brake hose banjo union connection at the caliper **(see illustration)**. Using a socket or ring spanner, unscrew and remove the banjo union bolt, and recover the two copper washers. Cover the banjo union and the orifice in the caliper, to prevent dirt ingress.

10 Remove the front brake pads as described in Section 4.

11 Extract the steel cap over the upper sliding pin bolt, and unscrew the upper bolt. Withdraw the caliper from the anchor bracket.

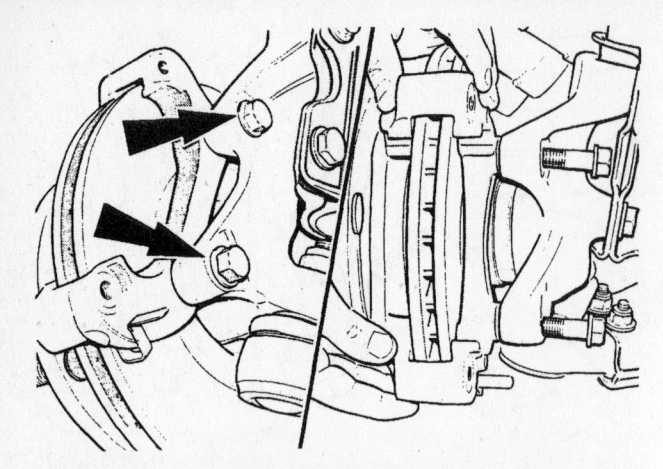

5.12 Undo the two bolts (arrowed) securing the sliding pin type caliper anchor bracket to the stub axle. Lift off the anchor bracket, and remove the two bolts

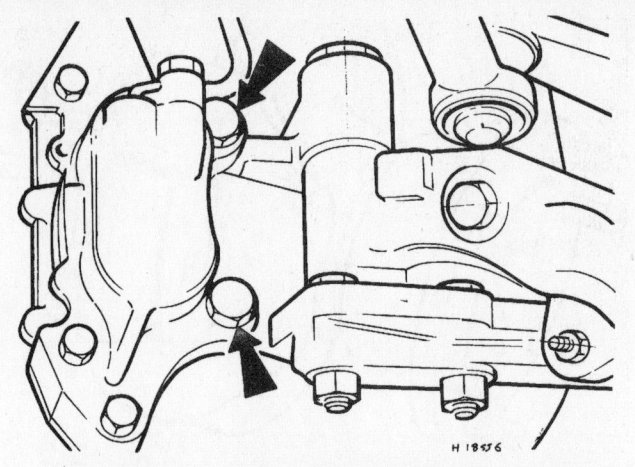

5.18 Undo the two bolts (arrowed) securing the opposed-piston fixed type caliper assembly to the stub axle, and withdraw the caliper

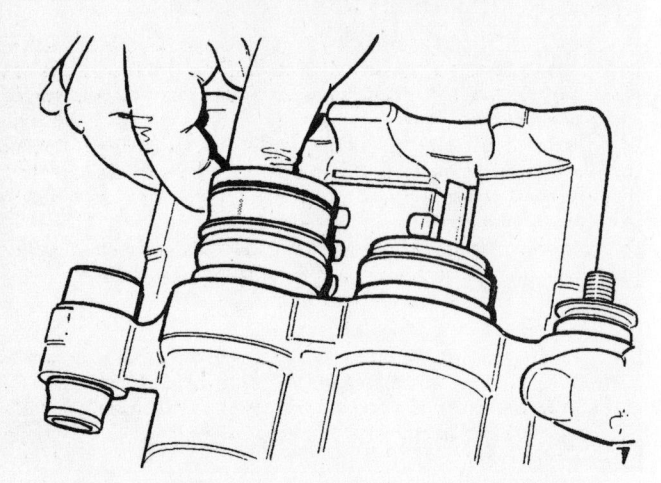

6.2 Removing the caliper pistons from the piston housing

6.4 Check the condition of the sliding pin bushes in the caliper piston housing

12 Undo the two bolts securing the caliper anchor bracket to the stub axle. Note that the upper bolt will not come fully out, due to the close proximity of the shock absorber, but it will unscrew sufficiently to allow removal of the anchor bracket. Lift off the anchor bracket, and remove the two bolts **(see illustration)**.
13 Refitting is a reversal of the removal sequence. Tighten all retaining bolts to the specified torque. On completion, release the brake hose clamp, and bleed the hydraulic system as described in Section 2. If the flexible hydraulic hose was clamped as described, it should only be necessary to bleed the brake being worked on.

Opposed-piston fixed type caliper

14 Apply the handbrake, loosen off the front roadwheel nuts, then jack up the front of the vehicle and support it on axle stands. Remember that on pre-1992 model year vehicles with six-stud wheels, the wheel nuts on the left-hand side have a **left-hand thread** - ie they unscrew **clockwise**. Remove the front roadwheels.
15 Clamp the caliper flexible hydraulic brake hose using a proprietary brake hose clamp, to reduce brake fluid loss from the master cylinder.
16 Wipe clean the area around the brake hose banjo union connection at the caliper. Using a socket or ring spanner, unscrew and remove the banjo union bolt, and recover the two copper washers. Cover the banjo union and the orifice in the caliper, to prevent dirt ingress.
17 Remove the front brake pads as described in Section 4.
18 Undo the two bolts securing the caliper assembly to the stub axle, and withdraw the caliper **(see illustration)**.
19 Refitting is a reversal of the removal sequence. Tighten all retaining bolts to the specified torque. On completion, release the brake hose clamp, and bleed the hydraulic system as described in Section 2. If the flexible hydraulic hose was clamped as described, it should only be necessary to bleed the brake being worked on.

6 Front brake caliper - overhaul

Note: *Before starting work, refer to the warning at the beginning of Section 2 concerning the dangers of hydraulic fluid, and to the warning at the beginning of Section 4 concerning the dangers of asbestos dust.*

1 Remove the front brake caliper as described in Section 5. Note that under no circumstances should the two halves of the opposed-piston fixed type caliper be separated, as they are specially bolted together during manufacture.
2 Position a piece of wood inside the caliper across the faces of the pistons, then use low air pressure (from a foot pump for example) applied to the fluid inlet port to force the pistons from the housing. Once the pistons have been partially ejected, they can be removed completely by hand **(see illustration)**. Suitably identify each of the pistons as to their location in the housing.
3 Using a non-metallic instrument such as a knitting needle, carefully remove the piston seals, seal retainers and dust covers, as applicable.
4 Clean the pistons and housing with methylated spirit, and allow to

Chapter 9 Braking system

7.2 Using a micrometer to measure the thickness of the brake disc

7.3 Using a dial gauge and stand set-up to check the brake disc run-out

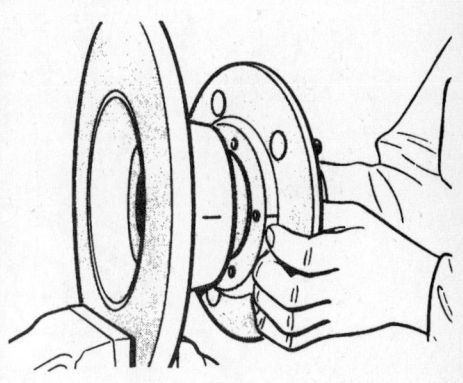

7.6 If the original disc and hub are to be reassembled to each other, make alignment marks as an aid to reassembly

dry. Examine the surfaces of the piston and housing for wear, damage and corrosion. If the piston surface alone is unserviceable, obtain a repair kit which includes new pistons and seals; if the housing is unserviceable, renew the caliper complete. If both the pistons and housing are in satisfactory condition, obtain a repair kit of seals. Where applicable, check the condition of the sliding pin bolts and bushes, and renew these components as necessary **(see illustration)**. The bushes can be removed and refitted into the housing using mandrels of suitable diameter as drifts.

5   Dip the internal components in clean brake fluid, then fit the new seals to the caliper bores - use your fingers only for this (no tools).

6   Locate the seal retainers or dust covers as applicable, lubricate the caliper bores with brake fluid, and carefully insert the pistons. If the original pistons are being refitted, ensure that they are fitted into their original bores. With the pistons in place, engage the dust covers (where fitted) with the grooves in the caliper.

7   Refit the caliper as described in Section 5.

7   Front brake disc - inspection, removal and refitting

Note: *To prevent uneven braking, BOTH front brake discs should be renewed or reground at the same time.*

Inspection

1   Remove the brake pads as described in Section 4.

2   Scrape any corrosion from the disc. Rotate the disc, and examine it for deep scoring, grooving or cracks. Using a micrometer, measure the thickness of the disc in several places **(see illustration)**. Light wear and scoring is normal, but if excessive, the disc should be removed, and either reground by a specialist, or renewed. If regrinding is undertaken, the minimum thickness must be maintained. Obviously, if the disc is cracked, it must be renewed.

3   The disc should be checked for run-out, but before doing this, the front hub bearings must be checked and if necessary adjusted as described in Chapter 10. The run-out is best checked with a dial gauge, although using feeler blades between the face of the disc and a fixed point will give a satisfactory result. The check should be made on both sides of the disc, at the mid-point of the brake pad contact area. Rotate the disc, noting the variation in measurement as the disc is rotated **(see illustration)**. The difference between the minimum and maximum measurements recorded is the disc run-out.

4   If the run-out is greater than the specified amount, check for variations of the disc thickness as follows. Mark the disc at eight positions 45° apart, then using a micrometer, measure the disc thickness at the eight positions, 15 mm in from the outer edge. If the variation between the minimum and maximum readings is greater than the specified amount, the disc should be renewed.

Removal

5   Remove the caliper and, where applicable, its anchor bracket with reference to Section 5, but do not disconnect the hydraulic brake hose. Suitably suspend the caliper assembly, taking care to avoid straining the brake hose.

6   Refer to Chapter 10, and remove the front wheel hub unit complete with brake disc. If the original disc and hub are to be reassembled to each other, make alignment marks as an aid to reassembly **(see illustration)**.

7   Using a screwdriver, bend back the locktabs (where fitted) and unbolt the disc from the hub assembly in diagonal sequence.

Refitting

8   Refitting the front brake disc is a reversal of the removal procedure, but the following additional points should be noted:
   a) Clean the mating surfaces of the disc and hub assembly before reassembling, and ensure that the alignment marks are adjacent to each other.
   b) Always use new locktabs (where fitted) to secure the disc retaining bolts.
   c) Adjust the hub bearings as described in Chapter 10.

8   Rear brake shoes - renewal

Note: *The following procedure entails removal of the rear hub for access to the brake shoes. Refer to Chapter 8 for further specific details of the various axles, and identify the unit being worked on before proceeding. A special hub nut removal tool may be required, depending on axle type.*

Warning: *Brake shoes must be renewed on BOTH rear wheels at the same time - NEVER renew the shoes on only one wheel, as uneven braking may result. Dust created by wear of the brake shoes may contain asbestos, which is a health hazard. Never blow it out with compressed air, and don't inhale any of it. An approved filtering mask should be worn when working on the brakes. DO NOT use petrol or petroleum-based solvents to clean brake parts. Use brake cleaner or methylated spirit only. DO NOT allow any brake fluid, oil or grease to contact the brake shoes or drum.*

1   Remove the rear hub on each side, as described in Chapter 8, Section 10 or 11 according to axle type.

2   With the rear brake assemblies now accessible, and working on one side at a time, brush the dust and dirt from the brake drum, backplate and brake shoe components. **Do not** inhale the dust, as it is a health hazard.

3   Check the brake drums for excessive wear, or signs of damage. The drums must be renewed (or alternatively, machined) if extensive wear has taken place.

9-10   Chapter 9 Braking system

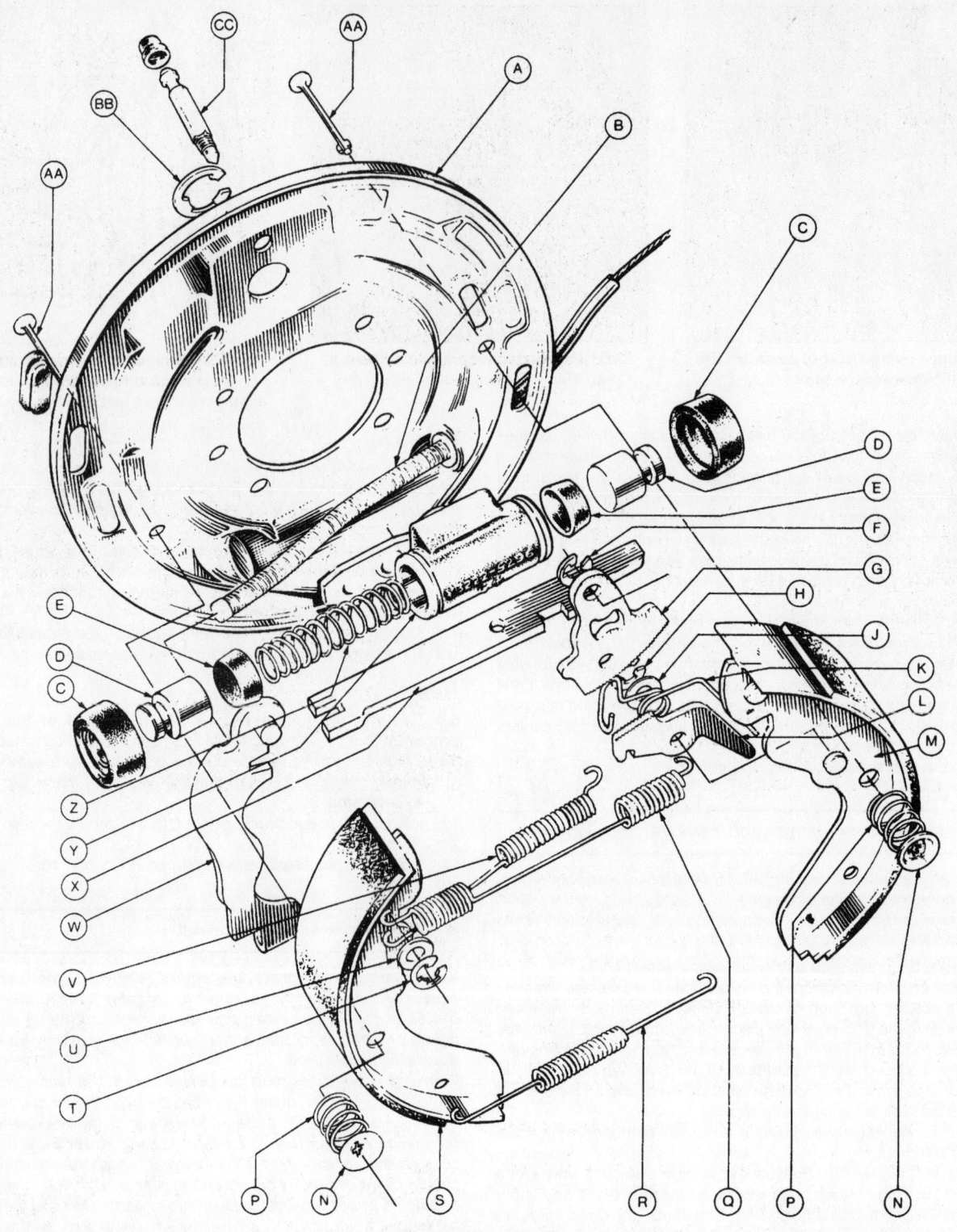

8.4 Rear brake components

A	Backplate	K	Spring	U	Washer
B	Handbrake cable	L	Ratchet	V	Retaining spring
C	Wheel cylinder dust cover	M	Brake shoe	W	Handbrake lever
D	Wheel cylinder piston	N	Spring cup	X	Spacer strut
E	Piston seal	P	Holding-down spring	Y	Wheel cylinder
F	Pivot pin clip	Q	Upper return spring	Z	Piston spring
G	Ratchet	R	Lower return spring	AA	Holding-down pin
H	Pivot pin clip	S	Brake shoe	BB	Wheel cylinder retaining clip
J	Washer	T	Pivot pin clip	CC	Bleed nipple

Chapter 9 Braking system 9-11

8.6a Upper return spring location on leading shoe

8.6b Upper return spring location on trailing shoe

8.7 Lower return spring and attachment points

8.8 Removing the leading brake shoe

8.10 Disconnecting the handbrake cable (arrowed) from the trailing shoe

4 Check the brake shoe lining thickness and, if it is below the minimum limit given in the Specifications, or if the lining rivets are flush with the lining surface, it will be necessary to renew all four rear brake shoes. Renewal is also necessary if the linings are contaminated with oil or hydraulic fluid. In this case, the source of contamination must also be rectified **(see illustration)**.

5 To remove the brake shoes, first remove the holding-down spring from the leading shoe by depressing the cup, turning it through 90° and withdrawing the washers, spring, and pin from the backplate.

6 Note the position of each brake shoe return spring, and mark the outer surface of the shoe webs to indicate their front and rear locations **(see illustrations)**.

7 Unhook the lower return spring from both shoes, using a pair of pliers **(see illustration)**.

8 Pull the lower end of the leading shoe away from the abutment, and unhook it from the upper return spring; detach the return spring from the trailing shoe **(see illustration)**.

9 Remove the holding-down spring from the trailing shoe, using the procedure described in paragraph 5.

10 Pull the upper end of the trailing shoe away from the wheel cylinder, pull the handbrake cable spring back, and disconnect the handbrake cable from the handbrake lever. The trailing shoe can now be removed from the backplate **(see illustration)**.

11 The self-adjusting mechanism must now be removed from the leading shoe by prising the two clips from the pivot pins. Note the correct position of the ratchet spring **(see illustration)**.

12 Finally remove the handbrake lever and spacer strut from the trailing shoe by pulling the lever and twisting the strut, and then

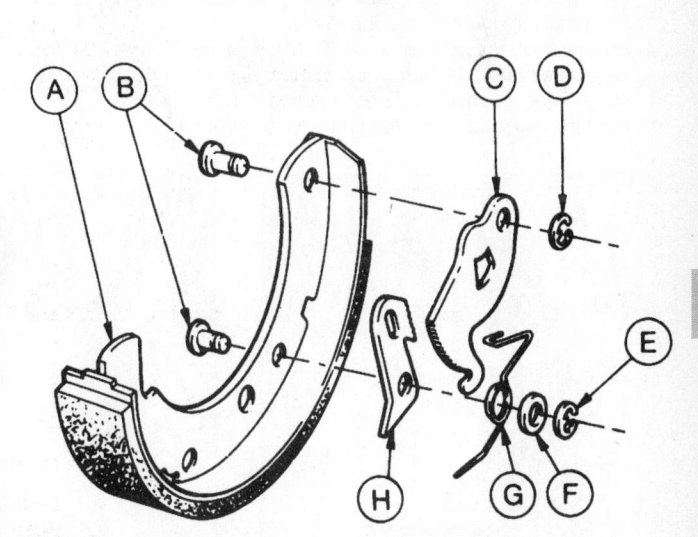

8.11 Exploded view of the self-adjusting mechanism

A	Leading brake shoe	E	Pivot pin clip
B	Pivot pins	F	Washer
C	Large ratchet	G	Spring
D	Pivot pin clip	H	Small ratchet

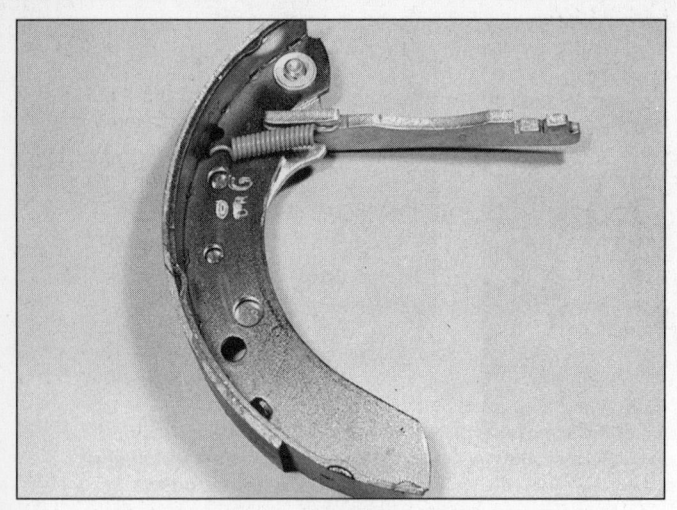

8.12a Trailing shoe and handbrake lever attachments - outboard side

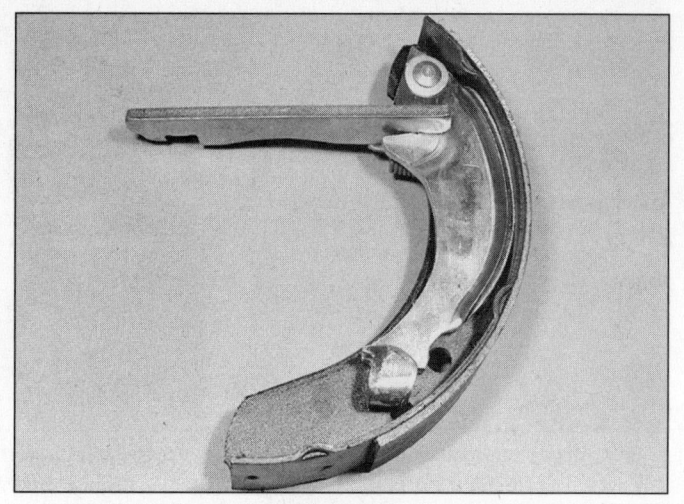

8.12b Trailing shoe and handbrake lever attachments - inboard side

unhooking the retaining spring. Prise the pivot pin clip out of its groove, and remove the handbrake lever and washers from the trailing shoe **(see illustrations)**.

13 With the brake shoes removed, locate an elastic band around the wheel cylinder to prevent the pistons from coming out. Take care not to depress the footbrake pedal whilst the brake shoes and drums are removed.

14 Thoroughly clean all traces of lining dust from the shoes and backplate, but **do not** inhale the dust, as it is hazardous to health.

15 Check that the wheel cylinder pistons are free to move in their bores. Check the wheel cylinder dust covers for damage, and the wheel cylinders and brake pipe unions for hydraulic fluid leaks.

16 Check the handbrake components and self-adjusting mechanism for wear, and renew any items as necessary.

17 Refitting of the rear brake shoes is a reversal of the removal procedure, but the following additional points should be noted:

a) When refitting the brake shoes, note that the leading shoe is the one with the thicker lining.
b) Apply a smear of high-melting-point brake grease to the brake shoe contact areas on the backplate, but take care not to allow the grease to contact the shoe linings.
c) Ensure that the spacer strut its fitted at right-angles to the handbrake lever. The adjuster ratchets should be positioned as shown **(see illustrations)** prior to fitting the leading shoe.
d) Refit the rear hubs using the procedures described in Chapter 8.

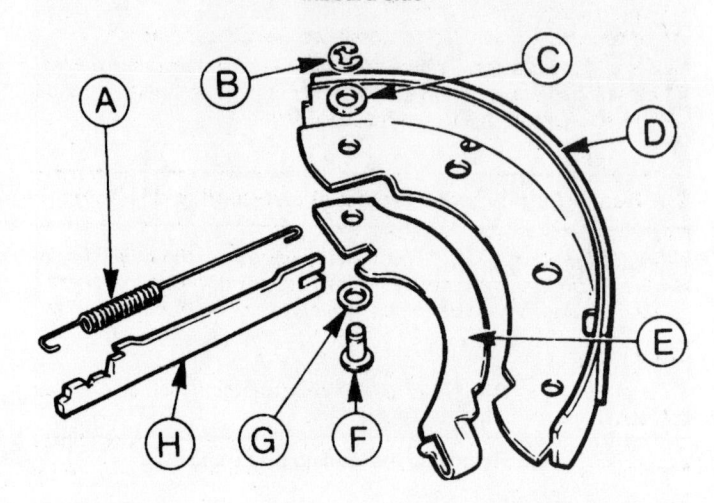

8.12c Rear brake shoe and handbrake components

A Spring	E Handbrake lever
B Pivot pin clip	F Pivot pin
C Washer	G Washer
D Trailing brake shoe	H Spacer strut

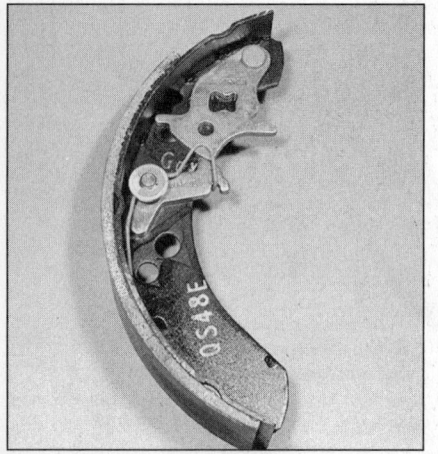

8.17a Self-adjusting mechanism positioning prior to refitting the brake shoes - inboard side

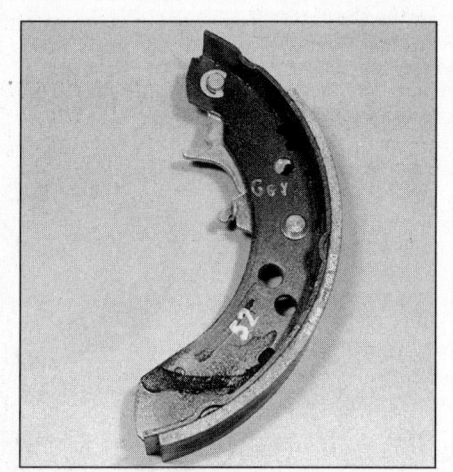

8.17b Self-adjusting mechanism positioning prior to refitting the brake shoes - outboard side

9.3 Brake pipe union connection and bleed nipple (arrowed) at the rear of the wheel cylinder

Chapter 9 Braking system

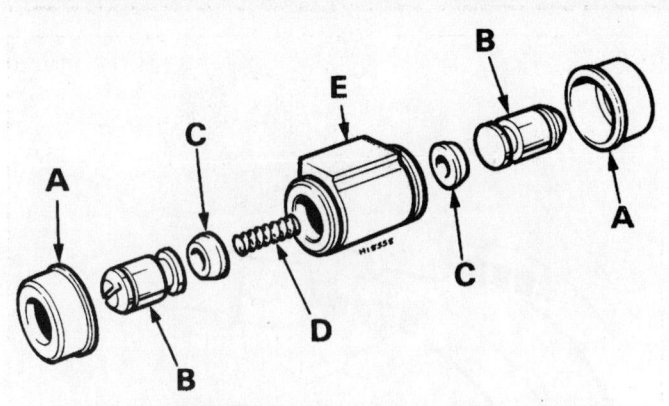

9.9 Exploded view of the rear wheel cylinder assembly

A Dust cover
B Pistons
C Seals
D Spring
E Cylinder body

e) On completion, depress the footbrake several times to operate the self-adjusting mechanism.
f) If necessary, adjust the handbrake as described in Section 14.

18 Finally, road-test the vehicle to check the operation of the brakes. If new linings have been fitted, the efficiency of the brakes may be slightly reduced until the linings have bedded-in.

9 Rear wheel cylinder - removal, overhaul and refitting

Note: *Before starting work, refer to the warning at the beginning of Section 2 concerning the dangers of hydraulic fluid, and to the warning at the beginning of Section 8 concerning the dangers of asbestos dust.*

Removal

1 Remove the rear brake shoes as described in the previous Section.
2 Using a proprietary brake hose clamp, clamp the flexible brake hose forward of the rear axle. This will minimise brake fluid loss during subsequent operations.
3 Wipe away all traces of dirt around the brake pipe union at the rear of the wheel cylinder, then using a split ring spanner if possible, unscrew the union nut. Plug or tape over the disconnected pipe end, to prevent dirt ingress **(see illustration)**.
4 Unscrew and remove the bleed nipple from the rear of the wheel cylinder.
5 Either prise the retaining clip from the rear of the wheel cylinder using a screwdriver, or undo the two retaining bolts, according to cylinder type. Remove the cylinder from the brake backplate.

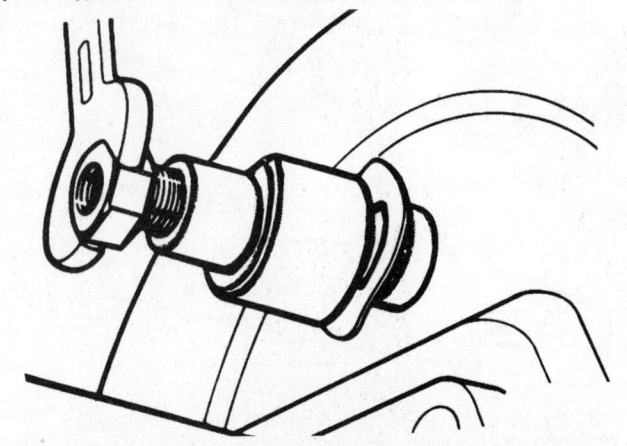

9.15 A special tool is useful when fitting the retaining clip to the wheel cylinder

Overhaul

6 Clean the external surfaces of the cylinder, then pull free the dust cover from each end of the cylinder.
7 The pistons and seals will probably shake out, but if not, use a foot pump to apply air pressure through the hydraulic union and eject them. Recover the spring fitted between the pistons.
8 Note their fitted direction, then remove the seals from the pistons.
9 Clean the pistons and the cylinder by washing in fresh hydraulic fluid or methylated spirits (not petrol, paraffin or any other mineral-based fluid). Examine the surfaces of the pistons and the cylinder bores, looking for any signs of rust, scoring or metal-to-metal rubbing, which if evident, will necessitate renewal of the wheel cylinder unit **(see illustration)**.
10 Reassemble by lubricating the first piston in clean hydraulic fluid, then manipulating its new seal into position so that its raised lip faces away from the brake shoe bearing face of the piston.
11 Insert the piston into the cylinder from the opposite end of the cylinder body, and push it through to its normal location in the bore.
12 Insert the spring into the cylinder, then fit the second new seal into position on the second piston (as described for the first) and fit the second piston into the wheel cylinder. Take care not to damage the lip of the seal as the piston is inserted into the cylinder - additional lubrication and a slight twisting action may help. Only use your fingers (no tools) to manipulate the piston and seal into position.
13 Fit the new dust covers to each end of the piston and cylinder body.

Refitting

14 Clean the wheel cylinder location on the backplate.
15 Refitting the rear wheel cylinder is a reversal of the removal procedure, but the following additional points should be noted:

a) On wheel cylinders secured by a retaining clip, fit a new clip to each time it is removed.
b) A special tool is useful when fitting the retaining clip to the wheel cylinder **(see illustration)**. If the tool is not readily available, a short length of tubing, a threaded stud, a nut, and washer can be made into a suitable tool quite easily.
c) It is important to ensure that the location peg on the wheel cylinder locates with the hole in the backplate.
d) After refitting the brake shoes, brake drum and wheel hub components, bleed the braking system as described in Section 2, and then depress the brake pedal several times to actuate the self-adjusting mechanism.
e) Adjust the handbrake, if necessary, as described in Section 14.

10 Master cylinder - removal and refitting

Note: *Before starting work, refer to the warning at the beginning of Section 2 concerning the dangers of hydraulic fluid.*

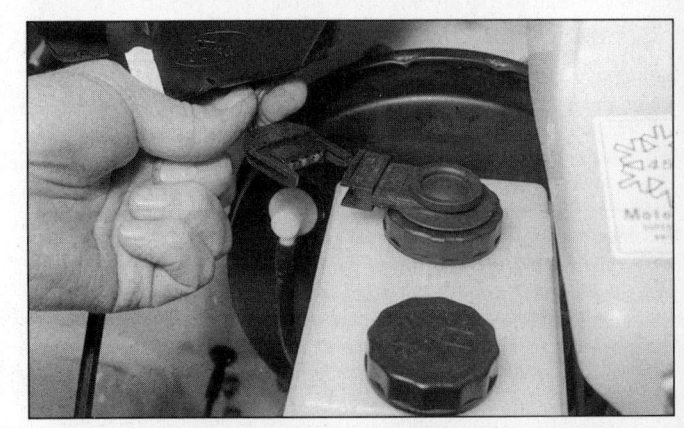

10.1 Detach the brake fluid level warning indicator wiring connector from the master cylinder reservoir

9•14 Chapter 9 Braking system

10.3a Identify each brake pipe and its connection to the master cylinder before removal

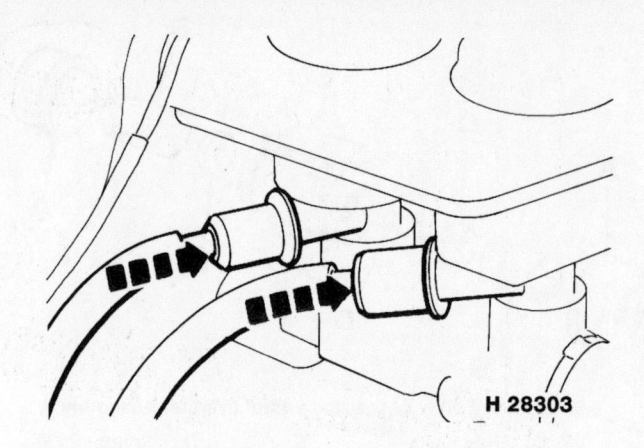

10.3b On models with ABS, press the fluid return pipe retaining boss into the reservoir and pull free the fluid line

Removal

1 Working in the engine compartment, detach the brake fluid level warning indicator wiring connector from the master cylinder reservoir **(see illustration)**.
2 Wipe clean the area around the reservoir filler cap, then remove the cap. The reservoir should now be emptied by drawing off the fluid with a syringe. Alternatively, open a convenient bleed screw, and pump the fluid into a suitable container.
3 Identify each brake pipe and its connection to the master cylinder **(see illustration)**. Unscrew the pipe-to-master cylinder union nuts, and disconnect the brake pipes. On models with ABS, when disconnecting the fluid return pipes from the reservoir, press the retaining boss into the reservoir, then pull free the fluid line **(see illustration)**. Plug the connections, and tape over the pipe ends to prevent the entry of dirt.
4 On models with ABS, ensure that the servo vacuum is exhausted by depressing the brake pedal several times with the engine switched off.
5 Unscrew the mounting nuts, and withdraw the master cylinder from the servo unit **(see illustration)**. Recover the gasket fitted between the cylinder and the servo unit.

Refitting

6 Refitting is a reverse of the removal sequence. If a replacement master cylinder is to be fitted, it will be necessary to lubricate the seals before fitting to the vehicle, as they have a protective coating when originally assembled. Remove the blanking plugs from the hydraulic pipe union seatings. Inject clean hydraulic fluid into the master cylinder, and operate the primary piston several times so that the fluid spreads over all the internal working surfaces.
7 When reattaching the fluid pipe unions, they should be loosely assembled until all are located. The master cylinder should also be loosely attached, to allow the pipe connections to be engaged easily and without the danger of cross-threading. With all pipes connected, tighten the fittings and the master cylinder retaining nuts.
8 Top-up the hydraulic reservoir fluid level, and bleed the system as described in Section 2.

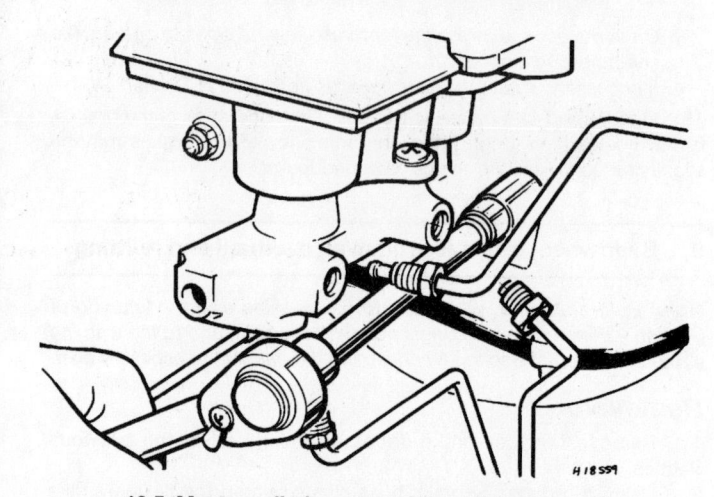

10.5 Master cylinder removal from the servo unit

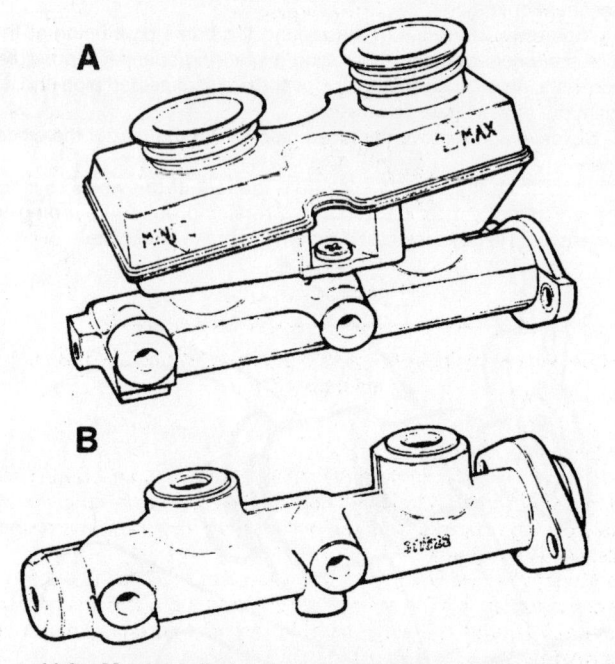

11 Master cylinder - overhaul

Note: *The following procedure is applicable to vehicles with standard braking systems only. Overhaul of the master cylinder fitted to ABS-equipped vehicles should not be attempted. Before starting work, refer to the warning at the beginning of Section 2 concerning the dangers of hydraulic fluid.*

1 Remove the master cylinder as described in the previous Section.
2 Remove the reservoir filler cap and the brake fluid level warning indicator cap and indicator assembly. Invert the cylinder, and drain off

11.3a Master cylinder and reservoir type identification
A Cylinder with screw fixing reservoir
B Cylinder with push-fit reservoir

Chapter 9 Braking system

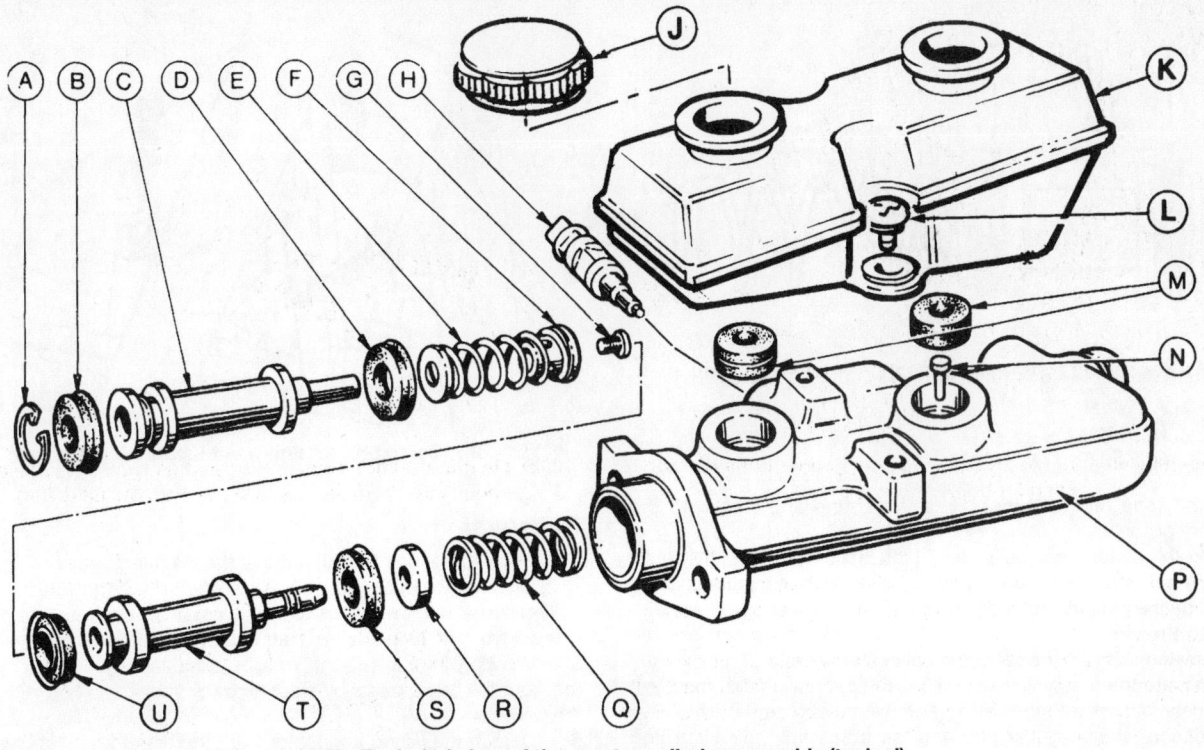

9-15

11.3b Exploded view of the master cylinder assembly (typical)

A	Circlip	F	Retainer	K	Reservoir	Q	Spring
B	Seal	G	Screw	L	Screw	R	Retainer
C	Primary piston	H	Brake fluid warning light switch (where fitted)	M	Seal	S	Seal
D	Seal			N	Piston stop pin	T	Secondary piston
E	Spring	J	Reservoir cap	P	Cylinder body	U	Seal

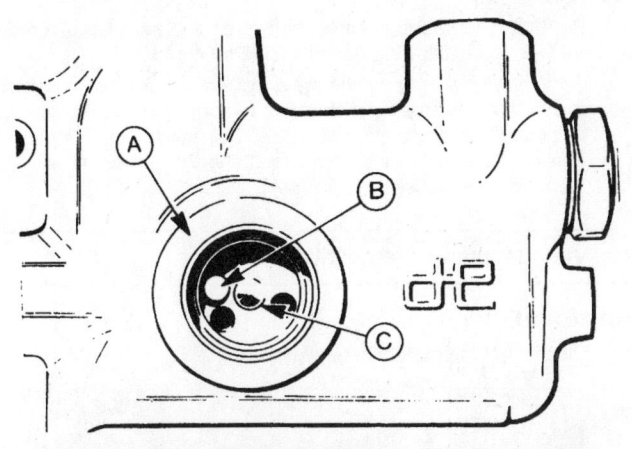

11.4 Master cylinder (A), piston stop-pin (B) and secondary inlet port (C)

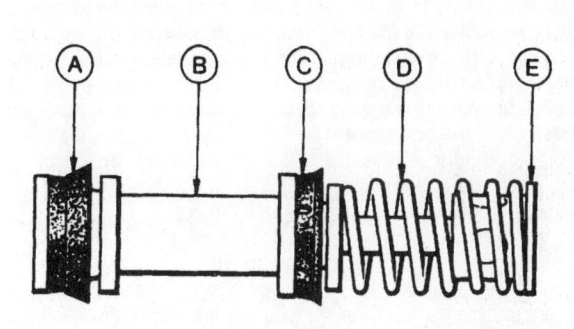

11.8a Primary piston components - assembled position

A	Seal	D	Spring
B	Piston	E	Retainer
C	Seal		

any fluid remaining in the reservoir.

3 Detach the reservoir from the master cylinder by unscrewing the two retaining screws. On some models, the reservoir is removed by simply pulling upwards from the cylinder and removing the rubber seals **(see illustrations)**.

4 Mount the cylinder in a soft-jawed vice, then use a length of dowel rod to depress the primary piston. With the piston held down, locate and remove the stop-pin from the front reservoir inlet **(see illustration)**.

5 Extract the circlip from the mouth of the cylinder, and withdraw the internal components. Place them on a clean surface in the exact order of removal; tap the cylinder on a wooden block if necessary to remove the secondary piston assembly.

6 Carefully remove the spring and sleeve and the fluid seals from the secondary piston.

7 Wash all components in clean hydraulic fluid and methylated spirit. Examine the pistons and cylinder bore surfaces for scoring, scratches, or bright wear areas; if any are evident, renew the master cylinder as a complete unit. If the surfaces of the cylinder are in good condition, obtain a repair kit comprising primary piston assembly and new secondary piston seals.

8 Dip the new seals in clean hydraulic fluid, and manipulate them into position on the secondary piston. Use your fingers only for this operation (no tools), and ensure that the seals are fitted the correct

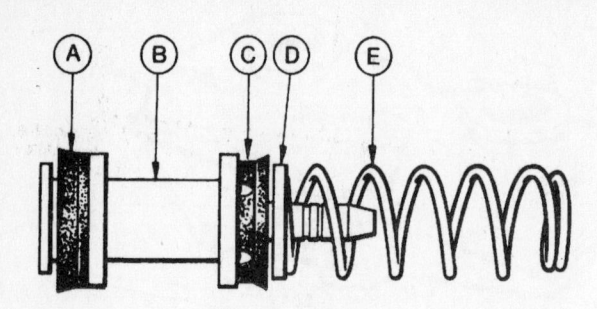

9•16 Chapter 9 Braking system

11.8b Secondary piston components - assembled position

- A Seal
- B Piston
- C Seal
- D Retainer
- E Spring

way round **(see illustrations)**. Refit the spring and sleeve to the secondary piston.
9 With the piston assemblies well-lubricated with clean hydraulic fluid, fit them into the master cylinder bore, secondary piston first, followed by the primary piston.
10 Refit the circlip to the mouth of the cylinder, then depress the primary piston and refit the secondary piston stop-pin.
11 Lubricate the reservoir seals with clean hydraulic fluid, then refit the reservoir (secure with the two screws, where applicable).
12 Refit the reservoir filler cap and the brake fluid level warning indicator assembly.
13 Refit the master cylinder as described in the previous Section.

12 Vacuum servo unit - testing, removal and refitting

Testing

1 To test the operation of the servo unit, with the engine switched off, depress the footbrake four or five times to exhaust the vacuum. Start the engine while keeping the footbrake depressed. As the engine starts, there should be a noticeable "give" in the brake pedal as vacuum builds up. Allow the engine to run for at least two minutes, and then switch it off. If the brake pedal is now depressed, again, it should be possible to detect a hiss from the servo when the pedal is depressed. After about four or five applications, no further hissing will be heard and the pedal will feel considerably firmer.
2 If the servo does not operate as described, check all vacuum connections at the servo and vacuum pump. Check the vacuum hose and non-return valve for condition and operation. If these checks do not reveal any problems, then the servo is at fault and renewal will be necessary.

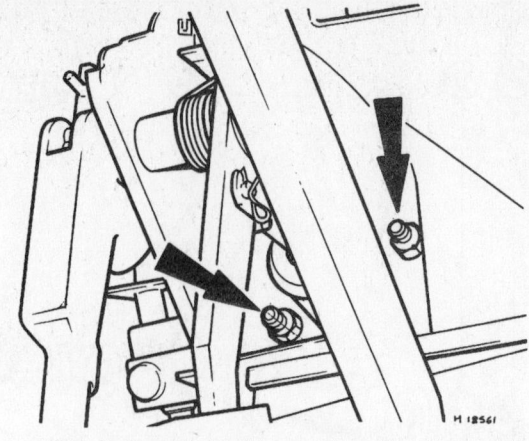

12.7 Servo unit retaining nut locations (arrowed)

Removal

3 Refer to Section 10 and remove the master cylinder.
4 Disconnect the vacuum hose at the servo non-return valve by pulling it free. If it is reluctant to move, assist it by prising it free using a screwdriver with its blade inserted under the elbow flange.
5 Working from inside the vehicle, disconnect the servo operating rod from the brake pedal by extracting the spring clip and withdrawing the clevis pin.
6 Detach the wiring connector from the brake stop-light switch on the brake pedal bracket, then twist the switch through 90° and remove it from the bracket.
7 Unscrew and remove the two nuts retaining the servo unit to the bulkhead, and remove the servo unit from the vehicle **(see illustration)**.
8 The servo unit is not repairable, and therefore it must be renewed if it is defective.

Refitting

9 Refitting the vacuum servo unit is a reversal of the removal procedure, but the following points should be noted:
 a) Tighten the retaining nuts to the specified torque wrench setting.
 b) Ensure that the stop-light switch is securely clipped into position, and that the wiring connection is securely made.
 c) Refer to Section 10 for details on refitting the master cylinder, and then top-up and bleed the hydraulic system (Section 2).

13 Vacuum pump - removal and refitting

Removal

1 Disconnect the battery negative lead.

13.2 Vacuum hose and oil feed pipe locations (arrowed) at the rear of the vacuum pump

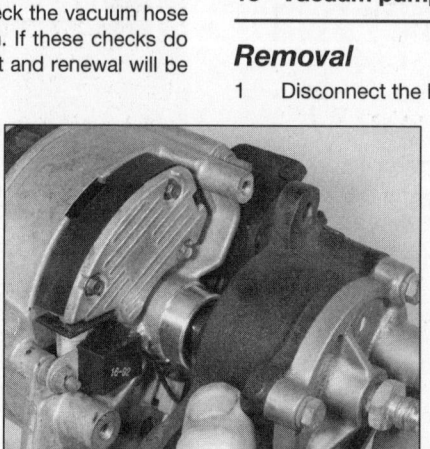

13.3a Withdraw the vacuum pump from the alternator splined shaft . . .

13.3b . . . and recover the pump-to-alternator O-ring seal

Chapter 9 Braking system 9-17

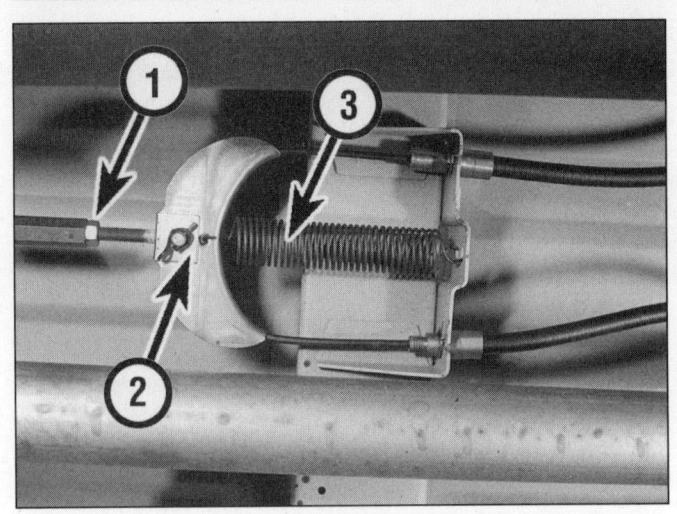

14.3a Handbrake cable adjuster (1), equaliser (2) and return spring (3)

2   Place a drip tray or bowl beneath the alternator, then unscrew the vacuum hose and the oil feed and return pipes from the rear of the pump (see illustration).
3   Undo the three bolts securing the vacuum pump to the rear of the alternator. Withdraw the pump from the alternator splined shaft, and recover the pump-to-alternator O-ring seal (see illustrations).

Refitting
4   Refitting is a reversal of the removal procedure.

14 Handbrake - adjustment

1   Normally, the self-adjusting rear brakes will also remove any excess handbrake lever movement, but where the handbrake cable has stretched, it will be necessary to carry out the following adjustment.
2   Chock the front wheels, then jack up the rear of the vehicle and support it adequately with suitable stands.
3   Fully release the handbrake lever and then working underneath the vehicle, loosen off the cable adjuster locknuts. (One locknut has a left-hand thread). Turn the adjuster until all tension is removed from the operating rods and cable, and then clean and lubricate the adjuster threads thoroughly (see illustrations). Operate the footbrake pedal several times to ensure that the rear brakes are adjusted, then pull the handbrake lever up three notches.
4   Retighten the adjuster until it is hand-tight but no more, and then tighten the locknuts against the adjuster; the threads each side of the adjuster should be of equal length, and the threads should be visible through the adjuster holes.
5   Under normal operation, the handbrake should be effective when applied three to five notches. Release the handbrake fully and check that the rear wheels are free to turn, then re-apply the handbrake and lower the vehicle to the ground.

15 Handbrake lever and primary rod - removal and refitting

Handbrake lever
Removal
1   Chock the front wheels, and then fully release the handbrake.
2   Prise free the handbrake lever gaiter from the floor, and ease it up the lever out of the way (see illustration).
3   Extract the spring clip, then withdraw the clevis pin from the

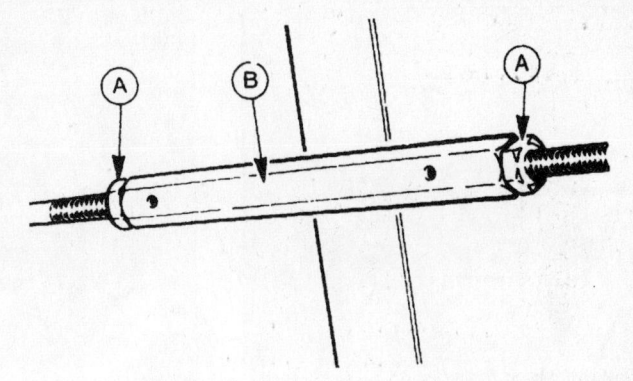

14.3b Handbrake cable adjuster locknuts (A) and adjuster (B)

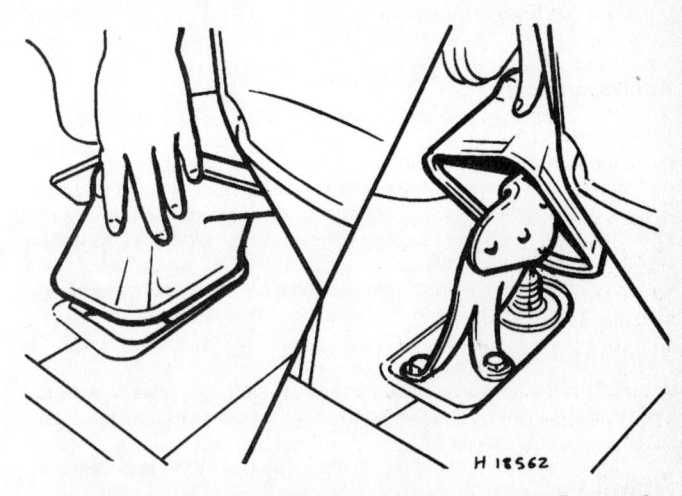

15.2 Prise free the handbrake lever gaiter from the floor, and ease it up the lever

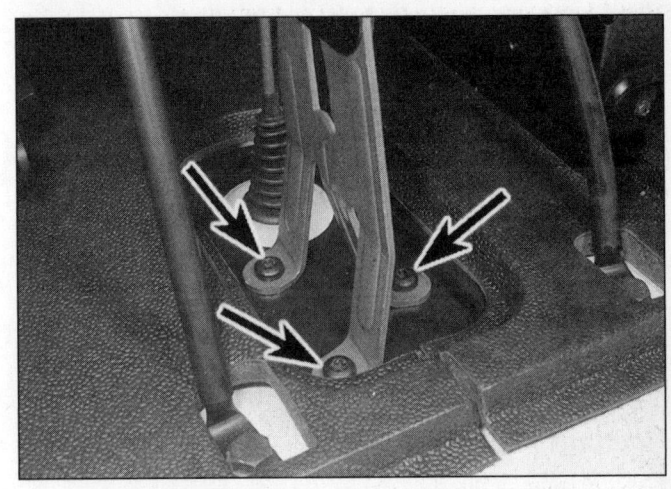

15.4 Handbrake lever retaining bolts (arrowed)

lever-to-relay link rod connection.
4   Undo the lever-to-floor mounting bolts, and remove the lever (see illustration).

Refitting
5   Refit in the reverse order of removal. Renew the clevis pin if it is excessively worn (also the spring clip if necessary), and lubricate the pin as it is fitted. On completion, check and if necessary adjust the handbrake as described in Section 14.

15.7 Handbrake primary rod-to-relay lever connection

16.6 Handbrake cable entry into brake backplate

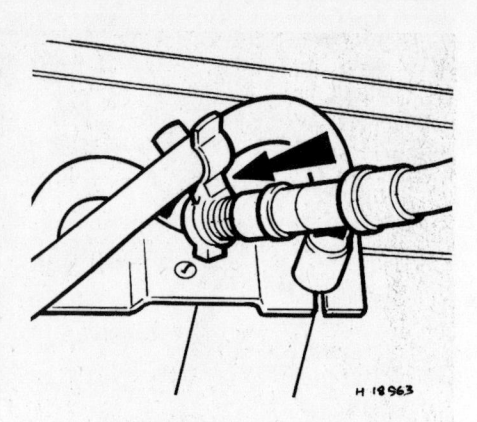

16.7 On short-wheelbase models, engage the handbrake cables in the clips (arrowed) at their crossing points

Primary rod

Removal

6   Chock the front roadwheels, release the handbrake, then raise and support the vehicle at the rear on axle stands.
7   With the handbrake fully released, disconnect the primary rod from the relay lever by extracting the spring clip and withdrawing the clevis pin **(see illustration)**.
8   Detach the primary rod from the cable equaliser unit by removing the spring clip and clevis pin. Remove the primary rod.

Refitting

9   Refit in the reverse order of removal. Renew the clevis pins if they are excessively worn, also the spring clips if necessary. Lubricate the clevis pins as they are fitted.
10   On completion, check and if necessary adjust the handbrake as described in Section 14.

16 Handbrake cable - removal and refitting

Removal

1   Chock the front wheels, slacken the rear wheel nuts, then raise the vehicle at the rear and support it on axle stands.
2   Release the handbrake, then working from underneath the vehicle, detach the handbrake primary rod from the equaliser by removing the clevis pin and clip.
3   Detach the return spring from the equaliser.
4   Remove the rear brake drums as described in Section 8.
5   Detach the brake cable from the brake shoe mechanism operating lever, by pulling on the cable return spring so that the cable can be disengaged from the lever.
6   Detach the cable from the location bracket on the backplate, and withdraw the cable **(see illustration)**.

Refitting

7   Refit in the reverse order of removal. Refer to Section 8 to refit the brake drum. On short-wheelbase models, engage the cables in the clips at their crossing points **(see illustration)**.
8   Before lowering the vehicle, check and if necessary adjust the handbrake as described in Section 14.

17 Brake pressure control valve - description, removal and refitting

Note: *Before starting work, refer to the warning at the beginning of Section 2 concerning the dangers of hydraulic fluid.*

17.2 Brake pressure control valve

Description

1   Certain models are fitted with a brake pressure control valve, the purpose of which is to regulate the hydraulic pressure applied to the rear brakes, regardless of vehicle loading. This then prevents the wheels "locking up" when heavy brake pressure is applied.
2   The valve assembly is mounted on the underside of the vehicle, attached to the inboard side of the right-hand chassis member, opposite the fuel tank **(see illustration)**.
3   The valve operation is fully automatic, and it cannot be adjusted or repaired. If defective, it must therefore be renewed.

Removal

4   To remove the pressure control valve, first chock the front wheels, then raise and support the vehicle at the rear end on axle stands. Allow a suitable working clearance underneath.
5   Wipe clean and then remove the brake fluid reservoir filler cap. Place a clean piece of polythene sheet over the filler neck, and secure with an elastic band. This will minimise brake fluid loss when the hydraulic pipes are detached from the valve.
6   Clean the hydraulic pipe connections at the control valve, then unscrew the union nuts and detach the pipes from the valve. Plug or tape over the pipe ends, to prevent fluid loss and the ingress of dirt.
7   Withdraw the valve retaining clip, and withdraw the valve from its bracket.

Refitting

8   Refit in the reverse order of removal. As the valve is fitted to the

Chapter 9 Braking system

18.2 Load-apportioning valve

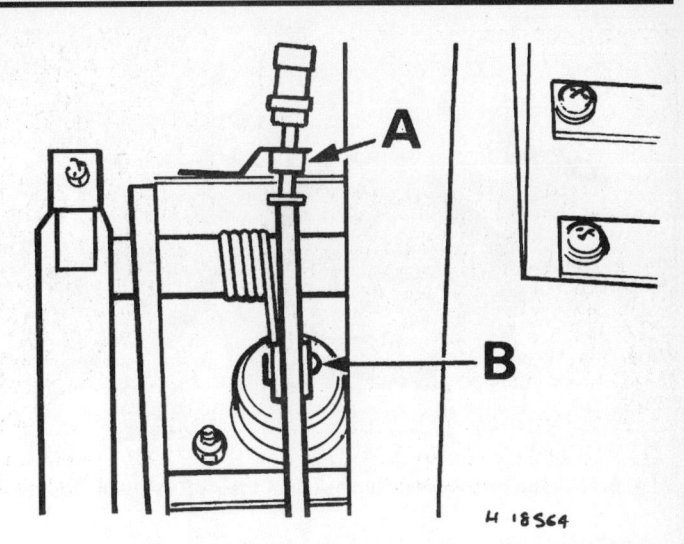

19.1 Brake pedal-to-servo pushrod clevis pin (B) and brake stop-light switch (A)

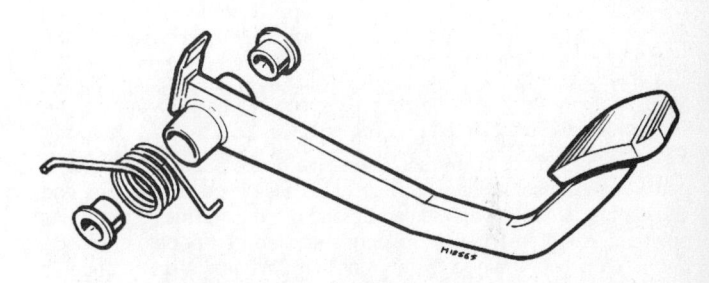

19.3 Brake pedal and associated fittings

bracket, align the cut-out. When the valve is refitted, top-up the hydraulic fluid, and bleed the rear brakes as described in Section 2. Once the rear brakes are bled, have an assistant slowly depress the brake pedal whilst you slacken the brake pipe union on the pressure control valve. Only slacken the pipe union slightly to allow the fluid past. As soon as fluid is seen coming from the valve, retighten the union.

9   Lower the vehicle to complete.

18 Load-apportioning valve (LAV) - general

The function of this device is similar in certain aspects to that of the brake pressure control valve described in the previous Section, but operates according to vehicle loading rather than hydraulic pressure. The load-apportioning valve is only fitted to certain models, and differs in design and location.

The LAV unit is mounted on the chassis in front of the rear axle, and is operated by a lever and load-sensing spring interconnected between the valve and the axle **(see illustration)**.

The only time that the LAV unit will need removal is if the valve is defective or the axle is to be removed, in which case the valve unit can be left in position, but the coil spring will have to be detached (refer to Chapter 8, Section 8).

The valve may have to be re-adjusted if the assembly is removed. This requires the use of specialised equipment, and reference to several graphs depending on the vehicle body type. The removal and refitting of this unit should therefore be entrusted to a Ford dealer.

19 Brake pedal - removal and refitting

Removal

1   Detach the brake pedal-to-servo pushrod by extracting the spring clip and withdrawing the clevis pin **(see illustration)**.
2   Detach the wiring connector from the brake stop-light switch, then twist the switch through 90° and withdraw it from the bracket.
3   Unhook and remove the spring clip securing the brake pedal shaft on the brake side, then press the pedal towards the clutch so that the brake pedal is released **(see illustration)**.
4   Press or drive out the pedal bushes, and remove the spring.

Refitting

5   Refit in the reverse order of removal. Align the cut-out in the shaft with the pedal box as they are reassembled.

20 Anti-lock braking system (ABS) - general information

An electrically-operated anti-lock braking system is available on certain models in the range. The system only becomes operational at speeds in excess of 7 mph (4 kph). It comprises an actuation unit (servo unit and special type tandem master cylinder), hydraulic unit, electronic module, brake pedal travel sensor, and a wheel speed sensor on each front and rear wheel hub.

The hydraulic unit consists of a twin-circuit electric pump which is controlled by a speed sensor and modulator twin valve block (one valve for each channel).

The electronic module is located inside the vehicle in the glove compartment, and serves four main functions: to control the ABS system; to measure the vehicle speed; to monitor the electric components in the system; and to provide "on-board" system diagnosis. The electrical functions of the ABS module are continuously monitored by two microprocessors, and these also periodically check the solenoid-operated valves by means of a test pulse during the operation of the system. The module checks the signals sent by the system sensors to provide a fault diagnosis; in the event of a fault occurring in the ABS system, a warning light on the instrument panel will come on and remain on until the ignition is switched off. A particular fault is represented by a two-digit code system stored within the module memory. A "STAR" type tester is required to analyse the fault diagnosis system, and in the event of a fault being indicated, the vehicle must be entrusted to a Ford garage for analysis.

The ABS system functions as follows. During normal braking, pressure from the brake pedal (and the servo unit) closes the master cylinder valves, and hydraulic pressure is applied through the brake circuits in the conventional manner. When a wheel starts to lock up under heavy braking, the circuit inlet valve in the hydraulic unit is closed off, to prevent further pressure being applied through that

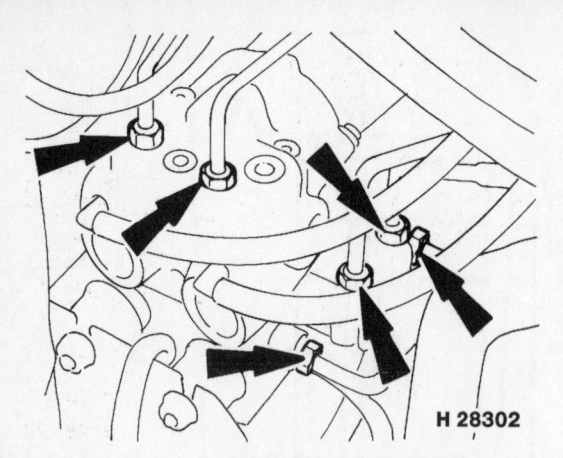

9•20 Chapter 9 Braking system

21.4 Brake pipe connections (arrowed) at the ABS hydraulic unit

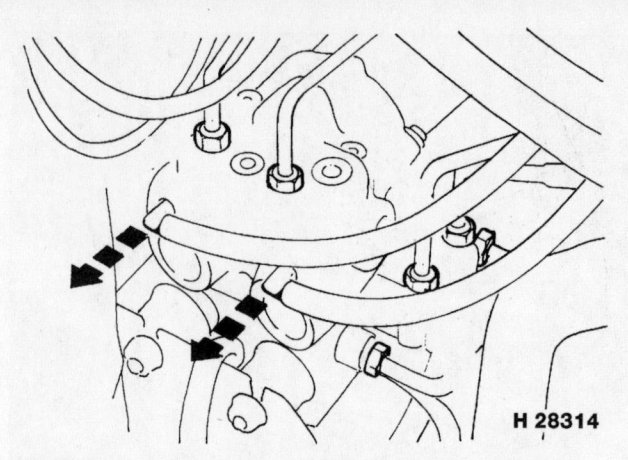

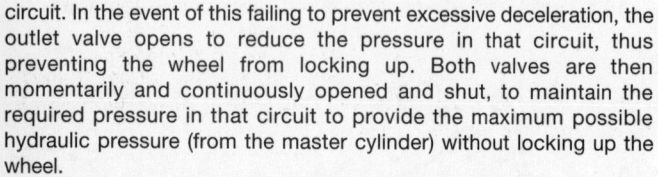

21.5 Detach the low-pressure fluid return pipe connectors at the ABS hydraulic unit

circuit. In the event of this failing to prevent excessive deceleration, the outlet valve opens to reduce the pressure in that circuit, thus preventing the wheel from locking up. Both valves are then momentarily and continuously opened and shut, to maintain the required pressure in that circuit to provide the maximum possible hydraulic pressure (from the master cylinder) without locking up the wheel.

Slight pulsations will be felt through the brake pedal when the ABS is functioning. To reduce excessive brake pedal pulsations, a pedal travel sensor monitors any slight increase in pedal pressure, and causes the pump to be switched on and off; this maintains the pedal position. When emergency braking is applied, the pedal is pressed back to a predetermined "safety position". When the brake pedal is released, the ABS mode is automatically cancelled.

21 Anti-lock braking system components - removal and refitting

Hydraulic unit

Note: *Before starting work, refer to the warning at the beginning of Section 2 concerning the dangers of hydraulic fluid.*

Removal

1 Disconnect the battery negative lead.
2 Wipe clean the area around the master cylinder reservoir filler cap, and remove the cap. The reservoir should now be emptied by drawing off the fluid with a syringe, or by opening a convenient bleed screw and pumping the fluid into a suitable container.
3 Place absorbent rags around the hydraulic unit, and be prepared for hydraulic fluid spillage as the various pipes are disconnected.
4 Identify each brake pipe and its connection to the hydraulic unit, then unscrew the union nuts and disconnect them **(see illustration)**. Plug or tape over the pipe ends, to prevent fluid loss and the ingress of dirt.
5 Detach the low-pressure fluid return pipes at the hydraulic unit **(see illustration)**.
6 Disconnect the motor wiring multi-plug at the hydraulic unit, and the valve block multi-plug at the connector adjacent to the battery.
7 Undo the three nuts securing the hydraulic unit to the mounting bracket, and withdraw the unit from the engine compartment.

Refitting

8 Refitting is a reversal of removal. On completion, bleed the complete hydraulic system as described in Section 2.

Electronic module

Removal

9 Disconnect the battery negative lead.
10 Release the fastening catch, and lower the module mounting tray from the roof of the glove compartment.
11 Unclip the module, and slide it out of its location in the tray **(see illustration)**.
12 Disconnect the wiring multi-plug and remove the module.

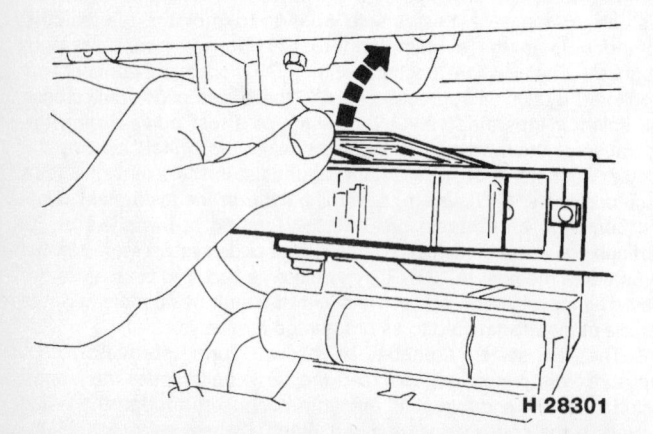

21.11 Unclip the ABS electronic module, and slide it out of its location in the tray

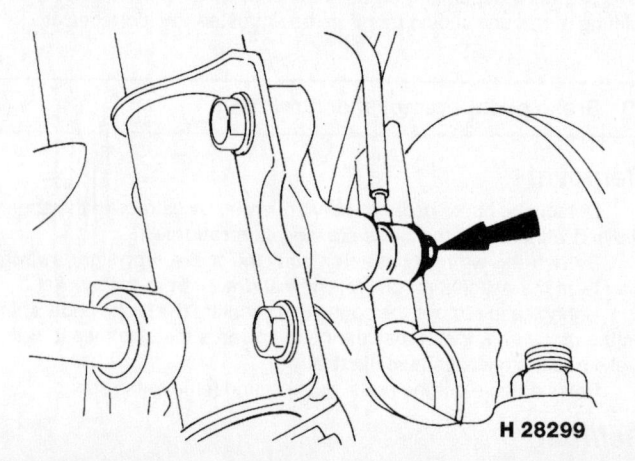

21.15 Unscrew the retaining bolt (arrowed) and withdraw the ABS front wheel speed sensor from its location in the stub axle

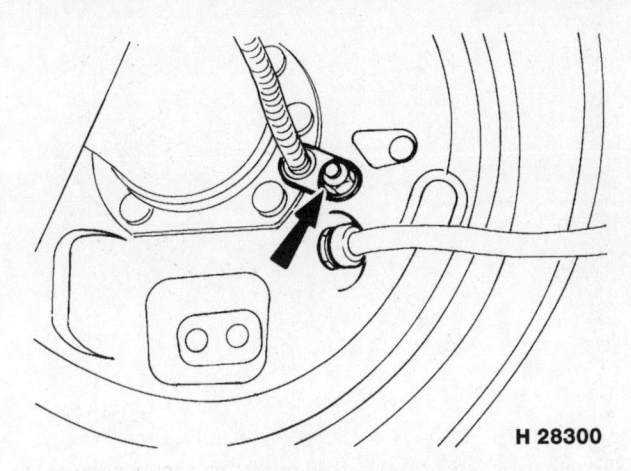

Chapter 9 Braking system

21.20 Unscrew the ABS rear wheel speed sensor retaining bolt (arrowed), and withdraw the sensor from its location in the brake backplate

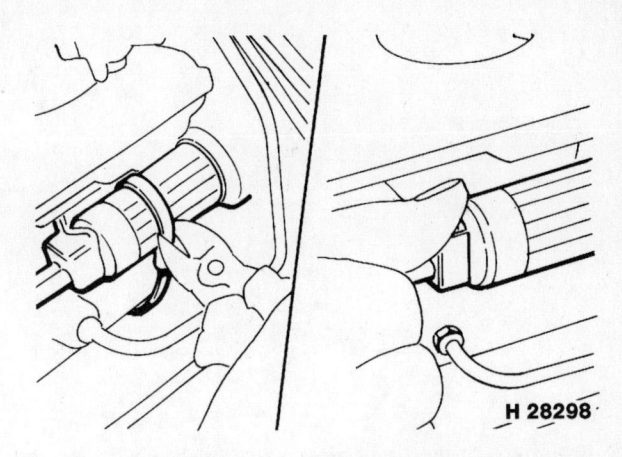

21.24 Cut off the ABS brake pedal travel sensor cable securing tie, and disconnect the wiring multi-plug

Refitting
13 Refitting is a reversal of removal.

Front wheel speed sensor

Removal
14 Apply the handbrake, loosen off the front roadwheel nuts, then jack up the front of the vehicle and support it on axle stands. Remove the front roadwheels.
15 Unclip and detach the sensor cable from the wiring loom **(see illustration)**.
16 Unscrew the retaining bolt, and withdraw the sensor from its location in the stub axle. Remove the sensor and lead from the vehicle.

Refitting
17 Refitting is a reversal of removal. When inserting the sensor into position, ensure that the mating surfaces are clean, and free from oil or grease. Also check that the locating tag on the sensor is correctly positioned. Feed the cable through the wheel arch, and ensure that it is clipped in position. Secure the cable with any ties provided. On completion, turn the steering from lock-to-lock, and ensure that the sensor lead does not foul on any steering or suspension components before lowering the vehicle to the ground.

Rear wheel speed sensor

Removal
18 Chock the front wheels, then jack up the rear of the vehicle and support it on axle stands.

19 Unclip and detach the sensor cable from the wiring loom.
20 Unscrew the retaining bolt, and withdraw the sensor from its location in the brake backplate **(see illustration)**. Remove the sensor and lead from the vehicle.

Refitting
21 Refitting is a reversal of removal. When inserting the sensor into position, ensure that the mating surfaces are clean, and free from oil or grease. Ensure that the cable is correctly routed and clipped in position. Secure the cable with any ties provided.

Brake pedal travel sensor

Removal
22 Disconnect the battery negative lead.
23 Ensure that the vacuum in the brake servo is exhausted by depressing the brake pedal several times with the engine switched off.
24 Cut off the sensor cable securing tie, and disconnect the wiring multi-plug **(see illustration)**.
25 Extract the retaining circlip, and carefully withdraw the sensor from the servo unit. As the sensor is withdrawn, take care that the O-ring seal does not drop into the interior of the servo unit. If this happens, the O-ring **must** be extracted before the sensor is refitted.

Refitting
26 Refitting is a reversal of removal. Ensure that the O-ring seal is in place on the sensor body prior to refitting, and secure the cable to the sensor body using a new cable-tie.

Notes

Chapter 10 Suspension and steering

Contents

	Section
Front anti-roll bar (beam axle type) - removal and refitting	18
Front anti-roll bar (IFS) - removal and refitting	10
Front beam axle - removal and refitting	15
Front beam axle leaf spring - removal and refitting	16
Front coil spring - (IFS) - removal and refitting	5
Front hub assembly (beam axle type) - removal, refitting and adjustment	12
Front hub assembly (IFS) - removal, refitting and adjustment	2
Front hub bearings (beam axle type) - renewal	13
Front hub bearings (IFS) - renewal	3
Front shock absorber (beam axle type) - removal and refitting	19
Front shock absorber (IFS) - removal and refitting	11
Front stub axle (beam axle type) - removal and refitting	14
Front stub axle (IFS) - removal and refitting	4
Front suspension and steering check	See Chapter 1
Front suspension bump stop (beam axle type) - removal and refitting	17
Front suspension lower arm balljoint (IFS) - removal and refitting	9
Front suspension lower arm bracket bush (IFS) - renewal	8
Front suspension lower arm bush (IFS) - renewal	7
Front suspension lower arm (IFS) - removal and refitting	6
Front wheel alignment check	See Chapter 1
General information	1

	Section
Power steering fluid level check	See Chapter 1
Power steering gear unit - removal and refitting	33
Power steering pipes and hoses - removal and refitting	34
Power steering pump - removal and refitting	32
Power steering pump drivebelt check, adjustment and renewal	See Chapter 1
Power steering system - bleeding	35
Rack-and-pinion steering gear unit - removal, overhaul and refitting	25
Rear axle leaf spring - removal and refitting	20
Rear shock absorber - removal and refitting	21
Steering column - dismantling, overhaul and reassembly	24
Steering column - removal and refitting	23
Steering gear rubber gaiters - renewal	27
Steering wheel - removal and refitting	22
Track rod end balljoint - removal and refitting	26
Wheel and tyre maintenance and tyre pressure checks	See Chapter 1
Wheel alignment and steering angles - general information	36
Worm-and-nut steering gear - removal, overhaul and refitting	28
Worm-and-nut steering gear - rocker shaft pre-load adjustment	29
Worm-and-nut steering gear drag link - removal and refitting	31
Worm-and-nut steering gear drop arm - removal and refitting	30

Specifications

Independent front suspension (IFS)
Type .... Independent "hybrid" MacPherson strut, with coil springs and telescopic shock absorbers. Anti-roll bar fitted to certain models.

Hub bearing adjustment (see text):
   Pre-1990 model year:
      Initial tightening of bearing adjuster nut .... 23 to 33 Nm
      Final bearing endfloat .... 0.025 to 0.13 mm
   1990 model year onwards:
      Initial tightening of bearing adjuster nut .... 27 to 40 Nm
      Final bearing endfloat .... 0.002 to 0.050 mm

Beam axle front suspension
Type .... Forged steel "I" section beam axle with semi-elliptic leaf springs and telescopic shock absorbers. Anti-roll bar fitted to certain models.

Stub axle-to-beam axle clearance .... 0.025 to 1.0 mm
Shim sizes .... 3.3 to 4.6 mm in 0.1 mm increments
Hub bearing adjustment (see text):
   Initial tightening of bearing adjuster nut .... 23 to 33 Nm
   Final bearing endfloat .... 0.025 to 0.13 mm

Rear suspension
Type .... Solid rear axle supported on semi-elliptic leaf springs with telescopic shock absorbers.

Steering

Type.. Rack-and-pinion (Independent front suspension) or worm-and-nut (beam axle front suspension). Power steering available on both suspension types.

Rack-and-pinion steering
Pinion turning torque.. 0.9 to 1.8 Nm
Steering gear lubricant... Grease to Ford spec. SLM-1C-9110A
Lubricant capacity.. 180 grams

Worm-and-nut steering
Steering shaft turning torque... 0.3 to 0.8 Nm
Rocker shaft pre-load... 2.5 to 3.0 Nm
Steering gear lubricant... Grease to Ford spec. SLM-1C-9110A
Lubricant capacity.. 200 grams

Power steering
Type:
   Vehicles with independent front suspension................................ ZF
   Vehicles with beam axle front suspension.................................... Bendix
Fluid type.. Automatic transmission fluid to Ford spec. ESP-M2C-166H (Duckhams Uni-Matic)

Wheel alignment and steering angles
Note: *The figures for camber, castor and steering axis inclination are dependent on model year and vehicle type. Consult a Ford dealer for exact specifications.*

Toe setting
   Independent front suspension... 2.0 mm (toe-in) to 2.0 mm (toe-out)
   Beam axle front suspension.. 0 to 1.60 mm (toe-in)

Roadwheels
Type... Five- or six-stud fixing, steel
Size.. 14 x 5, 14 x 5.5, 15 x 5.5, 15 x 6

Note: *Vehicles with six-stud wheels have **left-hand thread** wheel nuts on the left-hand side up to the 1992 model year. From 1992 onwards, conventional right-hand thread nuts are used on both sides.*

Tyres
Tyre sizes (dependent on model).. 185 R14 Rein, 185 R14C 6PR, 185 R14C 8PR, 195 R14C 6PR, 195 R14C 8PR, 205/70 R14 Rein, 185 R15C 6PR, 215/70 R15C 8PR, 225/70 R15C 6PR, 225/70 R15C 8PR
Tyre pressures... See Chapter 1 Specifications

Torque wrench settings

	Nm	lbf ft
Roadwheels		
Wheel nuts:		
Five-stud wheels	85	63
Six-stud wheels	168	124
Independent front suspension		
Anti-roll bar-to-crossmember bolts	20 to 28	15 to 21
Anti-roll bar link rod nuts	20 to 28	15 to 21
Crossmember to chassis	70 to 90	52 to 66
Hub bearing adjuster nut:		
Stage 1:		
Pre-1990 model year	23 to 33	17 to 25
1990 model year onwards	27 to 40	20 to 30
Stage 2	Slacken to give specified endfloat	
Lower arm bracket-to-chassis nuts:		
Pre-1992 model year	88 to 113	65 to 83
1992 model year onwards	144 to 201	106 to 148
Lower arm bracket-to-crossmember bolts	26 to 32	19 to 24
Lower arm balljoint-to-stub axle nut:		
Pre-1992 model year	130	96
1992 model year onwards	200	148
Lower arm balljoint-to-lower arm nuts	40 to 51	30 to 38
Lower arm-to-front bracket pivot bolt nut:		
Pre-1992 model year	88 to 113	65 to 83
1992 model year onwards	144 to 201	106 to 148

Chapter 10 Suspension and steering

Lower arm-to-crossmember pivot bolt nut (see text):
  Clamping torque:
    Pre-1992 model year 100   74
    1992 model year onwards 220   162
  Fully slacken... -   -
  Snug torque:
    Pre-1992 model year 70   52
    1992 model year onwards 200   148
  Torque angle:
    Pre-1992 model year .... 90°   90°
    1992 model year onwards .... 45°   45°
Shock absorber-to-stub axle bolts.. 40 to 57   30 to 42
Shock absorber upper retaining nut .... 40 to 51   30 to 38
Shock absorber insulator nuts.. 40 to 57   30 to 42

Beam axle front suspension
Anti-roll bar anchor plate nuts .... 70 to 97   52 to 72
Anti-roll bar link nuts .... 70 to 97   52 to 72
Hub bearing adjuster nut:
  Stage 1 .... 23 to 33   17 to 25
  Stage 2 .... Slacken to give specified endfloat
Shock absorber upper nuts.. 40 to 51   30 to 38
Shock absorber lower nuts.. 70 to 90   52 to 66
Spring bump stop nut .... 40 to 51   30 to 38
Spring front eye bolt nut .... 156 to 196   115 to 145
Spring shackle nuts .... 70 to 90   52 to 66
Spring U-bolt nuts:
  Stage 1 .... 35 to 45   26 to 33
  Stage 2 .... 75 to 85   55 to 63
  Stage 3 .... 114 to 146   84 to 108

Rear suspension
Spring front eye bolt nut:
  "H" axle 177   131
  "G" axle 186   137
Spring shackle nuts:
  "H" axle 84   62
  "G" axle 186   137
Spring U-bolt nuts:
  "H" axle 94   69
  "G" axle 125   92

Rack-and-pinion steering
Column tube to bulkhead 23   17
Column tube upper mounting 23   17
Pinion bearing cover 85   63
Steering gear to crossmember 50   37
Steering wheel nut 45   33
Universal joint clamp plate bolt 35   26
Universal joint to pinion shaft pinch-bolt 30   22
Track rod inner balljoint to steering rack 103   76
Track rod end balljoint locknut 80   69
Track rod end balljoint to steering arm 60   44
Yoke plug:
  Stage 1 10   7
  Stage 2 .... Slacken by 30°   Slacken by 30°

Worm-and-nut steering
Column tube to bulkhead 23   17
Column tube upper mounting 23   17
Drag link balljoint to drop arm 60   44
Drag link balljoint to steering arm 60   44
Drag link balljoint locknut 80   69
Drop arm-to-steering shaft nut 270   199
Rocker shaft adjustment screw locknut 35   26
Rocker shaft side cover 21   16
Steering gear to chassis 84   62
Steering wheel nut 45   33
Thrust bearing adjuster locknut 135   100

Chapter 10 Suspension and steering

Worm-and-nut steering (continued)

Track rod end balljoint to steering arm	60	44
Track rod end balljoint clamp bolt nut	24	18
Transfer tube clamp plate screws	6	4
Universal joint clamp plate bolt	35	26

Power steering and associated systems (where different from above)

Bendix steering gear to chassis	70 to 97	52 to 72
Drag link balljoint to drop arm	115	84
Drag link balljoint to steering arm	115	84
Pump bracket to cylinder block	52 to 64	38 to 47
Pump mounting bolts:		
M10	41 to 58	30 to 43
M12	21 to 28	16 to 21
Pump pulley bolts	21 to 28	16 to 21
Track rod end balljoint to steering arm:		
Bendix steering gear	115	84
ZF steering gear	60	44
ZF steering gear to crossmember	50	37

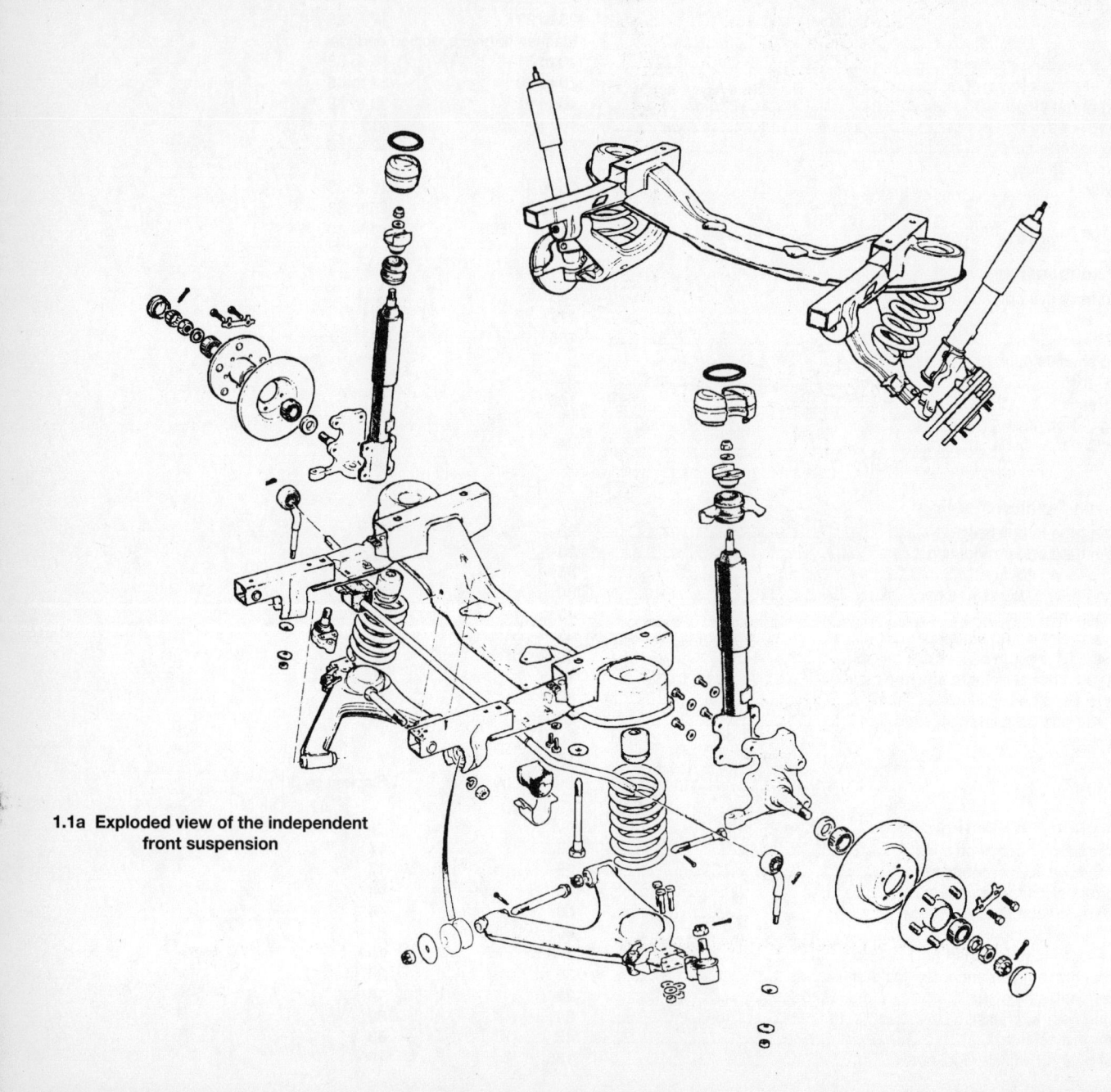

1.1a Exploded view of the independent front suspension

Chapter 10 Suspension and steering

1 General information

On pre-1992 model year vehicles, the front suspension system will be of either independent (IFS) type, fitted to short-wheelbase models, or beam axle type, fitted to long-wheelbase and 100L models **(see illustrations)**. From the 1992 model year onwards, all models are fitted with independent front suspension.

The independent front suspension system comprises a coil spring, a lower arm and a telescopic double-acting shock absorber each side. The beam axle suspension comprises a single taper leaf spring and a double-acting telescopic shock absorber each side.

An anti-roll bar is fitted to the front suspension system on some models.

The rear suspension system comprises single or multiple semi-elliptic leaf springs and telescopic double-acting shock absorbers.

The steering system fitted will be either rack-and-pinion type (IFS models), or worm-and-nut type (beam axle models) **(see illustrations)**. The steering column used is common to all models. Power steering is available with both suspension types.

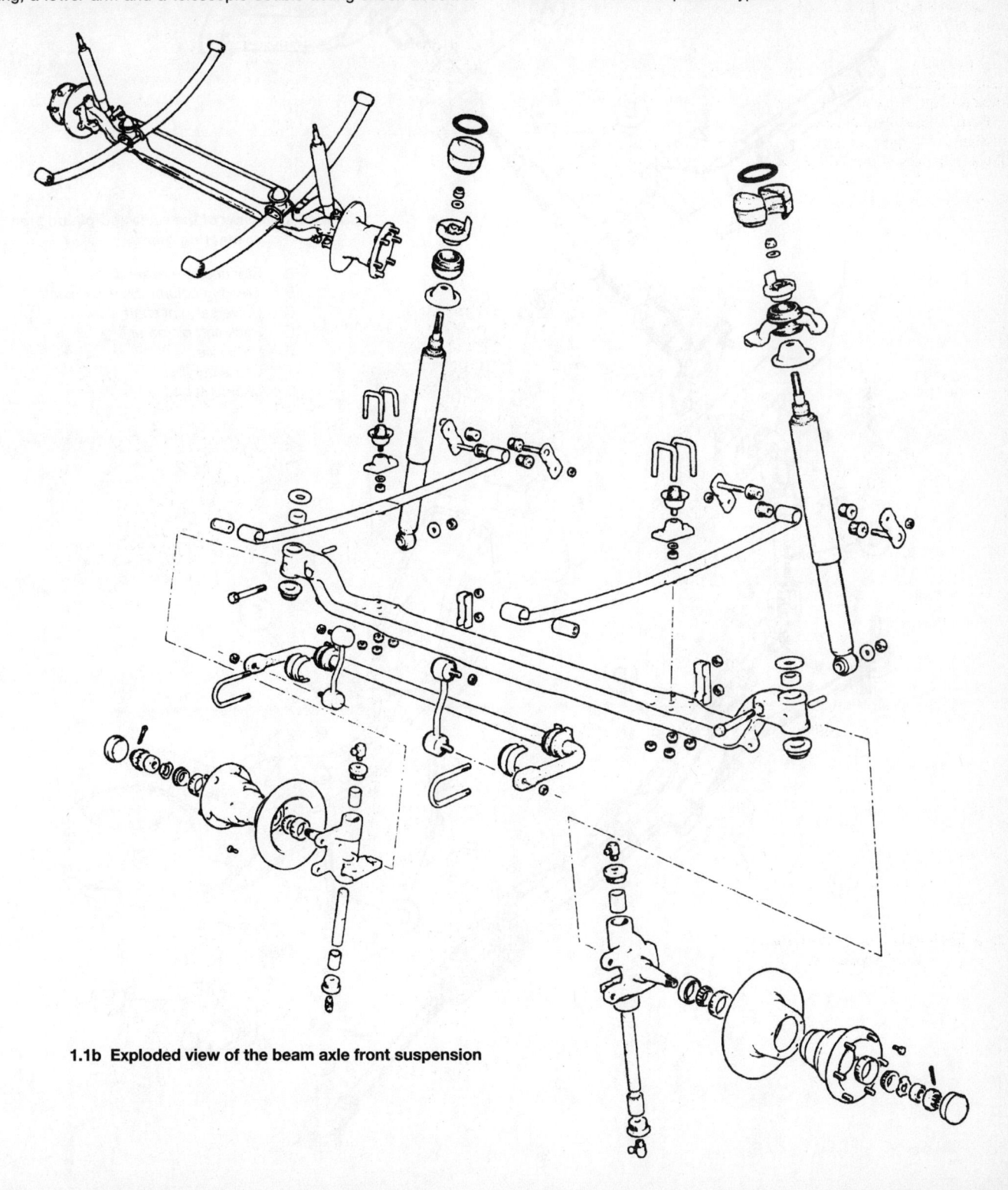

1.1b Exploded view of the beam axle front suspension

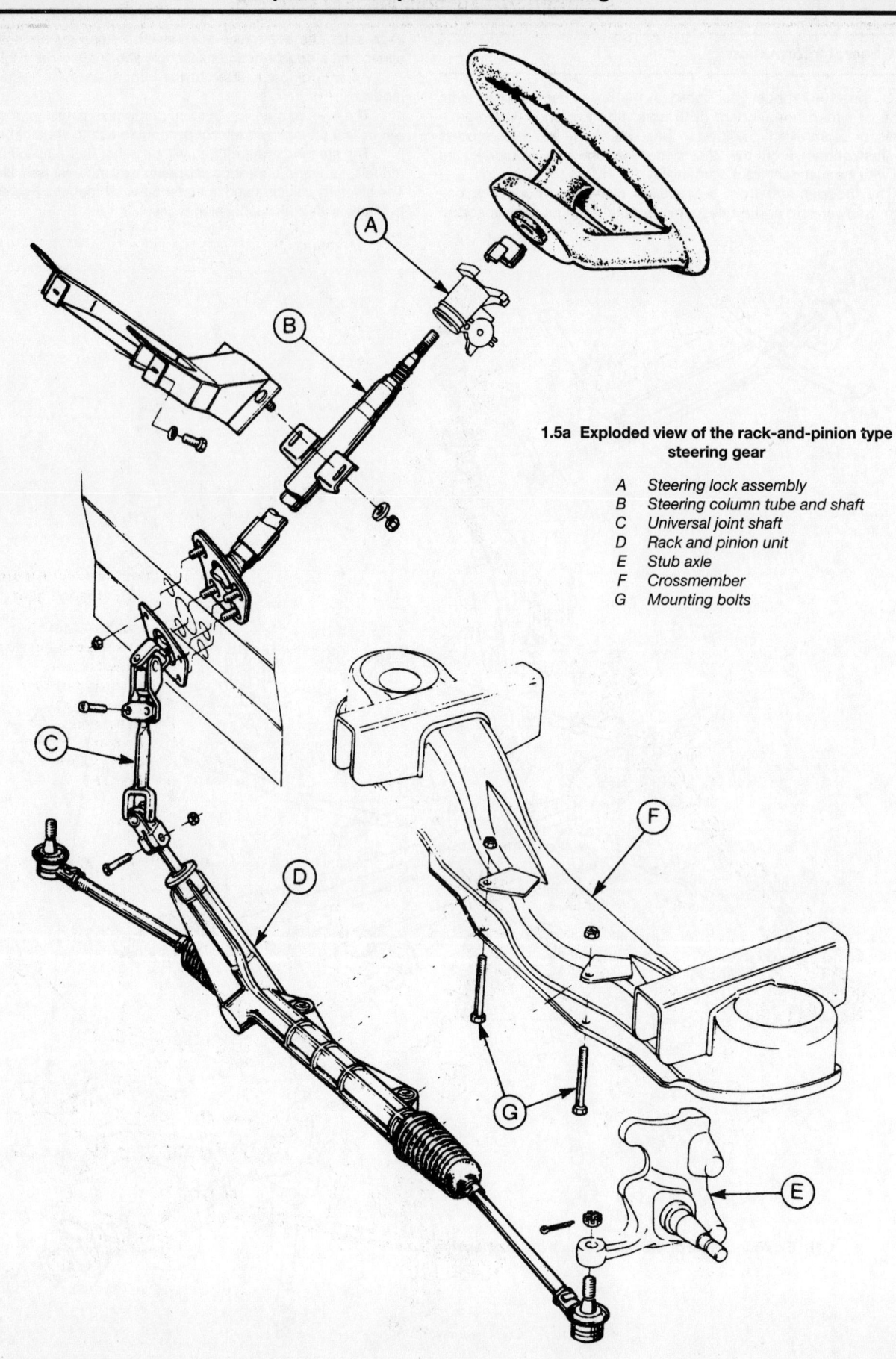

1.5a Exploded view of the rack-and-pinion type steering gear

- A Steering lock assembly
- B Steering column tube and shaft
- C Universal joint shaft
- D Rack and pinion unit
- E Stub axle
- F Crossmember
- G Mounting bolts

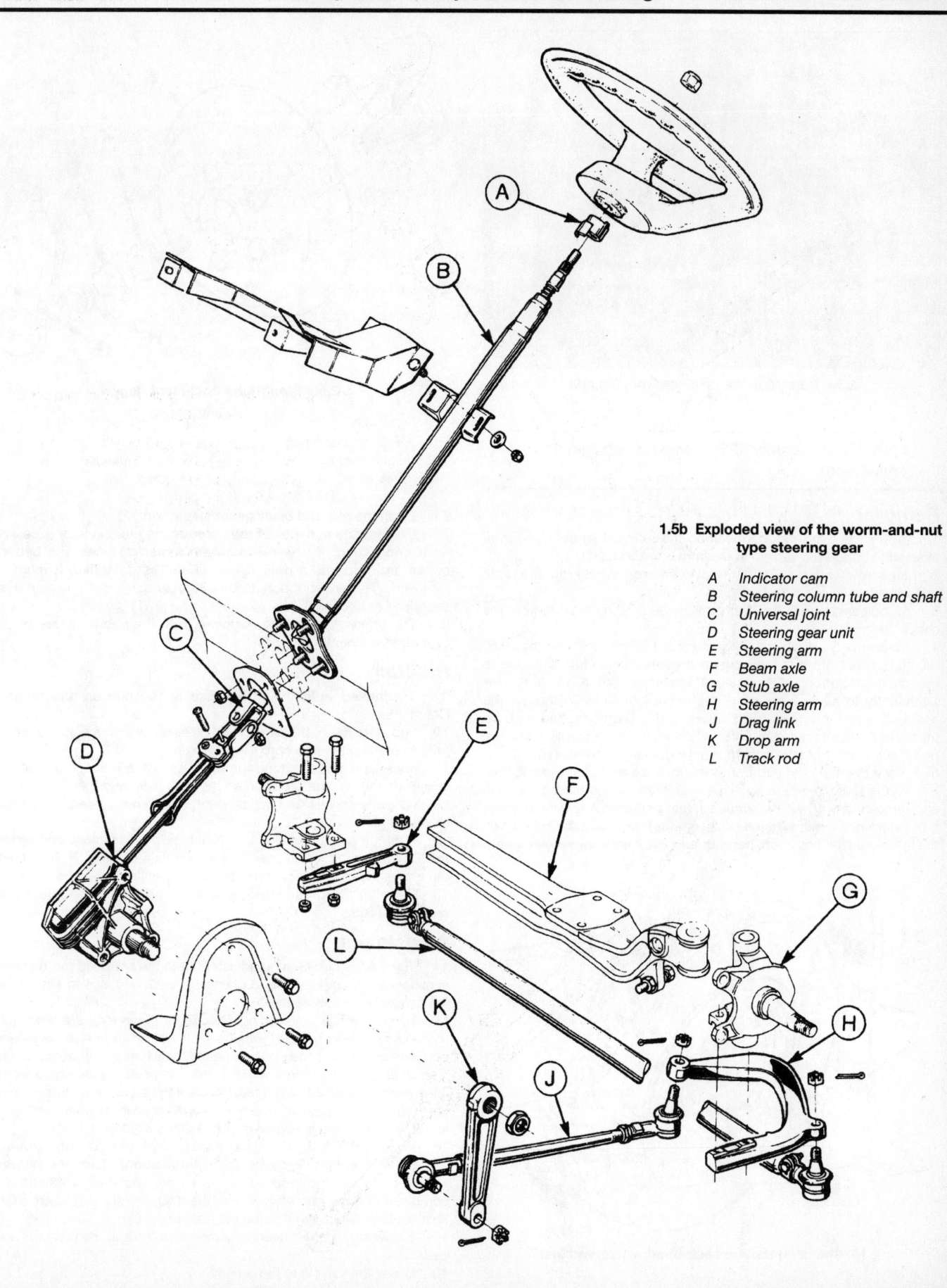

Chapter 10 Suspension and steering

10-7

1.5b Exploded view of the worm-and-nut type steering gear

- A   Indicator cam
- B   Steering column tube and shaft
- C   Universal joint
- D   Steering gear unit
- E   Steering arm
- F   Beam axle
- G   Stub axle
- H   Steering arm
- J   Drag link
- K   Drop arm
- L   Track rod

10

10-8 Chapter 10 Suspension and steering

2.5a Removing the dust cap from the hub

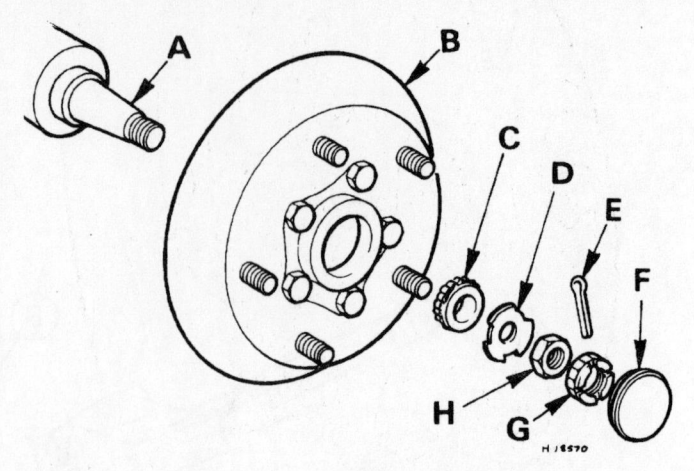

2.5b Front hub attachment details

A	Stub axle	E	Split pin
B	Hub/disc assembly	F	Dust cap
C	Outer bearing	G	Nut retainer
D	Washer	H	Hub nut

2 Front hub assembly (IFS) - removal, refitting and adjustment

Removal

1 Apply the handbrake, loosen off the relevant wheel nuts, then raise and support the vehicle at the front on axle stands.
2 Unscrew the nuts and remove the roadwheel on the side concerned.
3 Unbolt and detach the front brake hose location bracket from the shock absorber.
4 Undo the two bolts securing the brake caliper anchor bracket to the stub axle. Note that the upper bolt will not come fully out, due to the close proximity of the shock absorber, but it will unscrew sufficiently to allow removal of the anchor bracket. Withdraw the anchor bracket, complete with caliper and brake pads, and tie it up from a convenient place under the wheel arch. The hydraulic hose can be left attached, but take care to avoid stretching or twisting it.
5 Prise free the dust cap from the hub, wipe away the grease, then extract the split pin and remove the nut retainer. Unscrew the hub nut, and remove its washer. Withdraw the hub unit complete with its outer bearing from the stub axle **(see illustrations)**. Note that the hub nut on the left-hand side has a **left-hand thread** - ie it unscrews **clockwise**.

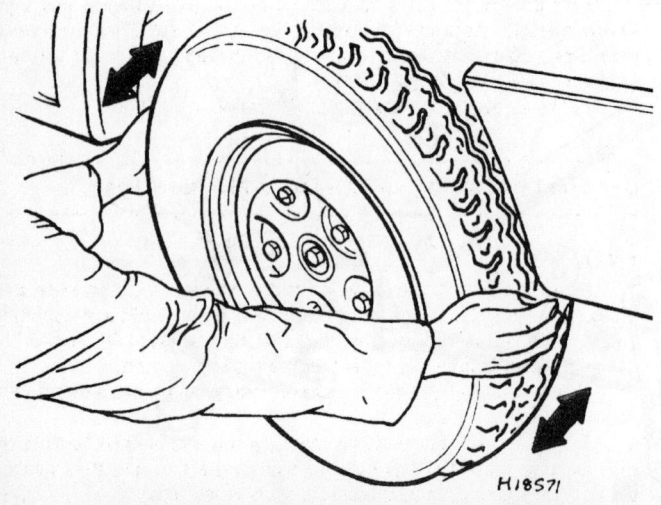

2.15 Checking the front hub bearings for endfloat

6 Clean the hub and bearings for inspection.
7 Examine the surfaces of the outer bearing for signs of excessive wear and pitting. If new bearings are required, renew the bearing cones and cups as a pair. If the oil seal is defective, it must be renewed. To renew the hub bearings and oil seal, proceed as described in Section 3.
8 The brake disc can be removed from the hub if necessary, as described in Chapter 9.

Refitting

9 If removed, refit the brake disc to the hub as described in Chapter 9.
10 Lubricate the hub bearings and oil seal lips with a suitable grease prior to refitting the hub onto the stub axle.
11 Take care when refitting the hub unit not to damage the oil seal lips. Slide the unit into position on the stub axle, and then fit the outer bearing cone, washer and adjuster nut, but do not tighten the nut fully at this stage.
12 Refit the anchor bracket and brake caliper assembly, and tighten the retaining bolts to the specified torque (see Chapter 9). Reconnect the brake hose to the location bracket on the shock absorber.
13 Refit the front roadwheel, and tighten the retaining nuts to the specified torque.

Adjustment

14 Tighten the hub bearing adjuster nut to the specified torque whilst simultaneously spinning the roadwheel in each direction to ensure that the bearings are fully seated.
15 Loosen off the adjuster nut by one flat, then rock the roadwheel by hand to further seat the bearings. Now hold the wheel at diagonally-opposite points, and then pull and push the wheel in and out to feel for a small amount of endfloat which should be present **(see illustration)**. If the required endfloat is not felt, unscrew the adjuster nut further, then try again. Do not apply a rocking motion to the wheel when testing for endfloat or a false impression may possibly be gained.
16 An accurate hub bearing endfloat check should now be made using a dial indicator gauge **(see illustration)**. Turn the bearing adjuster nut as required to achieve the specified endfloat. On completion, fit the nut retainer over the adjuster nut, and insert a new split pin to secure the nut in the set position.
17 Smear some wheel bearing grease over the nut, then refit the dust cap.
18 Lower the vehicle to the ground.

Chapter 10 Suspension and steering

2.16 Checking the front hub bearing endfloat using a dial gauge

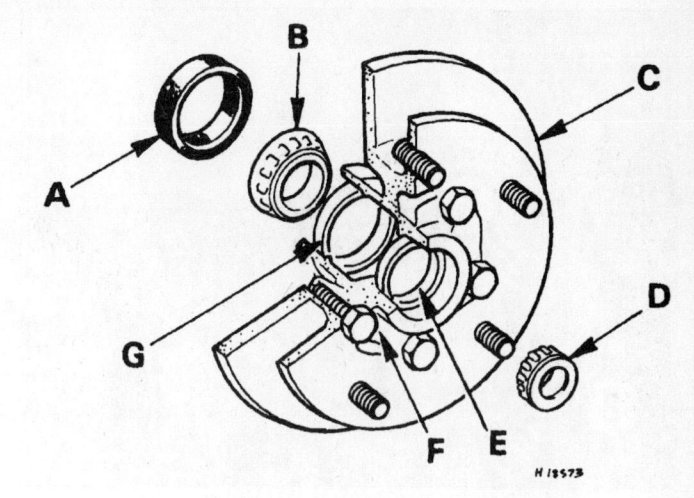

3.3 Exploded view of the front hub bearings

- A Oil seal
- B Inner bearing cone
- C Hub/disc assembly
- D Outer bearing cone
- E Outer bearing cup
- F Disc retaining bolt lock tab
- G Inner bearing cup

3 Front hub bearings (IFS) - renewal

Note: *Always renew both inner and outer bearing assemblies at the same time, and ensure that each bearing cup and cone is from the same manufacturer.*

1 Remove the front hub assembly from the stub axle as described in the previous Section.
2 Withdraw the inner oil seal from the hub by levering it out with a suitable screwdriver or similar tool.
3 Extract the inner and outer bearing cones **(see illustration)**.
4 Remove the bearing cups by driving them out of the hub using a suitable soft metal drift. Take care not to damage the bore of the hub during this operation.
5 Drive the new bearing cups into their housings using a suitable tube drift, whilst supporting the hub unit. Ensure that the cups are driven fully home and in contact with their abutment faces in the hub.
6 Lubricate the bearing cones and cups with wheel bearing grease, then fit the cones. The outboard cone can be left until later for fitting if required (after the hub is refitted onto the stub axle).
7 Drive a new oil seal into position in the hub on the inboard side.
8 Refit the front hub assembly as described in the previous Section, and adjust the endfloat.

4 Front stub axle (IFS) - removal and refitting

Removal

1 Remove the front hub assembly from the stub axle as described in Section 2.
2 Extract the split pin securing the track rod end balljoint to the stub axle steering arm. Unscrew the castellated retaining nut, then release the balljoint taper using a suitable balljoint separator.
3 Position a jack or axle stand under, and in contact with, the suspension lower arm.
4 Undo the four bolts, and detach the shock absorber from the stub axle **(see illustration)**.
5 Extract the split pin (where fitted), then unscrew the nut securing the lower arm balljoint to the stub axle. If the balljoint shank turns as the nut is being undone, push down hard on the stub axle. This will lock the taper of the balljoint shank, preventing rotation. On later models, a 9 mm Allen key can be inserted into the top of the balljoint shank to allow the shank to be held stationary as the nut is undone.
6 With the nut removed, release the balljoint taper using a suitable balljoint separator or two-legged puller, but take care to avoid damaging the balljoint dust cover.
7 Withdraw the stub axle from the balljoint shank and remove it from the vehicle.

Refitting

8 Where the lower arm balljoint is secured by a castellated nut and split pin, to facilitate fitment of the new split pin, turn the balljoint shank so that the split pin hole is at 90° to the stub axle spindle.
9 Ensure that the tapers are clean, then locate the stub axle over the balljoint shank.
10 Refit the retaining nut, and tighten to the specified torque while preventing rotation of the balljoint as previously described.
11 Where applicable, secure the retaining nut using a new split pin. If necessary, tighten the nut further to align the slots in the nut with the split pin hole in the balljoint shank.
12 Attach the shock absorber to the stub axle, refit the four bolts and washers, and tighten to the specified torque. Ensure that the brake caliper anchor bracket upper retaining bolt is in place in its hole before attaching the shock absorber. Remove the jack or axle stand under the suspension lower arm.
13 Refit the track rod end balljoint to the stub axle steering arm, then screw on the retaining nut and tighten to the specified torque. If necessary, tighten the nut further to align the slots in the nut with the split pin hole in the balljoint shank.
14 Refit the front hub assembly as described in Section 2.

5 Front coil spring - (IFS) - removal and refitting

Removal

1 Apply the handbrake, loosen off the wheel nuts, then raise and support the vehicle at the front end on axle stands. Allow a minimum clearance between the crossmember and the ground of 500 mm.
2 Remove the front roadwheel on the side concerned.
3 Unbolt and detach the front brake hose location bracket from the shock absorber.
4 Extract the split pin securing the track rod end balljoint to the stub axle steering arm. Unscrew the castellated retaining nut, then release the balljoint taper using a suitable balljoint separator.
5 Where applicable, disconnect the anti-roll bar from the suspension lower arm (see Section 10).

10•10 Chapter 10 Suspension and steering

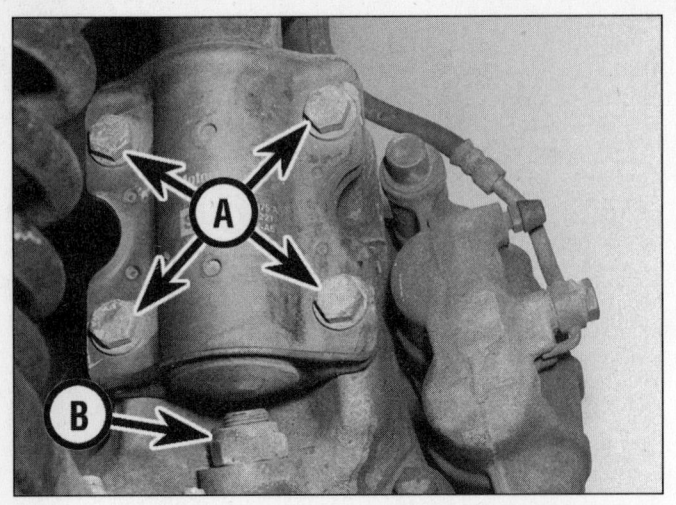

4.4 Shock absorber-to-stub axle retaining bolts (A) and lower arm balljoint-to-stub axle retaining nut (B)

6 Position a jack under the suspension arm, and raise it to just support the weight of the arm.
7 Unscrew the four bolts, and detach the shock absorber from the stub axle. Support the stub axle assembly, so as not to place undue strain on the lower arm balljoint.
8 Slowly lower the jack under the suspension arm, and allow the arm to drop. Remove the coil spring and its upper rubber pad.
9 Examine the upper rubber pad, and renew it if it shows any sign of damage or deterioration.

Refitting

10 Locate the rubber pad onto the top end of the coil spring, and locate the spring into position between the crossmember and the suspension arm. Engage the spring end into the slot in the pad. Ensure that the lower end of the spring engages in the recess in the suspension arm.
11 Raise the suspension arm using a suitable jack. Align the stub axle-to-shock absorber bolt holes, and insert the bolts. Tighten the bolts to the specified torque. Remove the jack under the suspension arm.
12 If applicable, reconnect the anti-roll bar link to the suspension arm (see Section 10).
13 Refit the track rod end balljoint to the stub axle steering arm, screw on the retaining nut and tighten to the specified torque. If necessary, tighten the nut further to align the slots in the nut with the split pin hole in the balljoint shank.
14 Reconnect the brake hose to the location bracket on the shock absorber.
15 Refit the roadwheel, and lower the vehicle to the ground.
16 Tighten the wheel nuts to the specified torque.

6 Front suspension lower arm (IFS) - removal and refitting

Removal

1 Remove the front coil spring on the side concerned, as described in the previous Section.
2 Straighten the retaining split pins in the bolts of the suspension arm to crossmember and front bracket, then withdraw the pins. Unscrew the retaining nuts, remove the washers, and withdraw the pivot bolts **(see illustrations)**.
3 Lower the suspension arm from its location, and remove it.
4 Check the condition of the suspension arm bushes, and renew them as described in Sections 7 and 8 as applicable if they show any signs of deterioration. Renew the suspension arm if there is any sign of damage or distortion.

6.2a Suspension lower arm to front bracket pivot bolt, nut, washer and bushes

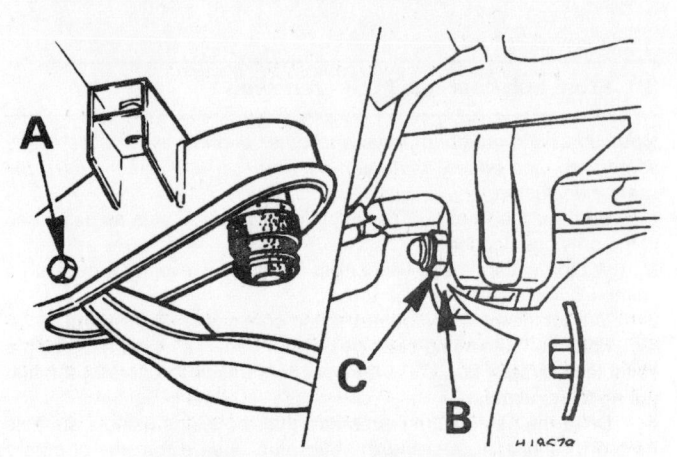

6.2b Suspension lower arm attachments

A Suspension arm-to-crossmember pivot bolt
B Dished washer (inset shows orientation)
C Suspension arm-to-front bracket retaining nut

Refitting

5 Engage the suspension arm in the crossmember and front bracket, and insert the pivot bolts. Fit the dished washer so that its convex face is towards the bush of the front bracket. Do not fully tighten the retaining nuts at this stage. They must be fully tightened when the vehicle is standing on its wheels.
6 Refit the front coil spring as described in the previous Section.
7 With the vehicle standing on its wheels, the lower suspension arm retaining nuts can now be tightened to the specified torque, and new split pins fitted to secure. When tightening the nut securing the rear pivot bolt to the crossmember, the following tightening sequence must be adopted. First tighten the nut to the clamping torque figure given in the Specifications, then slacken the nut fully. Tighten it again to the "snug" torque figure, then tighten further through the specified angle of rotation.

7 Front suspension lower arm bush (IFS) - renewal

1 Remove the front suspension lower arm as described in the previous Section.
2 If the suspension arm bush is worn or perished, it can be withdrawn from the suspension arm eye using a simple puller

Chapter 10 Suspension and steering

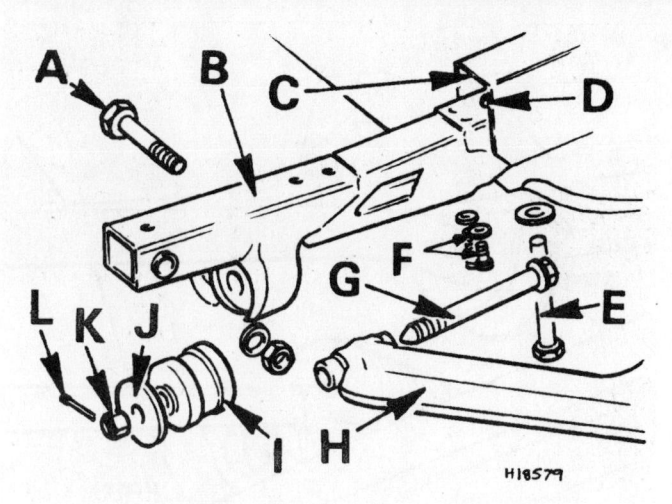

8.3 Front suspension lower arm and front bracket components

- A Front bracket-to-chassis securing bolt
- B Front bracket
- C Crossmember
- D Dowel
- E Front bracket/crossmember securing bolt
- F Torx bolts
- G Suspension lower arm-to-front bracket bolt
- H Suspension lower arm
- I Front bracket bush
- J Dished washer
- K Nut
- L Split pin

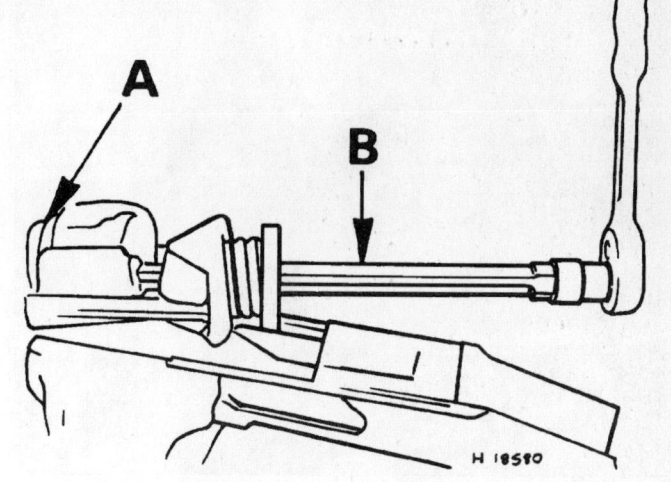

8.6 Front suspension lower arm bracket bush (A) removal using a two-legged puller (B)

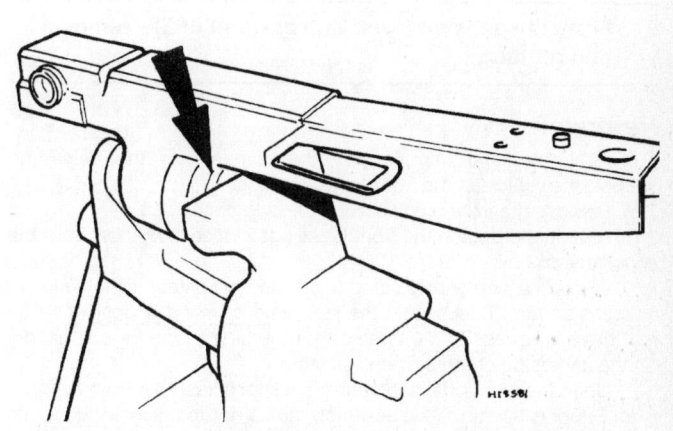

8.7 Press the lower arm bracket bush (arrowed) into position using a vice and spacer tube

comprising a metal tube of suitable diameter, (just less than that of the arm eye inside diameter), washers, and a long bolt and nut. Alternatively (and preferably), if a press is at hand, the bush can be pushed out using a suitable rod or a length of tube of suitable diameter.

3   If the suspension arm has been damaged or distorted in any way, it must be renewed.

4   To ease the fitting of the new bush into the suspension arm, lubricate the bush and the eye in the arm with engine oil, then press or draw (as applicable) the bush into the arm so that the bush lips are seated correctly.

5   Wipe off any excess oil, then refit the front suspension lower arm as described in the previous Section.

8 Front suspension lower arm bracket bush (IFS) - renewal

Note: *Before starting, it should be noted that if both the right-hand and left-hand side bracket bushes are to be renewed, remove and refit one bracket at a time. If both brackets are removed at the same time, the suspension geometry will be disturbed, and will require checking and possibly adjustment by a Ford dealer on completion.*

1   Apply the handbrake, then raise and support the front of the vehicle on axle stands.

2   Where applicable, disconnect the anti-roll bar from the suspension arm (see Section 10).

3   Unscrew and remove the front bracket-to-chassis securing nut and washer **(see illustration)**. Position a jack under the bracket and raise it to support its weight, then withdraw the bolt. The jack can then be lowered and removed.

4   Extract the split pin, and unscrew the lower arm-to-front bracket nut. Remove the washer and the bolt.

5   Unscrew and remove the two Torx bolts which secure the suspension bracket to the crossmember, then remove the retaining bolt. The front suspension bracket can now be detached and removed from the crossmember (on which it is located on dowels).

6   To extract the bush from the bracket, locate the bracket in a vice fitted with protective jaws so that the bush is uppermost, then press out the bush using a two-legged puller. Alternatively, draw the bush out using a long bolt, spacer tube, washers and nut **(see illustration)**.

7   Clean out the eye in the bush before inserting the new bush. Lubricate the eye and bush with engine oil, then press the bush into position using the vice and a spacer tube **(see illustration)**. Ensure that when fitted, the bush lips protrude each side of the bracket.

8   Refit the front bracket to the chassis, and reconnect the associated items in the reverse order of removal, but note the following additional points:

a) Ensure that the bracket is fully engaged with the location dowels before tightening the retaining nuts and bolts.

b) The suspension arm pivot washer must be fitted so that its convex side is facing the suspension bush. Do not tighten the retaining nut to the specified torque until after the vehicle is lowered and is free standing on its wheels. A new split pin can then be inserted to secure.

c) The crossmember-to-chassis bolt and the two Torx bolts should only be hand-tightened initially. The bracket-to-chassis bolts are then fitted, (jack under the bracket to align the bolt holes) and tightened. Remove the jack, and tighten the crossmember-to-chassis bolts to the specified torque.

d) Refer to Section 10 to reconnect the anti-roll bar (where fitted).

9.6 Lower arm balljoint-to-stub axle and lower arm retaining nuts

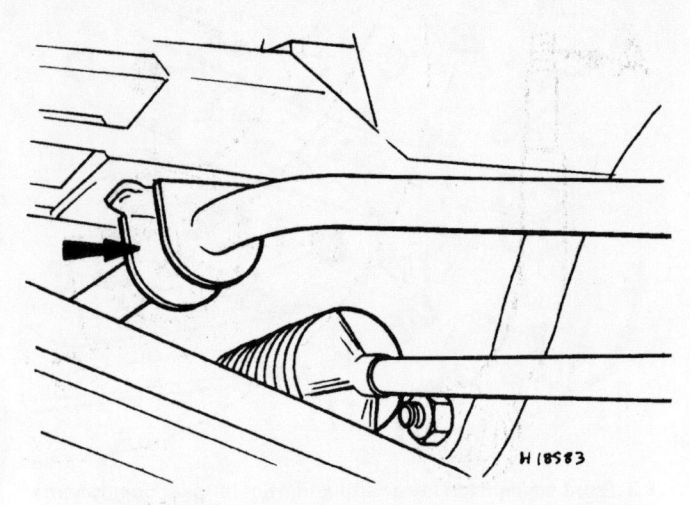

10.2a Anti-roll bar-to-crossmember mountings (arrowed)

9 Front suspension lower arm balljoint (IFS) - removal and refitting

Removal

1 Apply the handbrake, loosen off the wheel nuts, then raise and support the vehicle at the front on axle stands.
2 Remove the front roadwheel on the side concerned.
3 Unbolt and detach the front brake hose location bracket from the shock absorber.
4 Position a jack or axle stand under, and in contact with, the lower suspension arm. Ensure that the jack head or stand is positioned so that there is access to the three balljoint retaining nuts (or bolt heads) on the underside of the suspension arm.
5 Undo the four bolts, and detach the shock absorber from the stub axle. Support the stub axle assembly, so as not to place undue strain on the lower arm balljoint.
6 Extract the split pin (where fitted), then unscrew the nut securing the lower arm balljoint to the stub axle **(see illustration)**. If the balljoint shank turns as the nut is being undone, push down hard on the stub axle. This will lock the taper of the balljoint shank, preventing rotation. On later models, a 9 mm Allen key can be inserted into the top of the balljoint shank, to allow the shank to be held stationary as the nut is undone.
7 With the nut removed, release the balljoint taper using a suitable balljoint separator or two-legged puller, but take care to avoid damaging the balljoint dust cover. Lift the stub axle from the balljoint shank.
8 Unscrew the three retaining nuts, remove the bolts, and withdraw the balljoint stub from the suspension arm.

Refitting

9 Insert the balljoint stub into the suspension arm. Take care not to damage the balljoint dust cover when inserting the stub; If it is inserted too far, the cover can easily be damaged.
10 Refit the three balljoint retaining bolts, screw on the nuts and tighten to the specified torque.
11 Where the balljoint is secured to the stub axle by a castellated nut and split pin, to facilitate fitment of the new split pin, turn the balljoint shank so that the split pin hole is at 90° to the stub axle spindle.
12 Ensure that the tapers are clean, then locate the stub axle over the balljoint shank.
13 Refit the retaining nut, and tighten to the specified torque while preventing rotation of the balljoint as previously described.
14 Where applicable, secure the retaining nut using a new split pin. If necessary, tighten the nut further to align the slots in the nut with the

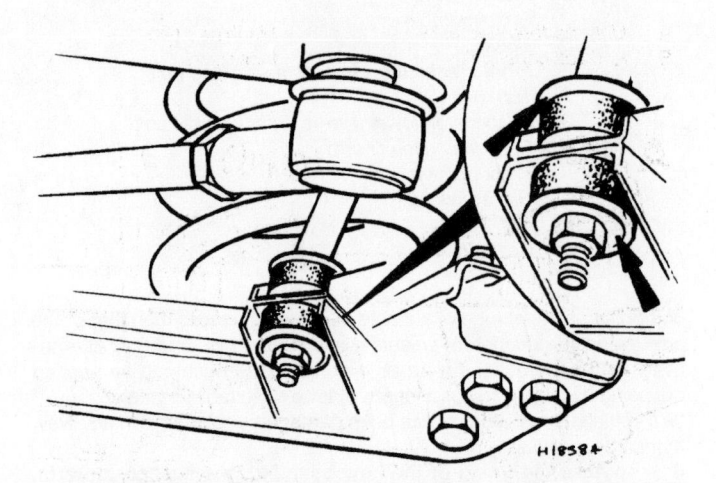

10.2b Anti-roll bar link rod and bushes. Note the dished washers (arrowed) fitted with their convex sides toward the bushes

split pin hole in the balljoint shank.
15 Attach the shock absorber to the stub axle, then refit the four bolts and tighten to the specified torque. Remove the jack or axle stand under the suspension lower arm.
16 Reconnect the brake hose to the location bracket on the shock absorber.
17 Refit the roadwheel, and lower the vehicle to the ground.
18 Tighten the wheel nuts to the specified torque.

10 Front anti-roll bar (IFS) - removal and refitting

Removal

1 The anti-roll bar and its connecting link rods are best removed and refitted with the vehicle free standing, therefore if possible, position it over an inspection pit, or run it onto ramps at the front end.
2 To remove the anti-roll bar, undo the retaining bolts and detach the bar from the crossmember on each side, then undo the retaining nuts and detach it from the suspension arms (complete with link rods) **(see illustrations)**.
3 The link rods can be removed from the anti-roll bar if necessary, by extracting the spring clip at each end, then tapping them off using a drift. Alternatively, use a small puller. Refit the link rods so that the two

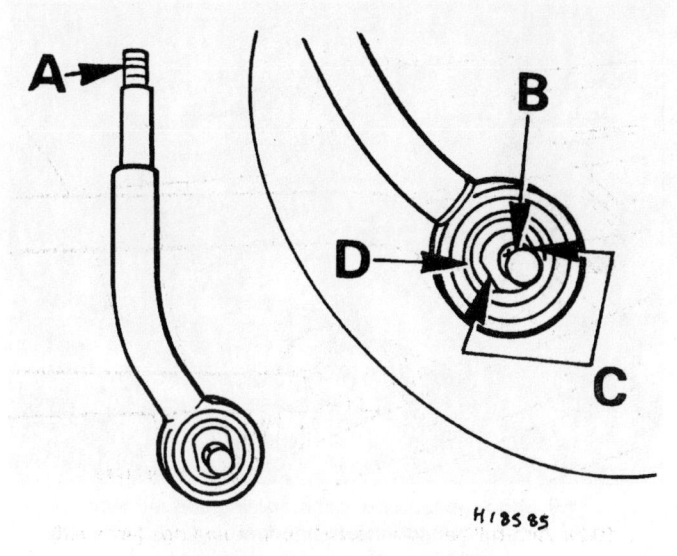

Chapter 10 Suspension and steering   10•13

10.3 Anti-roll bar link rod details

- A Link rod threaded end
- B Anti-roll bar shank
- C Machined flats
- D Inner bush

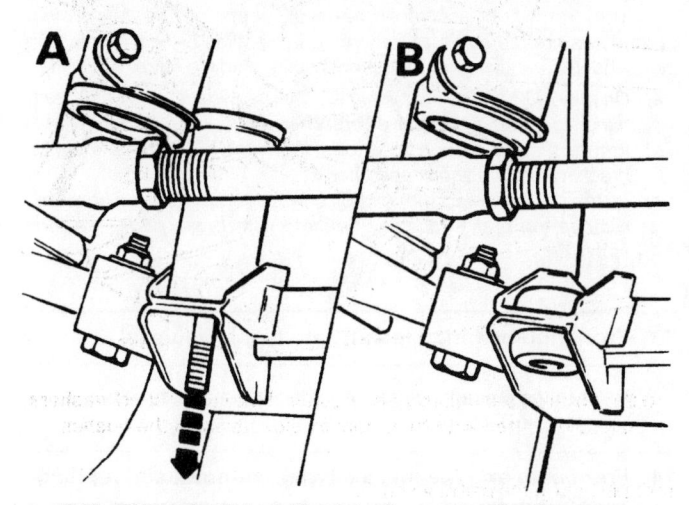

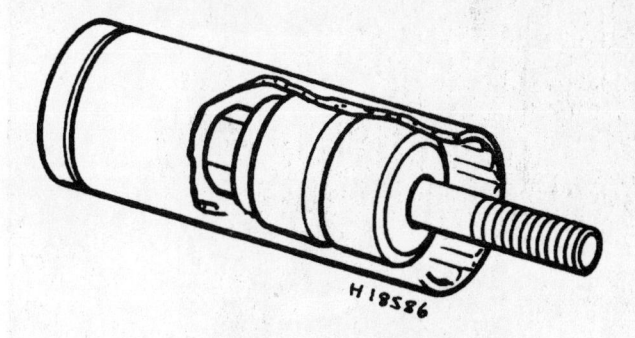

10.5a Link rod bush assembly located in fitting tube

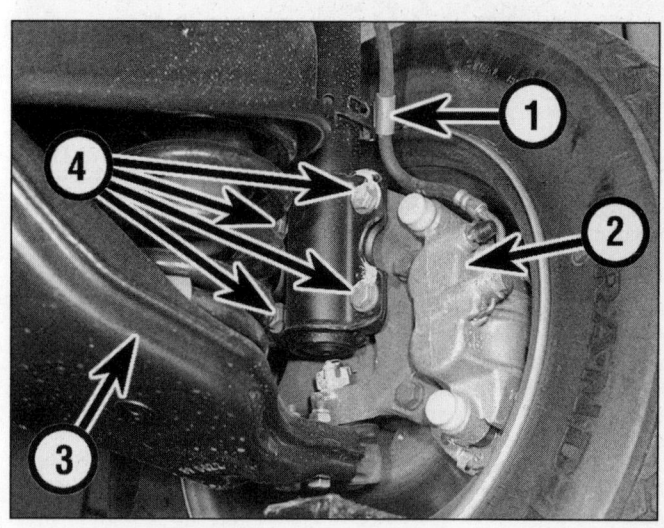

10.5b Fitting the link rod bush to the suspension lower arm

- A Fitting bolt
- B Bush fully fitted

11.2 Front shock absorber and related component attachments

1. Brake hose location bracket
2. Brake caliper
3. Suspension lower arm
4. Shock absorber-to-stub axle retaining bolts

machined flats on the anti-roll bar are approximately in line with the threaded end of the link rod, and secure with the spring clips **(see illustration)**.

4 Inspect the anti-roll bar insulator rubbers and link rod bushes, and renew them if they are perished or worn. Cut or prise free the link rod bush from the lower suspension arm.

5 To fit the link rod bush to the suspension arm, first lubricate the bush and its location in the suspension arm with washing-up liquid, then insert an M8 x 70 mm bolt fitted with a flat washer into the bush. Locate the bush and bolt into the bore of a 25 mm extra-deep socket, or a tube of suitable dimensions **(see illustration)**. Insert the bolt through the hole in the suspension arm, and then pull on the bolt using a suitable self-gripping wrench or similar, and draw the bush through the eye and into the arm. Keep the socket (or tube) flush against the arm whilst pulling the bush through. When the bush is inserted, remove the bolt and then renew the bush on the opposite side of the vehicle in the same manner, (it is not good practice to renew the bush on one side only) **(see illustration)**.

6 To renew the insulator rubbers, first check that the left-hand side insulator engages on the protruding locator on the anti-roll bar. Locate the right-hand side insulator onto the bar, and ensure that both insulators are fitted with their joints to the rear.

Refitting

7 Locate the anti-roll bar, and engage the insulator bracket lugs into their slots in the crossmember each side. Locate the retaining bolts, and tighten them to the specified torque.

8 Refit the anti-roll bar link rods each side, ensuring that the dished washers are fitted with their convex side towards the bushes. Refit and tighten the retaining nuts.

11 Front shock absorber (IFS) - removal and refitting

Removal

1 Apply the handbrake, loosen off the front wheel nuts, then raise the front of the vehicle and support it on axle stands. Remove the roadwheel on the side concerned.

2 Undo the retaining bolt, and release the brake hose location bracket from the front shock absorber **(see illustration)**.

3 Position a jack under the suspension lower arm, and raise it to just support the weight of the arm.

10-14 Chapter 10 Suspension and steering

11.4 Shock absorber upper mounting and retaining nut on pre-1992 model year vehicles

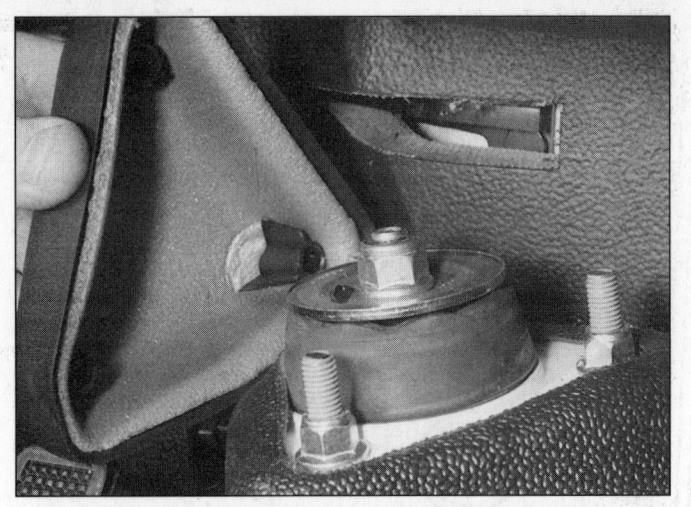

11.5 Shock absorber upper mounting and retaining nut on later models

4 On pre-1992 model year vehicles, prise free the rubber retaining ring from the shock absorber top cover inside the cab, then separate and remove the cover half-sections **(see illustration)**. Unscrew and remove the shock absorber upper retaining nut, then withdraw the washer and retainer.
5 On later models, remove the shock absorber cover from inside the cab **(see illustration)**. Unscrew the shock absorber upper retaining nut, then withdraw the dished washer. Hold the shock absorber piston with a 6 mm Allen key while undoing the retaining nut.
6 Unscrew the four bolts, and detach the shock absorber from the stub axle. Support the stub axle assembly, so as not to place undue strain on the lower arm balljoint.
7 If the shock absorber unit is leaking, or defective in any way, it must be renewed (it cannot be repaired). To check the action of the shock absorber, mount it in a vice, and then operate the piston rod a few times through its full stroke. If the action is noticeably weak or there is an uneven resistance, the unit is in need of replacement. It is advisable to renew both front shock absorbers at the same time, or the handling characteristics of the vehicle could well be adversely affected.
8 Before refitting the shock absorber, check the condition of the insulator bush in the body. If perished or worn, it should be renewed.
9 On pre-1992 model year vehicles, to remove the insulator bush, prise it free (failing this, carefully cut it out). Clean the aperture in the body panel prior to fitting the replacement. On later models, undo the three retaining nuts, and remove the complete insulator assembly.

Refitting

10 If the insulator was removed on pre-1992 model year vehicles, lubricate the new insulator and the location bore with washing-up liquid, then insert the insulator by pressing and twisting it into position. On later models, locate the insulator assembly, and secure with the three nuts tightened to the specified torque.
11 Smear the inside of the insulator and the shock absorber upper end with washing-up liquid to ease fitting, then insert it up through the insulator and fit the retainer, washer and nut (early models), or dished washer and nut (later models).
12 Align the lower mounting holes of the shock absorber with the corresponding holes in the stub axle, and then insert the retaining bolts.
13 Tighten the upper retaining nut to the specified torque. Refit the upper cover, and secure with the retaining ring (where fitted).
14 Tighten the four shock absorber-to-stub axle retaining bolts to the specified torque. Remove the jack or axle stand under the suspension lower arm.
15 Reconnect the brake hose location bracket to the shock absorber.
16 Refit the roadwheel, and lower the vehicle to the ground.
17 Tighten the wheel nuts to the specified torque.

12 Front hub assembly (beam axle type) - removal, refitting and adjustment

The front hub assembly removal, refitting and adjustment procedures are the same as described in Section 2, for vehicles with independent front suspension, but bearing in mind the following points:
a) On pre-1992 model year vehicles, the roadwheel bolts on the left-hand side have a **left-hand thread** - ie they unscrew **clockwise**.
b) Ignore the instruction to unbolt the front brake hose location bracket from the shock absorber.
c) Instead of removing the anchor bracket, undo the two bolts and remove the brake caliper, complete with brake pads, from the stub axle.

13 Front hub bearings (beam axle type) - renewal

Refer to the procedures contained in Section 3 of this Chapter.

14 Front stub axle (beam axle type) - removal and refitting

Removal

1 Remove the front hub assembly as described in Section 12.
2 Unscrew the nuts, and remove the steering arm-to-stub axle retaining bolts. Remove the steering arm from the stub axle **(see illustration)**.
3 Unscrew and remove the kingpin upper and lower grease nipples and cap nuts **(see illustration)**.
4 Drive out the kingpin retaining cotter pin from the beam axle, and remove the kingpin. You may have to use a suitable press or drift to extract the pin, which may in turn entail removal of the beam axle.
5 Remove the stub axle and shim.
6 Assuming that the stub axle is being overhauled, remove the grease seal from the upper bore, and push out the stub axle bottom bearing.
7 Remove the opposite stub axle in the same manner, but keep the respective right- and left-hand components separate.
8 Do not remove the steering lock stop-bolts unless absolutely necessary, as these are adjusted for position, and will require special tooling to reset them when they are refitted. This will have to be done by a Ford dealer.
9 Thoroughly clean the stub axle beam axle locations with paraffin, and dry them with a lint-free cloth. Examine both for signs of distortion or

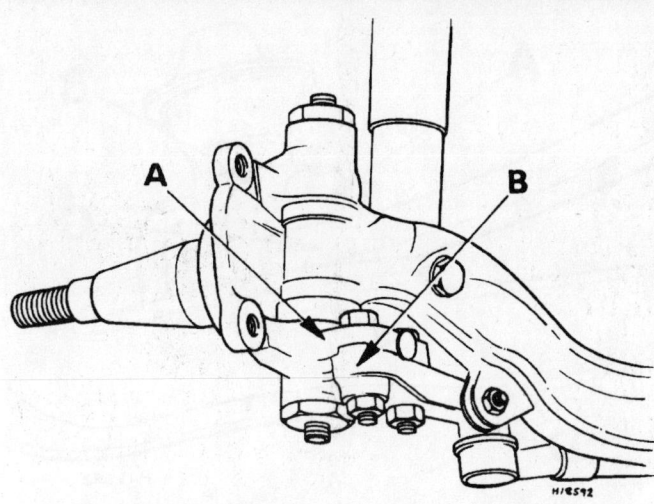

Chapter 10 Suspension and steering

10-15

14.2 Stub axle (A) and steering arm (B) showing retaining bolts

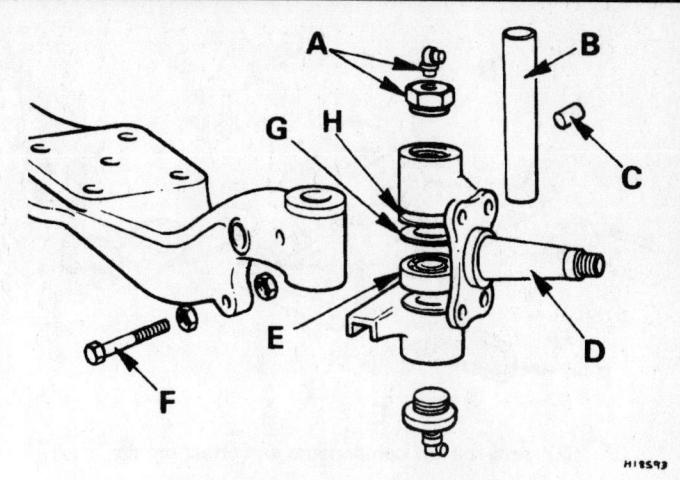

14.3 Exploded view of the stub axle

A   Grease nipple and cap nut   E   Bottom bearing
B   Kingpin   F   Steering lock stop-bolt
C   Cotter pin   G   Shim
D   Stub axle   H   Grease seal

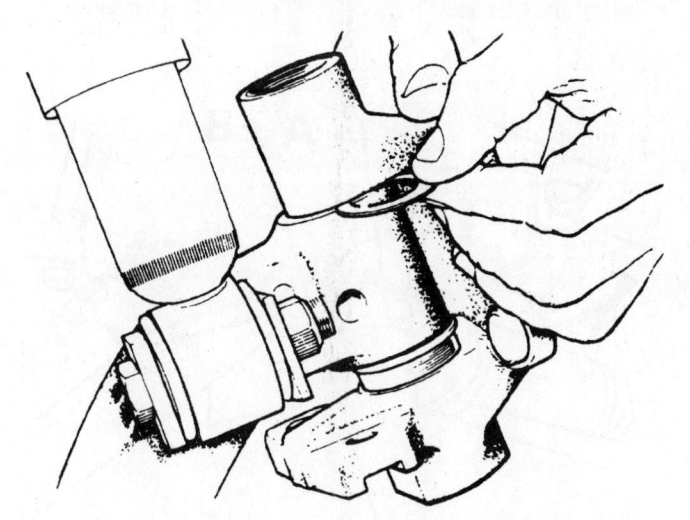

14.11 Select and insert a new shim of the required thickness

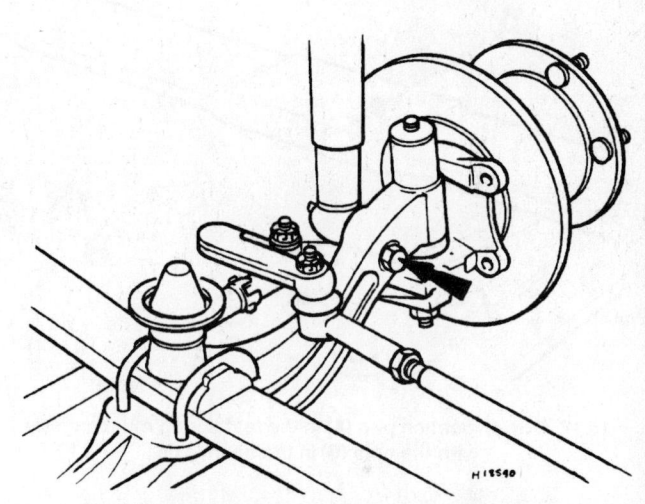

15.4 Shock absorber-to-stub axle retaining bolt

damage. If in doubt regarding the condition of the beam axle or stub axle, have your Ford dealer make an inspection and renew as necessary.
10 Assuming that the kingpin is to be renewed, the stub axle pivot bushes will also have to be renewed. As the bush removal and refitting procedure requires the use of specialised equipment, their replacement is best entrusted to your Ford dealer, who will also ream the newly fitted bushes to suit the kingpin.

Refitting

11 With the new bushes fitted and the lower bearing and grease seal in place, locate the stub axle unit to the beam axle. Select and insert a new shim of the required thickness between the upper face of the beam axle eye and the bottom face of the upper stub axle eye **(see illustration)**. Measure the required shim thickness using a feeler blade, and select a shim which will provide the specified stub axle-to-beam axle clearance.
12 Lightly smear the kingpin with grease, then push it downwards just past the shim location. Insert the shim, then push the kingpin back up and align the cut-away section with the cotter pin hole in the axle.
13 Insert a new cotter pin, and drive it home so that it is flush with the axle case.
14 Refit the upper and lower cap nuts and grease nipples. Lubricate the kingpin at each end, and then check its turning action. If it is excessively tight, a thinner shim is probably required. If it is excessively loose in its feel, it may need a thicker shim. Recheck the clearance

between the stub axle and the beam axle.
15 Refit the steering arm to the stub axle, and tighten the retaining nuts to the specified torque.
16 Refit the hub assembly as described in Section 12, and check/adjust the endfloat as given.

15 Front beam axle - removal and refitting

Removal

1 The front beam axle can be removed in a fully-assembled state or partially dismantled; if the kingpins are seized, it will be advantageous to remove the beam first, and press them out with a hydraulic press.
2 Apply the handbrake, then loosen off the front wheel nuts, (note that the nuts on the left-hand side have a **left-hand thread** - ie they unscrew **clockwise**). Raise and support the vehicle at the front on axle stands placed beneath the chassis side members. Support the beam axle with a trolley jack and stands.
3 Unscrew the nuts and remove the front roadwheels.
4 Unscrew and remove the nuts securing each front shock absorber to the beam axle. Note that the bolts are withdrawn from the front **(see illustration)**.

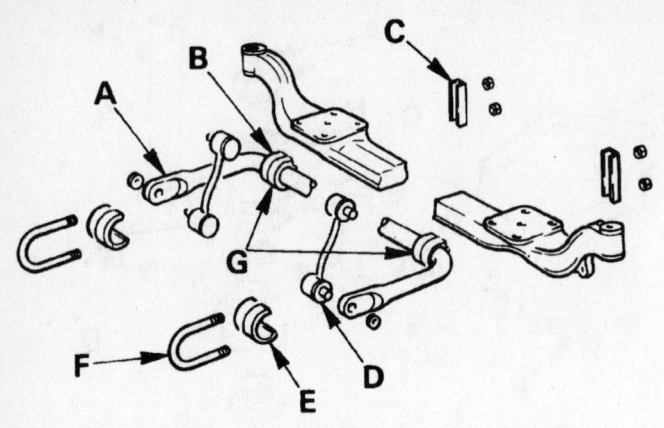

15.7 Anti-roll bar components and attachments

A Anti-roll bar	E Insulator clamp
B Insulator	F U-bolt
C Anchor plate	G Insulator inner faces
D Link	for dimension setting

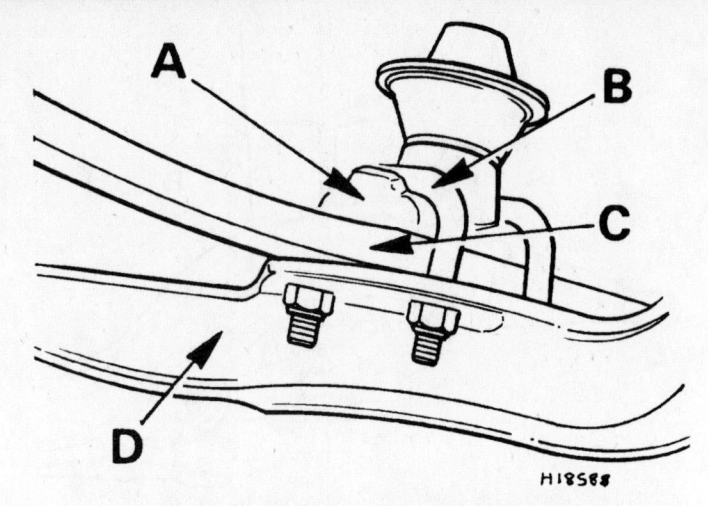

15.8 Beam axle-to-spring attachments

A Top plate	C Leaf spring
B U-bolt	D Beam axle

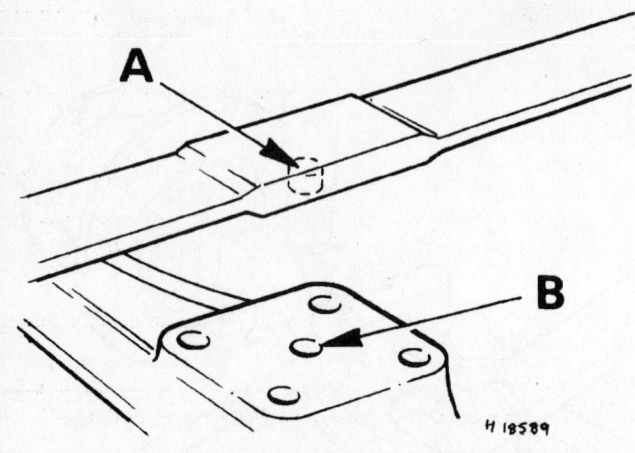

15.12 Dowel location peg (A) in the leaf spring must engage with the hole (B) in the beam axle

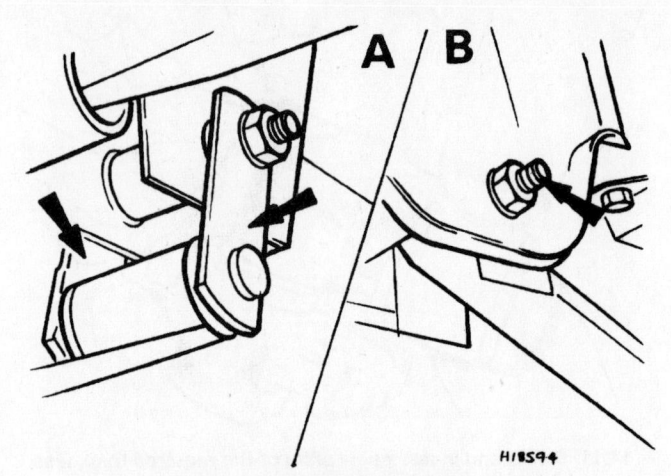

16.3 Leaf spring shackle plates at rear of spring (A) and eye-bolt (B) at the front

5 Extract the split pin, then unscrew the castellated nut securing the drag link to the stub axle steering arm. Release the drag link using a suitable balljoint separator.

6 Unscrew the brake caliper retaining bolts and withdraw the calipers, complete with brake pads, from the stub axles. The hydraulic hoses can be left attached to the calipers, but suspend or support each caliper so that the hose is not stretched or deformed.

7 Where applicable, unscrew the retaining nuts and remove the anti-roll bar anchor plates, clamps and U-bolts **(see illustration)**.

8 Unscrew the retaining nuts, and remove the axle to spring U-bolts and top plates. Ensure that the axle is well-supported each side before detaching the U-bolts **(see illustration)**.

9 Enlist the aid of an assistant to help steady the axle, then lower and withdraw the unit from under front of the vehicle.

10 If required, the beam axle can be further dismantled by referring to the appropriate Sections of this Chapter.

11 If distortion of the axle is suspected, it should be checked by a suitably-equipped garage, and renewed if necessary.

Refitting

12 Refitting is a reversal of removal, but the following additional points should be noted:

a) When raising the axle into position, engage it with the dowel location peg in the spring **(see illustration)**, then fit and tighten the U-bolts and nuts to the specified torque, (the nuts should be tightened in three stages, as specified at the start of this Chapter).

b) Ensure that the shock absorber retaining bolts are fitted with their heads to the front.

c) If an anti-roll bar is fitted, set the insulators 620 mm apart, measured from the inner face of each insulator, and an equal distance from the anti-roll bar cranked ends.

d) Tighten all fastenings to the specified torque, then further to the nearest split pin hole alignment position (where applicable). Always use new split pins to secure.

16 Front beam axle leaf spring - removal and refitting

Removal

1 Apply the handbrake, then raise and support the vehicle at the front on axle stands placed beneath the chassis side members. Support the beam axle with a trolley jack and stands.

2 Unscrew and remove the U-bolt nuts, then slowly lower the jack under the axle. Disengage the U-bolts and top plate from the spring. The jack should be lowered to the point where the axle/spring location dowel is clear.

3 Unscrew and remove the self-locking nuts from the spring shackles, then, using a soft metal drift, drive out the shackle pins and plates, and extract the rubber bushes **(see illustration)**.

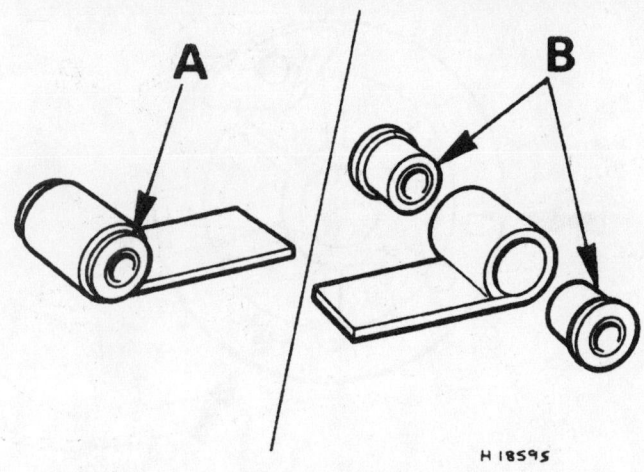

Chapter 10 Suspension and steering

10-17

16.6 Leaf spring eye bush (A) and rear rubber bushes (B)

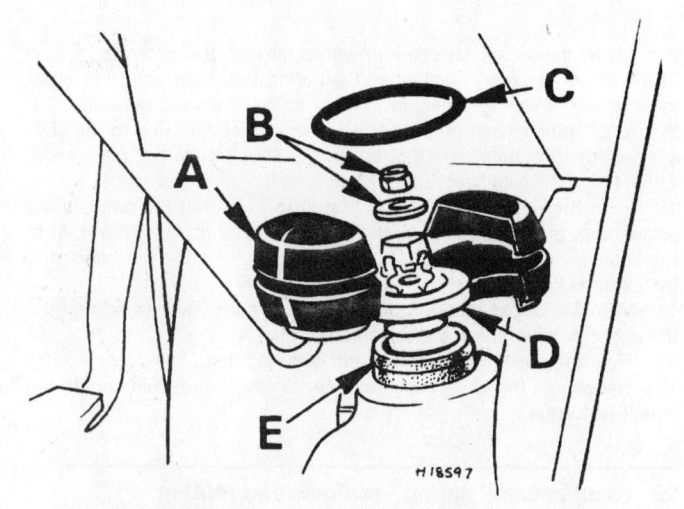

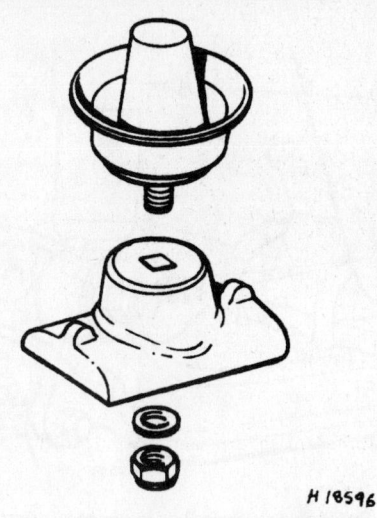

17.2 Bump stop and top plate components

19.1 Front shock absorber top mounting and cover

A Cover half-sections
B Nut and washer
C Rubber retaining ring
D Upper retainer
E Insulator

4 Unscrew and remove the front mounting nut and washer, and drive out the bolt whilst supporting the spring.
5 Lift the spring away from the axle and mountings.
6 Examine the front and rear mounting bushes, and check the condition of the shackle, U-bolts and bump stop **(see illustration)**. Renew any worn or damaged components.
7 The spring eye bush can be renewed by pressing, drawing or cutting out the old bush, according to the facilities available. Whatever method is employed to remove and refit the bush, take care not to damage the spring eye.
8 When fitting the new bush, ensure that when installed there is an equal amount of bush protruding each side of the spring eye. Support the spring, to avoid the possibility of damage and distortion.

Refitting

9 Refitting is a reversal of removal, but the following additional points must be noted:
a) Assemble the spring to the chassis, but do not tighten the shackle bolts to the specified torque until after the vehicle is lowered to the ground, and is standing on its wheels.
b) When assembling the spring to the axle, ensure that the location dowel engages in the hole in the axle platform.
c) Centralise the top plate on the spring before fitting the U-bolts and tightening the retaining nuts to the specified torque.

17 Front suspension bump stop (beam axle type) - removal and refitting

Removal

1 Proceed as described in paragraphs 1 and 2 in the previous Section, and remove the top plate from the spring.
2 Unscrew and remove the bump stop retaining nut and washer, then remove the bump stop from the top plate **(see illustration)**.

Refitting

3 Refitting is a reversal of removal. Tighten the bump stop retaining nut to the specified torque.

18 Front anti-roll bar (beam axle type) - removal and refitting

Removal

1 Apply the handbrake, then raise and support the vehicle at the front on axle stands placed beneath the chassis side members.
2 Unscrew the anti-roll bar link-to-chassis mounting nuts.
3 Unscrew the retaining nuts, and detach the anchor plates, the insulator clamps and the U-bolts. Disconnect the anti-roll bar, and remove it from the vehicle.
4 Renew the insulators and any other items which are worn or damaged **(see illustration 15.7)**.

Refitting

5 Refitting is a reversal of removal, but note the following additional points:
a) When refitting the anti-roll bar insulators, they must be positioned 620 mm apart. Measure this distance from the inner face of each insulator. When set, the insulators must be equally distanced each side from the cranked ends of the anti-roll bar.
b) Tighten the retaining nuts to the specified torque.

19 Front shock absorber (beam axle type) - removal and refitting

Removal

1 Working within the cab, prise free the rubber retaining ring from the shock absorber top cover, then separate and remove the cover half-sections **(see illustration)**.

10•18 Chapter 10 Suspension and steering

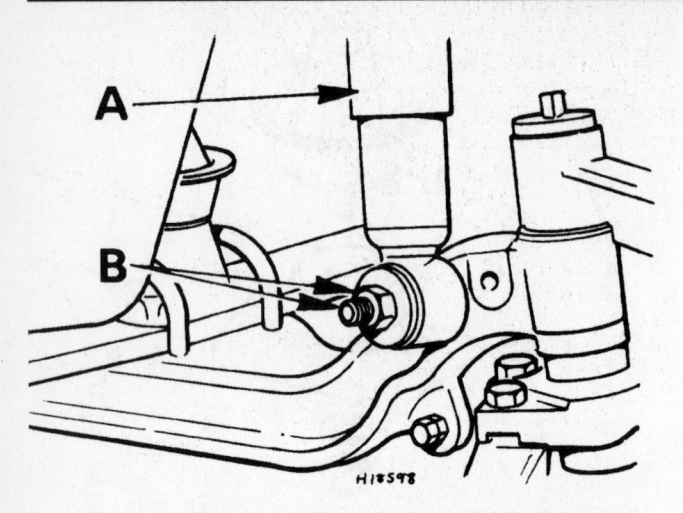

19.3 Front shock absorber lower mounting to beam axle

A Shock absorber
B Nut, washer and bolt

2 Unscrew and remove the shock absorber upper retaining nut and washer, then remove the upper retainer (and insulator if necessary).
3 Working underneath the front end of the vehicle, unscrew and remove the shock absorber bottom end retaining nut and washer. Withdraw the bolt, and then lower and remove the shock absorber unit **(see illustration)**.
4 If the shock absorber unit is leaking or is defective in any way, it must be renewed. To check the action of a shock absorber, mount it in a vice and operate the piston rod a few times. If the action is weak or there is an uneven resistance, it is in need of renewal. It is advisable to renew both front shock absorbers at the same time. The renewal of one only can adversely affect the steering and handling.
5 The insulator bush should be inspected for wear in the bottom eye. If necessary, this can be pressed or driven out for renewal. Smear the new bush with washing-up liquid to ease fitting, then press it into position so that it protrudes an equal amount each side of the eye.
6 If the upper insulator is still in position in the body, inspect it for signs of perishing or excessive wear. To remove it from the panel, prise or if necessary, cut it free.

Refitting

7 Clean the upper insulator aperture in the body, then lubricate the new insulator with washing-up liquid, and insert it by pressing and twisting it into position.
8 Locate the lower retainer over the top of the shock absorber unit, engaging the "D"-shaped hole over the flat on the piston rod.

20.3 Rear spring and shackle

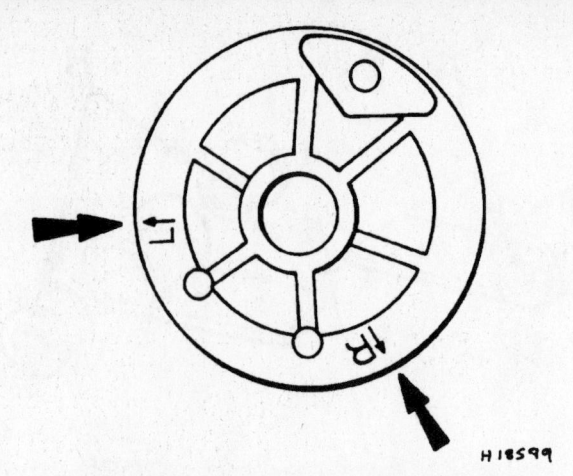

19.10 Shock absorber upper retainer positional marks ("L" and "R")

9 Insert the shock absorber upwards through the body panel, and fit the upper retainer, washer and securing nut. Lubricate the upper retainer with washing-up liquid to ease fitting. It should be noted that the upper retainer can only be fitted in one direction, due to the "D"-shaped location hole, and the flat on the shock absorber piston rod. When fitting the retaining nut, hand-tighten it only at this stage.
10 Turn the upper retainer and piston rod, so that the appropriate arrow mark on the top face of the retainer points towards the front of the vehicle - "R" for the right-hand side, or "L" for the left-hand side **(see illustration)**.
11 With the upper retainer and piston rod correctly aligned, tighten the upper retainer nut to the specified torque.
12 Refit the cover half-sections and securing ring.
13 Reconnect the lower mounting, and tighten its retaining nut to the specified torque.

20 Rear axle leaf spring - removal and refitting

Removal

1 Chock the front wheels, then loosen off the rear wheel nuts on the side concerned. Raise and support the vehicle at the rear on axle stands placed beneath the chassis side members. Support the rear axle with a trolley jack.
2 Unscrew the nuts and remove the rear roadwheel(s).
3 Unscrew and remove the spring shackle retaining nuts, and withdraw the plate and shackle pins, using a soft metal drift as necessary **(see illustration)**.
4 Unscrew and remove the front mounting retaining nut and washer, and drive out the mounting bolt with a soft metal drift **(see illustration)**.
5 Unscrew and remove the U-bolt nuts, and detach the U-bolts together with the clamp plate; the rear spring can now be lifted from the rear axle and withdrawn from beneath the vehicle **(see illustration)**.
6 Examine the front and rear mounting bushes, and check the condition of the shackle U-bolts and spring leaves; renew any faulty components. Always renew the self-locking nuts once they have been removed.

Refitting

7 Refitting is a reversal of removal, but note the following additional points:
 a) The shackle pins and nuts must not be fully tightened until after the vehicle is lowered to the ground.
 b) When fitting the spring to the axle, engage the centre locating bolt fully before fitting the U-bolts and clamp plates

Chapter 10 Suspension and steering

10-19

20.4 Rear spring front mounting bolt

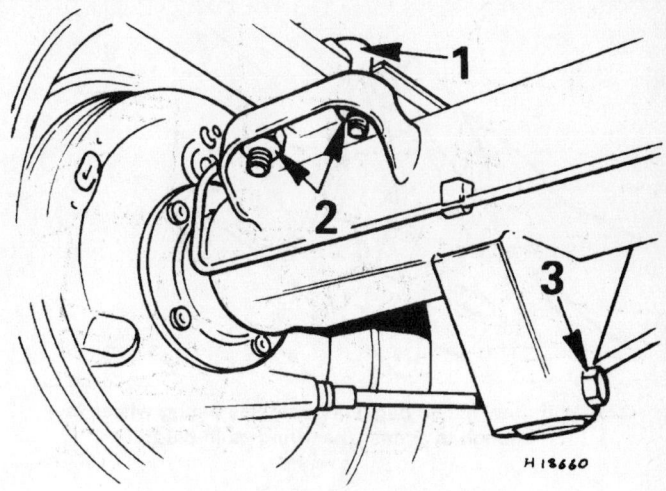

20.5 Rear spring-to-axle attachments

1 U-bolt
2 U-bolt nuts
3 Shock absorber lower mounting bolt

c) Tighten all nuts and bolts to the specified torque.
d) On models with a load-apportioning valve in the braking system, have the setting checked by a Ford dealer at the earliest opportunity.

21 Rear shock absorber - removal and refitting

Removal

1 Chock the front wheels, then raise and support the vehicle at the rear on axle stands placed beneath the chassis side members.
2 Undo the retaining nut, and withdraw the shock absorber lower mounting bolt **(see illustration)**.
3 Unscrew the upper mounting bolt to the underbody, and then remove the shock absorber **(see illustration)**.
4 To test the shock absorber for efficiency, grip the upper or lower mounting eye in a vice, and then pump the piston repeatedly through its full stroke. If the resistance is weak or is felt to be uneven, the shock absorber is defective and must be renewed. It must also be renewed if it is leaking fluid. It is advisable to renew both rear shock absorbers at the same time, or the handling characteristics of the vehicle could be adversely affected.

Refitting

5 Refitting is a reversal of removal. Ensure that the mounting bolts are tightened securely.

22 Steering wheel - removal and refitting

Removal

Models without air bag

1 Centralise the front roadwheels so that they are in the straight-ahead position. Prise free the centre pad from the steering wheel **(see illustration)**.
2 Unscrew the steering wheel retaining nut, then pull free the steering wheel from the shaft. The wheel is located on the shaft by a master spline.

Models with air bag

Warning: *Handle the air bag unit with extreme care as a precaution against personal injury, and always hold it with the cover facing away from the body. If in doubt concerning any proposed work involving the air bag unit or its control circuitry, consult a Ford dealer or other qualified specialist.*

3 Disconnect the battery negative lead.
4 **Warning:** *Before proceeding, wait a minimum of 15 minutes, as a precaution against accidental firing of the air bag unit. This period ensures that any stored energy in the back-up capacitor is dissipated.*
5 Turn the steering wheel as necessary so that one of the air bag unit retaining bolts becomes accessible from the rear of the steering

21.2 Rear shock absorber, showing lower mounting bolt (arrowed)

21.3 Rear shock absorber upper mounting to the underbody

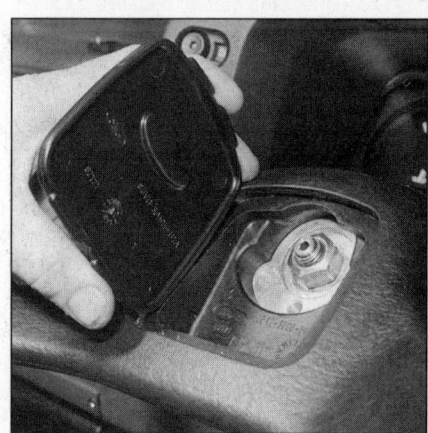

22.1 Prise free the centre pad from the steering wheel, then unscrew the steering wheel retaining nut

10

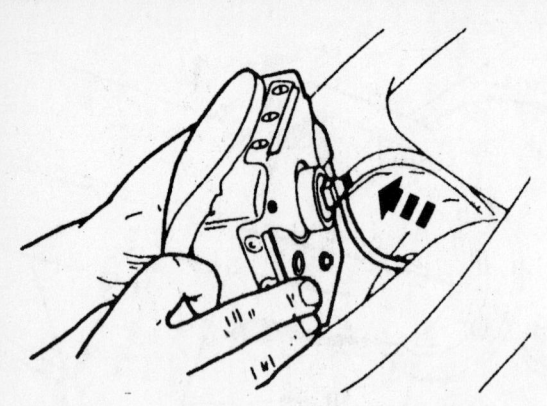

10•20 Chapter 10 Suspension and steering

22.6 Withdraw the air bag unit from the steering wheel, far enough to access the wiring multi-plug

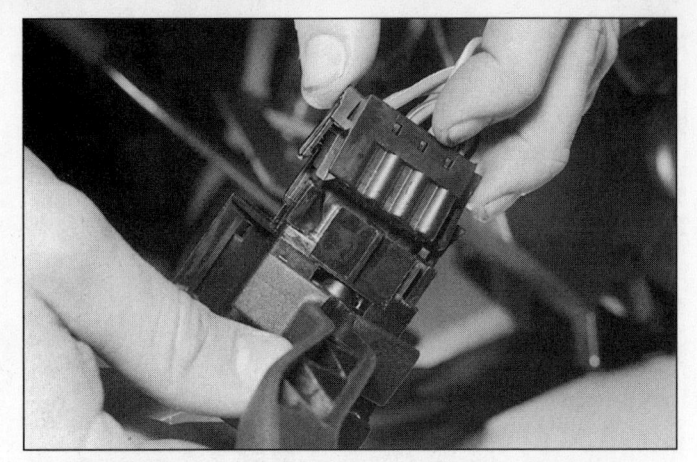

23.4 Disconnect the wiring loom multi-plug connectors from the column switches

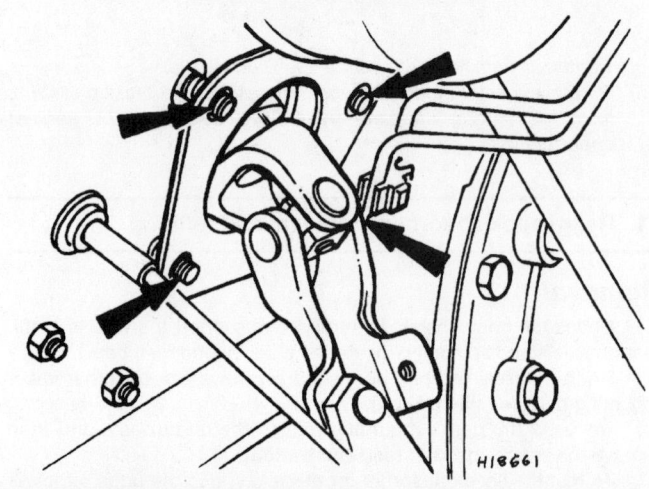

23.6 Steering column to bulkhead attachment points (arrowed)

23.7 Steering column upper retaining nuts

wheel. Undo the bolt, then turn the steering wheel again until the second bolt is accessible. Undo this bolt also.
6 Withdraw the air bag unit from the steering wheel, far enough to access the wiring multi-plug **(see illustration)**.
7 Disconnect the multi-plug from the rear of the unit, and remove it from the vehicle. **Warning:** *Position the air bag unit in a safe place, with the mechanism facing downwards as a precaution against accidental operation.*
8 **Warning:** *Do not attempt to open or repair the air bag unit, or apply any electrical current to it. Do not use any air bag which is visibly damaged, or which has been tampered with.*
9 Centralise the front roadwheels so that they are in the straight-ahead position.
10 Unscrew the steering wheel retaining nut, then pull free the steering wheel from the shaft. The wheel is located on the shaft by a master spline.

Refitting

All models

11 Refitting is a reversal of removal. Align the master spline in the steering wheel hub with the shaft master spline, and push it firmly into position. Tighten the retaining nut to the specified torque. Refit the air bag unit or the centre pad, as applicable, then reconnect the battery negative lead.

23 Steering column - removal and refitting

Removal

1 Disconnect the battery negative lead.
2 Remove the steering wheel as described in Section 22.
3 Undo the retaining screws, and remove the upper and lower column shrouds.
4 Disconnect the wiring loom multi-plug connectors from the column switches, and release the loom-to-column retaining straps **(see illustration)**.
5 Working from the engine compartment side, unscrew the universal joint clamp plate bolt, and move the clamp plate aside. Note that a new clamp plate bolt will be required when refitting. Separate the universal joint from the lower universal joint shaft or steering gear shaft, as applicable.
6 Unscrew the four nuts which secure the steering column tube to the bulkhead **(see illustration)**.
7 From inside the vehicle, support the weight of the column, then undo the two upper retaining nuts. Withdraw the column unit from within the vehicle **(see illustration)**.

Refitting

8 Refitting is a reversal of removal, but note the following additional points:

a) *Ensure that both the steering column and roadwheels are centralised when refitting the universal joint to the steering gear shaft, and secure with a new clamp plate bolt.*
b) *Tighten all fastenings to the specified torque. Loosely tighten the column-to-bulkhead nuts, followed by the upper column nuts, then fully tighten the column-to-bulkhead nuts, followed by the two upper column nuts.*
c) *Refit the steering wheel with reference to Section 22.*

Chapter 10 Suspension and steering

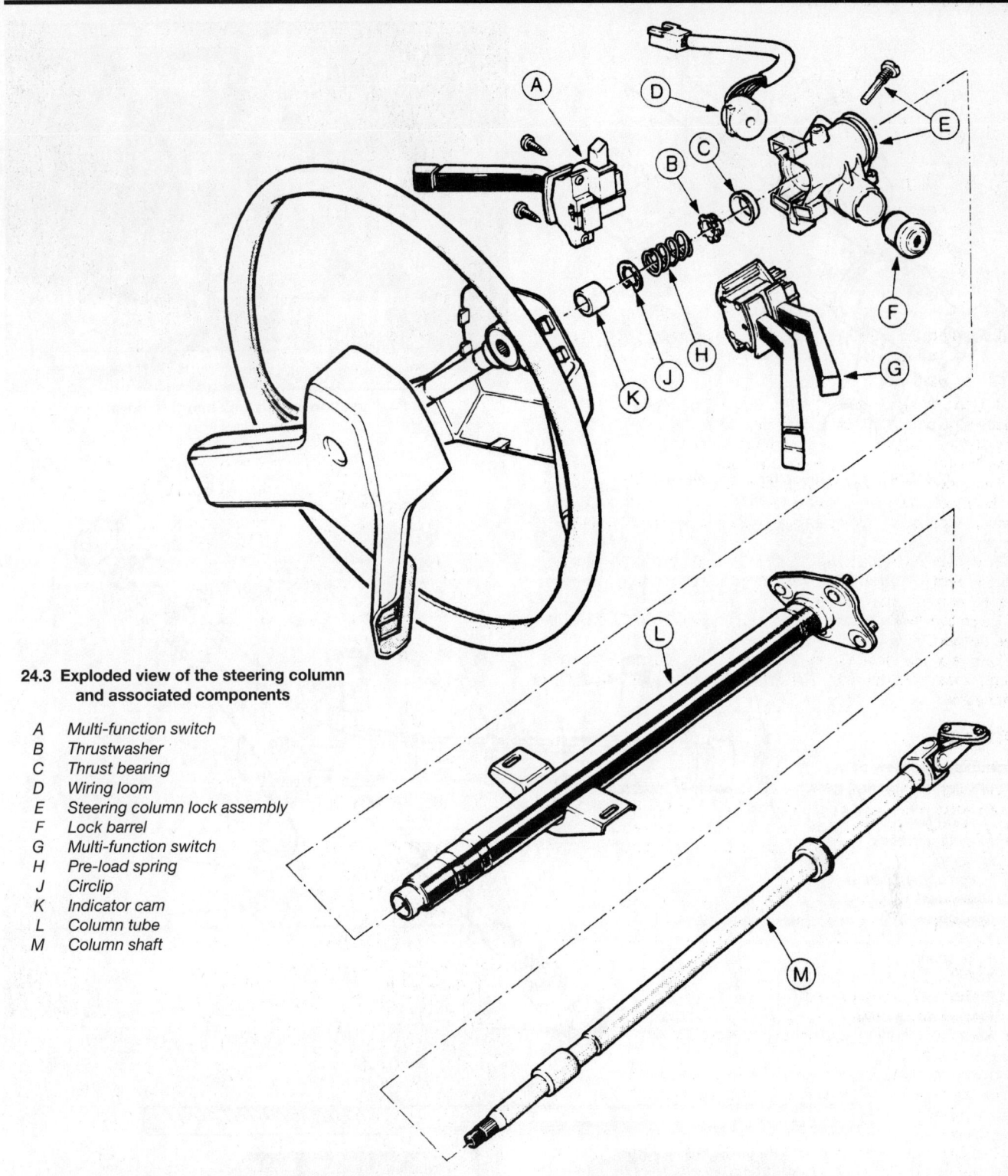

24.3 Exploded view of the steering column and associated components

- A Multi-function switch
- B Thrustwasher
- C Thrust bearing
- D Wiring loom
- E Steering column lock assembly
- F Lock barrel
- G Multi-function switch
- H Pre-load spring
- J Circlip
- K Indicator cam
- L Column tube
- M Column shaft

d) Ensure that all wiring loom connections are securely made, and fit new loom retaining straps. Check the operation of the various switches before refitting the column shrouds.

24 Steering column - dismantling, overhaul and reassembly

Dismantling

1 Remove the steering column from the vehicle as described in the previous Section, then support the column in a vice fitted with soft jaw protectors.

2 If not already removed, withdraw the steering wheel from the column as described in Section 22.

3 Remove the indicator cam, and then prise free the star washer. Withdraw the spring and upper thrustwasher **(see illustration)**.

4 Fit the ignition key into its switch, and turn it to position "II". The steering column shaft can now be withdrawn.

5 Undo the screws securing the column multi-function switches, and remove the switches.

6 To remove the steering column lock unit, drill out the tube-to-lock

10-22 Chapter 10 Suspension and steering

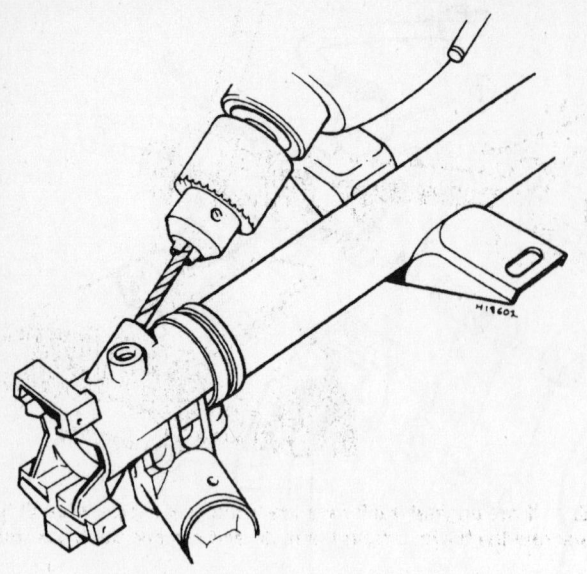

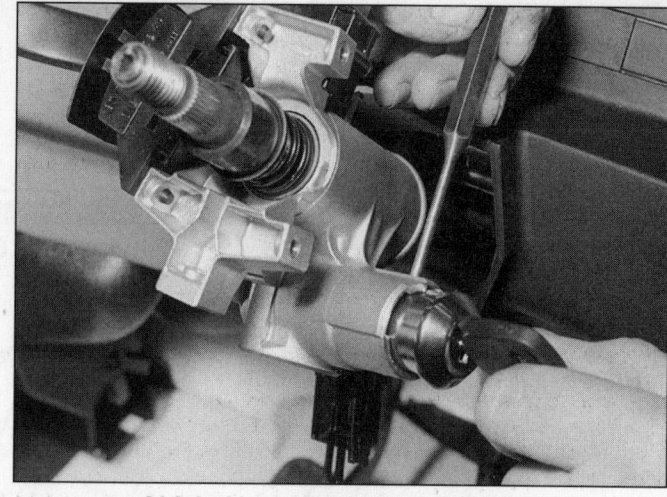

24.9 Ignition switch lock barrel removal

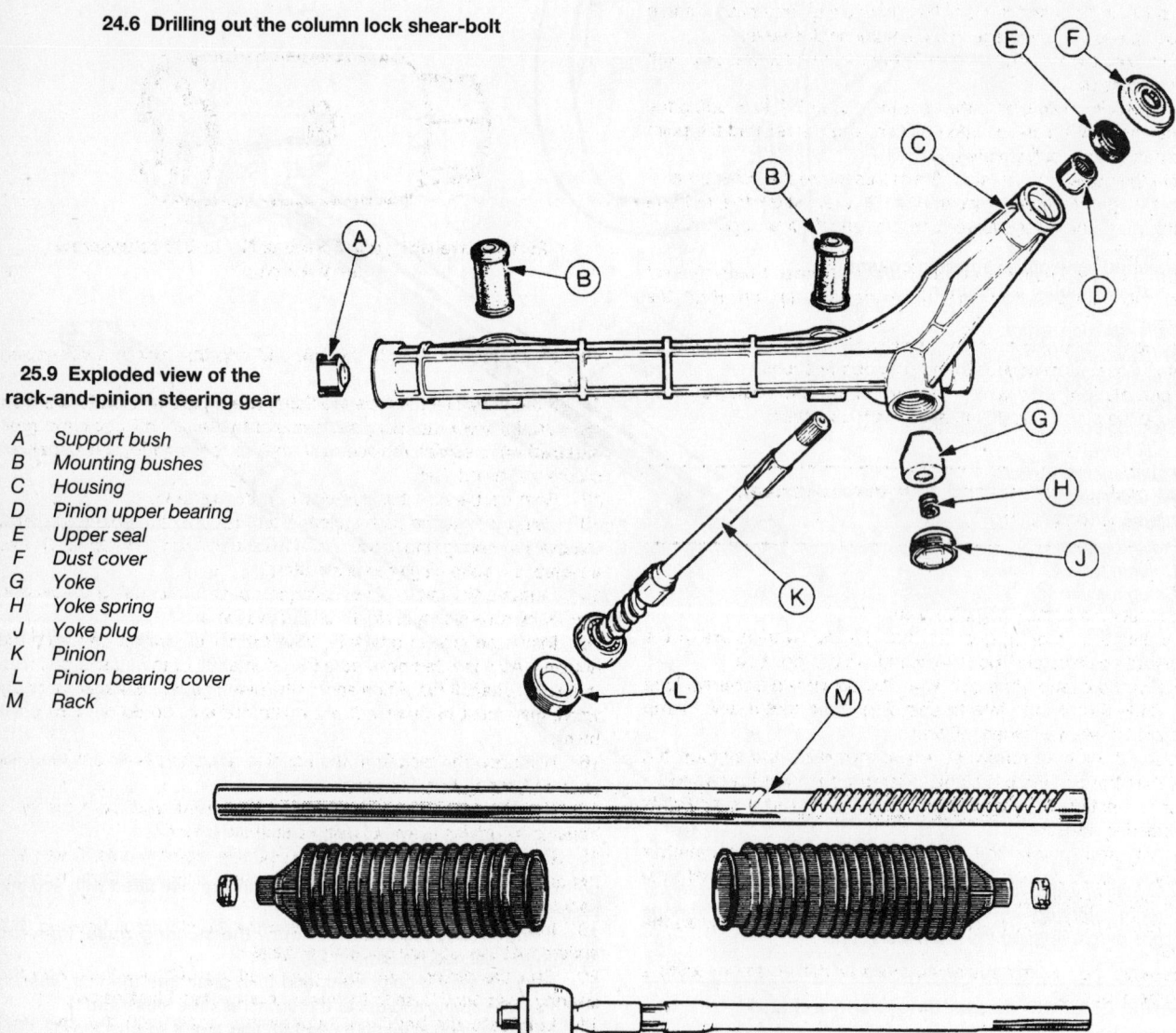

24.6 Drilling out the column lock shear-bolt

25.9 Exploded view of the rack-and-pinion steering gear

- A Support bush
- B Mounting bushes
- C Housing
- D Pinion upper bearing
- E Upper seal
- F Dust cover
- G Yoke
- H Yoke spring
- J Yoke plug
- K Pinion
- L Pinion bearing cover
- M Rack

Chapter 10 Suspension and steering

shear-bolt using a 3/16 in diameter drill, and then carefully tap the lock unit free **(see illustration)**.
7 The upper column support bearing is removed by prising it out.
8 Undo the two grub screws to remove the ignition switch loom plate from the lock housing.
9 To remove the ignition switch lock barrel, turn the key to position "I", then insert a small-diameter punch into the hole in the lock housing, and release the lock barrel **(see illustration)**.

Overhaul

10 Carefully inspect the condition of the steering column and column shaft, checking for any signs of deformation or distortion.
11 Check for free play, which would indicate excessive wear in the universal joint.
12 Check for excessive movement of the column shaft in the column tube, indicating wear in the upper support bearing.
13 Renew any defective or obviously-worn components. If the column has been damaged in any way, it must be renewed as an assembly.

Reassembly

14 Commence reassembly by refitting the lock unit. With the ignition key set in position "I", insert the lock into its housing, and push it home until the lock pin is felt to engage in the column lock sleeve.
15 Turn the key to position "0" then fit the loom plate, securing with the two grub screws.
16 Push the lock housing onto the column tube until it is abutting the tube. Screw the new shear-bolt into position, and tighten it to the point where the head of the bolt shears off.
17 Locate the upper column shaft thrust bearing to the outer tube.
18 Turn the ignition key to position "II", then slide the column through the tube, locate the lower bearing, and fit the upper thrust-washer and spring.
19 Locate the star washer over the shaft, and drive it onto its seat using a suitable tube drift so that it secures the spring. Refit the indicator cam.
20 Refit the multi-function column switches, then refit the column and steering wheel as described in the previous Sections.
21 On completion, check the operation of the multi-function switches and the steering lock for satisfactory operation.

25 Rack-and-pinion steering gear unit - removal, overhaul and refitting

Removal

1 Disconnect the battery negative lead.
2 Centralise the steering gear so that the roadwheels are in the straight-ahead position, and lock the column in this position.
3 Unscrew the clamp plate bolt from the column-to-universal joint coupling. Slide the clamp plate to one side. Note that a new clamp plate bolt will be required when refitting.
4 Loosen off the front roadwheel bolts, then raise and support the vehicle at the front end on axle stands. Remove the front roadwheels.
5 Refer to Section 26, and disconnect the track rod end balljoints from the steering arms.
6 Unscrew and remove the steering gear unit-to-crossmember retaining bolts, and then withdraw the steering gear unit downwards to disengage the universal joint from the column.
7 Unscrew the pinch-bolt, and remove the universal joint from the pinion shaft.
8 To remove the mounting bushes, press or drift them out using a suitable tube or socket.

Overhaul

9 Mount the steering gear unit in a vice fitted with protective jaws. Cut free the rubber gaiter retaining clips, and slide the gaiters down the track rods. Remove the pinion dust cover **(see illustration)**.

25.11 If the original track rods are fitted, use a pipe wrench to unscrew the balljoint from the rack, and remove the track rod

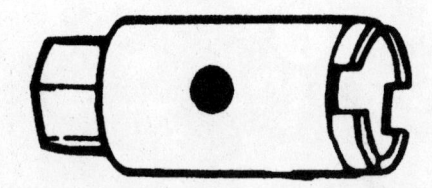

25.13 If available, use Ford tool No 13-011 to unscrew the yoke plug

10 Move the rack fully to the left, and grip the rack in a soft-jawed vice.
11 If the original track rods are fitted, use a pipe wrench to unscrew the balljoint from the rack, and remove the left-hand track rod **(see illustration)**. If service replacement track rods are fitted, use a spanner on the machined flats.
12 Remove the right-hand track rod in the same way.
13 Using a hexagon key, unscrew and remove the yoke plug, and remove the spring and yoke. If available, use Ford tool No 13-011 to unscrew the yoke plug **(see illustration)**.
14 Remove the lower pinion bearing cover, again using a hexagon key, or by reversing tool No 13-011 (if available).
15 Move the rack to one side, then extract the pinion unit from the housing. As it is withdrawn, note the orientation of the master spline of the pinion shaft. If the pinion and/or the bearings are damaged or badly worn, they must be renewed as a combined unit, so do not dismantle them.
16 Withdraw the rack from the housing. Carefully lever out the rack support bearing from the housing.
17 The pinion bearings and seal can be removed from the gear housing by driving them out using a suitable punch.
18 Clean, inspect and renew any defective components. Clean any old sealant from the yoke plug and housing. Clean off and dress the rack tube staking before reassembly.
19 Insert the rack support bush into the steering rack housing, but ensure that the lugs are correctly engaged.
20 Drift the pinion seal and upper bearing into position, with the bearing positioned flush to the seal shoulder **(see illustration)**.
21 Lubricate the bearings, bushes and seals with the specified grease, and then slide the rack into its housing and position it so that all of its teeth are visible.
22 Refit the pinion and bearing unit. Press the rack along its housing, and engage the pinion so that when the rack is in its central location in

10-24 Chapter 10 Suspension and steering

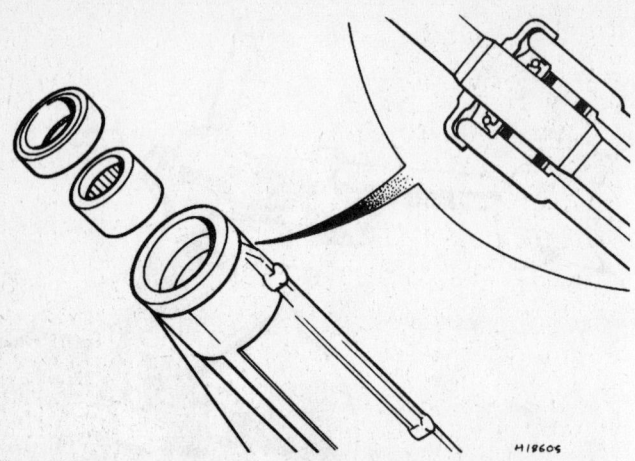

25.20 Drift the pinion seal and upper bearing into position, with the bearing positioned flush to the seal shoulder

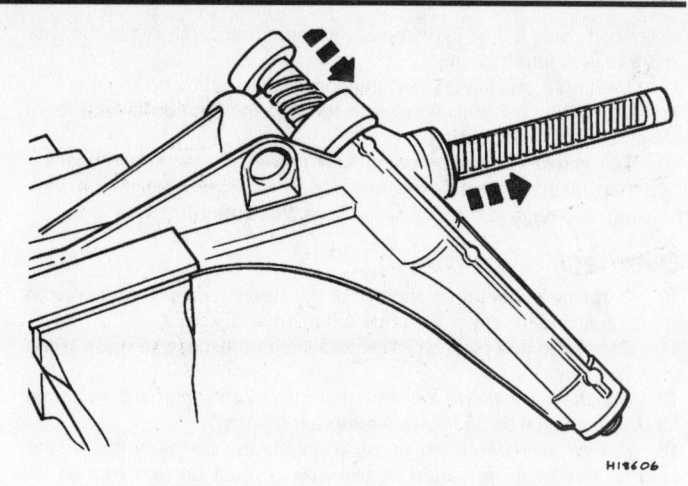

25.22 Refitting the pinion and bearing unit

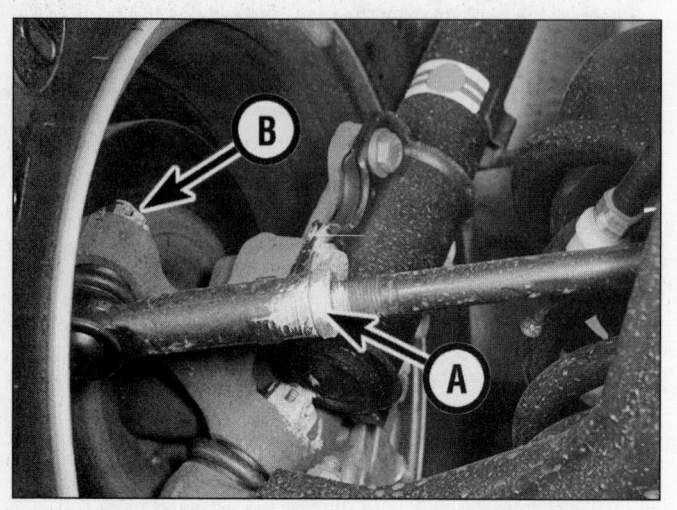

26.3 Track rod end locknut (A) and balljoint-to-steering arm nut (B) on rack-and-pinion steering gear

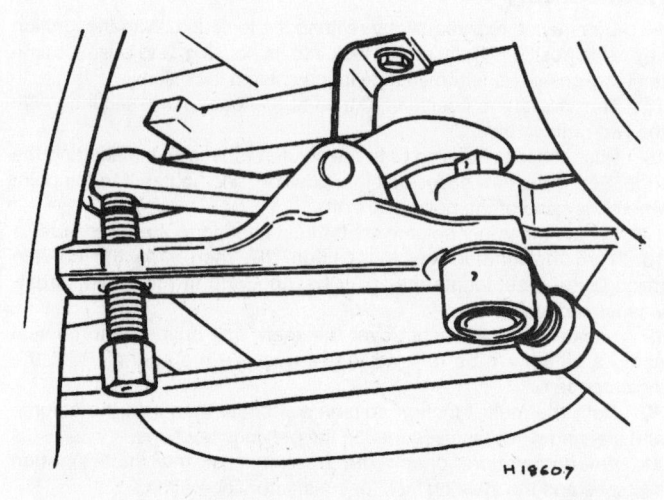

26.5a Using a balljoint separator tool, release the track rod end from the steering arm

the housing, the pinion master spline is positioned as noted during removal **(see illustration)**.
23 Fill the pinion and rack housing with the specified grease, refit the pinion bearing cover, and tighten it to the specified torque. Stake the cover and housing using a suitable punch or chisel.
24 Centralise the steering rack (halve the pinion rotations lock to lock) and clean any grease from the housing and plug threads.
25 Refit the rack yoke and spring into the housing, smear the plug thread with a sealant solution, then fit and tighten the plug to the specified torque. Move the rack through five full operating movements in each direction to settle it, then back off the plug by 30°.
26 Using a suitable torque wrench or pre-load gauge, check the pinion turning torque. Centralise the rack, turn the pinion one turn anti-clockwise, then clockwise two turns, and note the turning torque. Further turn it one turn anti-clockwise. The turning torque through the centre of travel must be as given in the Specifications. If required, the yoke plug can be turned a further 5° in either direction (from the minus 30° position). When loading the rack against the spring, no free play between the back of the rack and the yoke should be felt.
27 Stake the yoke plug and the pinion plug to the housing to secure, in three equidistant positions.
28 Slide the rack to one side to expose the teeth, then relocate the gear unit in the vice, clamping the rack teeth securely in protective jaws.
29 Screw the track rod balljoint units to the rack, and tighten them securely. Stake the joint flange into the rack groove to lock. If a pipe wrench was used to tighten the units, remove any burrs by filing them smooth.
30 Relocate the steering gear rubber gaiters, and secure with new clips.
31 Fill the pinion dust cover with the specified grease, then slide it over the pinion shaft onto the housing so that it is in contact with the upper seal lip.

Refitting

32 Refitting is a reversal of the removal procedure, but before reconnecting the column universal joint coupling, set the steering wheel and front wheels in the straight-ahead position. If a new steering gear unit is being fitted, the straight-ahead position can be ascertained by halving the number of turns necessary to move the rack from lock-to-lock. Use a new clamp plate bolt to secure the universal joint coupling. Tighten the nuts and bolts to the specified torque, and fit new split pins (where applicable). Finally, check and if necessary adjust the front wheel toe setting, as described in Section 36.

26 Track rod end balljoint - removal and refitting

Removal

1 Chock the front wheels, loosen off the front wheel nuts, then raise and support the vehicle at the front on axle stands.

Chapter 10 Suspension and steering   10-25

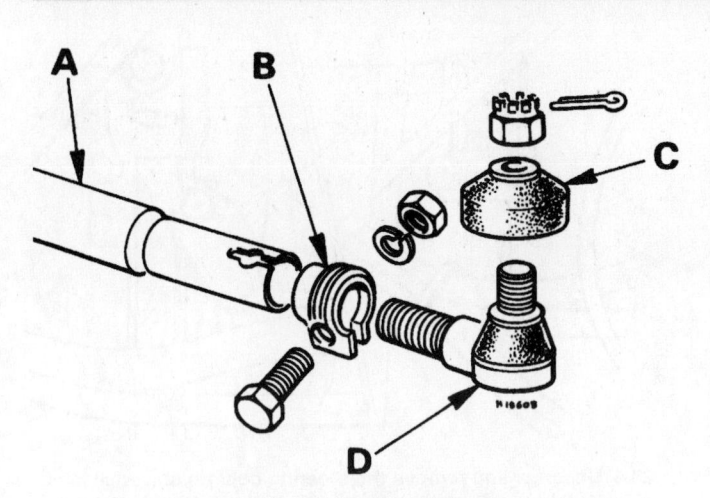

26.5b Track rod end component details on the worm and-nut steering gear

A Track rod
B Clamp
C Dust cap
D Track rod end

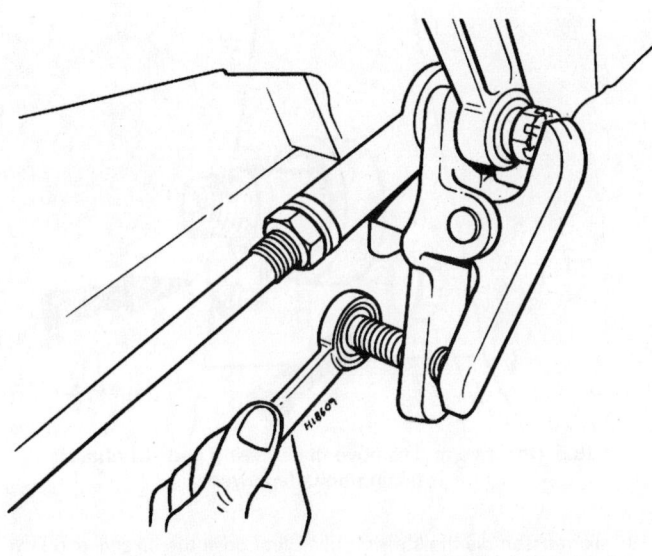

28.2 Using a balljoint separator, release the tapered balljoint shank, and separate the drag link from the drop arm

2 Remove the relevant front roadwheel.
3 Mark the track rod and track rod end in relation to each other, then loosen the locknut a quarter of a turn, or slacken the clamp bolt nut, according to steering gear type (see illustration).
4 Extract the split pin, and unscrew the balljoint-to-steering arm nut.
5 Using a balljoint separator tool, release the track rod end from the steering arm (see illustrations).
6 Unscrew the track rod end from the track rod, noting the number of turns necessary to remove it. Note that on beam axle models, the track rod ends have left- or right-hand threads, depending on the side concerned - ie the left-hand track rod end unscrews *clockwise*.

Refitting

7 Screw the new track rod end onto the track rod the exact number of turns as noted during removal.
8 Engage the track rod end balljoint shank in the steering arm, and screw on the retaining nut. Tighten the nut to the specified torque, and

27.5 Fit and tighten the clips on the steering gear rubber gaiter, ensuring that the gaiter is not twisted

secure with a new split pin. Tighten the nut further, if necessary, to align the split pin holes.
9 Tighten the track rod end locknut or clamp bolt nut, according to steering gear type.
10 Refit the roadwheel, and lower the vehicle to the ground.
11 Tighten the roadwheel nuts to the specified torque.
12 Check and if necessary adjust the front wheel toe setting, as described in Section 36.

27 Steering gear rubber gaiters - renewal

1 Remove the track rod end balljoint as described in Section 26.
2 Note the position of the track rod end locknut by counting the number of threads from the nut face to the end of the track rod. Record this figure, then unscrew and remove the locknut.
3 Remove the clips, and slide the gaiter from the track rod and steering gear housing.
4 Slide the new gaiter over the track rod, and onto the steering gear. Where applicable, make sure that the gaiter locates in the cut-outs provided in the track rod and steering gear housing.
5 Fit and tighten the clips, ensuring that the gaiter is not twisted (see illustration).
6 Screw the track rod end locknut onto the track rod, and position it with the exact number of threads exposed as noted during removal.
7 Refit the track rod end balljoint as described in Section 26.

28 Worm-and-nut steering gear - removal, overhaul and refitting

Removal

1 Apply the handbrake, then raise the vehicle at the front end and support it on axle stands. Centralise the steering (roadwheels in the straight-ahead position).
2 Extract the split pin, and unscrew the nut securing the drag link balljoint to the drop arm. Using a balljoint separator, release the tapered balljoint shank, and separate the drag link from the drop arm (see illustration).
3 Unscrew and remove the drop arm-to-steering gear retaining nut. If no master spline is visible, mark the fitted position of the drop arm on the steering shaft, by scribing an alignment mark across the two end faces. Withdraw the drop arm from the shaft using a puller (see illustration).

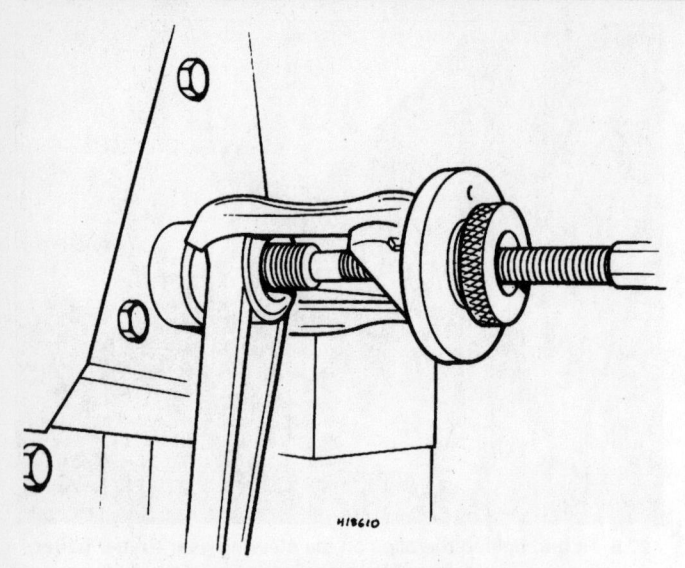

10-26   Chapter 10 Suspension and steering

28.3 Withdrawing the drop arm from the steering shaft using a puller

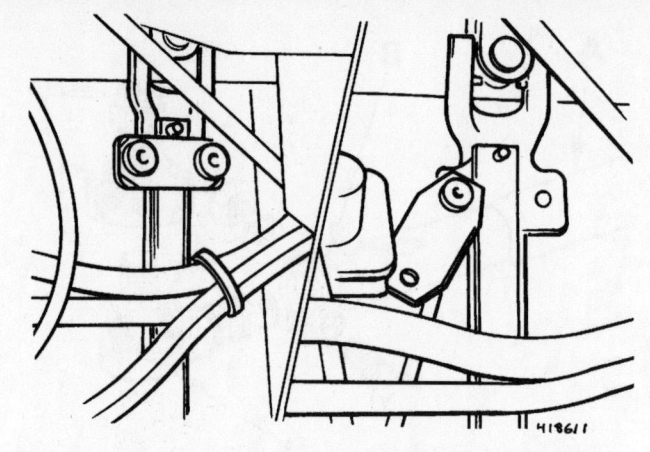

28.4 Unscrew and remove the steering column universal joint clamp plate pinch-bolt, and move the clamp plate to one side

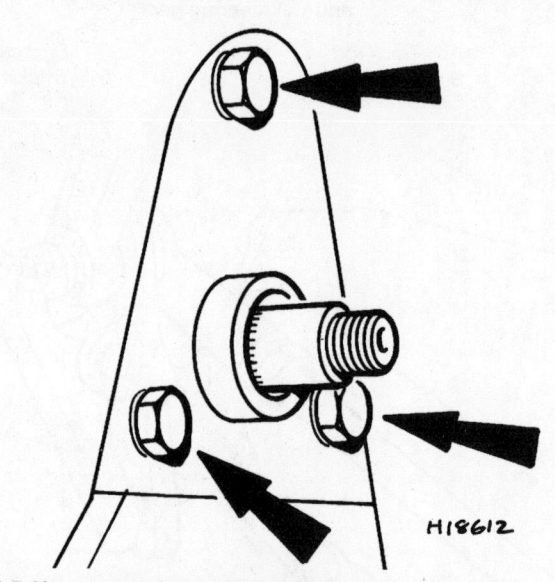

28.5 Unscrew and remove the steering gear-to-chassis retaining bolts (arrowed)

4 Unscrew and remove the steering column universal joint clamp plate pinch-bolt, and move the clamp plate to one side **(see illustration)**. Note that a new clamp plate bolt will be required when refitting.
5 Unscrew and remove the steering gear-to-chassis retaining bolts, and remove the steering gear unit **(see illustration)**.

Overhaul

6 Clean the exterior of the steering gear with paraffin, and thoroughly dry it.
7 Loosen the locknut which secures the rocker shaft adjustment screw, then unscrew and remove the three bolts which retain the rocker shaft housing side cover in position. Remove the side cover, gasket and rocker shaft assembly **(see illustration)**.
8 Remove the adjustment locknut, and unscrew the side cover from the adjustment screw. Slide the adjustment screw and spacer out of the rocker shaft location slot **(see illustration)**.
9 Straighten the tabs of the lockwasher retaining the thrust bearing adjuster locknut, and unscrew and remove the locknut; a special C-spanner is required to do this, which should be available from a tool agent **(see illustration)**. Remove the lockwasher from the housing, and drive out the roll pin from the steering shaft.
10 Unscrew and remove the thrust bearing adjuster, and carefully withdraw the steering shaft together with the upper and lower bearings.
11 Using a suitable drift, drive the upper and lower thrust bearing cups out of the adjuster and steering box.
12 Hold the worm nut in a soft-jawed vice, unscrew the transfer tube clamp plate retaining screws, and remove the clamp plate **(see illustration)**.
13 Remove the transfer tubes and the 62 balls from the worm nut. Note that the steering shaft, worm nut and balls are a matched assembly, and are not available separately.
14 Prise the oil seal from the drop arm end of the steering box.
15 Thoroughly wash all components in paraffin, and dry them with a lint-free cloth.
16 Examine all the components for damage, fractures, and excessive wear. Fit the rocker shaft temporarily in the steering box bush, and check that there is no excessive clearance, then inspect the teeth of the rocker shaft and for wear. Check the bearing races and balls for pitting and signs of wear, and inspect the bush in the side cover for wear. New bushes should be drifted into position where necessary, but if the rocker and steering shafts need renewal, it will probably be more economical to obtain a reconditioned steering gear.
17 Obtain a new oil seal, side cover gasket and thrust bearing adjuster lockwasher.

18 To reassemble the steering gear, first drive the oil seal and lower thrust bearing cup into the steering box, making sure that they are fitted squarely. Similarly, using suitable diameter tubing, drive the upper thrust bearing cup into the bearing adjuster.
19 Slide the worm nut onto the steering shaft ensuring correct orientation, and press the steel balls into each of the four holes until all 62 are in position. It will be necessary to shake the assembly to settle the balls in their grooves, but take care not to allow the balls to fall between the worm, nut and ball tracks.
20 Refit the transfer tubes, align the transfer holes, then fit and tighten the clamp plate and retaining screws.
21 Grease the caged thrust bearing races, position them in the bearing cups, then locate the worm nut and steering shaft into the steering box. Screw the thrust bearing adjuster into the housing. Using a suitable torque wrench or a pre-load gauge, tighten the thrust bearing adjuster to achieve the steering shaft turning torque given in the Specifications.
22 Fit the new lockwasher and the thrust bearing adjuster locknut, and tighten it with the special tool. Bend one tab into the locknut slot, and the remaining tab over the housing **(see illustration)**.
23 Fit the adjuster screw to the rocker shaft location slot, and select a spacer to give a clearance of 0.05 mm between the screw head and the contact face of the rocker shaft. Remove the screw, fit the spacer, and refit the screw.

Chapter 10 Suspension and steering

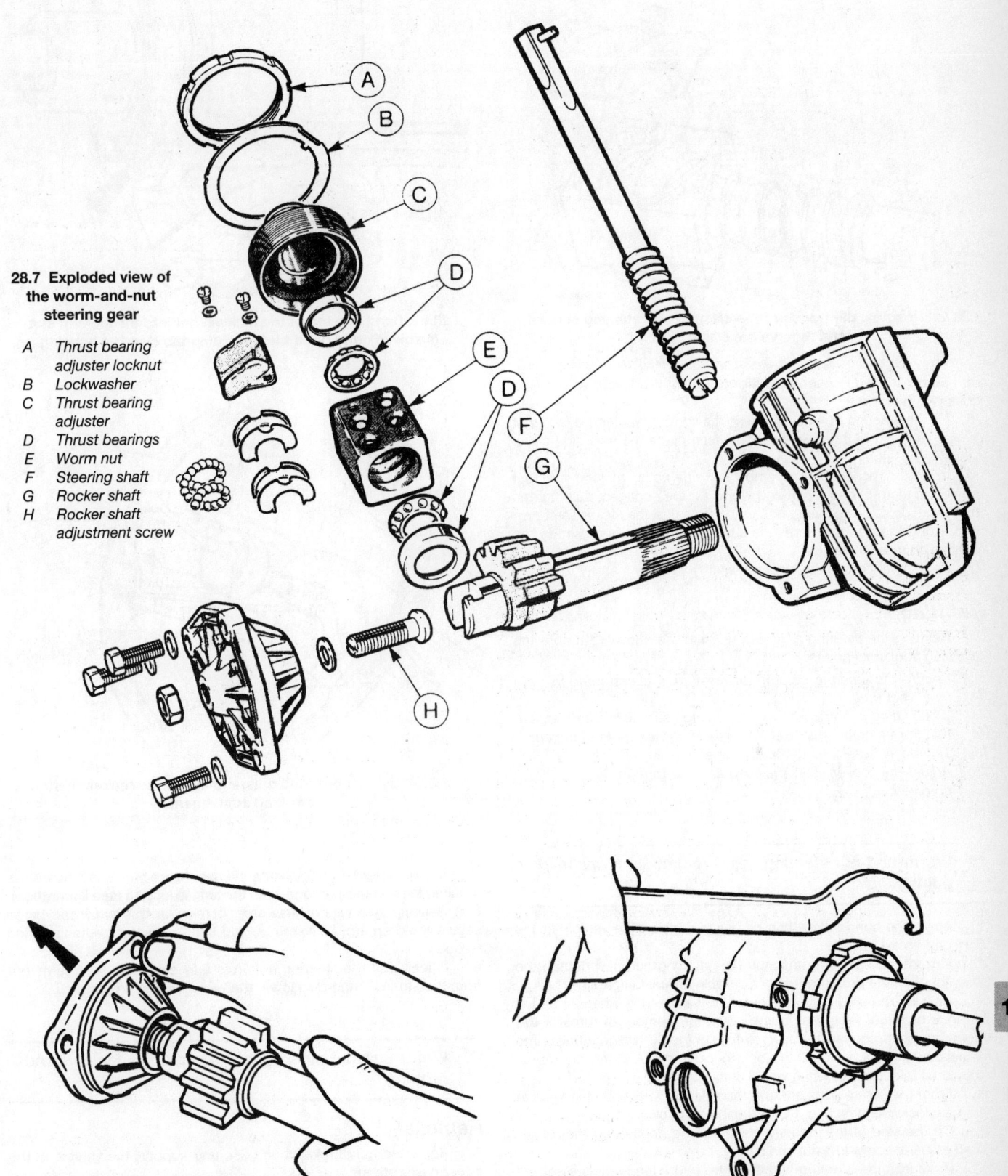

10-27

28.7 Exploded view of the worm-and-nut steering gear

- A Thrust bearing adjuster locknut
- B Lockwasher
- C Thrust bearing adjuster
- D Thrust bearings
- E Worm nut
- F Steering shaft
- G Rocker shaft
- H Rocker shaft adjustment screw

28.8 Slide the side cover with adjustment screw and spacer out of the rocker shaft location slot

28.9 Unscrew the thrust bearing adjuster locknut using a C-spanner

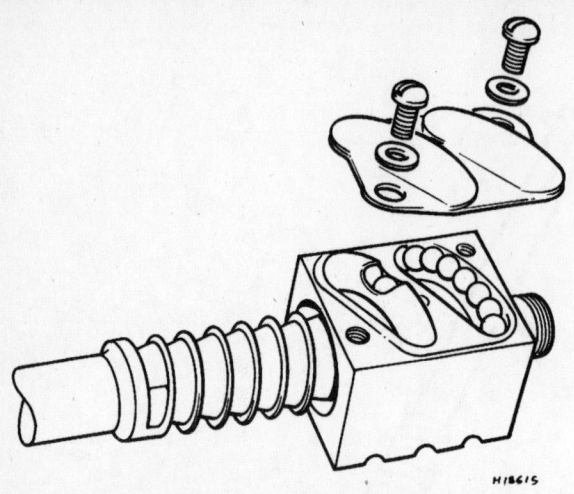

10-28 Chapter 10 Suspension and steering

28.12 Unscrew the transfer tube clamp plate retaining screws, and remove the clamp plate

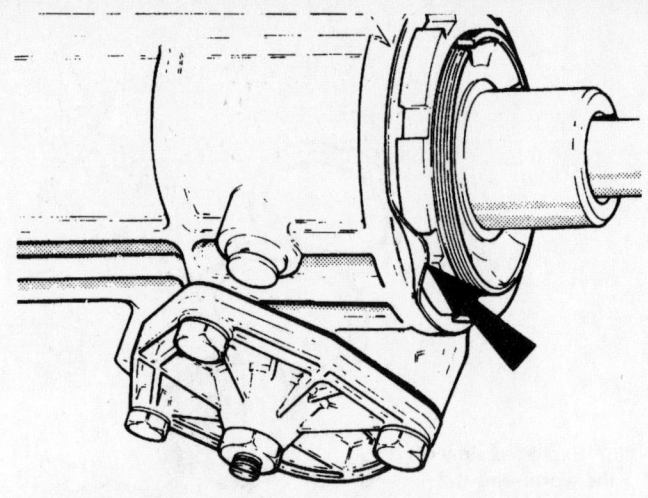

28.22 Bend one tab of the lockwasher into the locknut slot (arrowed), and bend the remaining tab over the housing

24 Screw the side cover onto the rocker shaft adjuster screw, and loosely fit the locknut.
25 Fill the steering box housing with the correct type and quantity of grease as given in the Specifications, then place the new side cover gasket in position.
26 Insert the rocker shaft assembly and side cover, making sure that the centre teeth of both shaft and worm nut are engaged, then tighten the three side cover retaining bolts. Adjustment of the rocker shaft pre-load, using the adjuster screw, is carried out later, after refitting the steering gear to the vehicle.
27 Refit the roll pin to the steering shaft.

Refitting

28 Refitting the steering gear is a reversal of removal, but note the following additional points:

a) Secure the steering column universal joint clamp plate using a new pinch-bolt.
b) When fitting the drop arm to the steering gear rocker shaft, ensure that the alignment marks and/or master splines are in alignment.
c) Tighten all fastenings to their specified torque settings.
d) Adjust the rocker shaft pre-load as described in Section 29 on completion.

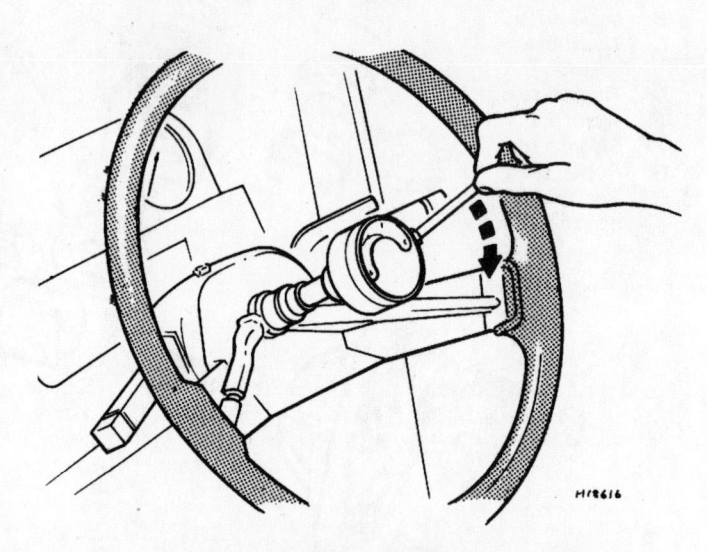

29 Worm-and-nut steering gear - rocker shaft pre-load adjustment

1 Apply the handbrake, then raise and support the vehicle at the front end on axle stands.
2 Extract the split pin, unscrew the retaining nut, and detach the drag link from the drop arm using a suitable balljoint separator.
3 Release the steering lock, then turn the steering wheel to its full left lock position. From this point, count the number of turns of the steering wheel required to move to full right lock. Now centralise the wheel by moving it back half the lock-to-lock turns. A slight "high spot" should be felt on the steering wheel at this point.
4 From the centre position, turn the steering wheel two full turns in an anti-clockwise direction, then proceed as follows.
5 On the side of the steering gear housing, loosen off the rocker shaft adjuster screw locknut and screw.
6 Prise free the steering wheel centre pad. Connect up a socket extension and a suitable torque wrench or pre-load gauge, and then turn the steering wheel clockwise four complete turns to measure the turning torque required. The turning torque should be as given in the Specifications (rocker shaft pre-load) **(see illustration)**.

29.6 Using a pre-load gauge to check the rocker shaft pre-load adjustment

7 If adjustment is necessary, adjust the rocker shaft screw as required to meet this pre-load, then tighten the locknut **(see illustration)**.
8 Reassemble in the reverse order of renewal. Use a new split pin to secure the drop arm balljoint nut, and tighten the nut to the specified torque.
9 Check that the steering action is fully satisfactory by turning it from lock-to-lock, and then lower the vehicle to the ground.

30 Worm-and-nut steering gear drop arm - removal and refitting

Removal

1 Apply the handbrake, then raise and support the vehicle at the front on axle stands.
2 Extract the split pin, unscrew the retaining nut, and detach the drag link from the drop arm using a balljoint separator tool **(see illustration 28.2)**.
3 Unscrew and remove the nut securing the drop arm to the

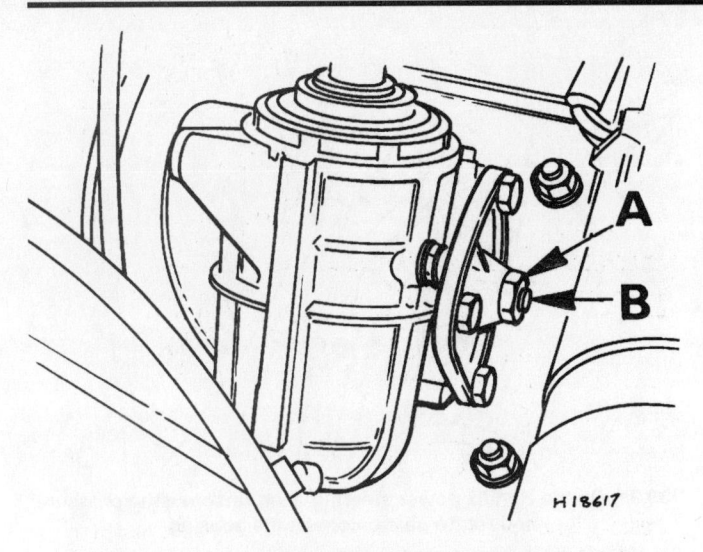

Chapter 10 Suspension and steering

29.7 Steering gear rocker shaft pre-load adjuster screw (B) and locknut (A)

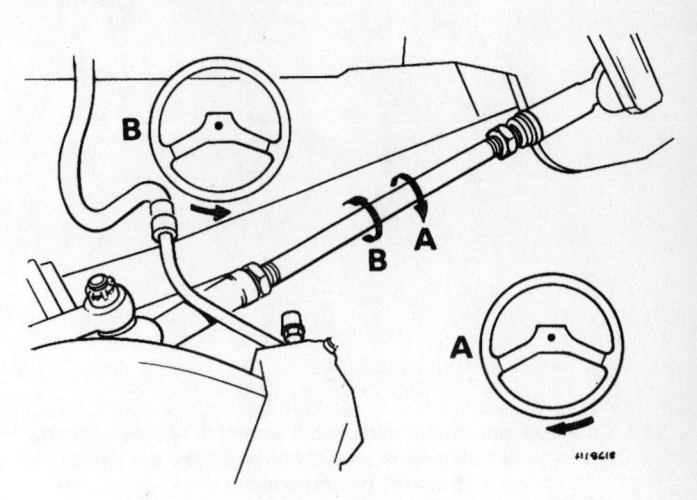

31.6 Adjust the drag link as required to centralise the steering wheel

steering box rocker shaft. If no master spline is visible, make an alignment mark across the face of the shaft and arm, to indicate their relative positions for refitting. Withdraw the drop arm from the shaft using a suitable puller **(see illustration 28.3)**.

Refitting

4 Refitting is a reversal of the removal procedure, but note the following additional points:
 a) Centralise the steering before reconnecting the drop arm, and ensure that the master spline or alignment marks made during removal align.
 b) Tighten the retaining nuts to the specified torque, and insert a new split pin to secure the drag link castellated nut.
 c) On completion, check that the steering action is satisfactory lock-to-lock, and also that the front wheels are in the straight-ahead position when the steering wheel is centralised. If required, the drag link can be adjusted to achieve this, as described in Section 31.

31 Worm-and-nut steering gear drag link - removal and refitting

Removal

1 Apply the handbrake, then raise and support the vehicle at the front on axle stands.
2 Straighten and extract the split pins from the balljoint nuts at each end of the drag link, then unscrew and remove the nuts. Using a universal balljoint separator, release the balljoints and withdraw the drag link.
3 To remove the drag link balljoints, loosen the locknuts and unscrew the balljoints, noting that they have left- and right-hand threads, according to side - ie the left-hand balljoint nut unscrews **clockwise**.

Refitting

4 Screw the new balljoints onto the drag link an equal number of turns each, so that the ballpin centres are approximately 455.0 mm apart.
5 Refit the drag link, tighten the balljoint nuts, and fit new split pins.
6 With the roadwheels in the straight-ahead position, the steering gear must be at the centre of its travel with the steering wheel in the straight-ahead position. Adjust the drag link accordingly, and then tighten the balljoint locknuts **(see illustration)**.
7 Lower the vehicle to the ground.

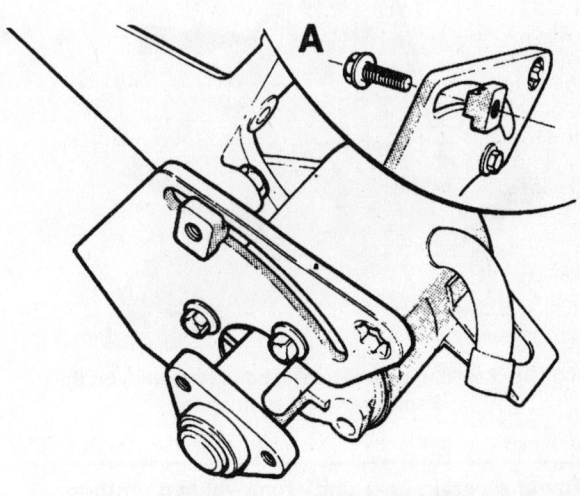

32.4 Power steering pump and mounting bracket, showing adjuster bolt and nut (A)

32 Power steering pump - removal and refitting

Removal

1 Disconnect the battery negative lead.
2 Remove the power steering pump drivebelt as described in Chapter 1, then undo the retaining bolts and remove the pump pulley.
3 Place a suitable container under the power steering pump, disconnect the fluid pipes, and drain the fluid. Cover the pipe ends and the pump orifices after disconnection. Where applicable, unscrew the clamp bolt securing the high-pressure hose to the rear of the pump bracket.
4 Remove the pump bracket bolts, and withdraw the pump assembly **(see illustration)**.

Refitting

5 Refitting is a reversal of removal, but tighten the nuts and bolts to the specified torque. Refit and tension the drivebelt as described in Chapter 1. Refill the power steering system with fluid, and bleed it as described in Section 35.

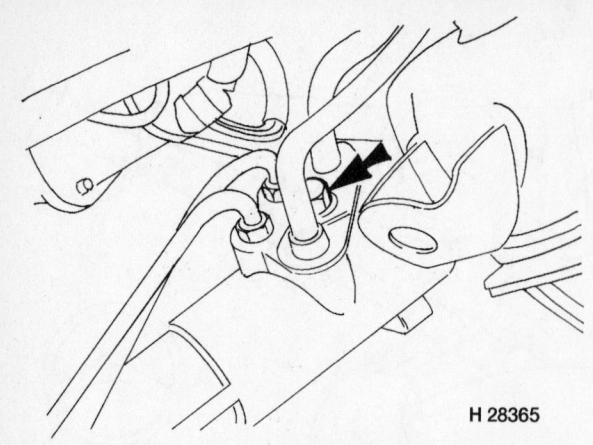

10•30 Chapter 10 Suspension and steering

33.1 On the ZF power steering gear, unscrew the power steering pipe locking plate bolt (arrowed) and withdraw the pipes from the pinion housing

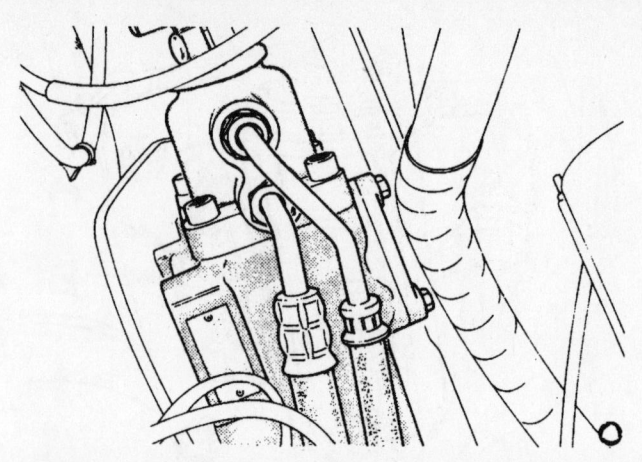

33.3a On the Bendix power steering gear, unscrew the pressure and return pipe unions at the housing

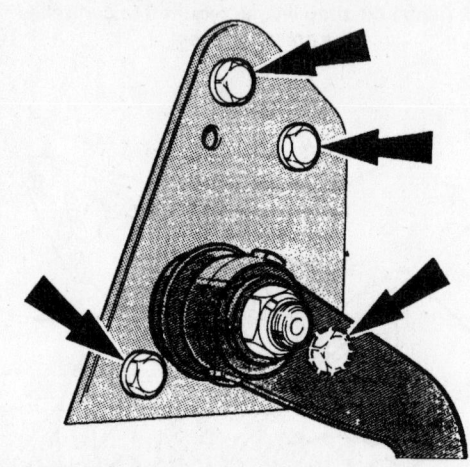

33.3b Steering gear retaining bolts (arrowed) on the Bendix power steering gear

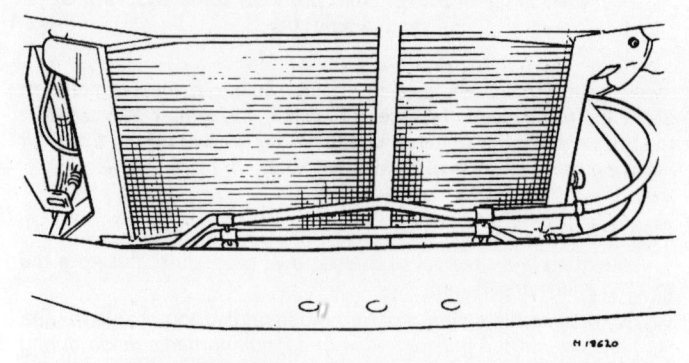

34.2 On pre-1995 models, unscrew and remove the hydraulic hose clamp bolts from the front panel

33 Power steering gear unit - removal and refitting

Removal

Vehicles with independent front suspension

1 The power steering gear unit fitted to vehicles with independent front suspension is of the ZF rack-and-pinion type. The removal procedure is as essentially given for the manual steering gear unit in Section 25, but in addition, the hydraulic lines will need to be detached. To do this, place a container beneath the steering gear, then unscrew the pipe locking plate and withdraw the pipes from the pinion housing **(see illustration)**. Allow the fluid to drain into the container as the pipes are released. Cover the pipe ends and steering gear orifices after disconnection, to prevent the ingress of foreign matter.

2 In addition, it will be necessary to detach the pipes from their attachments on the steering gear housing prior to removal. Further information on the power steering pipes and hoses is given in Section 34.

Vehicles with beam axle front suspension

3 The removal procedure for the Bendix type power steering gear fitted to vehicles with beam axle front suspension is essentially as given for the manual steering gear unit in Section 28, but in addition, the hydraulic lines will need to be detached. To do this, place a container beneath the steering gear, then unscrew the pressure and return pipe unions, and drain the power steering fluid **(see illustration)**.

Cover the pipe ends and steering gear orifices after disconnection, to prevent the ingress of foreign matter. Note also that there are four steering gear retaining bolts, rather than three as on manual types **(see illustration)**.

Refitting

All models

4 The refitting procedure is a reversal of removal, but note the following additional points:

a) When reconnecting the steering gear hydraulic connections, take care not to over-tighten the unions.
b) Refill and bleed the power steering system as described in Section 35.

34 Power steering pipes and hoses - removal and refitting

Removal

1 Disconnect the battery negative lead.

2 On pre-1995 model year vehicles, detach and remove the radiator grille (Chapter 11), then unscrew and remove the hydraulic hose clamp bolts from the front panel **(see illustration)**.

3 Where applicable, unscrew the clamp bolt securing the high-pressure hose to the rear of the power steering pump bracket.

4 Locate suitable container(s) under the steering gear and pump units, then disconnect the hoses from each. On later vehicles with rack-and-pinion type power steering, undo the bolt securing the locking plate to the pinion housing, then remove the locking plate and

Chapter 10 Suspension and steering

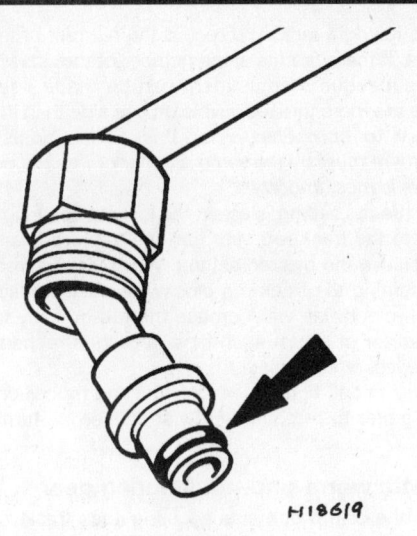

34.7 O-ring seal (arrowed) on high-pressure fluid hose connector

withdraw the hoses. Clean the area around the hose unions, and plug them to prevent further fluid leakage and the possible ingress of dirt.
5   Disconnect the hoses from the fluid reservoir. On later vehicles, the hose connections incorporate quick-release connectors to minimise fluid loss from the reservoir. To release these hoses, depress the connector releasing clips and withdraw the hose.
6   Where applicable, release the pipes from the clamps on the rack-and-pinion steering gear.
7   If the hose(s) and/or their union O-ring seals are perished or damaged, they must be renewed. The O-ring seal is only available with a new hose, so treat it with care if they are to be re-used **(see illustration)**.

Refitting

8   Refitting is a reversal of removal. Ensure that all connections are clean, and do not over-tighten the unions.
9   On completion, top-up the system fluid level (do not re-use the old fluid) and bleed the system as described in Section 35.

35 Power steering system - bleeding

1   If the power steering system has been emptied of fluid, first top-up the fluid level, using the specified type of fluid (see Chapter 1). Apply the handbrake, then raise and support the vehicle at the front so that the front wheels are clear of the ground. Turn the steering wheel from lock-to-lock twice (engine switched off). As the wheels are being turned, top-up the reservoir fluid level as necessary. Lower the vehicle to the ground.
2   Start up the engine and allow it to run at its normal idle speed whilst the above procedure is repeated, again keeping the reservoir topped-up to the required level.

36 Wheel alignment and steering angles - general information

1   Accurate front wheel alignment is essential to provide positive steering and prevent excessive tyre wear. Before considering the steering/suspension geometry, check that the tyres are correctly inflated, that the front wheels are not buckled, and that the steering linkage and suspension joints are in good order, without slackness or wear.
2   Wheel alignment consists of four factors **(see illustration)**:
Camber is the angle at which the front wheels are set from the vertical when viewed from the front of the vehicle. "Positive" camber is the amount (in degrees) that the wheels are tilted outward at the top of the vertical.

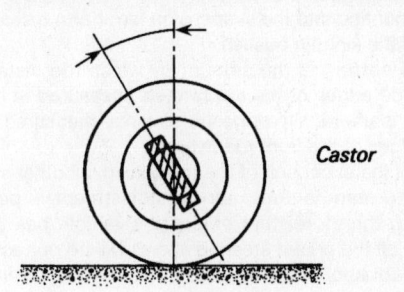

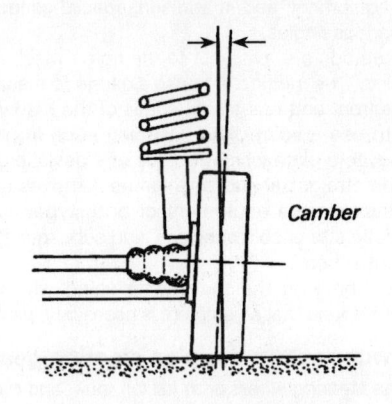

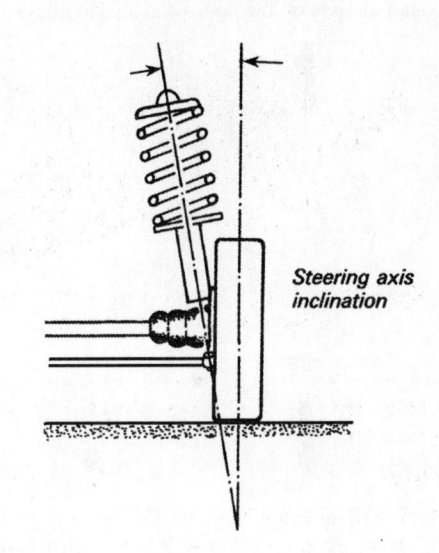

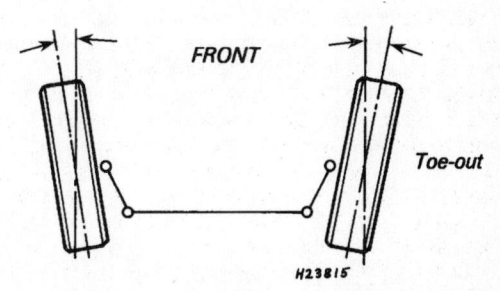

36.2 Wheel alignment and steering angle measurements

Castor is the angle between the steering axis and a vertical line when viewed from each side of the car. "Positive" castor is when the steering axis is inclined rearward at the top.
Steering axis inclination - also known as **kingpin inclination** is the angle (when viewed from the front of the vehicle) between the vertical and an imaginary line drawn through the suspension strut

upper mounting and the suspension lower arm balljoint, or through the centre of the kingpin bushes.

Toe setting is the amount by which the distance between the front inside edges of the roadwheels (measured at hub height) differs from the diametrically-opposite distance measured between the rear inside edges of the front roadwheels.

3   With the exception of the toe setting, all other steering angles are set during manufacture, and no adjustment is possible. It can be assumed, therefore, that unless the vehicle has suffered accident damage, all the preset steering angles will be correct. Should there be some doubt about their accuracy, it will be necessary to seek the help of a Ford dealer, as the specification varies considerably according to model and equipment, and in addition, special gauges are needed to check the various angles.

4   Two methods are available to the home mechanic for checking the toe setting. One method is to use a gauge to measure the distance between the front and rear inside edges of the roadwheels. The other method is to use a scuff plate, in which each front wheel is rolled across a movable plate which records any deviation, or scuff, of the tyre from the straight-ahead position as it moves across the plate. Relatively inexpensive equipment of both types is available from accessory outlets to enable checking, and subsequent adjustments, to be carried out at home.

5   If, after checking the toe setting using whichever method is preferable, it is found that adjustment is necessary, proceed as follows.

Vehicles with rack-and-pinion steering gear

6   Turn the steering wheel onto full left lock, and record the number of exposed threads on the right-hand steering track rod. Now turn the steering onto full right lock, and record the number of threads on the left-hand side. If there are the same number of threads visible on both sides, then subsequent adjustment can be made equally on both sides. If there are more threads visible on one side than the other, it will be necessary to compensate for this during adjustment. *After adjustment, there must be the same number of threads visible on each track rod. This is most important.*

7   To alter the toe setting, slacken the locknut securing the track rod end balljoint to the track rod, and turn the track rod using a self-grip wrench to achieve the desired setting. When viewed from the side of the vehicle, turning the track rod clockwise will increase the toe-out, turning it anti-clockwise will increase the toe-in. Only turn the track rods by a quarter of a turn each time, and then recheck the setting using the gauges, or scuff plate.

8   After adjustment, tighten the locknuts and reposition the steering gear rubber gaiter to remove any twist caused by turning the track rods.

Vehicles with worm-and-nut steering gear

9   Slacken the clamp bolt nuts securing each track rod end to the track rod, and turn the track rod using a self-grip wrench to achieve the desired setting. The track rod ends have left and right-hand threads, therefore turning the track rod in one direction increases its length, and turning it in the other direction decreases it. Increasing the length of the track rod increases the toe-in; decreasing the length increases the toe-out. Only turn the track rod by a small amount each time, and then recheck the setting using the gauges, or scuff plate.

10   Tighten the track rod end clamp bolt nuts on completion of the adjustment.

Chapter 11 Bodywork and fittings

Contents

	Section
Bonnet - removal, refitting and adjustment	6
Bonnet release cable and latch - renewal	7
Bonnet safety catch - removal and refitting	8
Door trim panels - removal and refitting	9
Exterior mirrors and associated components - removal and refitting	24
Facia - removal and refitting	29
Front bumper - removal and refitting	25
Front door - removal, refitting and adjustment	11
Front door fittings - removal and refitting	10
Front door quarter glass - removal and refitting	19
Front door window and regulator - removal and refitting	18
Front grille - removal and refitting	27
General information	1
Headlining - removal and refitting	31
Interior trim - removal and refitting	30
Maintenance - bodywork and underframe	2
Maintenance - upholstery and carpets	3

	Section
Major body damage - repair	5
Minor body damage - repair	4
Opening rear quarter window - removal and refitting	22
Rear bumper - removal and refitting	26
Rear door fittings - removal and refitting	14
Rear doors - removal, refitting and adjustment	15
Seat belt components - removal and refitting	33
Seats - removal and refitting	32
Sliding side door - removal, refitting and adjustment	13
Sliding side door fittings - removal and refitting	12
Sliding window glass and frame - dismantling and reassembly	21
Sliding window glass and frame - removal and refitting	20
Tailgate - removal, refitting and adjustment	17
Tailgate fittings - removal and refitting	16
Underbody and general body check	See Chapter 1
Windscreen and fixed windows - removal and refitting	23
Windscreen grille - removal and refitting	28

Specifications

Torque wrench settings

	Nm	lbf ft
Bench seat pivot bolt	6 to 8	4 to 6
Seat track-to-floor bolts	21 to 25	16 to 19
Seat frame-to-seat track nuts	21 to 25	16 to 19
Seat belt upper anchor bolts	38 to 53	28 to 39
Seat belt stalks to floor	38 to 53	28 to 39
Seat belt inertia reel mountings	38 to 53	28 to 39
Seat belt pre-tensioner and stalk bolts	38 to 53	28 to 39

Chapter 11 Bodywork and fittings

1 General information

The body and chassis on all versions of the Transit is of all-steel construction. Three basic chassis types are available: short-wheelbase, long-wheelbase and extended-wheelbase models.

The three main body types are Van, Bus and Chassis Cab. Twin opening rear doors or a tailgate are fitted and, on some models, side opening door(s) are available. The bodyshell is as aerodynamic in shape as possible, to promote economy and reduce wind noise levels.

During manufacture, each body is carefully prepared for painting, given a zinc phosphate treatment, sprayed with a polyester primer, which is then oven-baked and finally, two top finisher coats of enamel are applied. The body cavities are wax-injected to prevent corrosion.

Inertia reel seat belts are fitted to the front seats and, on later vehicles, the front seat belt stalks are mounted on automatic tensioners (also known as "grabbers") **(see illustration)**. In the event of a serious front impact, a spring mass sensor releases a coil spring, which pulls the stalk buckle downwards and tensions the seat belt. It is not possible to reset the tensioner once fired, and it must therefore be renewed.

Due to the large number of specialist applications of this vehicle range, information contained in this Chapter is given on parts found to be common on the popular factory-produced versions. No information is provided on special body versions.

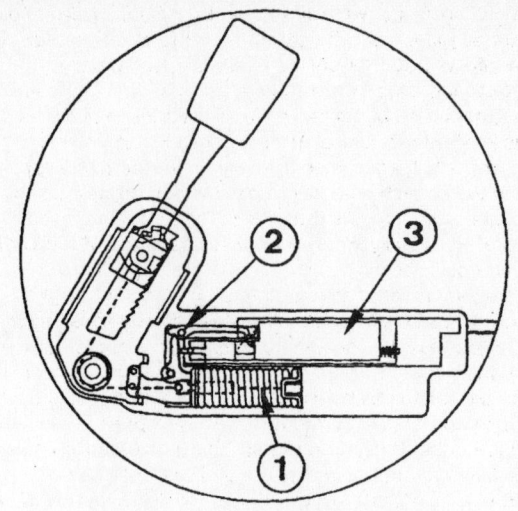

1.4 Automatic seat belt tensioner

1 Coil spring
2 Lever system
3 Spring mass sensor

2 Maintenance - bodywork and underframe

The general condition of a vehicle's bodywork is the one thing that significantly affects its value. Maintenance is easy, but needs to be regular. Neglect, particularly after minor damage, can lead quickly to further deterioration and costly repair bills. It is important also to keep watch on those parts of the vehicle not immediately visible, for instance the underside, inside all the wheel arches, and the lower part of the engine compartment.

The basic maintenance routine for the bodywork is washing - preferably with a lot of water, from a hose. This will remove all the loose solids which may have stuck to the vehicle. It is important to flush these off in such a way as to prevent grit from scratching the finish. The wheel arches and underframe need washing in the same way, to remove any accumulated mud which will retain moisture and tend to encourage rust. Paradoxically enough, the best time to clean the underframe and wheel arches is in wet weather, when the mud is thoroughly wet and soft. In very wet weather, the underframe is usually cleaned of large accumulations automatically, and this is a good time for inspection.

Periodically, except on vehicles with a wax-based underbody protective coating, it is a good idea to have the whole of the underframe of the vehicle steam-cleaned, engine compartment included, so that a thorough inspection can be carried out to see what minor repairs and renovations are necessary. Steam-cleaning is available at many garages, and is necessary for the removal of the accumulation of oily grime, which sometimes is allowed to become thick in certain areas. If steam-cleaning facilities are not available, there are some excellent grease solvents available, such as Holts Engine Degreasant, which can be brush-applied; the dirt can then be simply hosed off. Note that these methods should not be used on vehicles with wax-based underbody protective coating, or the coating will be removed. Such vehicles should be inspected annually, preferably just prior to Winter, when the underbody should be washed down, and any damage to the wax coating repaired using Holts Undershield. Ideally, a completely fresh coat should be applied. It would also be worth considering the use of such wax-based protection for injection into door panels, sills, box sections, etc, as an additional safeguard against rust damage, where such protection is not provided by the vehicle manufacturer.

After washing paintwork, wipe off with a chamois leather to give an unspotted clear finish. A coat of clear protective wax polish like the many excellent Turtle Wax polishes, will give added protection against chemical pollutants in the air. If the paintwork sheen has dulled or oxidised, use a cleaner/polisher combination such as Turtle Wax Hard Shell to restore the brilliance of the shine. This requires a little effort, but such dulling is usually caused because regular washing has been neglected. Care needs to be taken with metallic paintwork, as special non-abrasive cleaner/polisher is required to avoid damage to the finish. Always check that the door and ventilator opening drain holes and pipes are completely clear, so that water can be drained out. Brightwork should be treated in the same way as paintwork. Windscreens and windows can be kept clear of the smeary film which often appears, by the use of proprietary glass cleaner like Holts Mixra. Never use any form of wax or other body or chromium polish on glass.

3 Maintenance - upholstery and carpets

Mats and carpets should be brushed or vacuum-cleaned regularly, to keep them free of grit. If they are badly stained, remove them from the vehicle for scrubbing or sponging, and make quite sure they are dry before refitting. Seats and interior trim panels can be kept clean by wiping with a damp cloth and Turtle Wax Carisma. If they do become stained (which can be more apparent on light-coloured upholstery), use a little liquid detergent and a soft nail brush to scour the grime out of the grain of the material. Do not forget to keep the headlining clean in the same way as the upholstery. When using liquid cleaners inside the vehicle, do not over-wet the surfaces being cleaned. Excessive damp could get into the seams and padded interior, causing stains, offensive odours or even rot. If the inside of the vehicle gets wet accidentally, it is worthwhile taking some trouble to dry it out properly, particularly where carpets are involved. *Do not leave oil or electric heaters inside the vehicle for this purpose.*

4 Minor body damage - repair

Note: *For more detailed information about bodywork repair, Haynes Publishing produce a book by Lindsay Porter called "The Car Bodywork Repair Manual". This incorporates information on such aspects as rust treatment, painting and glass-fibre repairs, as well as details on more ambitious repairs involving welding and panel beating. The colour photographic sequence accompanying this Section illustrates the operations described below.*

Repairs of minor scratches in bodywork

If the scratch is very superficial, and does not penetrate to the metal of the bodywork, repair is very simple. Lightly rub the area of the scratch with a paintwork renovator like Turtle Wax Color Back, or a very fine cutting paste like Holts Body+Plus Rubbing Compound, to remove loose paint from the scratch, and to clear the surrounding bodywork of wax polish. Rinse the area with clean water.

Apply touch-up paint to the scratch using a fine paint brush; continue to apply fine layers of paint until the surface of the paint in the scratch is level with the surrounding paintwork. Allow the new paint at least two weeks to harden, then blend it into the surrounding paintwork by rubbing the scratch area with a paintwork renovator or a very fine cutting paste, such as Holts Body+Plus Rubbing Compound or Turtle Wax Color Back. Finally, apply wax polish from one of the Turtle Wax range of wax polishes.

Where the scratch has penetrated right through to the metal of the bodywork, causing the metal to rust, a different repair technique is required. Remove any loose rust from the bottom of the scratch with a penknife, then apply rust-inhibiting paint such as Turtle Wax Rust Master, to prevent the formation of rust in the future. Using a rubber or nylon applicator, fill the scratch with bodystopper paste like Holts Body+Plus Knifing Putty. If required, this paste can be mixed with cellulose thinners such as Holts Body+Plus Cellulose Thinners, to provide a very thin paste which is ideal for filling narrow scratches. Before the stopper-paste in the scratch hardens, wrap a piece of smooth cotton rag around the top of a finger. Dip the finger in cellulose thinners, and quickly sweep it across the surface of the stopper-paste in the scratch; this will ensure that the surface of the stopper-paste is slightly hollowed. The scratch can now be painted over as described earlier in this Section.

Repairs of dents in bodywork

When deep denting of the vehicle's bodywork has taken place, the first task is to pull the dent out, until the affected bodywork almost attains its original shape. There is little point in trying to restore the original shape completely, as the metal in the damaged area will have stretched on impact, and cannot be reshaped fully to its original contour. It is better to bring the level of the dent up to a point which is about 3 mm below the level of the surrounding bodywork. In cases where the dent is very shallow anyway, it is not worth trying to pull it out at all. If the underside of the dent is accessible, it can be hammered out gently from behind, using a mallet with a wooden or plastic head. Whilst doing this, hold a suitable block of wood firmly against the outside of the panel, to absorb the impact from the hammer blows and thus prevent a large area of the bodywork from being "belled-out".

Should the dent be in a section of the bodywork which has a double skin, or some other factor making it inaccessible from behind, a different technique is called for. Drill several small holes through the metal inside the area - particularly in the deeper section. Then screw long self-tapping screws into the holes, just sufficiently for them to gain a good purchase in the metal. Now the dent can be pulled out by pulling on the protruding heads of the screws with a pair of pliers.

The next stage of the repair is the removal of the paint from the damaged area, and from an inch or so of the surrounding "sound" bodywork. This is accomplished most easily by using a wire brush or abrasive pad on a power drill, although it can be done just as effectively by hand, using sheets of abrasive paper. To complete the preparation for filling, score the surface of the bare metal with a screwdriver or the tang of a file, or alternatively, drill small holes in the affected area. This will provide a really good "key" for the filler paste.

To complete the repair, see the Section on filling and respraying.

Repairs of rust holes or gashes in bodywork

Remove all paint from the affected area, and from an inch or so of the surrounding "sound" bodywork, using an abrasive pad or a wire brush on a power drill. If these are not available, a few sheets of abrasive paper will do the job most effectively. With the paint removed, you will be able to judge the severity of the corrosion, and therefore decide whether to renew the whole panel (if this is possible) or to repair the affected area. New body panels are not as expensive as most people think, and it is often quicker and more satisfactory to fit a new panel than to attempt to repair large areas of corrosion.

Remove all fittings from the affected area, except those which will act as a guide to the original shape of the damaged bodywork (eg headlight shells, etc). Then, using tin snips or a hacksaw blade, remove all loose metal and any other metal badly affected by corrosion. Hammer the edges of the hole inwards, in order to create a slight depression for the filler paste.

Wire-brush the affected area to remove the powdery rust from the surface of the remaining metal. Paint the affected area with rust-inhibiting paint such as Turtle Wax Rust Master; if the back of the rusted area is accessible, treat this also.

Before filling can take place, it will be necessary to block the hole in some way. This can be achieved by the use of aluminium or plastic mesh, or aluminium tape.

Aluminium or plastic mesh, or glass-fibre matting, is probably the best material to use for a large hole. Cut a piece to the approximate size and shape of the hole to be filled, then position it in the hole so that its edges are below the level of the surrounding bodywork. It can be retained in position by several blobs of filler paste around its periphery.

Aluminium tape should be used for small or very narrow holes. Pull a piece off the roll, trim it to the approximate size and shape required, then pull off the backing paper (if used) and stick the tape over the hole; it can be overlapped if the thickness of one piece is insufficient. Burnish down the edges of the tape with the handle of a screwdriver or similar, to ensure that the tape is securely attached to the metal underneath.

Bodywork repairs - filling and respraying

Before using this Section, see the Sections on dents, scratches, rust holes and gash repairs.

Many types of bodyfiller are available, but generally speaking, those proprietary kits which contain a tin of filler paste and a tube of resin hardener are best for this type of repair, like Holts Body+Plus or Holts No Mix, which can be used directly from the tube. A wide, flexible plastic or nylon applicator will be found invaluable for imparting a smooth and well-contoured finish to the surface of the filler.

Mix up a little filler on a clean piece of card or board - measure the hardener carefully (follow the maker's instructions on the pack), otherwise the filler will set too rapidly or too slowly. Alternatively, Holts No Mix can be used straight from the tube without mixing, but daylight is required to cure it. Using the applicator, apply the filler paste to the prepared area; draw the applicator across the surface of the filler to achieve the correct contour and to level the surface. As soon as a contour that approximates to the correct one is achieved, stop working the paste - if you carry on too long, the paste will become sticky and begin to "pick-up" on the applicator. Continue to add thin layers of filler paste at 20-minute intervals, until the level of the filler is just proud of the surrounding bodywork.

Once the filler has hardened, the excess can be removed using a metal plane or file. From then on, progressively-finer grades of abrasive paper should be used, starting with a 40-grade production paper, and finishing with a 400-grade wet-and-dry paper. Always wrap the abrasive paper around a flat rubber, cork, or wooden block - otherwise the surface of the filler will not be completely flat. During the smoothing of the filler surface, the wet-and-dry paper should be periodically rinsed in water. This will ensure that a very smooth finish is imparted to the filler at the final stage.

At this stage, the "dent" should be surrounded by a ring of bare metal, which in turn should be encircled by the finely "feathered" edge of the good paintwork. Rinse the repair area with clean water, until all of the dust produced by the rubbing-down operation has gone.

Spray the whole area with a light coat of primer, either Holts Body+Plus Grey or Red Oxide Primer - this will show up any imperfections in the surface of the filler. Repair these imperfections with fresh filler paste or bodystopper, and once more smooth the surface with abrasive paper. If bodystopper is used, it can be mixed with cellulose thinners, to form a really thin paste which is ideal for filling small holes. Repeat this spray-and-repair procedure until you are satisfied that the surface of the filler, and the feathered edge of the paintwork, are perfect. Clean the repair area with clean water, and allow to dry fully.

The repair area is now ready for final spraying. Paint spraying must be carried out in a warm, dry, windless and dust-free atmosphere. This condition can be created artificially if you have access to a large indoor working area, but if you are forced to work in the open, you will have to pick your day very carefully. If you are working indoors, dousing the floor in the work area with water will help to settle the dust which would otherwise be in the atmosphere. If the repair area is confined to one body panel, mask off the surrounding panels; this will help to minimise the effects of a slight mis-match in paint colours. Bodywork fittings (eg chrome strips, door handles etc) will also need to be masked off. Use genuine masking tape, and several thicknesses of newspaper, for the masking operations.

Before commencing to spray, agitate the aerosol can thoroughly, then spray a test area (an old tin, or similar) until the technique is mastered. Cover the repair area with a thick coat of primer; the thickness should be built up using several thin layers of paint, rather than one thick one. Using 400-grade wet-and-dry paper, rub down the surface of the primer until it is really smooth. While doing this, the work area should be thoroughly doused with water, and the wet-and-dry paper periodically rinsed in water. Allow to dry before spraying on more paint.

Spray on the top coat using Holts Dupli-Color Autospray, again building up the thickness by using several thin layers of paint. Start spraying in the centre of the repair area, and then, using a circular motion, work outwards until the whole repair area and about 2 inches of the surrounding original paintwork is covered. Remove all masking material 10 to 15 minutes after spraying on the final coat of paint.

Allow the new paint at least two weeks to harden, then, using a paintwork renovator or a very fine cutting paste such as Turtle Wax Color Back or Holts Body+Plus Rubbing Compound, blend the edges of the paint into the existing paintwork. Finally, apply wax polish.

Plastic components

With the use of more and more plastic body components by the vehicle manufacturers (eg bumpers. spoilers, and in some cases major body panels), rectification of more serious damage to such items has become a matter of either entrusting repair work to a specialist in this field, or renewing complete components. Repair of such damage by the DIY owner is not really feasible, owing to the cost of the equipment and materials required for effecting such repairs. The basic technique involves making a groove along the line of the crack in the plastic, using a rotary burr in a power drill. The damaged part is then welded back together, using a hot air gun to heat up and fuse a plastic filler rod into the groove. Any excess plastic is then removed, and the area rubbed down to a smooth finish. It is important that a filler rod of the correct plastic is used, as body components can be made of a variety of different types (eg polycarbonate, ABS, polypropylene).

Damage of a less serious nature (abrasions, minor cracks etc) can be repaired by the DIY owner using a two-part epoxy filler repair material, such as Holts Body+Plus or Holts No Mix, which can be used directly from the tube. Once mixed in equal proportions (or applied directly from the tube in the case of Holts No Mix), this is used in similar fashion to the bodywork filler used on metal panels. The filler is usually cured in twenty to thirty minutes, ready for sanding and painting.

If the owner is renewing a complete component himself, or if he has repaired it with epoxy filler, he will be left with the problem of finding a suitable paint for finishing which is compatible with the type of plastic used. At one time, the use of a universal paint was not possible, owing to the complex range of plastics encountered in body component applications. Standard paints, generally speaking, will not bond to plastic or rubber satisfactorily, but Holts Professional Spraymatch paints, to match any plastic or rubber finish, can be obtained from dealers. However, it is now possible to obtain a plastic body parts finishing kit which consists of a pre-primer treatment, a primer and coloured top coat. Full instructions are normally supplied with a kit, but basically, the method of use is to first apply the pre-primer to the component concerned, and allow it to dry for up to 30 minutes. Then the primer is applied, and left to dry for about an hour before finally applying the special-coloured top coat. The result is a correctly-coloured component, where the paint will flex with the plastic or rubber, a property that standard paint does not normally posses.

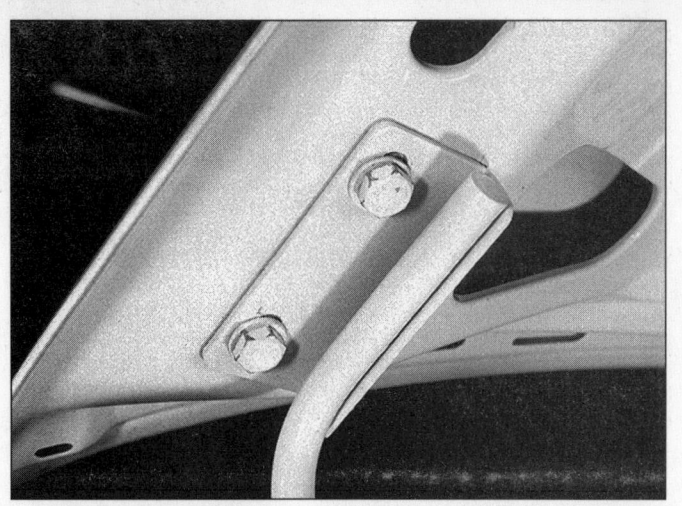

6.2 Mark around the bonnet hinges, to show the outline of their fitted positions for correct realignment on assembly

5 Major body damage - repair

With the exception of Chassis Cab versions, the chassis members are spot-welded to the underbody, and in this respect can be termed of monocoque or unit construction. Major damage repairs to this type of body combination must of necessity be carried out by body shops with welding and hydraulic straightening facilities.

Extensive damage to the body may distort the chassis, and result in unstable and dangerous handling, as well as excessive wear to tyres and suspension or steering components. It is recommended that checking of the chassis alignment be entrusted to a Ford agent with specialist checking jigs.

6 Bonnet - removal, refitting and adjustment

Removal

1 Open the bonnet, and support it with its stay rod.
2 Mark around the bonnet hinges, to show the outline of their fitted positions for correct realignment on assembly **(see illustration)**.
3 Have an assistant support the bonnet whilst you unscrew and remove the hinge retaining bolts, then lift the bonnet clear.

Refitting

4 Refitting is a reversal of removal. Tighten the hinge bolts fully when bonnet alignment is satisfactory.

Adjustment

5 Further adjustment of the bonnet fit is available by loosening the hinges and the locknuts of the bump stops on the front crossmember. The bonnet can now be adjusted to give an even clearance between its outer edges and the surrounding panels. Adjust the front bump stops to align the edges of the bonnet with the front wing panels, then retighten the locknuts and hinge bolts.

7 Bonnet release cable and latch - renewal

Release cable

1 Open and support the bonnet. If the cable is broken, release the latch by reaching up from the underside, and release it by hand using a suitably-shaped rod (welding rod may suffice).
2 Where fitted, undo the screws and remove the plastic cover from the front panel for access. Release both the cable nipple from the

Chapter 11 Bodywork and fittings   11-5

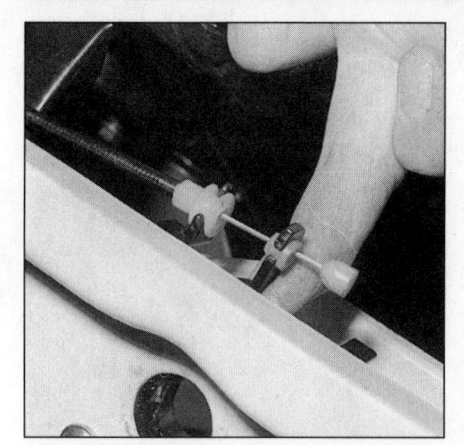

7.2 Bonnet release cable attachments at the latch

7.3 Detach the bonnet cable from the release handle

7.6 Removing the bonnet latch from the front panel

8.2 Bonnet safety catch

9.1a Prise free the trim from the window regulator handle, undo the retaining screw . . .

9.1b . . . then withdraw the handle . . .

latch, and the outer cable from the inner face of the front panel **(see illustration)**.
3   Detach the cable from the release handle by sliding it sideways **(see illustration)**.
4   Withdraw the cable through from the engine compartment side, complete with the bulkhead grommet.
5   Refitting is a reversal of removal. Check for satisfactory operation on completion.

Bonnet latch

6   Detach the cable from the latch as described previously, then undo the three retaining screws. Remove the latch from the front panel **(see illustration)**.
7   Refitting is a reversal of removal.

8   Bonnet safety catch - removal and refitting

Removal

1   Open the bonnet, and support it with its stay rod.
2   Make an alignment mark around the fitted position of the safety catch to the bonnet, with a pencil or marker pen. Undo the catch retaining bolts and the release lever Torx screw, then remove the two items complete with the connecting rod **(see illustration)**.

Refitting

3   Refitting is a reversal of removal, but note the following additional points:

a)   Align the catch with the markings made when removing the catch.
b)   When tightening the release lever screw, tighten it slowly until secure. When tightened, check that the lever movement is satisfactory, and that it does not bind.
c)   Take care not to overtighten the catch or release lever securing bolts/screw, or the safety catch may stick in the open or closed position.

9   Door trim panels - removal and refitting

Front doors

Removal

1   On pre-1995 model year vehicles, prise free the trim from the window regulator handle, undo the retaining screw, note the fitted position of the handle on its shaft (with the window fully raised), then withdraw the handle and the escutcheon plate **(see illustrations)**.
2   On 1995 model year onwards vehicles, fitted with manual window regulators, fully shut the window, note the position of the regulator handle, then release the spring clip and withdraw the handle. The clip can be released by inserting a clean cloth between the handle and the door trim, and pulling the cloth back against the open ends of the clip to release its tension, whilst simultaneously pulling the handle from the regulator shaft splines.
3   On vehicles with electric window regulators, remove the switches as described in Chapter 12, Section 4.

11-6 Chapter 11 Bodywork and fittings

9.1c ... and escutcheon plate

9.4 Undo the retaining screw and remove the remote release handle surround

9.6a Prise back the trim covers from the door pull handle ...

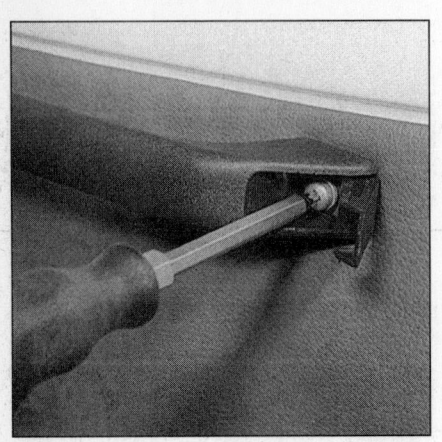

9.6b ... then undo the retaining screws

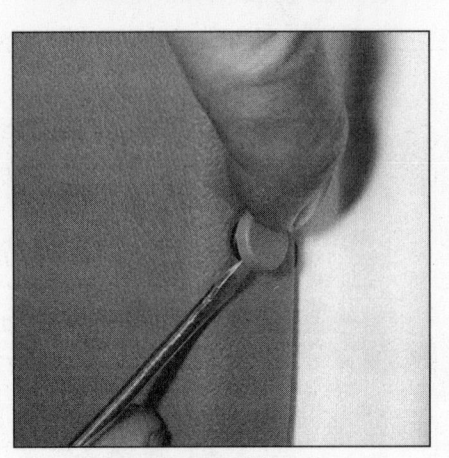

9.7a On later models, prise off the trim caps ...

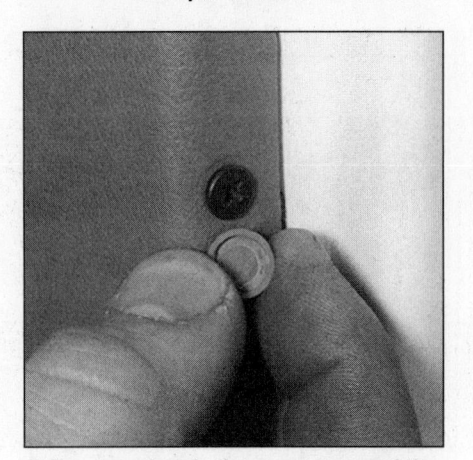

9.7b ... and undo the screws around the periphery of the door trim panel

4 Undo the retaining screw, and remove the remote release handle surround **(see illustration)**.
5 Where fitted, remove the door bin by prising up the two trim covers (one at each upper edge) and removing the screws.
6 Prise back the two trim covers from the door pull handle using a suitable screwdriver or a similar tool. Undo the two retaining screws, and remove the handle **(see illustrations)**.
7 On early models, carefully prise free the door trim panel, prising with a suitable tool between the panel around its outer and lower edges at the fixing points. On later models, prise off the trim caps and undo the screws around the periphery of the panel **(see illustrations)**. Remove the panel.
8 If the panel has been removed for access to the door internal components, the plastic insulation sheet will have to be locally removed for access. To do this, cut through the adhesive securing the plastic sheet to the door using a sharp knife. Now carefully peel back the insulation sheet as necessary. Do not attempt to peel back the sheet without first cutting through the adhesive, and take care not to touch the adhesive after the sheet has been removed. If care is taken, the existing adhesive will re-bond the sheet on completion.

Refitting

9 Refitting is a reversal of removal.

Rear doors and tailgate

Removal

10 Remove the inner handle trim surround (where applicable) by sliding it sideways.
11 The rear door trim panels are secured by plastic retaining clips, the removal of which requires the use of a suitable forked tool **(see illustration)**. These clips are easily broken, so take care when prising them free. Remove the trim panel.

Refitting

12 Refitting is a reversal of removal. Align the panel, and press the clips into position.

Sliding side door

Removal

13 Undo the retaining screws and remove the bump stop **(see illustration)**.
14 Undo the retaining screw and remove the inner lock escutcheon **(see illustration)**.
15 Carefully prise free the plastic retaining clips using a suitable forked tool **(see illustration 9.11)**, then remove the panel.

Refitting

16 Refitting is a reversal of removal.

10 Front door fittings - removal and refitting

Exterior handle (pre-1995 model year)

Removal

1 Remove the door inner trim panel as described in the previous Section.
2 Working through the access apertures in the inner panel, undo the two Torx screws and remove the handle **(see illustration)**.

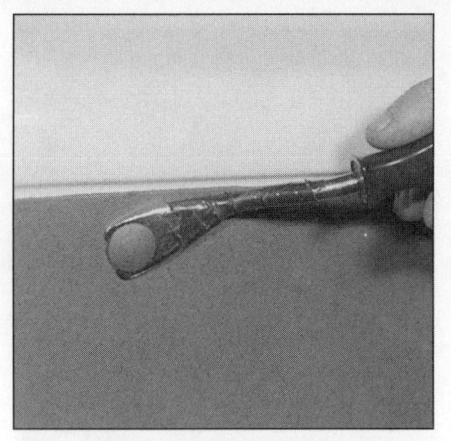

Chapter 11 Bodywork and fittings

9.11 Using a forked tool to release the trim panel retaining clips

9.13 Undo the retaining screws and remove the sliding side door bump stop

9.14 Sliding side door inner lock

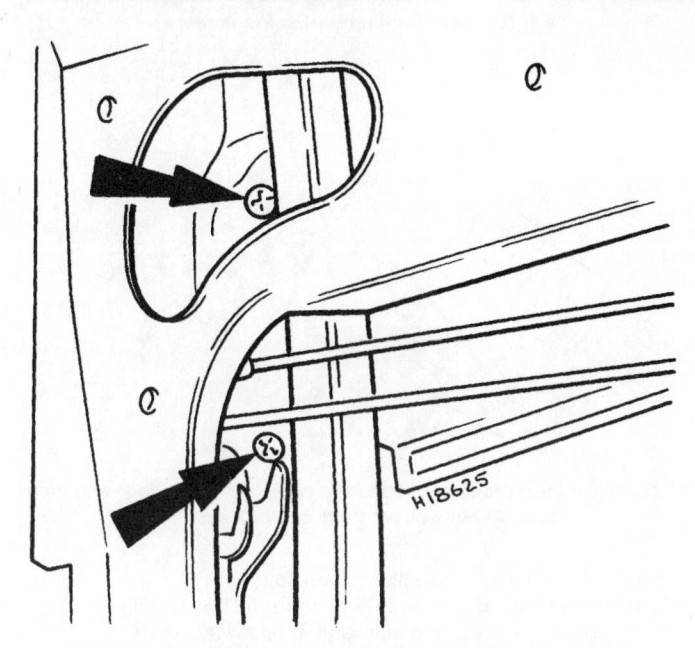

10.2 Undo the two Torx screws (arrowed) and remove the front door exterior handle

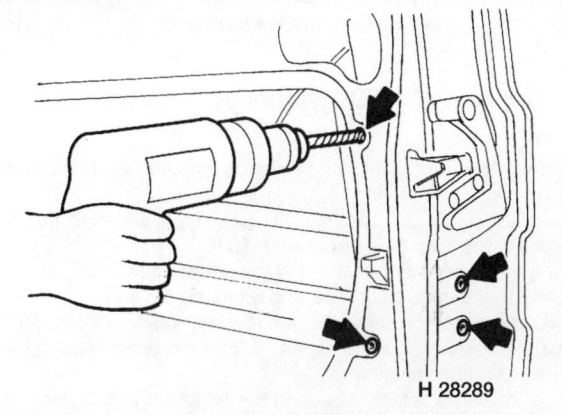

10.5 Drill out the four rivets (arrowed) securing the door lock shield panel to the door

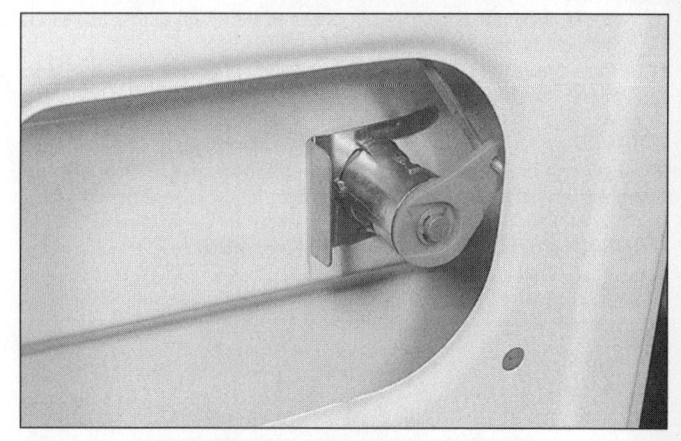

10.12 Door lock barrel and securing clip

Refitting
3 Refitting is a reversal of removal.

Exterior handle (1995 model year onwards)
Removal
4 Remove the front door window and regulator as described in Section 18.
5 Using a suitable drill, drill out the four rivets securing the lock shield panel to the door **(see illustration)**.
6 Using a sharp knife, cut through the adhesive securing the lock shield panel to the outer door skin, and withdraw the panel.
7 Undo the screw securing the window rear guide channel to the door, pull the channel down to release it from the upper locating clip, and remove the guide channel.
8 Undo the three screws securing the lock unit to the door, and slightly withdraw the lock for access.
9 Undo the two screws and remove the exterior handle.

Refitting
10 Refitting is a reversal of removal. Use new rivets to secure the lock shield panel to the door.

Door lock barrel (pre-1995 model year)
Removal
11 Remove the door inner trim panel as described in the previous Section.
12 Prise free the lock barrel securing clip using a suitable screwdriver as a lever, withdraw the lock unit and detach the operating rod **(see illustration)**.

Refitting
13 Refitting is a reversal of removal.

11-8 Chapter 11 Bodywork and fittings

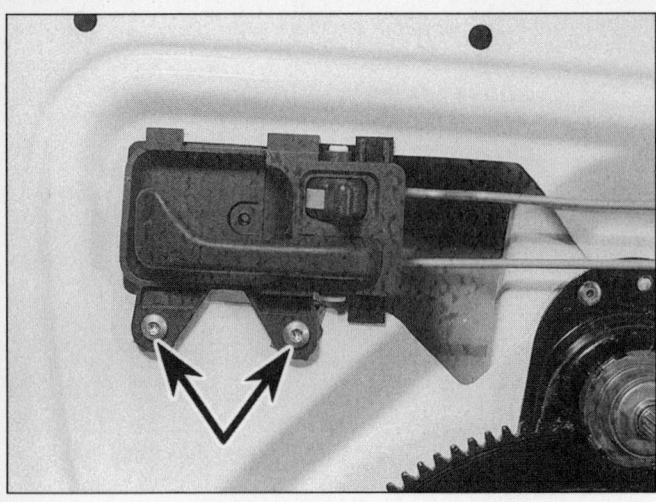

10.24 Detach the door lock remote release handle by unscrewing the two Torx screws (arrowed)

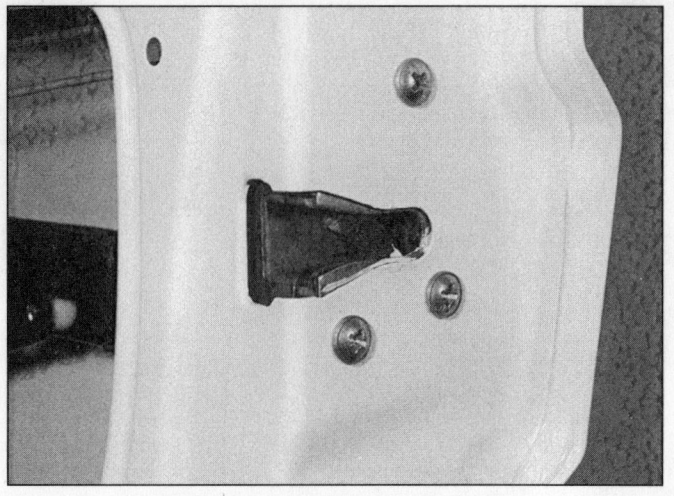

10.25 Door lock unit retaining screws

Door lock barrel (1995 model year onwards)

Removal

14 Remove the front door window and regulator as described in Section 18.
15 Using a suitable drill, drill out the four rivets securing the lock shield panel to the door **(see illustration 10.5)**.
16 Using a sharp knife, cut through the adhesive securing the lock shield panel to the outer door skin, and withdraw the panel.
17 Undo the screw securing the window rear guide channel to the door, pull the channel down to release it from the upper locating clip, and remove the guide channel.
18 Undo the three screws securing the lock unit to the door, and slightly withdraw the lock for access.
19 Release the retaining clip, and disconnect the operating rod from the lock barrel.
20 Where applicable, disconnect the central locking set/reset switch from the lock barrel.
21 Prise free the lock barrel securing clip using a suitable screwdriver as a lever, and withdraw the lock barrel.

Refitting

22 Refitting is a reversal of removal. Use new rivets to secure the lock shield panel to the door.

Door lock unit (pre-1995 model year)

Removal

23 Remove the door inner trim panel as described in the previous Section.
24 Detach the remote release handle by unscrewing the two Torx screws **(see illustration)**.
25 Undo the three retaining screws, and remove the door lock complete with connecting rods and the inner remote release unit **(see illustration)**. Detach the connecting rods from their retaining clips as the assembly is removed from the door.

Refitting

26 Refitting is a reversal of removal. Do not fully tighten the door lock screws until after the inner remote release unit and the connecting rods are secured.

Door lock unit (1995 model year onwards)

Removal

27 Remove the front door window and regulator as described in Section 18.
28 Using a suitable drill, drill out the four rivets securing the lock

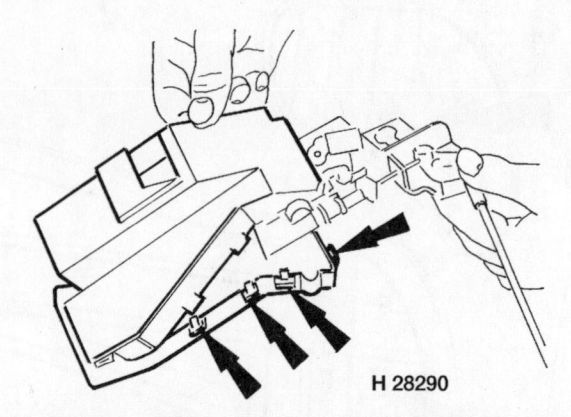

10.33 On later models, release the clips (arrowed) and remove the protective cover from the lock assembly

shield panel to the door **(see illustration 10.5)**.
29 Using a sharp knife, cut through the adhesive securing the lock shield panel to the outer door skin, and withdraw the panel.
30 Undo the screw securing the window rear guide channel to the door, pull the channel down to release it from the upper locating clip, and remove the guide channel.
31 Undo the three screws securing the lock unit to the door, and slightly withdraw the lock assembly for access. Where fitted, disconnect the central locking wiring multi-plug.
32 Release the retaining clip and disconnect the operating rod from the lock barrel.
33 Withdraw the lock assembly, then carefully release the clips and remove the protective cover **(see illustration)**.
34 Disconnect the inner remote release unit cable from the lock assembly, and remove the lock from the door **(see illustration)**.
35 If required, the central locking motor (where fitted) may be removed from the lock assembly by undoing the two screws and twisting the motor to detach the operating rod.

Refitting

36 Refitting is a reversal of removal. Use new rivets to secure the lock shield panel to the door.

Inner remote release unit and cable (1995 model year onwards)

Removal

37 Remove the door inner trim panel as described in the previous Section.

Chapter 11 Bodywork and fittings

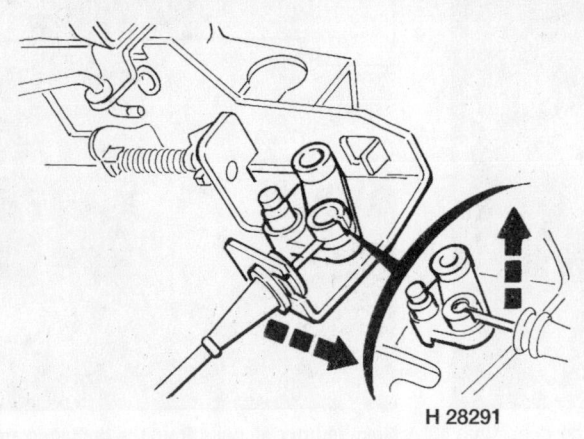

10.34 Disconnect the inner remote release unit cable from the lock assembly as indicated

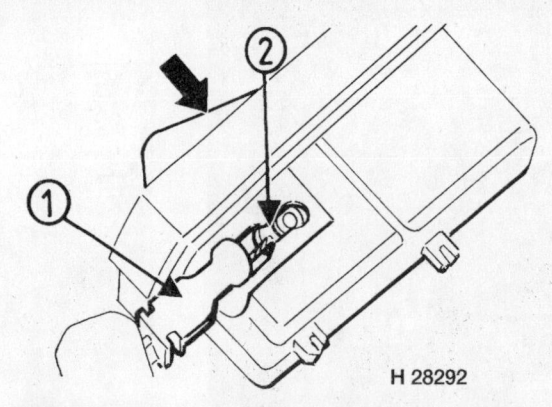

10.40 Detach the release cable plastic outer cable end and blanking piece (1) from the release unit. Apply light inwards pressure to the release handle when in the locked position, to align the cable end with the release slot (2)

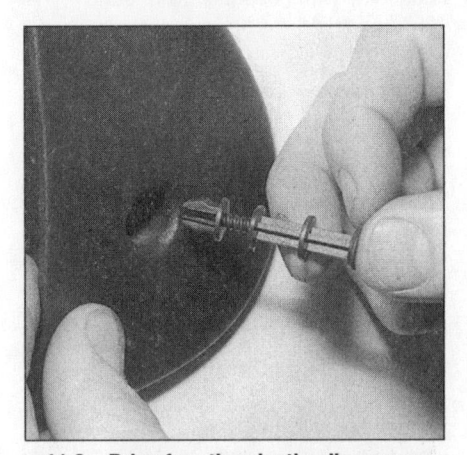

11.2a Prise free the plastic clip covers from the door upper hinge cover

11.2b Removing the hinge cover inner retaining clip

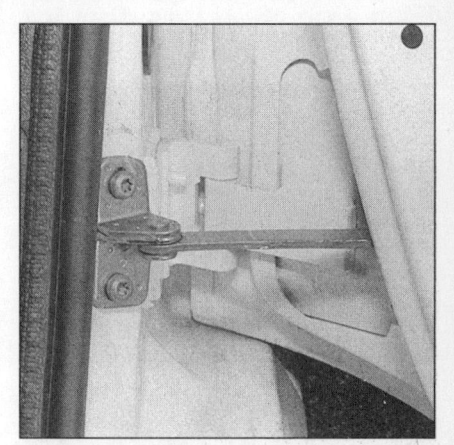

11.3 Undo the two Torx screws securing the door check strap

38 Undo the screw securing the inner remote release unit to the door.
39 Withdraw the release unit, and remove the plastic shroud.
40 Detach the release cable plastic outer cable end and blanking piece from the release unit. Apply light inwards pressure to the release handle when in the locked position, to align the cable end with the release slot **(see illustration)**.
41 Push down on the cable end to disconnect it from the release unit, then remove the unit.
42 To remove the cable completely, remove the door lock unit as described previously, and disconnect the other end of the cable from the lock.

Refitting

43 Refitting is a reversal of removal.

11 Front door - removal, refitting and adjustment

Pre-1995 model year
Removal
1 Open the door, and position a suitable padded jack or support blocks underneath it; don't lift the door, just take its weight.
2 Prise free the plastic clip covers from the door upper hinge cover, then remove the screws and the cover **(see illustrations)**.
3 Undo the two Torx screws securing the door check strap **(see illustration)**.

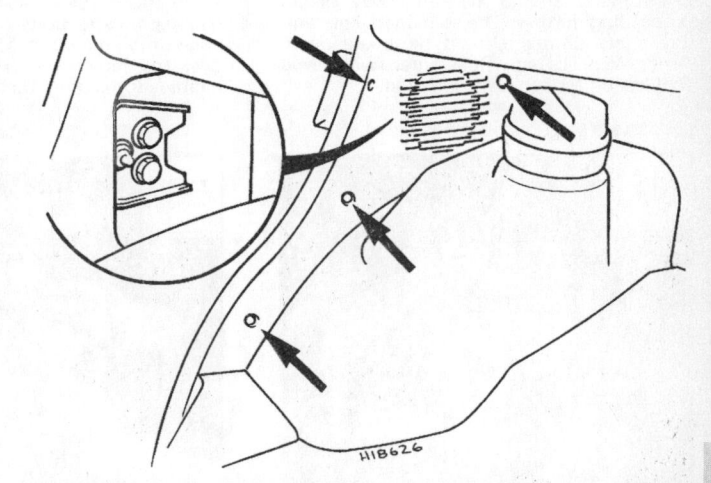

11.4a Remove the front footwell trim (clips arrowed) for access to the door lower hinge bolts

4 Undo the four retaining screws, and remove the front footwell trim for access to the door lower hinge bolts **(see illustration)**. Have an assistant support the door, then unscrew the two retaining bolts and single nut from the lower hinge, and the three retaining bolts from the upper hinge **(see illustration)**. Carefully remove the door.

1. This photographic sequence shows the steps taken to repair the dent and paintwork damage shown above. In general, the procedure for repairing a hole will be similar; where there are substantial differences, the procedure is clearly described and shown in a separate photograph.

2. First remove any trim around the dent, then hammer out the dent where access is possible. This will minimise filling. Here, after the large dent has been hammered out, the damaged area is being made slightly concave.

3. Next, remove all paint from the damaged area by rubbing with coarse abrasive paper or using a power drill fitted with a wire brush or abrasive pad. 'Feather' the edge of the boundary with good paintwork using a finer grade of abrasive paper.

4. Where there are holes or other damage, the sheet metal should be cut away before proceeding further. The damaged area and any signs of rust should be treated with Turtle Wax Hi-Tech Rust Eater, which will also inhibit further rust formation.

5. *For a large dent or hole* mix Holts Body Plus Resin and Hardener according to the manufacturer's instructions and apply around the edge of the repair. Press Glass Fibre Matting over the repair area and leave for 20-30 minutes to harden. Then ...

5A. ... brush more Holts Body Plus Resin and Hardener onto the matting and leave to harden. Repeat the sequence with two or three layers of matting, checking that the final layer is lower than the surrounding area. Apply Holts Body Plus Filler Paste as shown in Step 5B.

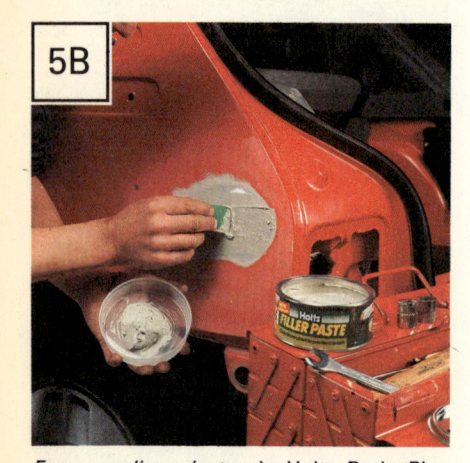

5B. *For a medium dent*, mix Holts Body Plus Filler Paste and Hardener according to the manufacturer's instructions and apply it with a flexible applicator. Apply thin layers of filler at 20-minute intervals, until the filler surface is slightly proud of the surrounding bodywork.

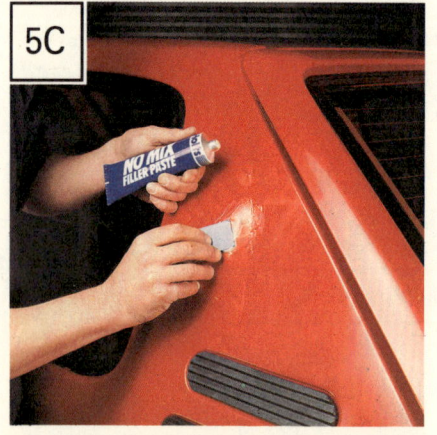

5C. *For small dents and scratches* use Holts No Mix Filler Paste straight from the tube. Apply it according to the instructions in thin layers, using the spatula provided. It will harden in minutes if applied outdoors and may then be used as its own knifing putty.

6. Use a plane or file for initial shaping. Then, using progressively finer grades of wet-and-dry paper, wrapped round a sanding block, and copious amounts of clean water, rub down the filler until glass smooth. 'Feather' the edges of adjoining paintwork.

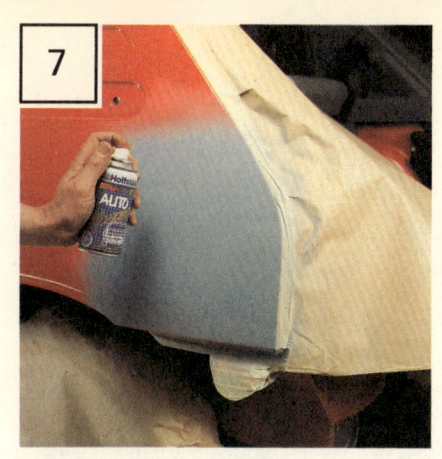

7 Protect adjoining areas before spraying the whole repair area and at least one inch of the surrounding sound paintwork with Holts Dupli-Color primer.

8 Fill any imperfections in the filler surface with a small amount of Holts Body Plus Knifing Putty. Using plenty of clean water, rub down the surface with a fine grade wet-and-dry paper – 400 grade is recommended – until it is really smooth.

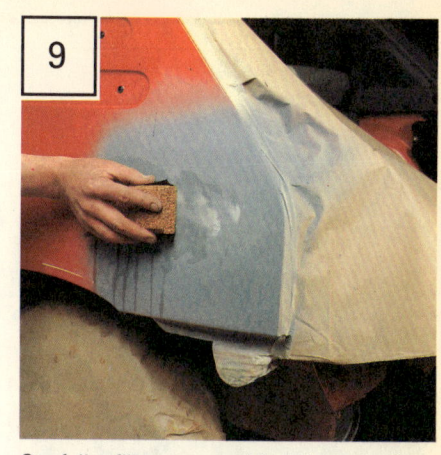

9 Carefully fill any remaining imperfections with knifing putty before applying the last coat of primer. Then rub down the surface with Holts Body Plus Rubbing Compound to ensure a really smooth surface.

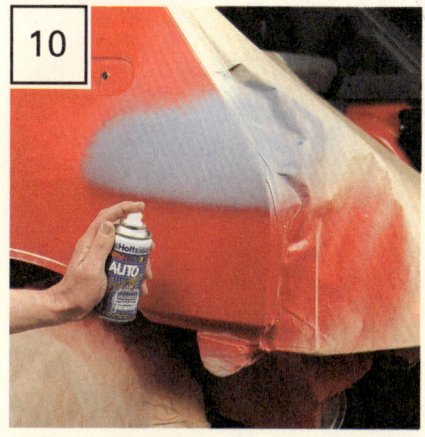

10 Protect surrounding areas from overspray before applying the topcoat in several thin layers. Agitate Holts Dupli-Color aerosol thoroughly. Start at the repair centre, spraying outwards with a side-to-side motion.

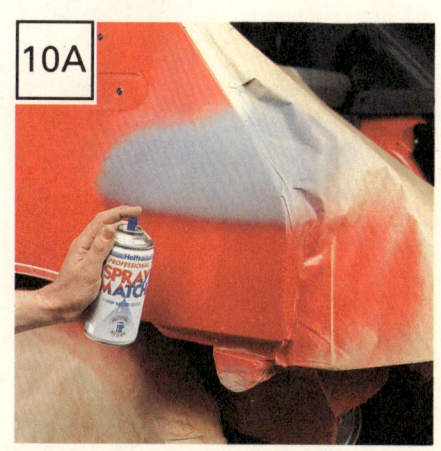

10A If the exact colour is not available off the shelf, local Holts Professional Spraymatch Centres will custom fill an aerosol to match perfectly.

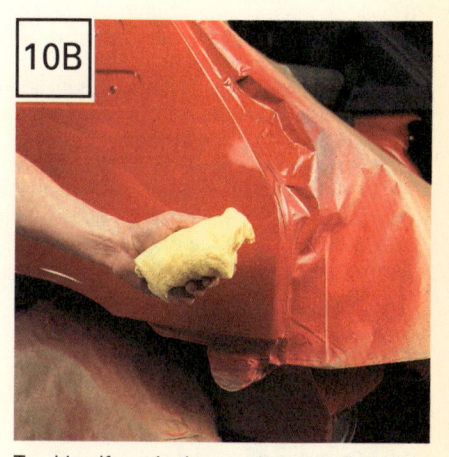

10B To identify whether a lacquer finish is required, rub a painted unrepaired part of the body with wax and a clean cloth.

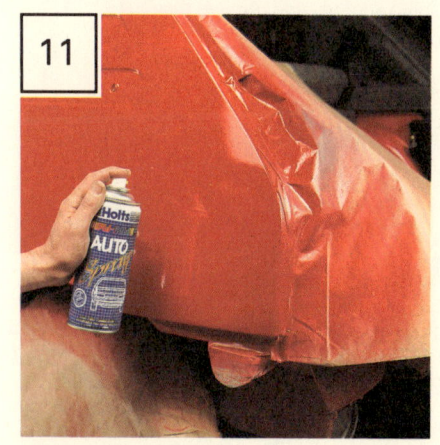

11 If *no* traces of paint appear on the cloth, spray Holts Dupli-Color clear lacquer over the repaired area to achieve the correct gloss level.

12 The paint will take about two weeks to harden fully. After this time it can be 'cut' with a mild cutting compound such as Turtle Wax Minute Cut prior to polishing with a final coating of Turtle Wax Extra.

14 When carrying out bodywork repairs, remember that the quality of the finished job is proportional to the time and effort expended.

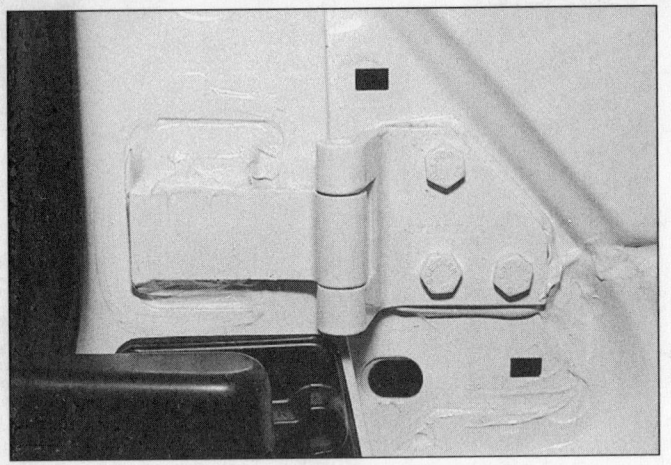

11-10　Chapter 11　Bodywork and fittings

11.4b Door upper hinge retaining bolts

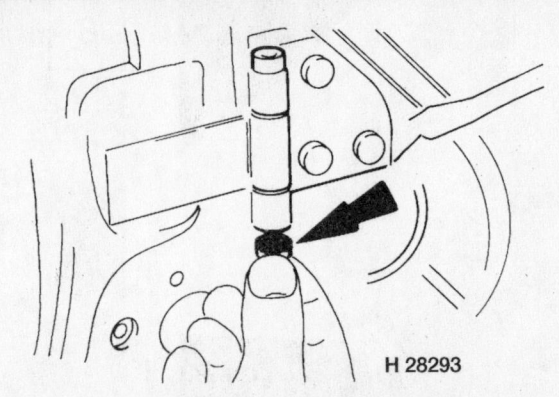

11.16 On later models, remove the hinge pin retaining clips (arrowed) and push out the hinge pins

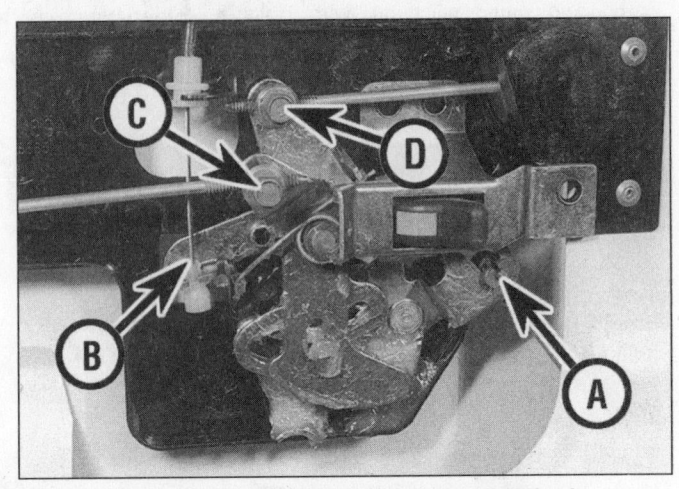

Refitting and adjustment

5 Align the retaining stud of the lower hinge, and insert a retaining bolt in the upper hinge. Hand-tighten the bolt to secure the upper hinge and door.
6 Fit and hand-tighten the remaining upper and lower hinge bolts.
7 Reconnect the door check strap, then shut the door and align it in its aperture so that it has an even clearance all round. When satisfied, tighten the upper hinge bolts from within the cab.
8 Tighten the lower hinge bolts and retaining nut, then open the door and shut it to ensure that it does not bind with the body aperture at any point. Adjust the door striker plate if necessary, then refit the footwell and hinge trims to complete.

1995 model year onwards
Removal
9 Disconnect the battery negative lead.
10 Undo the four retaining screws, and remove the front footwell trim for access to the door lower hinge.
11 Open the door, and position a suitable padded jack or support blocks underneath it; don't lift the door, just take its weight.
12 Undo the two screws, and release the wiring multi-plug support bracket. Disconnect the door harness wiring multi-plug.
13 Squeeze the grommet on the "A" pillar, and withdraw the grommet complete with wiring harness.
14 Undo the two Torx screws securing the door check strap.
15 Prise free the plastic clip covers from the door upper hinge cover, remove the screws and the cover.
16 Have an assistant support the door, then remove the hinge pin retaining clips, push out the two hinge pins, and remove the door **(see illustration)**.

Refitting and adjustment
17 Refitting is a reversal of removal. Open and shut the door to ensure that it does not bind with the body aperture at any point. Adjust the door striker plate if necessary, then refit the footwell and hinge trims to complete.

12 Sliding side door fittings - removal and refitting

Handle
Removal
1 Remove the door inner trim as described in Section 9.
2 Detach the outer handle operating rod, then undo the retaining nuts, remove the washers and withdraw the handle.

Refitting
3 Refitting is a reversal of removal.

12.11 Sliding side door lock remote control unit

A Lock rod and clip　　C Latch rod
B Handle cable　　　　D Handle rod

Lock unit
Removal
4 Remove the door inner trim panel as described in Section 9.
5 Slide the door partly open, then detach the latch operating rod.
6 Undo the three retaining screws, and remove the lock unit.

Refitting
7 Refitting is a reversal of removal.

Lock remote control unit
Removal
8 Remove the door inner trim panel as described in Section 9.
9 Remove the caps and unscrew the door latch release handle retaining screws.
10 Detach the inner and outer operating cable, and remove the handle and cable.
11 Detach the lock barrel operating rod. Loosen off the latch and outer handle operating rod screws, release the shorter handle rod clip, and remove the rod **(see illustration)**.
12 Carefully drill out the lock remote control unit retaining rivets, and remove the unit from the door.

Refitting
13 Refit in the reverse order of removal. When offering the unit to the door, check that the latch rod fits into the lower retaining boss, and engage the outer handle rod. Align the unit with the rivet holes and fit new rivets.

Chapter 11 Bodywork and fittings   11•11

12.17a Undo the centre rail retaining screw at the leading edge . . .

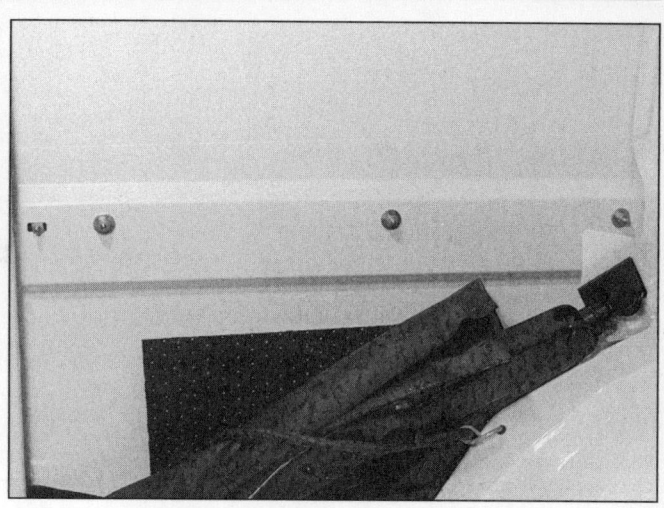

12.17b . . . and the stud nuts on the inside

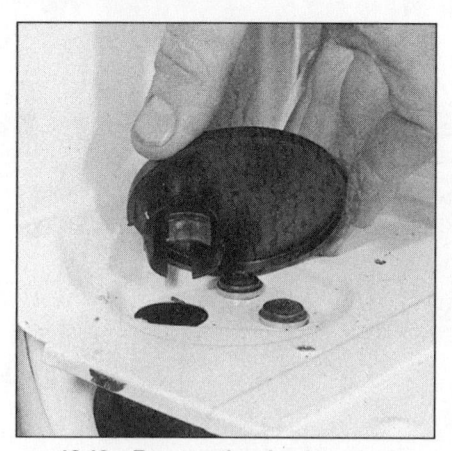

12.19a Remove the circular cover from the step . . .

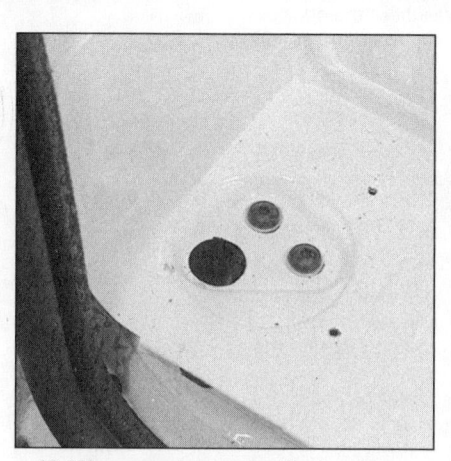

12.19b . . . and unscrew the two lower rail retaining screws

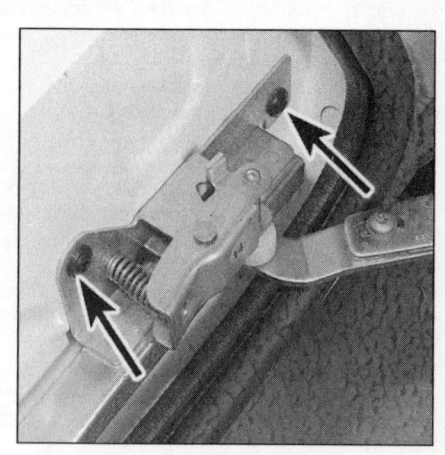

12.20 Undo the two screws (arrowed) and detach the lower guide support from the body

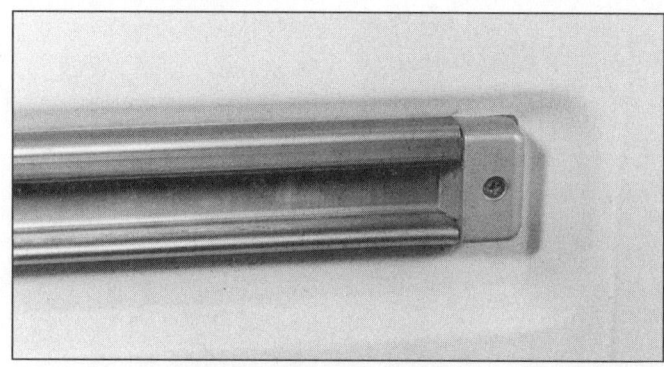

13.1 Undo the retaining screw, and remove the sliding side door end stop from the centre rail

14 Adjust the latch and lock rods to suit, then fit the inner handle cable and the lock barrel rod. Refit the trim.

Guide rails

Upper rail

15 Open the door, then undo the retaining screws and detach the upper guide support. Drill out the pop-rivets and remove the rail. Refit in the reverse order of removal. Adjust the upper guide rail to suit, then tighten the screws.

Centre rail

16 Remove the side door as described in Section 13.
17 Undo the retaining screw at the leading edge, and the stud nuts on the inside, then remove the rail **(see illustrations)**. Note that the rear nut is an expansion nut which also secures the end (stopper) cap.
18 Refitting is a reversal of removal.

Lower rail

19 Open the side door, remove the circular cover from the step, and unscrew the two retaining screws **(see illustrations)**.
20 Undo the two screws and detach the lower guide support **(see illustration)**.
21 Undo the retaining screws, and remove the lower rail complete with the lower latch unit.
22 Refitting is a reversal of removal. Check that the door operates smoothly and closes securely.

13 Sliding side door - removal, refitting and adjustment

Removal

1 Undo the retaining screw, and remove the end stop from the centre rail **(see illustration)**.
2 Slide the door open, and unscrew the Torx screws securing the door lower guide support **(see illustration)**.

11•12 Chapter 11 Bodywork and fittings

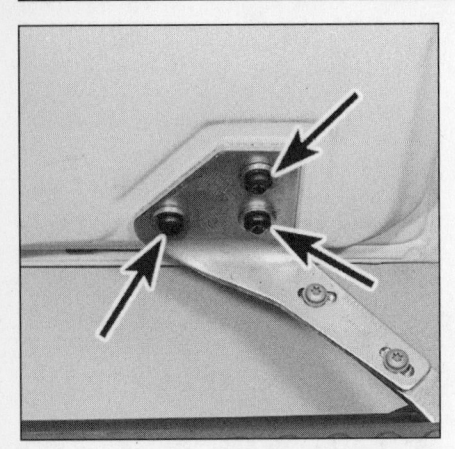

13.2 Unscrew the Torx screws (arrowed) securing the door lower guide support

13.3 Remove the Torx screws securing the upper guide support

13.6 Sliding side door lower guide support flush-fitting adjuster screws (arrowed)

3 Enlist the aid of an assistant to support the weight of the door on the centre rail, then remove the Torx screws securing the upper guide support **(see illustration)**.
4 Support the door at each end, slide it to the rear, and remove it from the vehicle.

Refitting
5 Refitting is a reversal of removal. Align the door and engage it onto the centre track, then reconnect the fittings.

Adjustment
6 Check the door for satisfactory flush-fitting adjustment. Adjust if necessary by loosening off the lower support adjuster screws to reposition the door as required, then tighten them and recheck the fitting **(see illustration)**.
7 To adjust the height, loosen off the upper support locknut, turn the adjuster bolt as required, then retighten the locknut to secure **(see illustration)**.
8 When fitted, and in the closed position, the door should be aligned flush to the surrounding body, and should close securely. If required, adjust the striker plate position to suit **(see illustration)**.

14 Rear door fittings - removal and refitting

1 In most instances, the door trim panel will need to be removed to provide access to the item concerned. Refer to Section 9 for details.

Lock barrel
Removal
2 Detach the lock lever rod and where fitted, disconnect the central locking set/reset switch from the lock barrel. Remove the barrel retaining plate, and then withdraw the lock barrel.

Refitting
3 Refitting is a reversal of removal.

Upper latch unit
Removal
4 Undo the two retaining bolts, detach the connecting rod, and remove the latch **(see illustration)**.

Refitting
5 Refitting is a reversal of removal.

Lock and rod unit
Removal
6 Hold the upper connecting rod so that the clips can be detached

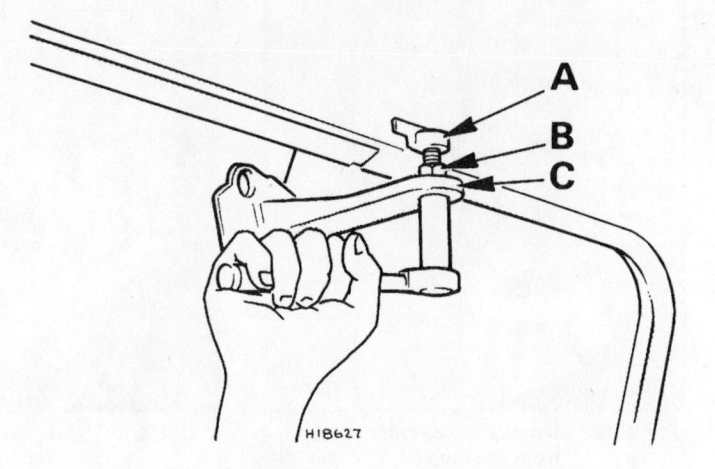

13.7 Sliding side door height adjustment at the upper guide support

A Roller unit
B Lock nut
C Upper support

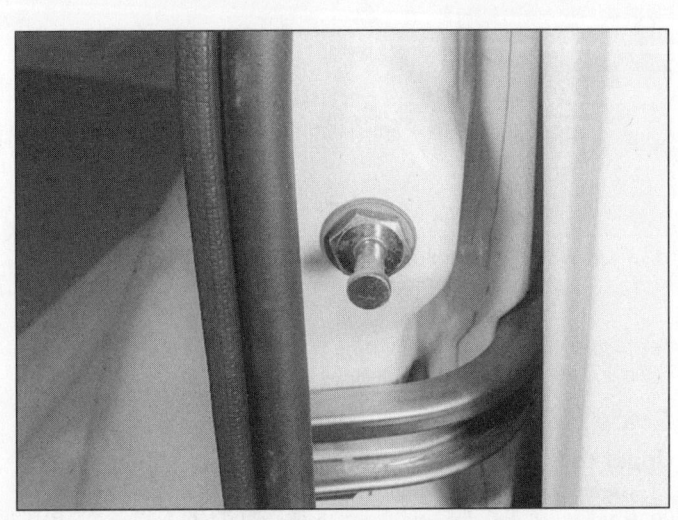

13.8 Sliding side door striker plate

Chapter 11 Bodywork and fittings

14.4 Rear door upper latch unit removal

from their rods and the rods disconnected from the lock unit.
7 Undo the three retaining screws, and remove the lock unit. Where applicable, disconnect the central locking wiring multi-plugs.

8 If required, the central locking motor (where fitted) may be removed from the lock assembly by undoing the two screws and twisting the motor to detach the operating rod.

Refitting
9 Refitting is a reversal of removal.

Lock release and lock unit
Removal
10 Undo the retaining screw **(see illustration)** and then partially withdraw the release handle, twisting it to detach the connecting rod.
11 Disconnect the operating rods from the outer handle and lock barrel, and the upper latch rod from the latch. Undo the three retaining screws and remove the latch unit.
12 If required, the lock barrel can be removed by prising free the retaining clip and withdrawing the lock barrel **(see illustrations)**.

Refitting
13 Refitting is a reversal of removal. Check the operation of the lock and latch before refitting the inner trim panel.

Inner release handle and striker assemblies
Removal
14 To remove the handle, undo the Torx screws and detach the striker rods (upper and lower) **(see illustration)**.

14.10 Rear door inner lock release unit and retaining screw

14.12a Rear door lock barrel and retaining clip

14.12b Rear door lock barrel removal

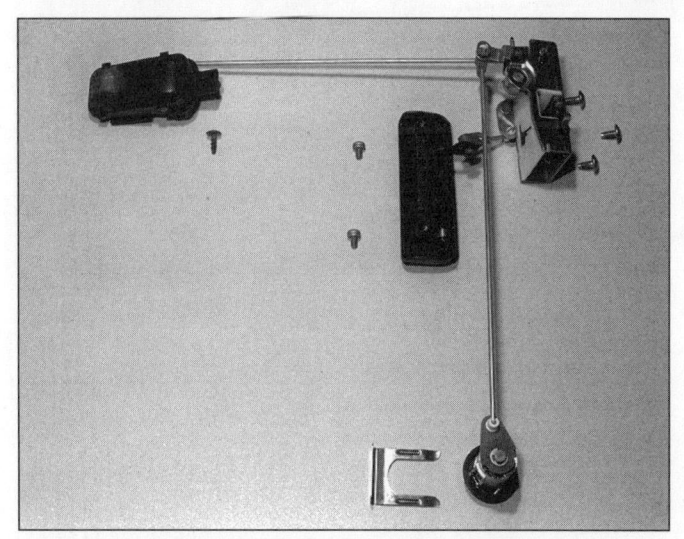

14.12c Rear door release handle, latch and lock unit showing connecting rods and securing screws

14.14 Rear door release handle

11-14 Chapter 11 Bodywork and fittings

14.15a Rear door upper striker rod (arrowed)

14.15b Rear door lower striker rod (arrowed)

14.15c Rear door lower striker guide plate

14.15d Rear door upper striker wedge plate

14.15e Rear door lower striker wedge plate

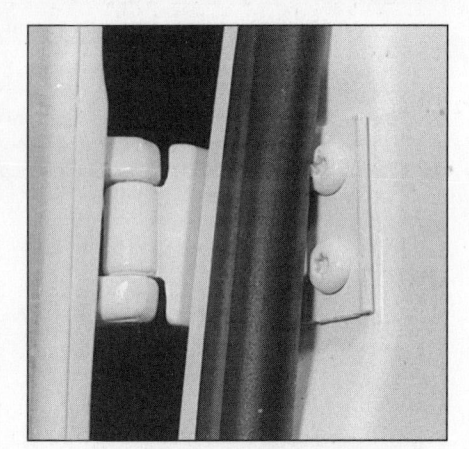

15.3a Rear door hinge attachment screws to door

15 The striker rod guide plates at the upper and lower corners can be removed by unscrewing their retaining screws, as can the striker plates **(see illustrations)**.

Refitting
16 Refitting is a reversal of removal, but adjust the strikers to suit.

15 Rear doors - removal, refitting and adjustment

Removal
1 Open the rear doors. If removing the left-hand rear door, remove its inner trim panel (Section 9).
2 Detach the check strap from the door. Disconnect the wiring from the appropriate fitting(s) in the door (as applicable), and withdraw the loom from the door. On later vehicles, remove the interior vent trim from the "D" pillar, and disconnect the wiring multi-plugs in the vent aperture. Release the pillar grommet, and pull the wiring harness out of the pillar.
3 Mark around the periphery of each door hinge with a suitable marker pen, to show the fitted position of the hinges when refitting the door. Have an assistant support the door, undo the retaining screws/nuts from each hinge, and withdraw the door **(see illustrations)**.

Refitting and adjustment
4 Refitting is a reversal of removal. Align the hinges with the previously-made marks, then tighten the bolts. Ensure that the check strap is central with the door when reconnected **(see illustration)**.
5 Open and shut the doors, and ensure that they don't bind with the body aperture at any point. Adjust the door hinges if necessary, to provide an even clearance all round.

15.3b Rear door hinge attachment nuts to body

16 Tailgate fittings - removal and refitting

Outer handle
Removal
1 Disconnect the latch cover plate or remove the trim panel (Section 9).
2 Remove the handle cover nuts **(see illustration)**. Detach the

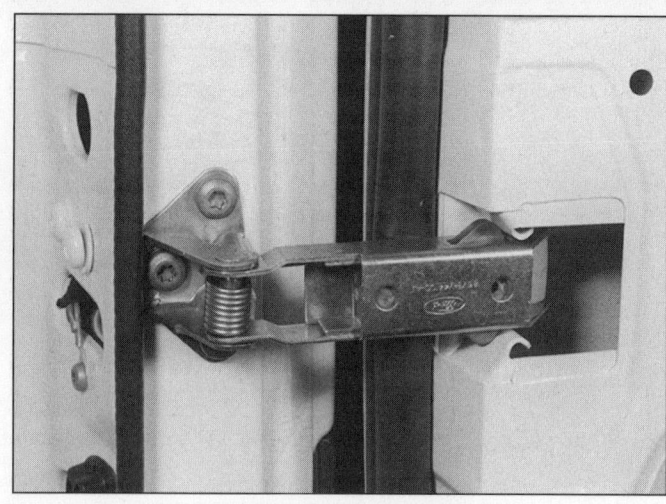

Chapter 11 Bodywork and fittings

15.4 Rear door check strap

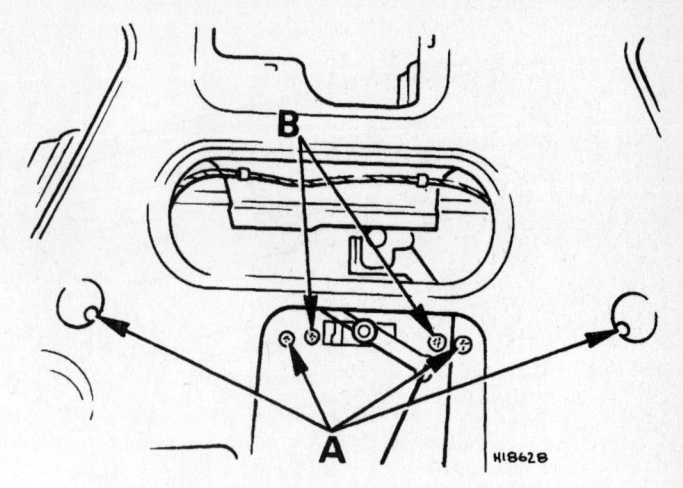

16.2 Tailgate cover nuts (A) and handle screws (B)

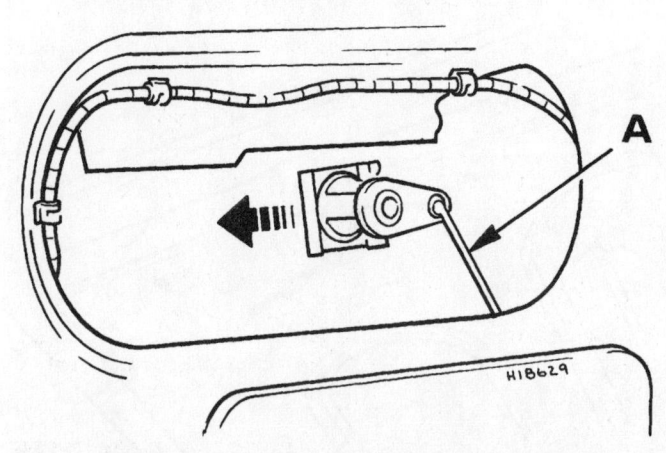

16.7 Detach the lock operating rod (A) then release the U-shaped retaining clip to withdraw the tailgate lock barrel

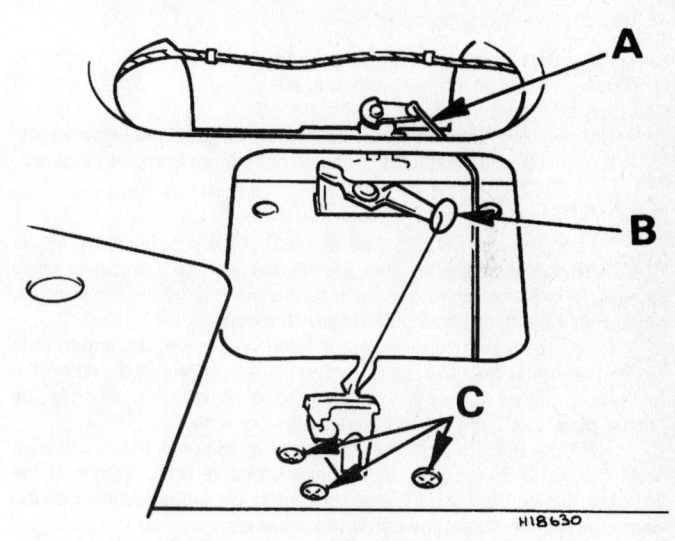

16.11 Tailgate lock operating rod (A) handle rod (B) and latch securing screws (C)

number plate light wiring, and remove the cover.
3 Disconnect the operating rod from the handle, then undo the two retaining screws and remove the outer handle.

Refitting

4 Refitting is a reversal of removal.

Lock barrel

Removal

5 Remove the trim panel (Section 9).
6 Release the retainer, and detach the lock operating rod. Where applicable, disconnect the central locking set/reset switch from the lock barrel.
7 Prise free the U-shaped retaining clip, and withdraw the lock barrel (see illustration).

Refitting

8 Refit in the reverse order of removal, but ensure that the lock is fitted with the barrel drain hole facing down.

Latch unit

Removal

9 Remove the latch cover (three screws) or the trim panel (Section 9).
10 Detach the latch operating rods, and (where applicable) disconnect the central locking wiring multi-plug.
11 Undo the three latch retaining screws, and lock the latch rotor.

Remove the latch and rods from the tailgate. If a new latch unit is being fitted, detach the operating rods from the old unit, and fit them to the replacement latch. Note that although the retaining clip tags may break off during removal, the clips can still be used (see illustration).
12 If required, the central locking motor (where fitted) may be removed by undoing the two screws and twisting the motor to detach the operating rod.

Refitting

13 Refitting is a reversal of removal. Check the operation of the latch before refitting the latch cover (or trim panel as applicable).

17 Tailgate - removal, refitting and adjustment

Removal

1 The aid of two assistants will be required to support the tailgate as it is removed. First open the tailgate, then support it in the open position and detach the wiring harness at the multi-plug connectors in the body. Pull the wiring loom through the body, and leave it attached to the tailgate.
2 Where applicable, disconnect the rear window washer hose.
3 Loosen off the tailgate hinge bolts, and have the two assistants support the weight of the tailgate (see illustration).

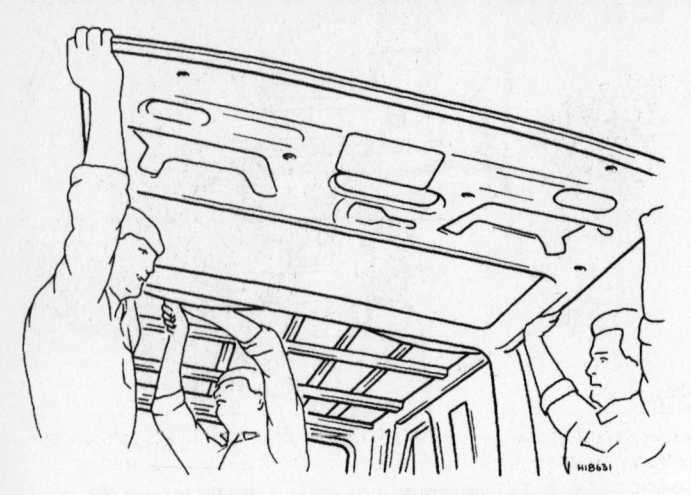

11-16 Chapter 11 Bodywork and fittings

17.3 Supporting the tailgate during removal and refitting

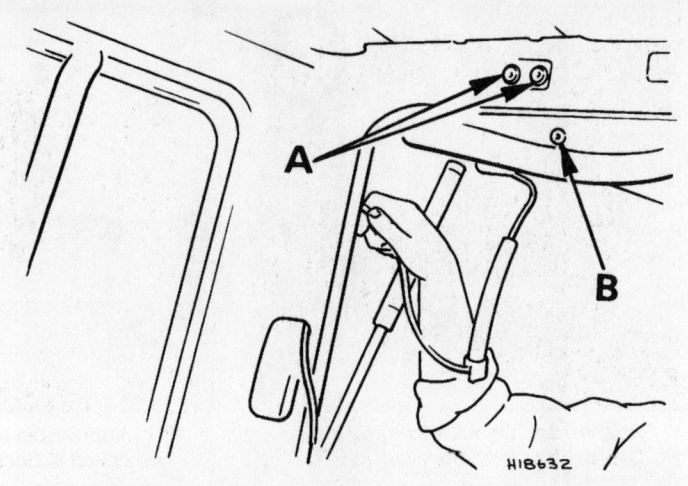

17.5 Tailgate hinge-to-body bolts (A) and hinge-to-tailgate bolts (B). Pull the disconnected wiring loom through as shown

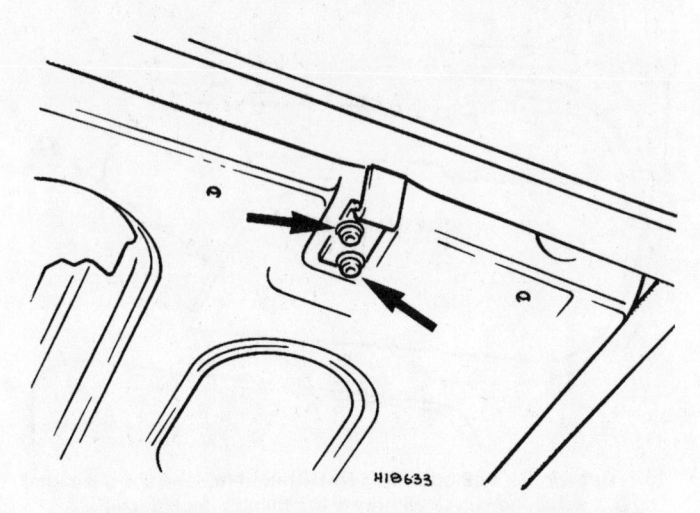

4 Prise up the retaining clips securing the tailgate strut balljoints, and detach the balljoint from the stud each side. Take care not to lift the clips by more than 4 mm.
5 Unscrew the hinge bolts and remove the tailgate **(see illustration)**.
6 If required, the weatherstrip can be pulled free from the tailgate.

Refitting

7 To refit the weatherstrip, first ensure that the joint faces are clean, then feed the weatherstrip onto the tailgate. Locate it first over each corner, then press it home at each centre point between the corners, and push it by thumb pressure towards the corners.
8 When the weatherstrip is fully located on the tailgate, engage the small sealing lip over the flange of the tailgate (if required). When the tailgate is refitted, it may be necessary to re-adjust the position of the striker plate to enable the tailgate to close correctly.
9 Refit the tailgate in the reverse order of removal. Press the strut balljoints onto their studs, using hand pressure only. Note that the struts are gas-filled, and therefore cannot be repaired. If renewing them, be sure to obtain the correct replacements.

Adjustment

10 When the tailgate is refitted, check its adjustment and if necessary re-adjust as follows.

Height adjustment

11 Loosen off the hinge retaining bolts, and reset the tailgate at the required height to suit the latch/striker engagement and the body aperture, then fully retighten the bolts.

Side clearance adjustment

12 Loosen off the tailgate side bump guides, the striker plate and the hinge bolts. Centralise the tailgate in its aperture, then retighten the hinge bolts. If required, re-adjust the position of the striker plate so that the tailgate closes securely. Now adjust the position of the side bump guides so that they only just contact the "D" pillar bumpers when the tailgate is set at the safety catch position, and only make full contact when the tailgate is closed **(see illustration)**.

18 Front door window and regulator - removal and refitting

Pre-1995 model year

Removal

1 Raise the window, then remove the door trim panel as described in Section 9.

17.12 Tailgate side bump guide retaining screws (arrowed)

2 Detach the door lock rod clips from the vertical stay bar **(see illustration)**.
3 Remove the upper stay bar bolt, and pivot the bar towards the front of the door.
4 Remove the screw securing the extension channel from the latch end of the door, then pull the extension channel from the fixed channel **(see illustration)**.
5 Prevent the window from dropping by wedging it up with a suitable block of rubber (or have an assistant support it), then drill out the four rivets securing the regulator unit (4.5 mm drill). Withdraw the regulator unit from the door **(see illustration)**.
6 Lower the door glass, tilt it out at the top (with the lock rods behind it) then withdraw it from the door **(see illustration)**.
7 If a new window is being fitted, locate the regulator channel so that it is 90 mm from the front edge of the glass. Ease assembly of the channel by lubricating it with washing-up liquid or French chalk.
8 If required, the door weatherstrip can be removed by gripping it at its top corner and pulling it free from the door. When refitting the channel, first locate it in the front lower corner, then fit it progressively to the sides and top of the frame.

Refitting

9 Refitting is a reversal of removal. Before refitting the door trim panel, raise and lower the window to ensure that it operates in a satisfactory manner.

Chapter 11 Bodywork and fittings   11•17

18.2 Detach the door lock rod clips (arrowed) from the vertical stay bar

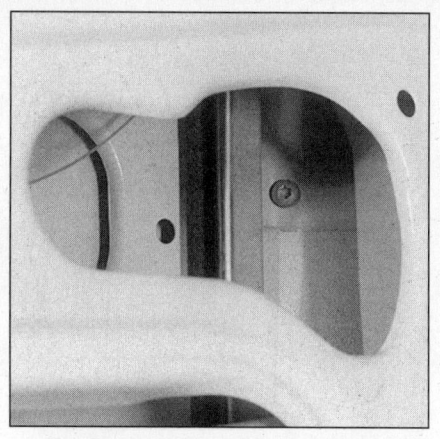

18.4 Remove the screw securing the extension channel from the latch end of the door

18.5 Drill out the four rivets (arrowed) securing the regulator unit

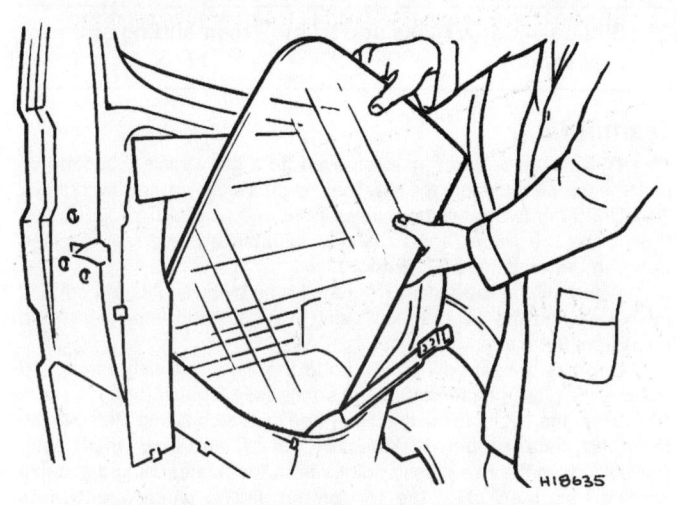

18.6 Withdraw the window glass from the door

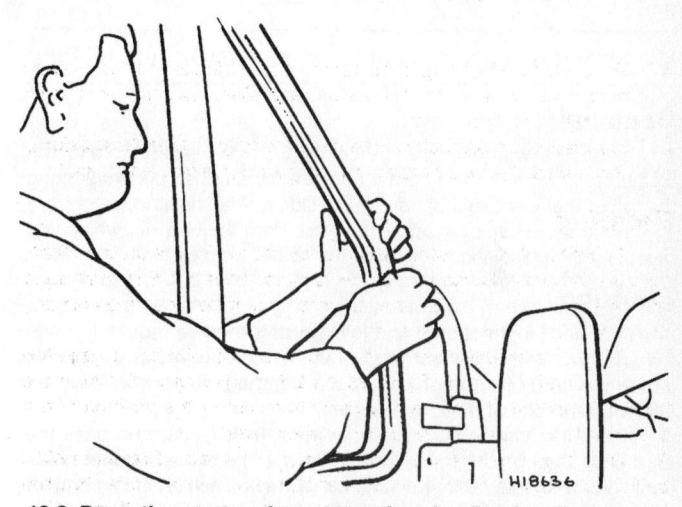

19.2 Press the quarter glass outwards using firm hand pressure, whilst simultaneously pulling free the rubber weatherstrip

1995 model year onwards

Removal

10 Lower the window, then disconnect the battery negative lead.
11 Remove the door trim panel as described in Section 9.
12 Undo the screw securing the inner remote release unit to the door.
13 Starting from the top centre and working around the window aperture, pull the complete weatherstrip from its location, and remove it from the door.
14 Wedge the window to prevent it dropping further, then drill out the four rivets securing the regulator unit using a 4.5 mm drill.
15 Slide the regulator arm from the window glass channel, and remove the regulator unit from the door. If electric windows are fitted, disconnect the wiring multi-plug.
16 Using a 4.5 mm drill, drill out the four rivets securing the door brace bracket at the top and bottom. Unclip the wiring harness multi-plugs if central locking is fitted, and remove the door brace bracket.
17 Lower the glass into the bottom of the door, and carefully manoeuvre it out of the guide channel. Remove the glass from the door.

Refitting

18 Refitting is a reversal of removal. Use new rivets to secure the door brace bracket and regulator unit. When refitting the weatherstrip, engage the front lower corner first, then work round ensuring correct seating. Before refitting the door trim panel, raise and lower the window to ensure that it operates in a satisfactory manner.

19 Front door quarter glass - removal and refitting

Removal

1 Prise free the plastic caps from the door mirror trim fasteners, then unscrew and remove the four fasteners. Lift and remove the trim.
2 Press the glass outwards using firm hand pressure, whilst simultaneously pulling free the rubber weatherstrip from the top corner **(see illustration)**. As the glass is extracted from the door, push it firmly, in a progressive manner, clear along its edges from the inside out until finally it can be removed.

Refitting

3 First loop a length of strong cord into the weatherstrip groove, so that the cord ends are at the lower corners. Passing the cord through the aperture of the window, locate the lower edges of the weatherstrip over the flange of the aperture, then press the glass inwards and simultaneously pull the cord to progressively locate the weatherstrip over the window aperture flange. Apply a progressive and continuous pressure until the window and weatherstrip are fully engaged in the aperture, at which point the cord will pull free **(see illustration)**.

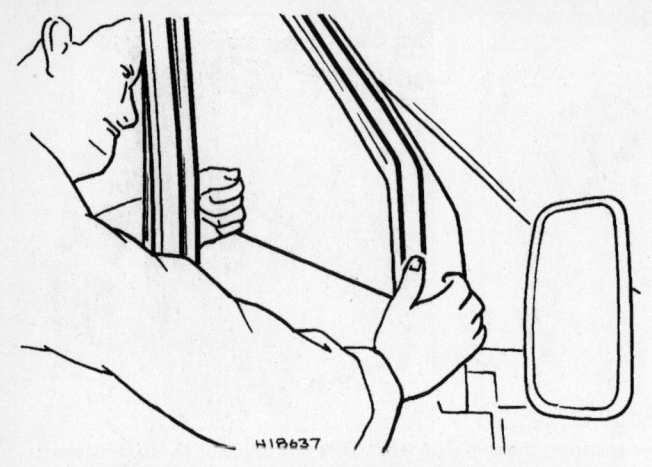

11-18 Chapter 11 Bodywork and fittings

19.3 Installing the door quarter glass, using the cord to locate the weatherstrip

20.4 Installing the sliding window glass and frame assembly

20 Sliding window glass and frame - removal and refitting

Removal
1 Slide the window open. Working from the inside, press the weatherstrip from the top corner aperture flange, then continue along the top of the aperture and down each side to free the strip.
2 Have an assistant support the glass from the outside, whilst you press out the glass and frame from the inside.

Refitting
3 A strong length of cord and two assistants will be required to refit the window. With the weatherstrip in position around the window, locate the cord into the groove of the weatherstrip so that the cord ends cross at one of the lower corners.
4 Offer the assembly to the door from the outside, and pass the cord ends through the frame aperture. Have the two assistants press firmly on the window from the outside, whilst you pull on the cord at an angle of 90° to the glass, so that the weatherstrip progressively unfolds over the aperture flange. As the cord moves around the aperture, the assistants should apply the pressure at the point adjacent to the cord as it unfurls the seal of the weatherstrip **(see illustration)**.
5 When the glass is in position, tap the weatherstrip with the flat of the hand all round to seat the seal against the door panel.

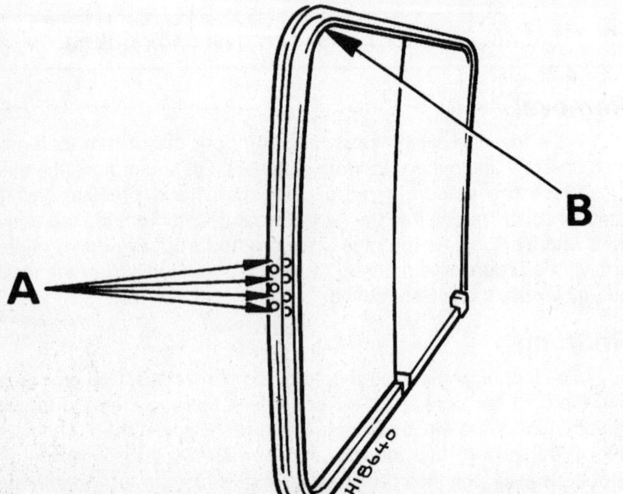

21 Sliding window glass and frame - dismantling and reassembly

Dismantling
1 With the glass and frame removed from the vehicle (Section 20), pull free the weatherstrip, then lay the unit on a cloth-covered work area.
2 Undo the two retaining screws from one side of the joint frame, then prise the frame apart using a suitable screwdriver inserted between the joints **(see illustration)**.
3 Withdraw the fixed glass from the frame by pulling its top edge. If necessary, cut the silicone seal using a suitable knife to release the glass from the frame.
4 Depress the window catch, undo the pawl retaining screw and remove the pawl, catch, button and spring **(see illustration)**.
5 Undo the two screws, and twist free the catch cover. Remove the threaded plate, rubber gasket and O-rings, and keep them safe. Carefully drive the two plastic guides from the runner using a suitable screwdriver, then pivot the top of the sliding window outwards (window runner disengaged) and withdraw the glass.
6 Withdraw the silent channel from the frame by pulling it free.
7 Undo the retaining screw, and remove the end seal and block.
8 Clean all of the old sealant from the fixed glass, renew any parts as necessary, and have some clear silicone sealant at hand during the reassembly.

Reassembly
9 Reassembly is a reversal of the dismantling procedure, but note

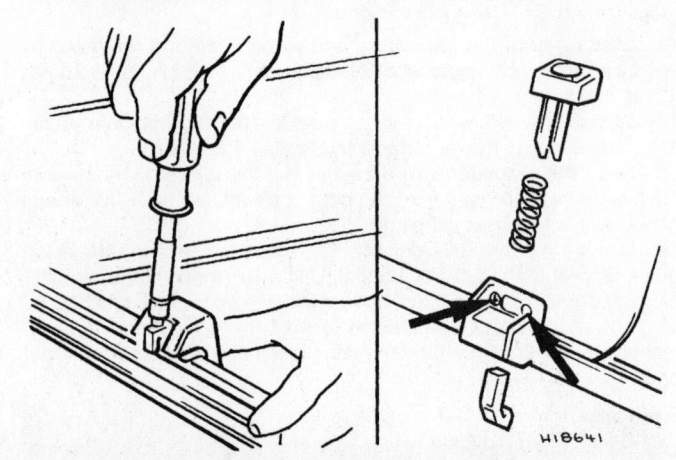

21.2 Sliding window assembly joint screws (A) and end seal block screw (B)

21.4 Remove the screws to dismantle the sliding window catch pawl and cover assembly

Chapter 11 Bodywork and fittings

the following points:
a) *Clean the frame and glass of grease and old sealant with methylated spirit prior to fitting. Apply a thin bead of clear sealant around the edges of the fixed glass before inserting it into position.*
b) *When fitting the window catch, ensure that the O-rings and the rubber gasket are correctly fitted.*
c) *When refitting the weatherstrip, align the drain holes in the strip with the corresponding holes in the frame.*

22 Opening rear quarter window - removal and refitting

Removal
1 Unscrew and remove the two catch-to-"D" pillar retaining screws, partly open the window, and then pull on the glass to detach the hinge leaves. Withdraw the glass **(see illustration)**.
2 The weatherstrip can be pulled free from the frame flange if required. The catch and studs can be removed from the glass by detaching the five screw caps, then undoing the special retaining nuts.

Refitting
3 Refitting is a reversal of removal, but note the following additional points:
a) *Ensure that the weatherstrip and frame flange joint surfaces are clean. When fitting the weatherstrip, ensure that the drain holes align.*
b) *Use new rubber seal washers when reassembling the catch and hinge studs.*

23 Windscreen and fixed windows - removal and refitting

The windscreen, tailgate and fixed side windows are direct glazed to the body, using special adhesive. Purpose-made tools are required to remove the old glass and fit the new glass, and therefore this work is best entrusted to a specialist.

24 Exterior mirrors and associated components - removal and refitting

Pre-1995 model year
Glass renewal
1 If the mirror glass is to be renewed, carefully prise free the outer trim retainer using a suitable screwdriver as a lever. Remove the retainer and glass **(see illustrations)**.

22.1 Removing the opening rear quarter window glass

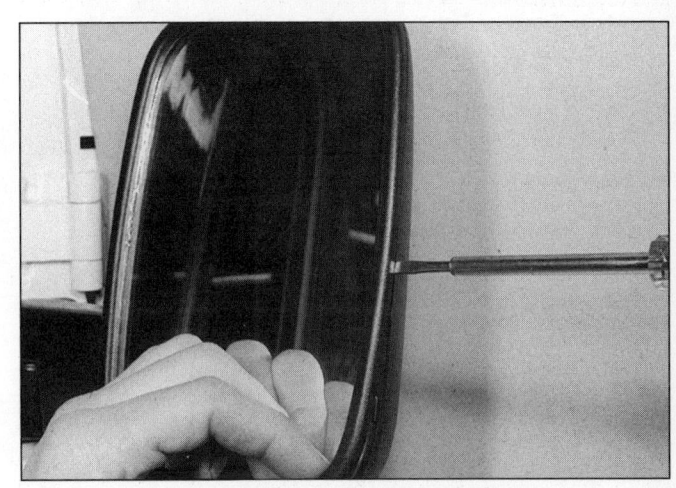

24.1a Prise free the mirror outer trim retainer . . .

2 To refit the glass, insert it into the retainer, then carefully press the rim of the retainer into position around the rim of the mirror.

Mirror assembly
3 Prise free the plastic caps from the mirror trim fasteners, then unscrew and remove the four fasteners. Lift and remove the trim **(see illustrations)**.

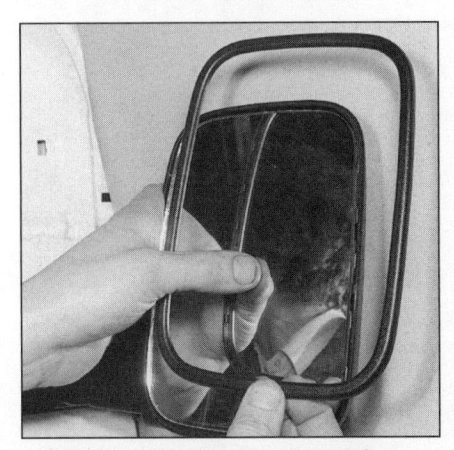

24.1b . . . then remove the retainer and glass

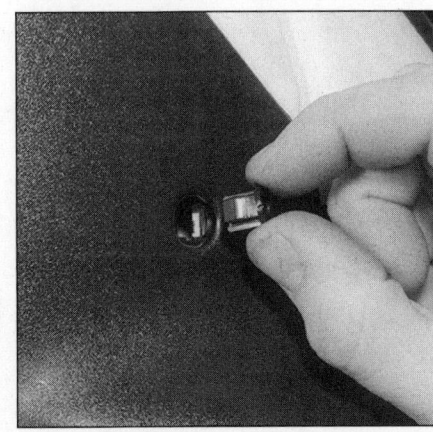

24.3a Prise free the plastic caps from the mirror trim fasteners . . .

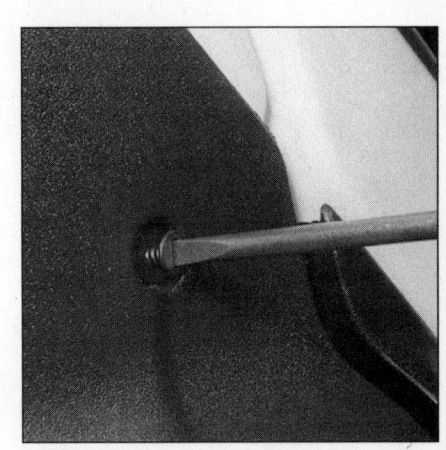

24.3b . . . then unscrew and remove the four fasteners

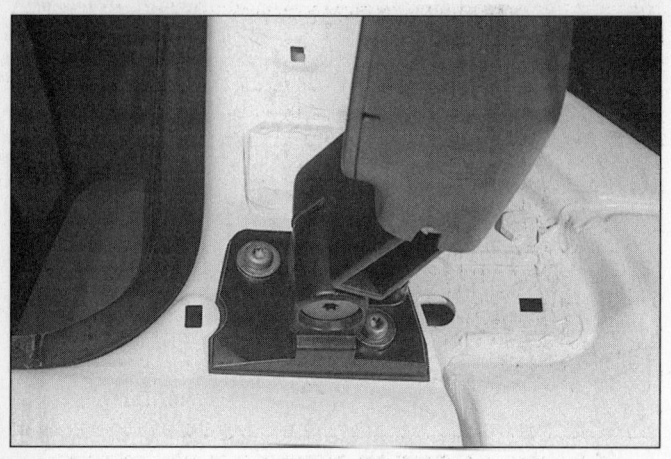

11•20 Chapter 11 Bodywork and fittings

24.4 Undo the two Torx retaining screws, and remove the mirror

24.7 Prising free the plastic caps from the mirror trim fasteners as fitted to later models

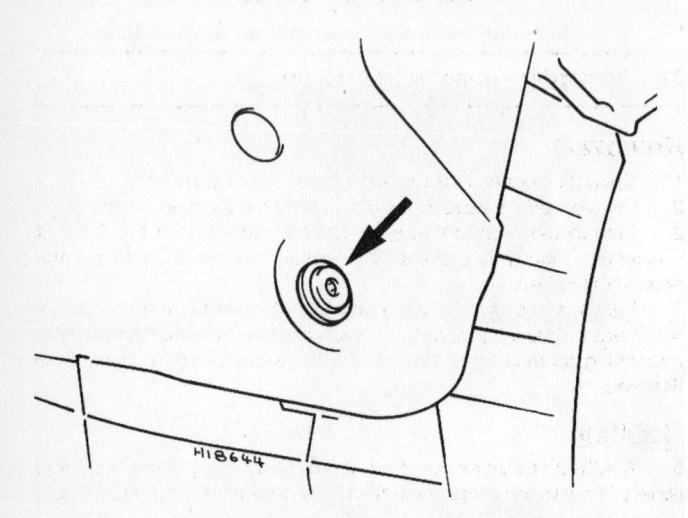

25.1 Remove the single Torx bolt (arrowed) retaining the front bumper end under each wheel arch

removed and refitted as a complete assembly. Replacement of the mirror glass separately is not possible.
7 Prise free the plastic caps from the mirror trim fasteners, then unscrew and remove the three fasteners **(see illustration)**.
8 Withdraw the mirror and frame assembly from the door and, if electric mirrors are fitted, disconnect the wiring multi-plug.
9 Refitting is a reversal of removal, but ensure that the gasket and guide pins are positively located as the mirror is positioned on the door.

25 Front bumper - removal and refitting

Pre-1995 model year

Removal

1 Unscrew and remove the single Torx bolt retaining the bumper end under each wheel arch **(see illustration)**.
2 Detach and remove the front number plate from the bumper.
3 Prise free the plastic retaining screw covers, then unscrew the bumper retaining screws. Withdraw the front bumper **(see illustrations)**.

Refitting

4 Refitting is a reversal of removal. Align the bumper correctly before fully tightening the retaining screws.

4 Undo the two Torx retaining screws, and remove the mirror **(see illustration)**.
5 Refitting is a reversal of removal.

1995 model year onwards

Mirror assembly

6 From the 1995 model year onwards, the mirror can only be

1995 model year onwards

Removal

5 From under the wheel arch on each side, remove the front brace and side attachments to the front panel and wing.

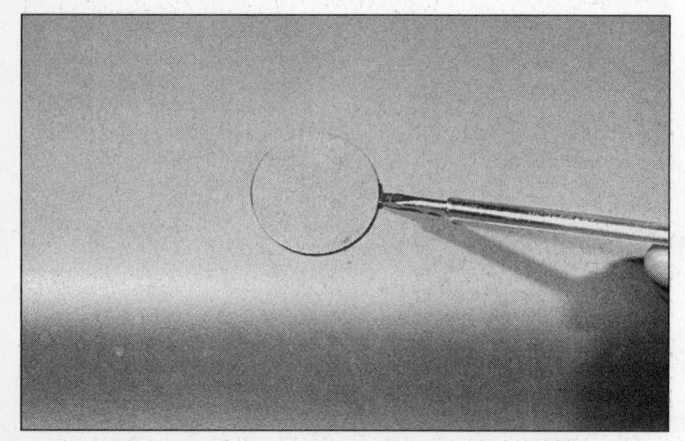

25.3a Prise free the plastic retaining screw covers . . .

25.3b . . . then unscrew the bumper retaining screws at the sides . . .

25.3c ... and at the front (arrowed)

6 Prise free the plastic caps from the outer attachments on each side, and undo the retaining screws.
7 If necessary, remove the front number plate for access, then undo the two centre retaining screws.
8 Pull the bumper forwards to release the side brackets, and remove the bumper from the vehicle.

Refitting

9 Refitting is a reversal of removal. Align the bumper correctly before fully tightening the retaining screws.

26 Rear bumper - removal and refitting

Removal

Note: *If a tow bar is fitted, its wiring harness will need to be detached before removing the bumper.*
1 Working from the underside of the vehicle at the rear, unscrew and remove the two bumper retaining nuts and bolts each side **(see illustration)**.
2 Give the plastic end caps a sharp pull to disengage them from the retainers. Withdraw the bumper rearwards from the vehicle.
3 If required, the plastic end caps can be removed from the bumper by detaching the retaining clips, then sliding the caps free.

Refitting

4 Refitting is a reversal of removal. Align the bumper correctly before fully tightening the retaining bolts and nuts.

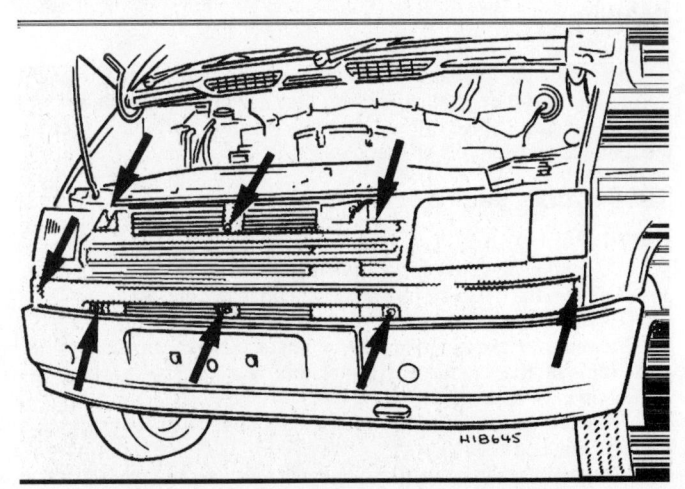

27.4 Front grille panel fastener locations (arrowed)

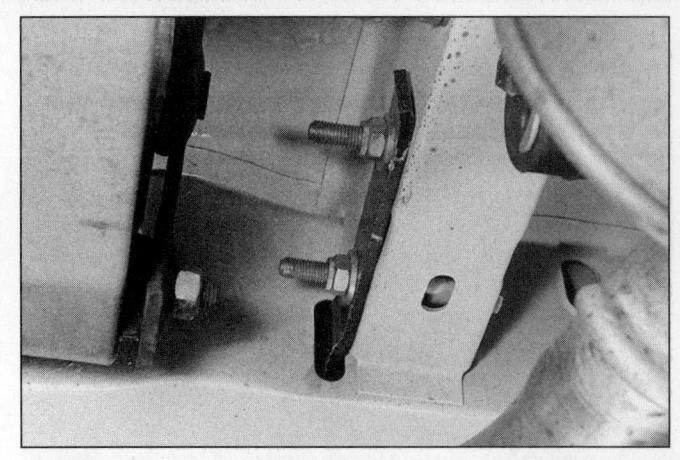

26.1 Unscrew and remove the two rear bumper retaining nuts and bolts each side

27 Front grille - removal and refitting

Removal

1 Open the bonnet, and support it in the raised position.
2 Unscrew and remove the retaining screw at each end of the grille.
3 Detach the headlight washer hose (if fitted) from the T-piece connector. Plug it to prevent fluid leakage, or tie it up above the reservoir fluid level.
4 Prise free the caps from the fasteners, then either turn the plastic fasteners a quarter of a turn to release them, or undo the screws, depending on method of attachment. Withdraw the grille panel **(see illustration)**.

Refitting

5 Refitting is a reversal of removal. Insert the plastic fasteners (where fitted) by simply pushing them into position, then fit their caps.

28 Windscreen grille - removal and refitting

Removal

1 Remove the windscreen wiper arms as described in Chapter 12.
2 Unscrew and remove the plastic retaining nut from the wiper arm centre pivot housing **(see illustration)**.
3 Where fitted, remove the plastic caps, then extract the plastic

28.2 Unscrew and remove the plastic retaining nut from the wiper arm centre pivot housing

11-22   Chapter 11   Bodywork and fittings

28.3 Windscreen grille plastic fastener removal

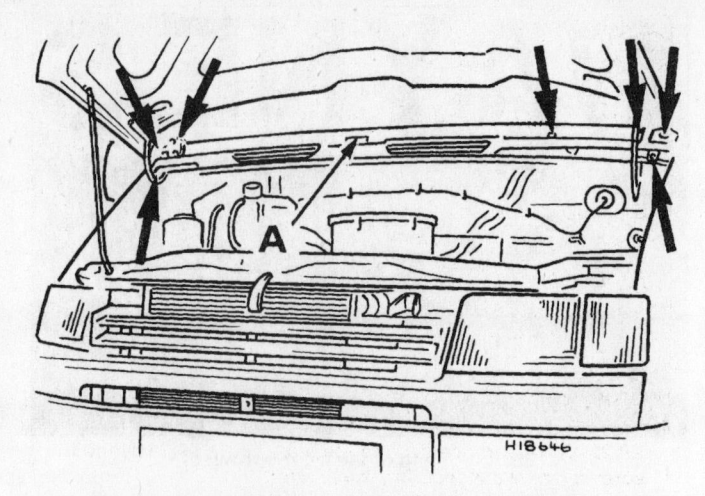

28.4 Windscreen grille fastener and retainer locations (arrowed) and centre pivot housing plastic nut (A)

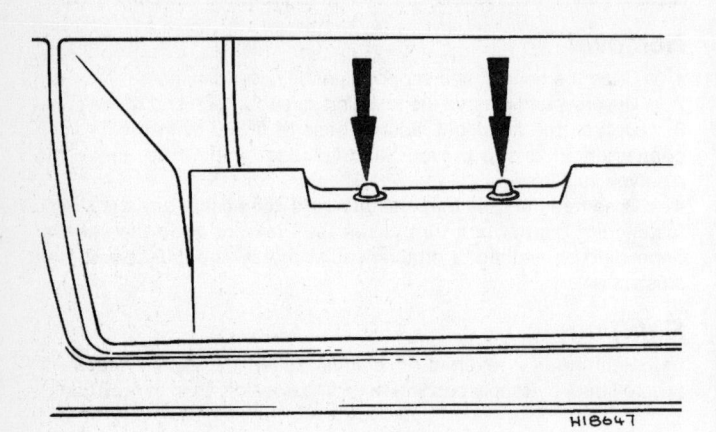

29.7a Release the two facia quarter-turn fasteners (arrowed) in the glovebox

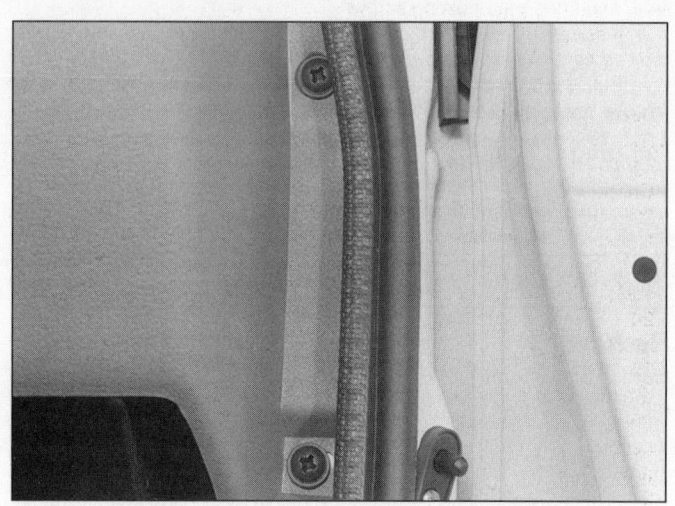

29.7b Facia side retaining screw locations

fastener and retaining screw from the cowl end pieces and remove them **(see illustration)**.
4 Detach the remaining fasteners, withdraw the grille panel and disconnect the washer hoses **(see illustration)**.

Refitting

5 Refitting is a reversal of removal. Check the windscreen washers for satisfactory operation on completion.

29 Facia - removal and refitting

Pre-1995 model year
Removal
1 Disconnect the battery negative lead.
2 Remove the steering wheel as described in Chapter 10.
3 Remove the steering column switches as described in Chapter 12.
4 Remove the instrument panel or tachograph as described in Chapter 12.
5 Undo the four screws retaining the heater facia panel, detach the switch wiring plug, and remove the panel.
6 Undo the two retaining nuts, and withdraw the heater control panel. Detach the heater warm-air ducts.

7 Release the two quarter-turn fasteners in the glovebox. Unscrew the four facia retaining screws (two each side) and then release the three quarter-turn fasteners from the facia top edge. Withdraw the facia unit from the vehicle **(see illustrations)**.

Refitting
8 Refitting is a reversal of removal.
9 Refer to the respective Chapters concerned for the relevant component refitting details. Ensure that all wiring connections are securely made. Check the operation of the various switches, instruments and controls on completion.

1995 model year onwards
Removal
10 Disconnect the battery negative lead.
11 Remove the "A" pillar trim as described in Section 30.
12 Remove the steering wheel as described in Chapter 10.
13 Remove the passenger's side air bag as described in Chapter 12.
14 Remove the instrument panel and radio/cassette player as described in Chapter 12.
15 Remove the screws and withdraw the upper and lower shrouds from the steering column.
16 Remove the crosshead screws, and withdraw the multi-function switch assembly from the steering column.
17 Disconnect the wiring multi-plug, and remove the switch assembly.

Chapter 11 Bodywork and fittings   11•23

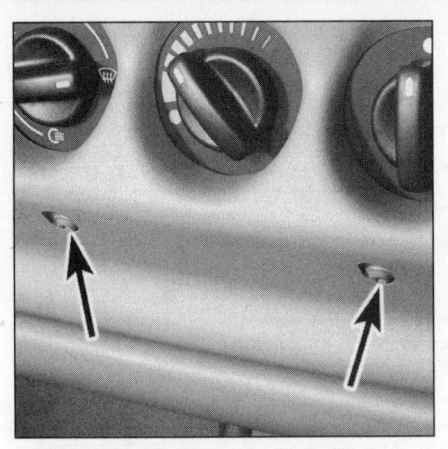

29.22 On later models, undo the two screws (arrowed) securing the heater control panel to the facia

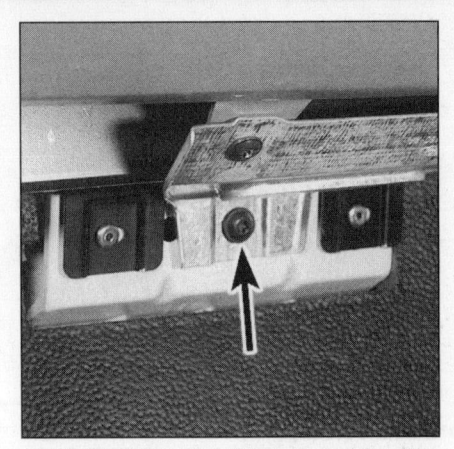

29.24 Undo the glovebox support bracket retaining screw (arrowed)

29.25 Prise out the screw covers, and undo the screws along the facia top edge

18 Undo the two screws, and withdraw the radio/clock surround from the facia.
19 Disconnect the wiring multi-plug, and remove the surround.
20 Undo the two screws, and remove the driver's side vent/switch bezel. Disconnect the switch wiring multi-plugs, and remove the bezel.
21 Remove the remaining switches, warning lights and the cigarette lighter, as applicable, with reference to the procedures contained in Chapter 12.
22 Undo the two screws securing the heater control panel to the facia **(see illustration)**.
23 Working within the instrument panel aperture, unscrew the steering column bracket retaining nut.
24 From under the facia, undo the glovebox support bracket retaining screw **(see illustration)**.
25 Prise out the screw covers, and undo the retaining screws along the top edge of the facia **(see illustration)**.
26 Undo the two screws at each end of the facia. For access to the screws, pull the front door weatherstrip from its location in the area around the facia ends **(see illustration)**.
27 With the aid of an assistant, withdraw the facia from its location, and detach any remaining vents, cables or wiring multi-plugs as necessary. Remove the facia assembly from the vehicle.

Refitting

28 Refitting is a reversal of removal. Refer to the respective Chapters concerned for the relevant component refitting details. Ensure that all wiring connections are securely made. Check the operation of the various switches, instruments and controls on completion.

30 Interior trim - removal and refitting

Door trim panels
1 Refer to the procedures contained in Section 9.

Front footwell trim
2 Open the front door, and undo the four footwell trim retaining screws.
3 Disconnect the loudspeaker wiring (where applicable) and remove the trim.
4 Refitting is a reversal of removal.

Rear quarter trim panel
5 The rear quarter trim panels are secured by a combination of screws and plastic retaining clips, the removal of which requires the use of a suitable forked tool **(see illustration 9.11)**. These clips are easily broken, so take care when prising them free.

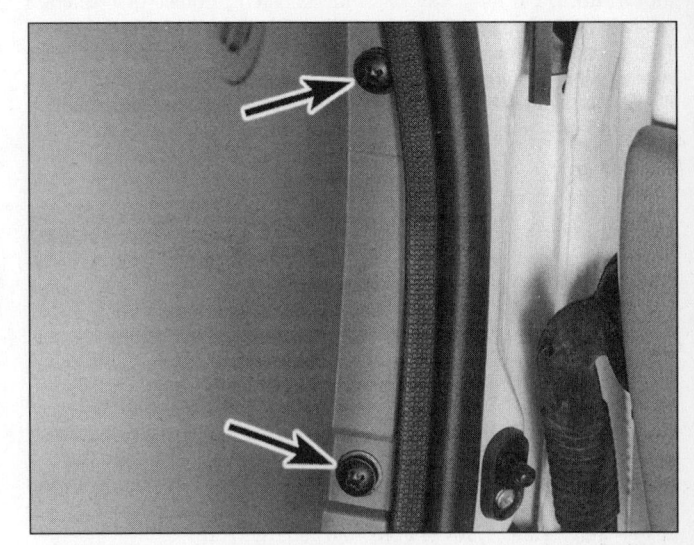

29.26 Undo the two screws at each end of the facia (arrowed)

6 Remove the rear seats, where applicable, for access to the panel attachments.
7 Release the panel retaining clips and screws, and withdraw the panel.
8 Depending on model, remove the plastic covers from the base of the "C" pillar on the sliding door side, and also remove the rear window washer bottle.
9 Refitting is a reversal of removal.

"A", "B", "C", and "D", pillar trim
10 The pillar trim is secured by screws, rivets, or a combination of both. In some areas, the screws will be concealed beneath plastic caps, which are simply prised off with a small screwdriver. Where rivets are encountered, it will be necessary to drill these out using a 4.5 mm drill, and to use new rivets to secure when refitting.

31 Headlining - removal and refitting

Removal
1 Unscrew the retaining screws, and pull free the "A" pillar trims.
2 Detach and remove the sunvisors. Also remove the interior light unit (Chapter 12).
3 Have an assistant support the headlining, then undo the retaining

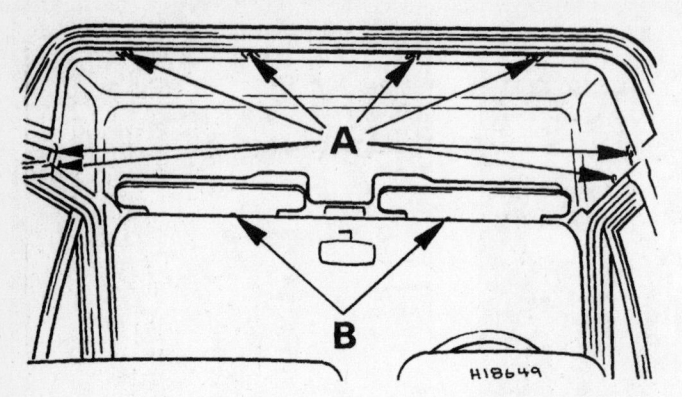

11•24 Chapter 11 Bodywork and fittings

31.3 Headlining retaining screw clips (A) and sunvisors (B)

screw clips and remove the headlining from the vehicle **(see illustration)**. On later models, the headlining panels are retained entirely by plastic push-fit retaining clips, the removal of which requires the use of a suitable forked tool **(see illustration 9.11)**. These clips are easily broken, so take care when prising them free.
4 If required, the centre and rear headlining sections can be detached and removed in the same manner (where applicable).

Refitting

5 To refit the headlining, locate it in position and secure it at the rear with screw clips (push them into position), feed the interior light wires through the headlining at the front, and then secure it in position along with the front and sides.
6 Refit the interior light and the "A" pillar trims to complete.

32 Seats - removal and refitting

Warning: *On vehicles fitted with seat belt pretensioning stalks, be careful when handling the seat; the tensioning device ("grabber") contains a powerful spring, which could cause injury if released in an uncontrolled fashion. The tensioning mechanism should be immobilised by inserting a safety "transit clip", available from Ford parts stockists.*

Front bucket seat

Removal

1 On later vehicles fitted with side trim panels, undo the screws at the front and rear, and remove the side trim.
2 If seat belt pre-tensioners are fitted, immobilise the tensioning mechanism by inserting the transit clip, then detach the inner and outer cable from the seat rails.

32.6 Front bucket seat retaining nuts (arrowed)

3 On vehicles with electrically-operated or electrically-heated seats, disconnect the seat wiring multi-plugs.
4 Move the seat to the fully forward position, then where fitted, unscrew and remove the two Torx bolts from the seat track.
5 Move the seat to the rearmost position, then where fitted, unscrew and remove the four Torx bolts.
6 Undo the four retaining nuts, and lift out the seat **(see illustration)**.

Refitting

7 Refitting is a reversal of removal. Tighten the bolts to the specified torque setting.

Front bench seat

Removal

8 On later vehicles fitted with side trim panels, undo the screws at the front and rear, and remove the side trim.
9 If seat belt pre-tensioners are fitted, immobilise the tensioning mechanism by inserting the transit clip.
10 Unscrew and remove the four, six or seven bolts (depending on model) which secure the seat to the floor **(see illustrations)**.
11 Where applicable, cut free the plastic outer seat belt buckle-to-frame ties, and detach the seat restrainer strap **(see illustrations)**.
12 Remove the seat, passing the seat belt webbing and stalk through as it is withdrawn.

Refitting

13 Refitting is a reversal of removal. Tighten the retaining bolts to the specified torque setting.

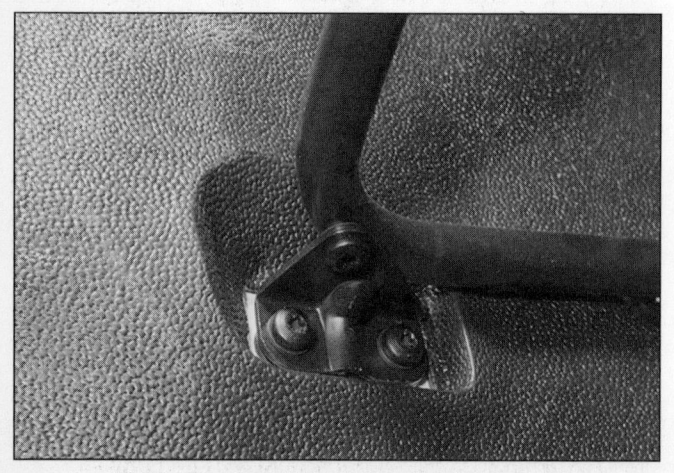

32.10a Bench seat front mounting bracket . . .

32.10b . . . and rear mounting bracket

Chapter 11 Bodywork and fittings

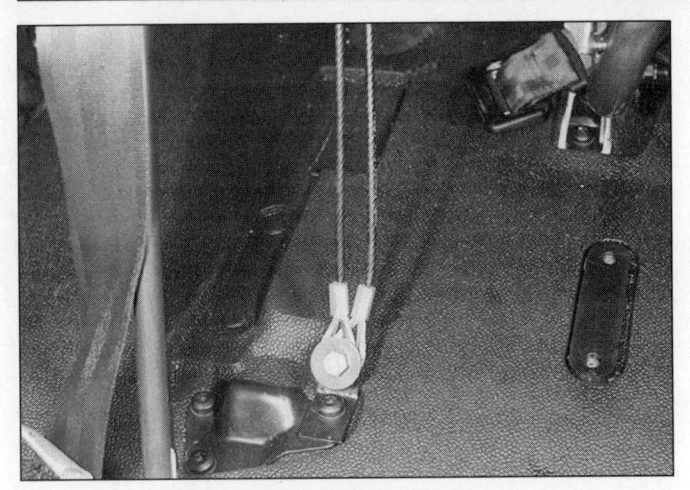

32.11a Bench seat restrainer strap

Rear seats

14 Various combinations of rear seats may be fitted, according to vehicle type and specification. The removal and refitting procedures are essentially the same as those described previously for the front bench seat, but ignore the references to the seat belt pre-tensioners.

33 Seat belt components - removal and refitting

Warning: *On vehicles fitted with seat belt pretensioning stalks, be careful when handling, as the tensioning device ("grabber") contains a powerful spring, which could cause injury if released in an uncontrolled fashion. The tensioning mechanism should be immobilised by inserting a safety "transit clip" available from Ford parts stockists. Note also that seat belts and associated components which have been subject to impact loads must be renewed.*

Front seat belt and stalk - pre-1995 model year

Removal

1 Remove the "B" pillar trim (Section 30), passing the webbing through the trim slot as it is withdrawn **(see illustration)**.
2 Unscrew the lower anchor bolt, but take care not to allow the webbing to retract into the reel.
3 Prise free the cover from the upper anchor bolt, and undo the bolt **(see illustration)**.
4 Unscrew and remove the lower retaining bolt **(see illustration)**.

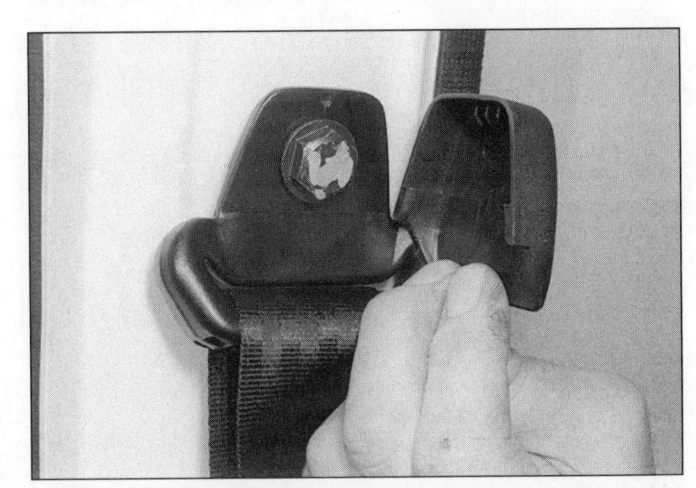

33.3 Prise free the cover from the seat belt upper anchor bolt

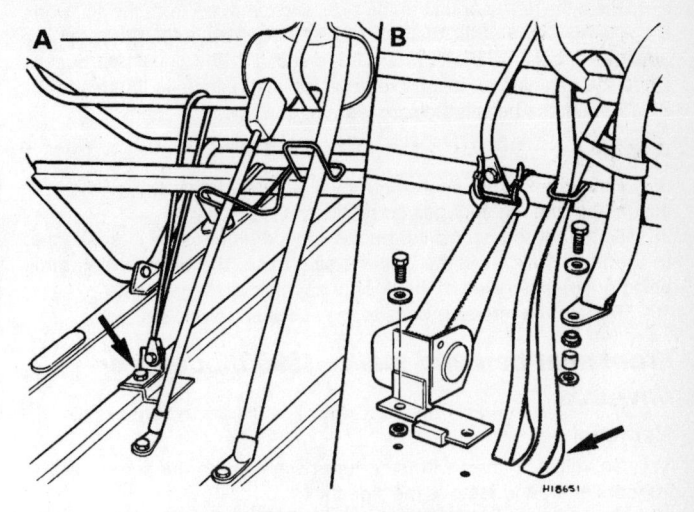

32.11b Typical seat restrainer types

A Double chassis cab strap fixing
B Single chassis cab strap fixing

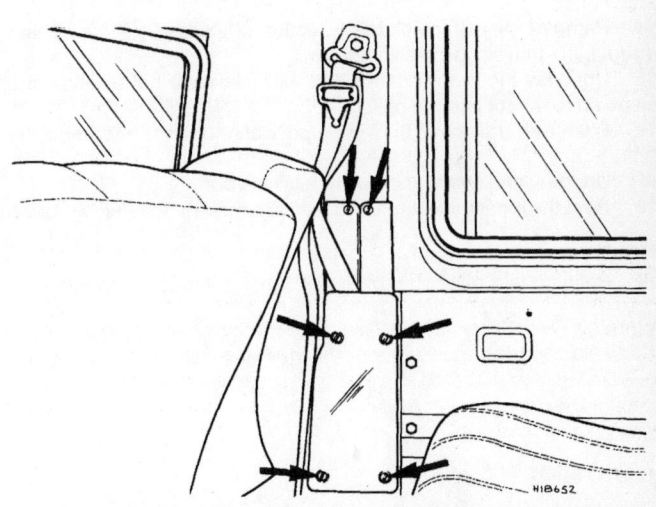

33.1 Remove the "B" pillar trim screws (arrowed), remove the trim, and pass the seat belt webbing through the trim slot as it is withdrawn

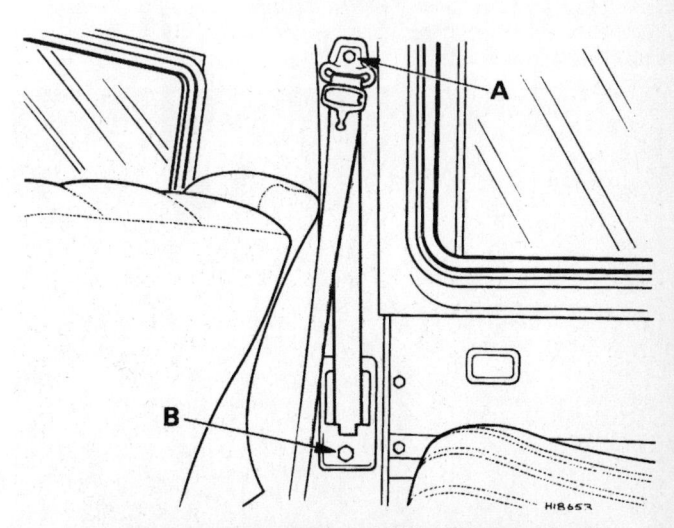

33.4 Seat belt upper anchor bolt (A) and lower retractor retaining bolt (B)

5 Pivot the retractor unit to the side, and remove it from the "B" pillar.
6 Remove the stalk-to-floor bolts to free the stalks, then where applicable, cut free the two tie-straps securing the outer belt buckle. Undo the retaining bolts, and remove the seat belts **(see illustration)**.
7 Renew the belts if they are worn or don't work properly.

Refitting
8 Refitting is a reversal of removal. When refitting the inertia reel, ensure that the tag engages correctly in the "B" pillar.
9 Note that the centre lap buckle tongue differs, and is connected to the floor stalk near the driver's seat base, the driver's belt stalk being on the inner side of the floor under the passenger seat.
10 Tighten the retaining bolts to the specified torque settings.

Front seat belt and stalk - 1995 model year onwards
Removal
11 On vehicles fitted with side trim panels, undo the screws at the front and rear, and remove the side trim.
12 If seat belt pre-tensioners are fitted, immobilise the tensioning mechanism by inserting the transit clip, then detach the inner and outer cable from the seat rails.
13 Remove the seat belt stalk from the pre-tensioning device attachment.
14 Remove the "B" pillar trim (Section 30) passing the webbing through the trim slot as it is withdrawn.
15 Unscrew the lower anchor bolt, but take care not to allow the webbing to retract into the reel.
16 Prise free the cover from the upper anchor bolt, and undo the bolt.
17 Unscrew and remove the lower retaining bolt.
18 Pivot the retractor unit to the side, and remove it from the "B" pillar.

Refitting
19 Refitting is a reversal of removal. When refitting the inertia reel,

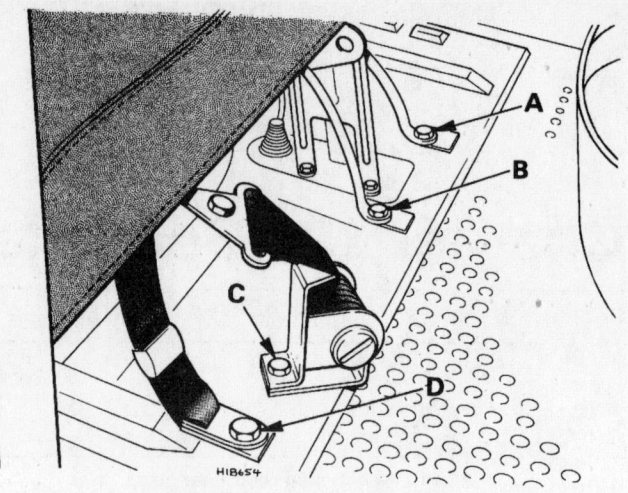

33.6 Typical seat belt floor fixings

| A | Lap belt buckle | C | Left-hand belt buckle |
| B | Right-hand belt buckle | D | Lap belt |

ensure that the tag engages correctly in the "B" pillar.
20 Tighten the retaining bolts to the specified torque settings.

Rear seat belts and stalks
21 Various combinations of rear seat belts may be fitted, according to vehicle type and specification. The removal and refitting procedures are essentially the same as those described previously for the front seat belts, but it will be necessary in some instances to remove the relevant interior trim for access. Refer to Section 30, if necessary, for interior trim details. Ensure that all attachment bolts are tightened to the specified torque when refitting.

Chapter 12 Body electrical systems

Contents

	Section
Air bag control module - removal and refitting	29
Air bag unit - removal and refitting	28
Battery check and maintenance	See Chapter 1
Battery - removal and refitting	See Chapter 5
Bulbs (exterior lights) - renewal	14
Bulbs (interior lights) - renewal	15
Cigarette lighter - removal and refitting	11
Clock - removal and refitting	12
Compact disc player - removal and refitting	24
Electrical fault-finding - general information	2
Exterior light units - removal and refitting	16
Fuel and temperature gauge (tachograph models) - removal and refitting	8
Fuses and relays - general information	3
General information and precautions	1
Headlight beam alignment - checking and adjustment	13
Horn - removal and refitting	17
Instrument panel components (non-tachograph models) - removal and refitting	6

	Section
Instrument panel (non-tachograph models) - removal an refitting	5
Loudspeakers - removal and refitting	27
Passive anti-theft system - general information and component renewal	30
Power amplifier - removal and refitting	26
Radio aerial - removal and refitting	25
Radio/cassette player - removal and refitting	23
Speedometer cable - removal and refitting	10
Switches - removal and refitting	4
Tachograph - removal and refitting	7
Tailgate wiper components - removal and refitting	22
Warning light cluster (tachograph models) - removal and refitting	9
Windscreen/headlight washer reservoir - removal and refitting	21
Windscreen/tailgate/headlight washer system check and adjustment	See Chapter 1
Windscreen/tailgate wiper blade check and renewal	See Chapter 1
Windscreen wiper motor and linkage - removal and refitting	19
Windscreen wiper pivot housing - removal and refitting	20
Wiper arms - removal and refitting	18

Specifications

Fuses (pre-1992 model year)

No	Rating (amps)	Circuit(s) protected
1	25	Headlight flasher, heater blower motor
2	10	Direction indicators
3	15	Windscreen wiper motor, windscreen washer pump (vehicles without headlight washers), intermittent wiper timer circuit
4	10	Reversing lights, brake lights, heated rear window
5	10	Fuel/temperature gauges, instrument panel warning lights
6	15	Tailgate wiper motor and washer pump
7	15	Dim-dip lighting
8 and 9	-	Spares
10	10	Right-hand side/tail lights, instrument panel illumination
11	10	Left-hand side/tail lights, number plate light
12	10	Right-hand headlight dipped beam
13	10	Left-hand headlight dipped beam
14	10	Rear foglights, headlight washer timer
15	-	Spare
16	10	Right-hand headlight main beam and main beam warning light
17	10	Left-hand headlight main beam
18	10	Front courtesy light, rear interior lights, clock/tachograph, radio, windscreen washer pump (vehicles with headlight washers)
19	20	Hazard warning lights, horn
20	25	Headlight washer pump, cigarette lighter
21	20	Heated rear window
22	10	Overdrive
23	-	Positions for five spare fuses

Chapter 12 Body electrical systems

Fuses (1992 to 1995 model year)

No	Rating (amps)	Circuit(s) protected
1	10	Right-hand headlight dip beam
2	10	Left-hand headlight dip beam
3	10	Right-hand side/tail lights, number plate light, high level marker lights, interior lighting
4	10	Left-hand side/tail lights, number plate light
5	20	Heated rear window relay
6	20	Headlight washer pump relay
7	20	Heated windscreen relay
8	3	Fuel system ECU (Turbo models)
9	20	Cigarette lighter
10	10	Interior lights, clock, radio memory, windscreen washer pump
11	20	Hazard flashers, horn
12	10	Headlight washer pump, rear foglights
13	10	Right-hand headlight main beam, main beam warning light
14	10	Left-hand headlight main beam
15	10	Heated seats, instrument panel illumination, heated screens
16	10	Stop-lights, reversing lights, automatic transmission inhibitor switch, water-in-fuel sensor, oxygen sensor (Turbo models)
17	10	Direction indicators
18	3	Anti-lock braking system
19	25	Heater motor
20	15	Windscreen wash/wipe switch, wiper motor
21	15	Automatic transmission downshift (kickdown) solenoid
22	15	Rear window wash/wipe
23	3	Power hold relay (Turbo models)
24	20	Dim-dip lighting
F1 and F2	-	Spare
F3 and F4	30	Anti-lock braking system

Fuses (1995 model year onwards)

No	Rating (amps)	Circuit(s) protected
1	30	Heater motor
2	15	Windscreen wiper motor
3	10	Rear window wiper motor
4	30	Electric windows
5	5	Anti-lock braking system
6	10	Anti-theft alarm system
7	10	Brake lights
8	10	Direction indicators
9	10	Anti-theft alarm system
10	30	Air conditioning
11	10	Interior lights
12	5	Electric door mirrors
13	20	Cigarette lighter
14	20	Horn, hazard flasher
15	10	Anti-theft alarm system, hazard flasher
16	20	Heated rear screen
17	20	Headlight washers
18	20	Heated windscreen
19	10	Right-hand side/tail lights
20	10	Left-hand side/tail lights
21	10	Right-hand headlight dipped beam
22	10	Left-hand headlight dipped beam
23	10	Right-hand headlight main beam
24	10	Left-hand headlight main beam
25	10	Rear foglights
26	-	Spare
27	10	Heated front seats
28	10	Electrical auxiliary heating
29	20	Front foglights
30	-	Spare
31	10	Ignition lock
32	5	Immobilisation system
33	5	Immobilisation system
34	5	Air bag
36	-	Spare
37	-	Spare

Chapter 12 Body electrical systems

Relays (pre-1992 model year)

Identification	Function
A	Automatic transmission inhibitor
B	Not used
C	Dim-dip lighting
D	Dim-dip lighting
E	Not used
F	Heated rear window
G	Direction indicator flasher (heavy-duty for trailer towing)
H	Headlight washer
I	Intermittent windscreen wiper
J	Intermittent tailgate wiper
K	Not used

Relays (1992 to 1995 model year)

Identification	Function
A	Dim-dip lighting
B	Headlight dipped beam
C	Not used
D	Not used
E	Power supply control
F	Main power supply
G	Power hold
H	Heated rear window
I	Not used
II	Not used
III	Not used
IV	Heated windscreen
V	Rear window wiper
VI	Downshift (kickdown) solenoid - automatic transmission
VII	Direction indicators
VIII	Headlight washer pump
IX	Windscreen wiper delay
X	Heater motor
XI	Not used
XII	Additional starting system circuit

Relays (1995 model year onwards)

Identification	Function
A	Dim-dip lighting
B	Headlight dipped beam
C	Not used
D	Left-hand side anti-theft alarm
E	Right-hand side anti-theft alarm
I	Ignition relay
II	Not used
III	Not used
IV	Direction indicators
V	Exterior light buzzer
VI	Not used
VII	Headlight washers
VIII	Heated windscreen
IX	Rear window wiper/delay
X	Windscreen wiper/delay
XI	Heated rear window and exterior mirrors
XII	Dim-dip lighting
XIII	Headlight main beam
XIV	Anti-theft alarm

Bulbs

	Wattage
Headlights	60/55
Sidelights	5
Direction indicator lights	21
Side direction indicator repeater lights	5
Brake lights (Chassis Cab models)	21
Tail lights (Chassis Cab models)	5
Brake/tail lights (Van and Bus models)	21/5
Reversing lights	21
Rear foglights	21

Bulbs (continued)

	Wattage
Number plate light (Chassis Cab models)	10
Number plate light (Van and Bus models with rear doors)	5
Number plate light (Van and Bus models with tailgate)	10
Interior lights	10

Torque wrench settings

	Nm	lbf ft
Windscreen wiper motor link arm nut	9 to 11	6 to 8
Windscreen wiper pivot housing nuts:		
Delco (plastic) housing	8 to 12	6 to 9
SWF (steel) housing	3	2
Windscreen grille panel plastic nut	15 to 20	11 to 15

1 General information and precautions

General information

The electrical system is of 12-volt negative earth type. Power for the lights and all electrical accessories is supplied by a lead/acid battery, which is charged by the alternator.

This Chapter covers repair and service procedures for the various electrical components not associated with the engine. Information on the battery, alternator, and starter motor can be found in Chapter 5.

All 1995 model year Transits are available with driver and passenger air bags, which are designed to prevent serious chest and head injuries in the event of serious impact. The sensor and electronic unit for the air bag is located behind the instrument panel inside the vehicle, and contains a back-up capacitor, crash sensor, decelerometer, safety sensor, integrated circuit and microprocessor. The driver's side air bag is inflated by a gas generator, which forces the bag out of the module cover in the centre of the steering wheel. A "clock spring" ensures that a good electrical connection is maintained with the air bag at all times - as the steering wheel is turned in each direction, the spring winds and unwinds. The passenger's air bag (where fitted) is located above the glovebox.

A Passive Anti-Theft System (PATS) is fitted on 1995 model year vehicles. This system disables the engine fuel system and starter motor unless a specific code, programmed into the ignition key, is recognised by the PATS transceiver.

Precautions

Warning: *Before carrying out any work on the electrical system, read through the precautions given in "Safety first!" at the beginning of this manual and in Chapter 5.*
Caution: *If the radio/cassette player fitted to the vehicle has an anti-theft security code (as does the standard unit fitted to later models), refer to the information given in the preliminary Sections of this manual before disconnecting the battery.*

Prior to working on any component in the electrical system, the battery negative lead should first be disconnected, to prevent the possibility of electrical short-circuits and/or fires.

2 Electrical fault-finding - general information

Note: *Refer to the precautions given in "Safety first!" and in Section 1 of this Chapter before starting work. The following tests relate to testing of the main electrical circuits, and should not be used to test delicate electronic circuits, particularly where an electronic control module is used.*

General

1 A typical electrical circuit consists of an electrical component, any switches, relays, motors, fuses, fusible links or circuit breakers related to that component, and the wiring and connectors which link the component to both the battery and the chassis. To help to pinpoint a problem in an electrical circuit, wiring diagrams are included at the end of this manual.

2 Before attempting to diagnose an electrical fault, first study the appropriate wiring diagram, to obtain a complete understanding of the components included in the particular circuit concerned. The possible sources of a fault can be narrowed down by noting if other components related to the circuit are operating properly. If several components or circuits fail at one time, the problem is likely to be related to a shared fuse or earth connection.

3 Electrical problems usually stem from simple causes, such as loose or corroded connections, a faulty earth connection, a blown fuse, a melted fusible link, or a faulty relay (refer to Section 3 for details of testing relays). Visually inspect the condition of all fuses, wires and connections in a problem circuit before testing the components. Use the wiring diagrams to determine which terminal connections will need to be checked in order to pinpoint the trouble-spot.

4 The basic tools required for electrical fault-finding include a circuit tester or voltmeter (a 12-volt bulb with a set of test leads can also be used for certain tests); an ohmmeter (to measure resistance and check for continuity); a battery and set of test leads; and a jumper wire, preferably with a circuit breaker or fuse incorporated, which can be used to bypass suspect wires or electrical components. Before attempting to locate a problem with test instruments, use the wiring diagram to determine where to make the connections.

5 To find the source of an intermittent wiring fault (usually due to a poor or dirty connection, or damaged wiring insulation), a "wiggle" test can be performed on the wiring. This involves wiggling the wiring by hand to see if the fault occurs as the wiring is moved. It should be possible to narrow down the source of the fault to a particular section of wiring. This method of testing can be used in conjunction with any of the tests described in the following sub-Sections.

6 Apart from problems due to poor connections, two basic types of fault can occur in an electrical circuit - open-circuit, or short-circuit.

7 Open-circuit faults are caused by a break somewhere in the circuit, which prevents current from flowing. An open-circuit fault will prevent a component from working.

8 Short-circuit faults are caused by a "short" somewhere in the circuit, which allows the current flowing in the circuit to "escape" along an alternative route, usually to earth. Short-circuit faults are normally caused by a breakdown in wiring insulation, which allows a feed wire to touch either another wire, or an earthed component such as the bodyshell. A short-circuit fault will normally cause the relevant circuit fuse to blow.

Finding an open-circuit

9 To check for an open-circuit, connect one lead of a circuit tester or the negative lead of a voltmeter either to the battery negative terminal or to a known good earth.

10 Connect the other lead to a connector in the circuit being tested, preferably nearest to the battery or fuse. At this point, battery voltage should be present, unless the lead from the battery or the fuse itself is faulty (bearing in mind that some circuits are live only when the ignition switch is moved to a particular position).

11 Switch on the circuit, then connect the tester lead to the connector nearest the circuit switch on the component side.

12 If voltage is present (indicated either by the tester bulb lighting or

Chapter 12 Body electrical systems

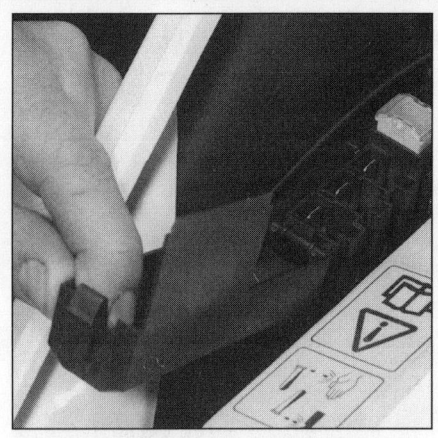

12-5

3.1a On later models, fusible links are contained in the battery junction box located next to the battery

3.1b Central electric box showing fuse and relay identification on the inside face of the lid

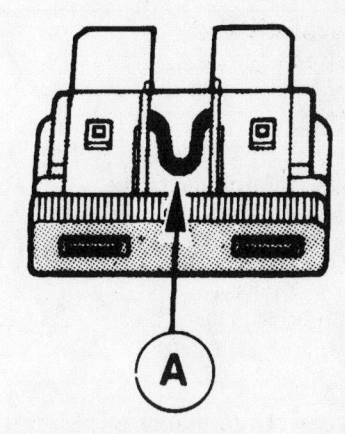

3.2 When inspecting a fuse, look for a break in the wire at (A)

a voltmeter reading, as applicable), this means that the section of the circuit between the relevant connector and the switch is problem-free.
13 Continue to check the remainder of the circuit in the same fashion.
14 When a point is reached at which no voltage is present, the problem must lie between that point and the previous test point with voltage. Most problems can be traced to a broken, corroded or loose connection.

Finding a short-circuit

15 To check for a short-circuit, first disconnect the load(s) from the circuit (loads are the components which draw current from a circuit, such as bulbs, motors, heating elements, etc).
16 Remove the relevant fuse from the circuit, and connect a circuit tester or voltmeter to the fuse connections.
17 Switch on the circuit, bearing in mind that some circuits are live only when the ignition switch is moved to a particular position.
18 If voltage is present (indicated either by the tester bulb lighting or a voltmeter reading, as applicable), this means that there is a short-circuit.
19 If no voltage is present during this test, but the fuse still blows with the load(s) reconnected, this indicates an internal fault in the load(s).

Finding an earth fault

20 The battery negative terminal is connected to "earth" - the metal of the engine/transmission and the vehicle body - and many systems are wired so that they only receive a positive feed, the current returning via the metal of the car body. This means that the component mounting and the body form part of that circuit. Loose or corroded mountings can therefore cause a range of electrical faults, ranging from total failure of a circuit, to a puzzling partial failure. In particular, lights may shine dimly (especially when another circuit sharing the same earth point is in operation), motors (eg wiper motors or the heater blower motor) may run slowly, and the operation of one circuit may have an apparently-unrelated effect on another. Note that on many vehicles, earth straps are used between certain components, such as the engine/transmission and the body, usually where there is no metal-to-metal contact between components, due to flexible rubber mountings, etc.
21 To check whether a component is properly earthed, disconnect the battery and connect one lead of an ohmmeter to a known good earth point. Connect the other lead to the wire or earth connection being tested. The resistance reading should be zero; if not, check the connection as follows.
22 If an earth connection is thought to be faulty, dismantle the connection, and clean both the bodyshell and the wire terminal (or the component earth connection mating surface) back to bare metal. Be careful to remove all traces of dirt and corrosion, then use a knife to trim away any paint, so that a clean metal-to-metal joint is made. On reassembly, tighten the joint fasteners securely; if a wire terminal is being refitted, use serrated washers between the terminal and the bodyshell, to ensure a clean and secure connection. When the connection is remade, prevent the onset of corrosion in the future by applying a coat of petroleum jelly or silicone-based grease, or by spraying on (at regular intervals) a proprietary water-dispersant lubricant such as Holts Wet Start.

3 Fuses and relays - general information

Fuses

1 The main fuses, relays and timers are located in the central electric box situated below the facia panel on the driver's side. Additionally, on later models, fusible links are contained in the battery junction box located next to the battery in the engine compartment **(see illustration)**. The fuses can be inspected and if necessary renewed, by opening the fusebox lid. The respective fuses and relays are identified on the diagram on the inside surface of the lid. Each fuse is also marked with its rating. The circuits that the fuses and relays protect are given in the Specifications at the start of this Chapter. Plastic tweezers are attached to the inside face of the lid to remove and fit the fuses **(see illustration)**.
2 To remove a fuse, use the tweezers provided to pull it out of the holder. Slide the fuse sideways from the tweezers. The wire within the fuse is clearly visible, and it will be broken if the fuse is blown **(see illustration)**.
3 Always renew a fuse with one of an identical rating. Never renew a fuse more than once without tracing the source of the trouble. The fuse rating is stamped on top of the fuse.
4 Fusible links are incorporated in the positive feed from the battery, their function being to protect the main wiring loom in the event of a short-circuit. When the links blow, all of the wiring circuits are disconnected, and will remain so until the cause of the malfunction is repaired and the link renewed.

Relays

5 A relay is an electrically-operated switch, which is used for the following reasons:
 a) A relay can switch a heavy current remotely from the circuit in which the current is flowing, allowing the use of lighter-gauge wiring and switch contacts.
 b) A relay can receive more than one control input, unlike a mechanical switch.
 c) A relay can have a timer function - for example an intermittent wiper delay.

12

12-6 Chapter 12 Body electrical systems

4.3a Unscrew the upper retaining screw ...

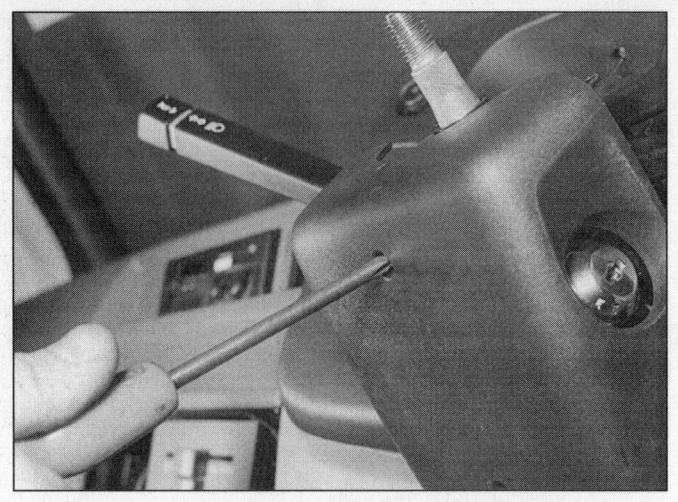

4.3b ... and the lower screws to remove the steering column shrouds

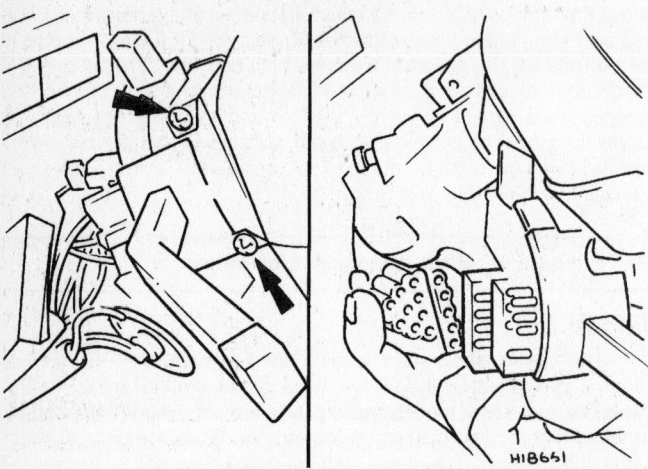

4.4 Remove the two screws (arrowed), withdraw the left-hand or right-hand multi-function switch assembly from the steering column, and disconnect the multi-plug

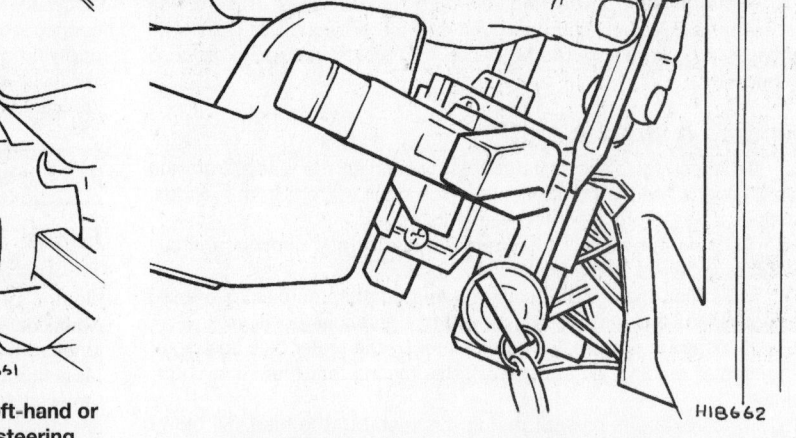

4.9 Depress the lock spring using a suitable rod or tool inserted through the access hole in the side of the cylinder, and withdraw the steering lock barrel

6   The relays and timers are located in the central electric box. The various relays can be removed from their respective locations by carefully pulling them from the sockets.
7   If a system controlled by a relay becomes inoperative and the relay is suspect, listen to the relay as the circuit is operated. If the relay is functioning, it should be possible to hear it click as it is energised. If the relay proves satisfactory, the fault lies with the components or wiring of the system. If the relay is not being energised, then it is not receiving a main supply voltage or a switching voltage, or the relay is faulty.

4 Switches - removal and refitting

Steering column multi-function switch

1   The steering column multi-function switch consists of left-hand and right-hand assemblies. The left-hand switch assembly comprises the headlight dip/flasher switch, the horn switch, the direction indicator switch, and the hazard flasher switch; the right-hand switch assembly comprises the light switch and the wiper/washer switch. The two halves can be removed and refitted independently of each other as follows.
2   Disconnect the battery negative lead.
3   Remove the screws, and withdraw the upper and lower shrouds from the steering column (see illustrations).
4   Remove the two crosshead screws, and withdraw the left-hand or right-hand switch assembly from the steering column (see illustration).
5   Disconnect the wiring multi-plug, and remove the switch assembly.
6   Refitting is a reversal of removal.

Ignition/starter switch and lock barrel

7   Disconnect the battery negative lead.
8   Remove the screws, and withdraw the upper and lower shrouds from the steering column.
9   Insert the ignition key, and turn it to position "I". Depress the lock spring using a suitable rod or tool inserted through the access hole in the side of the cylinder, and withdraw the steering lock barrel (see illustration). Slight movement of the key will be necessary in order to align the cam.
10   With the key fully inserted, extract the spring clip (taking care not to damage its location), then withdraw the key approximately 5 mm and remove the barrel from the cylinder.
11   Disconnect the wiring multi-plug, then remove the two grub screws and withdraw the ignition switch (see illustration).
12   Refitting is a reversal of removal, but check the operation of the steering lock in all switch positions.

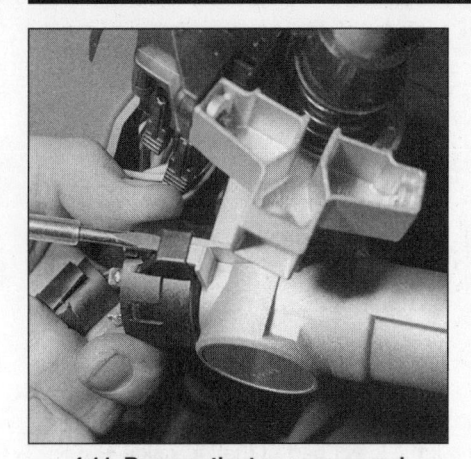

Chapter 12 Body electrical systems

4.11 Remove the two screws and withdraw the ignition switch

4.14 Courtesy light switch securing screw (arrowed) in the door pillar

4.20a Unscrew the retaining screws within the instrument panel surround . . .

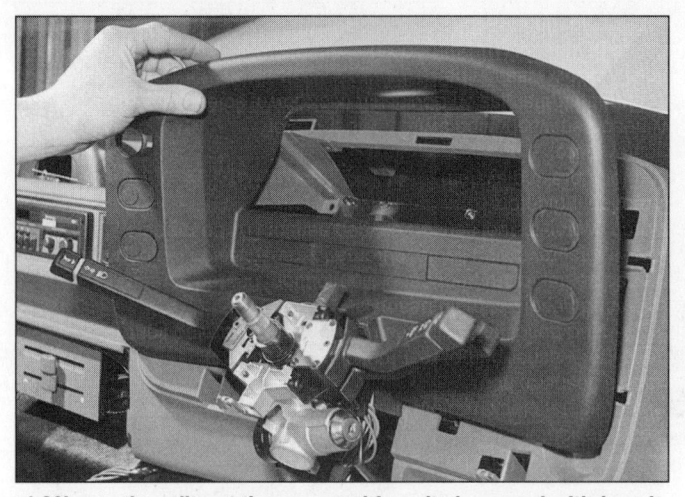

4.20b . . . then tilt out the surround from its base and withdraw it (steering wheel removed for clarity)

4.21 Press the appropriate switch from the panel, disconnect the wiring connector and remove the switch

Courtesy light switch

13 Disconnect the battery negative lead.
14 Open the door and unscrew the crosshead screw from the door pillar **(see illustration)**.
15 Remove the switch from the door pillar, and pull the wire out sufficiently to prevent it from springing back into the pillar. If necessary, tape the wiring to the door pillar while the switch is removed.
16 Disconnect the wire and remove the switch.
17 Refitting is a reversal of removal.

Instrument panel surround switches

Pre-1995 model year

18 Disconnect the battery negative lead.
19 Undo the retaining screws, and remove the upper and lower steering column shrouds.
20 Loosen off the upper steering column mounting nuts to slightly lower the column, then unscrew the retaining screws within the surround, tilt out the surround from its base, and withdraw it **(see illustrations)**.
21 Press the switch from the panel, then disconnect the wiring connector and remove the switch **(see illustration)**.
22 Refit in the reverse order of removal. Tighten the column upper mounting nuts to the specified torque setting (see Specifications in Chapter 10).

1995 model year onwards

23 Disconnect the battery negative lead.

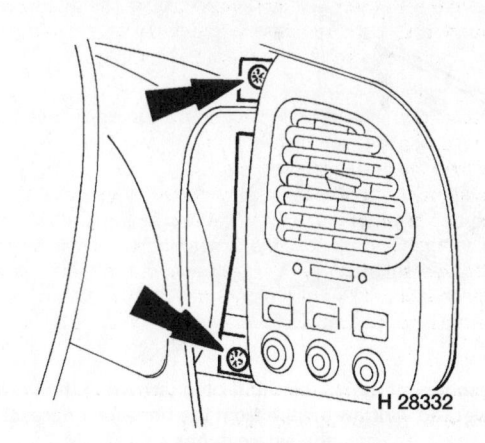

4.27 Undo the two screws (arrowed) securing the switch/vent panel, and withdraw the panel

24 Undo the retaining screws, and remove the upper and lower steering column shrouds.
25 Remove the left-hand and right-hand multi-function switches from the steering column, as described previously in this Section.
26 Undo the four instrument panel surround retaining screws, and withdraw the surround.
27 Undo the two screws securing the switch/vent panel, and withdraw the panel **(see illustration)**.

12-8 Chapter 12 Body electrical systems

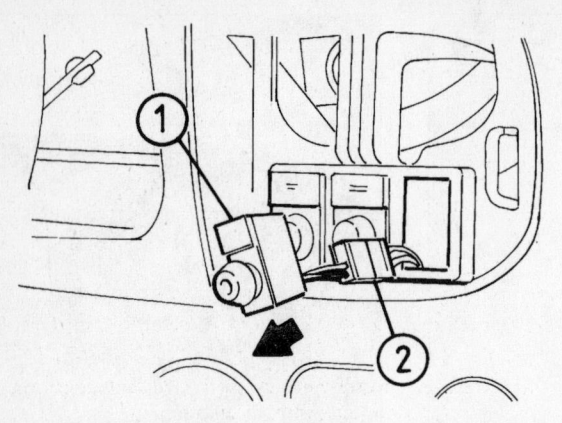

4.28 Carefully push out the switch (1) from behind, then disconnect the wiring connector (2)

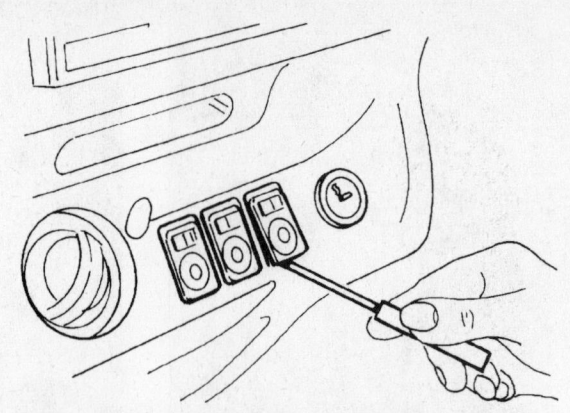

4.31 Carefully prise out the lower part of the facia side switch, and withdraw it from its location

4.33 Brake stop-light switch location in the pedal bracket

4.37 Removing the heater control panel retaining screws

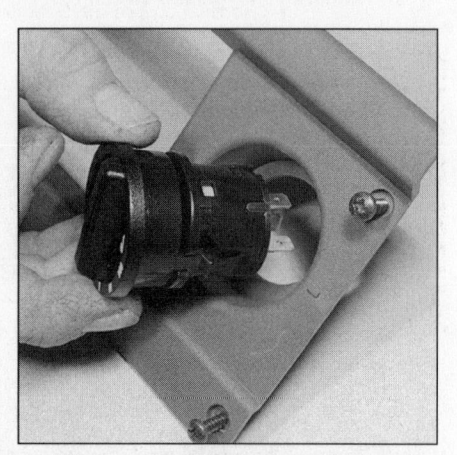

4.38 Compress the retainer tabs and withdraw the blower motor switch from the panel

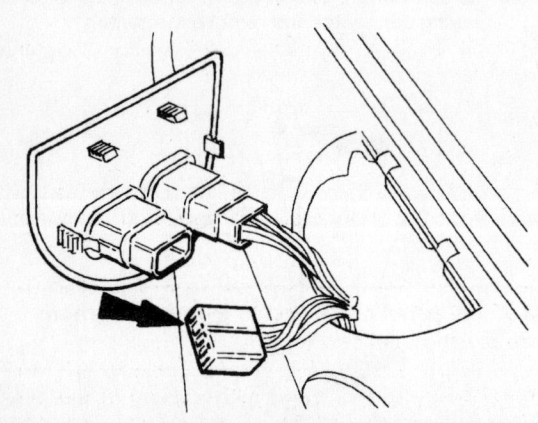

4.43 Disconnect the wiring multi-plug (arrowed) then remove the electric window switch from the bezel by depressing the side catches

28 Carefully push out the relevant switch from behind, then disconnect the wiring connector and remove the switch **(see illustration)**.
29 Refit in the reverse order of removal.

Facia side switches (1995 model year onwards)

30 Disconnect the battery negative lead.
31 Using a small screwdriver, carefully prise out the lower part of the switch from the facia **(see illustration)**. When the switch is released, withdraw it from its location and disconnect the wiring plug.
32 Refit in the reverse order of removal.

Brake stop-light switch

33 Disconnect the wiring connector from the switch unit, then twist the switch anti-clockwise and remove it from its retaining bracket **(see illustration)**.
34 To refit the switch, connect the wiring connector, and insert the switch into the retaining bracket.
35 Hold the brake pedal in the "at rest" position, push the switch down to depress the plunger, then twist the switch clockwise until it locks in position.

Heater blower motor switch

Pre-1995 model year

36 Disconnect the battery negative lead.
37 Undo the four screws retaining the heater control panel to the facia, and partially withdraw the panel to allow access to the rear of the switch **(see illustration)**.
38 Detach the switch wiring connector, then compress the retainer tabs and withdraw the switch from the panel **(see illustration)**.
39 Refit in the reverse order of removal.

1995 model year onwards

40 Refer to "Heater/ventilation components - removal and refitting" in Chapter 3.

Electric window switch

41 Disconnect the battery negative lead.
42 Carefully prise out the switch bezel from the door.
43 Disconnect the wiring multi-plug, then remove the switch from the bezel by depressing the side catches **(see illustration)**. Where two

Chapter 12 Body electrical systems

5.4 Removing the instrument panel left-hand retaining screws on pre-1995 models

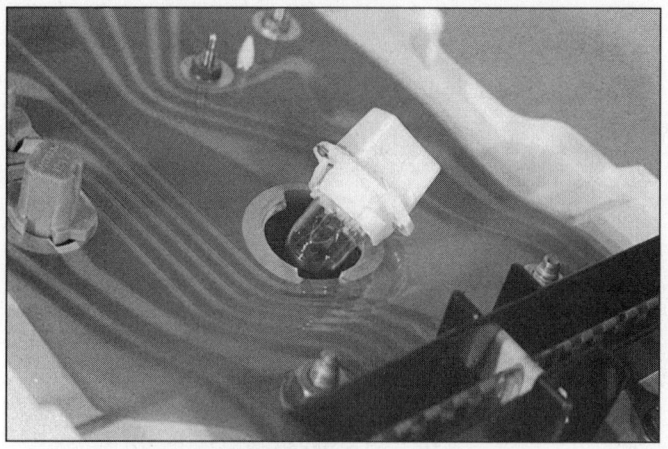

6.2 Instrument panel bulbholder removal

5.7 On later models, undo the five screws (arrowed) securing the instrument panel to the facia

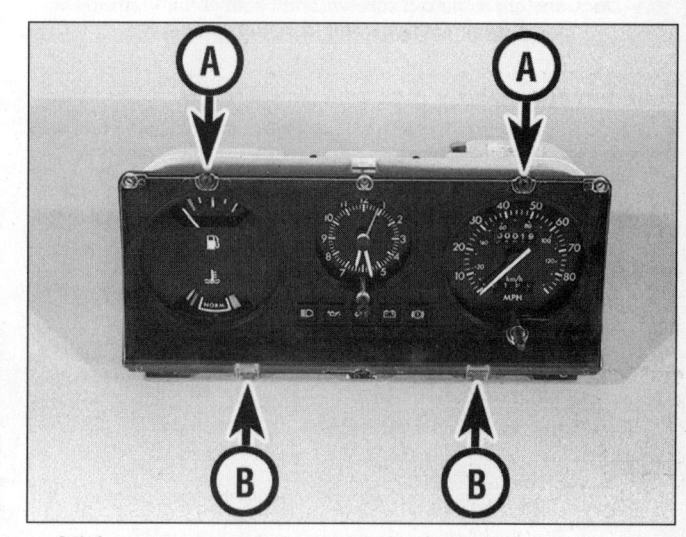

6.4 Instrument panel glass retaining screws (A) and clips (B)

switches are fitted to the bezel, mark the wiring multi-plug positions if both switches are to be removed.
44 Refit in the reverse order of removal.

5 Instrument panel (non-tachograph models) - removal and refitting

Removal

Pre-1995 model year

1 Disconnect the battery negative lead.
2 Undo the retaining screws, and remove the steering column shrouds.
3 Loosen off the upper column mounting nuts, and allow the column to drop a fraction. Undo the instrument panel surround retaining screws, tilt the panel out at the bottom, and withdraw the surround. Disconnect the switch wiring connectors to remove the surround.
4 Unscrew and remove the four instrument panel retaining screws, then withdraw the panel sufficiently to enable the speedometer cable and the wiring block connectors to be detached from the rear of the panel **(see illustration)**. Remove the instrument panel.

1995 model year onwards

5 Remove the steering column multi-function switch as described in Section 4.
6 Undo the four screws and withdraw the instrument panel surround.
7 Undo the five screws securing the instrument panel to the facia **(see illustration)**. Withdraw the panel slightly, disconnect the

speedometer cable and the two wiring multi-plugs from the rear, then remove the instrument panel.

Refitting

All models

8 Refit in the reverse order of removal. Check for satisfactory operation of the various instruments and associated components on completion.

6 Instrument panel components (non-tachograph models) - removal and refitting

1 Remove the instrument panel as described in the previous Section. When handling the instrument panel and removing or refitting its components, take care not to damage the printed circuit. Avoid knocking or dropping the unit, as it can easily be damaged.

Pre-1995 model year

Warning and illumination bulbs

2 Untwist the bulbholder, and withdraw it from the rear face of the panel. Remove the bulb from its holder **(see illustration)**.
3 Refit in the reverse order of removal.

Panel glass

4 Undo the two retaining screws at the top, and detach the two retaining clips at the bottom, then remove the glass **(see illustration)**.
5 Refit in the reverse order of removal.

12-10 Chapter 12 Body electrical systems

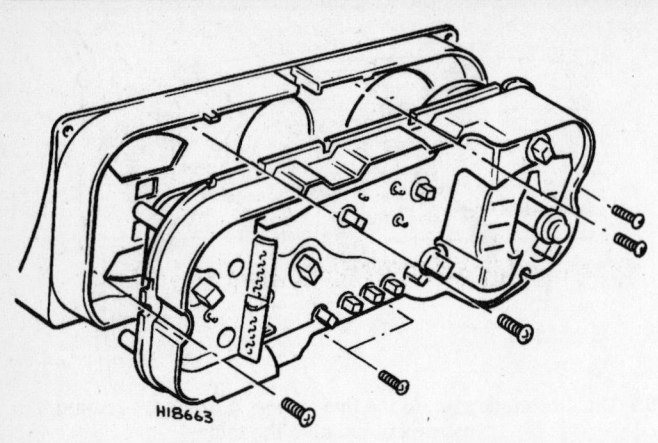

6.6 Undo the six retaining screws, and remove the instrument panel front surround unit from the main unit

Speedometer head

6 Undo the six retaining screws, and remove the front surround unit from the main unit (see illustration).
7 Undo the two retaining screws, and withdraw the speedometer head from the panel (see illustration).
8 Refit in the reverse order of removal.

Fuel gauge

9 Undo the six retaining screws, and remove the front surround unit from the main unit.
10 Unscrew the four retaining nuts, and remove the washers. Withdraw the fuel/temperature gauge unit from the front face side of the unit (see illustration).
11 Refit in the reverse order of removal.

Clock

12 Undo the six retaining screws, and remove the front surround unit from the main unit.
13 Unscrew the three retaining nuts, and withdraw the clock from the main unit.
14 Refit in the reverse order of removal.

Printed circuit

15 Remove the bulbholders, the clock and the fuel/temperature gauge.
16 Detach the multi-plug connector block, then carefully remove the printed circuit (see illustration).
17 Refit in the reverse order of removal.

1995 model year onwards

Warning and illumination bulbs

18 Untwist the bulbholder, and withdraw it from the rear face of the panel. Remove the bulb from its holder.
19 Refit in the reverse order of removal.

Panel glass

20 Carefully release the five retaining lugs, and remove the panel glass and frame from the main unit (see illustration).
21 Note the fitted positions of the symbol diffusers, and withdraw them from the front of the main panel.
22 Refit in the reverse order of removal.

Speedometer head

23 Remove the panel glass, then undo the three screws and withdraw the speedometer head from the main panel (see illustration).
24 Refit in the reverse order of removal.

Tachometer

25 Remove the panel glass, then undo the single screw and withdraw the tachometer from the main panel.
26 Refit in the reverse order of removal.

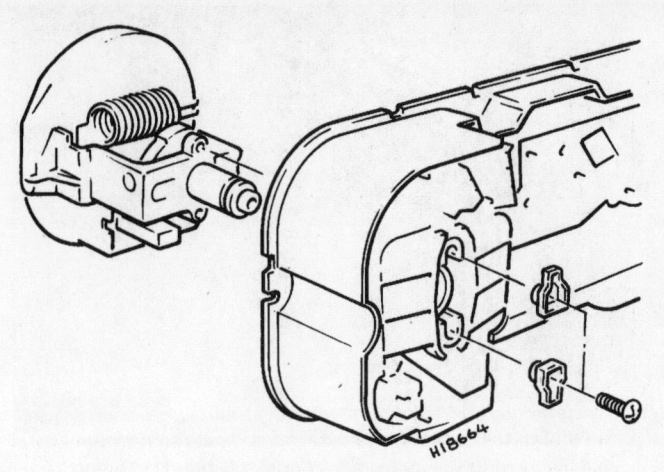

6.7 Speedometer head removal

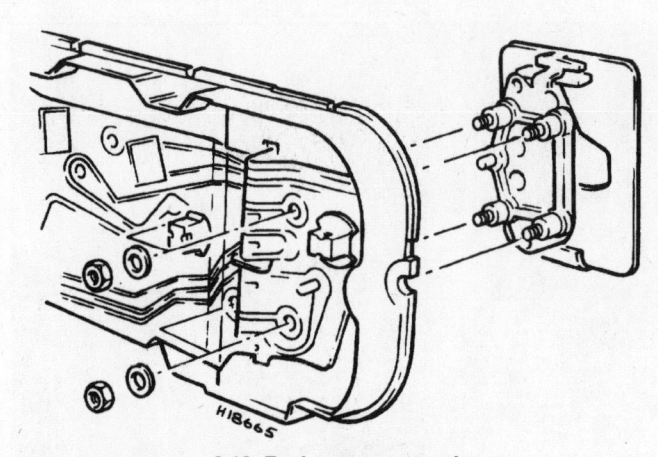

6.10 Fuel gauge removal

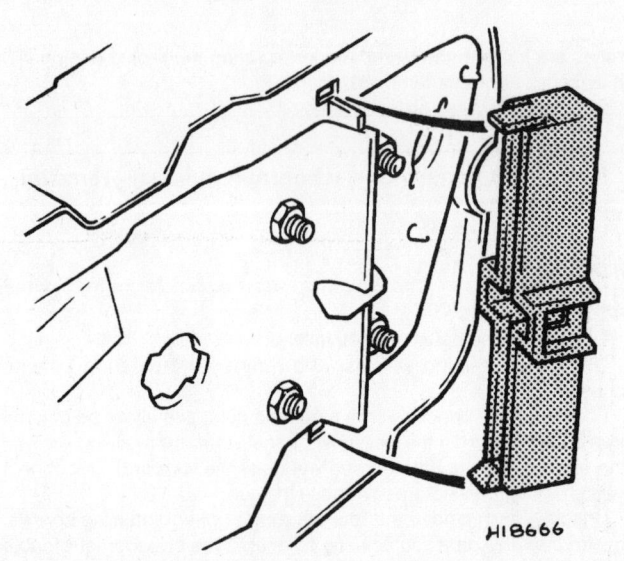

6.16 Detach the multi-plug connector block, then carefully remove the printed circuit

Fuel and temperature gauges

27 Remove the panel glass, then undo the single screw securing each gauge. Withdraw the fuel or temperature gauge, as applicable, from the main panel.
28 Refit in the reverse order of removal.

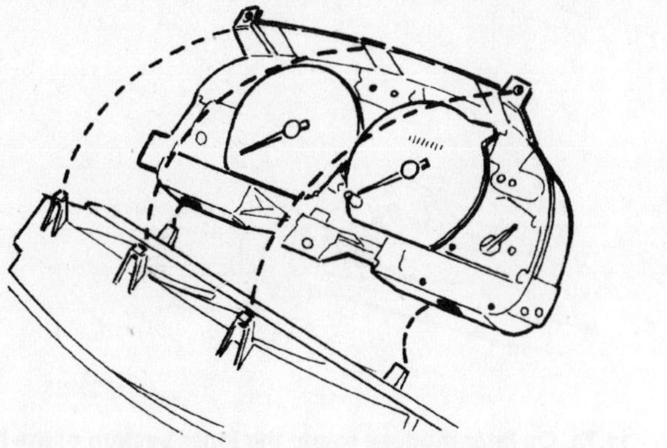

Chapter 12 Body electrical systems

6.20 On later models, release the five retaining lugs, and remove the instrument panel glass and frame from the main unit

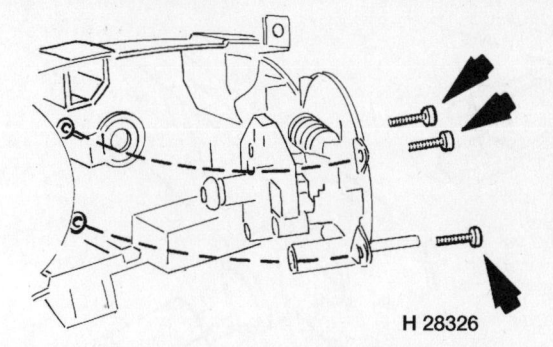

6.23 Undo the three screws (arrowed), and withdraw the speedometer head from the main panel

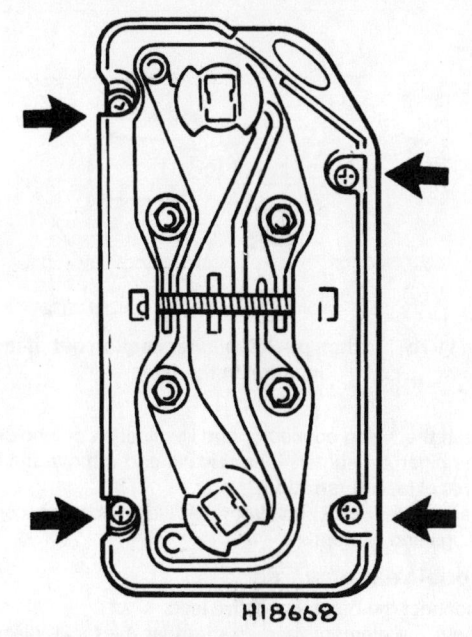

8.3a Fuel/temperature gauge housing screws (arrowed) on tachograph models

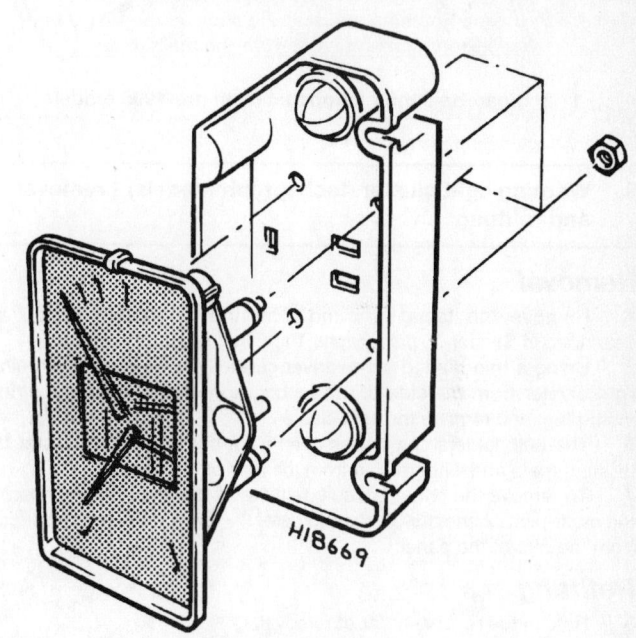

8.3b Removing the fuel/temperature gauge from the housing on tachograph models

Printed circuit

29 Remove the bulbholders, instruments and gauges as previously described.
30 Remove the gauge and instrument pin contacts from the printed circuit.
31 Using a thin flat-nosed punch, push in the pins to release the multi-plug connector block retainers, and remove the connector blocks.
32 Carefully lift the printed circuit off the locating dowels, and remove it from the rear of the instrument panel.
33 Refit in the reverse order of removal.

7 Tachograph - removal and refitting

Removal

1 Disconnect the battery negative lead.
2 Undo the retaining screws, and remove the upper and lower shrouds from the steering column.
3 Pull free the heater control switch knob, and where fitted, the intermittent wiper control knob.
4 Undo the four retaining screws, and remove the facia surround from the instrument panel sufficiently to detach the switch wires.
5 Disconnect the switch wire connectors. Untwist the illumination bulbs to remove them. Remove the panel.
6 Undo the four retaining bolts, and withdraw the tachograph assembly. Disconnect the wiring multi-plug, and remove the tachograph assembly.
7 Undo the two nuts and remove the tachograph from the mounting bracket.

Refitting

8 Refit in the reverse order of removal.

8 Fuel and temperature gauge (tachograph models) - removal and refitting

Removal

1 Remove the facia surround from the instrument panel as described in Section 7, paragraphs 1 to 5 inclusive.
2 Push out the combined fuel and temperature gauge assembly from behind the panel, and disconnect the wiring multi-plug.
3 Undo the four retaining screws, and remove the front gauge housing. Undo the four nuts and remove the gauge assembly from the rear housing **(see illustrations)**.

Refitting

4 Refit in the reverse order of removal.

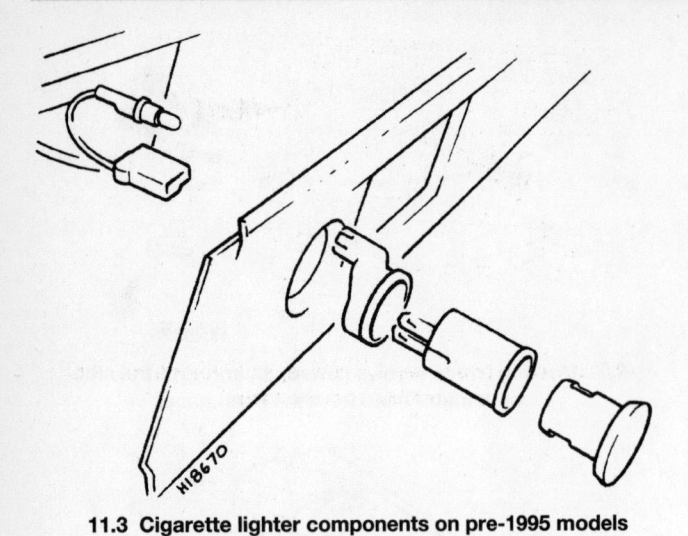

11.3 Cigarette lighter components on pre-1995 models

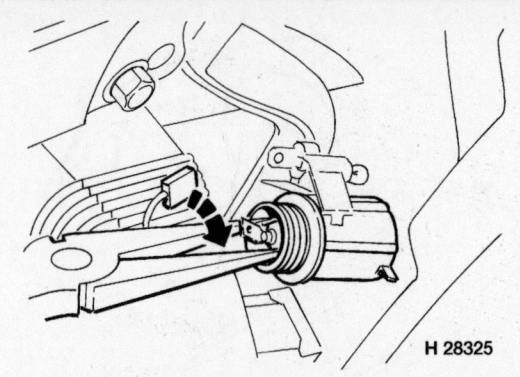

11.7a On later models, rotate the inner section of the lighter assembly clockwise to release it from the outer casing . . .

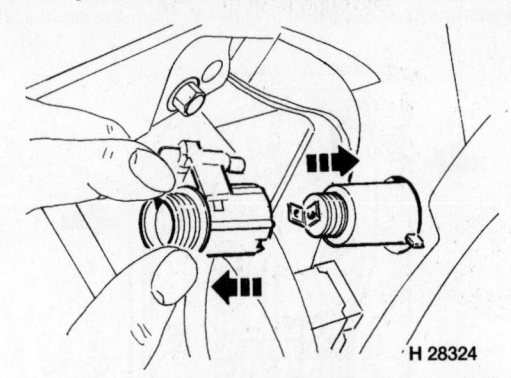

11.7b . . . then push the inner section out of its location in the facia

9 Warning light cluster (tachograph models) - removal and refitting

Removal
1 Remove the facia surround from the instrument panel, as described in Section 7, paragraphs 1 to 5 inclusive.
2 Using a thin bladed screwdriver carefully prise out the warning light cluster from the side of the tachograph. Disconnect the wiring multi-plug, and remove the light cluster.
3 The bulbholders can be removed from the rear of the cluster by twisting them and withdrawing from the rear of the panel.
4 To remove the printed circuit, remove all the bulbholders, release the multi-plug connector block, and carefully remove the printed circuit from the rear of the panel.

Refitting
5 Refit in the reverse order of removal.

10 Speedometer cable - removal and refitting

Removal
1 Remove the instrument panel as described in Section 5.
2 Apply the handbrake, then raise the vehicle at the front and support it securely on axle stands.
3 Working underneath the vehicle, undo the bolt, withdraw the retaining plate, and withdraw the cable from the transmission.
4 Withdraw the cable through the bulkhead, and remove it from the engine compartment.

Refitting
5 Refit in the reverse order of removal. When inserting the cable through the bulkhead, pass it through the grommet and align the colour band on the cable with the grommet. Re-route the cable so that it is clear of any moving parts on which it could chafe, and do not bend it too much.

11 Cigarette lighter - removal and refitting

Removal
Pre-1995 model year
1 Disconnect the battery negative lead.
2 Undo the four retaining screws, and remove the heater control panel from the facia sufficiently to allow access to the rear of the unit.
3 Detach the wiring connector and illumination bulbholder from the rear of the cigarette lighter, then release and remove the lighter unit from the panel (see illustration).
4 To remove the lighter unit from the illumination ring, compress the retaining lugs and withdraw the unit.

1995 model year onwards
5 Disconnect the battery negative lead.
6 Pull out the element then, from under the facia, disconnect the wiring connections at the rear of the lighter assembly.
7 Rotate the inner section of the lighter assembly clockwise to release it from the outer casing, then push the inner section out of its location in the facia (see illustrations).
8 If required, the bulb can be withdrawn from the outer casing for renewal.

Refitting
All models
9 Refit in the reverse order of removal. Check for satisfactory operation of the lighter on completion.

12 Clock - removal and refitting

Removal
Pre-1995 model year
1 Refer to the procedures contained in Section 6.

1995 model year onwards
2 Disconnect the battery negative lead.
3 Remove the radio/cassette player (or compact disc player, as applicable) as described in Section 23 or 24.
4 Remove the steering column multi-function switch as described in Section 4.
5 Undo the four screws and withdraw the instrument panel surround.

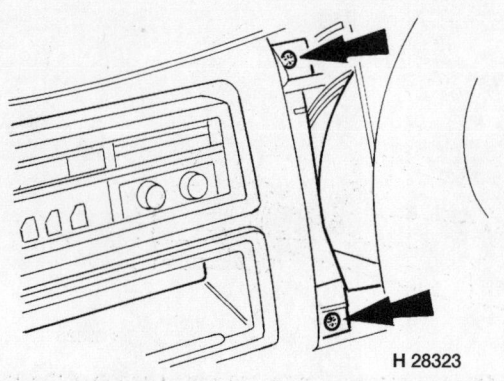

Chapter 12 Body electrical systems

12-13

12.6 Undo the two screws, and withdraw the radio/clock surround from the facia

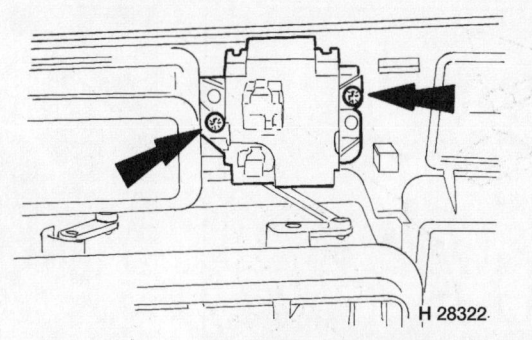

12.8 Undo the two screws (arrowed) and remove the clock assembly from the facia

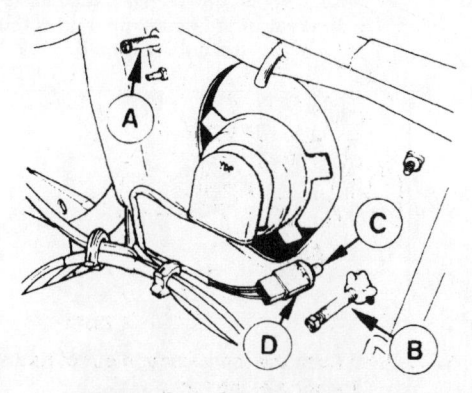

13.2a Rear view of early-type headlight unit

- A Horizontal beam adjustment screw
- B Vertical beam adjustment screw
- C Sidelight bulb
- D Sidelight bulbholder

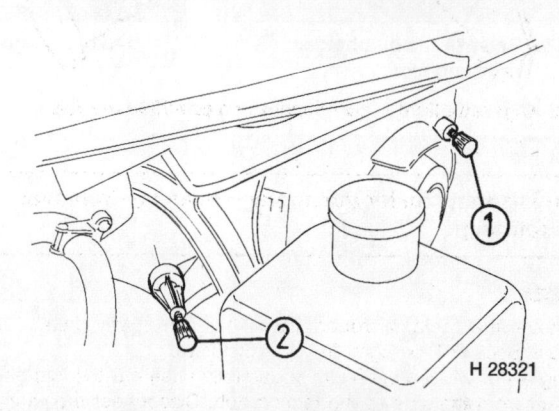

13.2b Rear view of later-type headlight unit

1. Horizontal beam adjustment screw
2. Vertical beam adjustment screw

13 Headlight beam alignment - checking and adjustment

1 Accurate adjustment of the headlight beam is only possible using optical beam-setting equipment, and this work should therefore be carried out by a Ford dealer or service station with the necessary facilities.
2 Temporary adjustment can be made when the headlight unit has been removed and refitted, or to compensate for normal adjustment whenever a heavy load is being carried. Turn the adjustment screws at the rear of the headlight unit to make the adjustment (see illustrations).
3 Before making any adjustments to the headlight settings, it is important that the tyre pressures are correct, and that the vehicle is standing on level ground. Bounce the front of the vehicle a few times to settle the suspension. Ideally, somebody of average size should sit in the driver's seat during the adjustment, and the vehicle should have a full tank of fuel.
4 Whenever temporary adjustments are made, the settings must be reset as soon as possible once the vehicle is in normal use.

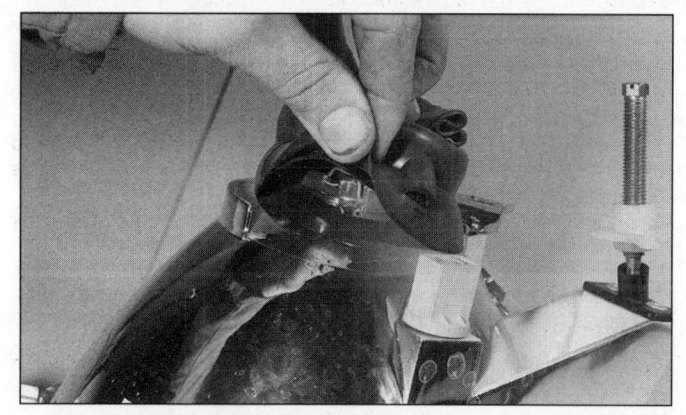

14.1 Disconnect the wiring multi-plug from the rear of the headlight unit, and remove the rubber cap

6 Undo the two screws, and withdraw the radio/clock surround from the facia (see illustration).
7 Disconnect the wiring multi-plug, and remove the surround. If required, the illumination bulbholder can be removed by twisting it anti-clockwise.
8 Undo the two screws, and remove the clock assembly from the facia (see illustration).

Refitting
All models
9 Refitting is a reversal of removal.

14 Bulbs (exterior lights) - renewal

Note: *Ensure that all exterior lights are switched off before disconnecting the wiring connectors to any exterior light bulbs. The headlight, front sidelight and direction indicator bulbs are removable from within the engine compartment with the bonnet raised.*

Headlight

1 Disconnect the wiring multi-plug from the rear of the headlight unit, and remove the rubber cap (see illustration).
2 Release the bulbholder retaining clip, and withdraw the bulb (see illustrations).

12

12-14   Chapter 12 Body electrical systems

14.2a Release the bulbholder retaining clip...

14.2b ...and withdraw the bulb

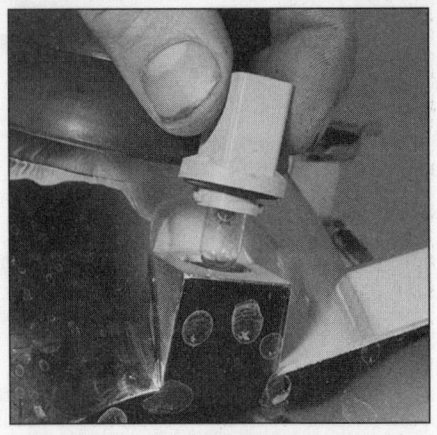

14.5 Untwist the sidelight bulbholder from the rear of the headlight, and withdraw the bulb and holder

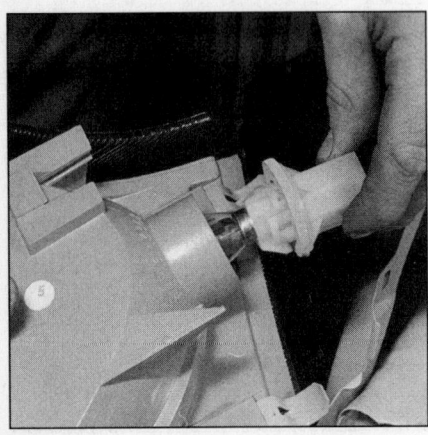

14.8 Removing the bulbholder from the rear of the direction indicator light unit

14.11 Front direction indicator side repeater location

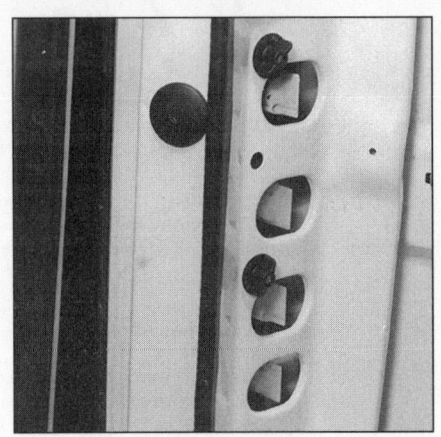

14.13a On early models, the rear light cluster bulbs are accessible through the apertures in the body pillar

3   Fit the new bulb using a reversal of the removal procedure. Do not touch the bulb glass with the fingers, as this will cause the bulb to fail. If it is touched, wipe it clean with a tissue soaked in methylated spirit.

4   Holts Amber Lamp is useful for temporarily changing the headlight colour to conform with the normal use when driving in France.

Front sidelight

5   Untwist the sidelight bulbholder from the rear of the headlight, and withdraw the bulb and holder **(see illustration)**.

6   Remove the bulb from the bulbholder.

7   Fit the new bulb using a reversal of the removal procedure. Check for satisfactory operation on completion.

Front direction indicator

8   Reach down and untwist the bulbholder from the rear of the direction indicator unit **(see illustration)**.

9   Remove the bulb from the bulbholder.

10   Fit the new bulb using a reversal of the removal procedure. Check for satisfactory operation on completion.

Front direction indicator side repeater

11   Pull the bulbholder from the rear of the light unit, then remove the bulb from its holder **(see illustration)**.

12   Fit the new bulb using a reversal of the removal procedure. Check for satisfactory operation on completion.

Rear light cluster

Van and Bus models

13   On early models, remove the cover flap (where fitted) from the rear body corner to gain access to the light cluster. Untwist and withdraw the appropriate bulb and holder from the light unit. Press and untwist the bulb to remove it from its holder **(see illustrations)**. On later models, undo the two plastic wing nuts, and remove the light unit. Compress the lower lugs followed by the upper lugs, and separate the bulbholder from the light unit. Press and untwist the bulb to remove it from its holder.

14   Fit the new bulb(s) using a reversal of the removal procedure. Check for satisfactory operation on completion.

Chassis Cab models

15   Release the lens retaining clip, and move the lens out of the way. Remove the appropriate bulb from the holder in the light unit.

16   Fit the new bulb(s) using a reversal of the removal procedure. Check for satisfactory operation on completion.

Rear number plate light bulb

Double rear door models

17   Prise free the light cap using a suitable screwdriver, then remove the bulb from its holder by pulling it free **(see illustrations)**.

18   Fit the new bulb using a reversal of the removal procedure. Check for satisfactory operation on completion.

Chapter 12 Body electrical systems

14.13b Untwist and withdraw the appropriate bulb and holder from the light cluster

14.17a On double rear door models, prise free the number plate light cap using a screwdriver . . .

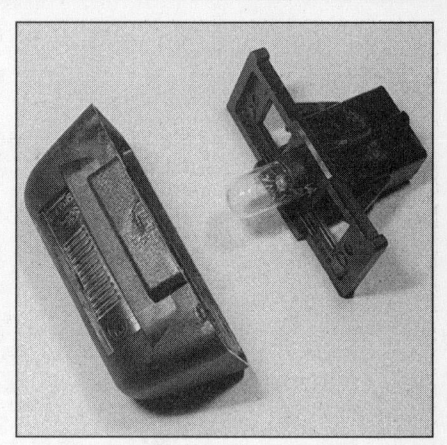

14.17b . . . then remove the bulb from its holder by pulling it free

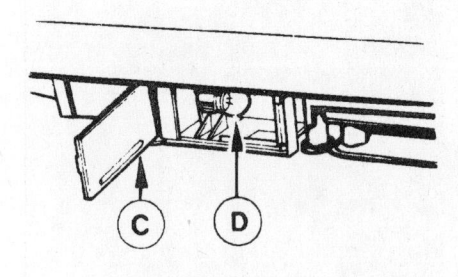

14.19 Rear number plate lens (C) and bulb (D) on Tailgate models

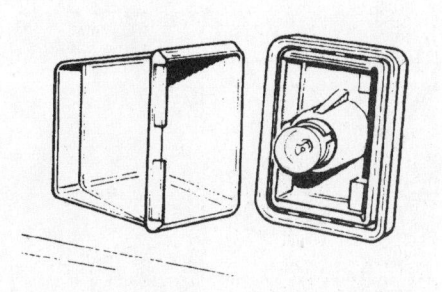

14.21 Rear number plate light assembly on Chassis cab models

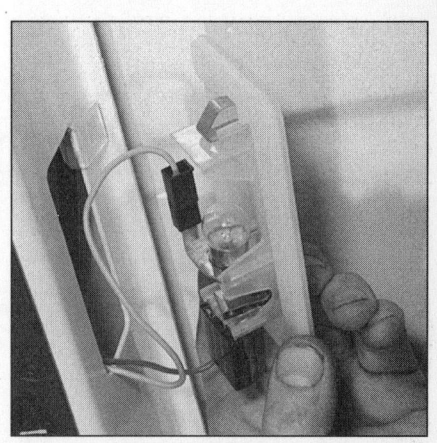

15.1 Carefully prise free the courtesy light unit for access to the bulb

Tailgate models

19 Slide the light lens to the left, and pivot it out of the way. Push and untwist the bulb to remove it from its holder **(see illustration)**.
20 Fit the new bulb using a reversal of the removal procedure. Check for satisfactory operation on completion.

Chassis Cab models

21 Pull free the light cap and lens, then press and untwist the bulb to remove it from its holder **(see illustration)**.
22 Fit the new bulb using a reversal of the removal procedure. Check for satisfactory operation on completion.

15 Bulbs (interior lights) - renewal

Courtesy lights

1 Insert a small electrical screwdriver blade into the indent in the light unit, and carefully prise it free **(see illustration)**.
2 Press and untwist the bulb from its holder. The rear courtesy light has a festoon-type bulb, and this type is simply prised free from its holder.
3 Fit the new bulb using a reversal of the removal procedure. Check for satisfactory operation on completion.

Hazard warning switch

4 Pull free the hazard warning switch lens/button, then remove the bulb **(see illustration)**.

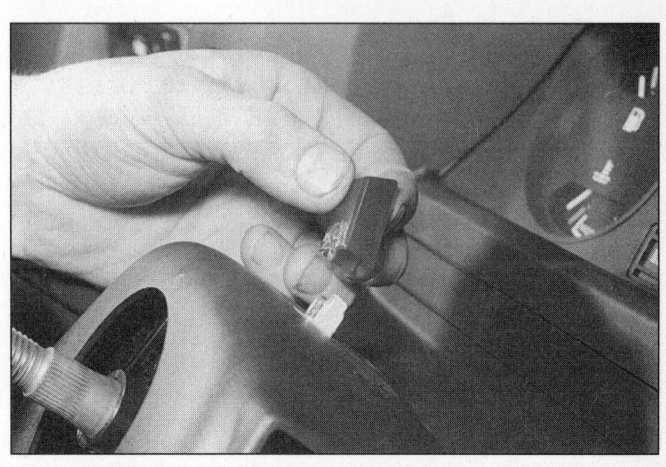

15.4 Pull free the hazard warning switch lens/button, then remove the bulb

5 Fit the new bulb using a reversal of the removal procedure. Check for satisfactory operation on completion.

Instrument panel illumination and warning lights

6 Procedures for renewal of the panel illumination and warning light bulbs are contained in Section 6 for non-tachograph models, and Section 9 for models fitted with tachographs.

16.4a On early models, turn the two plastic headlight retainers a quarter of a turn . . .

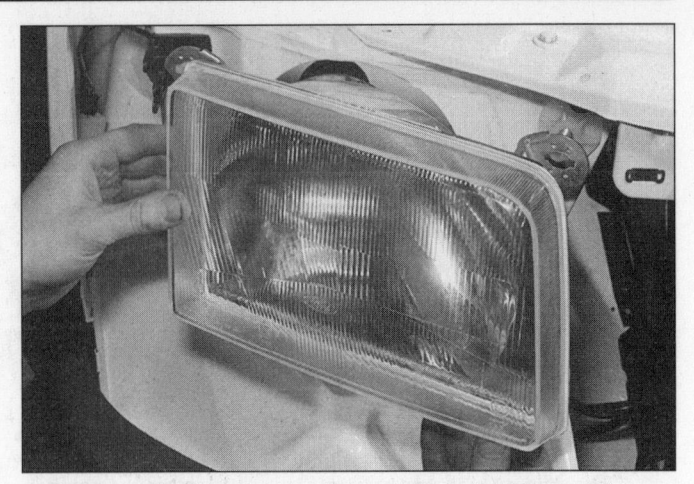

16.4b . . . withdraw the headlight unit from the top mountings, and disengage it from the lower adjuster

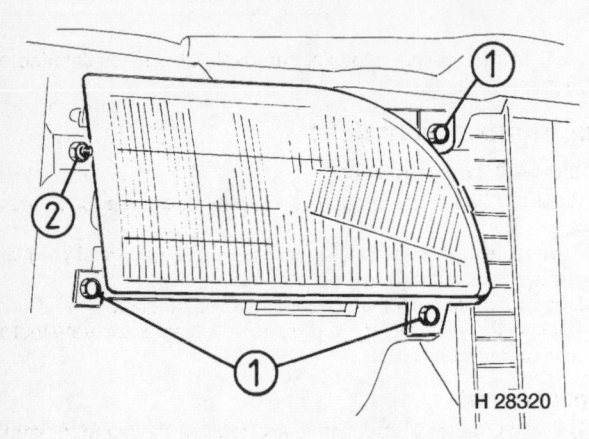

16.10 On later models, undo the three bolts (1) and one nut (2) to remove the headlight unit

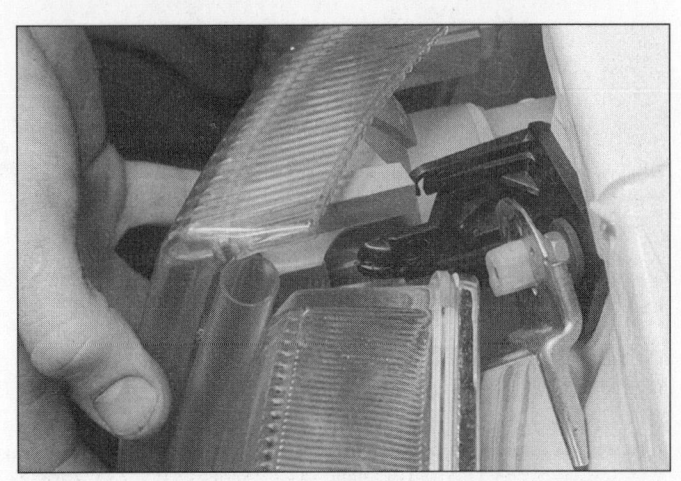

16.13 Front direction indicator unit removal on early models

Automatic transmission selector quadrant

7 Undo the two screws, and lift off the gear selector lever cover.
8 Twist the bulbholder anti-clockwise to detach it from the cover.
9 Remove the bulb from the holder.
10 Fit the new bulb using a reversal of the removal procedure. Check for satisfactory operation on completion.

16 Exterior light units - removal and refitting

Headlight unit

Pre-1992 model year

1 Remove the front direction indicator unit as described later in this Section.
2 Pull off the protective cap from the rear of the headlight, and disconnect the headlight multi-plug.
3 Twist the sidelight bulbholder anti-clockwise, and withdraw it from the headlight unit.
4 Using suitable pliers, turn the two plastic headlight retainers a quarter of a turn. Withdraw the headlight unit from the top mountings, and disengage it from the lower adjuster (see illustrations).
5 Refit in the reverse order of removal. Refer to Section 13 for details on headlight beam alignment. Check the headlights and indicators for satisfactory operation on completion.

1992 model year onwards

6 Disconnect the multi-plug at the rear of the direction indicator light unit, release the indicator unit retaining spring, and remove the unit.

7 Remove the radiator grille as described in Chapter 11.
8 Pull off the protective cap from the rear of the headlight, and disconnect the headlight multi-plug.
9 Twist the sidelight bulbholder anti-clockwise, and withdraw it from the headlight unit.
10 Undo the three bolts and one nut, and remove the headlight unit (see illustration).
11 Refit in the reverse order of removal. Refer to Section 13 for details on headlight beam alignment. Check the headlights and indicators for satisfactory operation on completion.

Front direction indicator unit

Pre-1992 model year

12 Twist the direction indicator bulbholder anti-clockwise and withdraw it from the light unit.
13 Press the lock tongue of the plastic retaining clip at the top of the indicator unit to one side, and then use a suitable screwdriver to detach it. Withdraw the indicator unit from the front (see illustration).
14 Refit in the reverse order of removal. Check for satisfactory operation on completion.

1992 model year onwards

15 Twist the direction indicator bulbholder anti-clockwise, and withdraw it from the light unit.
16 Release the indicator unit retaining spring, and remove the unit.
17 Refit in the reverse order of removal. Check for satisfactory operation on completion.

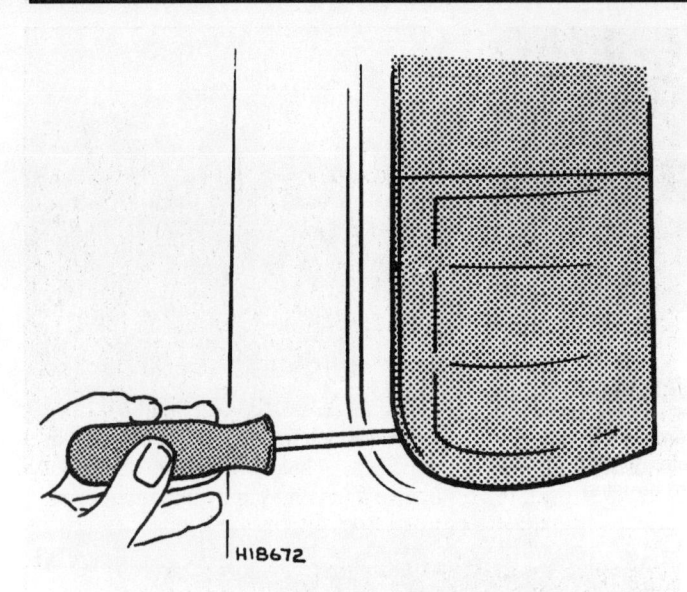

Chapter 12 Body electrical systems

12-17

16.22 Withdraw the rear light cluster as far as possible, then lift the lower plastic spring retainer using a screwdriver

17.1 Horn location and wiring connectors

Direction indicator side repeater

18 Pull the bulbholder from the rear of the light unit, then either depress the retaining lugs or turn the unit clockwise (according to fitting), and withdraw the unit from the front wing.
19 Refit in the reverse order of removal. Check for satisfactory operation on completion.

Rear light cluster

Pre-1992 model year Van and Bus models

20 Remove the cover flap (where fitted) from the rear body corner to gain access to the light cluster.
21 Unscrew the three plastic wing nuts securing the light cluster to the body.
22 Withdraw the light cluster as far as possible, then lift the lower plastic spring retainer using a screwdriver **(see illustration)**.
23 Disconnect the wiring multi-plug and remove the light cluster assembly.
24 Refit in the reverse order of removal. Check for satisfactory operation on completion.

1992 model year onwards Van and Bus models

25 Remove the cover flap (where fitted) from the rear body corner to gain access to the light cluster.
26 Unscrew the two plastic wing nuts securing the light cluster to the body.
27 Withdraw the light cluster assembly, and disconnect the wiring multi-plug.
28 With the assembly removed, compress the lower retaining lugs of the bulbholder, and release the bulbholder from the lens unit at the bottom. Compress the upper retaining lugs, and separate the bulbholder from the lens unit.
29 Refit in the reverse order of removal. Check for satisfactory operation on completion.

Chassis Cab models

30 Release the light cluster wiring loom from the clip on the rear crossmember, then disconnect the wiring multi-plug from its loom connection.
31 Unscrew the two nuts from the studs at the rear of the light cluster assembly.
32 Withdraw the light cluster assembly sideways and outwards, until the two studs and retaining clip are clear. Pull the wiring loom out of the crossmember, and remove the assembly.

33 Refit in the reverse order of removal. Check for satisfactory operation on completion.

Rear number plate light

Double rear door models

34 Refer to Chapter 11, Section 9, and remove the rear door interior trim panel.
35 Squeeze together the locking tabs on the wiring multi-plug, and push the light unit out of the rear door.
36 Disconnect the multi-plug and remove the light unit.
37 Refit in the reverse order of removal. Check for satisfactory operation on completion.

Tailgate models

38 Refer to Chapter 11, Section 9, and remove the rear door interior trim panel.
39 Disconnect the two wiring multi-plugs at the rear of the light unit, and unscrew the four light unit retaining nuts.
40 Remove the light unit from the tailgate.
41 Refit in the reverse order of removal. Check for satisfactory operation on completion.

Chassis Cab models

42 Pull free the light cap and lens from the light unit.
43 Disconnect the wiring multi-plug at the loom connector on the rear crossmember.
44 Withdraw the light unit rubber housing from the crossmember, pull out the wiring loom and remove the unit.
45 Refit in the reverse order of removal. Check for satisfactory operation on completion.

17 Horn - removal and refitting

Removal

1 The horn is located at the front of the vehicle, behind the radiator grille and underneath the left-hand headlight. Access is improved by removal of the radiator grille (Chapter 11, Section 27) **(see illustration)**.
2 Detach the two wiring connectors from the horn, then unscrew the horn mounting bracket bolt and withdraw the horn.
3 If required, the horn can be separated from the mounting bracket by undoing the retaining nut. The horn cannot be adjusted or repaired, and therefore if defective, it must be renewed.

Refitting

4 Refit in the reverse order of removal. Check for satisfactory operation on completion.

12-18   **Chapter 12 Body electrical systems**

18.2 Wiper arm-to-spindle retaining nut

19.3 Unscrew and remove the wiper linkage plastic retaining nut from the centre pivot housing

19.6 Detach the wiring multi-plug from the wiper motor

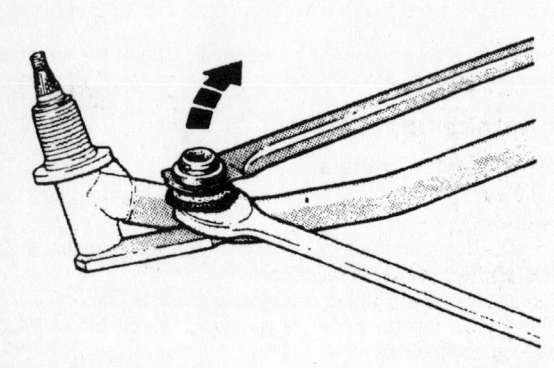

19.8a Prise the linkage balljoints off the pivot housing shaft . . .

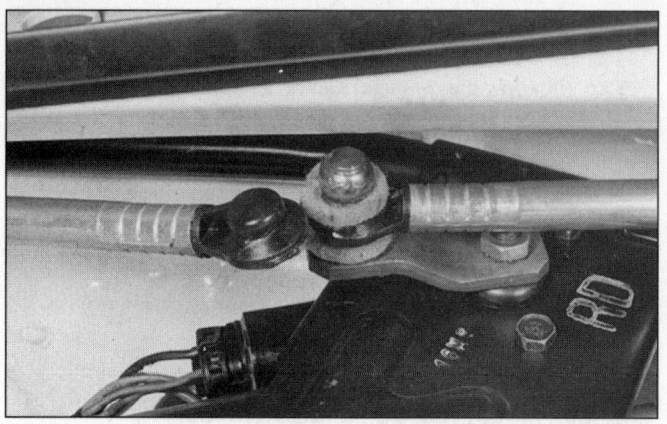

19.8b . . . and link arm ballpins using an open-ended spanner

18 Wiper arms - removal and refitting

Removal

1 Remove the wiper blades as described in Chapter 1.
2 Lift the hinged covers, and remove the nuts and washers securing the arms to the spindles **(see illustration)**.
3 Mark the arms and spindles in relation to each other, then prise off the arms using a screwdriver. Take care not to damage the paintwork.

Refitting

4 Refitting is a reversal of removal.

19 Windscreen wiper motor and linkage - removal and refitting

Removal

1 Disconnect the battery negative lead.
2 Remove the wiper arms as described in the previous Section.
3 Unscrew and remove the plastic retaining nut from the centre pivot housing **(see illustration)**.
4 Remove the windscreen grille panel as described in Chapter 11.
5 Undo the steel nut on each pivot housing, and remove it together with its shim.
6 Compress the locktab, and detach the wiring multi-plug from the wiper motor **(see illustration)**.
7 Undo the two bolts securing the wiper motor bracket to the bulkhead, and remove the complete motor and linkage assembly from the vehicle.
8 To remove the linkage, prise the linkage balljoints off the pivot housing shaft and link arm ballpins, using an open-ended spanner as a lever. Recover the felt washers, noting their fitted positions **(see illustrations)**.
9 Mark the relative positions of the wiper motor link arm and shaft, then unscrew the retaining nut and prise off the arm. Unscrew the three bolts to remove the wiper motor from its bracket.

Refitting

10 Refit in the reverse order of removal, but note the following points:
   a) Ensure that the motor link arm is correctly realigned as it is refitted to the drive shaft.
   b) One of two pivot housing types will be fitted, being of Delco or SWF manufacture. The Delco housing is plastic, the SWF steel. Depending on the type used, it is most important that the pivot nuts are correctly fitted and tightened to the specified torque wrench setting, according to type. On both types, it is important that the steel nuts which secure the pivot housings to the cowl are fitted first. The plastic nut, (which is very similar to the steel type in appearance), secures the windscreen grille panel. The Delco-type pivot housing steel nut must not be tightened in excess of 12 Nm (9 lbf ft).
   c) On completion, check the wipers for satisfactory operation.

20 Windscreen wiper pivot housing - removal and refitting

Removal

1 Remove the windscreen wiper motor and linkage as described in the previous Section. Prise the linkage balljoint off the pivot housing

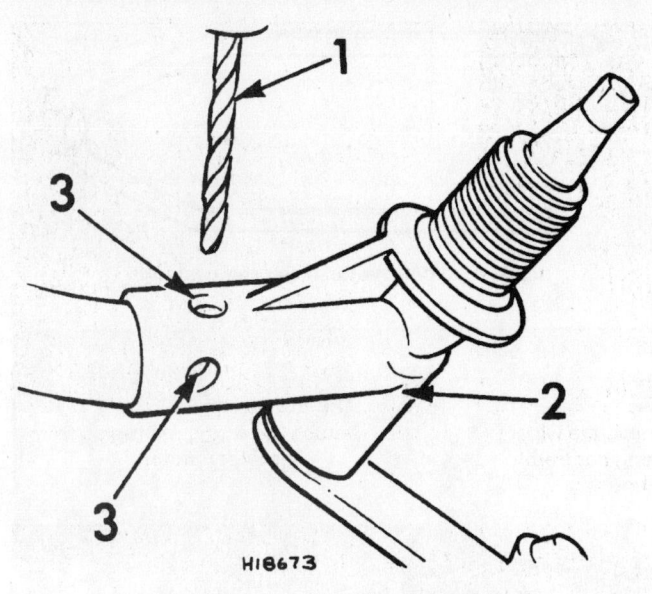

Chapter 12 Body electrical systems

20.2 Delco-type pivot housing removal

1 Drill
2 Pivot housing
3 10 mm deep hole

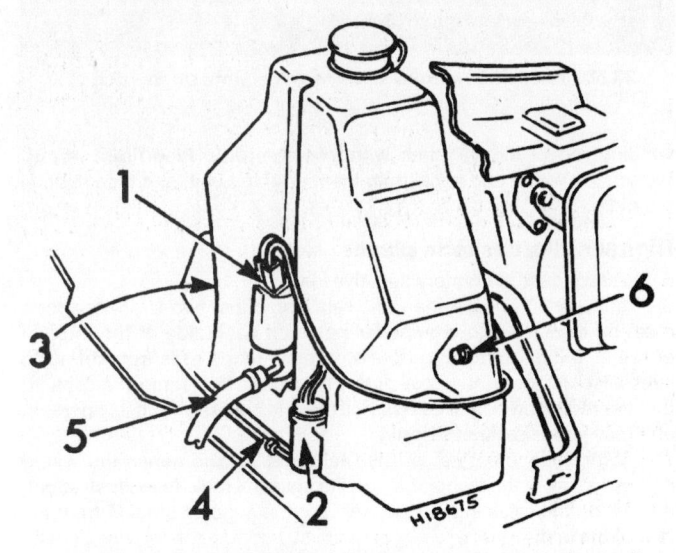

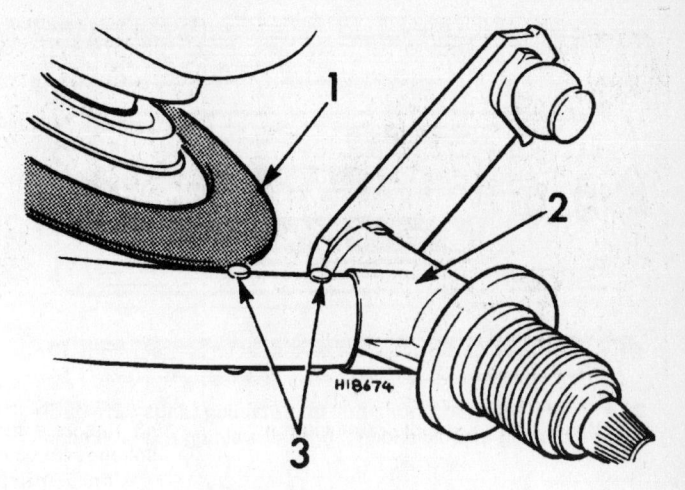

20.3 SWF-type pivot housing removal

1 Grinding disc
2 Pivot housing
3 Rivet heads

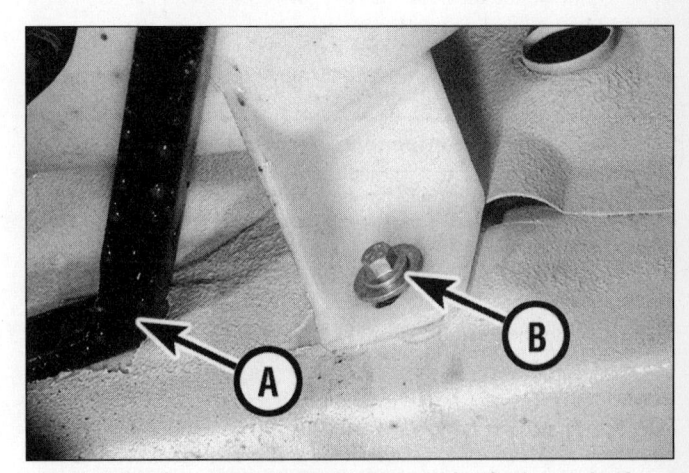

21.2 Washer reservoir attachments under the front wheel arch on later models

A Front bumper reinforcing bar
B Lower retaining bolt

21.1 Windscreen/headlight washer reservoir details (typical)

1 Headlight washer pump
2 Windscreen washer pump
3 Securing bolt
4 Windscreen washer hose
5 Headlight washer hose
6 Securing bolt

shaft ballpin, using an open-ended spanner as a lever. Recover the felt washers, noting their fitted positions.

2 To remove the Delco-type pivot housing, drill a 6.5 mm hole to a depth of 10 mm at the pre-marked points each side of the housing, and then separate the housing from the tube **(see illustration)**.

3 To remove the SWF-type pivot housing, carefully grind off the two rivet heads at the points shown, and then drive the rivets out using a suitable pin punch **(see illustration)**. Separate the housing from the tube.

Refitting

4 To reassemble the housing and tube on both types, slide the two together until the housing engages with the slot in the end of the tube. Where necessary, tap the housing home using a plastic hammer, and align the retaining pin or rivet holes (as applicable).

5 Install new rivets or suitable roll pins to secure. When fitted correctly, the pins should project slightly at each end.

6 Reconnect the linkage to the pivot housing shaft, then refit the assembly as described in the previous Section.

21 Windscreen/headlight washer reservoir - removal and refitting

Removal

1 Disconnect the wiring multi-plug(s) and washer hose(s) from the reservoir pump(s) **(see illustration)**.

2 On later models, remove the reservoir cover under the wheel arch, followed by the front bumper reinforcing bar **(see illustration)**.

3 Undo the retaining bolts and remove the reservoir.

4 If required, the pumps can be removed from the reservoir by prising them from their location. Recover the seal after removal of the pump.

12•20 Chapter 12 Body electrical systems

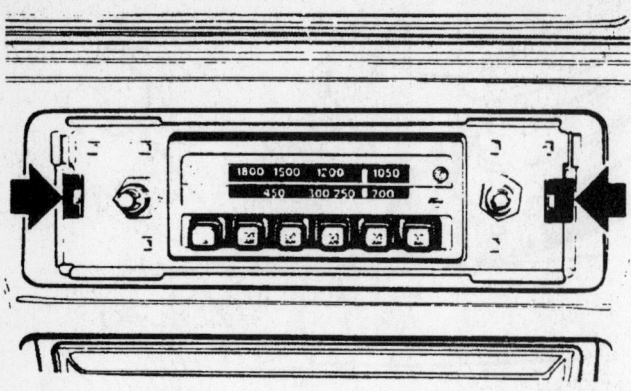

23.4 On the standard radio, pull the retaining tangs (arrowed) inwards, using a hook-ended length of welding rod or similar

23.6a Radio/cassette player removal tool

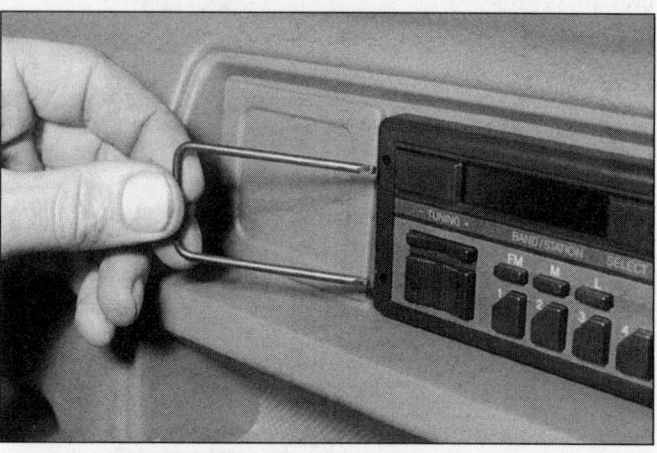

23.6b Insert the removal tools into the slots on the unit . . .

Refitting
5   Refit in the reverse order of removal. Lubricate the pump seal (if removed) with a little washing-up liquid, to ease fitting. On early models, engage the reservoir locating pin in the hole in the body side member as it is fitted.
6   On completion, top-up the reservoir with the required water/washer solution mix, and check for leaks and satisfactory operation.

22 Tailgate wiper components - removal and refitting

Removal
Wiper arm and blade
1   Proceed as described for the windscreen wiper arms and blades removal and refitting (Section 18). Note the position of the wiper arm in the parked position before removing it, to be sure of correctly repositioning it during refitting.

Wiper motor
2   Disconnect the battery negative lead, then remove the tailgate trim panel as described in Chapter 11, Section 9.
3   Remove the wiper arm and blade.
4   Detach the wiring connector from the wiper motor.
5   Undo the retaining screws and remove the wiper motor unit.

Washer reservoir
6   The procedure is similar to that for the removal and refitting of the windscreen/headlight washer reservoir described in the previous Section. Remove the right-hand rear interior trim panel for access, as described in Chapter 11, Section 30.

Refitting
7   Refit in the reverse order of removal, then check for satisfactory operation on completion.

23 Radio/cassette player - removal and refitting

Note: *The following applies only to radio or radio/cassette units fitted as original equipment by the manufacturer. Refer to "Radio/cassette unit anti-theft system" at the start of this manual, before proceeding.*

Removal
Standard radio
1   Disconnect the battery negative lead.
2   Pull free the radio control knobs, the plastic tone control lever, and the spacer from the tuning control.
3   Unscrew the two retaining nuts and remove the facia plate.
4   Pull the retaining tangs inwards, using a hook-ended length of welding rod or similar, then withdraw the radio **(see illustration)**. Detach the wiring and aerial from the rear of the unit, and then remove the radio.

Digital radio/cassette player
5   Disconnect the battery negative lead.
6   In order to release the radio retaining clips, two U-shaped rods must be inserted into the special holes on each side of the radio. If possible, it is preferable to obtain purpose-made rods from an audio specialist, as these have cut-outs which snap firmly into the clips so that the radio can be pulled out. Pull the unit squarely from its aperture, or it may jam **(see illustrations)**.
7   With the radio clear of the facia, detach the aerial and wiring connectors from the rear of the unit. Remove the radio **(see illustration)**.
8   Undo the retaining nut and remove the support bracket from the rear of the unit.

Refitting
9   Refitting is a reversal of removal bearing in mind the following points:
   a) With the standard radio, when it is fully installed, trim (tune) it for the best reception in an interference-free zone. Insert a small electrical screwdriver into the trim screw on the front face of the unit, and turn the screw progressively to obtain the best possible reception.
   b) With the digital radio/cassette player, when the leads are reconnected to the rear of the unit, press it into position to the point where the retaining clips are felt to engage.
   c) On all types with a security code, reactivate the unit in accordance with the code and the instructions given in the Ford Audio Operating Manual supplied with the vehicle.

24 Compact disc player - removal and refitting

The removal and refitting procedures for this unit (where fitted) are identical to those described for the radio/cassette player in the previous Section.

Chapter 12 Body electrical systems

12-21

23.6c ... and pull the unit from its aperture

23.7 Detach the aerial and wiring connectors from the rear of the unit

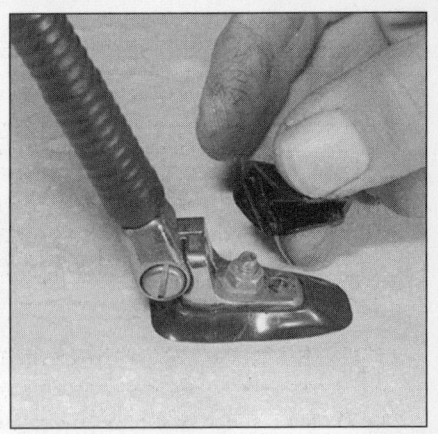

25.2 Prise free the retaining nut cover from the roof-mounted aerial, then unscrew the nut and remove the washer

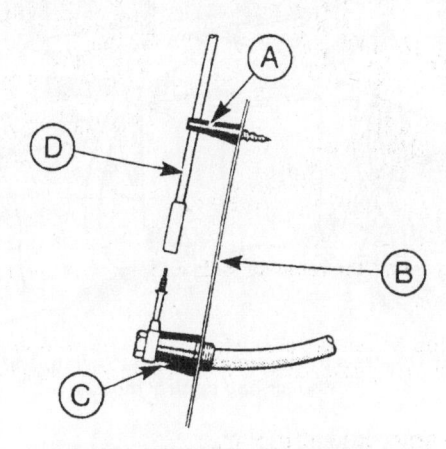

25.7 Side-mounted aerial details

A Aerial support
B Cab body
C Aerial base
D Aerial

25 Radio aerial - removal and refitting

Removal

Roof-mounted aerial

1 Refer to Chapter 11 and remove the cab headlining as necessary to gain access to the underside of the aerial.
2 From outside the vehicle, prise free the retaining nut cover from the aerial, unscrew the nut and remove the washer (see illustration).
3 Withdraw the aerial and spacer plate from the aerial lead stud.
4 To remove the aerial lead, remove the radio (Section 23) and detach the aerial from its rear face.
5 The aerial and lead can now be withdrawn from the vehicle. As the lead is routed up the windscreen "A" pillar, it is advisable to remove its trim and/or attach a length of strong cord to the aerial lead, and pull the lead through until clear, then detach the cord. Leave the cord in position, so that it can be re-attached to pull and guide the lead back through the original route.

Side-mounted aerial

6 This type of aerial is usually fitted to Luton body variants, to improve reception. Start by removing the radio from its aperture (Section 23) and disconnect the aerial lead from its rear face.
7 Unscrew and remove the aerial base mounting bolt, detach the aerial from the mounting, and pull the lead through. Withdraw the aerial downwards from the top support, then remove the aerial and lead (see illustration).

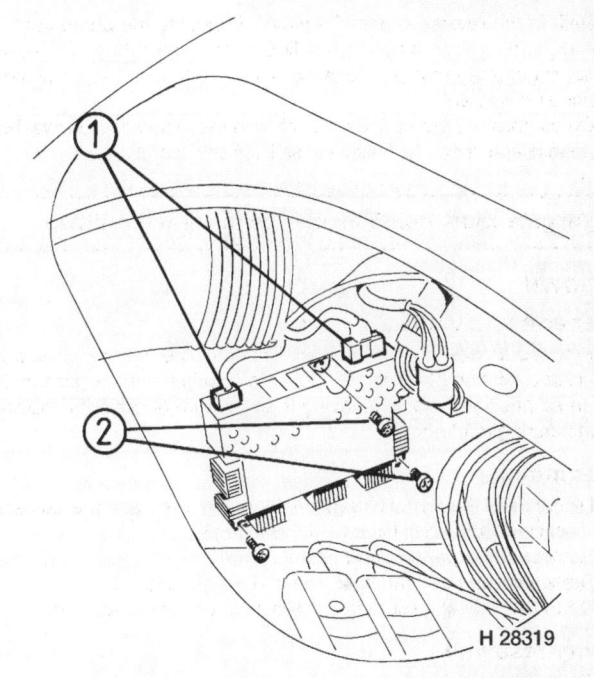

26.4 Power amplifier wiring multi-plugs (1) and retaining screws (2)

Refitting

8 Refit in the reverse order of removal. Ensure that the aerial lead is routed clear of any moving components.

26 Power amplifier - removal and refitting

Removal

1 This unit is fitted to certain Transit models from the 1995 model year onwards.
2 To remove the unit, first disconnect the battery negative lead.
3 Using a screwdriver and protective pad, prise out the stowage tray from the top of the facia.
4 Disconnect the two wiring multi-plugs, undo the three retaining screws, and remove the unit from its location (see illustration).

Refitting

5 Refitting is a reversal of removal.

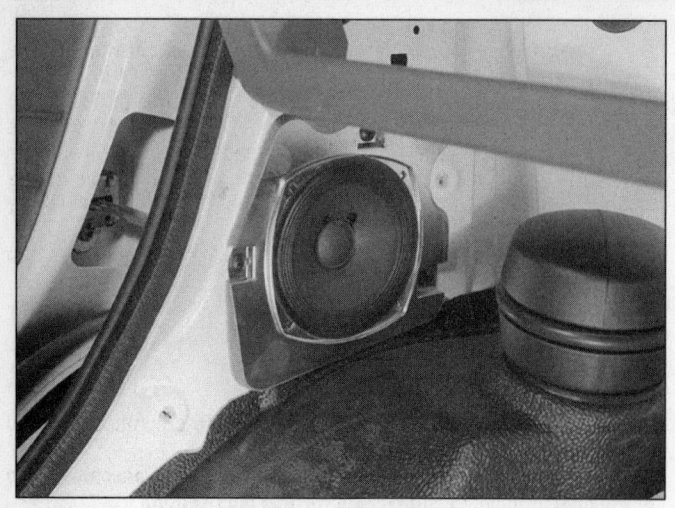

27.2 Standard speaker location behind the front trim panel

27 Loudspeakers - removal and refitting

Removal
1 Remove the appropriate trim panel for access to the speaker, as described in Chapter 11, Section 9 or 30.
2 Undo the retaining screws and withdraw the speaker unit (see illustration). Detach the wiring.

Refitting
3 Refit in the reverse order of removal.

28 Air bag unit - removal and refitting

Warning: *Handle the air bag unit with extreme care as a precaution against personal injury, and always hold it with the cover facing away from the body. If in doubt concerning any proposed work involving the air bag unit or its control circuitry, consult a Ford dealer or other qualified specialist.*

Removal

Driver's side air bag
1 Disconnect the battery negative lead.
2 **Warning:** *Before proceeding, wait a minimum of 15 minutes, as a precaution against accidental firing of the air bag unit. This period ensures that any stored energy in the back-up capacitor is dissipated.*
3 Turn the steering wheel as necessary, so that one of the air bag unit retaining bolts becomes accessible from the rear of the steering wheel. Undo the bolt, then turn the steering wheel again until the second bolt is accessible. Undo this bolt also.
4 Withdraw the air bag unit from the steering wheel, far enough to access the wiring multi-plug.
5 Disconnect the multi-plug from the rear of the unit, and remove it from the vehicle. **Warning:** *Position the air bag unit in a safe place, with the mechanism facing downwards as a precaution against accidental operation.*
6 **Warning:** *Do not attempt to open or repair the air bag unit, or apply any electrical current to it. Do not use any air bag which is visibly damaged, or which has been tampered with.*

Passenger's side air bag
7 Disconnect the battery negative lead.
8 **Warning:** *Before proceeding, wait a minimum of 15 minutes, as a precaution against accidental firing of the air bag unit. This period ensures that any stored energy in the back-up capacitor is dissipated.*

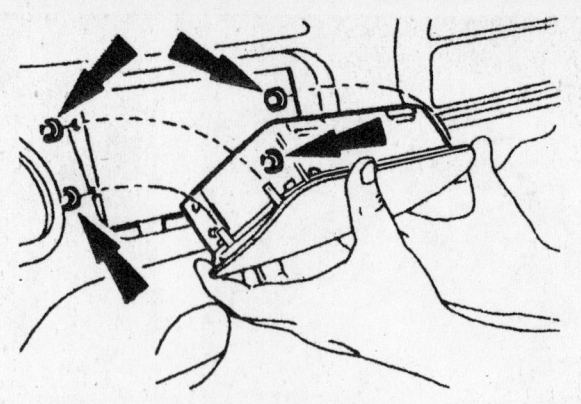

28.11 Undo the retaining nuts (arrowed) and ease the passenger's side air bag unit out of its location in the facia

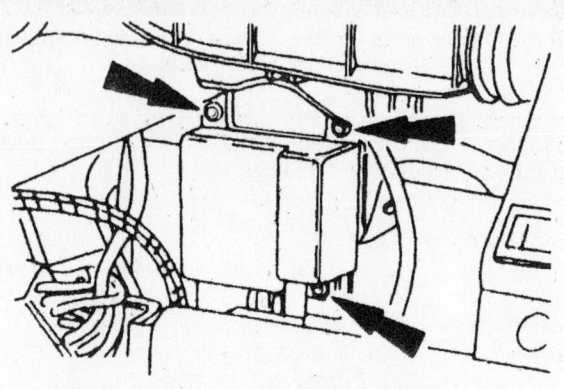

29.5 Unscrew the mounting bolts (arrowed) and remove the air bag control module

9 Using a screwdriver and protective pad, prise out the stowage tray from the top of the facia.
10 Working through the stowage tray aperture, disconnect the two wiring multi-plugs on the air bag unit.
11 Undo the retaining nuts, and ease the air bag unit out of its location in the facia (see illustration). **Warning:** *Position the air bag unit in a safe place, with the mechanism facing downwards as a precaution against accidental operation.*
12 **Warning:** *Do not attempt to open or repair the air bag unit, or apply any electrical current to it. Do not use any air bag which is visibly damaged, or which has been tampered with.*

Refitting
13 Refitting is a reversal of removal.

29 Air bag control module - removal and refitting

Removal
1 Disconnect the battery negative lead.
2 **Warning:** *Before proceeding, wait a minimum of 15 minutes, as a precaution against accidental firing of the air bag unit. This period ensures that any stored energy in the back-up capacitor is dissipated.*
3 Remove the instrument panel, according to type, as described earlier in this Chapter.
4 Disconnect the multi-plug from the module, by pressing the locking tab upwards and swivelling the retaining strap.
5 Unscrew the mounting bolts, and remove the module from the vehicle (see illustration).

Refitting
6 Refitting is a reversal of the removal procedure.

Chapter 12 Body electrical systems

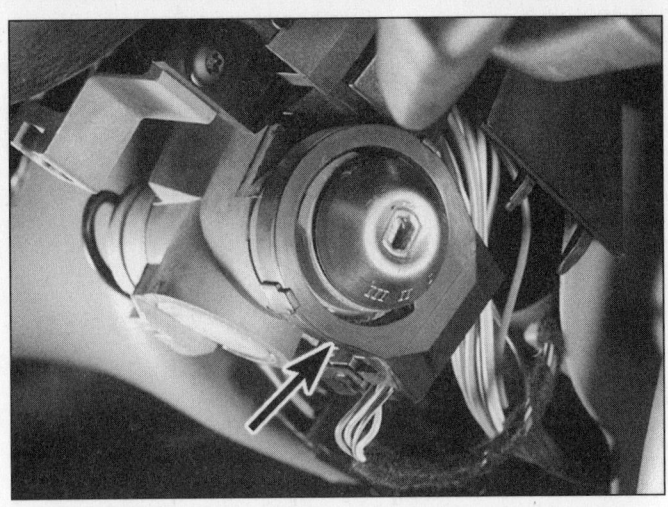

30.6 PATS transceiver location (arrowed) around the ignition switch/steering lock barrel

30 Passive anti-theft system - general information and component renewal

General information

1 For the 1995 model year, a Passive Anti-Theft System (PATS) is available on all models. This system is a vehicle immobiliser which prevents the engine from being started unless a specific code, programmed into the ignition key, is recognised by the PATS transceiver.
2 The PATS transceiver, fitted around the ignition/starter switch, decodes a signal from the ignition key as the key is turned from position "O" to position "II". If the coded signal matches that stored in the memory of the PATS module, the engine will start. If the signal is not recognised, the engine fuel system and starter motor will be disabled, preventing the engine from starting. For this reason, it is worth remembering to check the PATS for a possible fault if the vehicle will not start.
3 The PATS status is indicated by an LED control light in the instrument panel or facia.

Component renewal

PATS transceiver

4 Disconnect the battery negative lead.
5 Undo the screws, and remove the steering column upper and lower shrouds.
6 Undo the single screw, and withdraw the PATS transceiver from the ignition switch/steering lock barrel **(see illustration)**.
7 Release the wiring harness from the clips on the steering column, trace the harness below the steering column, and disconnect the wiring multi-plug. Remove the transceiver from the vehicle.
8 Refitting is a reversal of removal.

PATS module

9 Disconnect the battery negative lead.
10 Refer to Chapter 11 and remove the facia.
11 Disconnect the wiring multi-plug from the PATS module located on the bulkhead.
12 Pull the module downwards to remove it from the mounting bracket.
13 Refitting is a reversal of removal.

12-24 Chapter 12 Body electrical systems

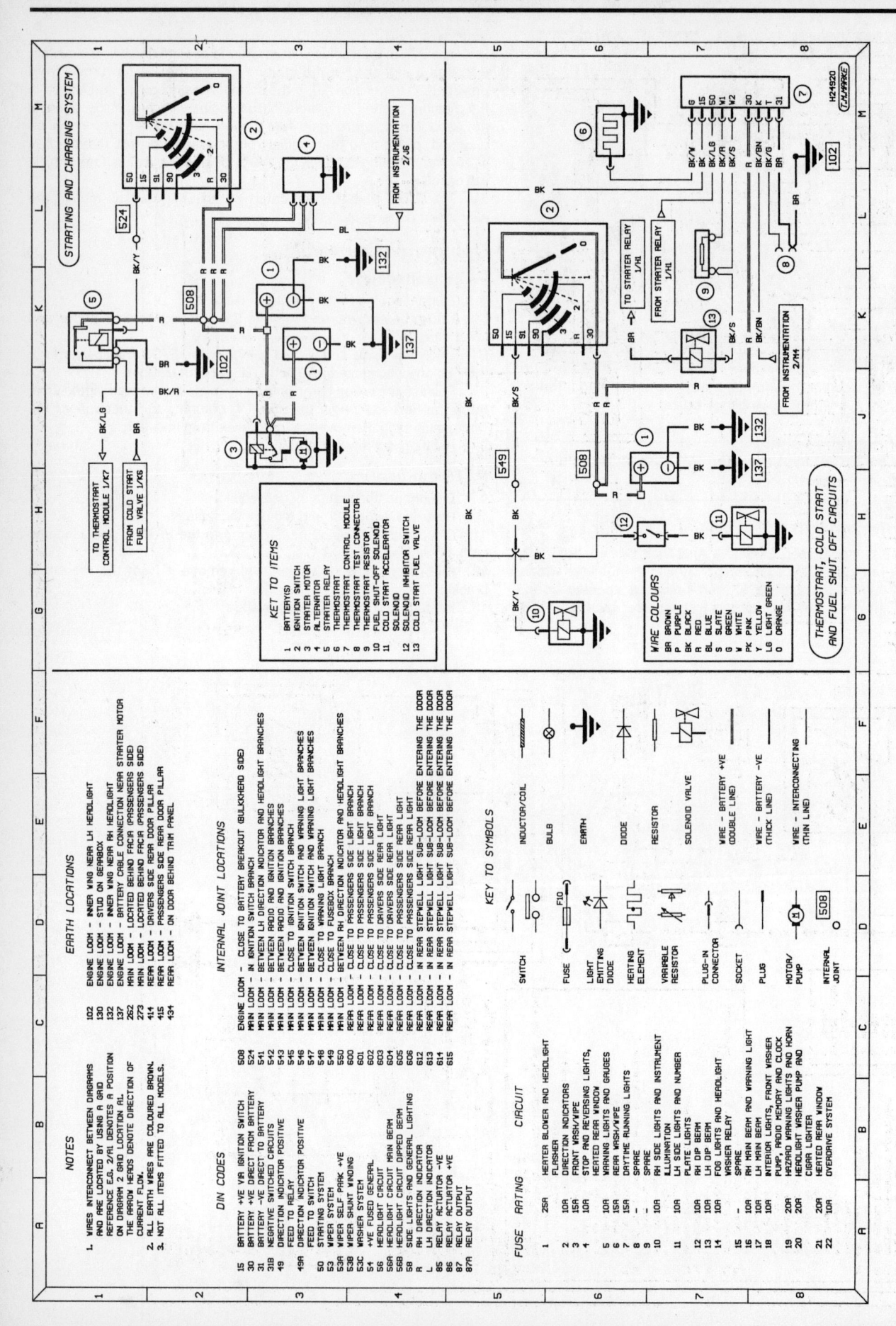

Diagram 1: Information for use of wiring diagrams, starting, charging and cold start system (models up to 1992)

Chapter 12 Body electrical systems

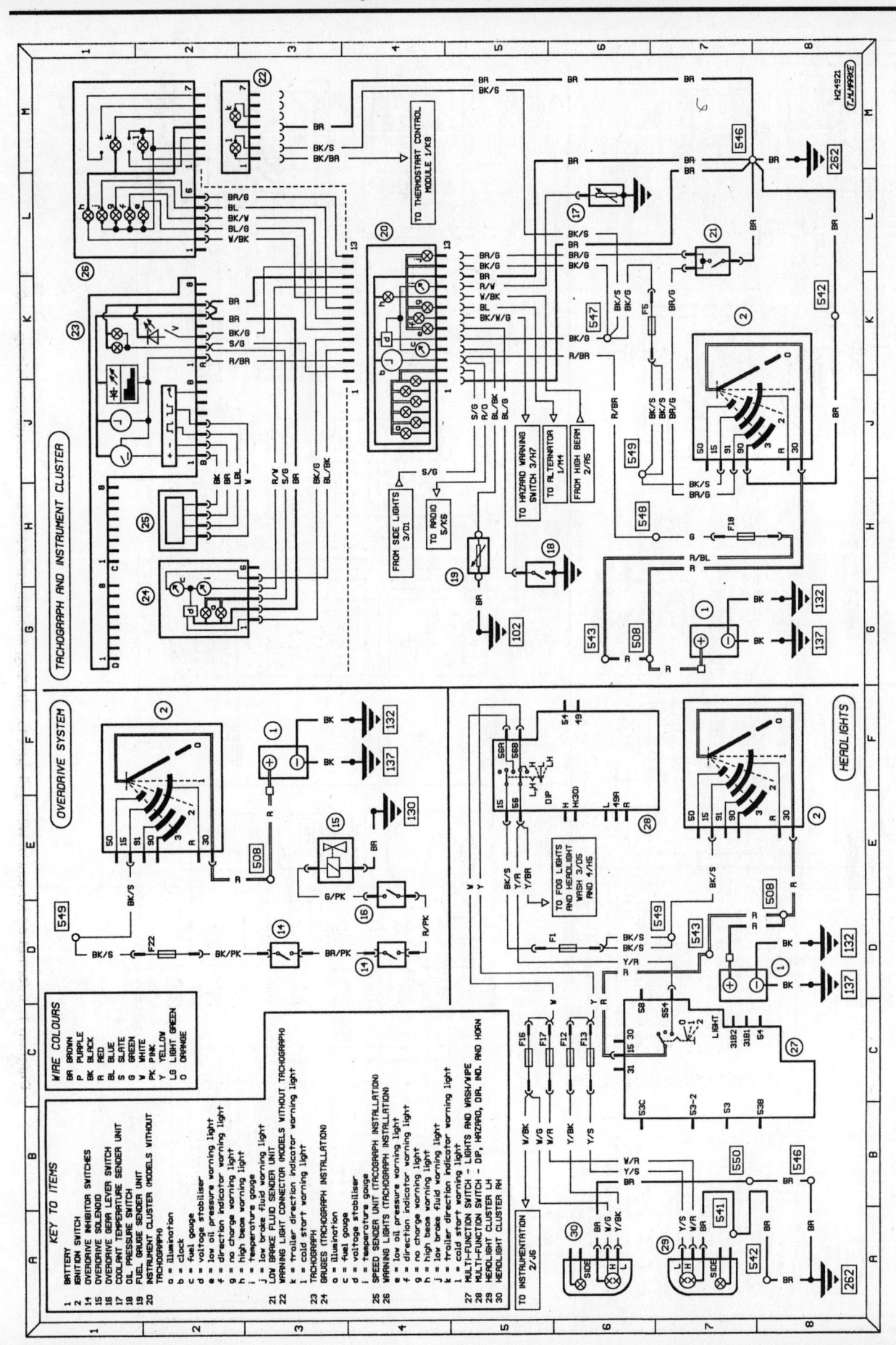

Diagram 2: Overdrive system, tachograph/instrument cluster and headlights (models up to 1992)

12-26   Chapter 12 Body electrical systems

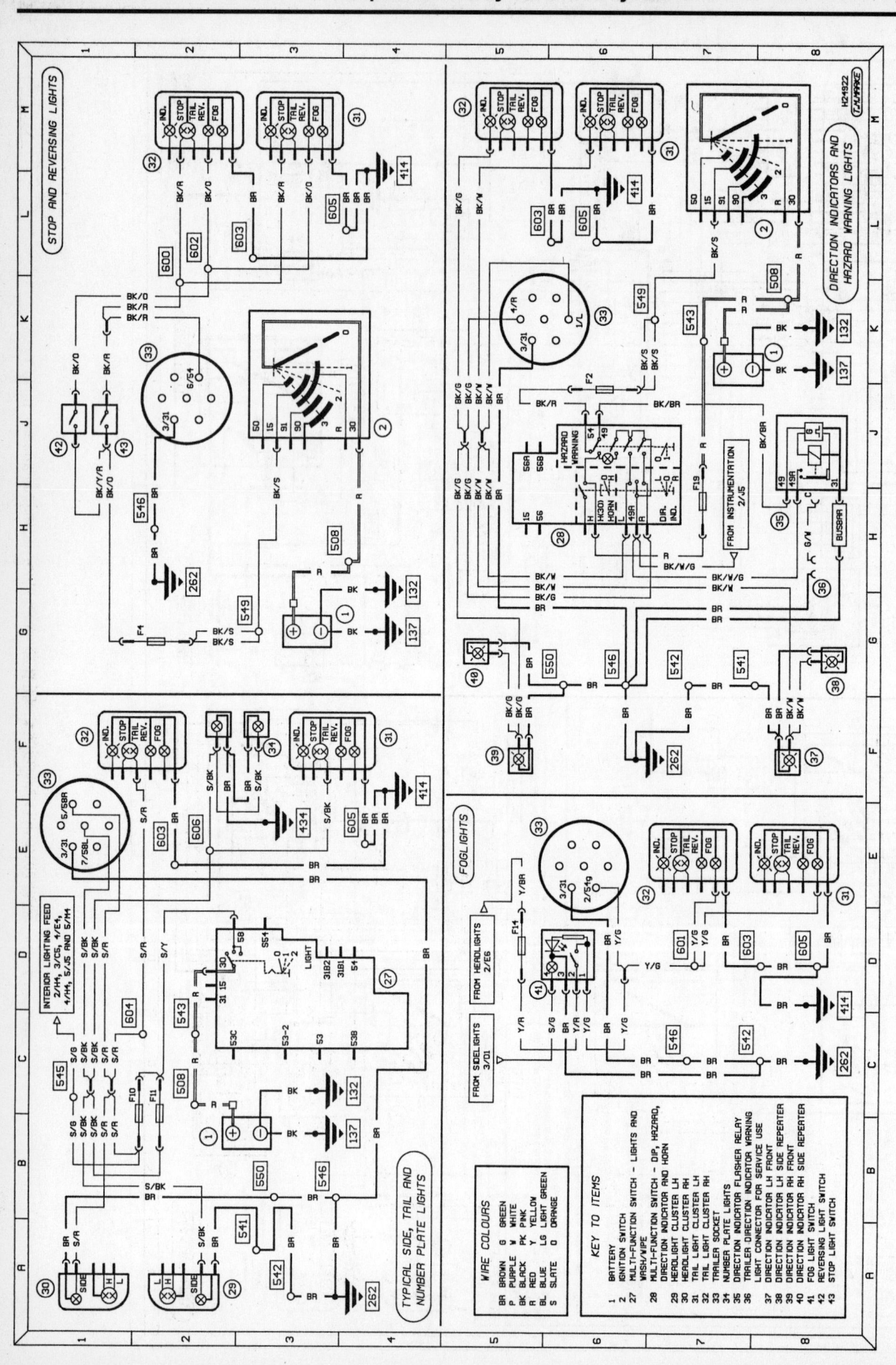

Diagram 3: Exterior lighting (models up to 1992)

Chapter 12 Body electrical systems

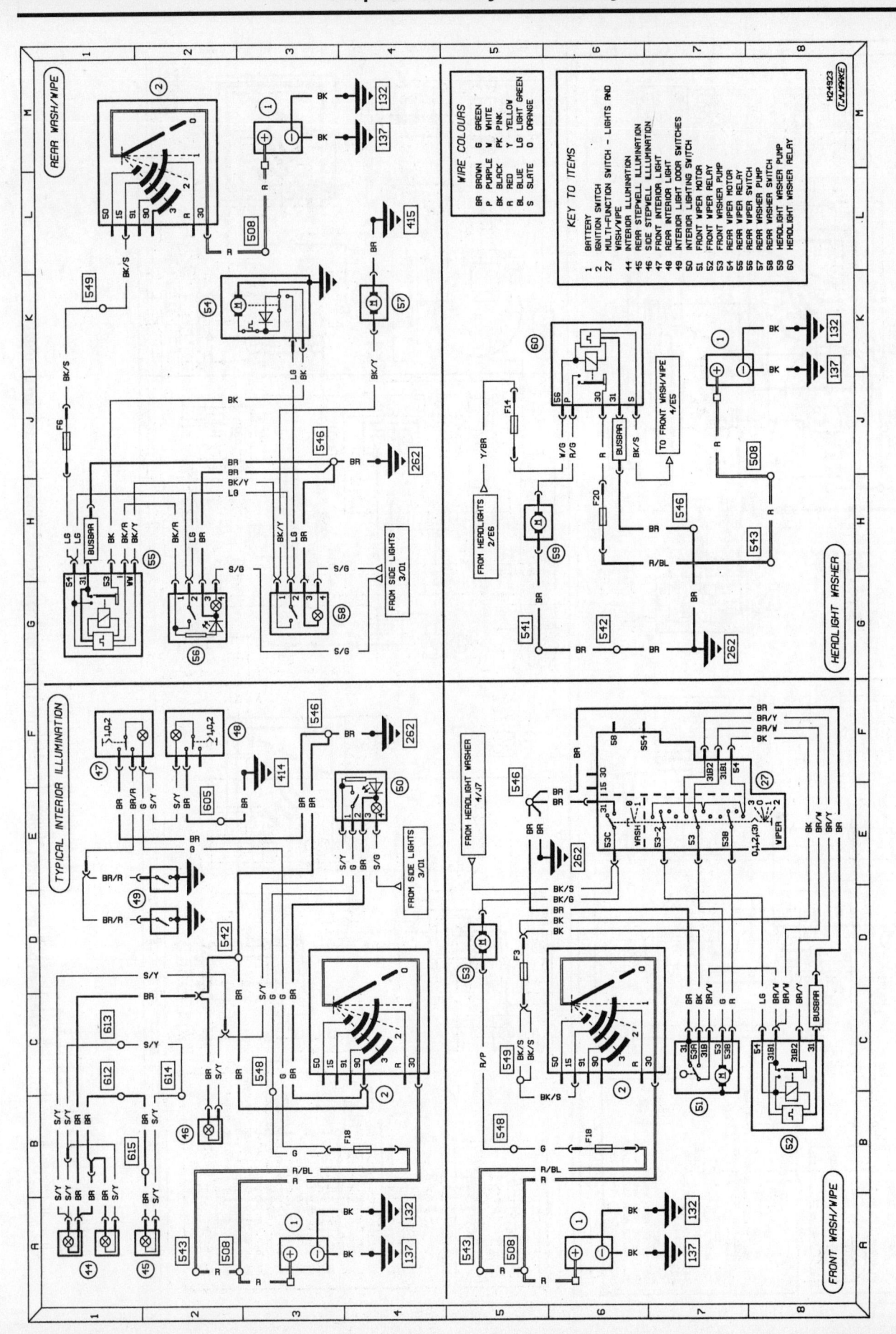

12-27

Diagram 4: Interior lighting and wash/wipe (models up to 1992)

Chapter 12 Body electrical systems

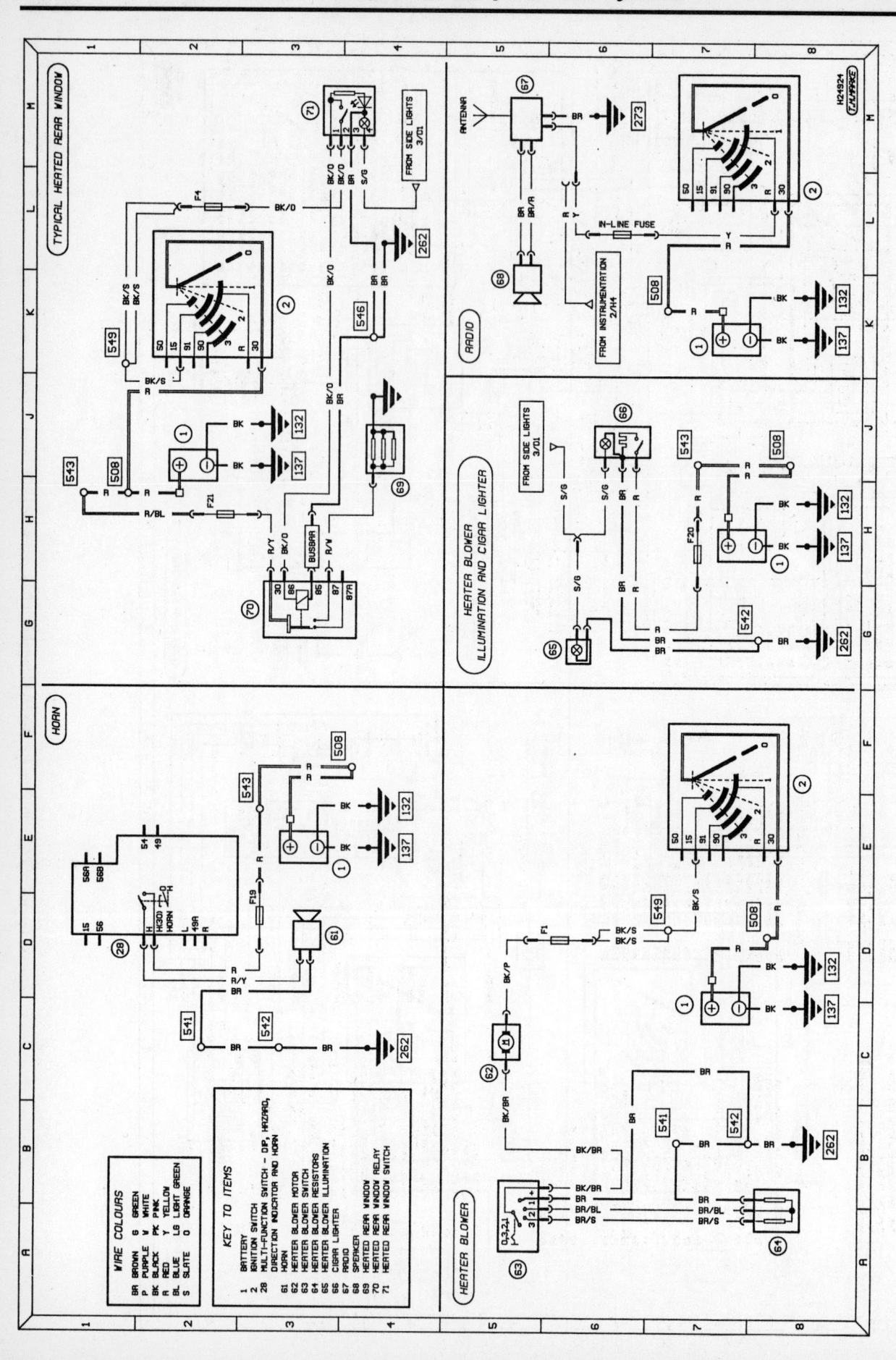

Diagram 5: Horn, heater blower, cigar lighter, radio and heated rear window (models up to 1992)

Chapter 12 Body electrical systems

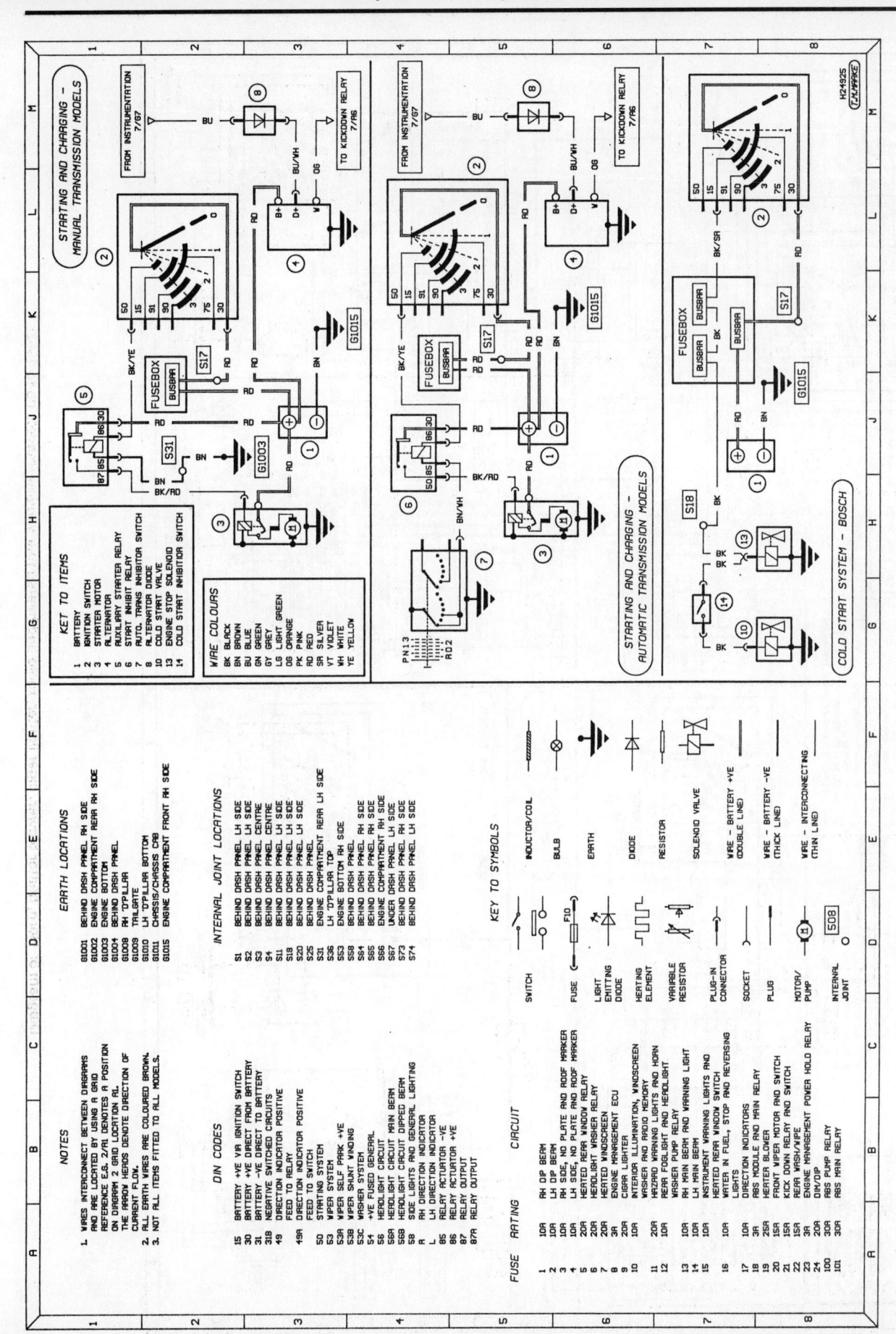

Diagram 6: Information for use of wiring diagrams, starting, charging and cold start system (models from 1992)

12-30 Chapter 12 Body electrical systems

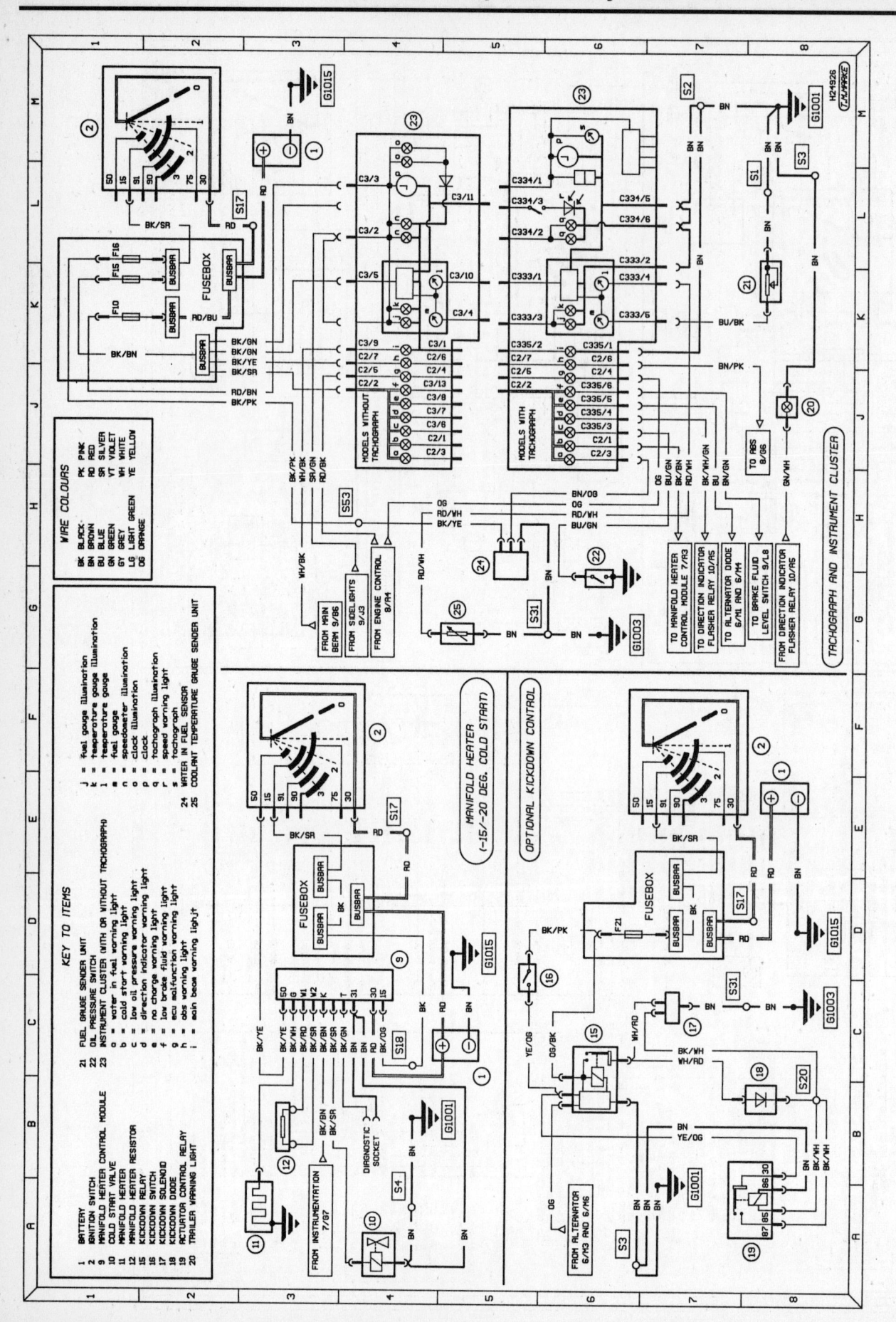

Diagram 7: Manifold heater, kickdown switch, tachograph and instrument cluster (models from 1992)

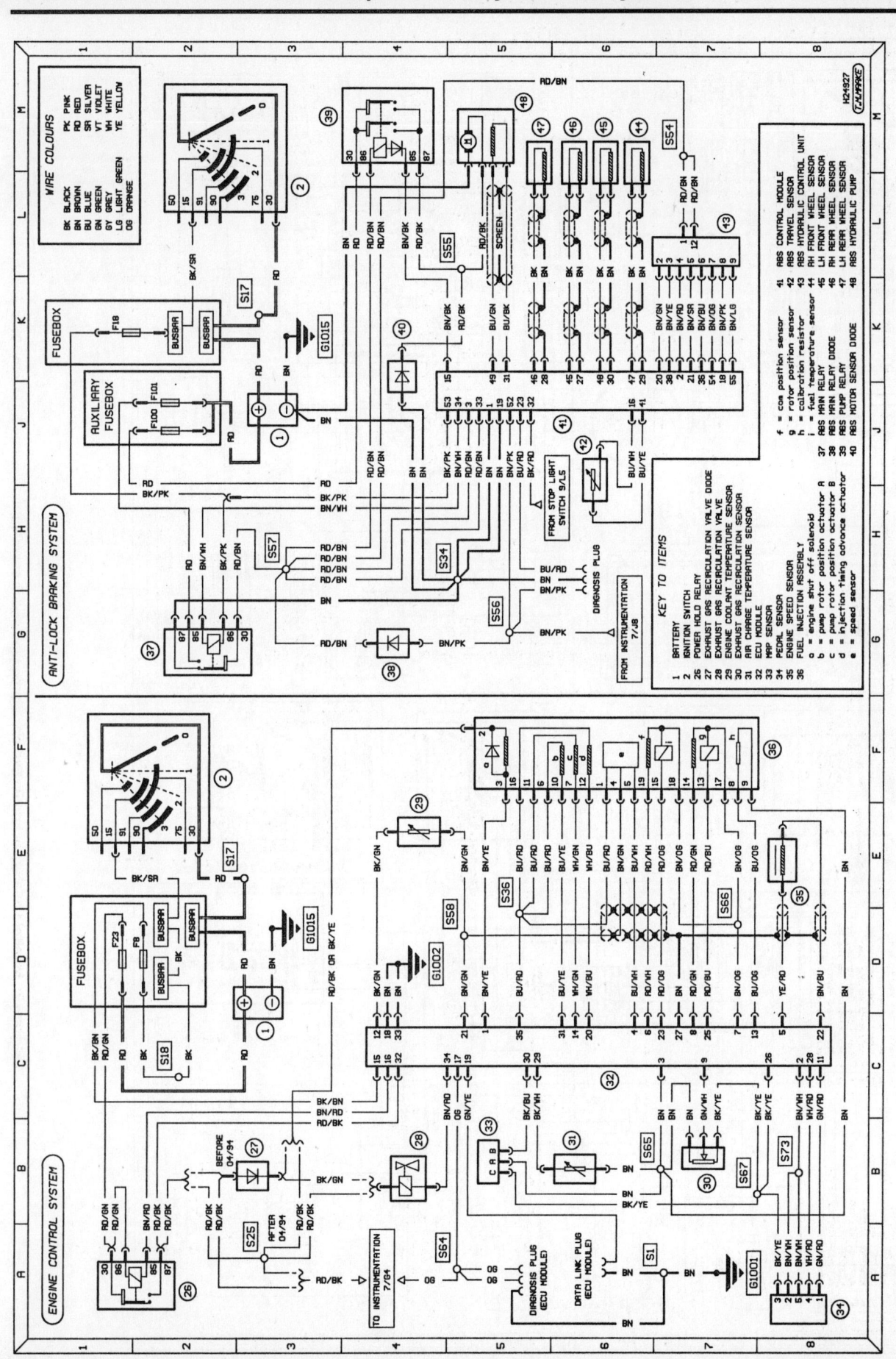

Chapter 12 Body electrical systems

Diagram 8: Engine control and anti-lock brakes (models from 1992)

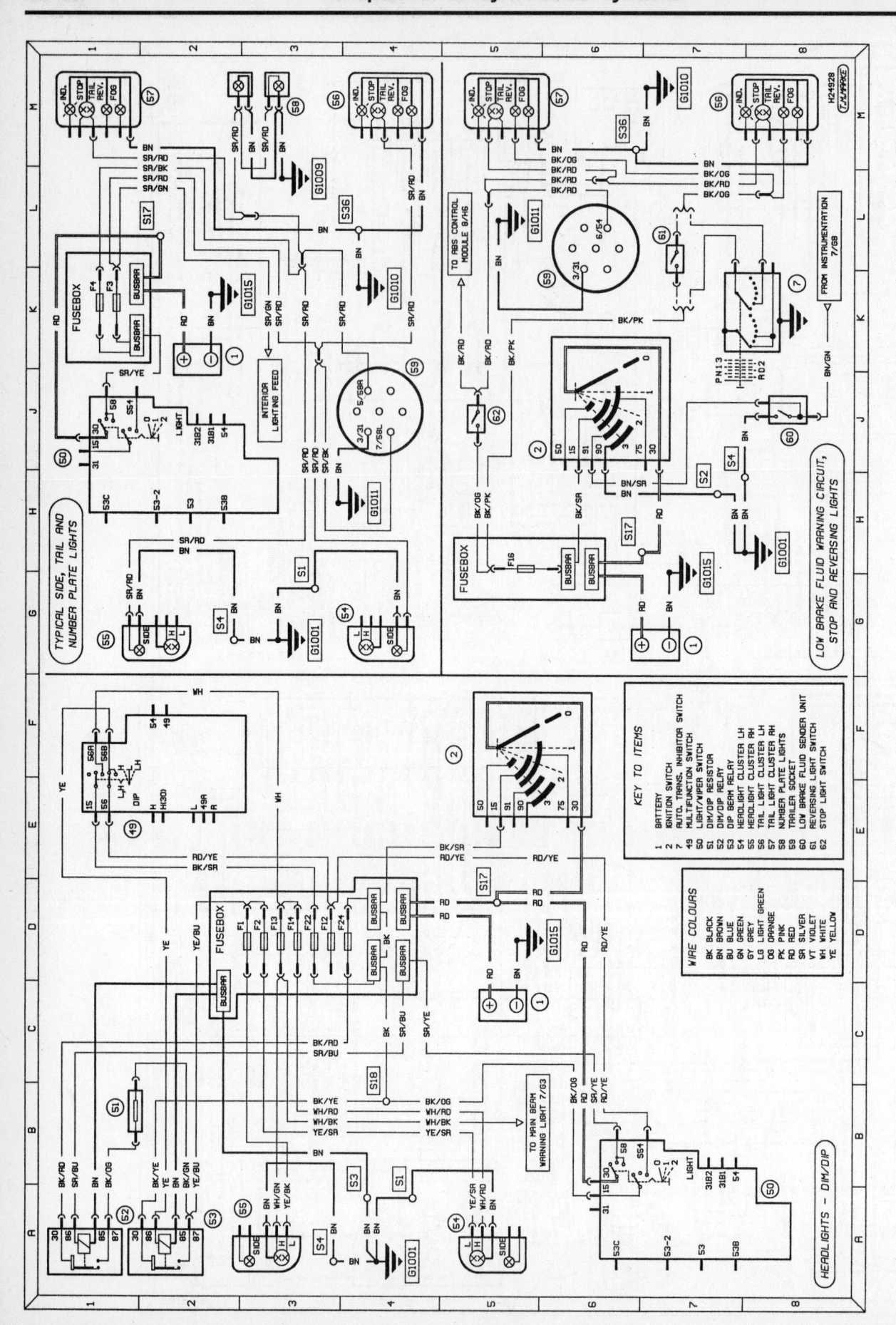

12-32　Chapter 12 Body electrical systems

Diagram 9: Exterior lighting (models from 1992)

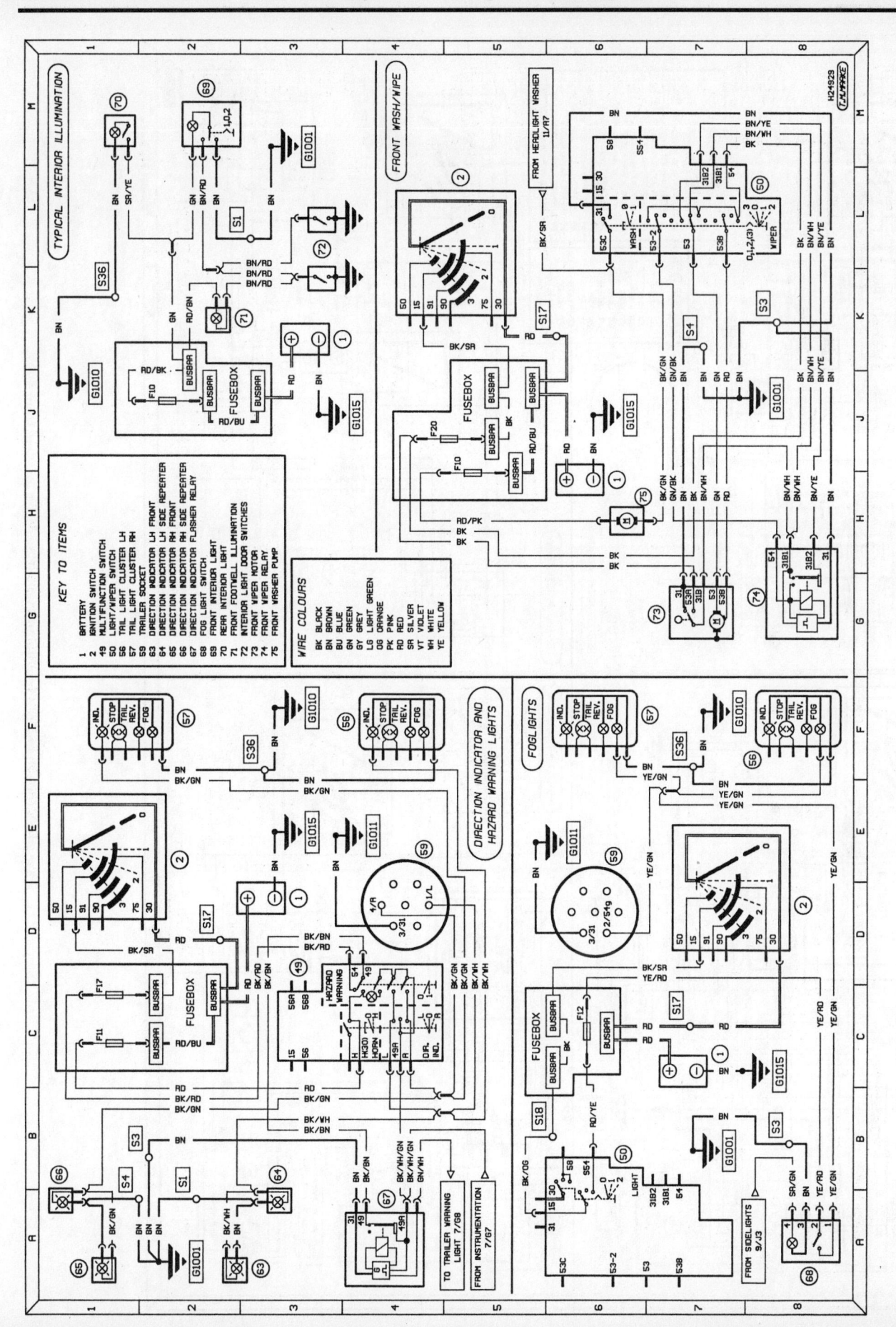

Chapter 12 Body electrical systems   12-33

Diagram 10: Exterior lighting (continued), interior lighting and windscreen wash/wipe (models from 1992)

12-34 Chapter 12 Body electrical systems

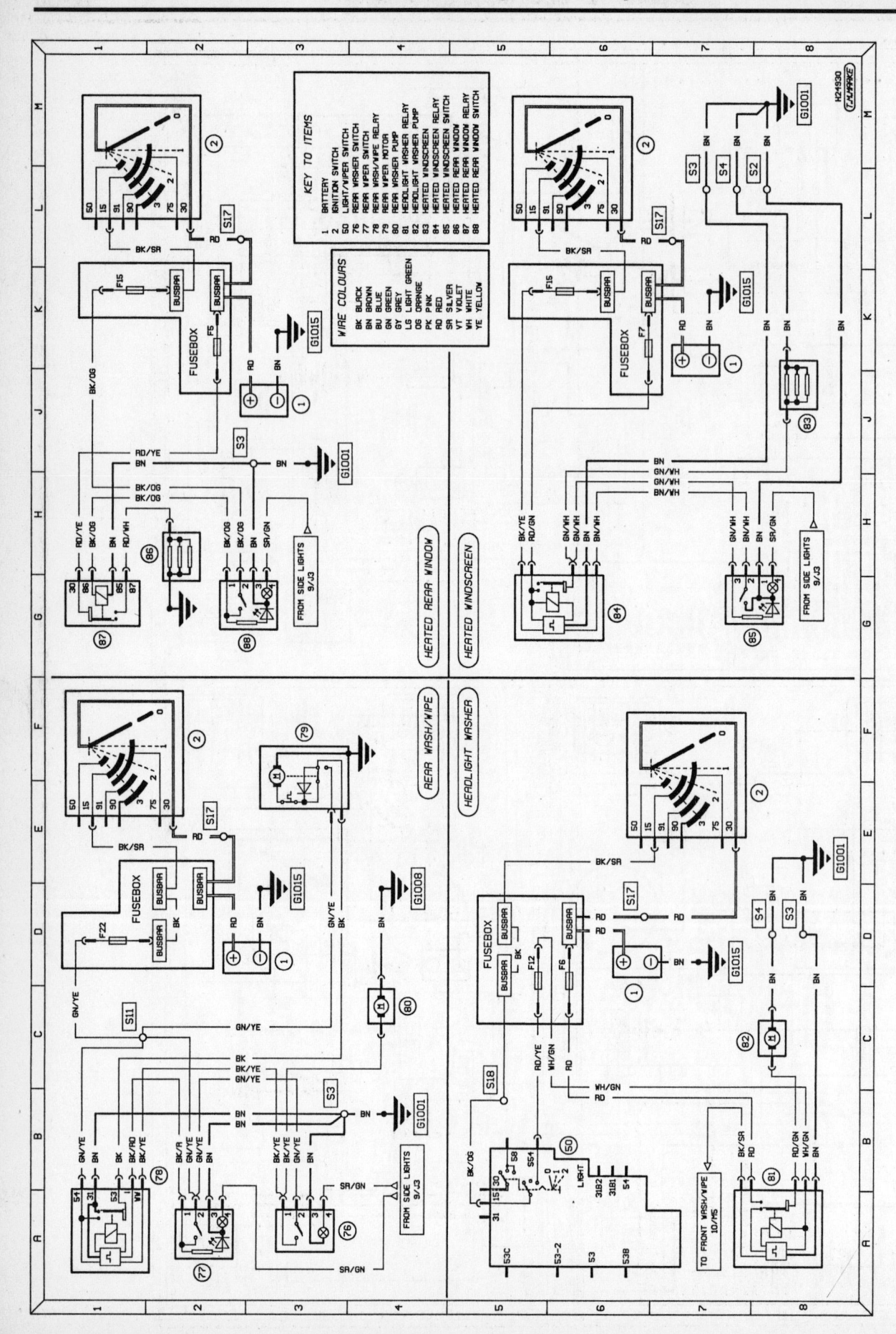

Diagram 11: Rear wash/wipe, headlight washer and heated screens (models from 1992)

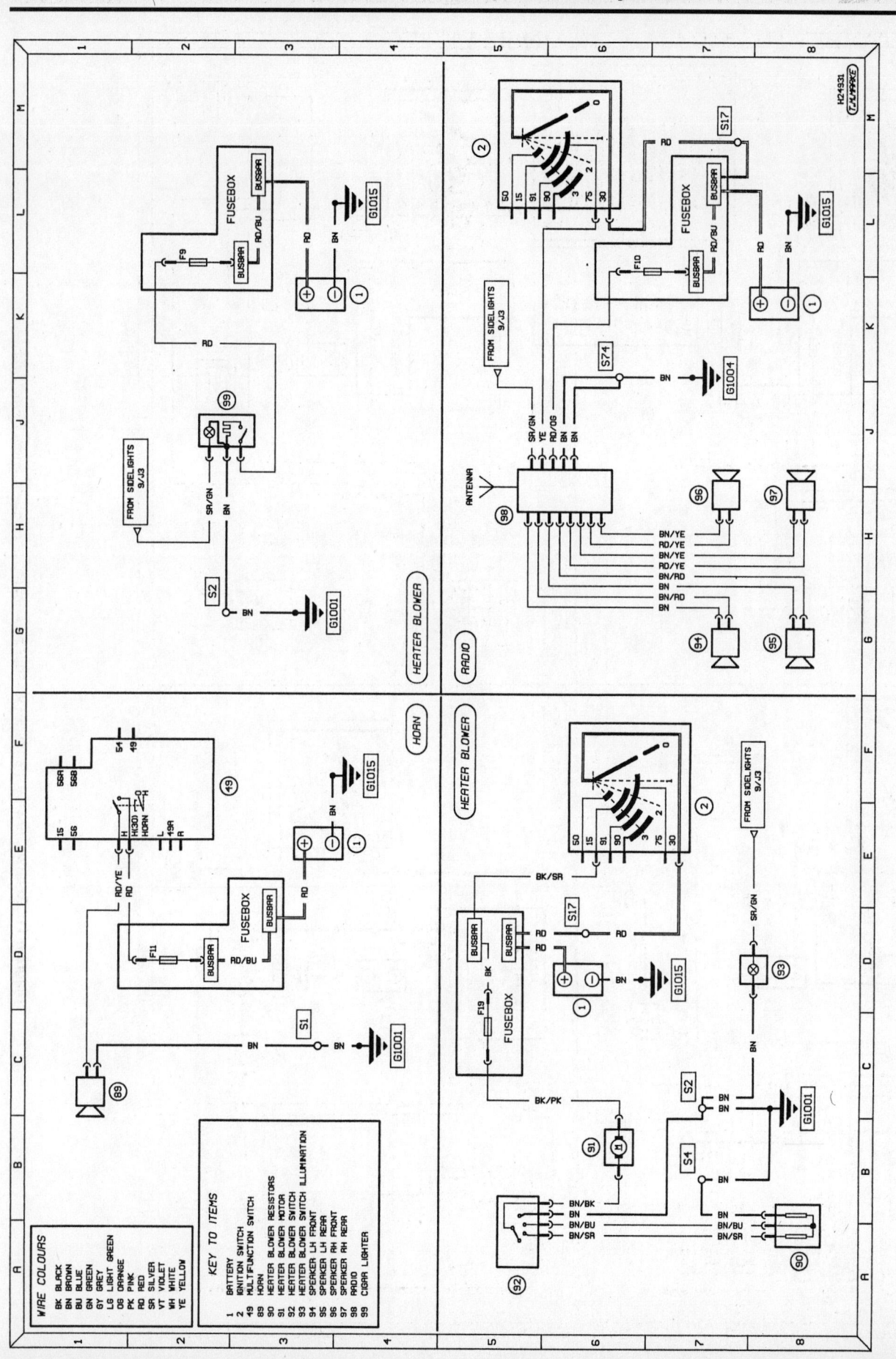

Chapter 12 Body electrical systems

Diagram 12: Horn, heater blower, cigar lighter and radio (models from 1992)

Notes

Index

Note: *References throughout this index relate to Chapter and page numbers, separated by a hyphen.*

A

A-pillar – 11-23
About this manual – 0-5
ABS – 9-19, 9-20
Accelerator – 4-12
Acknowledgements – 0-2
Aerial – 12-21
Air bag – 10-19, 12-22
Air cleaner – 1-1, 1-23, 4-3
Air conditioning – 1-18, 3-12
Alternator – 5-3, 5-4
   drivebelt – 1-13
Amplifier – 12-21
Anti-lock braking system (ABS) – 9-19, 9-20
Anti-roll bar – 10-12, 10-17
Anti-stall speed – 1-23
Anti-theft system – 12-23
Antifreeze mixture – 1-26
Automatic transmission – 7B-1 *et seq*
   fault diagnosis – 0-24
   fluid level check – 1-22
   linkage lubrication – 1-20
   removal – 2B-7, 2B-8
   selector quadrant bulb – 12-16

B

B-pillar – 11-23
Balljoints (track rod end) – 10-24
Battery
   check/charging – 1-12
   electrolyte level – 1-9
   flat – 0-19
   removal and refitting – 5-2
Beam axle (front) – 10-15, 10-16
Bearings
   big-end – 2B-20, 2B-23
   clutch release – 6-5
   engine – 2B-20, 2B-22
   main – 2B-20, 2B-22
   propeller shaft – 1-20, 8-4
   rear hub – 8-9, 8-12
Big-end bearings – 2B-20, 2B-23
Bleeding
   brake hydraulic system – 9-3
   fuel system – 4-3
   power steering – 10-31
Block – 2B-17
Blower (heater)
   motor – 3-9, 3-10
   switch – 12-8
Body damage – 11-2, 11-4
Body electrical system – 12-1 *et seq*
Bodywork and fittings – 11-1 *et seq*
Bonnet – 11-4, 11-5
   lubrication – 1-19
   release cable/latch – 11-4
Brake bands (automatic transmission) – 7B-2
Braking system – 1-17, 9-1 *et seq*
   caliper – 9-7, 9-8
   disc – 9-9
   drum – 9-9
   fault diagnosis – 0-25
   fluid – 1-10, 1-26
   light – 12-14, 12-17
   line check – 1-21
   master cylinder – 9-13, 9-14
   pads – 9-4
   pedal – 9-19, 9-21
   pipes and hoses – 9-4
   road test – 1-22
   shoes – 1-18, 9-9
   stop-light switch – 12-8
   vacuum pump – 9-16
   wheel cylinder – 9-13
Brushes
   alternator – 5-4
   starter motor – 5-5
Bulbs – 12-3, 12-9, 12-10, 12-13, 12-15
Bump stop (beam axle front suspension) – 10-17
Bumpers – 11-20, 11-21
Bush lubrication (steering) – 1-19
Buying spare parts and vehicle identification numbers – 0-9

Index

C

C-pillar – 11-23
Cables
   accelerator – 4-12
   bonnet release – 11-4
   clutch – 1-20, 6-2
   downshift (automatic transmission) – 7B-2, 7B-3
   handbrake – 9-18
   heater/ventilation control – 3-9
   kickdown (automatic transmission) – 7B-2, 7B-3
   selector (automatic transmission) – 7B-3
   speedometer – 12-12
Caliper (brake) – 9-7, 9-8
Camber – 10-31
Camshaft – 2B-12
   drivebelt – 2A-7 to 2A-8
   drivebelt covers – 2A-6
Capacities – 1-4
Carpets – 11-2
Castor – 10-31
Centre bearing check (propeller shaft) – 1-20
Charging system – 1-13, 5-3
Cigarette lighter – 12-12
Clock – 12-10, 12-12
Clutch – 6-1 *et seq*
   cable – 1-20, 6-2
   fault diagnosis – 0-23
   pedal – 6-3
   road test – 1-22
Coil spring (front suspension) – 10-9
Compact disc player – 12-20
Compression and leakdown test – 2A-4
Connecting rods – 2B-15, 2B-19, 2B-23
Contents – 0-3
Conversion factors – 0-20
Coolant
   level – 1-8
   renewal – 1-25
   temperature sender – 3-6
Cooling fan (radiator) – 3-5
Cooling, heating and ventilation systems – 3-1 *et seq*
   fault diagnosis – 0-23
   hoses – 3-3
Courtesy light – 12-7, 12-15
Crankcase – 2B-17
Crankcase emissions control – 4-20
Crankshaft – 2B-16, 2B-20, 2B-22
   oil seals – 2A-16
   sprocket – 2A-9
Cylinder block/crankcase – 2B-17
Cylinder head – 2A-10, 2A-11, 2B-9 to 2B-11
   cover – 2A-5

D

D-pillar – 11-23
Dents – 11-3
Differential – 8-14
Dimensions and weights – 0-6
Direction indicator – 12-14, 12-16, 12-17
Disc brakes – 1-18, 9-9
Doors – 11-5 to 11-14, 11-16, 11-17
   check and lubrication – 1-19
   inner trim panel – 11-5
   mirror – 11-19
   window glass – 11-16 to 11-19
Downshift cable (automatic transmission) – 7B-2, 7B-3
Drag link (steering gear) – 10-29
Drive pinion oil seal – 8-13
Drivebelt check – 1-13
Drivetrain road test – 1-22
Drop arm (steering gear) – 10-28
Drum brakes – 1-18, 9-9

E

Earth fault (finding) – 12-5
Electric window switch – 12-8
Electrical system (body) – 12-1 *et seq*
   check – 1-12
   fault diagnosis – 0-26
   road test – 1-22
Electrical systems (engine) – 5-1 *et seq*
Electrolyte level – 1-9
Electronic module (ABS) – 9-20
Electronic Programmed Injection Control system – 4-21, 4-23
Emissions control systems – 4-19, 4-20
Engine (in-car repair) – 2A-1 *et seq*
   fault diagnosis – 0-22
   mountings – 2A-19
   oil and filter change – 1-15
   oil level – 1-8
   removal – 2B-4, 2B-5, 2B-7, 2B-8
Engine compartment – 1-6
Environmental considerations – 0-14
Exhaust emissions control – 4-19, 4-20
Exhaust gas recirculation (EGR) system – 4-20
Exhaust manifold – 4-16
Exhaust system – 1-21, 4-19
Expansion tank (cooling system) – 3-3
Exterior lights – 12-16
Exterior mirror – 11-19

F

Facia – 11-22
   side switches – 12-8
Fan (radiator) – 3-5
Fast idle thermostatic sensor – 4-5
Fault diagnosis – 0-21
   automatic transmission – 0-24
   braking system – 0-25
   clutch – 0-23
   cooling system – 0-23
   electrical system – 0-26, 12-4
   engine – 0-22
   fuel and exhaust systems – 0-23
   manual transmission – 0-24
   propeller shaft – 0-25
   rear axle – 0-25
   steering – 0-25
   suspension – 0-25
Firing order – 2A-1
Flame plugs – 5-10
   fuel reservoir – 1-26
Flat battery – 0-19
Fluids – 1-3
   automatic transmission – 1-22
   brake – 1-10, 1-26
   leak check – 1-14, 1-21
   level checks – 1-8
   power steering – 1-11
   washers – 1-9
Flywheel – 2A-18
Footwell trim – 11-23
Front brake pad check – 1-18
Front sidelight bulb – 12-14
Fuel, exhaust and emissions control systems – 4-1 *et seq*
   fault diagnosis – 0-23
Fuel filter – 1-1, 1-16, 1-24, 4-11
Fuel gauge – 12-10, 12-11
   sender unit – 4-13
Fuel injection pump – 4-6
   sprocket – 2A-9
Fuel injectors – 4-9, 4-11
Fuel line check – 1-21
Fuel pump – 4-14

Index

Fuel tank – 4-13
Fuses – 12-1, 12-2, 12-5

G

Gaiters (steering gear) – 10-25
Gear lever (manual transmission) – 7A-3
Gear ratios
    automatic transmission – 7B-1
    manual transmission – 7A-1
Gearbox – See Manual transmission
Gearchange linkage (manual transmission) – 7A-3
Glass – 11-16 to 11-19
Glow plugs – 5-10
Grille – 11-21
Guibo joint (propeller shaft) – 8-5

H

Halfshaft – 8-8
Handbrake – 9-17
    cables – 9-18
    lever – 9-17
    lubrication and adjustment – 1-20
Handles (door) – 11-6, 11-7, 11-10, 11-13, 11-14
Hazard warning lights – 12-15
Headlight – 12-16
    beam alignment – 12-13
    bulb – 12-13
    washers – 1-9, 1-12, 12-19
Headlining – 11-23
Heater – 3-7
    blower motor – 3-9, 3-10
    blower switch – 12-8
Heating and ventilation systems – 3-1 et seq
Hinges and locks – 1-19
Horn – 12-17
    switch – 12-6
Hoses – 1-14
    cooling system – 3-3
    power steering – 10-30
Hub (front) – 10-8, 10-9, 10-14

I

Idle speed and anti-stall speed – 1-23
Ignition switch – 12-6
Indicators – 12-14, 12-16, 12-17
Inhibitor switch
    automatic transmission – 7B-4
    overdrive unit – 7A-10
Injection timing – 4-2, 4-8
Injectors – 4-9, 4-11
Inlet manifold – 4-15
Input shaft oil seal (manual transmission) – 7A-4
Instruments – 12-9
    illumination – 12-9, 12-10
    road test – 1-22
Instrument panel switches – 12-7
Interior light bulbs – 12-15
Interior trim – 11-23
Introduction to the Ford Transit Diesel – 0-5

J

Jacking, towing and wheel changing – 0-6
Jump starting – 0-19

K

Kickdown cable (automatic transmission) – 7B-2, 7B-3
Kingpin and bush lubrication – 1-19

L

Leaf spring
    front suspension – 10-16
    rear suspension – 10-18
Leakdown test – 2A-4
Light switch – 12-6
Load-apportioning valve (rear brakes) – 9-19
    check and adjustment – 1-22
Locks – 1-19
    door – 11-7, 11-8, 11-10, 11-12, 11-15
    steering column – 12-6
Loudspeakers – 12-22
Lower arm (front suspension) – 10-10 to 10-12
Lubricants and fluids – 1-3

M

Main and big-end bearings – 2B-20, 2B-22
Maintenance and servicing – 1-1 et seq
Manifolds – 4-15, 4-16
Manual transmission – 1-19, 7A-1 et seq
    fault diagnosis – 0-24
    removal – 2B-7, 2B-8
Master cylinder (brake) – 9-13, 9-14
Maximum speed – 4-1, 4-4
Mirrors – 11-19
MOT test checks – 0-28
Mountings
    engine – 2A-19
    transmission – 7A-7

N

Number plate light – 12-14, 12-17

O

Oils – 1-3
    change – 1-15
    check
        engine – 1-8
        manual transmission – 1-19
        rear axle – 1-21
Oil cooler – 2A-20
Oil filler cap check – 1-16
Oil filter – 1-1, 1-15
Oil pressure warning light switch – 5-10
Oil pump – 2A-14, 2A-16
Oil seals – 0-13
    automatic transmission – 7B-4
    crankshaft – 2A-16
    drive pinion (rear axle) – 8-13
    manual transmission – 7A-4
    overdrive unit – 7A-6
    speedometer drive pinion – 7A-6
Open-circuit (finding) – 12-4
Output shaft oil seal – 7A-5, 7B-4
Overdrive unit – 7A-10, 7A-11
    slipjoint lubrication – 1-20
    output shaft oil seal – 7A-6
Overhaul (engine) – 2B-1 et seq

P

Pads (brake) – 9-4
Paintwork damage – 11-2
Parking light bulb – 12-14
Parts – 0-9

Index

Pedals
   accelerator – 4-12
   brake – 9-19, 9-21
   clutch – 6-3
Pipes
   fuel – 4-11
   power steering – 10-30
Piston/connecting rod assemblies – 2B-15, 2B-19, 2B-23
Piston rings – 2B-21
Plastic components – 11-4
Power amplifier – 12-21
Power steering – 10-29 to 10-31
   fluid level check – 1-11
   pump drivebelt – 1-14
Preheating system – 1-26, 5-10
Pressure control valve (rear brakes) – 9-18
Priming fuel system – 4-3
Printed circuit – 12-10, 12-11
Propeller shaft – 8-1 et seq
   check – 1-20
   fault diagnosis – 0-25
   lubrication – 1-20
Punctures – 0-7

Q

Quarter panel – 11-23
Quarter window – 11-17, 11-19

R

Radiator – 3-3
Radio aerial – 12-21
Radio/cassette – 12-20
   anti-theft system – 0-19
Rear axle – 8-1 *et seq*
   fault diagnosis – 0-25
   oil level check – 1-21
Rear door – 11-12, 11-14
Rear hub – 8-9, 8-12
Rear light cluster – 12-14, 12-17
Regulator (alternator) – 5-4
Regulator (door window) – 11-16
Relays – 12-3, 12-5
Release bearing (clutch) – 6-5
Repair procedures – 0-13
Respraying – 11-3
Reversing light switch – 7A-6
Rings (piston) – 2B-21
Road test – 1-22
Roadwheel check – 1-17, 1-22
Rocker cover – 2A-5
Rocker gear – 2A-10
Roll bars – 10-12, 10-17
Routine maintenance and servicing – 1-1 *et seq*
   procedures – 1-8 et seq
   schedule – 1-4
Rubber gaiter (steering gear) – 10-25

S

Safety first! – 0-11
   air conditioning system – 3-11
   automatic transmission – 7B-2
   cooling system – 3-2
   electrical system – 12-4
   engine electrical – 5-2
   fuel and exhaust systems – 4-3, 4-21
Scratches – 11-2
Seat belts – 1-13, 11-25
Seats – 11-24
Selector (automatic transmission) – 7B-4
   cable – 7B-3

Sender units
   fuel gauge – 4-13
   coolant temperature – 3-6
Servicing – 1-1 *et seq*
Servo (automatic transmission) – 7B-5
Servo unit (braking system) – 9-16
Shock absorber
   front – 10-13, 10-17
   rear – 10-19
Shoes (brake) – 9-9
Short-circuit (finding) – 12-5
Side repeater – 12-14, 12-16
Sidelight bulb – 12-14
Sliding door – 11-10, 11-11
Sliding window – 11-18
Solenoid valve (overdrive unit) – 7A-10
Spare parts – 0-9
Speakers – 12-22
Special tools – 0-14, 0-17
Speedometer – 12-10, 12-10
   cable – 12-12
   drive
      automatic transmission – 7B-4, 7B-6
      manual transmission – 7A-6, 7A-7
Sprockets
   camshaft – 2A-8
   crankshaft – 2A-9
   fuel injection pump – 2A-9
   timing belt – 2A-8
Starter motor – 5-4, 5-5
Starter switch – 12-6
Starting and charging systems – 5-1 *et seq*
Steering – 10-1 *et seq*
   angles/alignment – 10-31
   check – 1-17, 1-19
   column – 10-20, 10-21, 12-6
      switches – 12-6
   fault diagnosis – 0-25
   gear – 10-23, 10-25, 10-28 to 10-31
   pump – 10-29
   road test – 1-22
   wheel – 10-19
Stop solenoid – 4-6
Stop-light – 12-8, 12-14
Stub axle – 10-9, 10-14
Sump – 2A-13
Suspension and steering – 10-1 *et seq*
Suspension
   check – 1-17
   fault diagnosis – 0-25
   front – 10-9 to 10-17
   lower arm (front) – 10-10 to 10-12
   rear – 10-18, 10-19
   road test – 1-22
Switches – 12-6
   blower (heater) – 12-8
   brake stop-light – 12-8
   cooling system – 3-6
   courtesy light – 12-7
   electric window – 12-8
   facia – 12-8
   heater blower – 12-8
   horn – 12-6
   ignition – 12-6
   inhibitor (automatic transmission) – 7B-4
   instrument panel – 12-7
   light – 12-6
   oil pressure warning light – 5-10
   overdrive unit – 7A-10
   reversing light – 7A-6
   starter – 12-6
   steering column – 12-6
   stop-light – 12-8
   window – 12-8
   wiper – 12-6

Index

T

Tachograph – 12-11
Tachometer – 12-10
Tailgate – 11-14, 11-15
   check and lubrication – 1-19
   washer – 1-9, 1-12, 12-20
   wiper motor – 12-20
Tappets – 2B-12
TDC (locating) – 2A-5
Temperature control system (air cleaner) – 1-24
Temperature gauge – 12-10, 12-11
   sender unit – 3-6
Tensioner (timing belt) – 2A-8, 2A-9
Thermostat (cooling system) – 3-6
Throttle cable – 4-12
Timing belt – 2A-7 to 2A-9
   cover – 2A-6
Toe setting – 10-2, 10-31
Tools and working facilities – 0-15
Top Dead Centre (locating) – 2A-5
Towing – 0-6
Track rod end balljoint – 10-24
Tracking – 10-2, 10-31
Transmission – See Manual or Automatic transmission
Trim panels
   door – 11-5
   footwell – 11-23
   pillars – 11-23
   rear quarter panel – 11-23
Turbocharger – 4-16, 4-17, 4-19
Tyre pressures – 1-2
Tyres – 1-10

U

Underbody – 11-2
   check – 1-21
   views – 1-6, 1-7
Universal joint check (propeller shaft) – 1-20
Upholstery and carpets – 11-2

V

Vacuum diaphragm (automatic transmission) – 7B-4
Vacuum governor (automatic transmission) – 7B-5, 7B-6
Vacuum pump (brakes) – 9-16
Vacuum servo unit (braking system) – 9-16
Valves – 2B-10
   clearances – 2A-1, 2A-10
Vehicle identification numbers – 0-9
Ventilation system – 3-7 to 3-11
Vents (ventilation system) – 3-11
Viscous cooling fan (radiator) – 3-5

W

Warning lights – 12-9, 12-10, 12-12
Washers – 12-19
   fluid level – 1-9
   system check – 1-12
Water pump – 3-7
   drivebelt – 1-13
Weights – 0-6
Wheel (steering) – 10-19
Wheels
   alignment – 10-2, 10-31
   bearings (front) – 10-9, 10-14
   changing – 0-7
   check – 1-17, 1-22
Wheel cylinder – 9-13
Wheel sensor (ABS) – 9-21
Window glass – 11-16 to 11-19
Window regulator – 11-16
Window switch – 12-8
Windscreen – 11-19, 11-21
   washers – 12-19
   wiper motor – 12-18
Wiper arms – 12-18
Wiper blades – 1-2, 1-12
Wiper motor
   tailgate – 12-20
   windscreen – 12-18
Wiper switch – 12-6
Wiring check – 1-18
Wiring diagrams – 12-24 *et seq*
Working facilities – 0-15